GESTALT THERAPY

History, Theory, and Practice

EDITORS

Ansel L. Woldt
Kent State University

Sarah M. Toman
Cleveland State University

SAGE Publications
Thousand Oaks ▪ London ▪ New Delhi

For information:

Sage Publications, Inc.
2455 Teller Road
Thousand Oaks, California 91320
E-mail: order@sagepub.com

Sage Publications Ltd.
1 Oliver's Yard
55 City Road
London EC1Y 1SP
United Kingdom

Sage Publications India Pvt. Ltd.
B-42, Panchsheel Enclave
Post Box 4109
New Delhi 110 017 India

Printed in the United States of America

Library of Congress Cataloging-in-Publication Data

Gestalt therapy : history, theory, and practice / edited by Ansel L. Woldt, Sarah M. Toman.
p. cm.
Includes bibliographical references and index.
ISBN 978-0-7619-2791-4 (pbk.)
1. Gestalt therapy. I. Woldt, Ansel L. II. Toman, Sarah M.
RC489.G4G4845 2005
616.89′143—dc22

2004019663

This book is printed on acid-free paper.

08 09 10 11 12 9 8 7 6 5 4 3

Acquiring Editor: Jim Brace-Thompson
Editorial Assistant: Karen Ehrmann
Production Editor: Sanford Robinson
Typesetter: C&M Digitals (P) Ltd.
Indexer: Molly Hall
Cover Designer: Glenn Vogel

Contents

Acknowledgments

This textbook would not have been possible without the contributions of talent, time, and tenacity of each chapter author and dialogue respondent. All brought their passion for Gestalt therapy to the printed page. We have established new friendships and enriched existing ones through the process of working together. All deserve an "A" for their genius, positive energy, and desire to make this a worthy contribution to the Gestalt literature.

We received much needed support and words of encouragement for this project from a variety of sources—our students, our colleagues, and our friends. We are especially appreciative of the support we received from our editor at Sage, James Brace-Thompson, who assisted us through each stage of the development and production of this book. Thanks, too, to the others at Sage who offered their technical expertise and assistance, including Karen Ehrmann, our editorial assistant, and Sanford Robinson, our production editor.

We greatly appreciate Phil Brownell's contribution to the appendix "Digital Gestalt: Online Resources for the Discipline of Gestalt Therapy," in which he detailed the history of "digital Gestalt" and assisted Ansel in assembling the list of Gestalt resources available on the Internet at the time of completing the manuscript. Phil's commitment to the Gestalt community is unwavering.

We also want to express our appreciation to two of the most generous, yet unpretentious supporters of Gestalt's development and maintenance around the world. Rarely seen or heard, due to their quiet presence, are Edwin Nevis and Sonia March Nevis, whose unwavering support is always there—encouraging, coaching, creating, challenging, contributing, and urging us (and literally thousands of others) on to higher ground. Edwin and Sonia have been central in the founding of two of the world's most prominent Gestalt centers—the Gestalt Institute of Cleveland nearly 60 years ago and, more recently, the "Gestalt Meeting House" at the Gestalt International Study Center on Cape Cod, located in a beautiful wooded setting adjacent to the National Seashore. Their continuing efforts and financial support for the Gestalt Writers' Conferences had a direct impact on our decision to create this textbook. Thank you, Sonia and Edwin!

The book is dedicated, though, to the two people who believed in this project from its fledgling beginnings through its phase of standing by for departure to takeoff. Without their support and encouragement, this book would not have been completed.

So, a GRAND THANK YOU to
Nancy Woldt
and
Doug Toman

ACKNOWLEDGMENTS

Prologue-Foreword

Ansel L. Woldt and Sarah Toman

ABOUT CREATING THIS TEXTBOOK

The idea for this textbook project originated with the Kent Gestalt Writers' Group—a small group of friends and colleagues living near Kent, Akron, and Cleveland, Ohio, most of whom had been doctoral advisees of Ansel, the senior author, at some time. Some of them are present in this textbook as chapter authors (as noted in their biographical sketches). For a time we gathered together monthly, and then on an irregular basis, to support each other's creative potential and writing spirit. Part of the fun in our gathering was that we rotated meetings from home to home and the host and/or hostess provided dinner or luncheon. Scrumptiously speaking, at some meetings there was more eating than writing. Interestingly, four books, two doctoral dissertations, some chapters in books, and several journal articles have emerged in 4 years since our inception, although not all of them were on Gestalt therapy.

The spirit of the writers' group caught hold of Sarah Toman during our early gatherings, and she presented a fantastic idea of creating a textbook for novices entering the world of Gestalt. At that time, she was proposing a new Advanced Counseling Theories course on Gestalt therapy for doctoral students at Cleveland State University and was in the Post-Graduate Training Program at the Gestalt Institute of Cleveland. This idea struck a particular note with me, Ansel, as I had been encouraged numerous times over the past three decades of teaching Gestalt therapy to use my course syllabi, lecture notes, class handouts, experiential activities, and other class materials to write an academically oriented textbook on Gestalt therapy. Support and encouragement from the writers' group naturally led to the idea's taking form and moving toward the creation of this "new gestalt"—the coming together of all the pieces where the whole is greater than and different from the sum of its parts—and, for us, truly an "aha" experience.

We would like to share some of the formative processes of creating this textbook using the Gestalt cycle of experience in Figure P.1. This diagram attempts to depict the flow of human processes of person-environment contact and the various Gestalt resistance processes that affect the various phases of contact. In the chapters that follow, this person-environment contacting process will be referred to as the cycle of experience, the Gestalt contact cycle, the Gestalt continuum of experience, and the Gestalt homeostasis cycle by the different authors. It is unfortunate that human contact is so poorly represented in one-dimensional figures such as this, for there is always much more going on in our moment-to-moment interactions than mere words and arrows can portray.

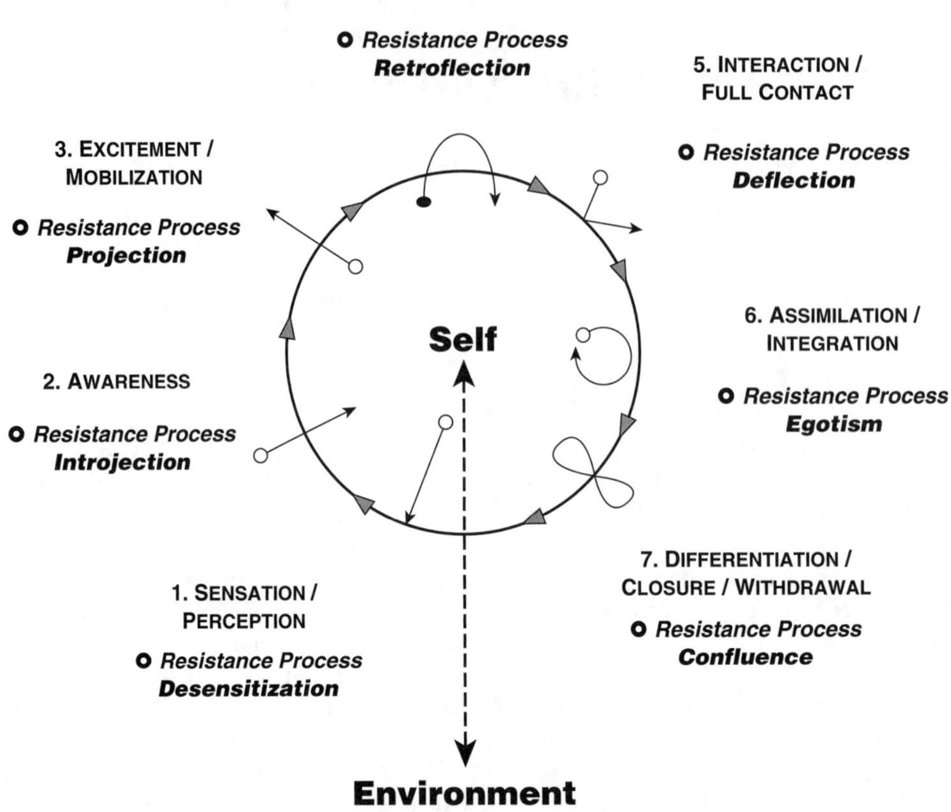

Figure P.1: Gestalt Cycle of Experience. This diagram depicts the primary "contacting" and "interrupting/resisting" processes a person uses in creatively adjusting and balancing personalized contact with her/his environment. It is an attempt to show what the potential interactive functions are at one's contact boundary—understanding that affect and cognition interface continuously as part of the ongoing parallel decision-making process.

Given the positive conditions in our "field"—which included the necessary internal, external, and interactive supports—the idea for the book flowed into and through the developmental phases of the cycle of experience. Beginning with <u>Sensation and Perception</u> (Position 1 in the figure), follow the arrows (→) to see how we moved from <u>Interested Awareness</u> *(great idea)* to → <u>Mobilization of Energy</u> *(excitement about writing and submitting a proposal to our potential textbook publisher)* to → <u>Encounter</u> *(meetings to design and outline possibilities)* to → <u>Action</u> *(preparing and sending a prospectus to the publisher)* to → <u>Interaction</u> (*creating dialogue with the publisher*) to → <u>Full and Immediate Contact</u> (*reaching agreement and signing the contract with Sage Publications*) to → <u>Assimilation, Synthesis,</u>

and Integration (*following through with the contractual terms and contacting prospective chapter authors and dialoguers*), which then led to Differentiation, New Perceptions, Sensations, and Awarenesses that have sustained us in various stages of Interaction → Contact → Assimilation → Integration → Differentiation → Closure → and Withdrawal. The book you hold in your hands is this well-formed "gestalt."

ABOUT THE INTENDED AUDIENCES: STUDENTS AND TEACHERS

Textbooks are intended for students and the faculty members who are charged with teaching them. We expect the audience for this textbook to be adult students, mostly professionals or people preparing for the helping professions who are novices to Gestalt therapy. It seems natural that students reading this book will have a strong desire to advance their understanding and application of Gestalt history, theory, and practice. So that the book may be valued by faculty members as well as by their students, we have written educational components for each chapter—Review Questions and Experiential Pedagogical Activities—not included in other Gestalt books.

ABOUT THE CHAPTER AUTHORS

We selected the chapter authors for their experience and knowledge of the theories and methods pertaining to each chapter's content. We were exceedingly pleased with the responses and encouragement we received from our invitations. The authors come from three continents, Europe, America, and Australia. Their level of knowledge, experience, and expertise is extensive, as the list includes the editors-in-chief of four Gestalt therapy journals, 14 present or former officers of Gestalt professional associations in Europe, Australia, and America, and several key faculty members from Gestalt institutes and training programs around the world. In addition to presenting photographs of the authors at the beginning of each chapter, we have provided brief biographical sketches. This follows the attempt of Gestalt pedagogy and therapy to provide various means of being in fuller contact (in this case with the authors and their dialogue respondents) by having a visual image and knowledge of some of their life experiences as you read their creations. We hope this adds to your experience of reading and favorably influences your learning process.

ABOUT THE DIALOGUE RESPONDENTS

One of the unique features of this textbook is the inclusion of dialogue respondents for each chapter. For this feature, we invited prominent Gestalt therapists and Gestalt therapy educators to dialogue with each chapter author. As with our invitations to the authors, the positive responses from those we invited to dialogue were positive and encouraging. In fact, so many folks volunteered that we didn't have enough room/chapters in our book for all their ideas.

Our goal in creating this feature was, first, to model Gestalt's valuing of different views by adding alternative voices. It is generally acknowledged in Gestalt circles that where two or more Gestalt therapists are gathered together there will be at least two different opinions about the same topic. Second, we wanted to "practice/demonstrate what we preach"—namely, the importance of dialogue in Gestalt therapy. The dialoguer was requested to read the assigned chapter, keeping in mind that his or her views on the subject might converge with, add to, or differ from the author's. After the dialoguer read the chapter, he or she was asked to contact the author and proceed with a "conversation" via phone or e-mail or in person. To our surprise, the dialoguers for three chapters were able to meet face-to-face with the authors. We hope you, the reader, will appreciate—and in some cases be challenged by—their comments, questions, and "alternative voices."

ABOUT THE EDITORS

Ansel Woldt is an Emeritus Professor at Kent State University and is in private practice as a psychologist in Kent, Ohio. He is a Diplomate in the American Psychotherapy Association and is recognized as the Gestalt Archivist by the Gestalt community. In over three decades as a Professor of Counseling Psychology and Counselor Education, he regularly taught graduate courses in Gestalt therapy. He also directed the doctoral dissertations for more than 100 students, over 74 of whom were Gestalt therapists who researched various aspects of Gestalt therapy; eight of them contributed to this textbook. His Gestalt education began in the 3-year Post-Graduate Program with the original faculty at the Gestalt Institute of Cleveland from 1970 to 1973, when the director of training was Erving Polster, the executive director was Bill Warner, and the faculty was composed of first-generation Gestalt therapists.

With a sincere interest in obtaining and preserving the history of Gestalt therapy, Ansel provided the leadership in creating the Gestalt Therapy Archives, featuring the Frederick and Laura Perls' Special Collection, which contains original manuscripts, documents, tapes, photographs, films, and so forth of the history of Gestalt therapy. He continues to be the collector for the archives, which are located in the Kent State University Library. Having been a regular participant and often a presenter at the annual Gestalt Journal Conferences, he encouraged the formation of a stronger Gestalt community by actively participating in town meetings and preconference and postconference sessions geared toward developing a Gestalt therapy association. He became the founding secretary and incorporating officer of the Association for the Advancement of Gestalt Therapy (AAGT) and has served continuously as an officer, currently as archivist/historian and continuing education officer. He has also been an associate editor of the *Gestalt Review* since its inception.

Sarah Toman is an associate Professor in the counseling program at Cleveland State University's College of Education, where she teaches graduate-level counseling and human growth and development courses, supervises counseling practicums and internships, and mentors doctoral students. She brings to the profession of psychology and psychotherapy a wealth of expertise from her research and writing in the area of vocational psychology. Sarah is a graduate of the Gestalt Institute of Cleveland's Post-Graduate Training Program and their specialty track in Child and Adolescent Therapy. She is a licensed psychologist in private practice in Medina, Ohio. During her graduate studies, she was Ansel Woldt's graduate research assistant and advisee. She is a founding member of the Kent Gestalt Writers Group, has participated in the Gestalt International Study Center's "Cape Cod Gestalt Writers Group," and has numerous textbook chapters and journal publications in the areas of career development, career counseling, and recently Gestalt therapy. She has served as membership co-chair and secretary of the Association for the Advancement of Gestalt Therapy, research chair of the National Career Development Association, and training consultant with National Career Assessment Services, Inc.

ABOUT THE FORMAT AND USING THIS TEXTBOOK

The primary purpose of this textbook is to provide an introduction to the history and fundamental concepts of Gestalt therapy along with the applications of and practices using these concepts in selected settings or with certain client systems. We envisioned that most of the readers would be faculty members and adult students who would be novices in the arena of the helping professions.

Of course, to achieve a satisfactory learning experience necessitates a secondary purpose, namely to recommend to faculty members what we believe to be instructional methods consistent with the philosophy and methodologies of Gestalt therapy. More than in teaching any other psychotherapeutic approach, in teaching Gestalt therapy it is important to "practice what we preach." By this we call for more than an academic familiarity with the information in the text. We urge a synthesis, integration, and application of a number of philosophical and methodological principles that guide Gestalt therapists, such as the following:

- Ongoing consideration and focusing on the "here-and-now" experience in the classroom, learning group, supervision, or mentoring setting.
- Ongoing contact with the "what and how" of the educational experiences of the students and faculty.
- Recognition of the importance of "experiencing" both theory and methods beyond reading, and far beyond memorizing, by incorporating "experiential activities" (we have identified some at the end of each chapter) that often provide the necessary support to move from a learning activity to a classroom experiment.
- Practice applying the "paradoxical theory of change" in a variety of ways so that students experience the real value inherent in Gestalt therapy.
- Creation of a learning environment that honors the "authentic encounter" of faculty with students and demonstrates the values inherent in both "I-It" and "I-Thou" relating.
- Use of the Gestalt cycle of experience or similar models in assessing and facilitating the transformational processes essential to "true" learning. This is where one learns how to flow along—or becomes aware of how one interrupts—one's experiential learning continuum that moves from sensation and perception to closure, differentiation, and withdrawal. It is especially valuable to use this model for students who experience "blocks" to their concentration and habitual interruptions in their attempts at studying and learning.
- Use of "process-oriented," "qualitative," and "formative" assessment, whereby feedback about behavior and functionality is valued more than statistically based evaluative and judgmental assessment. For example, in addition to exploring "what" students have learned in course "examinations," we attempt to help them look beyond the content and

explore their process of test taking—using Gestalt perspectives to focus on such things as examination anxiety, introjective test-taking habits, and retroflective exam behaviors.

To assist in achieving these objectives, we have attempted to design this textbook in a "Gestalt manner"—focusing on variables associated with good figure formation, particularly the contacting principles of awareness, mobilization, encounter, full contact, synthesis, assimilation, and integration. Our attempts to model the contacting processes central in Gestalt therapy theory in a manuscript may be feeble, but they are honest. By including such things as photographs of the contributors in the chapter headings, we hope that you, the reader, have more than the authors' words to associate with your new learnings or, if the learnings are not new, that you have fresh images to connect to previous learnings. Ansel's and Sarah's creation of experiential activities and review questions for every chapter is another effort to increase awareness and retention at a more meaningful level of conceptualization than mere words can convey.

Another feature of this textbook is the comprehensive reference list. A more traditional bibliography typically lists only those references cited in the book. Instead, we have chosen to provide a comprehensive bibliography by adding to the textbook citations all major books written in English on Gestalt therapy and other works that we have found useful for students, trainees, researchers, and other interested professionals. We were tempted to create another list of doctoral dissertations and master's theses that deal in part or whole with Gestalt therapy because copies of most of them are in a research collection at Kent State University Library. However, because that collection now numbers over 350, we decided it was too voluminous to include here. If it is impossible to personally visit the library, much can be discovered electronically about the kinds of books and research materials that have been accumulated at Kent State University by accessing the Web site www.kent.edu, then clicking on "Library and Media Services," then clicking on "Kent Link," and, under "Subject," typing in "Gestalt therapy." In addition to the general research holdings, there is a considerable collection of original manuscripts, books, audiotapes, videotapes, films, and other materials in the Library Archives and Special Collections, the listings of which are accessible at http://speccoll.library.kent.edu/other/gestalt.html.

We wish you interesting reading and experiencing of this new and unique introduction to Gestalt therapy.

Pre-Text

Gestalt Pedagogy: Creating the Field for Teaching and Learning

Ansel L. Woldt

Dialogue Respondent: Sarah M. Toman

INTRODUCTION

Pedagogy is an interesting word. Often, when I've used it, people ask, "Ped—? What—what's pedagogy?" When some hear the word, they think I'm referring to the medical treatment of foot disorders, mistaking it for *podiatry.* Well, I am not referring to the reparation of flat feet and bunions; instead, I use this "P" word to refer to what I consider it takes to be a truly remarkable educator. It is my desire to raise the awareness of pedagogy, what we do as teachers to benefit those developing as Gestalt practitioners. Ultimately, I hope that this textbook will reach Gestalt educators as well as students preparing to become Gestalt practitioners. At times when you are reading this Pre-Text, I will switch between addressing Gestalt teachers and students. I hope this is beneficial to both.

Authenticity, optimism, holism, health, and trust are important principles to consider when we approach teaching and learning from the perspective of Gestalt therapy theory. Like organismic self-regulation, learning is (optimally) a self-regulating process. In accordance with Gestalt therapy theory, Gestalt teaching and training (pedagogy) is based on the belief that people are by nature health seeking. We are more prone to respond positively to an "invitation to learn" than an "order" to learn. Learning from desire and internal motivating forces is far superior to mandated learning that is based on fear. Gestalt pedagogy, then, involves a statement of trust in the inherent ability of the organism/student to know his or her own needs, the way to go about satisfying these needs, and the order in which they should be dealt with. Like dialogical contact and experimental engagement of Gestalt therapists with clients, authentic Gestalt pedagogy is a trust-based endeavor that involves believing that the process will support the investigative procedure and that learning will occur.

To give a brief orientation to Gestalt therapy, for the sake of clarifying what we mean by "authentic Gestalt pedagogy," I quote Laura Perls from her "Comments on the New Directions" (of Gestalt therapy) (1976):

> The *actual experience* of any present situation does not need to be explained or interpreted; it can be directly contacted, felt and described here and now. Gestalt therapy deals with the obvious, with what is *immediately* available to the awareness of client or therapist and can be shared and expanded in the actual ongoing communication. The aim of Gestalt therapy is the *awareness continuum,* the freely ongoing gestalt formation where what is of greatest concern and interest to the organism, the relationship, the group or society becomes Gestalt, comes into the foreground where it can be fully experienced and coped with (acknowledged, worked through, sorted out, changed, disposed of, etc.) so that then it can melt into the background (be forgotten or assimilated and integrated) and leave the foreground free for the next relevant gestalt. (pp. 221–222, italics in original)

Sarah and I have both been (and still are) classroom teachers, counselors, psychologists, and professors of counseling psychology and counselor education. Our interest in Gestalt pedagogy is further supported by our experience in clinical supervision and consultation. I have often joked about "professing," "teaching," and "training." I put these three instructional functions in quotation marks because, by their very nature, they create contention and resistance from my perspective as Gestalt theorist and professional educator. According to Merriam-Webster (1991), to profess is "to declare in words or appearances only; . . . to practice or claim to be versed in a calling or profession" (p. 939), whereas "teaching applies to any manner of imparting information . . . or skill so that others may learn; instructing suggests methodical or formal teaching; . . . [and] training stresses instruction and drill with a specific end in view; to direct the growth of by bending, pruning, and tying; to form by instruction, discipline, or drill" (pp. 1209, 1251). When I think of training, my thoughts go to obedience classes for dogs, my parents' comments about the elephants and lions in Barnum and Bailey's circus being "so well trained," and visions of experimental psychology labs where my experimental psychology friends trained pigeons and primates, analyzing S-R (stimulus-response) data. I do not like to think of Gestalt education in these behavioristic terms. The words *training, trainer,* and *trainee,* so commonly used among Gestalt institute faculties, imply an authoritarian, "topdog–bottom dog" relationship between teachers and students and an assumption that students are "receptacles of knowledge." I believe that the terms *education, educate,* and *pedagogy* more closely approximate the values and processes of Gestalt therapy. According to Webster's dictionary (1991), "pedagogy is the art, science or profession of education" (p. 866), and "*educate* implies attempting to bring out latent capabilities" (p. 1209).

Like Gestalt therapy, Gestalt pedagogy is at least as much of an art as it is a science. In working with students, it has always been important to me to let them know my interest in offering them a learning experience that supports their developing a solid foundation in Gestalt therapy theory and clinical skills that are applicable to counseling and psychotherapy. To best understand and integrate the Gestalt approach, it is important for students to experience *in vivo* both the Gestalt therapy process and Gestalt methods of processing.

A general goal of Gestalt therapy education is to facilitate and support students to experience integrity in their personal and professional development, and from Gestalt's holistic perspective personal and professional development are inseparable. To accomplish this goal, we *invite* students to learn—which necessitates making contact with them and engaging them at our contact boundary. We attempt to "meet them where they are," not where we may want them to be or wish they could be. It has been our experience that treating students with the same kind of respect we show clients effectively engages them in a desire to learn.

We invite students to approach the Gestalt learning process with a fresh attitude about themselves as learners. They are responsible for their learning. By doing this, we make the educational experience a shared venture—it becomes "our" class. The invitation to experiment with Gestalt ways of learning helps students attune themselves to experiential processes while simultaneously learning Gestalt methods and knowledge of theory, practice, and ethics of the therapeutic relationship. Approaching students in this positive manner—with an invitation to learn—has typically yielded greater awareness, lively interest, enhanced motivation, authentic involvement, energized action, and significantly increased reading and engagement in outside learning activities. It creates a community atmosphere in the classroom without the traditional academic competitiveness, as well as integration of Gestalt principles with other therapeutic models.

Metaphorically, the invitation is for students to come to the table to dine, though we realize we cannot make them eat. Some will dive in, gobble up everything on the table, and go to the cupboard for more, never seeming to have their appetites satisfied. Others will nibble a bit here and there, leave some on their plate, swallow what tastes right, and spit out what doesn't taste right. Using this metaphor in class, I introduce students to the Gestalt lexicon (taken from psychoanalytic theory) by referring to the "introjective processes" that traditional approaches to teaching employ, expecting students to introject whatever the teacher thinks is important for them to learn. Introjection is a process by which ideas, like unchewed or underchewed food, are swallowed whole. Instead, the Gestalt method attempts to encourage, stimulate, model, process, attend, facilitate, self-disclose, feel, process, and intentionally create ambiguity by using paradox and frustration as growth-producing invitations to learning.

THE EXPERIENTIAL APPROACH TO TEACHING/LEARNING

In Gestalt circles, *experience, experiential,* and *experiment* are cherished words. We believe that "if a picture is worth a thousand words, an experience is worth a thousand pictures." To facilitate optimal learning, it is wise to create an experiential activity for every major (and minor) concept and application in Gestalt theory and methods. For example, I bring experiential learning into the Gestalt classroom by regularly employing paradox as a way to motivate students to read, by giving them *antiassignments.* Following is an excerpt from my Gestalt Therapy Syllabus that provides a paradoxical orientation to reading for the graduate course I have taught since 1970:

> I'd like to facilitate your introduction to Gestalt Therapy Literature, Philosophy, History, Principles, Methods, and Intervention Techniques by encouraging you to read a lot and engage actively in class activities, therapy demonstrations, and a variety of Gestalt-based learning experiences. To do this, I address your inner-self with an *antiassignment.* From

my years of teaching and mentoring graduate students, I know that reading assignments often engage you in a "top-dog versus bottom-dog" dialogue (Gestalt terminology *à la* Fritz Perls), internal argumentation, and even conflict as you go about addressing suggested readings. Much, if not most, of our class activity will be approached without exact reading assignments; however, you obviously will need to read in order to understand and participate in this class in a meaningful way. Therefore, I want you to begin by reading what *catches your eye,* what you are *curious about,* what *piques your interest,* what seems to *stand out from the background,* what you are *motivated to look at,* what you *feel like exploring,* what *your heart desires,* and what you *intuitively are drawn to, with the possibility that it may address or touch upon some unfinished business in your life.* If you find yourself not wanting to read, I suggest you experiment with delving into your resistance at the moment of awareness. In fact, you might consciously work at avoiding the book. If you engage in this experiment, pay attention to your inner processes and be willing to share your experiences with the class. In case you don't recognize it, this is a paradoxical approach to reading and learning—the principal approach to change in Gestalt therapy. Therefore, my real assignment for you, in this antiassignment, is to explore what it is like to not read assignments or things you are told you "should read." Then bring your reactions to this *antiassignment* to class for discussion. (Woldt, 2003, p. 2)

DIALOGUE AND ALTERNATIVE VOICES IN GESTALT EDUCATION

One fundamental pedagogical approach to model in a class dedicated to Gestalt theory and practice is dialogue. Understanding the role of dialogue in Gestalt therapy necessitates a basic orientation to the role of the therapist. In an early commentary from the *Counseling Psychologist* about the role of the therapist in Gestalt therapy, Lawrence Levin and Irma Lee Shepherd (1974) stated,

> Gestalt therapists are person/therapists who bring the full impact of their personality into the therapy room. They must be able and willing to encounter the other person(s) in the present—directly, honestly and spontaneously. Basically, the role of the Gestalt therapist is an alive, active, exciting, creative therapist who views the present therapy situation and interaction as the basis for change and experience. Therapy is seen as a microcosm of everyday life as it is the interaction, person to person, which forms the basis for and process through which therapeutic change occurs. Fritz Perls, among his many succinct definitions of Gestalt therapy, described the process as "I and Thou—Here and Now." . . . The role of the Gestalt therapist is to facilitate the development of self-support goals that are meaningful for the patient, and to find ways of working toward these goals. (p. 27)

One of the most prominent persons in the Gestalt community to have addressed the importance of dialogue is Lynne Jacobs (1989), who wrote,

> *Dialogic Relation*—The elements of what Buber calls "genuine dialogue"—the I-Thou *process* as it occurs between human beings—are (1) presence, (2) genuine and unreserved communication, and (3) inclusion. In therapy, these conditions become the prerequisites for a dialogic patient-therapist relationship.

Presence—The most basic element, and the most difficult, is *presence,* as opposed to seeming. One is present when one does not try to influence the other to see oneself only according to one's self image. . . . Presence cannot be legislated. . . . Where presence is difficult, many Gestalt therapists take the time to explore what their difficulty is, in order to foster greater ability to be present. Presence involves bringing the fullness of oneself to the interaction. Therapists must be willing to allow themselves to be touched and moved by the patient. . . . Being present also means being willing to be both power*ful* and power*less.* At crucial times the loving attitude of the therapist seems to provide an experience of grace for the patient. But ultimately the therapist is powerless to *change* the patient, and sometimes the pain of wanting to make the patient's life better but being powerless to do so is keenly felt. The therapist who is present brings this pain too to the meeting.

Genuine and Unreserved Communication—A corollary of this principle of presence is the requirement that one's participation in the dialogue be *genuine and unreserved.* . . . What must be "unreserved" is the person's willingness to be honestly involved, and to say what one believes *will* serve to create conditions for dialogue, or further the on-going dialogue, even if one is fearful of how they will be received. Unreserved communication does not preclude silence, but the silence must be a genuine responding and not based on protecting oneself or the other from one's self-expression. One must assume willing responsibility for the unreserved expression of that which occurs to one in the process of the dialogue. . . . [U]nreserved communication stemming from the therapist's authentic presence, conforms to the special circumstances of the therapy relationship. The need for unreserved communication is not a license for impulsive behavior; communication must be relevant to the task at hand. . . . Gestalt therapists do not confine themselves to a limited range of responses so

SARAH: Ansel, I really like your idea about including within each chapter some dialogue, or "conversations," between the chapter authors and others, as a way to model dialogue, rather than merely describing the dialogic process.

ANSEL: I agree, Sarah, this idea adds a dimension to our book that I've never seen or experienced in other books—especially textbooks. Your thoughts about this being a way to demonstrate Gestalt's inclusion of and valuing "different voices" have certainly come to life in reading the dialogue between some of our authors and dialoguers.

SARAH: Most textbook and academic journal readers are probably familiar with including alternative viewpoints as responses, but that style does not contain the potential for (a) presence, (b) genuine and unreserved communication, and (c) inclusion as described by Lynne Jacobs. I hope our authors and dialoguers experienced some of those notions during their "conversation" with each other.

ANSEL: Having worked with you on editing the dialogues between the authors and dialoguers, it's so interesting to see how Lynne Jacobs's description of dialogue is observable in the breadth of expressions throughout these chapters. It's pretty amazing how direct and honest our contributors were—whether complimentary or critical—and their integrity shows through in dialogue as we experience their true grit as Gestalt therapists.

SARAH: Well, not only their integrity but also their respect for each other and each other's viewpoints. In more academic-style responses, it often seems as if one writer is convinced that his or her view is the one and only "right" view, while in dialogue the dialoguers consider and take in multiple viewpoints—so fundamental to Gestalt ways of thinking and being.

that a transference can develop, as in the more traditional psychodynamic therapies. They are free to laugh and cry, to dance, yell, or sit quietly. . . . expect[ing] that by being present, and by communicating genuinely, the therapist will influence the patient. . . . *The artistry is in balancing one's presence in relation to the needs of the patient.* The paradox, that healing through meeting exposes what is possibly unhealed in the self, is only one of many paradoxes of therapy.

Inclusion and Confirmation—[Inclusion] is a concrete imagining of the reality of the other, in oneself, while still retaining one's own self-identity. In dialogue, there is a special insight or illumination in the personally experienced confirmation of oneself by another. Confirmation means that one is apprehended and acknowledged in one's whole being (Buber, 1965b). The act of confirmation requires that one enter into the phenomenological world of the other without judgment, while still knowing one's own being. . . . Gestalt therapy tends to focus on the *experiencing process,* or *how* one is experiencing. . . . [T]his difference stems from the Gestalt therapy emphasis on the awareness process. . . . The assumption is that patients can learn to deal with *what* they are experiencing, if they can learn *how* they experience, and *how* they interfere with their own experience. . . . Patients can be assisted in their attempts to enter dialogue by increasing awareness of their defensive structures. . . . The experience of being "made present," or included, in the eyes of another, has powerful healing potential in and of itself. . . . It is also an event which can contribute powerfully to restoring a derailed self-regulating process. . . . Patients use manipulative behavior when they do not have faith in their own processes of self-regulation. [T]he behavior might be described as a frightened attempt to get a need met. . . . [P]racticing inclusion while also confronting requires patience and confidence in the elasticity of one's own boundaries. . . .

ANSEL: As we're dialoguing about dialogue, I'm thinking back to a workshop I had with Rich Hycner in the 1980s while he was in the final stages of completing his manuscript for *Between Person and Person: Toward a Dialogical Psychotherapy* (1991). He was so excited about it and brought various aspects of it to life in an experiential-dialogical format—taking us through a range of "I-It" and "I-Thou" dyadic activities with a partner. Three things that I've remembered ever since then and used often in my classes and workshops are (a) that true healing in psychotherapy is in the "hyphen," that little dash ("-") in "I-Thou"; (b) that psychotherapy is a "paradoxical profession," by which he meant we are constantly fraught with tension between opposing polarities such as artist versus scientist, subjective versus objective presence with clients, personal versus professional presence, philosophical versus practical, and so forth; and (c) leaving us with this quote from Martin Buber (1923/1958) that Rich had us repeat five times, each time with the emphasis on a different word: "All real living is meeting" (p. 11). It was a very memorable learning experience for me, to say the least. I just became cognizant of the pedagogical awareness, that if it wasn't memorable it wouldn't have been learned and if it wasn't a learning experience it wouldn't be memorable.

SARAH: I can only hope that those using this textbook get half that much from our efforts and find our contact through this medium to create a memorable learning experience.

ANSEL: Amen and Hallelujah, Sarah! However, before signing off from this interchange, I want to add one last tribute or homage in our dialogue—in part to honor the little-known authors of another psychotherapy textbook that somehow found its way to me early in my career and became a reference point for future learning and action. Given their knowledge of therapeutic processes, I'm amazed never to have seen *Psychotherapy*

Dialogic Attitude—The dialogic attitude of the therapist is different from the dialogic relations of friendship: the dialogic assumed by the one—teacher or therapist—who is voluntarily engaged in furthering the learning of the other; and while the friendship is defined by fully mutual confirmation, the dialogic attitude of the therapist [or teacher] can be assumed independent of the inclinations of the patient [or student]. When both persons assume a dialogic attitude, then the fully mutual dialogic relation can accrue; but one can appreciate another in dialogue without mutuality. . . . The dialogic attitude is an expression of the latency of I-Thou; thus, the I-It phase . . . is embedded in the process that permits the possibility of the I-Thou moment between the two people. . . . Gestalt therapists do not demand that patients enter into such a relationship. They can only be present and authentic, and through the dialogic attitude refuse to forsake either their own "I" or the potential "I" of the other, while maintaining respect for the actuality of the other. (pp. 40–52, italics in original)

We hope this challenging oration about dialogue by the esteemed Gestalt therapist and theorist Lynne Jacobs serves to introduce you, the reader, to the dialogue box model employed throughout our book. The dialogue box for this introduction contains the conversational dialogue between my co-editor, Sarah Toman, and me about this very topic—dialogue.

GESTALT/CONFLUENT EDUCATION: A PEDAGOGICAL MODEL

Any discussion of Gestalt pedagogy would be remiss not to include the concept of "confluent education," which is consonant with the name of George Isaac Brown. In one of his writings, with the catchy title "Human Is As Confluent Does" (1975), he stated,

From the Center: A Humanistic View of Change and of Growth, by Rahe Corlis and Peter Rabe (1969), quoted or appearing as a reference in any readings of Gestalt, experiential, or other humanistic therapies. I loved their here-and-now approach and their view of change. For the students of counseling and psychotherapy who read our book, I'd like them to know something I learned when I was close to where these students are in their preparation, so I quote from Corlis and Rabe:

> How permanent is the change that occurs in therapy? . . . We don't know. . . . The only change which we want to effect in the exercise of psychotherapy is the ability to be able to change. . . . We want the patient to have his senses back, his feelings, and his muscle. We want him to have all of himself available once again, so that he can advance or retreat by his choice alone. . . . The work of becoming is the work of being alive. I cannot decide to take a deep breath and inhale once and for all. Instead there is the rhythm of breath, the rhythm of waking and sleeping, the rhythm of feelings that come forward and retreat. . . . We do not say that center is good and that periphery is bad. We say that to get stuck in either is arrhythmic and therefore not healthy. When we are well, we know our rhythm and move with it. Then we are the rhythm, we are center and periphery and the motion from one to the other is like the living breath. (pp. 120–121)

And one more sentence from them: "I had thought that my therapist would help me find my real self. Instead, I have found myself real" (Corlis & Rabe, 1969, p. 130). This reminds me of the dialogue between Skin Horse and the Velveteen Rabbit in one of my favorite stories (Bianco, 1994):

> "What is real?" asked the Rabbit one day. . . . "Does it mean having things that buzz inside you and a stick-out handle?"

> Confluent education is essentially the synthesis of the affective domain (feelings, emotions, attitudes, and values) and the cognitive domain (the intellect and the activity of the mind in knowing). Confluent education, however, also includes learning experiences wherein may exist an interplay between affectivity and cognition, where frustration and tension in appropriate degrees resulting from this interplay are seen as valued conditions, directly related to healthy growth and development. The unending interaction of self with universe inevitably produces an interplay sequence of (1) conflict, (2) confrontation, (3) persistence, and (4) some degree of resolution or finishing up. It is through this interaction that we grow, whether the self-universe interaction be immediate or an outgrowth of subsequent recollection and reflection. Interplay as a process may be subsumed under the taxonomical umbrella of integration. The description of confluent education always connotes a smooth and pleasurable series of lovely learning experiences where affective experience is interjected to add positive excitement to cognitive learning. The putting together of the affective and the cognitive through conscious teaching acts is an attempt to make both the educational process and its product, the student, more human. (p. 101)

There was a groundswell of activity throughout North America the 1960s and 1970s that focused on humanizing education by approaching teaching as the facilitation of learning from a holistic/gestalt perspective. As many have noted, this was the heyday of the human potential movement and the movement for humanizing the schools. During that time period, I constructed a handout as a reading list (see Table P-T.1) that contained the names of the authors and titles of several notable books (Woldt, 1980). In most cases it is self-evident from the titles of the books how they interfaced with and influenced Gestalt/confluent educators and education, as well as the reverse—being influenced *by* Gestalt therapy and confluent education.

> "Real isn't how you are made," said the Skin Horse. "It's a thing that happens to you. When a child loves you for a long, long time, not just to play with, but REALLY loves you, then you become Real." . . . "Does it happen all at once, like being wound up," he asked, "or bit by bit?" . . . "It doesn't happen all at once," said Skin Horse. "You become. It takes a long time. That's why it doesn't happen to people who break easily, or have sharp edges, or who have to be carefully kept. Generally, by the time you are Real, most of your hair has been loved off, and your eyes drop out and you get loose in the joints and very shabby. But these things don't matter at all, because once you are Real you can't be ugly, except to people who don't understand." "I suppose you are Real?" said the Rabbit. And then he wished he had not said it, for he thought the Skin Horse might be sensitive. But the Skin Horse only smiled. "The Boy's Uncle made me Real," he said. "That was a great many years ago; but once you are real you can't become unreal again. It lasts for always." (pp. 10–11)

In closing this dialogue, I want to thank you, Sarah—what a wonderful friend to have found yet another way to help me find myself "real." Though some days I feel shabby and loose in the joints, like Skin Horse, I feel loved and honored by you and can't become unreal again. It has been a true pleasure to have this time together as the co-editor and author of this loving piece of work and play. I am honored to share this space and place with you.

Table P-T.1 Books That Influenced and/or Were Influenced by Gestalt/Confluent Education

Year	Author/Editor(s)	Title of Publication
1951	Frederick Perls, Ralph Hefferline, & Paul Goodman	*Gestalt Therapy: Excitement and Growth in the Human Personality*
1951	Carl Rogers	*Client-Centered Therapy*
1952	Viktor Lowenfeld	*Creative and Mental Growth*
1953	Ruth Strang	*The Role of the Teacher in Personnel Work*
1953	Harry Stack Sullivan	*The Interpersonal Theory of Psychiatry*
1954	Carl Rogers & Rosalind Dymond (Eds.)	*Psychotherapy and Personality Change*
1954	Vivian Ross	*Handbook for Homeroom Guidance*
1955	Thomas Gordon	*Group Centered Leadership*
1955	George Kelly	*The Psychology of Personal Constructs*
1956	Clark Moustakas	*The Teacher and the Child*
1956	Henry Otto	*Social Education in Elementary Schools*
1957	Rudolph Dreikurs	*Psychology in the Classroom*
1958	Martin Buber	*I and Thou*
1959	Jacob Moreno	*Psychodrama: Foundations of Psychotherapy*
1960	Don Radler	*Success Through Play: How to Prepare Your Child for School Achievement and Enjoy It*
1961	Carl Rogers	*On Becoming a Person*
1962	Arthur Combs	*Perceiving, Behaving, Becoming*
1962	Eugene Gendlen	*Experiencing and the Creation of Meaning*
1963	Victor Frankl	*Man's Search for Meaning*
1963	Viola Spolin	*Improvisation for the Theatre*
1963	Laura Huxley	*You Are Not the Target*
1964	John Holt	*How Children Fail*
1964	Sydney Jourard	*The Transparent Self*
1964	Leland Bradford, Jack Gibb, & Ken Benne (Eds.)	*T-Group Theory and Laboratory Method: Innovation in Re-education*
1964	Virginia Axline	*Dibs: In Search of Self*
1965	Ruth Strang	*Helping Your Child Develop His Potential*
1965	Haim Ginnot	*Between Parent and Child: New Solutions to Old Problems*

(Continued)

Table P-T.1 (Continued)

Year	Author/Editor(s)	Title of Publication
1966	L. Raths, M. Harman, & S. Simon	*Values and Teaching: Working With Values in the Classroom*
1966	Michael Polanyi	*The Tacit Dimension*
1967	James Bugental	*Challenges of Humanistic Psychology*
1967	William Schutz	*Joy: Expanding Human Awareness*
1967	Richard De Mille	*Put Your Mother on the Ceiling: Children's Imagination Games*
1968	Carl Rogers	*Freedom to Learn*
1968	Abraham Maslow	*Toward a Psychology of Being*
1968	Herb Otto & John Mann	*Ways of Growth: Approaches to Expanding Human Awareness*
1968	George Leonard	*Education and Ecstasy*
1968	Bernard Gunther	*Sense Relaxation: Below Your Mind*
1968	Richard Jones	*Fantasy and Feeling in Education*
1968	Bob Rosenthal & Lenore Jacobson	*Pygmalion in the Classroom: Teacher Expectation and Pupils' Intellectual Development*
1969	Fritz Perls	*Gestalt Therapy Verbatim*
1969	Violet Oaklander	*Windows to Our Children: A Gestalt Therapy Approach to Children and Adolescents*
1969	Janet Lederman	*Anger and the Rocking Chair*
1969	William Glasser	*Schools Without Failure*
1969	Neil Postman & Charles Weingartner	*Teaching as a Subversive Activity*
1970	Joen Fagan & Irma Lee Shepherd (Eds.)	*Gestalt Therapy Now*
1970	Terry Borton	*Reach, Touch and Teach: Student Concerns and Process Education*
1970	Gerald Weinstein & Mario Fantini (Eds.)	*Toward Humanistic Education: A Curriculum of Affect*
1970	Gerald Egan	*Encounter: Group Processes for Interpersonal Growth*
1970	Kenneth Koch	*Wishes, Lies and Dreams*

Table P-T.1 (Continued)

Year	Author/Editor(s)	Title of Publication
1971	George I. Brown	*Human Teaching for Human Learning: An Introduction to Confluent Education*
1971	Harold Lyon	*Learning to Feel—Feeling to Learn*
1971	Abraham Maslow	*The Farther Reaches of Human Nature*
1971	Roberto Assagioli	*Psychosynthesis*
1971	June Shane, Harold Shane, Robert Gibson, & Paul Munger	*Guiding Human Development: The Counselor and the Teacher in the Elementary School*
1971	Albert Cullum	*The Geranium on the Window Sill Just Died, but Teacher You Went Right On*
1972	Virginia Satir	*Peoplemaking*
1972	Henry Cole	*Process Education*
1972	Moshe Feldenkrais	*Awareness Through Movement*
1972	Mary Greer & Bonnie Rubinstein	*Will the Real Teacher Please Stand Up?*
1972	Elizabeth Hunter	*Encounter in the Classroom: New Ways of Teaching*
1973	Janie Ryne	*The Gestalt Art Experience*
1973	Erving Polster & Miriam Polster	*Gestalt Therapy Integrated: Contours of Theory and Practice*
1973	Louis Rubin	*Facts and Feelings in the Classroom: The Role of Emotions in Successful Learning*
1973	Harold Bessell & Uvaldo Palomares	*Methods in Human Development: The Magic Circle Curriculum*
1974	Gloria Castillo	*Left-Handed Teaching: Lessons in Affective Education*
1974	Harold Bernard & Wesley Huckins	*Humanism in the Classroom: An Eclectic Approach to Teaching and Learning*
1974	Joel Latner	*The Gestalt Therapy Book*
1975	George I. Brown	*The Live Classroom: Innovation Through Confluent Education and Gestalt*
1975	Richard Schmuck & Patricia Schmuck	*Group Processes in the Classroom*
1975	Richard Curwin & Barbara Fuhrman	*Discovering Your Teaching Self*

(Continued)

Table P-T.1 (Continued)

Year	Author/Editor(s)	Title of Publication
1975	Larry Chase	*The Other Side of the Report Card: A How-to-Do-It Program in Affective Education*
1975	William Passons	*Gestalt Approaches in Counseling*
1975	James Ballard & Warren Timmerman	*Strategies in Humanistic Education Circle Book*
1975	Diane Read & Sidney Simon	*Humanistic Education Source Book*
1976	Jack Canfield & Harold Wells	*100 Ways to Enhance Self-Concept in the Classroom*
1976	John Miller	*Humanizing the Classroom*
1976	Andrew Fluegelman	*The New Games Book*
1976	Victor Daniels & Laurence Horowitz	*Being and Caring*
1977	Robert Valett	*Humanistic Education: Developing the Total Person*
1977	Joseph Zinker	*Creative Process in Gestalt Therapy*
1977	David Aspy & Flora Roebuck	*Kids Don't Learn From People They Don't Like*
1978	Shirley Heck & Jon Cobes	*All the Classroom Is a Stage: The Creative Classroom Environment*
1979	Barb Meister-Vitale	*Unicorns Are Real: A Right-Brained Approach to Learning*
1980	Bud Feder & Ruth Ronall	*Beyond the Hot Seat: Gestalt Approaches to Group*

CONCLUSION

Table P.-T.1 provides a glimpse of several pedagogical publications not typically represented in historical accounts of Gestalt therapy. Unfortunately, the concept of confluent education never really took hold except in specific locations, and even there the term has usually given way to concepts such as "affective education," "developmental guidance," "left-handed teaching," and "emotional intelligence." Though these approaches share some aspects of Gestalt/confluent education, they usually lack the interactive, experiential, and integrative qualities deemed central to George Brown's pedagogical models. Even further afield are the more prevalent approaches of the day that have at their core concepts from cognitive-behavioral (CBT) psychology. The CBT approaches are generally lacking in the affective domain and as such miss the mark with many students whose primary motivation derives more from feelings than from thinking, whereas confluent educators' way of being in the classroom is more "heart centered" than "mind centered." Their success with integrative learning derives more from the emotional aspects of living than from the cognitive aspects. The lively (or not so lively) interactions between the self and the universe—the person within his or her field—always involve various aspects of cognition, emotion, and behavior. This is the "holistic" core of Gestalt pedagogical theory and method—meeting and working with the "whole" person.

Because confluent education is so often overlooked in our chronologies, narratives, and histories, Sarah and I, as editors and authors of this book, hope that others will continue with this line of thinking and turn it into a "line of action" for and about Gestalt pedagogy. As editors of this textbook, we consider ourselves to be both educators and students of Gestalt theory, history, research, and practice. In this light, we offer here an enlarged picture of many of the pedagogical views, methods, and experiences that we hope will enliven and energize your classroom and your learning as you engage in the experiences ahead in this textbook.

Part I

FOUNDATIONS OF GESTALT THERAPY

CHAPTER 1

The History and Development of Gestalt Therapy

CHARLES E. BOWMAN

DIALOGUE RESPONDENT: EDWIN C. NEVIS

Charles E. Bowman is founder, co-president, and senior faculty of the Indianapolis Gestalt Institute in Indiana. A superb teacher and workshop facilitator, he has presented his "Interactive History of Gestalt Therapy" at Gestalt conferences on three continents. He is the author of several articles on Gestalt therapy and serves on the editorial board of *Gestalt Review* and *Electronic Gestalt Journal.* An organizational specialist and dynamic leader, he is Director of WorkLife Strategies at Verizon Communications and is former president of the Association for the Advancement of Gestalt Therapy.

Edwin C. Nevis is one of the original pioneers of Gestalt therapy. He is president of the Gestalt International Study Center. He was a founder of the Gestalt Institute of Cleveland, where he was president for 13 years and where he co-founded the International Gestalt Organization and System Development Program, which trains practitioners from over 20 countries. He was founding editor of Gestalt Press and (together with Joe Melnick) conceived the *Gestalt Review.* He is the author of several articles and books, including *Organizational Consulting: A Gestalt Approach* (1987), the editor of *Gestalt Therapy: Perspectives and Applications* (1992), and the coauthor of *Intentional Revolutions: A Seven-Point Strategy for Transforming Organizations* (1996) and *How Organizations Learn: An Integrated Strategy for Building Learning Capability* (1998). His career also includes 17 years on the faculty of the Massachusetts Institute of Technology Sloan School of Management.

It is highly instructive to learn something of the intensively tilled soil from which our virtues proudly emerge.

Paul Goodman, "The Father of the Psychoanalytic Movement"

The inevitability of identifying Gestalt therapy from one's own perspective has resulted in multiple definitions of Gestalt therapy and widely differing historical accounts. The typical narrative of Gestalt therapy history can be summarized in Carlyle's (Strouse & Strouse, 1993) famous maxim that all history is the biography of great men. The "great man" approach to history recounts the legend of a heroic figure (typically male) who individually changes the course of modern history, founds a school of thought, or introduces a new paradigm. In the history of Gestalt therapy, this approach details the contributions of Frederick Perls. Perls's name has been virtually synonymous with Gestalt therapy, along with his famous "empty chair" technique.

Numerous problems plague these traditional historical accounts. Discoveries are glamorized and multiple contributors are ignored. Embarrassing moments are omitted and disciplines are protected at the expense of truth. These "Fritz Perls" accounts are ethnocentric, sexist, shallow, and historically ignorant. They have left Gestalt therapy cemented in the zeitgeist of 1960s popular psychology. Unfortunately, most historical accounts ignore the richness of Gestalt therapy theory as the confluence of many contributions, from physics to feminism, Hasidism to Taoism, and radical individualism to relational psychology, to name just a few. Therefore, this chapter will present the history of Gestalt therapy from a field-theoretical perspective, identifying contributions to Gestalt therapy from an array of cultural, scientific, historical, and aesthetic components of human experience.

The broadest overview of Gestalt therapy identifies a changing weltanschauung as responsible for Gestalt therapy's development. *Weltanschauung* connotes more than the dictionary definition, "a shared worldview." It is how we apprehend the world—how we are involved in it, perceive it, and bring our personal history to

EDWIN: My first response to your chapter, Charlie, was to remember what it was like for me personally to fall into the world of psychology as a student in 1944. I was 18 years old and waiting to be drafted into the military service. My professors in the Psychology Department of the City College of New York introduced us to Wundt, Brentano, Lewin, Koffka, Köhler, Wertheimer, etc. Then, as a teaching assistant, I designed experiments to test Lewinian hypotheses (e.g., the Zeigarnik effect) and had the opportunity to meet Wolfgang Köhler, Kurt Goldstein, and others. I only realized years later how fortunate I was to have been in the presence of these pioneers and to have been exposed to them and their ideas. Imagine my delight about 7 years later to be introduced to Fritz Perls, Laura Perls, Isadore From, and Paul Goodman, and to be among the first to study with them as part of the founding group at the Cleveland Institute. You cannot imagine the excitement we experienced as part of a revolutionary, somewhat underground movement that was to revise and perhaps replace psychoanalysis as a therapy of choice.

CHARLIE: Another area that I would be interested in hearing about, Edwin, is what relationship, if any, existed between Gestalt psychology—Lewin, Köhler, and the gang—and Buber's approach (or reproach) towards psychotherapy. I am thinking, for instance, about any early connections between I-Thou and figure-ground.

bear on it. This collective perspective creates momentum and becomes an engine for change. In Gestalt therapy, the result has been movement (a) from deconstructive views of the world toward holistic models of existence; (b) from linear causality toward field theoretical paradigms; and (c) from an individualistic psychology toward a dialogical or relational perspective.

The following definition of Gestalt therapy reflects the influences of a field perspective on methodology:

> Gestalt therapy is a process psychotherapy with the goal of improving one's contact in community and with the environment in general. This goal is accomplished through aware, spontaneous and authentic dialogue between client and therapist. Awareness of differences and similarities [is] encouraged while interruptions to contact are explored in the present therapeutic relationship. (Bowman, 1998, p. 106)

This definition clearly outlines what a Gestalt therapist does in practice. Viewing the history of Gestalt therapy from a field theoretical perspective makes it possible to see how the various components in this definition have evolved. Understanding the changing weltanschauung adds texture and contour to an already colorful historical account of Gestalt therapy.

Gestalt therapy is celebrating over 50 years of existence, marking the publication of its first comprehensive text, *Gestalt Therapy: Excitement and Growth in the Human Personality* (Perls, Hefferline, & Goodman, 1951, 1994, hereafter referred to as *Gestalt Therapy*), and the birth of the first professional training group, the New York Institute for Gestalt Therapy. Though Frederick Perls looms large as the father of Gestalt therapy in the "great man" perspective, he invented neither the theory nor the subject matter, as he acknowledged (Perls, 1969b). The seeds of Gestalt therapy were planted well in advance of Frederick Perls and have fully germinated into a comprehensive theory of psychotherapy and a philosophical foundation for living.

EDWIN: I don't have any particular knowledge about the relationship between figure-ground and I-Thou in the thinking of the early folks. Buber was more focused on the interpersonal level than the intrapsychic one. I think of figure-ground as awareness phenomena and, as such, belonging to the early stages of contact.

With regard to the movement from Gestalt psychology to Gestalt therapy, I think this reflects the developing split between the practitioners and the scientists in the psychological world. In addition to Lewin's movement toward social action issues, key books on personality theory from a Gestalt perspective were written by Andra Angyal and Fritz Heider.

On a personal level, when my cohorts and I were exposed to Gestalt and field theory we were also encouraged to become practitioners who would change the world through our interventions. Only a handful of my age-group became Gestalt-oriented scientists (e.g., Leo Postman, Irvin Rock, and Mary Henle).

CHARLIE: Gestalt psychology was primarily relegated to Europe, while Gestalt therapy was germinated and flourished in the United States. I believe this was in part a result of the medical/psychiatric system established in the United States. A Veterans Administration position was a good-paying job for a psychologist or psychotherapist, as was an academic appointment. Gestalt therapy and theory made significant contributions in each realm. In an academic setting one would certainly have found Goodman. Likewise, in a clinical setting one would certainly have heard of the efficiency and success of this new form of therapy and, of course, of Dr. Perls. I am curious, Edwin, how this academic-clinical cleavage appeared to you as you moved from college to career.

EDWIN: The cleavage between academic and practitioner roles was just beginning, and effort developed to keep it from spreading. The concept of the "scientist/practitioner" was developed and continues to be advocated

An acquaintance with some of the early contributors in psychoanalysis, psychology, and philosophy only partially illuminates the theory labeled "Gestalt" in 1951. Victorian Europe, the dramatic impact of fascism and world war, the denouement of 1960s liberalism, and the subsequent conservative shift have all interacted to shape the landscape of Gestalt therapy.

today. However, the cleavage continued. It became a source of great conflict within the American Psychological Association. But it led to clinicians being elected as president of the APA and the growth of independent schools of professional psychology that grant a Doctor of Psychology degree, as opposed to the PhD, which remains a research/academic degree.

THE DESCENT OF GESTALT THERAPY IN PSYCHOANALYSIS

That Freud was a product of Victorian Europe and of nineteenth-century science needs no exegesis. Psychoanalytic theory was a revolutionary method for treating the ailments of a repressed and conservative society. Although Freud clearly identified society as responsible for these ills, his was not a social psychology; his enterprise was clearly medical. William Harvey's *On the Motion of the Heart and Blood in Animals* (1628/1993) had set the standard for medical research some 200 years earlier: Organismic functioning could be ascertained through dissection. Freud's advice to aspiring psychoanalysts illustrates his reliance on this model:

> I cannot advise my colleagues too urgently to model themselves during psychoanalytic treatment on the surgeon, who puts aside all his feelings, even his human sympathy, and concentrates his mental forces on the single aim of performing the operation as skillfully as possible. (quoted in Stepansky, 1999, p. 1)

Psychoanalytic dissection allowed classification of psychological functioning—for example, id, ego, and superego. Freud's careful observations and high degree of skepticism lent scientific credence to his "discoveries," which astonished Victorian Europe and the safe culture that had developed in Vienna. The world was forever changed.

Psychoanalysis was the starting point for Frederick and Laura Perls. Although their first treatise, *Ego, Hunger and Aggression* (Perls, 1947/1969a), originally carried the subtitle *A Revision of Freud's Theory and Method,* terms such as *mental metabolism, figure formation, gestalt/gestalten, organismic balance, zero point, holism, field theory, concentration therapy, face-to-face therapy, present-centered therapy, attending to the actual, undoing retroflections, body concentration, experience,* and *experiment* clearly indicated their departure. The 1969 Random House edition replaced the work's original subtitle with *The Beginning of Gestalt Therapy* and added, following Frederick Perls's name, the dubious credential "Associate Psychiatrist of the Esalen Institute."

Laura Perls authored two of the chapters in *Ego, Hunger and Aggression* (Rosenfeld, 1978a). This fact is seldom mentioned. Her interest in oral resistances and Fritz Perls's theory of dental aggression grew from her experiences of feeding and weaning her children (her phenomenological field). The book emerged from collaborative discussions between Frederick and Laura Perls. Although she was never cited as a coauthor, Frederick nominally acknowledged her contributions in the first edition of the book. This acknowledgment was deleted in the 1969 Random House edition.

The Perlses' departure from psychoanalysis began when Frederick Perls presented a paper at the 1936 Czechoslovakia Psychoanalytic Congress in Marienbad, disputing the "anal stage" of development as the origin of all resistance. The Perlses' theory of dental aggression was viewed as heresy and was summarily dismissed. This led the Perlses to reconsider their contributions as revisionist and ultimately to organize the new school of Gestalt therapy.

The "great man" account of the debacle of the 1936 Congress pitted Frederick Perls against Sigmund Freud and the orthodox psychoanalysts. Actually, Marie Bonaparte was the most outspoken critic of Perls's presentation of oral resistances. Later, as the figure of a new psychotherapy began to emerge, Frederick Perls (1947/1969a) said,

> I had studied with a number of psycho-analysts for years. With one exception—K. Laundauer—all those from whom I have derived any benefit have departed from the orthodox lines. . . . This proves, on the one hand, the tremendous stimulation which emanated from Freud but, on the other, it proved the incompleteness or insufficiency of his system. . . . While I was living entirely in the psycho-analytic atmosphere, I could not appreciate that the great opposition to Freud's theories might have some justification. (p. 81)

Frederick and Laura Perls studied psychoanalysis formally with first-generation analysts. The impact of these analysts is evident in the development of Gestalt therapy. Although Freud would marginalize many of his students for their challenge to the orthodoxy of classical analysis, the stage was set for alternatives to flourish. Rank was exploring the role of the "here and now" in the psychoanalytic setting, while Adler was exploring the role of paradox in therapy. Federn was developing preliminary concepts around ego boundaries, and Ferenzi was championing the active involvement of the analyst and emphasizing the subjective nature of interpretation. The renegade analyst who most directly contributed to Gestalt therapy was assuredly Wilhelm Reich.

Frederick Perls was in analysis with Reich and was attracted to a concept that would later develop into a central tenet of Gestalt therapy: organismic self-regulation. Further, Gestalt therapy borrowed heavily from Reich's general theory of "character armor." And Reich inadvertently made another major contribution to Gestalt therapy—bringing Paul Goodman into the fold. Commenting on Reich's work, Goodman (1945/1977c) published "The Political Meaning of Some Recent Revisions of Freud" in the journal *Politics,* and Frederick Perls was eager to meet the author upon arriving in Manhattan in 1946 (Stoehr, 1994).

Paul Goodman was more than interested in Reich. He was a patient of Alexander Lowen (one of Reich's students), and was an outspoken proponent of the same libertarian/anarchistic politics. Reich had completely abandoned his work on character and motoric involvement in psychoanalysis in favor of his discovery of the "orgone." Although this proved a deathblow to Reich, it was fortuitous for Gestalt therapy. "In effect Reich had left the field to them [Perls and Goodman,] and it was only necessary to clear the way to their own higher ground" (Stoehr, 1994, p. 45).

Gestalt therapy generally owes Freud, and the revolution he established, a debt of gratitude. Frederick Perls (1969c) expressed that gratitude in his autobiography:

> Freud, his theories, his influence are much too important for me. My admiration, bewilderment, and vindictiveness are very strong. I am deeply moved by his suffering and courage. I am deeply awed by how much, practically all alone, he achieved with the inadequate mental tools of association psychology and mechanistically-oriented philosophy. I am deeply grateful for how much I developed standing up against him. (p. 45)

Likewise, Goodman's debt of gratitude to Freud is measured in his comments dated September 24, 1939:

> The friendly man, our general friend, is dead. Now without a possible addition, in books we read his careful conjectures, first persuasive to the heart surprised, then recognized for even very true. He proved freedom and good conscience to all men (most to those who say the contrary but will be freed tomorrow). First he explored the flowery fields of hell, then the fierce deserts of heaven. An unfinished enterprise. His achievement is to be achieved. (quoted in Goodman, 1945/1977a, p. 6)

THE DESCENT OF GESTALT THERAPY IN EXPERIMENTAL PSYCHOLOGY

Wilhelm Wundt's (1874/1999) publication of *The Principles of Physiological Psychology* introduced the rigors of scientific inquiry and established psychology as a science. He defined psychology as the investigation of conscious processes, casting issues of mind and body back into the realm of philosophy. His aim was the reformation of psychological investigation, and his ammunition was the introduction of the experimental method. Though indirect, Wundt's impact on Gestalt therapy was profound, shaping the development of all psychological investigation and of psychotherapy specifically.

Freud's attempts to refine psychoanalysis as a method of scientific inquiry failed. Wundt's effort succeeded, launching the discipline of experimental psychology and gaining acceptance in the scientific community. For Gestalt therapy, its effects would be both beneficial and insidiously detrimental. The spirit and thoroughness of Wundt's inquiry into conscious processes benefited Gestalt therapy methodologically (as in the Gestalt therapeutic experiment). But the changing zeitgeist of the late twentieth century, marked by a conservative return to focused models of psychotherapy and the precise measurement of outcome and symptom alleviation, has revealed the more detrimental influence of this scientific approach to therapy.

The same year that Wundt's posthumous works were published, Franz Brentano (1874/1999) released *Psychology From an Empirical Standpoint.* His was a psychology sustaining philosophical roots yet building upon scientific method. Brentano and his students emphasized the unbiased description of inner experience as the basis of a scientific psychology. A student of Brentano, Christian von Ehrenfels, published "On Gestalt Qualities" ("Über "'Gestaltqualitaten'") (1890/1988) and coined the term *Gestalt* in developing a general theory of complex perception. The Gestalt school of psychology was born.

Gestalt psychology is generally remembered for the idea that "the whole is greater than the sum of its parts." Actually, the original wording, in a 1909 manuscript by Alexius Meinong, was "A thing is given in perception as the Gestalt quality of a sum of perceived characters" (quoted in Mulligan & Smith, 1988, p. 129). Kurt Lewin, a later descendant of the Brentanian school and student of Carl Stumpf, applied this idea to the mind, conceiving it as an amalgam of weak and strong *Gestalten* in constant communication. Lewin is a prominent figure in Gestalt therapy because of his development of field theory, action research, and systems dynamics.

In 1912, another student of Stumpf, Max Wertheimer, published his studies of perceptual grouping and the perception of movement. Together with Kurt Koffka and Wolfgang Köhler, they were considered "the Berlin school" of Gestalt psychology. In contrast to von Ehrenfels' work, which still relied upon reducing mental phenomena to elements, their work was revolutionary in identifying perception as a holistic process. The Berlin school attracted a number of students interested in a wide array of scientific endeavors. Among them were Kurt Lewin, Kurt Goldstein, and a doctoral student, Lore Posner (later, Laura Perls).

To identify Kurt Goldstein as a Gestalt psychologist is to dramatically understate his contributions to many fields in science and the humanities. Goldstein's astounding work *The Organism: A Holistic Approach to Biology Derived from Pathological Data in Man* (1939/1995) addressed not only his primary field of neurology but also the application of the phenomenological method in science, the generalizability of Gestalt perceptual psychology to the entire human condition, and the place of philosophy in medicine. His work challenged the linear, atomistic zeitgeist in science that suggested that theory formation based on empirical data would by itself lead to an adequate representation of reality. Studying the recovery of function after brain injury led him to realize "that only a method that placed the total organism of the individual in the foreground—in our interpretation of normal functioning or disturbances due to a defect—could be fruitful" (pp. 17–18).

Goldstein diverged from the Berlin school of Gestalt psychology in both the scope and the applicability of their concepts. Like Reich, Goldstein contributed to Gestalt therapy not only by synthesizing theory but also by connecting significant people. While completing her PhD in Gestalt psychology, Lore Posner studied for several years in Frankfurt at the Kurt Goldstein Center, where she met Frederick Perls, who was working at that time for Goldstein in his laboratory. Frederick Perls wed Lore Posner in 1929 (she would later anglicize her name to Laura). An exiled Goldstein would later seek a tutor in New York City to improve his English; the tutor would be Paul Goodman (Stoehr, 1994).

Several central tenets of Gestalt therapy are figural in this historical foray thus far. First is the Reichian concept of organismic self-regulation and the role of motoric functioning in psychotherapy. Second are Goldstein's concepts of the organism as a whole and the plasticity of the human organism in adapting to the environment in the face of adversity. Finally, from Lewin's work Gestalt therapy assimilated the concepts of the inseparability of the organism in the environment and the field theoretical perspective. The rigors of Wundtian investigation and Brentano's "act psychology" would provide sound methodological processes.

By the beginning of the twentieth century, science was clearly established as the method of choice for many endeavors traditionally considered philosophical. It was the weltanschauung in virtually all fields of investigation. But by the middle of the twentieth century, science itself was shifting. In the physical sciences, field theory was gaining recognition in concordance with the study of atomic structure. Einstein's theories of the interplay of time, matter, and energy were widely publicized. In this atmosphere, Goldstein's and Lewin's ideas also gained recognition.

The weltanschauung was changing from atomism to the holistic concepts prevalent today. While the Perlses were living in South Africa, their interest in holism was heightened by their exposure to the philosophical, scientific, and political ideas of Prime Minister Jan Christian Smuts, as exemplified in his book *Holism and Evolution* (1926/1996):

> Holism . . . underlies the synthetic tendency in the universe, and is the principle that makes for the origin and progress of wholes in the universe. . . . [T]his whole-making or holistic tendency is fundamental in nature . . . [and] has a well-marked ascertainable

> character. . . . Evolution is nothing but the gradual development and stratification of progressive series of wholes, stretching from the inorganic beginnings to the highest levels of spiritual creation. (p. v)

Today we understand that human health depends upon the interdependence of systems and that the delicate balance of nature depends on every aspect of the biosphere. In Gestalt therapy, we understand that "lives and collective systems intertwine and need to be considered together as a *unified field*" (Parlett, 1997, p. 16, emphasis in original). One could say that linear, atomistic investigation can reveal correlations but not causality.

THE DESCENT OF GESTALT THERAPY IN PHILOSOPHY

Before detailing the foundations of an aesthetically based psychotherapy, it is worthwhile to understand the consequences of maintaining these foundations during the current zeitgeist of conservatism. The insidious influence of Wundt's experimental psychology on Gestalt therapy can be seen in the approach to psychotherapy as a system, based on clinical epidemiology and evidence. As Haggbloom et al. (2002) have noted, "The discipline of psychology underwent a remarkable transformation during the twentieth century, a transformation that included a shift away from the European influenced philosophical psychology of the late 19th century to the empirical, research-based, American dominated psychology of today" (p. 139). But Laura Perls (1992a) has affirmed that "[t]he basic concepts of Gestalt therapy are philosophical and aesthetic rather than technical. Gestalt therapy is an existential-phenomenological approach and as such it is experiential and experimental" (p. 4). In an age where providers benefit from joining the pharmaceutical and third-party industries in delivering cost-based therapy, the philosophy of Gestalt therapy and of psychotherapy in general is in jeopardy.

The philosophical heritage of Gestalt therapy is simply too rich to ignore. Laura Perls's academic training included several years of study with Paul Tillich and thorough grounding in the philosophy of Kierkegaard, Heidegger, Husserl, and Scheler. She was also a student of Martin Buber and saw no conflict between the philosophy of Tillich, a German Protestant, and that of Buber, a German Jew and scholar of Hasidic Judaism. In fact, the similarities she found—in ideas of contact and presence—are cornerstones of Gestalt therapy (Rosenfeld, 1978a).

Laura Perls had met Edmund Husserl and studied his work on phenomenological reduction with Tillich. Husserl's phenomenological method would evolve into a solid foundation for Gestalt therapy methodology. Husserl was a student of Brentano, and Laura and Frederick Perls were exposed to their philosophies while working and studying with Goldstein. The weltanschauung allowed for the integration of philosophy and science, creating a breadth of

EDWIN: You position your thesis in relation to weltanschauung, and I want to elaborate on this. We Gestalt students were drawn to the approach not only because of the theory and method but also because of the implicit belief that we were going to change the world for the better. In the midst of a worldwide climate supporting democratic models, as opposed to authoritarian models, we saw a way to help liberate the restricted, conforming individual and to promote authenticity and individuality. As the third oldest Gestalt practitioner still alive (Erv Polster is a few years older than me), I must own up to having used the Gestalt approach to teach the people who created the liberation movements of the 1960s. But keep in mind that

attitude and affording abundant possibilities for the development of an existentially and phenomenologically based psychotherapy.

Frederick Perls was familiar with the philosophers referenced above, though only marginally so in comparison to Laura. He was, however, fascinated by the work of Salomo Friedlander. An obscure figure in philosophy, Friedlander (1918, cited in Clarkson & Mackewn, 1993, p. 5) posited a "zero-point" from which differences can emerge. Wulf (1996) acknowledged the compatibility of Friedlander's concepts with the figure-ground formulations of the Gestalt psychologists, Goldstein's homeostatic principles, and Eastern philosophy. For Gestalt therapy, Friedlander's philosophy would contribute to a method of integrating polarities, the concept of the "fertile void," and a more thorough understanding of the emergent gestalt. His philosophy of what he called "creative indifference" "eventually clarified for Frederick Perls Goldstein's term 'self-actualization' (used by Maslow thirty years later)" (Kogan, 1976, p. 241).

Paul Goodman, an itinerant man of letters, was well versed in philosophy and brought Aristotelian ideas into early Gestalt therapy. Crocker (1999) explains that Goodman made powerful connections between his studies with the American Aristotelian scholar Richard McKeon and the theory of perception posited in *Gestalt Therapy.* Isadore From was an acquaintance of Goodman who sought psychotherapy from Frederick Perls in 1946 after moving to New York City to study philosophy at the New School for Social Research (Rosenfeld, 1978b). From's love of philosophy would become his chalice for Gestalt therapy theory. The New York Institute for Gestalt Therapy was just being founded, and the philosophical basis of Gestalt therapy would be asserted and maintained there by Isadore From and Laura Perls until their deaths in 1990 and 1994, respectively. In the vernacular of "great man" historical accounts, if Frederick Perls was the father of Gestalt therapy, Laura Perls was certainly the first lady and Isadore From the dean of the school. From would earn this title not only because of the precision of his teaching and his devotion to Gestalt therapy theory but also because of Goodman's abandonment of Gestalt therapy and ultimately his

I am a very conservative person, not a revolutionary. I am an organization consultant and a one-time faculty member of MIT. We just accepted Paul Goodman's notion that a healthier individual would produce a more healthy society. Frederick Perls was mainly bent on changing psychoanalysis; whereas Goodman wanted to change society, and he saw what Fritz and Laura had created as a way of educating people.

CHARLIE: A weltanschauung of conservatism, unfortunately, leaves the liberation movement of the 1960s merely a historical glimmer in the sky. In many ways Goodman was as much the charismatic leader as Perls, and his radical approach to societal change was as costly to the growth of Gestalt therapy as Frederick Perls's antics at Esalen in terms of mainstream acceptance. I know that you have thought and written extensively about this sort of "mainstream acceptance" as antithetical to Gestalt therapy. Do you believe that maintaining that boundary has been costly to Gestalt therapy as a social movement?

EDWIN: It probably has done just that, and numerous older Gestalt therapists have said that we have lost our creative thrust. I wonder if that is an inevitable development as movements mature. On the other hand, I see continued experimentation among practitioners in both the clinical and organizational field. If we look at the broader context of society as a whole, we can see both strong forces for conservatism (highly ascendant in the U.S. national government at this time) and strong liberation movements. For example, it would have been unheard of as recently as 10 years ago to see open public debate about marriage between people of the same sex.

untimely death in 1972 at age 61. (The third author of *Gestalt Therapy*, Ralph Hefferline, a professor of psychology at Columbia University, conducted the book's Gestalt experiments with his students and recorded responses for use in the text. Once the book was published, Hefferline returned to behavioral psychology and maintained no ties with the Gestalt therapy community thereafter.)

The contributions of Martin Buber to Gestalt therapy deserve more discussion than can be offered here. Buber's treatises on presence and mutuality addressed the problems of fascism and utilitarianism in the mid-1900s. The Gestalt therapy values of presence, authenticity, dialogue, and inclusion are beholden to Buber's philosophy as outlined in *I and Thou* (1923/1958). Judith Brown (1980) summarized Buber's I-Thou contribution to Gestalt therapy as "the goal of every intervention in Gestalt therapy" (p. 55). Citing Buber's work as *the* most important influence on Gestalt therapy, Erhard Doubrawa (2001) identified the political implications of the I-Thou philosophy as a model for a utopian anarchy and a remedy for social ills.

It was virtually de rigueur among intellectuals in the 1940s to be well versed in Eastern thought, which had an obvious influence on Gestalt therapy. Paul Goodman immersed himself in Eastern philosophical literature. Frederick Perls would later go to Japan to study Eastern philosophy firsthand. Their differing responses exemplify a pattern that would always split the onetime collaborators—one the thinker and scholar, the other the actor and doer.

Philosophy has offered Gestalt therapy a system of values and method. From Husserl came a framework for investigating experience through the phenomenological method; from Kierkegaard, the belief that truth is subjective; and from Heidegger, the idea that "being" (*Dasein*) is more fundamental than consciousness. An operational summary of these existential contributions informs us that passionate choices, strong convictions, and personal experience compose an individual's "truth."

Gestalt therapy's roots in science *and* philosophy have given it the same flexibility and adaptability that the theory identifies in the human organism. "What has often gone unrecognized is the fact that because Gestalt therapy began with roots in both the research and experimental aspects of psychology as well as the more speculative, subjective approaches, it gained the strengths of each and thus has been able to avoid the pitfalls of the other" (Burley, 2001).

WORLD WAR AND THE RISE OF FASCISM

The rise of fascism, the Holocaust, and World War II were arguably the most influential factors in the development of Gestalt therapy since Freud and Breuer's development of the "talking cure." The list of indispensable contributors to Gestalt therapy who were forced to flee their homelands in search of safety and freedom from fascism is extensive—the Perlses, Buber, Lewin, Goldstein, Wertheimer, Koffka, Köhler, and Reich, to name but a few. Many lost entire families, and all lost loved ones and their worldly belongings. The trauma, impact, and magnitude of loss certainly dominated the weltanschauung of the World War II and postwar era. The profound impact of the Nazi empire and the suffering in its wake prompted two prominent Gestalt therapists, Cynthia Oudejans Harris and Gordon Wheeler, to translate into English *The Collective Silence: German Identity and the Legacy of Shame,* edited by Heimannsberg and Schmidt (1993).

Imagine the emotion and confusion associated with the terror of persecution coming after the prewar zeitgeist, which had been full of excitement and creativity. Wulf (1996) captured the zeitgeist of prewar Europe precisely:

> Expressionism at this time represented a reaction to the old, outdated bourgeois norms and the naïve belief in progress. The catastrophes brought about by the First World War, the destruction of humanity, were only too evident and too recent. Expressionists . . . were trying to create a new vision of the human being, one determined by social responsibility and compassion for others. Creative art was seen as evolving out of immediate inner experiencing and emotional dynamics. The basic themes were feelings, intuition, subjectivity, fantasy—themes that live on in Gestalt therapy.

For the Perlses, the war years were a time of sharp contrasts. Prosperity in Germany, with ties to Laura's wealthy family and thriving psychoanalytic practices, was followed by poverty and exile in Amsterdam. Flight to South Africa eventually brought prosperity once again with the reestablishment of their private practices and beginning the South African School for Psychoanalytic Studies in Johannesburg. They would experience a similar cycle again in Johannesburg with the juxtaposition of the creative freedom reminiscent of the prewar German Bauhaus culture and the subsequent flight to America in response to apartheid government. Frederick Perls had served in the German army as a medical corpsman in World War I and then as a psychiatrist in the South African army with the Allied Forces in World War II. Laura Perls moved from psychoanalyst to "washerwoman" and back. For the Perlses, these experiences affirmed the central role of Friedlander's theory of the "zero-point" and Smuts's views of holism and would later influence the Gestalt therapy theory of personality integration.

World War II proved a tipping point for Gestalt therapy, enriching the ground for a unified theory that would take form by 1951. It also produced what would become Gestalt therapy's biggest challenge—American clinical psychology. The establishment of the Veterans Administration and the significant monies available meant that medical centers would dominate and bureaucratize psychological and psychotherapy practice in the United States.

The war brought enormous casualties and need for psychological healing, but the psychoanalytic treatment available was ineffective in treating family, interpersonal, or occupational problems. American pragmatism would seize the day as behaviorism proved more effective in treating "shell shock" and the host of traumas accompanying the war. Clinical psychology had a foundation of Wundtian experiment in academe—a good fit with the emerging system of diagnostics that characterized American medicine.

The anarchistic roots of Gestalt therapy created friction between Gestalt practitioners and these established systems in medicine and academe. A healthy skepticism toward bureaucracies, born in response to fascism, is a major contribution of Gestalt therapy. One unfortunate result, however, has been the perception of Gestalt therapy as antiacademic, anti-intellectual, and antiestablishment. Richard Kitzler, in a trialogue with Laura Perls and E. Mark Stern (Stern, 1992) has pointed out that some practitioners, with their reliance upon technique and little else, have contributed to this misunderstanding of Gestalt therapy as marginalized not by choice but by ignorance. It is difficult work (which some have avoided) to assimilate holistic, philosophical, and scientific foundations, especially when the culture shifts away from many of the values inherent in the system.

From its inception, Gestalt therapy has had larger sociocultural implications than its modern reputation would suggest. For many early contributors to Gestalt therapy, anarchy was an antidote to fascism and the key to a more utopian society. Martin Buber had strong ties with this political orientation, as did Franz Koffka and Jan Christian Smuts. Goodman was a notable leader of the anarchist movement in the United States. He remained active through the student protest movements of the 1960s, and made numerous political literary contributions to anarchist publications such as *Politics*.

In his final years, Frederick Perls would flee Nixon-era America, fearing that prevalent fascist trends would result in the destruction of civil society and the disappearance of the individual freedom that he had enjoyed there. Less of a political spokesman for anarchy than Goodman, Perls would realize his rather reclusive dream of a Gestalt kibbutz in 1969. In Cowichan, British Columbia, he started a community where participants lived together, learning Gestalt therapy principles while practicing interdependence and Perls's own brand of utopian anarchy (Baumgardner & Perls, 1975; Shepard, 1975).

Other influences (too numerous to list here) also deserve note in Gestalt therapy history—for instance, the contributions of John Dewey and William James from American psychology and the impact of theater and avant-garde culture. Many elements of the weltanschauung colored Gestalt therapy, and this new approach spread rapidly after *Gestalt Therapy* was published. The history of Gestalt therapy illustrates field theory in action—a basic and necessary component of the therapy itself (Parlett, 1997; Yontef, 1993).

EVANGELIZING GESTALT THERAPY

In 1953, Marjorie Creelman invited Erving Polster to attend a workshop led by Frederick Perls in Cleveland (Wysong, 1979). By 1955, the members from the New York Institute for Gestalt Therapy who were conducting training in Cleveland included Paul Weiz, Laura Perls, Paul Goodman, and Isadore From. The New York Institute exported their collective teaching to an eager group of professionals seeking exciting alternatives to traditional psychotherapy training. In this way the Gestalt Institute of Cleveland began. The trainers for the first formal training program there in 1962 included Erving and Miriam Polster, Bill Warner, Richard Wallen, Sonia and Edwin Nevis, Joseph Zinker, Cynthia Harris, Rainette Fantz, Elaine Kepner, and Marjorie Creelman (Wysong, 1979). The program format evolved from weekend training to a "three-year intensive." In turn, the Cleveland faculty presented Gestalt therapy initially in Chicago and Boston and later throughout the world. Two paradigms for training emerged. Training might be led by a single individual—often a charismatic leader embarking on a "traveling road show,"—or it might employ a faculty approach, exposing students to various styles of assimilated Gestalt therapy theory.

Ever restless and with a strong propensity to bask in the style of the charismatic leader, Frederick Perls began a circuit of training in Gestalt therapy after the Cleveland school was established. His initial groups in the late 1950s were primarily lay groups. He was disappointed with the minor impact of lay training in the field of psychotherapy. This changed when he acquired "training appointments" in Columbus State Hospital in Ohio and Mendocino State Hospital in California (Shepard, 1975).

Wilson van Dusen had arranged for the appointment in Mendocino, which ultimately resulted in Perls's relocation to California and establishment of a training circuit on the West

Coast. By 1960 Perls was collaborating with James Simkin (one of his clinical psychology interns at William Allison White Institute and an early participant in the New York Institute group), and within a year two training groups were formed. The training institutes founded on the West Coast included the Gestalt Institute of San Francisco and the Gestalt Therapy Institute of Los Angeles. Like the Cleveland Institute staff, the training staff of the San Francisco and Los Angeles institutes (among them Walter Kempler, Robert Resnick, Janet Rainwater, Gary Yontef, Jerry Kogan, and Claudio Naranjo) carried word of Gestalt therapy to Mexico and South America and eventually around the world. Interest in Canada also grew as Harvey Freedman began training in Vancouver, British Columbia, in the early 1960s and then in Toronto with Harold Silver, Peter Brawley, and Jorge Rosner. Rosner and others would subsequently train Gestalt therapists in Scandinavia, Australia, and New Zealand (Solomon, 2000).

By the time Frederick Perls "settled" on the Pacific Rim in Big Sur, California, he reveled in his reputation as the founder of Gestalt therapy. Sales of *Gestalt Therapy* were steadily climbing and would exceed half a million copies by 1979 (Gaines, 1979). Perls appeared in popular magazines such as *Time* and *Life* and became a mainstay in the human potential movement—"Guru to the Hippies." He was a celebrity at the Esalen Institute in Big Sur from 1964 to 1969, where he provided professional training in Gestalt therapy as well as his weekend "circus." The "circuses" were large group demonstrations of Perls's skill and Gestalt technique—creating a reputation that would prove most damaging to Gestalt therapy. Nonetheless, as Jerry Kogan (1976) noted,

> This brilliant creation [Esalen] brought together thousands of people from all over the world, from street people to the most eminent men and women of letters and science. By 1965 the institute was the major center for humanistic psychology in America and by 1972 literally hundreds of growth centers through the United States and the world were operating on the Esalen model. (p. 253)

Renowned practitioners in various fields of human potential, including Alan Watts, Virginia Satir, Illana Rubenfeld, Ida Rolf, Will Schutz, and Sam Keen, were influenced by Perls at Esalen and contributed to Gestalt therapy without carrying its banner.

With the explicit goal of change and growth for "normals," the human potential movement was the subject of much scrutiny. The concern centered on emotional contagion and accusations that Gestaltists were revivalistic—essentially quasi-religious. A string of outcome studies in the early 1970s called into question their effectiveness as serious change agents (Garfield & Bergin, 1971; Lieberman, Yalom, & Miles, 1973; Yalom, 1975). Expressing a growing sentiment in psychology, James Hillman (1975) diagnosed the problem as follows: "Perhaps it [humanism] is the dominant *weltanschauung* of the mid-twentieth century and as such conceals the dominant pathology of that period: manic euphoria" (p. 241).

For Gestalt therapy specifically, the most unfortunate effect of Frederick Perls's circuses was a perception of Gestalt therapy as, ironically, significantly less than the sum of its parts. Gestalt therapy became known as a therapy of techniques, quick cures, or even gimmicks. It did not reflect Frederick Perls's years of training and practice, his knowledge of medicine and psychoanalysis, or certainly his brilliance. Due to the growing publicity from its association with the Esalen Institute, Gestalt therapy was flourishing and well-known. But it was gaining very different types of recognition. There were the "Fritzers," whom their opponents claimed followed Frederick Perls like groupies, introjecting each *technique du jour* as Perls explored his own creativity. There was the New York Institute, maintaining staunch adherence to the original theory as outlined in *Gestalt Therapy.* There were various blends of "Gestalt and . . . ," such as bioenergetics, transactional analysis, Buddhism, massage, and Jungian psychology.

Then there was the Gestalt Institute of Cleveland, holding fast to well-designed educational experiences in their postgraduate and intensive training programs while exploring wide areas of application and bringing new, and sometimes controversial ideas into Gestalt therapy theory. The tradition of Gestalt therapy at the Gestalt Institute of Cleveland has a strong foundation in Lewinian systems theory. This has sparked debate and research regarding the relationship between systems and field approaches. The Cleveland school pioneered the use of Gestalt therapy applications with interpersonal systems. Richard Wallen and Edwin Nevis were steeped in the work of Perls and Lewin—who by 1946 had spearheaded the beginnings of the NTL (National Training Laboratory) Institute in Bethel, Maine. Nevis and Wallen infused Gestalt training concepts, such as the "Gestalt cycle of experience," into the field of organization and systems development (Nevis, 1987). Joseph Zinker and Sonia Nevis have infused these structuralist ideas into their clinical work with couples and families, pioneering theory and practice with intimate systems.

Four very popular books of the 1970s came out of the Gestalt Institute of Cleveland (GIC) and remain popular in Gestalt therapy today. Erving and Miriam Polster published *Gestalt Therapy Integrated: Contours of Theory and Practice* in 1973. Their book emphasized that resistance in psychotherapy was not an inevitably pathological process but rather a process of creative adjustment. The book provided a sound, applicable theory for the process of personal growth and the experience of many in the human potential movement that "therapy is too good to be limited to the sick" (p. 7). The other highly readable book of the 1970s era that continues to enjoy popularity is Joseph Zinker's *Creative Process in Gestalt Therapy* (1977). Acclaimed by *Psychology Today* as one of the best books of 1977, Zinker reintroduced Gestalt therapy as an infinitely creative encounter between therapist and client. Like his close friends the Polsters, he specifically outlined the place of the Gestalt experiment in therapeutic work. Finally, Joel Latner's *Gestalt Therapy Book* (1973) was an erudite and elegant description of the state of Gestalt therapy in 1973. Latner was one of the first graduates of the Gestalt Institute of Cleveland.

After Frederick Perls died in 1970, these books did much to keep Gestalt therapy alive throughout the next decade and to cultivate the next generation of Gestalt therapists. Other lasting contributions included *Gestalt Therapy Now* (Fagan & Shepherd, 1970), *Gestalt Is* (Stevens, 1975), *The Growing Edge of Gestalt Therapy* (Smith, 1977), and a special issue of the American Psychological Association's *Counseling Psychologist* (1974) dedicated to Gestalt therapy and edited by Joen Fagan.

Several associations played prominent roles in setting the direction of Gestalt therapy in this era, either through collaboration, as in the case of the Association for Humanistic Psychology (AHP) and the American Group Psychotherapy Association, or by passive dissent, as in the case of the American Psychological Association. For example, AHP held special meetings for Gestalt therapists at its annual conferences in the 1970s and 1980s, out of which emerged the Gestalt Journal conferences. Perhaps the most significant professional relationship was that with the American Academy of Psychotherapists (AAP). As a result of the long-standing support of the academy, Ed Smith published a compendium of Gestalt articles that appeared in the academy's professional journal, *Voices,* from 1967 through 1989

(Smith, 1991). Fifty-seven articles were reprinted, 33 of which had appeared in *Voices* in the 1970s. Several respected Gestalt therapists have maintained their connections with Gestalt therapy through the academy, among them Irma Lee Shepherd, Joen Fagan, Sol Rosenberg, and Smith himself.

PUBLICATIONS, ORGANIZATIONS, AND PREDICTABLE ANARCHY

Currently no fewer than 200 training institutions are devoted to Gestalt therapy worldwide. In keeping with their anarchistic roots, Gestalt institutions invariably self-destruct and reconstitute. Training institutes differentiate into new organizations as a result of theoretical differences, practical considerations, or personality conflicts. As Richard Kitzler said in the trialogue with Laura Perls and E. Mark Stern, "Every organization ultimately dulls the charismatic call that quickened it. Integral to this process is bureaucracy as the organization wraps itself in the corruption of respectability" (Stern, 1992, p. 24).

In the late twentieth century, large membership organizations appeared that were devoted in one way or another to the propagation of Gestalt therapy. The Association for the Advancement of Gestalt Therapy (AAGT), the European Association for Gestalt Therapy (EAGT), Gestalt Australia New Zealand (GANZ), and the International Gestalt Therapy Association (IGTA) are prominent examples. There are corresponding examples in Mexico, South America, Russia, France, Germany, and Scandinavia, to name but a few. The most comprehensive list of associations, institutes, and journals is available in Appendix A (this volume) and on the World Wide Web at the Gestalt Therapy Megalist (http://enabling.org/ia/gestalt/gpass.html). The lively struggle that characterizes a Gestalt organization's search for novelty and contact guarantees that these organizations will continue to reconfigure themselves in the spirit of anarchical development.

The *Gestalt Journal* premiered in 1978 and was the first journal dedicated exclusively to Gestalt theory and practice. The *British Gestalt Journal* was founded in 1991, and today there are 11 professional journals in English alone. There are also hundreds of book titles. In 1991 Gordon Wheeler published *Gestalt Reconsidered,* calling into question the operationalization of several fundamental theoretical concepts of Gestalt therapy. In addition to eliciting significant responses (e.g., Yontef, 1992), this work ushered in a new era of authors collaborating and debating Gestalt therapy. The Gestalt International Study Center (GISC), founded by Edwin and Sonia Nevis, and the *Gestalt Review,* edited by Joseph Melnick, have dedicated significant resources to developing the body of Gestalt literature and research in a wide array of social, political, and professional applications.

INNOVATIVE TECHNOLOGY AND THE INFORMATION SUPERHIGHWAY

Since the 1960s, Gestalt therapy has used cutting-edge technology, evidenced by the early recording equipment that can be found at the Frederick and Laura Perls's Special Collections at the Kent State University Library Archives in Kent, Ohio. These Gestalt Archives contain manuscripts, photographs, early audiotapes, videotapes, and transcripts, side by side with the early equipment itself. Ansel Woldt has oversight of the Kent State collection, where he has also amassed the largest collection of academic dissertations on Gestalt therapy in the world and has served as the chair for 101 doctoral dissertations, most of them on some aspect of Gestalt therapy. From the "Gloria tapes," early videotapes that captured demonstrations of Frederick Perls, Carl Rogers, and Albert Ellis, to the creative work of Liv Estrup and her noteworthy multimedia presentation *What's Behind the Empty Chair* (2000), Gestalt therapists and institutions continue to explore digital, video, and distance learning technology as a relevant part of teaching and therapy.

Internet communication is dramatically increasing opportunities for contact and the further development of Gestalt therapy. Gestalt Global Corporation (www.g-gej.org/gestaltglobal/), chaired by Philip Brownell, hosts network resources, online and hard-copy publishing, discussion lists, innovative text-based technologies, and the online journal *Gestalt!* The growth of Gestalt therapy online has been remarkable:

> In the time span between the first appearance on-line of Gestalt therapists in 1995 to the writing of an article in *Gestalt Review* discussing field effects associated with internet technology (Brownell, 1998) there was at least a 500% growth in the quantity of Gestalt sites on the world wide web. That took place in approximately a two-year span. In the two years following that, the growth has continued so that now the increase measures approximately 1000%. (Brownell, O'Neill, & Goodlander, 1999)

CONCLUSION

So what does the history of Gestalt therapy tell us about becoming a Gestalt therapist? The first and foremost requirement is an ethos founded in deep reverence for the profound effects of the meeting of two human beings. Next is a dedication to awareness and the development of a weltanschauung that is widely informed and thoroughly considered. Finally, intense study and a commitment to understanding earlier contributions to the discipline is required. To paraphrase Isadore From, Beethoven was a brilliant composer, and he knew his Mozart well.

It is possible to practice Gestalt therapy solely from a "here and now" perspective or to work essentially with a limited tool kit of Gestalt experiments, or even to limit the focus to the dialogical relationship. To use these parts of Gestalt therapy exclusively, however, is to

EDWIN: I think it is important for students who read this book to realize that the underlying premise of the Gestalt model is to enable people to expand their awareness in order to see alternative choices for what is the best way not only to be true to themselves but also to be responsible members of society who are capable of making rich and powerful contact with others. I think it is also important for the student to know that Gestalt therapy emphasizes growth through the meeting of the therapist and client. It is an engagement therapy, not an interpretive one. It is a full articulation of what Buber had in mind by "I-Thou" connections. I am sure this will become clear in the later chapters.

CHARLIE: I couldn't agree more! Therapists-in-training seldom think of the experience of sitting in the therapist's chair in the consulting room 20 or 30 years from now. In my 20 years I have found Gestalt therapy continually renewing and lively for me as well as my clients. You mentioned beginning in 1944, Edwin. That's 60 years of living with Gestalt therapy. Congratulations and thank you!

unnecessarily limit the power of the method and the breadth of the theory. Laura Perls identified the necessity for the Gestalt therapist to bring his or her whole self into the therapeutic situation: "Gestalt therapy is existential, experiential and experimental. But what techniques you use to implement that and apply it, that depends to the greatest extent on your background, on your experiences professionally, in life, your skills and whatever" (quoted in Rosenfeld, 1978a, p. 24).

REVIEW QUESTIONS

1. In keeping with recent Gestalt theorists' focus on field theory, what were some of the cultural, theoretical, and historical elements present in the field as the early founders were constructing the principles of Gestalt therapy?

2. What were the contributions of Reich, Goldstein, Adler, and Lewin to the early central tenets of Gestalt theory?

3. Name Buber's notion that has been called "the goal of every intervention in Gestalt therapy" (Brown, 1980, p. 55), and *the* most important influence on Gestalt therapy and the remedy for social ills (Doubrawa, 2001). Describe how Buber's notion is useful, not only to Gestalt therapy theory, but also to the practice of Gestalt therapy.

4. Although the United States may have provided refuge to many contributors to Gestalt therapy theory during and following World War II, it also introduced some obstacles to the acceptance of the Gestalt approach among psychotherapists. What were some of those obstacles?

5. The 1960s and 1970s in the United States brought some unfortunate notoriety to Gestalt therapy, perhaps dimming its reputation as a viable psychotherapy approach. Name some of those events/circumstances and their influences on the reputation of Gestalt therapy theory.

EXPERIENTIAL PEDAGOGICAL ACTIVITIES

ACTIVITY 1: As described in this chapter, theory development is contextual and often dependent on chance meetings and collaborations. Design a time line of your own life, noting the contexts, events, and serendipitous circumstances and influences that have brought you to an interest in learning more about Gestalt therapy and theory.

ACTIVITY 2: Your chapter author describes the notion of the "great man" (or great woman) approach to history. In a small group or classroom setting, generate names of the "greats" in each decade who have made major contributions to world history in general. Discuss how those "greats" may also have influenced the development of psychological theories and practices, especially Gestalt therapy and theory.

ACTIVITY 3: Numerous resources are available to anyone interested in learning more about Gestalt therapy theory and practice. Your author lists several online resources, some of which distribute ongoing dialogues among the listed members. Log onto any of the Web sites listed in your chapter and critique their usefulness for your needs. Compare your critiques with those of your class peers.

ACTIVITY 4: Develop a skit for class in which you, as class members, take on the role of the pioneers of Gestalt therapy and of some of the psychoanalysts from whom they were breaking away. You might also include in your role-play skit some of the great minds that had a powerful influence on the founders, such as Aristotle, John Dewey, and Martin Buber. Role-play a skit for the class that includes some of the issues on which these people agreed and ones on which they differed.

CHAPTER **2**

Classical Gestalt Therapy Theory

MARGHERITA SPAGNUOLO LOBB

DIALOGUE RESPONDENT: PHILIP LICHTENBERG

Margherita Spagnuolo Lobb is founder and director of the Istituto di Gestalt (with training centers in Rome, Venice, Palermo, Ragusa, and Siracusa, Italy), a full member of the New York Institute for Gestalt Therapy, coeditor of *Creative License: The Art of Gestalt Therapy* (2003), and author of numerous articles in Gestalt journals. As visiting professor in universities and training centers in Italy and abroad and as the editor-in-chief of *Quaderni di Gestalt* and *Studies in Gestalt Therapy*, she has been vitally involved in creating and disseminating Gestalt therapy theory internationally. She is currently president of the Italian Federation of Associations of Psychotherapy and was formerly president of the European Association for Gestalt Therapy.

Philip Lichtenberg is the Mary Hale Chase Emeritus Professor at Bryn Mawr Graduate School of Social Work and Social Research and co-director of the Gestalt Institute of Philadelphia. He has published numerous articles and books, including *Community and Confluence: Undoing the Clinch of Oppression* (1994), *Getting Even: The Equalizing Law of Relationship* (1988), and *Encountering Bigotry: Befriending Projecting Persons in Everyday Life* (1997). He serves on the editorial board of the *Gestalt Review* and was previously an editor for the *Gestalt Journal*. He is a licensed and practicing psychologist and a member of the Gestalt Therapy International Network faculty.

What I'm going to offer here is my understanding of why and how Gestalt therapy was born: what drew the founders of our approach to search for new solutions to questions about psychotherapy in the middle of the 20th century and what developed from their answers. My primary point of reference is *Gestalt Therapy: Excitement and Growth in the Human Personality,* by Frederick Perls, Ralph Hefferline, and Paul Goodman (1951, 1994). Whereas Fritz and Laura Perls were the originators of the ideas that culminated in *Gestalt Therapy,* Paul Goodman is credited with writing most of the theoretical material in the book based on the Perlses' original thinking and writing as discussed and developed in the original group of founders in New York. Though I was not a witness of that time, I fell in love with Gestalt therapy as a student (in 1974), and since then I've looked for answers to many questions. In this chapter I will try to tell you some of what I have learned about the origins and classical elements of this theory.

Fifty years ago, the New Age movement supported personal growth as a way of emerging from the authoritarian model of the culture of that time. Our clinical approach also focused more on personal development and freedom from cultural schemas. Today, in the postmodern era, models of Gestalt therapy focus on various aspects of relational and field phenomena, the only experienced reality where a momentary truth can be found.

PHILIP: I like what you have written and can support what you say. However, I have a slightly different perspective on some of the issues that you raise and will put them forward for you to consider, and in this unique approach to teaching and learning about our favorite subject we get to dialogue about them.

I would like to take you down four paths to understanding the original thinking of our founders, the innovations that the Gestalt approach contributed to the general field of psychotherapy and culture, the consequences for our practice, and some current theoretical developments. First, I will address a methodological question: How should one approach reading the basic Gestalt therapy book, *Gestalt Therapy* (Perls et al., 1951, 1994)? This book is so sophisticated that it cannot be read in a naive way—a method is needed. Second, I will highlight the novelty of the founders' approach to psychology in their very first discussions, in both the questions they raised and the provisional answers they supplied. Third, I will show *how* these answers were developed in their discussions, filtered by the genius of Paul Goodman, and ultimately written and published as *Gestalt Therapy.* Finally, I will present two theoretical developments that are epistemologically coherent with classical Gestalt theory: the time dimension in the understanding of the contact process and explorations of what has been called the "between."

TO "MEET THE BOOK": A METHODOLOGICAL ISSUE

Our founding book, *Gestalt Therapy: Excitement and Growth in the Human Personality,* is strange and difficult to understand because it does not lend itself to rational categorizations, but it is provocative and intellectually challenging. It stimulates readers to reflect and generate new ideas. This effect is not dependent on culture or time or place; it happens any time one reads it—50 years ago or today. For this reason, it is often referred to as the "bible" of

Gestalt therapists. I'm referring in particular to the theoretical part of the book, which was written by Paul Goodman and based on a manuscript that Perls had given to him and on the reflections of the group of founders. This theoretical part was written in a style that cannot be introjected or swallowed whole. As the authors themselves wrote, "[W]e employ a method of argument that at first sight may seem unfair, but that is unavoidable and is itself an exercise of the gestalt approach" (Perls et al., 1994, p. 20). They called this method "contextual" and stated that it had been conceived to dissolve the chief neurotic dichotomies (Body and Mind; Self and External World; Emotional and Real; Infantile and Mature; Biological and Cultural; Poetry and Prose; Spontaneous and Deliberate; Personal and Social; Love and Aggression; Unconscious and Conscious). The aim of the book is therefore to create an experiment for readers while they read. This experiment is aimed to help readers experience how the above are not dichotomies but part of a figure/background structure.

What I say to my students to introduce them to *Gestalt Therapy* is to surrender themselves to its fascination and not to look for schematic understandings. The beauty of the book lies in its capacity to stimulate creative thought. For this reason, I suggest that my students read the book not at the very beginning of their training, when they look for certainties, but when they are relaxed enough to be curious about what elements of the book most fascinate them. I might tell them to keep a copy of *Gestalt Therapy* on their night table and freely read parts of it at the end of the day. The effect of this kind of reading is usually very strong. They are completely taken by the book and become excited, as if they have found a new way of seeing what they have always seen.

Gestalt Therapy encourages a "hermeneutic" process in its readers, as the authors themselves observed. According to Sichera (1997),

> The text is developed in a series of concentric circles, which oblige the reader to assume an active rather than a passive position. The knowledge of the text (like any authentic knowledge of the other) is at the same time a starting point and a destination. The reader is faced with the "impossible task: to understand the book he must have the 'Gestaltist' mentality, and to acquire it he must understand the book" (Perls et al., 1994, p. xxiv). The facts are seized only momentarily, and questions immediately arise again, in a circularity, which develops into a relationship with the book (this is called the hermeneutic logic of circularity). At times contradiction seems almost to have been deliberately invited into the heart of the text, almost as if to witness the necessary openness of every true thinking. (p. 10)

PHILIP: Yes, the "Goodman" volume of *Gestalt Therapy* is difficult to read and not open to easy introjecting. Partly, I agree, this is because it relies on persons placing theory on top of experience. But there is another reason, too. I have taught a study group on this text for the last 7 or so years, meeting once a month for 2 hours. We have covered only 80% of the book because we cover from one paragraph to three pages on a given evening. I have found that one important reason, not often enough acknowledged, is that the book both criticizes psychoanalysis and relies heavily on one variant of it. We have too long focused on its criticism and not enough on its continuation of that theory. Goodman approached Fenichel, the leader of the (politically) radical psychoanalysts and was rebuffed, but he learned a great deal. The one I have outlined is the radical version of psychoanalysis stemming from one of the two psychologies Freud wrote side by side throughout his career. Too few folks know psychoanalysis well enough, especially in its radical version, so the theory in the book escapes them. I will attend to a few issues from that theory in my response to you.

THE NOVEL CONTRIBUTION OF THE FOUNDERS: THEIR QUESTIONS

I have been told many things about the first gatherings of the founders. Isadore From told me about the psychoanalytic and generally well-informed background of the members of the group and the deconstructive method that characterized their questioning. Richard Kitzler (1999) recalled the informal and practical aim of those meetings. Members brought to the group their practical problems (like Shapiro's problems in helping difficult youth in the school he developed to function better in society). They expressed appreciation of the work of some Freudian dissidents, like Wilhelm Reich, and they used role-playing methods to approach clinical problems on the basis of the field-perspective belief that role-playing "the patient" allowed one to stay with the experience of the field.

What led the founders' research was the need to revise psychoanalysis (as the mainline psychotherapy model at that time) in a world that was now drastically changed after World War II. Through "chewing" contemporary philosophy, they integrated rich and stimulating new perspectives, from the views of dissident psychoanalysts (e.g., Karen Horney, Otto Rank, Wilhelm Reich) to phenomenology as a new way of looking at human experience.

They questioned whether, to say something new, it was necessary to invent a new model or whether it was enough to work at a metaclinical level. In other words, rather than questioning what did not work in the other clinical models (especially analytical and postanalytical ones), they were looking for what *did* work, according to a phenomenological analysis of successful therapeutic actions. I'm not saying that the founders accepted the ideas of their contemporary colleagues uncritically, but they were open to those ideas in their search for a key to understanding normality, the spontaneous regulation of the organism, and the healing relationship between human beings and nature and between the individual and the social group. Their dream was to build a theoretical model of spontaneous human functioning without devitalizing it in the process. They were well aware that their theories were necessary abstractions written in a code based on the logic of process, and for that very reason they could maintain and respect in its entirety the spontaneity of life.

The founders thus changed the direction of the usual theorizing and questioning from negative to positive, effecting a revolutionary change

PHILIP: In his radical version, Freud kept consciousness, id, ego, etc., as both internal organization and social relational organization. He did this where he wrote about instinctual impulses and perceptions as integrated in consciousness. So, too, where he developed id and ego as principles of organization, he included both internal and social organizing themes. (Conservative psychoanalysis did not see id as anything other than internal and posed ego against this, rather than seeing that both were concerned with how all drives were connected to each other and to the outer world.) Id, in its most advanced form in psychoanalysis, and in Gestalt therapy, refers to instigating background, both from within the organism and from the environment, either of which may be the initial instigating factor but both of which are integrated in developing figure formation.

Goodman (1994) posed a Faith-Security differentiation in referring to how the person lives in the present, either alive to the present in its fullness or repeating the past—the already achieved. "Accepting his concern and the object, and exercising the aggression, the creatively impartial man is excited by the conflict and grows by means of it, win or lose; he is not attached to what might be lost, for he knows he is changing and already identifies with what

from an epistemological point of view. As a matter of fact, to look at what an individual does as the best solution possible is the opposite of looking at what he or she does in terms of whether it accords with some universal "should." To believe in what we call self-regulation of the organism/environment field means to look at the world differently. We don't have to worry about what should be done, about seeing what doesn't work and inventing tools to repair the evil. Evil and good are part of the same whole. According to the founders,

> This book concentrates on and seeks to interpret a series of such neurotic dichotomies of theory, leading up to a theory of the self and its creative action. We proceed from problems of primary perception and reality through considerations of human development and speech to problems of society, morals, and personality. (Perls et al., 1994, p. 17)

The method the founders used to question reality and the answers they came up with are congruent with this basic principle of staying with what works and evolves, with what is, rather than falling into the trap of assessing reality, establishing what should or should not be. Goodman laid claim to an Aristotelian formulation when he stated that "[t]he standard of evaluation emerges in the act itself, and is, finally, the act itself as a whole" (Perls et al., 1994, p. 66).

he will become. With this attitude goes an emotion that is the opposite of the sense of security, namely faith: absorbed in the actual activity he does not protect the background but draws energy from it, he has faith that it will prove adequate" (p. 134). In psychoanalysis, Ferenczi proposed a comparable idea in his "magical omnipotence"; T. Benedek called it "confidence"; E. Erikson referred to this as "basic trust"; and I've called it "confident expectation."

MARGHERITA: After reading your note, Philip, I remain with the feeling that you are convinced that Gestalt therapy said nothing new or different from what you call radical psychoanalysis. Is this true? If yes, I wonder if your reaction here aims to demonstrate that Gestalt therapy theory says nothing relevant indeed, or you criticize a lack of development from a promising basis in Gestalt therapy.

PHILIP: I think Gestalt therapy developed some basic ideas, building on the platform of radical psychoanalysis but not departing sharply from it. So there is new and there is already established stuff. Neither psychoanalysis nor Gestalt therapy has done enough with the "confidence" or "faith" issue, a matter I have been developing. It is in both, and quite provocative. It is a personality function, Goodman's "readiness" or "attitude" and my "disposition."

THEORETICAL LINES OF GESTALT THERAPY

What answers did the founders obtain from their questioning? Basically, they asserted that life could be seen only at the contact boundary, in the experience of making and withdrawing from contact with the environment. Although there are many ways to present Gestalt theory, I will introduce it through five theoretical lines: (a) the organism/environment field; (b) the self; (c) the experience of contact and withdrawal from contact; (d) disturbances of functioning of self; and (e) the aim of psychotherapy.

The Organism/Environment Field

The expression *organism/environment field* is one of the most frequently used and meaningful terms in *Gestalt Therapy.* Although the influence of Kurt Lewin's field theory on the founders is evident, they implicitly kept their distance from it, focusing on contact making and withdrawal from contact between the organism and the environment rather than on the field (Perls et al., 1994, p. 4).

The founders conceived the relationship between organism and environment at both the anthropological and the sociopolitical level. The interaction of organism and environment has an obvious anthropological context, as it is related to Darwinian evolution. In fact, the human animal is considered the result of an evolutionary response to the environment, so the interaction of organism and environment is inherent in the matrix of evolution itself. The very concept of the organism's self-regulation (Goldstein, 1939/1995) is linked to the evolution of species. Fritz Perls's (1947/1969a) intuition regarding development in infancy and the concept of dental aggression was based on a theory of human nature as capable of self-regulation, a theory that is certainly more positive than the mechanistic conception pervading the Freudian theory current at the beginning of the twentieth century. The group that founded Gestalt therapy wanted, in effect, to show that individual needs cannot be considered in isolation from societal rules (Spagnuolo Lobb, Salonia, & Cavaleri, 1997; Spagnuolo Lobb, Salonia, & Sichera, 1996).

The field perspective in Gestalt therapy invites us to engage in nondichotomous thinking. For instance, if we see one partner of a couple visibly hurting the other, we can see the phenomenon in a linear way, attributing the cause of the hurt to that one partner. We can also see the same phenomenon in a field perspective, in which both hurting and being hurt are part of the field, and we can address our attention to those experiences of the partners that lead them to "call" the hurting and the being hurt into the field. Questions coming from a field perspective might be "How do I contribute to your hurting me?" and "How do I contribute to your being hurt?"

So, what is "the field" for Gestalt therapists? Is it the personal perception of one's own environment? How is thinking in terms of organism/environment field different from thinking in terms of systems? Obviously the field is not merely a subjective reality. The field perspective allows us to think of perception as a relational product that functions best when our thinking is totally centered on the contact boundary and thus grasping both what is internal and what is external—both the self's needs or experiences and the environment's demands or conditions. Specific to our theory is the notion that the self is *midway* between the organism and the environment and thus in a uniquely relational position. Many more examples and applications of field perspective could be cited, but I will leave that to Malcolm Parlett, who addresses them in the next chapter on contemporary theory.

For some time we have been witnessing a widespread attempt to bring the definition of the field in Gestalt therapy close to that of the system in systems theory. Although systems theory is certainly easier to use than a field perspective in that it offers the security of formal structure, it cannot do justice to the creative possibilities generated by being at the boundary of the unknown, with all its uncertainties and fears, or to the hopeful possibilities of human nature that the field perspective recognizes. The field in Gestalt therapy is a process, not a system (Hodges, 1997).

The Self—As Process, Function, and Boundary Event

According to *Gestalt Therapy,* what drove the group of founders to create a new theory of the self was a weakness in psychoanalytic theory about the ego:

> In the literature of psychoanalysis, notoriously the weakest chapter is the theory of the self or the ego. In this book, proceeding by not nullifying but by affirming the powerful work of creative adjustment, we essay a new theory of the self and the ego. (Perls et al., 1994, p. 24)

The self, the hinge on which all psychotherapeutic approaches turn, is conceived in *Gestalt Therapy* as the capacity of the organism to make contact with its environment—spontaneously, deliberately, and creatively. The function of the self is to contact the environment (called the "how" of human nature).

The view of the "self as function" is still a unique perspective among personality and psychotherapeutic theories. Gestalt therapy theory studies the self as a function of the organism-environment field in contact, not as a fixed structure. This approach rests, not on a rejection of the idea of contents or structures, but simply on the conviction that the task of anyone who studies human nature is to observe the criteria that produce spontaneity, not the criteria that allow human behavior to be schematized.

What does it mean to say that the self, as function, expresses a capacity or a process? Let us take an example: A newborn baby knows how to suck. This is a general capacity, or human function, whereas what it sucks is the content. The child's capacity to suck (and later to bite, chew, sit up, stand, walk, etc.) brings the child into contact with the world and fosters his or her spontaneity—or, in some cases, aversion. In fact, if the child is forbidden to suck (bite, chew, stand, walk, etc.), he or she must compensate by doing something else to make contact, thereby seeking a creative adjustment to the situation. For example, if a child is given soured milk or is punished for trying to crawl, stand, or walk, he is significantly influenced by this experience. However, Gestalt therapy is not interested in judging the quality of the milk or the parents' behavior; rather, we focus on how the child reacts. This allows us to focus on how the organism can be supported to claim its spontaneous functioning, which for us is the reason for which and the means by which it lives: contact brought about through various abilities. What helps clients recover their spontaneity is not only knowing what was not good but also experiencing new possibilities of making contact or rediscovering their functional spontaneity with a new creative adjustment—a new organization of the experience of the organism-environment field.

The Three Functions of Self

Having defined the self as the complex system of contacts necessary for adjustment in a difficult field, the authors of *Gestalt Therapy* identified certain "special structures" that the self creates "for special purposes" (Perls et al., 1994, pp. 156–157). These structures are clusters of experiences around which specific aspects of the self are organized. Although *Gestalt Therapy* uses psychoanalytic terms (the id, the ego, and the personality), it describes these concepts in experiential and phenomenological terms, conceiving them as capacities that function in an integrated mode in the holistic context of experience that constitutes the self. Id, ego, and personality are just three of the many possible experiential structures; they are understood as examples of the person's capacity to relate to the world. The id is the sensory-motor background of the experience, perceived as if "inside the skin"; the personality as assimilation of previous contacts; and the ego as the motor that moves the other two functions and chooses what belongs and what is alien to it. Next we will examine these three partial functions of the self.

The Id Function

The id function is defined as the organism's capacity to make contact with the environment by means of (a) the sensory-motor background of assimilated contacts; (b) physiological needs; and (c) bodily experiences and sensations that are perceived "as if inside the skin" (including past unfinished situations).

The Sensory-Motor Background of Assimilated Contacts

The various chapters of *Gestalt Therapy* present different definitions of *contact* that at times seem to conflict. For example, making contact is described as a constant activity of the self (the self being in continuous contact with the environment), but it is also described as a significant experience capable of changing the previous adjustment of the self. What, then, is contact? Is it like the experience of sitting on a chair (in which parts of the body are in physical contact with the chair) or something like making love for the first time with all the fullness of our being with a person with whom we are deeply in love? The authors of *Gestalt Therapy* refer to two kinds of contact: assimilated contact and contact with novelty, which leads to growth.

Ordinarily we feel no need to check every time we sit down whether the chair is strong enough to hold us or to reconstruct the whole series of proprioceptive and motor coordinations that permit us to sit on it. Only a destructuring event, such as the chair wobbling or creaking, reactivates the self at the contact boundary between our body and the chair. However, an infant must learn everything, and everything is a novelty to be experienced, destructured, and assimilated. A child experiences some relationship between crying and the mother's arrival (or lack thereof) and learns to regulate his or her inner sense of timing. When the mother does not respond, the child may experience the anguish of abandonment. The sensory-motor background of assimilated contacts, then, pertains to those specific acquisitions relating to the complexity of psychophysical development (Piaget, 1950) and of bodily experience (Kepner, 1987).

Physiological Needs

In the context of Gestalt therapy theory, where the self is a function of the field, physiological needs constitute the excitation of the self, coming from the organism. The self can be activated by an internal excitation (generated by the emergence of a physiological need) or by an external influence (received from an environmental pressure). This distinction, however, exists only in our minds, for the self is a function of the field, an integrated process where an environmental element may stimulate a physiological need in the same way that a physiological need may stimulate the perception of a part of the field not previously perceived. For example, seeing a fountain as we walk along under a blazing sun may remind us of thirst, just as thirst activates us to the search for water in the environment. These perceptual and relational dynamics were originally identified by the Gestalt psychology theorists and researchers Köhler (1940, 1947) and Koffka (1935).

To add a clinical example, seeing the therapist's beard may "remind" a client of some (frustrated) desire to express her sexual affection to her father, in the same way as the desire to release her own sexual energy may activate the patient to look for a perceptive (male) element in the therapist. The therapeutic process requires that the therapist be exactly at the boundary where the patient's physiological need meets his beard, as an environmental element, and it presupposes that the therapist is able to supply the specific support this client is seeking in order to develop more fully in this type of contact.

Bodily Experience and What Is Experienced "as If Inside the Skin"

This third aspect of the id function synthesizes the preceding two, providing a sense of integration in the self's experience of basic trust (or lack of trust) in making contact with the environment. This aspect reflects the delicate relationship between self-support and environmental support, between the sense of internal fullness and the sense that the environment can be trusted. The two experiences are interconnected: the more one feels able to trust the environment, the more one experiences an internal fullness as a relaxation of anguish or physiological desires. Vice versa, the more secure one feels internally, the more it is possible and functional to entrust oneself to the world. Laura Perls was particularly attentive to this interconnection in her clinical work. Her attention to patients' posture and gait enabled her to modulate her intervention, honoring the sense of self-support arising from the relationship with environmental support (Perls, 1976). Isadore From, on the other hand, connected psychotic experience to a strong anxiety that characterizes contact making through this aspect of self. For psychotics, the experience of what is "inside the skin" is highly anxiety producing and (still more important) is perceived as undifferentiated from or confused with what is "outside the skin." In other words, in psychotic disturbance we see the lack of perception of the boundary between the inside and the outside (see Spagnuolo Lobb, 2003a).

The Personality Function

Personality function expresses the capacity of the self to make contact with the environment on the basis of what one has become. "The Personality is the system of attitudes assumed in interpersonal relations. . . . [It] is essentially a verbal replica of the self" (Perls et al., 1994, p. 160). Thus personality function is expressed by the subject's answer to the question "Who am I?" It is the frame of reference and the basic attitudes of the individual (Bloom, 1997). In Gestalt therapy theory, personality represents a totally different concept than it does in psychoanalysis or transactional analysis, where personality is a normative aspect of the psychic structure, side by side with the impulsive (id) and regulatory (ego) aspects.

In Gestalt therapy, personality function expresses one's capacity to make contact with the environment on the basis of one's given definition of self. For example, if I think of myself as shy and inhibited, I set up a completely different kind of relationship with my environment than someone whose definition of self is daring and extroverted. This concept recalls the empirical "me" of G. H. Mead (1934), whose theory surely influenced Paul Goodman. Personality function, as a matter of fact, pertains to how we create our social roles (e.g., becoming a student or parent), assimilate previous contacts, and creatively adjust to changes imposed by growth and development.

Thus one of the basic aspects a therapist must look at is the functioning of the self at the level of personality. For example, an 8-year-old boy spontaneously uses language appropriate to his age. However, if he expresses himself in adult language, he may be viewed (by his manner of contacting the environment) as expressing a disturbance of personality function. The same may be said of a woman of 40 who talks like a 16-year-old, a mother who behaves like a friend or a sister toward her children, or a student who behaves like a professor, to say nothing of a client who defines him- or herself as a person who has no need of help.

The Ego Function

Ego function expresses a different capacity of the self in contact: the capacity to identify oneself with or alienate oneself from parts of the field (this *is* me, this *is not* me), the power to want and to decide that characterizes the uniqueness of individual choices. It is the will as a power, in the sense used by Otto Rank (1941, p. 50), that organizes autonomously, representing neither a biological impulse nor a social drive but rather constituting the creative expression of the whole person (Müller, 1991, p. 45).

Thus the ego function intervenes in the process of creative adjustment by making choices, identifying with some parts of the field and alienating itself from others. Ego is that function of the self that gives an individual the sense of being active and deliberate. The self spontaneously exercises this intentionality and carries it forward with strength, awareness, excitation, and capacity to create new figures. The ego function "is deliberate, active in mode, sensorically alert and motorically aggressive, and conscious of itself as isolated from the situation" (Perls et al., 1994, p. 157). According to *Gestalt Therapy,* these are precisely the characteristics that lead us to think of ego as the agent of experience. Once we have created this abstraction, we no longer think of the environment as a pole of experience but rather as a distant external world, and we see ego and environment as nondichotomous parts of a single event. Ego function works on the basis of the interchange of all the other structures of the self. The capacity to spontaneously deliberate is exercised in harmony with the capacity to contact the environment through what is perceived as being "inside the skin" (id function) and through the definition given to the "Who am I?" question (personality function). It is the capacity to introject, project, retroflect, and fully establish contact.

A clinical example seems in order here. An emotion normally experienced as a whole phenomenon can be described according to different functions of self. According to *the id function,* when one experiences the emotion, one perceives one's muscles as being relaxed or tense and experiences one's breathing as free and open or constricted. *The personality function* defines the emotion as one's own (e.g., "I'm the sort of person who feels these emotions"). *The ego function* allows the development of excitation connected with the emotion: for example, by introjecting (defining the experience as "I'm moved, it's okay with me"); projecting (noticing the excitation in one's environment too—for instance, saying something like "I can see that other people are moved too"); or retroflecting (avoiding full contact with the environment by pulling back or turning the energy inward, as in "I want to handle this experience alone").

Gestalt Therapy describes these ego functions both as capacities to make contact and as resistances to it (losses of ego functions). This double use of the above-mentioned terms reflects an important coherence with Gestalt therapy epistemological principles, yet it is often a source of confusion in that the same terms can be used to describe both normality and psychopathology.

THE EXPERIENCE OF CONTACT AND WITHDRAWAL FROM CONTACT

The attention to process in Gestalt therapy leads us to see the experience of contact as it develops, thus considering the time dimension. In fact, in an ordinary healthy experience,

> [o]ne is relaxed, there are many possible concerns, all accepted and all fairly vague—the self is a "weak Gestalt." Then an interest assumes dominance and the forces spontaneously mobilize themselves, certain images brighten and motor responses are initiated. At this point, most often, there are also required certain deliberate exclusions and choices. . . . That is, deliberate limitations are imposed in the total functioning of the self, and the identification and alienation proceed according to these limits. . . . And finally, at the climax of excitement, the deliberateness is relaxed and the satisfaction is again spontaneous. (Perls et al., 1994, p. 157)

The self is defined by the process of contact and withdrawal from contact, in which the self is drawn to the contact boundary with the environment and, after the fullness of the encounter, withdraws. The experience of contact is described in *Gestalt Therapy* as having four phases (*fore-contact, contact, final contact, postcontact*), each with a different stress on the figure/background dynamic.

The organism's self-activation is called *fore-contact,* the moment at which excitements emerge that initiate the figure/background process. As an example of the development of the self, let us take the need of hunger. In *fore-contact* the body is perceived as background, whereas the excitation (need of hunger) is the figure. In the following phase, that of *contact,* the self expands toward the contact boundary with the environment, following the excitation that, in a *subphase of orientation*, leads it to explore the environment in search of an object or a set of possibilities (food, various types of food). The desired object now becomes the figure, while the initial need or desire recedes to the background. In a second *subphase of manipulation,* the self

---

PHILIP: With respect to ego function, there is an ambiguity in Gestalt therapy theory. Isadore From spoke of the need to create a distinct "I" and a distinct "You" in contacting, and this necessitates not only looking at identifying and alienating what is for oneself but also helping the other identify and alienate what is for him or her. Are we responsible only for ourselves or for enabling the other to become open and real? And are we only agents of identifying and alienating, or also functions of the other who affects who we are and what we want?

MARGHERITA: I believe Isadore was the first who underlined the social perspective of ego and other self-functions in clinical practice. His theory very much focused on the relational perspective (the concept of contact boundary) and the field perspective (the concept of situation) that pervade the first volume of *Gestalt Therapy* (1994). For instance, he used to teach to Gestalt therapists his relational theory on dreams and lapses, etc.: For example, "How did I contribute to the telling of this dream to me?" This social aspect of self was included *in nuce* in Freud's theory; for sure it wasn't figural in his method but was developed later by his "dissident" students, when the cultural milieu was more open to this aspect.

PHILIP: There remains some ambiguity between Fritz's and Isadore's creating a distinct "I" and a distinct "You." With Fritz, the person is responsible only for the self (later appearing in his "Gestalt Prayer"), whereas in Isadore's approach, the person is also responsible for the other developing his/her distinctness. Both radical psychoanalysis and Gestalt therapy have a social aspect in clinical practice.

"manipulates" the environment, choosing certain possibilities and rejecting others (it chooses, for example, a savory, hot, soft food rich in protein), targeting certain parts of the environment and overcoming obstacles (it actively looks for a place, such as a diner, bakery, or restaurant, where the chosen food can be found). In the third phase, *final contact,* the final objective, the contact, is the figure, while the environment and the body are the background. The whole self is occupied in the spontaneous act of contacting the environment, awareness is high, the self is fully present at the contact boundary with the environment (the food is bitten, tasted, savored), and the ability to choose is relaxed because there is nothing to choose at that moment. It is in this phase that the nourishing exchange with the environment, with the novelty, takes place. This, once assimilated, will contribute to the growth of the organism.

In the last phase, *postcontact,* the self diminishes to allow the organism the possibility of digesting the acquired novelty so as to integrate it, without awareness, into the preexisting structure. The process of assimilation is always unaware and involuntary (as digestion is involuntary); it may come into awareness to the degree that there is a disturbance. The self, therefore, ordinarily diminishes in this phase, withdrawing from the contact boundary.

Clearly, this example cannot do justice to the complexity of the self's system of contact, for that system is constantly in action on various levels and constitutes the current experience of the individual. One may read a book (mental contact) lying in a hammock (largely assimilated contact unless the hammock overturns), listening to the birds singing (acoustic contact), smelling the scent of the flowers (olfactory contact), and relishing the warmth of the sun (kinesthetic contact). In this complex system of contacts, however, the organism is prevalently centered on one—the one it chooses and identifies with in order to grow. It may be reading the book if the most prominent need is linked to mental growth, or listening to the birds singing if this acoustic contact evokes emotions and thoughts that are prominent at that moment, or something else.

PHILIP: In respect to contacting and withdrawing, I have some thoughts. First, I believe our conception of the contact and withdrawing process derives from what Freud, early in his career, called the "experience of satisfaction," which influenced many concepts later in his career.

MARGHERITA: We have to consider that Freud lived in another time, with different cultural categories. The concept of "experience of making and withdrawing from contact" is a clinical declination of the philosophical movements, which started around 1920, when the concept of a unique truth itself was put into question by existentialism and the concept of experience became figural for phenomenologist researchers. So the concept of a contact and withdrawing process was the result of a comprehensive movement in culture and society. Every theoretician expresses the ideas of his or her time.

PHILIP: Freud was well ahead of his time when he was good and merely part of his time when he was not. Goodman found the advanced part of Freud.

DISTURBANCES IN THE FUNCTIONING OF SELF

"A strong error is already a creative act and must be solving an important problem for the one who holds it" (Perls et al., 1994, pp. 20–21). The first question in approaching the issue of psychopathology is: "How do we speak of psychopathology in Gestalt therapy?" (Robine,

1989). The basic understanding of resistances as creative adjustments leads us to think of psychopathology in a unique way. We believe that any symptom or behavior usually defined as pathological is a creative adjustment of the person in a difficult situation. The so-called losses of ego function are creative choices to avoid the development of excitation during various phases of the experience of contact with the environment because that development would cause the person to experience the anxiety linked to that excitement.

Habitual interruptions of contact lead to the accumulation of uncompleted situations (interrupted spontaneity leads to open gestalts and unfinished situations), which subsequently continue to interrupt other processes of meaningful contact. The anxiety accompanying the primary interruption of contact (which, as the situations are repeated, becomes habitual) is the consequence of excitation being inadequately supported by oxygen (adequate breathing) at the physiological level and by environmental response at the social level (Spagnuolo Lobb, 2001a, 2001b). This type of excitation cannot lead the organism to the spontaneous development of self at the contact boundary. Retroflection is the interruption most often seen in the patient's way of being with the therapist. The therapist must discover the primary interruption, or, as Perls put it, must "peel the onion."

Spontaneity means being fully present at the contact boundary, with full awareness of oneself and with full use of one's senses. This allows one to see the other clearly. A dancer moving spontaneously dances with grace but without knowing which foot moves first. When *spontaneity* is interrupted, excitation becomes anxiety to avoid; *intentionality* becomes distorted; and the *contacting* carries anxiety (of which one is unaware) and happens via introjecting, projecting, retroflecting, egotism, or confluence. For example, if a young girl spontaneously feels the desire to hug her father and she encounters his coldness, she stops her spontaneous movement toward him, but she doesn't stop her intentionality to contact him. The excitation of "I want to hug him" is blocked in an inhaling movement (where she holds her breath), and she becomes anxious. To avoid this anxiety, she learns to do other things and eventually may even forget the anxiety. What she does is establish contact via styles of interrupting or resisting spontaneity such as

- *Introjecting*: The development of excitement is interrupted using a rule or a premature definition (e.g., "You shouldn't be expansive" or "Fathers should not be hugged").
- *Projecting*: The development of excitement is interrupted by disowning it and attributing it to the environment (e.g., "My father is rejecting me" or "My expansiveness must be wrong for him").
- *Retroflecting*: The development of excitement is interrupted by being turned back inside instead of being allowed to lead to full contacting of the environment (e.g., "I do not need to, and it is not good for me to hug him").
- *Egotism*: Contact with the environment happens but gets finished too soon before the novelty brought by the environment is contacted and assimilated (e.g., the girl hugs her father but doesn't experience the novelty of this event, saying to herself, "I knew that to hug him wouldn't be anything new for me").
- *Confluence*: The girl's excitement doesn't develop because the process of differentiation of organism from environment doesn't even start (e.g., she takes her father's coldness as her own attitude and doesn't even think of the possibility of hugging her father).

Besides the above-mentioned losses of ego functions, we need to consider which function, among the personality and id functions, is mainly disturbed. When there is a disturbance of the personality function, a rigidity or anxiety toward a novelty in the field regarding social relationships disturbs the contact, and the ego loses certain abilities. One example might be that of becoming a mother, which requires not only a biological change but also a change in social relationships (being mother to one's child). What seems new is defined as "not for me" by the ego function (in that the support of the personality function is lacking), which cannot adapt to the changes in social relationships or in the cultural values or the language presented by the current situation. In conjunction with the id function, which organizes what is felt, personality function disturbances contribute to the loss of functioning of the ego and are at the root of neurotic disturbances.

> In contrast, in the case of psychoses, there is a serious disturbance of the id function: the ground of security arising from assimilated contacts is missing and the ego cannot exercise its capacity to deliberate on this ground. Thus contacting is dominated by sensations that invade a self, which, as we might say, "has no skin." All that happens on the outside is potentially experienced as happening also on the inside: the self moves without the clear perception of boundaries with the environment (confluence), in a state in which everything is anxiety-inducing novelty (it cannot be assumed that there will not be an earthquake) and nothing is effectively assimilable (because nothing can really be recognized as different, as new). This disturbed experience of the id function can be read in the breathing and posture, in the way the patient looks at others and in her/his manner of relating in general, as well as in her/his language. The body and the language are, indeed, for this very reason the most important tools of phenomenological reading for the therapist. For example, one might state his/her experience as "Your voice takes possession of my brain." "That glass of water has destroyed my stomach." "It wasn't the hero of the film who was bleeding, it was me, but you could see it on the screen." "When you smile I breathe easier." These examples remind us of the strict link between the outside and the inside, that we have to consider in treatment of psychosis. (Spagnuolo Lobb, 2002, 2003a)

The Aim of Psychotherapy: From Egotism to Relational Creativity

Among the losses of ego function Goodman included egotism, a neurotic structure that has been either ignored or debated because of its limited definition in *Gestalt Therapy* and because it is undeniably provocative. "For want of a better term, we call this attitude 'egotism,' since it is a final concern for one's boundaries and identity rather than for what is contacted" (Perls et al., 1994, p. 237).

Egotism is a contact interruption that the ego function carries out in the final phase: at the culminating moment of the contact experience. This occurs when there should be an exchange between the organism and the environment and all the willful abilities should be relaxed. Instead, the ego maintains control, making contact without allowing the environmental novelty to upset it. The person is aware of everything and often has something to say about everything.

> The typical example is the attempt to maintain erection and prevent the spontaneous development of the orgasm. By this means he proves his potency, that he "can," and gets a satisfaction of conceit. . . . He wards off the surprises of the environment . . . by seeking to isolate himself as the only reality. (Perls et al., 1994, p. 237)

Egotism, then, has to do with not surrendering oneself to the environment or trusting the vital novelty that the environment represents.

Isadore From was often heard saying that egotism is the illness that psychotherapists ("even Gestalt therapists," he would say humorously) communicate to their patients when they give them the capacity to know everything about themselves but cannot give them the trust necessary to plunge into life. The egotist can be the "recovered" patient who has learned everything about his or her contact interruption, even how to avoid it, but who still is not able to be in the fullness of life, accepting the risk that is implied in trusting the environment to allow for true spontaneity of contact.

The concept of egotism was at the leading edge of this new approach because it raised a question about the aim of psychotherapy: Is therapy purely a treatment of psychological functioning, or does it have more complex aspects? If it is the former, we have to consider egotist patients as "cured," for they have control and consciousness of their lives. And if this is the aim of psychotherapy, we have to consider as "healthy" a world made up of boring people who have something to say about everything but who prevent their own spontaneous development. Therefore, the concept of egotism brings us back to the initial challenge that the authors of *Gestalt Therapy* accepted when they set out to create a phenomenological model of psychotherapy that could support the organism's spontaneity in encountering its environment, an aim that implies more complex tasks.

Egotism entails withdrawing from the relational deliberateness proper to human beings; the egotist "make[s] sure that the ground possibilities are indeed exhausted—there is no threat of danger or surprise—before he commits himself" (Perls et al., 1994, p. 237). This concept raises two important questions for the psychotherapist. First, is the therapist's task to support the consciousness of being (make all that is id become ego, as Freud suggested) or to help clients reclaim their spontaneity in contacting the environment? Second, is psychotherapy a mere technical intervention, a clinically detached "art," or does it imply also a lifestyle and a social attitude in the person who applies it?

For Gestalt therapy, the aim of "the cure," so to speak, is surely not consciousness of self but the spontaneity of contacting the other, the committing of oneself to the spontaneity of making

PHILIP: Both Freud and Goodman resolved the dialectic of defining oneself (in contacting) and losing oneself in a unit larger than oneself (at final contact) where all is figure and the body and the other recede in their distinctness from each other. Along these lines, I believe that self diminishes at final contact, as Goodman suggests, not at postcontact. We lose self in separateness when we merge with the other or with the food and other nutriments we need. Egotism, then, would be the result of anxiety at final contact, the unwillingness to proceed to healthy confluence wherein one becomes a part of something bigger than self alone.

MARGHERITA: Then how do you explain retroflection?

PHILIP: I do not see a problem with the matter of retroflection in my analysis of the dialectic of defining self and losing self.

MARGHERITA: Maybe I could explain the last point on egotism and retroflection. What you define as egotism is what I call retroflection (a loss of ego function in the moment of full contact). Egotism happens for me a little further on, when contact has been made and the novelty brought by the other/environment is not taken in by the organism in a manner that enables it to be deconstructed. So growth cannot happen, since the novelty is not assimilated. Goodman writes that the egotist knows everything but remains with no spirit, no aliveness. The person is boring (as a critic of psychoanalysis, the psychoanalyzed knows everything but is not able to change his or her own life).

contact, which is the basis for creativity. Giving psychotherapy the task of restoring spontaneous awareness (distinct from consciousness) in contacting the environment means giving space and trust to the creativity that is natural for the human organism in relation, rather than giving space and trust to preestablished rules of social living. This spontaneous contact is the foundation of social living that integrates individual creativity and community rules (Spagnuolo Lobb et al., 1996). For this reason, the concept of egotism as one of the losses of ego function represents both an innovation and an important cultural and political effect of psychotherapy.

A second question is: Does our paying attention to egotism as a resistance to be cured define the role of the psychotherapist? The answer is "Yes," for we are interested in our relationship with the client and believe that that relationship is where treatment takes place. We don't pretend to know everything about the other or ourselves; instead, we use our knowledge as the background of our relationship with the client. If the self in *Gestalt Therapy* is epistemologically based on respect for the integrity and spontaneity of life, then this principle must be validated in the therapeutic relationship, and the therapist must integrate it into his or her own way of being.

RECENT THEORETICAL DEVELOPMENTS

In recent years, many theorists have broached new concepts that are consistent with Gestalt theory. But such developments can be our "Achilles' heel" if they are not in line with Gestalt therapy's unique epistemological frame of reference. Among the many creative theoretical developments from *our* roots of classical Gestalt theory, I select two examples for discussion here: (a) the dimension of time in the contact process and (b) the perspective of the "between."

The Dimension of Time in the Contact Process

The concept of time in the contact-withdrawal experience is not clearly defined in *Gestalt Therapy*. Specifically, it is not clear whether the four phases of contact-withdrawal express the *possible* development of the experience of contact, thus allowing space for the possibility that they will not be developed in every experience of contact, or whether, simply because the experience develops in time, the dimension of time in the experience of contact has to be understood in the Heideggerian sense, hence involving a meaning connected with the intentionality proper to each phase of the process. For example, if we consider relational meaning in the therapeutic process, every sentence the client utters takes on meaning in the context of time. A message from the client such as "I feel anxious" acquires different meanings according to the phase of the session in which it is uttered. In the first phase, it expresses fear of beginning the interaction; in the second phase, fear of being overwhelmed by the gradually emerging tension; in the central phase, fear of going deeper and of letting oneself go; and toward the end of the session, fear of detachment. Far from being a predetermined way of understanding the client, placing the patient's message in the context of time allows the relational meanings of his or her communications to be grasped more accurately (Salonia, 1992; Spagnuolo Lobb, 2003b).

We all know, for example, clients who begin to talk about important subjects during the last few minutes of the session and others who start before even sitting down. A client who arrives for the first time for a session and immediately tells the therapist about the most intimate part of his or her problem is clearly avoiding the experience of fore-contacting the environment (probably because it creates anxiety). We may therefore say that the anxiety that the client feels in fore-contact does not allow him or her to develop the process of contact spontaneously. The client then creates solutions that, through the loss of an ego function, enable him or her not to feel anxiety. A basic tool for the Gestalt therapist is to identify in which of the contact phases the client feels the anxiety of the relationship and interrupts contact with the therapist.

The Experience of the "Between"

A recent ongoing development in Gestalt theory concerns the social core of Gestalt therapy, the experience of the "between"—that is, the experiential space between the "I" and the "you," or between internal experience and environmental influence—and of the relational aspects of therapy, what many refer to as the "co-creation of the field." The editors of this book invited major proponents of field and relational Gestalt theory to address this topic in later chapters. Here I will simply comment on the connection of this aspect of our theory with the classical model.

Consistent with phenomenological thinking, Gestalt therapy states that we cannot know "reality" in itself but only the part of it that we experience in the here and now—in other words, the experience of contact and withdrawal as we interact with our environment. For Gestalt epistemology, contact is a boundary event in continuous evolution, which the Gestalt therapist looks on as a process of relational intentionality. The forming of the relationship is the place where the "I" and the "you" arrive at a new truth, a momentary configuration of harmony that immediately gives way to other figures. The ability to stay in the ceaseless equilibrium of the moment and to experience the uncertainty of the moment-to-moment truth of the relationship is a typical quality of a Gestalt therapist. The Gestalt method is one that allows things to happen, the ever-new creation of suitable solutions in the here and now of the therapeutic relationship, insofar as the self of every individual is present at the "contact boundary."

To move from the intrapsychic paradigm to that of the "between" means that the therapist observes him- or herself and the patient not as separate entities but as a "dialogical totality" in which the patient and the therapist are in dialogue with each other. Every communication from the patient is inscribed and receives its meaning from the gestalt of mutual perceptions, in which relational deliberateness is expressed. The following examples are adapted from my colleague Salonia (1992). When a client says, "I'm afraid at the moment. I don't know why," if the therapist intervenes using an intrapsychic approach, he or she will try to understand the kind of fear, past experiences, what the patient is afraid of, et cetera, and will ask questions like "Could you go deeper into what you are feeling?" or "Are you aware of anything right now that reminds you of a previous experience when you were afraid?" If instead the therapist applies the interpersonal paradigm of the "between" as a horizon of reference, he or she may ask questions such as "How do I frighten you?" or "In what way do you not feel protected by me?" In this case, the patient is likely to respond with "It has nothing to do with you, it's my problem." But if the therapist says, "Take your time. How am I frightening, or how have I frightened you?" the patient may timidly hint, "Maybe because you speak so loudly." At this point there is an opening that allows the renewal of a previously interrupted relational pattern. This kind of dialogue opens for the patient the possibility of overcoming the relational anxiety that he or she tried to avoid via the interruption of contact (and then forgot). At this point, after the relational intentionality has been brought to the contact boundary again, the therapist can use a variety of Gestalt interventions with the intention of bringing to awareness the here and now of the therapeutic dialogue.

CONCLUSION

To present the classical principles of Gestalt therapy theory, I first presented a methodological perspective—the hermeneutic logic of circularity—as a tool to read and refer to the founding text of this approach in a way that can stimulate your creativity. I then critically introduced the innovations that the founders of Gestalt therapy brought to the field of psychotherapy research and praxis, outlining the revolutionary change of epistemological view implied in looking at the normal spontaneity of human nature rather than trying to categorize it. I also summarized the core aspects of the classical Gestalt therapy theory in five main concepts: (a) the organism/environment field; (b) the crucial perspective on self as a process, a function, and a boundary event; (c) the development of the experience of contact and withdrawal from contact with the environment; (d) the unique theory of psychopathology in Gestalt therapy, with its concepts of resistance as creative adjustment, of losses of ego functioning, and of neurotic and psychotic experience; and (e) egotism, which I have critically appreciated as a concept representing a clinical and cultural transition from an earlier psychoanalytical perspective to a more modern idea of the aim of psychotherapy, and consequently of the attitude of the psychotherapist. I called this aim a shift "from egotism to relational creativity." Finally I presented, as examples of the developments that classical Gestalt theory can foster, two theoretical lines: one focused on a phenomenological consideration of the dimension of time in the experience of contact and the other starting from the dialogic perspective of the "between" and developing the concept of co-creating the therapeutic field. I hope that in this chapter I have given an idea of the depth, fascination, and usefulness of original Gestalt therapy theory and that readers will integrate it into their own personal and professional styles.

REVIEW QUESTIONS

1. What is meant by the author's statement that *Gestalt Therapy* encourages a "hermeneutic" process in readers and Sichera's statement that "the text is developed in a series of concentric circles"? How might a style of writing introduce the reader to "process" (an important element of the Gestalt approach)?

2. It has often been said that the theoretical volume of *Gestalt Therapy* was written so that readers could not introject it. What does this statement mean?

3. The author believes the founders of Gestalt therapy were looking for "a key to understanding normality, the spontaneous regulation of the organism, and the healing relationship between human beings and nature and between the individual and the social group." In what ways was their approach different from the mainstream therapeutic approach (psychoanalysis) of that time?

4. What is meant in Gestalt theory by the viewing of the self "as process, function, and boundary event"? How does this differ from other theories of self or personality theories?

5. When a symptom or behavior that is usually viewed as "pathological" is defined as "a creative adjustment of the person in a difficult situation" by Gestalt therapists, what does this mean?

EXPERIENTIAL PEDAGOGICAL ACTIVITIES

ACTIVITY 1: When you are ready (feeling curious), read any part of the theoretical volume of *Gestalt Therapy* (Vol. 1 in the 1994 edition, Vol. 2 in the 1951 edition), with an attitude of curiosity, and see what happens. Keep some notes on your processes, to be discussed in class.

ACTIVITY 2: This chapter introduced five of the basic Gestalt resistances or styles of interrupting contact—projecting, retroflecting, introjecting, confluence, and egotism. These are viewed as developing from creative adjustments to difficult life situations. Prepare a handout that describes the Gestalt resistances in more detail, and break into small groups of three to five students to discuss the definitions of each form of resistance. Develop a role-play "skit" that you can perform in front of the class. Let the situation develop, and note how in your skit you spontaneously use one of the contact interruptions mentioned. Good role plays usually take a few minutes to develop, attending to (a) the scene, (b) the characters, and (c) the situation. Try to assess what phase of contact (*fore-contact, contact, final contact, postcontact*) the form of resistance is interrupting, and note what form of resistance is being depicted. The whole role play should last about 5 to 10 minutes. After you finish the skit, the class will try to guess which resistances were demonstrated, the phase of contact, and how the resistance could be a creative adjustment to a situation. Compare what the class observed with the experiences of the persons involved.

ACTIVITY 3: Pair off with a classmate; one of you will role-play a therapist and the other a client. As therapist, experiment with the difference between an intervention based on the "individual/intrapsychic" focus (using questions like "What do you feel when you say that?" "What do you want?" "What are you doing?") and an intervention based on a contact boundary perspective (using questions like "How am I involved in this feeling of yours?" "You say that you are scared. How do I contribute to your being scared?").

ACTIVITY 4: Form subgroups of four to seven in class, and have each person assume the role of one of the founders of Gestalt therapy—for example, Fritz Perls, Laura Perls, Paul Goodman, Paul Weisz, Elliott Shapiro, Ralph Hefferline, or Isadore From. (Students will receive a handout that contains brief biographical sketches of the above founders.) In your small group, take 10 to 15 minutes to create a dialogue that represents the kind of interactive process you imagine took place when these people met in the late 1940s and wrote *Gestalt Therapy*. You will then be asked to play your "skit" before the class and will be encouraged to extend the drama in the role plays and discuss the experience with the class.

CHAPTER 3

Contemporary Gestalt Therapy: Field Theory

MALCOLM PARLETT

DIALOGUE RESPONDENT: ROBERT G. LEE

Malcolm Parlett's background in academic psychology and educational research has served him well as the founding editor of the *British Gestalt Journal* and as the author of numerous book chapters and articles on Gestalt therapy. He is currently a visiting professor at the University of Derby and a registered psychotherapist with the UK Council for Psychotherapy. He is active as an international consultant on Gestalt therapy and organizational development. Following training at the Gestalt Institute of Cleveland in the 1970s, he co-founded the Gestalt Psychotherapy and Training Institute in the United Kingdom.

Robert G. Lee is a licensed psychologist and Gestalt therapist in Massachusetts with a private practice in Cambridge. His special interest in research and treatment of shame issues with individuals, couples, and families has led to his extensive writing for Gestalt books and journals about this topic. He is the co-editor of *The Voice of Shame: Silence and Connection in Psychotherapy* (1996). In his latest collected work, *The Values of Connection: A Relational Approach to Ethics* (2004), he and other distinguished theorists and practitioners explore the relational values that derive from the Gestalt model as well as how these values offer field solutions to modern problems. He is a member of the visiting faculty of the Gestalt Institute of Cleveland, and he teaches and trains nationally and internationally.

INTRODUCTION: AN APPROACH GROUNDED IN THE IDEAS OF GESTALT'S FOUNDING BOOK

Gestalt therapy has not stood still. The first decades after its founding were a time of experiment in practice rather than of theory development. However, three Gestalt classics stem from that time (Latner, 1973; Polster & Polster, 1973; Zinker, 1977), all of which have stood the test of time. In the last quarter-century, theoretical writing has expanded dramatically. The numbers of new Gestalt books and professional journals indicate that there is growing interest worldwide in the theory and practice of Gestalt therapy, and part of what gives Gestalt therapy its contemporary relevance is its distinctive theoretical outlook.

One cannot appreciate the way Gestalt theory has developed without acknowledging the continuing influence of the founding text, *Gestalt Therapy: Excitement and Growth in the Human Personality,* by Frederick Perls, Ralph Hefferline, and Paul Goodman, first published in 1951 (a revised version appeared in 1994 and is now the definitive edition). Their text remains the starting point for any contemporary Gestalt theorist. Some writers stay close to its language, concepts, and theoretical priorities, whereas others stretch the original ideas in new directions and change the language. All agree that the book was years ahead of its time in its conception of human beings in society and in pointing the way for therapy.

Obviously, the wider world of psychology and psychotherapy has undergone huge changes since *Gestalt Therapy* was first published. Gestalt therapists have integrated insights, concepts, and methods, such as the developmental work of Daniel Stern (1985), and have acknowledged other movements, such as that within psychoanalysis toward a more intersubjective view of therapy (see Jacobs, 1992). At the same time, too much susceptibility to influences from outside has also prompted unease. There is a constant tension—especially for authors and editors of journals and books—between what is new and exciting

---

BOB: Malcolm, it is with pleasure that I join you in a conversation around your eloquently written and comprehensive chapter on Gestalt field theory. As to what you have presented above, supporting and even celebrating differences has always been a hallmark of Gestalt therapy. So, as you say, it is not surprising that there are differences in understanding of basic theory. Equally important is the emphasis in Gestalt therapy on dialogue between differences. Reflecting on what you have said about the enduring quality of Gestalt theory, for myself, a major attraction of Gestalt theory is its basic conceptualization of a person meeting his/her environment, called contact, which is the crucible for living, evolving, and thriving. This basic theoretical stance has always made it easy for me to assimilate my life experience into how I understand what it means to be human and to work with others. It places people in a field context from the start and makes possible an understanding of field properties and dynamics, which you are about to explore with us, and which are not so understandable from other theoretical perspectives.

MALCOLM: I like very much your comment about contact—that it is "the crucible for living, evolving, and thriving." I recall Carl Hodges remarking that "contact organizes the field," and we are doing that here, in this first exchange between us—we are organizing the field of "Bob-Malcolm-dialogue." There is the field of the reader, the book, the ideas of this chapter, and now there is the field of you, Bob, and me—a field within a field. But we are leaping ahead here. I look forward to co-creating the temporary field of our dialogue.

---

and necessary to attend to and what is essential for the preservation of Gestalt therapy as a distinct tradition.

Famously, Laura Perls (1992c), co-founder of the approach with Fritz Perls and Paul Goodman, encouraged therapists to draw on "whatever life experience and professional skills" they have "assimilated and integrated in [their] background" (p. 133). Given this "permission" for Gestalt therapists and theorists to pursue their own directions, it is not perhaps so surprising that there is also diversity in what theory has focused on. As Robine (2001) pointed out, there are significant inconsistencies worldwide in what is understood as basic theory. However, for all the variation, there are also areas of convergence that have become more apparent in the last 20 years, and I will focus on them in this chapter. I appreciate that others are likely to disagree with the "version" I am presenting.

A DEFINING PERSPECTIVE

The foremost convergence that I discern centers on the concepts of "field" and "field theory." Two editions of a popular textbook devoted to Gestalt therapy that appeared in the 1980s did not even have "field" in the indexes (Van de Riet, Korb, & Gorrell, 1980/1989). But almost all writing today includes and discusses field theory, the field perspective, the relational field, or the field paradigm. *Field* has become one of the most frequently used terms in current Gestalt literature. Though hard to define precisely (and there is variation from author to author), the concept of the field has become both indispensable and theoretically central. The field is the medium in which therapy takes place and is inseparable from it. The field is the entire situation of the therapist, the client, and all that goes on between them. The field is made and constantly remade. When we talk of the "atmosphere changing," we are talking about the field. When we acknowledge that the therapist's and client's "overall level of trust and ease with each other" has developed (increased or decreased) over time, we are reflecting on a development of the overall field. The communication has changed, as have the individuals, as has the scope of what is possible for the two parties to do together. Something occurs in the overall organization of what is happening. What I am describing may be difficult to pin down, but every experienced practitioner learns to pay attention to this overall organization, the situation as a whole—that is, to the field. This degree of focus on the field does not appear to have affected the thinking of any other major psychotherapeutic approach to the same extent, and it suggests that Gestalt therapy's "field perspective" is critical in defining the approach. That the essential ideas were extensively prefigured in *Gestalt Therapy* (Perls et al., 1951) underlines how influential was the founding orientation.

In this chapter we shall be returning again and again to the field perspective as a linking theme that lends overall coherence to the distinctive, widely shared outlook of contemporary Gestalt therapists.

THE "UNITARY" PERSPECTIVE IN GESTALT THERAPY

One of the major influences on Gestalt therapy, the school of Gestalt psychology, emphasized that human perception and thinking were structured and patterned and should not be "reduced" in an atomistic way into component parts. If psychology was to have relevance to people's experiences, to how people lived and thought and perceived, then psychologists needed to be observing patterning and relationship, whole configurations and complex interactions, rather than chopping up nature and experience into underlying sensations or stimulus-response units in the manner of reductionist science.

Likewise, the founders of Gestalt therapy sought to do justice to the complex, indivisible world of phenomenological experience in "holistic" fashion. That is, a person's familial and social world, organizations and culture, as well as his or her biological nature, had to be considered together, not as if they existed in separate compartments. Human beings were not to be regarded in isolation from their natural settings, each individual alone with his or her "intrapsychic" psychological processes. As Latner (1992) wrote,

> Most psychological theories are . . . of this type. They look for the individual and the individual's psychological properties, ego states, cognition, tendencies to self-realization or to individuation. These are objects, the equivalents of a planet in a Newtonian universe. Alternatively, the new [field] perspective looks at the dimensions of interplay in time and space, the effects of relatedness over time. (p. 21)

In Gestalt therapy, the "unitary" outlook, the relationship between parts and whole, and the balancing of connecting with others while also maintaining a separate identity have been central preoccupations. The concept of field as a unitary, encompassing concept appealed to the authors of *Gestalt Therapy.* They wrote as follows:

> In any psychological investigation whatever, we must start from the interacting of the organism and its environment. . . . Let us call this interacting of organism and environment in any function the "*organism/environment field,*" and let us remember that no matter

---

BOB: As you say, Gestalt's holistic stance enables a fuller, more integrated understanding of people's experience. The simplicity and complexity of this concept can be illustrated in what you are starting to say and what you further present later about the complex, layered nature of the "field." The term *field* can have several different meanings and is often used interchangeably between these meanings, frequently within the same article. It is difficult to do otherwise. *The field* can be used to refer to the many environmental conditions and influences that conceptualize our existence, relating to all or specific elements of family, culture, gender, friendship network, nationality, economic conditions, spirituality, geographical location, political atmosphere, occupation, physical health, and so much more. In this vein, we all exist in multiple "fields" simultaneously. But our own personal qualities, such as our hopes, fears, skills, limitations, emotional state, energy, needs, and style, our accumulated experience and beliefs, our sense of our possibilities for connection and disconnection, these are part of our "field" as well. And to return to where I started, as you have presented, these two parts of our "field" are not separate. They are intimately intertwined, inextricably interwoven into wholes of perception and involvement.

MALCOLM: As you say, there is no question that exact definitions of the field, or even precise descriptions of any particular field, are very difficult. Physicists have the same difficulty in elaborating field concepts in the physical realm. They are elusive, slippery, and difficult to pin down. Yet field concepts are necessary, certainly when speaking of human beings and the nature of our experience; we need them to describe holistic processes, the intimate interplay between human beings and their experienced worlds, the milieu in which they exist, forming part of the scene themselves. Of course, there is a potential difficulty in that the field can become so inclusive as to

how we theorize about impulses, drives, etc., it is always to such an *interacting field* that we are referring, and not to an isolated animal. (Perls et al., 1994, p. 4, italics added)

The signal achievement, in the 1940s and 1950s, was for Perls and Goodman to have predated insights that have since become commonplace. Today, in biology, anthropology, developmental psychology, and numerous other areas of human inquiry, it is taken for granted that to study separately animals and habitats, mothers and babies, ecosystems and land-use patterns is to set off on the wrong path: They need to be seen as indivisibly connected and inseparable and studied in a "unitary" way.

The radical outlook proposed by Goodman and Perls was not altogether or easily assimilated, even by Gestalt therapists themselves: Wheeler (1990), for example, argued that Fritz Perls himself lacked an emphasis on field in his later writing. In the contemporary era, in much of medicine and psychology, reductive tendencies and a dualistic biomedical outlook still predominate. Even in much psychological treatment and therapy as practiced today, an individual's problems are seen as primarily a matter of "personal psychopathology," something to do with "what is going on inside" him or her, and to be diagnosed and treated by a detached clinician who does not "get involved." The Gestalt therapy idea is different: One must begin by regarding the "whole field" of the therapy. This includes, as has already been said, the experiences of both the client and therapist separately and together, their patterns of contact and engaging with each other, and the multiple complexities of the relationship between them as manifested moment by moment—and cumulatively over time (Shub, 1992).

The "unitary perspective" is hard to acquire in an intellectual culture that is so dualistic and compartmentalized. The founders of Gestalt therapy thought not only that this way of thinking and perceiving reality was important for understanding human behavior but that dualistic thinking helped to destroy a sense of wholeness in people's lives.

include anything and everything: It is important to differentiate the "relevant ground" that goes with the figure of interest and to be specific without being exclusionary or fixed. In discussing the "principle of possible relevance"—about including too much (Parlett, 1991)—I wrote, "[W]hat is most relevant and pressing is readily discoverable in the present. Instead of exhaustively documenting what is in the field, there is attention to what is momentarily or persistently relevant or interesting—and this will show how the field is organized" at any one time. The unitary approach I describe is in contrast to what happens usually when human beings try and describe reality: They chop it up, divide it into parts, split things up, rather than keeping them together and seeking to describe the seamless continuity, which is how we experience actual lived life. It is as if fences are erected and then people think the land is not one continuous land any more—but it is, of course. As you say, we exist in many fields simultaneously, but they are not neatly differentiated and separated. As I said earlier, the field of our conversation exists within the field of the chapter content, author, and reader but is not entirely separate from it.

BOB: Yes, as you have referred to in the chapter, people's chopping up their experience is reflective of what works, is accepted or appropriate in their culture and in sync with how they are defined by others. For example, people are often told in our culture that if they are to succeed they must develop "self" confidence, as if this task were solely up to them. This perspective breaks the unitary, seamless continuity of their relational experience and puts the focus solely on them. What people actually develop when they develop so-called "self" confidence is confidence in others' interest in and ability to respond to them, which is achieved relationally, not solely individually. And this is only one of the many examples of how our culture expects people to split their experience.

"We believe that the Gestalt outlook is the original, undistorted, natural approach to life, that is, to man's thinking, acting, feeling. The average person, having been raised in an atmosphere of splits, has lost his Wholeness, his Integrity" (Perls et al., 1994, p. xxiv). Gestalt therapy was about restoring the sense of a unity or wholeness of experience and of living.

FIELD THEORY AND THE INFLUENCE OF KURT LEWIN

Gestalt therapists, wishing to take further the field-related ideas of the founding book, have increasingly looked to the work of Kurt Lewin (1890–1948). Of the previous generation of Gestalt psychologists, he was the one who had elaborated ideas of field most extensively. His ambition was to establish ideas of field in scientific terms.

The term *field* was an importation from physics. Michael Faraday and James Maxwell had introduced the word into physics in the 1840s to mean the magnetic field. The word itself was originally taken from the name given to the background in heraldic shields. The magnetic field is demonstrated in the elementary physics experiment where iron filings are sprinkled on paper placed on top of a magnet. The specific patterns displayed are a representation of the magnetic field and the configuration of forces within it. Change the position of the magnet and the whole pattern shifts. Put a second magnet or metal object under the paper, and the field and the pattern of iron filings are altered drastically (see Experiential Activity #1).

Lewin's (1952) idea was that in psychology, too, various forces, vectors, and "influences" act together to produce a specific, unique outcome in a particular situation at a particular time. Each force affects the others in a complex interactive relationship. Lewin called the ideas and thinking that surround the central concept of field "field theory." The field is an informing metaphor to help in describing complex interrelating events, both "external" social forces and "internal" personal drives and needs that in practice are all interacting and affecting each other. They "come together," and trying to take them apart and study them one at a time and independently means falling into the reductionist trap.

In general, conceptual terms, *field* in Gestalt therapy can be defined as "a totality of mutually

BOB: However, as McConville (2001a) says, "There is no field . . . unless we are referring to a field that includes, as a co-constitutive pole, an engaged subjectivity. Fields cannot be spoken of properly as existing in themselves, in nature, apart from a co-constitutive human subjectivity" (pp. 200–201). And to reflect a bit more on the difficulty of characterizing or speaking about the "field," this means that in any given situation there is not just one "field" of one person, who exists in many "fields" simultaneously. Instead, in another sense, there are as many "fields" as there are participants and observers. And these "fields" are not isolated "fields" but are, again as you present, highly influenced by each other and with any given event or series of events will contain much shared co-constructed material. This just illustrates the difficulty of conceptualizing the "field." But for the purpose of addressing a particular field, I like your notion that what is most relevant and pressing about any field is readily discoverable in the present. For those of our readers who would like further clarification of this complex, layered nature of the field, I suggest your article (Parlett, 1997) and Lynne Jacobs's article (2003).

MALCOLM: We are back to the slippery definitions and difficulty in pinning down what a field actually *is,* where it begins and ends, and so forth. It really does mean that care needs to be exercised in how the concept is used, not as

influencing forces that together form a unified interactive whole" (Yontef, 1993, p. 297). However, in using such a broad and inclusive general concept, it is also necessary to "define" the field that one is talking about at the time. As Yontef (2001) asserts, "[A] field can only be defined in relation to its parts and to the larger field of which it is part" (p. 84), and "[T]he field is defined according to your purpose" (p. 85). In other words, a lot of the meaning has to be derived from the context of use. This matter of the usage of the term *field* is itself a good example of how the "figure" makes sense only when the wider context or "ground" is made clear as well, the figure and ground together composing "the field" that needs to be appreciated as a whole.

a catch-all general category but in connection with precise descriptions of phenomena. I shall go on later to point out that some theorists consider that fields may have an independent physical existence, albeit not one that can be measured within the present paradigms of scientific knowledge. However, we are at the limits of knowledge here, and I would agree with McConville that an "engaged subjectivity" is necessary to *register* or *experience* a field of the kind that we are talking about here.

THEORY INTO PRACTICE: FIELD THEORY PRINCIPLES THAT INFORM CLINICAL METHOD

"Field theory can hardly be called a theory in the usual sense," said Kurt Lewin (1952, p. 45). Rather, it is a set of principles, an outlook, a method, and a whole way of thinking that relates to the intimate interconnectedness between events and the settings or situations in which these events take place. So *theory* in this case denotes a general theoretical outlook or way of appreciating reality that involves, in Lewin's words, "looking at the total situation" (p. 288) and being willing to address and investigate the organized, interconnected, interdependent, interactive nature of complex human phenomena. There are many features of the field perspective in Gestalt therapy, and they have fundamental implications for how therapists practice.

1. The therapist, or "observer," is not detached, objective, separated from the field but rather a part of it.

As Latner (1992) wrote,

> The field includes those who study or observe it. Since all the aspects of the field are related, there is no way to know a field except within it, as a part of it. Thus, studying the field means including yourself in your study. . . . Therapy includes the therapist. What takes place in therapy is created by both the therapy and the person or persons who come to therapy, and the therapeutic work is the work done by all the individuals in the room. (pp. 20–21)

In the simplest case of two individuals meeting, something comes into existence that is a product of neither of them exclusively. Beaumont (1993) pointed out that

> contact is clearly a creative process. . . . When we contact one another we *gestalt* ourselves and also the other. Contact is not passive perception of a fixed objective reality, but rather

> the *creation* of a phenomenal experimental reality. . . . Contact is . . . a mutually creative interaction. Each participates in the creation of the other. (p. 90)

With this "co-created" reality, a shared field comes into existence. We can use the analogy of a dance: Each dancer has a repertoire of preferred sequences, movements, rhythms, or dance steps. Two dancers create a dance together that is a product of each dancer's creativity and self-regulation in light of the other dancer's dance. At a particular time, the dance seems to "take over." The field itself, once organized and structured, begins to "regulate the dancers" (Parlett, 1991, p. 76).

These ideas link with those about the dialogic relationship in therapy (Yontef, 1993), in which the therapist is enjoined to be authentic, a real person acting in a "horizontal" relationship, rather than to take up the more "vertical" position of the professionally removed expert. He or she cannot stand outside the relationship but is co-creating what happens within it. (We shall return to this theme later.)

2. The field is organized, and therapy involves the mutual investigation of how it is organized.

Lewin (1952) wrote,

> Whether or not a certain type of behavior occurs depends not on the presence or absence of one fact or a number of facts as viewed in isolation, but upon the constellation (the structure and forces) of the specific field as a whole. The "meaning" of the single fact depends upon its position in the field. (p. 150)

Meaning derives from looking at the total situation, the totality of coexisting facts. Further,

> [e]verything is interconnected and the total situation needs to be taken into account. Properties of things are ultimately defined by their context of use. Thus, a table can be used as a surface for writing or for serving a meal upon. It can be sat on and becomes a seat or turned upside-down can represent a boat for a child playing. In other words, rather than thinking in terms of the enduring properties of objects which are held to be constant, their characteristics are defined by a *wider organization of overall meaning,* which emphasizes interdependence. (p. 149, italics in original)

The development of field theory is partly an attempt to put into some coherent and rational-sounding form what many sensitive, socially aware, and intelligent human beings do anyway—that is, respond to the total circumstances pertaining to a situation in ways that are creative and effective. Gestalt therapists learn to be skilled in observing the situation as a whole and "noticing the process." This means realizing, for instance, when "the time is right to propose something new," when it is time to change the activity or take a break, or when collective energy is beginning to drop within a group discussion. These observations are "felt" or "sensed" rather than "worked out"—they come, not from application of a rule or theory, but as total human responses that the majority of people are well able to make and that are raised to high prominence in the training of Gestalt therapists (and Gestalt organizational consultants; see Nevis, 1987). Awareness of the field that one is in, and of the different conventions and tacit assumptions that operate in that field, is the development of sensitivity to context and to what is "appropriate" or "called for" in a situation. Gestalt therapists are to be skilled in recognizing how the field is organized.

Present-day Gestalt therapy recognizes the importance of having many different ways of working, according to the circumstances and contextual background that are part of the present field. The general shift in direction away from anything like "fixed techniques" is an indication of the need to attend to the organization of the field as it is encountered in the moment. Mackewn (1997) expressed it well:

> Gestalt is a field approach; so there is no "right way" of intervening; no "right intervention." This is not the same as saying that any intervention will do. Some interventions are certainly better than others, at certain points. The choice of approach or intervention depends upon all the field conditions at the time and is a matter of fine discrimination. Factors affecting the choice include the personality type and ego strength of the client and counselor, the length and aims of the counseling, the circumstances in which the counseling takes place, the holistic energetic process of the client, the recent present and past life experiences of the client, the stage of the counseling process and so on. Developing the ability to be aware of and take account of all these field conditions requires a native interest in and talent for fine observation, experiential and theoretical training, lots of practice and plenty of professional support. (p. 219)

3. Gestalt therapists work in the "here and now" and explore the immediate, present field.

The field is not a static entity but is in constant flux. A new piece of information, a sudden realization, a momentary mismatch between therapist and client, can "alter everything." A field can change dramatically in a moment. The therapist attends both to the subtle and often rapid changes that can occur and to relatively stable field configurations. In "analyzing" the field, no particular special causal status is accorded to events in the past, which in many therapy systems may be thought of as "determinants" of what is happening now. Likewise, future events, planned or fantasized, are not given special status (as "goals" or "incentives") but again are seen as part of what is occurring in the present. In other words, it is the constellation of influences in the present field that both "explains" behavior and constitutes the actual present experience of the client (and the therapist) that is being investigated. As part of the present, there may be times of "recollecting last week" or "planning for next week."

Staying with the unfolding of here-and-now experience is one of the well-recognized central features of Gestalt therapy. Yet its basis in a field

BOB: A question that comes to me here is, How do Gestalt therapists make their way in this discovery of the organization of the field, of which they are an integral part? For me, it is following the energy in the field, particularly highlighted through the signs of shame, belonging, and yearning (which are not just individual characteristics but field variables), that guides me through the maze of field information. This points the way both to areas where people's sense of connection is based on a sense of belonging and areas where people's attempts, or lack of attempts, at connection are informed by a sense of isolation, mistrust, despair, desperation, hopelessness, or uncertainty. In the latter cases, in which there is insufficient perceived support for yearnings, what is usually seen are people's attempts to cope with the

outlook is not always appreciated. The field's constant change means that the therapist needs to be fully attentive and "present." As Zinker (1987) wrote: "Presence implies being here fully, with all of one's body and soul—open to all possibilities" (p. 5). Spagnuolo Lobb (2003b) emphasized the importance of the "improvisational" element in Gestalt therapy. Describing a therapy sequence in some detail, she concluded that the therapist "feels there is a strong emotional involvement between them [the therapist and the client] and has to take a decision on how to use it therapeutically." She continued:

> This is the phase that Stern et al. (1998) called the "now moment; . . . now moments are like the ancient Greek concept of *Kairos*, a unique moment of opportunity that must be seized, because your fate will turn on whether you seize it and how" (p. 991). This is the crucial moment in the therapeutic session. . . . Therapeutic co-creation works on an improvisational basis: it cannot happen thanks to premeditated, known, schematic, knowledgeable processes. . . . [I]t is similar to the sophisticated ability of the jazz player who has all the musical knowledge in her/his blood and is able to be fresh, strong, contactful and unique in her/his playing.

4. The therapist attends to exploring different parts of the field.

Wheeler (1991) has argued that Gestalt therapy has sometimes focused too much on what is "figural" to the detriment of ongoing structures of the field. He reminds us that crucial parts of present experience are based on "organized features" that endure "across situations and over time" and that "infuse and constrain the figures of contact themselves." Psychotherapy is "always a matter of reorganization of these structures of ground over time." The work can be "hampered by (an) over-emphasis on figure" as opposed to the wider field from which figures emerge (p. 3).

shame that covers their yearnings. Interventions aimed at only controlling or changing people's "troublesome" or "inappropriate" behavior that can manifest in such cases, without understanding the field nature of, and condition of support for, the underlying yearning(s), are most often doomed to failure in the long run. People may not even be aware of their needs and yearnings if they do not perceive sufficient support for them. So discovering the organization of the field, of which I am a part, is an ongoing process that continues with each interaction/intervention. (For our readers, see Lee, 2004; Wheeler, 2003a. Also see Lee, 2001, for a case study illustrating the above approach.)

MALCOLM: You raise many points that are of importance in therapy. My own answer to your question about "how Gestalt therapists discover the organization of the field when they are part of it" is that we need to pay attention to our overall experience, particularly as mediated through our bodily reactions, feeling states, sensations. Unless we are attuned and aware, we are likely to miss some major parts of our potential experience. We experience the field through all our senses. So "following the energy in the field" requires a whole-being response, *felt* and *sensed* as much as (or more than) *thought about*. This said, what do I look for that reveals the field organization? The answer is many things: what appears unfinished, awkward, unsaid; what puzzles or alarms me, or sends me to sleep; what I feel I am being led to notice, and what I am being led away from noticing; what the client or patient is doing, not doing, stops him/herself from doing; and, of course, how I am experiencing the client's apparent experiencing of me—the whole intersubjective, co-created nature of the therapy as it is happening now, and the mutual influencing that is taking place between us, in both explicit and implicit ways. I certainly attend to issues of shame, fear, agency, etc., but I do want to emphasize *how*

Others who worry that some of the original formulations of Gestalt therapy theory were overly simple echo Wheeler's cautions. For instance, Fodor (1998) wrote: "Gestalt therapy highlights awareness and uses the medium of therapeutic dialogue (contact) to facilitate the awareness process. A basic assumption is that awareness itself is the curative factor in therapy" (p. 62). She suggests it is important to move

> beyond awareness itself as the goal of therapy to a focus on *knowledge acquisition* as the focus of our therapeutic work. . . . Awareness-enhancing work will continue to be essential, but more attention [could] be given to the ways we gain knowledge, make decisions, and structure experience. (p. 62)

The various points made are indicative of the ways contemporary Gestalt therapists practice. In Mackewn's (1997) words, these are not

these are appreciated—primarily in the sensing-feeling modality. I realize how big and important is the question you raise!

BOB: I fully support with you the whole-being stance that is needed to explore and take in information in a field. You have eloquently captured this process, which I jumped over. Still, for me a large part of discovering the organization of the field involves how I organize what I become aware of in my exploration of both my sensations and other material that is available to notice in the field. With each of the possibilities that you mention (i.e., "what appears unfinished, awkward"), my own style is to become curious in how that might be an expression of belonging and/or an expression of a disconnect in the field. But I realize that I am getting ahead of things a bit here, as you touch on this subject, as well as other things that I have referred to here, later in the chapter.

> bound by tracking or staying with the *client's figure* but may make any aspect of the field figural. In shuttling attention between different aspects of the field, we will constantly be reconfiguring the field as we make new elements figural and others ground. (p. 179)

The field perspective calls us to consider human behavior and experience in a much wider context, being open to long-term patterns and persistent styles of self-organization. The client is seen within his or her family context, and in some cases in relation to social, economic, or other "impersonal" forces with which individual beings have to grapple and that they are likely to reflect and embody (Parlett, 2000).

In short, there has been a significant movement in Gestalt therapy practice away from short-term work in which the directive to focus on the immediate "here and now" was, with mistaken zeal, interpreted far too literally. The "there-and-then" reality of, say, a restimulated childhood trauma, or "here-and-then" attention to, for instance, how the client is "still resentful towards the therapist from last week's session," or the "there-and-now" reporting of some significant contemporary event in the person's work or home life all have their place. These different field configurations can be subsumed within the overall "here-and-now" field of the present session—as "subfields" or fields within fields. The field can be thought of as "laminated," and as therapists we can move between layers and levels, switching frames or positions according to what "carries energy" or has been long ignored (because it does not "carry energy"). Thus we, as therapists, can reach deeply into the past in a regressive reenactment on one occasion, whereas at another time, in different conditions, we can insist on looking at the present relationship with the therapist, today in this room now. We can switch the emphasis from reality to role play, from experiencing something at a physical bodily level to visual fantasy, to searching for a metaphor, to telling the story. We can notice not just the immediate figure that is present but ongoing features, the structures and repetitive patternings arising in the field. And, as Kepner (1995) pointed out, a past figure can be relocated against a present ground—often essential in recovery from traumas in the past.

In other words, the versatility and power of the therapist to engage fully and deeply with the client and his or her reality are often enhanced by "movement within the field" as well as by "reconfiguring the field." This may entail changing the ground (as Kepner said, from past to present) or reframing experience (e.g., "What are the benefits that come from this disaster?"), or changing what is figure and what is ground (e.g., "I notice that I have been attending to your distress, and now I am acknowledging your courage").

THE THERAPEUTIC FIELD

Gestalt therapy began as an offshoot of psychoanalysis and in reaction to it. Mid-20th-century psychoanalysis was still espousing a view of human beings as led by instincts. Unconscious needs and characterological defenses "explained" human behavior. The therapist was a would-be scientific observer, detached and supposedly uninvolved personally. His or her world and experience in therapy were separate, and patients' reactions to the analyst were the subject of "transference interpretations."

We have already seen that the Gestalt therapy focus on unraveling the present field of experience and exploring the co-created relationship between therapist and client is a fundamentally different approach. However, just as Gestalt therapy has moved on, so has much of the psychoanalytic movement. The work of major psychoanalytic theorists, notably Kohut (1984) and Stolorow and Atwood (1992), has led to a convergence with that of dialogic Gestalt therapists such as Gary Yontef and Lynne Jacobs. The latter, an experienced Gestalt therapist (who, interestingly, has also trained as an analyst), describes a new-shared emphasis. "The perspective of understanding that every phenomenon that happens in the therapeutic encounter is variably co-created by the therapist and patient together, never just by the patient" (Jacobs, 2000b, p. 106), is an idea that has already been referred to as central in field theory thinking.

Yontef (2001) has pointed out that the dialogic perspective

> has to do with an emphasis on meeting the patient without aiming. The first principle is inclusion, which is putting yourself so much into the patient's experience, trying to feel the patient's experience as intensely as if you could feel it in your own body—without giving up your separate sense of self. [The final] authority on whether the empathic or the inclusion statement is accurate is that the patient tells you whether it is accurate or inaccurate. A principle I have come to is that, if the patient says [to me as a therapist] "you don't understand," you don't. (pp. 86–87)

In other words, in a therapeutic field where there is a shared, mutually constructed relationship, the whole approach of the therapist toward the client becomes critically important. Yontef continued:

> A related principle is confirmation. We want not only to accept the person but confirm our sense of his or her existence and potential. . . . If we practice inclusion and confirmation,

> it requires a faith that by identifying with the present state of the person, the person can grow. It requires faith in the process. (pp. 87–88)

In an important statement, he added: "You can't really practice inclusion without being emotionally present. One aspect of presence that we don't talk a lot about that I think is very powerful is described with words like compassion, kindness, equanimity, humility" (p. 88).

Jacobs (2000b) pointed out that "patients have to develop the confidence [that] as they lose their habitual form, or fixed patterns, as they trip and fall, as they sink into despairing silence, the therapist is still trying to stay in touch with them" (p. 106). This requires that the field of therapy have a

> dimension wherein the therapist's responses are experienced as consolidating, affirming, enhancing of the self-esteem of the patient, lending self-coherence to the patient. The therapist is deeply involved and engaged in . . . the holding, outline-defining, containing function while patients experiment with unfamiliar de-stabilizing ways of organizing their own experience. (p. 106)

The movement in Gestalt therapy, then, was first a greater appreciation of dialogue, the relationship and "the between," and since then has been a further development to "conversation with attuned, calibrated presence. Therapists now need to learn even more sensitive listening to the patient" (Jacobs, 2000b, p. 107). Her advice is: "Listen from the patient's perspective what it's like to be the patient and what it's like to be in relationship to me the therapist" (p. 107).

A Shift in Paradigm

What we notice, in the thinking of both Yontef and Jacobs, is a fundamental *relational* stance—an emphasis on the mutuality and co-created, co-regulated nature of therapy, where, as therapists, we are part of organizing the mutual reality or shared field and in turn are created and organized by it. As I have written previously (Parlett, 1991):

> A provocative idea for therapists follows from the notion of reciprocal influence, namely that change in the client may be achieved by the therapist changing her or himself. Since it is a co-created field, a function of what the therapist brings to it as well as what the client brings, a change in the way a therapist acts or feels towards his/her client and interrelates with him, will affect the mutual field and have consequences for the client. . . . It strongly endorses the view that in the impeccable practice of Gestalt therapy there has to be a central place for continuing supervision, as well as daily attention to our fitness-to-practice. . . . If we are to act congruently and authentically as therapists, we have to acknowledge that the way we are and the way we live cannot be entirely separated from our work as professional Gestalt therapists. Everything in our phenomenal field becomes part of the matrix from which we co-create fields with others. (p. 78)

Robine (2001) also wrote of the way in which patient and therapist become implicated with each other:

> When a patient sits in front of me and tells me that he is anxious, I can choose to listen to his words not only as words *in* a certain situation, but also as words *of* the situation, *as if* these words were belonging to an undifferentiated field which has to be explored, instead of to an individual, the one who tells them. The individualist classical position would focus, as I used to do during many years, upon the patient's anxiety: how does he feel it, where does it come from, what does it remind him of, which projections organise it, etc. From this position the therapist comes to consider that he gets a more and more definite knowledge of his patient. . . . Another choice . . . is to look at this anxiety as belonging "first" to the situation. Maybe this anxiety is his response to seeing me? Maybe I am making him anxious? Maybe I am making him anxious as a reaction to my seeing him? Or to our meeting? Maybe "his" anxiety is actually mine? Or may it only be the atmosphere which is being created between us? (pp. 101–102)

The view that therapists can be so implicated in the therapeutic experiences of their patients or clients is a far cry from "the detached expert" view of the therapist. It follows, however, from the wholesale shift in thinking that has been referred to, notably by Wheeler (1997), as a shift from the "individualist" to the "field paradigm."

The term *paradigm shift,* now in wide use, means a revolutionary change in basic assumptions, methods, and outlook that can occur in any area of knowledge and in science marks a major turning point (as, for instance, occurred with the arrival of Einstein's theory of relativity, which overturned the centuries-old Newtonian model of the universe). Major expansions of human understanding rarely occur without some kind of revolution that changes the generally accepted ideas of the day.

As we have seen, within therapy—and more widely in psychology and medicine—ideas of the field represent a revolutionary development in how human beings are seen in relation to each other; hence the acknowledgment that a paradigm shift is under way. Newton, Descartes, and Bacon were influential in promoting a particular view of "scientific objectivity" that grew up in parallel with development of the "machine age." It resulted in human beings' being treated as if they were objects. The tendency to objectify others and subtly to dehumanize them, denying or demeaning their subjective experience, was part of what Gestalt therapy reacted against. With its emphasis on exploring experience through phenomenological inquiry, dialogue, and experiment, Gestalt therapy honored the validity of the individual's unique, subjective experience and valued authenticity, personal responsibility, and the capacity of human beings to question orthodoxy and resist social pressures to conform. It was a humanistic agenda in line with existentialist ideas and constituted a vigorous defense of the individual in the face of "antihuman" trends within society, such as state oppression, mass conformity, and other restrictions on human freedom.

However, as Wheeler (2000) and others have pointed out, the assertive "individualist" emphasis within Gestalt therapy, though it may have been in tune with the spirit of the 1960s and 1970s, seems out of tune now, not only with the present era, but with some of the original key ideas in *Gestalt Therapy* published in 1951. Specifically, Wheeler suggested that Gestalt therapy needs to amplify and reconsider selfhood from a field or relational standpoint—an idea that was present in the founders' ideas but has not been fully worked out since.

Many writers—including Lichtenberg (1994), Polster (1995), Crocker (1999), Wheeler (2000), and Philippson (2001)—have addressed the Gestalt theory of the self, and although there are different emphases and academic-style disputes, there is also a substantial area of agreement. This is based on the idea, first spelled out in *Gestalt Therapy,* that the self arises in contact and is a "process" and not "a thing": "Let us call the 'self' the system of contacts at any one moment. As such, the self is flexibly various . . . [It] is the contact-boundary at work" (Perls et al., 1951, p. 235). Others have added to this revolutionary idea. As Spagnuolo Lobb (2001a) wrote, the self is "put in neither an intrapsychic nor an environmental position. . . . [I]t acts and is acted upon" (p. 51). Or as Crocker (1999) stated, "The self, as a complex power of the human organism, is an integral element in the environmental situation, and is recurrently responsive to, and active in, the events in the surrounding environment and inside the organism" (pp. 171–172).

"The self is best understood," wrote Wheeler (2000, pp. 103–104), as a "natural process of unifying the experiential field, the synthesizer or 'gestalt-maker' of experience (or better still, the gestalt-making process itself)." The process has even been called "selfing." Thus Wolfert (2000) wrote that "selfing is an activity, a dynamic relation which is ever-moving, ever-changing—an organization shaped by and shaping experiences in the play of the forces of the field" (p. 77).

Values and Ethics

The implication of *the view of self espoused in Gestalt therapy* is that the self changes as a function of changes in the field as a whole, where "the self is the figure/background process" or "the power that forms the gestalt in the field" (Perls et al., 1994, p. 152). In other words, the self is to be understood as a function of field and as contacting what is "other" in the field. As Wheeler and others have pointed out, this means that human beings are inextricably tied up in other people's fates and that there is no absolute and sharp cutoff point between the field of self and the field of others. As Lee (2002) pointed out, "If you and I are significant to each other, you are part of my construction of 'self' and I am part of your construction of 'self'" (p. 36).

Affirming as central the intersubjective, co-created, interdependent nature of human existence and experience means that particular ethical, political, or value positions are given support, with implications for therapy priorities. A central interest for Gestalt therapists must be how individuals manage their lives. Specifically, for therapists "what concerns us . . . in this ever-changing field are the ever-changing constellations of the ever-changing individual" (Perls, 1976, p. 25). Addressing this previously, I argued that

> [t]he ability to "adjust creatively" is necessary for health and well being in a complex and changing world. Conversely, inability in this realm results in dis-ease (alienation, isolation, etc.). The focus of a more field-based therapy could be on *promoting an active process of learning and practising abilities of creative adjustment.* (Parlett, 2000, p. 20, italics in original)

Moreover, a heightened concern for the "health" of the field itself is called for.

> If it is our evolved nature to be whole-field-integrative, relational, and intersubjective . . . and if our full development of that nature is dependent on a healthy field of other healthy selves . . . then it follows that an ethical perspective . . . must be based on the criterion of *which actions, which attitudes most foster that healthy development of the whole*

> *field.* Such a criterion simultaneously aims toward taking care of both "our own interest" *and* the interest of the whole field. No longer are the two things inherently opposed—self *versus* other. (Wheeler, 2000, pp. 379–380, italics in original)

The same principles lead to a view of professional ethical problems that arise in all forms of therapy, including Gestalt therapy. Lee (2002) explained the need to

> [f]ind solutions to ethical problems that serve both the individual and the larger field, ones that lead to and support healthy self/other development. Ideally when these ethics are considered by its members to be part of the ground of the field, such that we all understand that my internal experience is part of your internal experience and yours is part of mine . . . wouldn't there be much less need of an externally enunciated and enforced code of ethics? (p. 47)

Lee may sound idealistic, though he acknowledged that there would still be "conflicts and mistakes." He went on:

> Conflicts and mistakes would be handled with enough support provided by the people involved and the surrounding community, rather than being handled in an individualistically administered process in which participants are seen as adversaries and the name of the game is to discredit, blame, humiliate the other and the most powerful individual or group wins. (p. 48)

A FIELD VIEW OF DEVELOPMENT

Rethinking Gestalt therapy theory from a more "field-influenced" conceptual base has taken writers into areas that earlier Gestalt therapists have written little about. One of these contemporary themes is human development—child, adolescent, adult. In 1993,Yontef observed that "[t]he Gestalt therapy concept of human development is that it is always a function of biological maturation, environmental influences, interaction of the individual and the environment, and creative adjustment by the unique individual" (p. 272).

In other words, development is a function of the whole field. Yet the implications were still not fully explored. Wheeler (1998) expressed many Gestalt therapists' and researchers' keenly felt discomfort with standard clinical models of development—all involving "stages" in a process of personal maturation: "With these models the developing child is viewed too much in isolation, as if human development were something purely 'inner' or biologically driven" (p. 115).

Gillie (1999) and others have suggested that the seminal research of Daniel Stern (1985) provides a basis for a more specifically Gestalt theory on infant development. Specifically, "Stern draws four key significant conclusions." *First,* infants "differentiate themselves from the start"—replacing ideas of "fusion with mother" (p. 109). *Second,* "development proceeds through increasingly complex phases [that] do not take the place of their predecessor" (p. 109). *Third,* "infants organize their experience from the beginning" (p. 109)—in other words, they are field sensitive and begin "selfing" from the start. *Fourth,* "the developing 'sense of self' is a co-creation between the infant and environment . . . and self-regulation is a function of what happens between the infant and the carer(s)" (p. 109).

Wheeler (1998) expanded on the idea that "*development always and necessarily means the development of a whole field*—not just development *in* a field or context, but development *of* that field or context" (p. 117, italics in original). In short,

> [t]he environment that is integrated into the child's evolving self-process must itself evolve over time, in some organized harmony with the biological and experiential growth of the child. . . . [T]he parents that the four-year-old needs are "different parents" from the ones that the infant needed, or that the 20-year-old will need later. Parents themselves have to grow and develop. (p. 117)

McConville (2001b), writing about adolescent development, also explored the question of "what develops?" and again looked to a deeper understanding of "the biological, psychological, and social as dimensions of an integrated field, which Lewin called the *life space*" (p. 30). McConville quoted Yontef (1993): "Using the field approach one thinks of living, moving, changing, energetic interacting. . . . [T]he forces of a field are of a whole and *develop over time*" (p. 301, emphasis added by McConville). McConville concluded, "A field approach to human behavior is by definition an implicit model of development. The child-environment system is in a state of . . . tension of movement or *becoming*" (p. 30). There is an "unfolding (or the interruption of an unfolding) . . . that orients that field in a certain developmental direction" (p. 30).

Writing about the ongoing development of adults, I pointed out that "new conditions foster developmental shifts. Changed circumstances and novel situations require the individual—challenging him or her—to experiment and extend his/her range" (Parlett, 1997, p. 25). In this, I liken the structure of a Gestalt experiment (see, e.g., Zinker, 1977) to the experience of a "change in life circumstances" (like taking a new job, leaving home, giving birth). "Major shifts require a particular kind of calibrated support and challenge in the field, . . . enough accompanying support in the field, linked to a compelling invitation to 'risk doing something differently'" (p. 25).

THE PHENOMENOLOGY OF SHAME AS A FIELD EXPERIENCE

"Risks" and "supports" are mentioned frequently in discussions of shame. As a specific topic, condition, and emotion, shame has become much discussed in the last 10 years. Many Gestalt writers have addressed it, including Lee (1995), Yontef (1996), Wheeler (1996), Resnick (1997), and Fuhr and Gremmler-Fuhr (1997). Resnick (1997) summarized points of agreement and of contention. There is agreement, for instance, about (a) much of the reported and described experience of shame—feeling "bad," "weak," "worthless," "acutely embarrassed"; (b) its difference from guilt (about *being* wrong as opposed to *doing* wrong); (c) how "shame of being ashamed" is

BOB: The process of the work that Gordon Wheeler and I engaged in around how shame and belonging regulate the relational field is a prime example of the intersubjective nature of the field. We came to the process from seemingly different tracks, me from my study of and research on shame as well as my belief that Gestalt theory was talking about shame without mentioning it by name, and he from his long-time interest in the nature of "self" process. And we discovered we were in the same place. The atmosphere that existed between Gordon and me led to many, many awarenesses. For

common; (d) how shame is used in social control; and (e) how therapists and many therapy interventions can be inadvertently shaming for the patient.

Wheeler (1997), in collaboration with Robert Lee, made a persuasive case that shame in particular might be best regarded as a field phenomenon:

> In personal terms, what parts of myself, what urges and desires, what thoughts and feelings, can be *received and connected within my social environment* . . . ? What parts will meet with resonance and energetic response (including at times energetic opposition), and . . . which parts will be met with a pulling away, a disconnect, often in an overtly belittling or punishing form? (pp. 233–234, italics in original)

Shame, he suggested, is the "*affect of that disconnect in the field*" (p. 234, italics in original).

What Wheeler (1997) called the "disconnect in the field" involves an absence of support from, or loss of connection with, others—or worse, acts of hurtful rejection, sarcasm, mockery, or public exposure. But he was at pains to remind us that

> the field we are talking about . . . is not just my "environment" . . . in the sense of something "outside myself." It is also "my world," in the same sense that my inner world is "mine," and an "*essential and integral part of my self.*" (p. 234)

example, I remember where I was sitting in Gordon's kitchen when I realized the awareness that shame is "felt as a break in the cohesiveness of the self" and then saying that to Gordon, which enabled him to make a further discovery about the condition of the environmental field that must exist in order for that to occur. The quality of intersubjective support in our field, together, led to a product that could not have resulted from just an individual.

MALCOLM: Yes, this is a great example. Close professional collaborations, like other intense one-to-one relationships, are wonderful models for seeing field phenomena at work. The whole co-regulated, mutually constructed, relational field has distinct qualities; it changes over time; it is different from being the sum of the parts (the two selves); a third entity comes into existence, with a life of its own. Sometimes it becomes difficult to say "who thought what first," so intertwined and co-created is the field (or third entity) that is formed between people in close relationship who are each affecting the other. Interestingly, you describe an "atmosphere"—that is how people often describe an energetic field that is created.

BOB: And with regard to what you say about people in close relationships, this intersubjective nature of the field, in the context of sufficient safety and caring, is the essence of what we commonly refer to as intimacy.

This means (as he wrote elsewhere; Wheeler, 1995) that the "disconnect" is "*felt as a break in the cohesion of the self*" (p. 82, italics in original).

Wheeler was seeking here, as elsewhere in his writings, to demonstrate again that the Gestalt view of self—being *in* the field, part *of* the field, and integrator of the field, all at the same time—enables a definitive shift away from an intrapsychic position. The experience of shame can be written about as if it were a pathological state of an individual alone, even though shaming arises clearly within relationships and social settings. Thus Kaufman, a psychoanalyst renowned for his writing about shame, wrote, "Shame is felt as an inner torment, as sickness of the soul. It is the most poignant experience of the self by the self. . . . Shame is a wound felt from the inside, dividing us both from ourselves and from one another" (quoted in Wheeler, 1995, p. 82). The language here is very different and does not carry the sense of human beings located always and inevitably within, and forming part of, a wider relational field, with "self-other" being more the focus of study than the experiences of an individualized self.

Fuhr and Gremmler-Fuhr (1997) pointed out that Robine (1991) also regarded shame from a field perspective. Robine (1991) described shame as a "serious break of confluence with the environmental field. . . . Any major developmental process . . . requires a major break of confluence with our environmental field in some respect" (p. 251). They added that shame "cannot be generally avoided and . . . there is nothing sacred about shame feelings" (p. 252). By this Fuhr and Gremmler-Fuhr appear to have meant that shame feelings are a commonplace part of human experience and are bound to occur—whereas others had implied that they were devastating and to be avoided at all costs. Treating them as "sacred" implies giving them too much solemn attention when they should be treated in a more robust and matter-of-fact way.

Writers, it must be said, differ in their emphasis in writing about shame. Some incline toward a more robust attitude, recognizing the existence and importance of shame reactions and the need to learn to tolerate them. Others tend to draw most attention to the need for exceptional levels of sensitivity when working with issues of shame and the need for high levels of support. The different emphases are indicative of wider theoretical and ideological tensions within the Gestalt community. Faced with study of "an organism/environment field," some incline to emphasizing the organism's autonomy, capacity for choice, inner-directedness, and personal responsibility, albeit within the field; others lean more toward emphasizing connection, the need for environmental support, and inevitable relatedness. These tensions exist both within "the field of Gestalt therapy" and within the lives and thinking of many practitioners in this field.

THE "FIELD" AND ITS MYSTERY

It is appropriate to return to the "field of Gestalt therapy" in bringing together final thoughts regarding contemporary theory. Though this account has drawn upon a range of writers and ideas, the actual variation is far wider. I have noted areas of convergence and identified the field perspective as the core of present-day Gestalt therapy theory. Those with good knowledge of today's professional Gestalt therapy field internationally will have a sense of the complexity of the subdivisions, training allegiances, and ideological fissures that are present in the field generally and that energize parts of the theoretical debate.

In focusing on the concept of the field and the field perspective, I am aware of the degree of selection I have had to exercise. Moreover, I realize that many questions about the field remain unanswered. In particular, are we any closer to understanding the exact nature of "the field"? What is its precise status? Spagnuolo Lobb (2001a) suggested that

BOB: I continue to be in awe of, and surprised by, what I know and am continuing to learn about field phenomena. As you quote from Spagnuolo Lobb, we are reaching for an understanding of what has been ungraspable, particularly from other theoretical perspectives. But the rewards for progressing in this direction are great. The knowledge of field properties and dynamics that I have acquired from a Gestalt relational perspective has made such a difference in how I live my own life as well as how I am able to understand and to be with others. As to the field that we have been co-creating here together with our readers, bringing forward the

> the founders of Gestalt therapy tried to make a theory of human nature that does not categorize, or put human behavior into schemas. . . . They tried to grasp the ungraspable, to catch the uncatchable, they tried to make a theory of what is not theorizeable. (p. 50)

Are our ideas of "field" equally elusive?

A particular question eventually becomes unavoidable. Is "the field" ultimately just a metaphor, a useful science-derived concept and framework that can be used to explain what is difficult to explain? Or is "something there" in the form of an explicit energy field in "the space between"? Kepner (2003a), an experienced Gestalt therapist with a strong interest in physical process, described the field as follows:

diverse history and body of ideas that you have so competently presented, I have enjoyed our interchange, and I find myself curious as to what it will stir in our readers.

MALCOLM: Thanks, Bob, for stirring me. I just hope that the conversation between us gives extra flavor to the interesting and complex issues that always come up when considering field phenomena. Ultimately, like all concepts and theories in Gestalt, ideas about the field need to be chewed and digested, discovered as being relevant to one's own life and experience. They have to make the transition from words on a page to something lived and embodied, known intimately, and recognized as valid because they ring true for us at a deep level.

> [T]he energetic field of the therapist, group and environment [is] crucial to support or mitigate certain kinds of experience. This concept is not part of standard Gestalt therapy theory, nor part of our western education, but I have come to understand as essential to understanding how experiential fields are created. (p. 8)

He offered the example of how "some facilitators seem to be able to create a 'magic' that is more than the sum of their intellectual knowledge" and how a therapist with a strong and well-developed energy field in a particular frequency literally vibrates the client's field into more of that frequency, making it easier for the client to access that kind of experience (p. 9).

Roberts (1999a) also argued that the field is not just an imaginary construct. He pointed to the field having its own "laws," or "orders," which have been described, for instance, by Boszormenyi-Nagy and Krasner (1986) and other family systems therapists such as Hellinger (see Beaumont, 1998, for a Gestalt-related discussion). Roberts wrote, "The *field as a whole* determines what is needed in any given situation—and implies the appropriate action if we listen to it. By helping the client attend to her experiencing process, we enable her to access the intelligence of the field" (p. 42). He goes on to cite dreams as an example:

> If we try to understand the dream as a *field event*—an emergent property of the whole field—we see that it need not be understood exclusively as some kind of "private message" sent from an inner Self. . . . Indigenous cultures everywhere have long considered that dreams harbour messages for the *community,* not the individual. . . . They reflect an order which transcends the shared social reality, and are *not* considered the exclusive property of the dreamer. A field theoretical understanding has more in common with these perspectives on dreaming than with those of most 20th century psychological theories. (pp. 43–44)

Questioning the extreme subjectivist view that there is no field other than the one we construct, other writers (e.g., Parlett, 1991; Robine, 1996) have pointed out that many "mysterious" phenomena well-known to therapists are altogether inexplicable within the usual frameworks of mainstream scientific knowledge. Robine (1996) wrote:

> It is well known, at least among psychoanalysts and psychotherapists, that it is no accident that we get certain patients and not others, that they bring up certain themes and not others, and that this happens at certain moments and not others. Whether we call it "coincidence," "synchronicity," "communication at an unconscious level," or "transference/countertransference," . . . all clinicians experience the same frustration at their limited ability to explain this phenomenon. (p. 15)

No discussion of the field in the specialized and relatively small-scale arena of Gestalt therapy should ignore the general scientific beliefs of the day. However, there is much upheaval and "mystery" in contemporary science. For instance, in the wake of developments in quantum physics and brain research, and using sophisticated computer technology that was not available in the early days of studying "paranormal phenomena" and "extrasensory perception," extraordinary developments are occurring in these specialist subjects. As never before, there is an increasing focus for legitimate scientific study of these phenomena funded by the National Aeronautics and Space Administration (NASA) and conducted in universities such as Princeton and Stanford by scientists from the mainstream. There are widespread speculations that something like an information-carrying general field exists and that the brain is "holographic" and "analyzes frequencies" of this field (see, e.g., Pribram, 1991; Radin, 1997; Sheldrake, 1995).

It would be ironic if Gestalt therapists were to turn their backs on these developments, suggestive as they are of a forthcoming scientific revolution—and one, if (or when) it comes, that might well confirm Gestalt therapy's increasing "field emphasis" as inquiry along essential lines. As was the case with our founders in 1951, Gestalt therapists may need courage to be "ahead of their time" in taking present-day ideas of field theory a lot further yet.

REVIEW QUESTIONS

1. The author, Malcolm Parlett, explains how working in the "here and now" has a broader definition in contemporary Gestalt therapy than merely staying present focused. Define and describe the more sophisticated notion of working in the here-and-now that the addition of a field theory approach has brought to the practice of working from a Gestalt perspective.

2. The therapist's role in the therapeutic setting has changed over the past hundred years. First, describe the differences noted in the chapter between psychoanalysis and Gestalt therapy. Next, outline and define the roles, responsibilities, and function of the therapist when working from a contemporary Gestalt field approach.

3. Explain why retaining a supervisor is especially important when working with clients from a field theory orientation.

4. What is the definition of the "self" in Gestalt therapy theory, and what is meant by the term *selfing*?

5. What is meant by the notion that shame is a "disconnect" or a "major break of confluence"? Give an example of shame and disconnect or break in confluence.

EXPERIENTIAL PEDAGOGICAL ACTIVITIES

ACTIVITY 1: Iron filings and magnets: This is an experiment that many people have done as children. But it is worth doing again to get a visual sense of field phenomena. Place iron filings on a stiff piece of paper and put a magnet under the paper. Notice how the magnet organizes the whole field. Notice what happens when a second magnet is placed under the paper and is moved slowly. Then notice what happens when a third magnet is placed under the paper. (Activity designed by Robert Lee.)

ACTIVITY 2: Drawing with partners: Divide into pairs, with each dyad getting a large piece of paper and some crayons or magic markers. Within the dyads, decide who will go first. Then, without talking, the first person draws something, a line, a figure, anything he or she wishes. After a short time, the first person stops and the second person adds to the drawing in the way he or she wishes. Continue to take turns drawing, without speaking, until both agree, nonverbally, that the drawing is finished. Change partners and repeat this process several times. Have participants talk in small groups as to what stood out to them about the experience. And have them note how their experience of their own participation, what they contributed, and possibly their sense of themselves varied in different dyads. (Activity designed by Robert Lee.)

ACTIVITY 3: The field in which each of us is immersed is not a two-dimensional entity easily depicted on paper. In fact, the field is better represented in three dimensions. However, for the sake of this activity, you are asked to simplify the notion of field by drawing one on paper. First, depict yourself (as a picture, symbolic representation, figure, etc.). Select what you consider to be your primary field (although the fields in which we reside at work, at home, and in organizations may overlap with each other and be embedded in the larger field of the universe, select one for this exercise). Around the picture of yourself, depict the other people, structures, animals, material possessions, experiences, and influences that exemplify the field from your own unique perspective. Next, consider entering into a new therapeutic relationship with a Gestalt therapist. That individual now also becomes a component of your field. As you walk into the therapy office, you carry with you representations, like your drawing, of various fields in your life. As you can see, the therapist has much to learn about you and about being with you in your field.

ACTIVITY 4: The author of this chapter writes about Gestalt therapy as an improvisational activity, quoting Spagnuolo Lobb's (2003b) description of what Stern (2004) called "now moments," unique opportunities or once-in-a-lifetime moments that must be seized. To help you get a sense of the potential impact of such turning-point moments in the therapeutic setting, reflect back into your own life and identify one such "now moment" or unique decisional point. In journal format, briefly describe your selected moment, and then generate an outline of the alternative paths not taken. Flesh out each of your alternative paths by writing paragraphs describing how your life could have changed if you had made each of those alternative choices. In the way that your alternative paths could have changed your life, "now moments" in the therapeutic setting can change the course of the therapeutic moment or the unit of work.

ACTIVITY 5: Your chapter author quotes Roberts (1999a) as stating that dreams are a "field event—an emergent property of the whole field—we see that it need not be understood exclusively as some kind of "private message" sent from an inner Self. . . . Indigenous cultures everywhere have long considered that dreams harbour messages for the *community,* not the individual" (pp. 43–44). In journal format, narrate one of your recently recalled dreams from your perspective as the dreamer. Next, go back and rewrite a description of the dream events as if they have implications for the field in which you reside, the community, or the world. Note any differences in the process of generating the multiple perspectives of your dream and of any awarenesses you experience as a result of considering your dreaming as having potential implications for others than yourself.

CHAPTER **4**

Phenomenology, Existentialism, and Eastern Thought in Gestalt Therapy

SYLVIA FLEMING CROCKER

DIALOGUE RESPONDENT: PETER PHILIPPSON

Sylvia Fleming Crocker is highly regarded as a Gestalt therapist, trainer, consultant, and author. Following her early career as a philosophy professor, she studied Gestalt therapy with Erving and Miriam Polster and later with the faculty of the Gestalt Therapy Institute of Los Angeles after earning another graduate degree in counseling. Her book *A Well-Lived Life: Essays in Gestalt Therapy* (1999) is widely read, as are her many articles in Gestalt therapy journals. She has a private practice in Laramie, Wyoming, where she works with individuals, couples, and families. She has become well-known for her talents in conducting experiential workshops—teaching and training internationally, often combining elements of psychodrama, dream work, and spirituality with Gestalt therapy.

Peter Philippson is well-known for his contributions in Gestalt journals and conferences. He is the author of *Self in Relation* (2001) and coauthor of *Gestalt: Working With Groups* (1992). He is co-founder of the Manchester Gestalt Centre in the United Kingdom; a faculty trainer and supervisor for the Gestalt Psychotherapy and Training Institute, United Kingdom; a full member of the New York Institute of Gestalt Therapy; and core faculty for the Gestalt Therapy International Network.

GESTALT: A HOLISTIC APPROACH

PETER: I am glad to be involved in this process with you, Sylvia. I value and enjoy your interest in putting Gestalt therapy on a sound philosophical foundation and the clarity with which you express your understanding of the links between the philosophy and the practical action of therapeutic work.

SYLVIA: Thanks, Peter; I enjoy our dialoguing, too; very stimulating and enjoyable!

Many threads make up the tapestry of Gestalt therapy's theory and its methods, the most important of which are the psychoanalysis of Freud, Horney, Rank, and Reich; the holism of Goldstein and the Gestalt psychologists; Lewin's humanistic development of field theory; the experimental and problem-solving approaches of the pragmatists Dewey and James; the philosophy of Aristotle and Kant; the phenomenology of Husserl; the existentialism of Heidegger, Kierkegaard, Tillich, and Buber; and several important ideas from the Chinese nature philosophy/religion of Taoism and its elaboration in Zen Buddhism.

Theoretically, Gestalt therapy is an example of the Aristotelian paradigm, a way of understanding that focuses upon concrete and specific individuals, situations, and events, seen in their environmental contexts, and attempts to understand the nature of change and how things—particularly living things—come to be as they are and to behave as they do. This is a marked contrast to the more familiar Platonic paradigm, which focuses on unchanging universal essences that are imperfectly exemplified in the changing world.

Paul Goodman, who, along with Laura Perls, was the intellectual "powerhouse" in the development of Gestalt therapy's theory, was well schooled in the philosophy of Aristotle (Stoehr, 1994). Goodman's theoretical elaboration of Gestalt therapy in Perls, Hefferline, and Goodman (1951, hereafter referred to simply as *Gestalt Therapy*) clearly shows the profound influence on him of Aristotle's ways of thinking (see Crocker, 1999). Gestalt therapy's point of departure—the field of the organism-environment—resulted from field considerations in physics and the biological focus of the pragmatists James and Dewey, as well as from Goodman's interest in Aristotle's biological and ethical writings.

INFLUENCE OF PHENOMENOLOGY AND EXISTENTIALISM

The phenomenology of Husserl (Spinelli, 1989) is concerned with epistemological issues rather than problems of living and acting in everyday life. Husserl's point of departure is the Kantian-Brentano position that it is impossible to know reality as it really is, apart from our own organizing perceptions and understandings of it. All we can ever know are the *appearances* of real things because we are forever unable to break through our own peculiarly *human* ways of knowing. However, human beings cannot tolerate meaninglessness and will impose meaning upon all experiences, whether these meanings accurately reflect either the world "out there" or appearances. Although all humans, being of the same species, probably experience what is revealed to them in similar ways, every person has at least somewhat different perceptions and interpretations of the shared world. These idiosyncratic interpretive elements are routinely imposed on the data of experience.

Husserl developed the phenomenological method as a way of separating experiential invariants from interpretational elements that are imposed on experiential data (Spinelli, 1989). Phenomena show regularities that appear in repeated combinations and sequences. These can be described, and models can be constructed intellectually that offer explanations of them and often lead to prediction and control. Scientific knowledge deals only with the regularities of phenomena plus intellectually constructed models that attempt to explain those regularities. It is impossible to transcend our own ways of knowing and to compare the appearances (*phenomena*) with the things as they are in themselves (*noumena*). Modern research scientists essentially use the phenomenological method as they "operationalize" their theories by describing verification procedures in experiential terms so that their results can be replicated by other investigators.

Three rules operate in a phenomenological process (Spinelli, 1989). First, and most important for Gestalt therapy, is the rule of the *epoche*: Bracket the question of the truth or falsehood of any and all interpretations of reality. Second is the rule of description: Provide a dispassionate description of the immediate and concrete impressions of what happened, as opposed to any interpretations of that experience—in other words, "describe," don't "interpret." Third is the horizontalization or equality rule: Avoid any hierarchical assumptions as to which described element is more important than any other. By separating as much as possible the experience from its interpretation, and by considering in detail the descriptions of a given experience, one can carefully weigh all of the evidence and entertain a variety of hypotheses that, in turn, will allow one to affirm the hypothesis that best explains all the data. If this method is followed, the explanations of experience will result from a close consideration of experience and thus be "experience near," as opposed to interpretations that are "experience far" and/or merely speculative. By being open to our experience in this way, we also become theoretically flexible: We regard any theoretical

---

PETER: I would like here to focus on Husserl's phenomenology, which interests both of us, where we make different aspects figural and then end up in a different area of thinking. Husserl's hope was to follow in the footsteps of Descartes and find if there was something solid and indubitable from which to proceed with surety. Husserl's method was to bracket, describe, and horizontalize, as you, Sylvia, described: first of all applying the method to the phenomena as they appeared and then going beyond Descartes to apply the method to the phenomenological process itself, to transcend the "I" who is bracketing, describing, and horizontalizing. His wish was to discover whether there is anything left. Why is this important for Gestalt therapists? I believe that Husserl has a great deal to say about our theory and method, and that it is precisely his second, transcendental, reduction that is most pertinent, as Gestalt theory of self similarly questions the "I" we think we know.

SYLVIA: I agree that how/when/if the self exists is an important question among Gestalt theorists, and that Husserl's second reduction raises this question also, but that there is no consensus about whether the self does or does not endure through time. Goodman's theory of the self owes, in my opinion, far more to Kant and Aristotle than it does to Husserl. Husserl can be understood as using his method to find out about what really exists, or he can be understood as looking at the evidence in experience for the beliefs we hold. The first is an ontological inquiry; the second is strictly epistemological. Both Kant and Goodman asserted that the self does *not* appear an as object; rather, each person has a subjective sense of agency and of possession of these experiences. From this view, the self is the subject of all awareness and has a subjective sense of itself as being present and owning all of its experiences, and it is this subjective sense that is the basis of our belief in the enduring life of the

construct as having only transitory validity—that is, being valid only as long as it is the most comprehensive and consistent explanation of the facts as they appear.

In Gestalt therapy, this method undergoes a transformation into Gestalt's therapeutically fruitful phenomenological method. Whereas the goal of Husserl's phenomenology is *knowledge*, the primary goal of Gestalt phenomenology is *practical*: the processes of healing and growth for concrete individuals, groups, and institutions. The therapist's manner and responsiveness give evidence that the therapist actively welcomes the client's revelation of his own personal truth, his own personal ways of being. The "descriptive" requirement of Husserl's phenomenology thus takes the following form: The therapist observes closely how in particular the client reveals himself: his choice of words as he tells his story, his body language, changes in voice tone, manifestations of his emotional reactions to what he is saying, and so on. In response to what the client reveals, the therapist suggests several possible experiments and explorations that can amplify certain aspects of that revelation, can give a variety of perspectives to that aspect, and can bring to light some of its connections to other parts of the client's experience.

The phenomenological principle of the *epoche*, or bracketing of interpretive elements along with questions of truth and falsehood, is the most important of the three principles, both in phenomenology and in Gestalt therapy. However, its Gestalt form is significantly different, especially with regard to questions of truth or falsehood. The Gestalt therapist's concern is not to find out whether the client is telling the truth as she tells her story but to understand the *meanings the client gives* to the people and events in her life. The therapeutic task thus becomes, in part, *hermeneutic*.

self. I think Husserl's influence is greater in the practicalities of the phenomenological method, not the theory of the self.

PETER: I agree there are all sorts of ideas in the Gestalt community about "self." Yet on any reading of *Gestalt Therapy,* the theory of self as arising from contact comes out as central to both the theory and the therapy. This is explicitly stated in Chapter 11, Section 1: "Thus the theory of the self develops directly with the therapy of the self" (Perls et al., 1994, p. 166). It is precisely in bracketing the tired "known," describing the experience in the moment, the here and now, and moving beyond our standard hierarchy of what is important (horizontalization) so that the new can come about. I do not take the *epoche* to be merely about bracketing my assumptions and meaning making to find the meaning the client gives. I would want, along with the client, to put aside for the moment all the assumptions *both* of us make about what is here, to face together the void, and to find something whose meaning arises out of our present contacting, the co-creation of self and other in the field. If self is, as in Gestalt therapy, the contacting process itself, then we are interested in the client's truth, not in an interpretive way, but as it arises in the truth of our contact.

SYLVIA: The meaning the client has given a situation and experimenting with other ways of approaching it can occur in the therapeutic practice of exploration. What I would not do is tell the client to put aside his or her understanding of the situation, but I myself would regard it as "true for the client"—a version that is highly mutable through the therapeutic processes.

Hermeneutics is a method of interpretation in which something is understood on its own terms, without having imported meanings imposed upon it. The process of hermeneutics in Gestalt therapy is one of discovering the meanings the client has given situations and people in her experience and tracing the impact of these meanings on how the client lives through time and circumstances.

The phenomenological method in Gestalt therapy involves a process that seeks to discover how the client's beliefs, and her understanding of the events and persons in her life, function in the client's own organization of experience, and therefore how they function as the *ground* of her cognitive, emotional, and behavioral responses to current and ongoing situations. As these things come more clearly into the client's awareness during the therapeutic process, and as she experiments with and explores aspects of life that had seemed fixed (though, in fact, they were intrinsically dynamic and mutable), her internal organization begins to "loosen," to become less stuck and more fluid as she begins to rethink old beliefs and try new behaviors. As this process goes on over time, healthy change becomes possible. Whether a person's father was just as the client has internalized him or whether the father has remained the same or has become a different person is not of primary importance in the therapy. What matters most is the how the *perceived and understood* "father" affects the client's ongoing life, apart from what the father was "really" like or how he is now.

How Gestalt therapists employ the phenomenological principle of "horizontalization" or "equality" is more problematic. As we have seen, in Husserl's phenomenology, the phenomenological data are to be given equal importance, but although it *may* be possible, at least to some degree, to do this in the pursuit of scientific knowledge, it is neither possible nor desirable in a therapeutic process. If the therapist gave equal importance to every aspect of the client's (verbal and nonverbal) revelations in therapy and made no discriminating evaluations, she would not be able to make sense of what was happening with the client or to fruitfully intervene. Therefore, although a Gestalt therapist employs the principle of horizontalization, she does so with an interesting therapeutic twist.

A Gestalt therapist brings to the meeting with a client a ground of personal and professional understanding, experience, and skill that greatly influences responses to the client. The therapist

---

PETER: Husserl started his exploration with a critique of what he called the "natural attitude," the sense of a continuing human being in a known and continuous world. In Gestalt therapy terms, we could see this as an activity of what Goodman called "personality function," a relatively fixed set of attitudes and ways of being that would form the basis for our description of ourselves. This fixity can be used to support ongoing contact if it is open to modification when the situation we are in changes; it can also be a defensive fixation, used to prevent contact in areas that we fear through either their associations or their unknownness.

SYLVIA: This also ties in with Taoist and Buddhist ideas that fixity is only an illusion, that what-is is dynamic, fraught with constant change. Many people believe that at a certain point in their lives their "character" is basically fixed—"you can't teach an old dog new tricks"—when in fact such fixity involves only an unwillingness to change. Gestalt therapy rejects the idea of fixity, and it does not move the client toward fixed goals. The goals that are achieved are discovered improvisationally in the dance between client and therapist.

I do agree that it is important to bracket, as you stated earlier, "the tired 'known,' describing the experience in the moment, the here and now, and moving beyond our standard hierarchy of what is important (horizontalization) so that the new can come about." However, Peter, here is where I think we have a significant difference. I do not believe that all of a client's patterns of contacting can be replicated in the relationship between client and therapist. Therefore, I think it is important for therapist and client to look together at the problematic situations in the client's ongoing life that have brought him into therapy, paying attention not only to the content but to the nonverbal manner of the telling. In this regard, it is also important for the therapist to help the

pays attention to some things that seem more significant than others; some aspects of the way the client tells his story pique curiosity and suggest ways of exploration, whereas others do not. Some phenomena suggest preliminary assessments that will either be revised and enriched or discarded in the light of the therapist's ongoing experience with the client. During the course of the therapeutic process, the therapist is aware of "wisps of theory" that weave in and out of her awareness and entertains "working hypotheses" and hunches as the client tells his story. The therapist *holds lightly* all these insights, hunches, working hypotheses, and meanings made of the results of suggested explorations and experiments. She does not cling to any of these thoughts or become fixed on any provisional diagnostic category, specific procedure, or agenda. Rather, the therapist constantly revises the assessment of the client as he reveals himself more and at greater depth.

In contrast to the Husserlian phenomenologist, the therapist considers everything she thinks about and does with the client in terms of *use* value, not *truth* value. Everything is done for the sake of helping a client discover his own unique truth as he learns how he actually lives, and for the sake of his becoming increasingly clear about how he wants to express that truth as his life goes on. Because the primary goal of the therapeutic process is healing and growth and not epistemological truth, it is phenomenologically legitimate to employ any thought, entertain any hunch or hypothesis, or suggest any variety of experiments and explorations that will, in a sense, "separate" the functional from the dysfunctional, the healthy from the destructive, the authentic from the inauthentic in how the client lives his life. The work of a Gestalt therapist, as the phenomenological method is employed, has the character of an improvisational dance: Being prepared with a ground of understanding and skill, the therapist meets the client in the space they share with a welcoming openness—and then they make up the dance together.

The transformation of Husserlian phenomenology into Gestalt's phenomenological method was accomplished, in part, under the influence of Heidegger's (1949) existentialist version of phenomenology, as well as Buber's (1923/1958) assertion of the primacy of the

client explore the meaning he has already imposed on his situation and to explore other ways of seeing and responding. In this way, both client and therapist become aware of, and can begin to explore and experiment with, the patterns of contact that are typical for the client as he lives through time and circumstances.

PETER: I know we disagree here. For me, the fixed, stuck patterns will be replicated, and these are the ones we concern ourselves with. I don't think GT is a problem-solving therapy. I do agree that an exploration can start with some situation the client brings from outside, but the clinical aim is to find a way to bring this into the room.

SYLVIA: While I believe that sometimes the contact between client and therapist is the primary focus of the session, I think it would be more accurate to say of the overall therapeutic enterprise that, by using the phenomenological approach, both client and therapist face what-is in the client's life—as the client reveals it in the here and now with the therapist. The prevailing attitude in this process—in the therapist throughout, and gradually in the client—is an equanimical openness and curiosity and a willingness to form a fresh understanding of the important situations that are of concern to the client, paying careful attention also to his patterns of response to them as these are revealed in the therapeutic process.

I-Thou meeting with the "Other" and the life of dialogue. Kierkegaard's (1954) understanding of the faith relationship between God and the individual, and of the uniqueness of every person's authentic truth, played an important role in the thought of all of these thinkers.

Laura Perls was familiar with the works of Husserl, Heidegger, Kierkegaard, and Buber as a result of having studied philosophy with the Protestant philosopher/theologian Paul Tillich (Stoehr, 1994). The influence of these men's ideas on Goodman resulted both from his association with Laura and from his own reading. Fritz Perls knew of Husserl through Laura and Goodman but did not have a direct familiarity with Husserl's work.

Heidegger's (1962) approach to phenomenology, with its more humanistic bent, significantly influenced Gestalt phenomenology. For Heidegger, Western thought had moved so far away from the lived experience of ordinary human beings that it was necessary to begin again with the experiential foundations of important concepts. Heidegger attempted (unsuccessfully) to give a phenomenological account of Being by beginning with a phenomenological account of *human* being, which Heidegger defined descriptively as a *Dasein,* a being (*Sein*) who is there (*da*). As with Heidegger, the Gestalt approach begins with the field of the organism-environment. For Heidegger, human beings have a sense of being thrown into the situations in which they find themselves; these situations seem to be the result of an accident of birth and to have no other apparent meaning. One of the great tasks of each person's life is to create life's meaning by how it is lived in the concrete situations of life. As people develop, they discover several other kinds of beings: Some things are *vorhanden* (objects that are merely *there* in the environment, without any particular purpose or usefulness), and others are *zuhanden* (objects that are *at hand* and can be used). We are free to employ any of these as we enact the meanings of our lives, or we can "lose" ourselves in "busy-ness" to avoid the task of personal meaning making.

We find, in addition to *vorhanden* and *zuhanden,* other beings like ourselves, each of whom is also a *Dasein.* We cannot be indifferent to others like ourselves, for each of us is thrown into the world and faced with the same existential task. Though each person is as unique as this-here-now-human-being, we are inescapably thrown together and have real relationships with each other, which in turn have important implications for our attitudes and behaviors toward each other. Each of us is, in actual fact, a *Mitsein,* a being (*Sein*) whose being is also being-with (*mit*). Though we may regard nonhuman things as merely useful, taking such an attitude toward another *Mitsein* is inappropriate—rather, we owe every *Mitsein* an attitude of care (*Sorge*) and concern (Heidegger, 1962).

Heidegger (1962) employed Kant's distinction between things, which have value primarily by being useful, and persons, who, because they are *originating sources of value,* cannot legitimately be reduced to the level of mere things having only "use value." Buber (1923/1958), following this same tradition, distinguishes between relations (i.e., ways of being) of the "primary word" *I-Thou* and the "secondary word" *I-It.* For him, the fundamental fact of human life is that it is relational: "All real living is meeting" (p. 11), and the primary way of living, I-Thou, is a word that "can only be spoken with the whole being" (p. 10). In the relationship of I-Thou, each receives the unique revelation of the other. A few years after Buber published *I and Thou* (1923/1958), he elaborated his ideas in an essay he called "Dialogue" (1926), published in his book *Between Man and Man* (1926/1965a). Here Buber stated, "The basic movement of the life of dialogue is the turning towards the other . . . [in which] this one person steps forth and becomes a presence" (p. 22). Again, "He who is living the life of dialogue receives in the ordinary course of the hours something that is said and feels himself approached for an answer . . . [and thereby] receives . . . a harsh and strengthening sense of reciprocity" (p. 20).

This meeting is not, however, one in which one person seeks to use the other, for that would be an instance of I-It relating. It is important to note that for Buber I-It relating plays an important role in our everyday living because we must deal with the world and with each other in "I-It" ways in order to survive. There is nothing amiss in that. But to regard other persons, animals and things in nature, and even nature as a whole as *merely* useful is to depart from the fundamental motions of one's humanity. Being constantly open to the revelation of Thou, whenever and from wherever it comes—even while being busy in the workings of I-It—and being willing to reveal oneself as Thou to an Other's I when the opportunity presents itself—that is being faithful to oneself as a person. For Buber, in such meetings the unique individuality of the Other is revealed and received, and from this mutual process arises true community and thus the fulfillment of life.

In Gestalt therapy, the fundamental attitude of the therapist to the client is a caring and welcoming openness, a willingness to be there in ways that encourage the client to reveal his own personal truth, and a respectfulness of the primacy of the client's experience. In this sense, the fundamental movement between therapist and client is the presence of an I to a Thou. Yet here is a paradox, expressed by Arnold Beisser (1970) as the *paradoxical principle of change*: The overarching purpose of the therapeutic process is the client's desire for change that will relieve his pain, coupled with the therapist's willingness to place herself, her experience, knowledge, and skill, at the service of the client and his needs. However, the processes of Gestalt therapy require looking *away* from this goal and focusing instead on the *letting-be-of-what-is*. The paradoxical principle is that change cannot happen unless we first affirm and embrace what-is. Just as happiness cannot be found by aiming directly at it, but by engaging in activities that produce happiness as a by-product, so healthy human change can be achieved by giving *what-is* its due, by facing it squarely and with clarity. Both happiness and healthy functioning are by-products of the way we live, and we cannot learn to live in healthy and more functional ways unless we first become aware of the truth of how we *actually* exist. The processes of Gestalt therapy—through which clients become vividly aware of *what-is* in their own lives—are the very processes that initiate the course of, or pathway to, change and lead toward more functional and satisfying living. The paradox is that *what-is-wished-for* can be accomplished *only* if it recedes into the background and if *what-is-now* takes "center stage." Otherwise, the client will remain stuck.

Although the dominant movement in Gestalt therapy is I-Thou, to be therapeutically effective the therapist must move in and out of moments of I-It as she makes practical evaluations and suggestions about the client's ongoing process. The therapist often suggests experiments and explorations of something noticed in the client as he tells his story, and these spring from an attitude of practicality, an application of methods and principles, that belongs to I-It. Many responses to that revelation are a mixture of the I-Thou's disinterested (nonpractical) curiosity and the I-It of interventions. Buber (1923/1958) himself speaks of such a mixture when he says: "The *It* is the eternal chrysalis, the *Thou* the eternal butterfly—except that situations do not always follow one another in clear succession, but often there is a happening profoundly twofold, confusedly entangled" (pp. 17–18). The therapeutic relationship and its interactions between the Gestalt therapist and client are just such a mixture of I-Thou and I-It. All of the therapist's interventions are motivated by a caring curiosity and concern to help the client reveal more and more of himself, and to do so at greater depth. However, regard for the client as a Thou is preeminent, and it is the motivating source of the therapist's I-It movements in relations with the client. These interventions are not undertaken to "get somewhere"—that is, to achieve a specific practical outcome—but to further the client's process of self-discovery and self-revelation. The Gestalt therapist accepts whatever the client reveals, in whatever way he reveals himself. The I-Thou of the Gestalt therapist is embodied in this very attitude or nonjudgmental acceptance of the client's self-revelation. The Gestalt therapist must be able to be present for and engage with the client in ways that begin to "retune," reorganize, or, in a significant sense, re-create the ways in which the client experiences himself and others in everyday life.

INFLUENCE OF TAOISM AND ZEN

Organismic Self-Regulation

In both its theory and its practice, Gestalt therapy is a biological and educational model. We view the human being as an organism that is part of nature, living in natural cycles of contact and withdrawal. Human beings, like all other natural organisms, regulate themselves in changing circumstances (whether internal or external). As a result, the natural tendency is to adapt in ways that bring about organismic balance, either within the organism or within the larger field of the organism-environment. The organism, in other words, regulates itself in ways that enable it to develop that natural stature and those powers that, in turn, enable it to function in ways natural to mature members of the species. The term *organismic self-regulation* was developed by the authors of *Gestalt Therapy* to express this naturalistic adaptive process (Perls et al., 1951).

Within this theoretical framework, the Gestalt therapist regards the client as always possessing innate principles of healthy functioning, even though the client's personal experiences in her own environmental circumstances may have resulted in survival adaptations that, in turn, interfere with and distort the working of these principles. The task of the therapist is, therefore, to facilitate the client's returning to healthy ways of living freely guided by natural principles. In contrast to the psychoanalyst, the Gestalt therapist is not required to be a "fount of wisdom" or to "put into" the client correct interpretations of her experience. Indeed, the therapeutic task is not essentially cognitive—though cognition is involved—but experiential and transformative of both awareness and patterns of behavior. Just as the client's dysfunctional patterns of living involve the whole person (mind, feelings, desires, body, habitual patterns of behavior, and varieties of relationships with others), so also must the processes that lead to healing and growth engage the whole person in the many dimensions of living. The work of the therapist is thus a holistic task.

Goodman brought to the writing of the theoretical volume of *Gestalt Therapy* not only his own synthesis of Aristotle's ethical and biological writings and the biological and problem-solving bent of the pragmatists Dewey and James but also a number of Taoist philosophical principles of nature. Goodman, like many other intellectuals of his time, was very familiar with the Taoist ideas of "going *with* nature." This is apparent in his 1947 book *Kafka's Prayer,* in which he employed Taoist principles in his analysis of some of Kafka's work. A few years later, in the early days of the New York Institute, one of the courses Goodman taught used the *Book of Tao* (Lao Tzu, 1963) as one of the texts to be studied (Stoehr, 1994).

A central theme running throughout the *Book of Tao* is the assertion that the wise and virtuous person learns the ways of nature and lives in accordance with nature's ways. That this belief was fundamental in Goodman's thinking is clear in one of his favorite sayings: *Natura sanat non medicus* (only nature heals) (Goodman, 1977b). Thus the task of the Gestalt therapist is to engage the client in ways that allow nature to do the healing and the growing. Perls et al. (1951) are clear and specific in how this approach helps the client "[t]o observe [his] self in action—ultimately to observe [his] self *as* action—[which] calls for techniques strikingly different from those [he] may have tried already and found wanting; in particular, introspection" (p. 3). In contrast to essentially cognitive approaches ("talking cures"), the Gestalt "clinician has sought ever more intimate *contact* with the activities of the human organism as *lived* by the human organism" (p. 21).

> The patient is taught to *experience himself.* "Experience" derives from the same Latin source *experiri,* to try, as does the word "experiment," and the dictionary gives precisely the sense that we intend here, namely, "the actual living through an event or events." (Perls et al., 1951, p. 15)

Here the therapist is a kind of catalyst, "an ingredient which precipitates a reaction which might not otherwise occur" (p. 15), so that how the person actually functions in certain situations is enacted in the here and now of the therapeutic situation. By experimenting with these processes, ultimately the client "has tools and equipment to deal with problems as they may arise" and experiences a sense of "heightened vitality and more effective functioning" (p. 15).

This Taoist principle of "going with nature" is clearly expressed in the following passages from the *Tao Te Ching,* the *Book of Tao* (Lao Tzu, 1963):

> The sage manages affairs without action
> and spreads doctrine without words.
> He acts but does not rely on his own ability. (#2)
> By acting without action, all things will be in order. (#3)
> [The great rulers]
> . . . accomplish their task; they complete their work
> . . . they simply follow Nature. (#14)
> Tao invariably takes no action,
> and yet there is nothing left undone. (#37)

Oriental martial arts have been strongly influenced by the *Book of Tao.* The point of these arts is to understand the nature of motion and to employ the opponent's own force in such a way as to deflect the attack, often to turn that force back on the attacker. It is because the martial artist understands how to work *with* natural processes that a tiny man or woman can defeat an opponent who is much larger and stronger. In this way, the martial artist acts without acting: That is, he "does not rely on his own ability." Seen in this light we can regard Gestalt therapy as a kind of "martial art"—the art of using the client's own natural processes in the service of her healing and growth. The therapist "does not rely on his own ability" but helps the client learn to live by the healthy principles of nature. At the very end of the theoretical section of *Gestalt Therapy,* Goodman says of a client who is living well:

> In its trials and conflicts the self is coming to be in a way that did not exist before. In contactful experience the "I," alienating its safe structures, risks this leap and identifies with the growing self, gives it its service and knowledge, and at the moment of achievement stands out of the way. (Perls et al., 1951, p. 466)

In Goodman's words, the "I" *lets nature heal.*

Here-and-Now Focus—Just Seeing, Just Being

At one point, Fritz Perls went to Japan to learn about Zen, a synthesis of Mahayana Buddhism and Taoist principles. Zen meditation is a process of emptying the mind in order to experience satori, or enlightenment. No philosophical discourses are involved in Zen training. Rather, the Zen master directly points to the "Buddha nature," by pointing to what-is, or answers a question about the Buddha nature with a seeming non sequitur: "two pounds of flax." Like koans, riddles that do not make sense to ordinary ways of thinking (e.g., "What is the sound of one hand clapping?"), meditation, direct pointing, and seemingly nonsense statements are ways of emptying the mind of ordinary thought processes so it may become able to perceive the "suchness," the "thisness" (Watts, 1957, p. 127), of what-is in the present moment. A person who can perceive "this" will be "instantaneously enlightened" and experience satori.

No doubt this is the source of Fritz's famous exhortation to Gestalt therapists and clients to lose their minds and come to their senses. In his view as a trained psychoanalyst, the problem with the psychoanalytic approach was that it played directly into neurotics' problem, which was to *substitute* thinking for action, and thus contributed to their remaining "stuck." In contrast, Gestalt therapy is not a talking approach, although it uses language: Language is merely the medium of experimentation, of actively exploring how clients actually perform their acts of living. Because Gestalt is an experimental and holistic approach to "what-is," the experiences in therapy are not "about" what-is but are actual lived experiences that have the power to alter how clients live their lives beyond the therapeutic context.

One of the major ways in which Zen has had an enduring influence on Gestalt therapy is, therefore, in the emphasis on the primacy of the here and now. The Zen archer effortlessly lets go of the arrow without *trying* to hit the target, without deliberately breaking down the motions into lifting the bow, pulling back the arrow in the string, aiming at the target, and releasing. Rather, it is all one seamless and spontaneous act. It is as if the arrow shot itself. "In walking, just walk. In sitting, just sit. Above all, don't wobble" (Watts, 1957, p. 135)—which is to say, in effect, don't reflect on the process, just do it. Alan Watts emphasized,

> Zen is not merely a cult of impulsive action. The point . . . is not to eliminate reflective thought but to eliminate "blocking" in both action and thought, so that the response of the mind is always like a ball in a mountain stream—"one thought after another without hesitation." (p. 150)

This ability to live in the present moment and to give ourselves fully to whatever we are engaged in is the sign of an "awakened mind." Watts (1957) said that such a "mind responds immediately, without calculation" (p. 83). The "liberated" person fully embraces whatever is happening in *this* place and in the *present moment.*

The embrace of what-is, concretely and specifically, in the present is not limited to the embrace of what is of monumental importance, but it is the single-minded embrace of "nothing special" (Watts, 1957, p. 126). Zen spirituality is not about thinking about God when one is peeling potatoes; it is being fully engaged in peeling the potatoes. Indeed, Zen teaches that all daily activities can be done with the same kind of undivided presence in the moment, where we give ourselves wholly to whatever we do, without second-guessing ourselves, without self-consciously observing how we are doing what we are doing, without being double-minded. One of the Zen masters said:

> Before I had studied Zen for thirty years, I saw mountains as mountains, and waters as waters. When I arrived at a more intimate knowledge, I came to the point where I saw that mountains are not mountains, and waters are not waters. But now that I have got its very substance I am at rest. For it's just that I see mountains once again as mountains, and waters once again as waters. (Watts, 1957, p. 126)

Similarly, in Gestalt therapy we focus on the concrete and specific events of a client's life. We do not reserve our energies for her "big problems" but help our client notice, to become aware of how she *actually lives* in the everyday affairs of her life—without *trying* to change anything but simply to become mindfully aware. It is clear how this point of view harmonizes with "the paradoxical principle of change." Change does not occur when we strain to make it happen, or even when we have the present intention to work at change. It happens when we allow the issue of change to recede into the background as we single-mindedly focus on what-is. Of course, the therapist employs his understanding and therapeutic skills to encourage deeper and fuller revelations of what-is in the client's living, but not directly with the goal of achieving future changes in the client's living. Rather, the therapeutic process is itself a full engagement with the *present moment.* The entire therapeutic process is done in the present, and the client's self-revelation, her letting-what-is-stand-out-in-the-open, happens *only* in the present, in the here and now. Such present engagement often leads somehow (mysteriously) to the breaching of the barriers to transformation, not by trying but by simply wholly embracing present experience. This is one of the great contributions of Zen to Gestalt therapy.

The Fertile Void

Another contribution by both Taoism and Zen is the idea of the fertility of "the void." As indicated above, Zen meditation is a way of emptying the mind of ordinary thought processes in order to become in tune with the fertility of nonbeing or no-mind. Although being (sky energy, maleness, activity) and nonbeing (earth energy, femaleness, passivity) are one in the Tao, nonbeing is ontologically prior to (more fundamental than) being. In Taoism and in Zen, nonbeing is the source of all creativity; it is the void that is always fertile. Though both principles exist together eternally in what-is (the Tao), the superiority of nonbeing over being is one of the major themes in the *Book of Tao* (Lao Tzu, 1963). This is clear from the following passages:

> Weakness is the function of Tao.
> All things in the world come from being.
> And being comes from non-being. (#40)
> Tao is empty [like a bowl]. It may be used but its capacity is never exhausted.
> It is bottomless, perhaps the ancestor of all things. (#4)
> The Spirit of the valley never dies.
> It is called the subtle and profound female.
> The gate of the subtle and profound female is the root of Heaven and Earth.
> It is continuous, and seems to be always existing.
> Use it and you will never wear it out. (#6)
> Thirty spokes are united around the hub to make a wheel,
> but it is on its non-being that the utility of the carriage depends.
> Clay is molded to form a utensil,
> but it is on its non-being that the utility of the utensil depends.

> Doors and windows are cut out to make a room,
> but it is on its non-being that the utility of the room depends.
> Therefore turn being into advantage, and turn non-being into utility. (#11)

Through the practice of the highest form of *zazen,* namely *schikan-taza,* "just sitting," Fritz learned the value of silence: the willingness to "just sit" with silence and to experience a kind of emptiness, which in Zen is called nonbeing or no-mind and in Taoism is called nonbeing, the void, or the feminine. This often provides the key to a person's breaking through to a kind of new awareness that has a liberating effect—that is, satori (Greaves, 1976). Perls called this the experience of "the fertile void," and it has become an integral part of the Gestalt approach.

In Gestalt therapy, silence is often important in the therapeutic process, for important things that have been out of awareness are thereby given an opportunity to emerge into consciousness, where they can be explored and effectively dealt with. As long as the time is always "filled" with talking, by either the therapist or the client, some of those elements in the client's ground that support important behaviors are not given space to come into awareness. It is important for the therapist to be comfortable with silence so that she can resist the urge to "say something" when the client falls silent.

Similarly, it is important for the therapist to encourage a client to "stay with" being confused or at a loss to know "what to do next." This is another version of the experience of the "fertile void." By attentively waiting in the silence or asking the client to stay with the confusion, the therapist supports the client in ways that can lead to a breakthrough in the client's understanding of his situation. This "attentive waiting" is one of the ways in which Gestalt therapy facilitates the client's letting-be-of-what-is. Just as the empty spaces in Chinese and Japanese landscape painting are integral to the design and significance of the whole, so is staying with the silence and the confusion that is sometimes an intrinsic element in the Gestalt therapeutic process.

Polarities

From a Taoist point of view, even though nonbeing is ontologically superior to being, experience testifies to their ultimate inseparability. Polarities are found throughout nature, including human life. Therapists often see the natural occurrence of polarities in their clients' everyday life, especially when clients feel internally conflicted about taking one of several possible courses or when they have ambivalent feelings toward other people and/or situations. These inner conflicts frequently have a confusing, sometimes paralyzing, effect on their ability to function. The Gestalt therapist helps the client explore each side of the polarity, often taking an experimental approach by asking the client to give a voice to each of the poles. As a result of this experimental exploration, the client either discovers the reconciling ground and thus moves beyond the conflict to some form of resolution or discovers a way to live with the polarity.

CONCLUSION: THE SINGULARITY OF WHAT-IS

The Tao that can be told of is not the eternal Tao.

Lao Tzu, The Book of Tao, #1

In contrast to cognitive behavioral (CBT) and rational-emotive (RET) therapies, Gestalt therapy and many varieties of psychoanalysis acknowledge the powerful role of the therapeutic relationship in the success of the therapy itself. However, there is a watershed difference between psychoanalysis and the Gestalt approach. Psychoanalysis continues to emphasize the analyst's interpretation of the client's experience, which the analyst gives by listening to the client's story in ways that permit the analyst to access certain psychological categories (such as projection, Oedipal issues, separation issues), which are, in turn, given to the client as explanations of his experience. Here the analyst subsumes the themes of the client's story under a complex of psychological categories that can be discussed and intellectually understood by the client and that the client can "work through" with the analyst. In contrast, Gestalt therapy uses the phenomenological method to help the client explore and experiment with the concrete specific events of life. In so doing, the therapist guides the client in paying close attention to what actually happens in his life and how he typically responds to it.

By learning how to "let-what-is-stand-out-in-the-open," the client begins to reveal his own unique personal truth, both to himself and to the therapist. Through this process, the client in Gestalt therapy becomes more focused on the here and now in daily life and more and more discovers how he actually lives his life—and, gradually over time, how he *wants* to live it. Increasingly, the client is able to express his own unique truth beyond the therapeutic situation and in his daily living. The meaning of the client's story is not imposed upon his experience by the therapist but emerges through the therapeutic processes of self-discovery and self-revelation. Therefore, although it is possible for the therapist and the client to discuss some aspects of the changes that are happening in the client's living, such *lived truths* are unique to the person—and ultimately can only be *witnessed to,* never fully verbalized. Because this truth is *lived* truth and is not essentially cognitive, it can readily lead to transformative changes in how the client feels, thinks, and acts—which, of course, is the ultimate aim of psychotherapy.

PETER: In the therapeutic setting, I stay as much as possible with the givens of our experience together. I am not looking for choices. As awareness develops, the dilemma pushes for completion and closure. My interest is in the truth of the unique situation, what is authentic to experience, to the "principles of nature," as you say at one point. That truth is not one person's interpreted truth, but the truth we are creating together. Sometimes something happens that neither I nor the client understand but that is the only real response to the situation.

SYLVIA: I believe, too, that by means of the Gestalt therapeutic processes clients can learn how to have livelier contact with others, can learn how to speak and act in ways in which there is greater congruence between thought, feeling, intention, and behavior, and can gradually come to an empowered understanding of how they want to live their lives, and that this readily translates into the manner of clients' everyday lives. However, most of the meanings a person lives by are not essentially those created together by client and therapist but those created by a client and the people and situations with which she has contact in everyday life.

PETER: As I've written about in my recent book, *Self in Relation* (Philippson, 2001), for me the image of this therapy is of people facing each other, neither of whom knows what will happen next, but one of whom, the therapist, is grounded in the knowledge of having done this many times before and knowing that something new has the power to emerge that can promote major changes in the client's life and possibly also in the therapist's.

In *Gestalt Therapy* (Perls et al., 1951), the paradigmatic human process of doing business with the world involves taking an interest in a situation to be dealt with, going through a discovery process to find alternative approaches to the problem, "identifying with" one of these and "alienating" the others, then acting on that alternative and thus dealing with the problem. Ideally, the person would live holistically enough so that he would "give himself" fully to whatever course of action seemed best to him and with which he had identified, and thus his actions would be performed spontaneously and naturally. Unfortunately, such naturalness is rare, and its absence creates a variety of difficulties that bring people into therapy. Among the many sources of these difficulties is a client's inability to move from thought into action, or his being ambivalent or "of two minds" about the course of action he has decided on but has not *fully* identified with. The formulation in *Gestalt Therapy* of this ideal process—and the methods that have been developed to address the many issues that interrupt and distort it—shows the impact on Gestalt therapy of the strands of thought that have been the focus of this chapter, namely Taoism/Zen and existentialism/phenomenology.

The existentialists stress the paramount importance of the unique individual's choices and the actions that flow naturally from them. The emphasis in all of these approaches is on doing what is "appropriate" to the situation, what the situation "calls for" and what "belongs" to it. Ideally, such actions express the individual's unique response to the "call" to her of what-is in the present situation in which she finds herself. The "call" is unique to her and sometimes requires actions that are for her alone to do. The authentic person takes responsibility for how she answers that call. What she responds to can be another person who addresses her, as in Buber, or a significant situation that is developing around her. In her response to what-is in a given time and place, the "liberated" person expresses her own personal truth, a truth that is uniquely lived out by her in a given time and in a specific place. She responds as a singular individual, not as one for whom there can be adequate "substitutes." Because what is revealed is unique, it cannot be expressed fully in words because the meanings of words have to do with *shared* characteristics.

This is precisely the ideal in Zen. The liberated person "goes with nature" while wholly embracing "what-is"—in this *place* and in this *now.* His response is without internal conflict or any apparent process of deliberation and decision. Like Kierkegaard's "knight of faith," who makes difficult leaps without the least indication of a loss of balance, the person who lives naturally "just does it," whatever is called for in that concrete situation. In his identifying embrace of what-is and what-is-to-be-done, he acts responsibly with a completely spontaneous naturalness. From a Taoist/Zen perspective, such a person is doing "nothing special," he is simply allowing what-is in the present moment to reveal itself to him and out of that receptivity is responding with "no-mind." According to the *Tao Te Ching* (Lao Tzu, 1963), such a person:

> Manages affairs without action
> And spreads doctrine without words.
> . . . He acts but does not rely on his own ability. (#10)

Persons who follow nature

> . . . accomplish their task; they complete their work
> . . . they simply follow Nature. (#17)

REVIEW QUESTIONS

1. Crocker cites three rules that operate in a phenomenological process. Define each rule: (a) the rule of *epoche;* (b) the rule of *description;* and (c) the rule of *horizontalization or equality.* How is each rule useful to Gestalt theory?

2. The term *organismic self-regulation,* as defined in *Gestalt Therapy* (Perls et al., 1951, 1994) and in this chapter, has implications for the tasks of therapy. How is the term useful in describing the therapeutic process?

3. What is the likely source of influence for Fritz Perls's declaration that to be vital and healthy it is good "to lose your mind and come to your senses"?

4. What are the relationships and differences between therapeutic work existing in the here and now and Zen spirituality?

5. What is the therapeutic purpose of exploring polarities?

EXPERIENTIAL PEDAGOGICAL ACTIVITIES

ACTIVITY 1: Read an opinion column on the editorial page of a newspaper. In reading it, distinguish between what is "public fact" and what is the "author's opinion." Next, read a news account on the front page and see if it is a report of observable facts or a mixture of opinions and reported facts. Start noticing what other people reveal to you and your interpretations of what they say and do. Discuss your findings and observations with a classmate, including how these "fact versus opinion" differences pertain to therapeutic dialogue.

ACTIVITY 2: Invite a tai chi master to attend your class as a guest to demonstrate and explain the martial arts exercise of *push hands.* After each class member learns the basics of *push hands,* discuss how this is a useful metaphor of therapy from a Gestalt perspective.

ACTIVITY 3: In the Hollywood film *Raiders of the Lost Ark,* the hero must make a leap of faith when stepping on an invisible bridge crossing a gorge. As Crocker describes the leap of faith in this chapter, "The person who lives naturally 'just does it,' whatever is called for in that concrete situation. . . . From a Taoist/Zen perspective, such a person is doing 'nothing special,' he is simply allowing what-is in the present moment to reveal itself to him." After viewing this excerpt from *Raiders of the Lost Ark,* discuss in small groups other events of your own life or your clients' lives that have required leaps of faith and what supports helped make them possible.

ACTIVITY 4: Zen meditation includes the experience of just sitting with silence and experiencing no-mind. If you have not practiced meditation before, begin by sitting and being aware of quieting your thoughts for a short time. Quieting thoughts is not as easy as it sounds, and you may find you begin this exercise with mere seconds of no-mind. As you practice quieting your thoughts every day for a week, take note of the process in a journal. You may want to document increases in time spent with no-mind, or you may want to catalogue those thoughts that invade the quietness.

CHAPTER 5

Gestalt Therapy Theory of Change

GARY M. YONTEF

DIALOGUE RESPONDENT: REINHARD FUHR

Gary M. Yontef is a fellow of the Academy of Clinical Psychology and a diplomate (ABPP) in both clinical psychology and clinical social work. He has been a Gestalt therapist since training with Frederick Perls and James Simkin in 1965. Formerly on the Psychology Department faculty of the University of California, Los Angeles, and chairman of the Professional Conduct Committee of the Los Angeles County Psychological Association, he is now in private practice in Santa Monica. He is a past president of the Gestalt Therapy Institute of Los Angeles and for 18 years was chairman of their faculty. He is an editorial board member of the *International Gestalt Journal* (formerly the *Gestalt Journal*) and the *Gestalt Review* and is an editorial adviser of the *British Gestalt Journal.* He was the first chairman of the International Gestalt Therapy Association and is a faculty member of the Gestalt Therapy International Network (GTIN). He is co-founder and co-director of the Pacific Gestalt Institute. He has written 39 articles and chapters on Gestalt therapy theory, practice, and supervision and is the author of *Awareness, Dialogue and Process: Essays on Gestalt Therapy* (1993), which has been published in Spanish, German, Portuguese, and Korean.

Reinhard Fuhr, PhD, is a Gestalt therapist, trainer, and senior lecturer at the University of Goettingen, Germany. He and his wife, Martina, are co-directors of the Gestalt Zentrum Goettingen (Gestalt Institute). He is associate editor of *Gestalt Review* and co-editor of the German journal for transpersonal psychology and psychotherapy but is perhaps best known for co-editing and -authoring (with his wife) the gigantic (1,245 pages) pedagogical *Handbuch der Gestalttherapie* (2001) and three other books on the Gestalt approach.

inexorable. From conception to .e are constantly changing. The itself is constantly changing, as are events and structures in the universe. Even when there appears to be no change, slow and subtle shifts are always taking place. Apparently unchanging events are events that change so slowly that they merely appear to be static; some processes appear to change so slowly that they take on the attributes of unchanging structure. A standing wave looks as if it is not changing when it is actually a repeating process that creates a static appearance by the repetition. A person who resists change and stays relatively static still changes in relation to surroundings. The rest of the field does not stop changing because some individual has slowed to the point of appearing static.

The central question is not whether there will be change but whether human change will be toward growth or deterioration, or whether there will be apparent lack of change, in which the person grows or deteriorates so slowly in comparison with the surrounding world that it appears as stasis. The central question for Gestalt therapy theory and practice is: How do individuals and their societies, including psychotherapists, influence and support change in the direction of healing, growth, and wholeness, and how do they interfere with healing, growth, and wholeness—or even precipitate deterioration?

REINHARD: I am glad to have been invited to communicate with you on your chapter. When reading it, as well as other recent Gestalt writings, I noticed that my perspective is no longer strictly a Gestalt perspective. I think I have transcended (some would say "betrayed") the original Gestalt theory by integrating many other alternative theories and metatheories. I will therefore suggest a few extensions and alternatives to the views you offer and ask some questions.

GARY: From my perspective, introducing new information, theories, techniques, and perspectives into Gestalt therapy is not a betrayal of Gestalt therapy. On the contrary, it is in the finest Gestalt therapy tradition. Optimally, I would hope such additions expand Gestalt therapy rather than transcend it. A central issue is whether the novelty introduced is truly assimilated or just introjected and added on. If it is assimilated, it goes through a process of creative adjustment: The new information is modified by the interaction with the Gestalt therapy system, and the Gestalt therapy system is modified by that same interaction.

In Gestalt therapy theory, the therapist is not a change agent that makes change happen. The Gestalt therapist is an agent in the quest to create conditions that maximize conditions for growth, conditions that allow growth to happen when it has been arrested or limited, conditions that focus attention where needed for healing and growth. Gestalt therapy trusts organismic self-regulation more than therapist-directed change attempts. Rather than aiming to move the patient to be different, the Gestalt therapist believes in meeting patients as they are and using increased awareness of the present, including awareness of figures that start to emerge (thoughts, feelings, impulses, etc.) that the person might or might not allow to organize new behavior. With this present-centered awareness, change can happen without the therapist aiming for a preset goal.

THE PARADOXICAL THEORY OF CHANGE

The paradoxical theory of change is at the core of the Gestalt therapy change theory. The paradox is that the more one tries to be who one is not, the more one stays the same

(Beisser, 1970). When people identify with their whole selves, when they acknowledge whatever aspect arises at a moment, the conditions for wholeness and growth are created. When people do not identify with parts of who they are, inner conflict is created, and all of a person's resources cannot go into needed interactions of self and other. When people identify with their mode of restraint and disown their basic feelings, they disown that which is needed for motivating energy and direction. When people identify with their impulses and disown their mode of restraint, they disown what they need for safe, sane, and healthy behavior.

The more people try not to change—the more they resist natural or necessary changes in the self or the environment—the more they will change in relation to the changing conditions of the environment. Psychological health is largely a matter of identification with the whole self and maximum use of the whole self for necessary tasks in the lived environment. The paradoxical theory of change is closely related to the fundamental principles of Gestalt therapy: phenomenology, field theory, and dialogic existentialism. It is also strongly influenced by Zen, as described by Sylvia Crocker in Chapter 4.

The Gestalt therapist focuses on the patient's being aware and his or her increasing ability to be aware, as needed, of whatever forces are operating in the person/environment field. To be aware of these forces, to own them, is to own the choices made. The Gestalt therapist prefers to create the conditions for self-awareness that will support natural change rather than to become an agent of programmatic behavior change.

In the Gestalt therapy model of change, significant increase in awareness occurs by virtue of dialogic contact. The Gestalt therapist strives to establish contact as a whole person with the person of the patient—as the patient experiences him- or herself. Out of this existential meeting, new awareness and growth occur. In turn, the growth in awareness supports further contact.

REINHARD: Change! Your position is, as far as I have grasped it, that change in Gestalt therapy happens by natural and self-regulated processes. We just have to care for the conditions that make the process of change possible and to remove obstacles by becoming aware of them in an accepting way. I would completely agree—as one pole of a polarity. I would, though, complement this position (which has been corroborated by much of what systems theorists have discovered) by the other pole—the intentionality of change, the sometimes very rational decision in favor of particular changes. Both would form a unit for me—the trust in the process on the one side and the goal-oriented and planned (programmed) change on the other side. Therefore, I would not argue against "programmatic behavior change" as such, though I would definitely argue against the lopsided or even exclusive use of this approach in psychotherapy as anywhere else.

GARY: If you interpret my writing as excluding systematic programmatic work, intentional change, perhaps I have not been clear enough. Phenomenological experimentation and establishing the field conditions for growth include systematic experimentation with new behavior. The issue for me is whether goal-directed and planned change is done from a phenomenological and dialogic perspective consistent with the paradoxical theory of change—or is merely behavior modification based on a person's self-rejection. If it is not the former, it is better done in a behaviorist framework where data are collected systematically and the therapist takes responsibility for the results. In the Gestalt therapy framework, programs are established and mutually regulated by the joint direction of the therapist and patient and are structured according to phenomenological principles.

ORGANISMIC SELF-REGULATION IN THE ORGANISM-ENVIRONMENT FIELD

The Organism-Environment Field

The paradoxical theory of change is based on a trust in the ability of human beings to self-regulate in a manner that achieves the best possible adjustment in the context in which they live. Gestalt therapy is a holistic theory that believes that people are inherently self-regulating and oriented toward growth and that they cannot be validly understood apart from their environment.

In Gestalt therapy theory, people are always a part of an organism-environment field. This contrasts with the conventional viewpoint that people exist separately but also have relations with others. The Gestalt therapy view is that this conventional isolated person is only an abstraction out of the field, the organism-environment field. People exist only as part of a relational field—they are "of the field." From the conventional viewpoint, relations with others are added and dispensable considerations. From the conventional viewpoint, it can be meaningful to consider people without considering their context. In Gestalt therapy, people can live and be meaningfully understood only in relationship to their context. People exist, are born, grow, deteriorate, and die as part of the organism-environment field.

Self as a Phenomenon of the Field

The whole field determines change, or stasis. The basic sense of self is a phenomenon of the field—it is co-constructed by the individual and the environment. The individual and the environment co-create each other. Identity is formed and maintained, expanded and contracted, by the whole field, by the mutual construction of the individual and the rest of the organism-environment field.

The sense of "I" is formed by contact with and differentiation from the rest of the organism-environment field by the processes of the contact boundary. Self and other create a boundary that connects people to other people and also maintains autonomous identities. Martin Buber (1926/1965a, 1923/2000) stated that "I" exists only as a relationship of I-Thou or I-It. Similarly, Winnicott (1960) stated that there is no mother or child; there is only the mother-child unit. In therapy, that field is largely the therapist and the patient, though it often includes others, such as other members of the group, spouses, families, people at work, and the agency delivering service.

FIELD THEORY PRINCIPLES AND THE THEORY OF CHANGE

Field theory is essential for understanding the Gestalt therapy theory of change, the organism-environment field, the paradoxical theory of change, and the holistic faith in organismic self-regulation. Gestalt therapy field theory, discussed in Chapter 3 of this book, is a viewpoint on how the world is organized, how it works, how to observe this organization, and how change happens. Here we will consider only how it relates to the theory of change in Gestalt therapy. The following principles of field theory are an integral part of the theory of change:

1. *Change is a function of the whole context in which a person lives.* Therefore, the awareness work in therapy must attend to the whole context in which the patient lives and the whole

context of the therapy. Gestalt therapy is interested in all of the factors that determine the course of human change. These include the maturation of genetic/biological processes, psychobiosocial development as a function of interpersonal relations throughout life, family and cultural influences, and the conditions at work and in the community. Change or lack of change in therapy is a result of the whole patient-therapist field (Perls, Hefferline, & Goodman, 1951, 1994; Jacobs, 1995a, 1995b).

2. *Change anywhere in the field affects all subsystems of the field.* The elements of the field are interdependent and subordinate to the whole and are regulated by their function in the whole. Although individuals function separately in some sense, they are always dependent on each other and on the whole. Any change in the complex relational events that compose the organism-environment field affects all other parts of the field. A change in one member of a family or group will affect every other member of the family or group. In the field of the therapist and patient, a change in one will affect the other (Yontef, 1993).

3. *Gestalt therapy focuses on the subjective awareness of the patient, the interactions in session, and an understanding of the whole context of forces that is the background of the everyday life of the patient.* Where the past experiences of a person are still affecting the current field, the operation of these processes of thought, affect, and habit must also be a part of the achieved understanding.

4. *Change in Gestalt therapy is seen as a time/space process.* The forces of the field are in flux, movement, change—and this change in time and space has to be part of our understanding. *Process* refers to the dynamics of that change in time and space. Change is not just a change in structure, a spatial viewpoint, nor is it just a change in dynamics, a temporal viewpoint. A purely spatial viewpoint that does not take into account the temporal dimension—for example, a viewpoint that sees a phenomenon as a thing or structure—is not field theoretical. These forces are events that happen and move through time and space. This means that change happens as a function of the whole field, all of the forces that compose the field, and happens over time and space (Yontef, 1993).

5. *All observation is from a particular place, time, and perspective.* This is a phenomenological viewpoint: That is, all reality is interpreted, and there is no knowable "objective" reality. Nor is any awareness only subjective, for all awareness does point to ("intend toward") something. The therapist has neither an objective nor an uninterpreted viewpoint. All events happen in a particular time and space, and all "observations" are interpretations from a particular time and space. I observe a patient on a particular day in my office, and this is a particular day in the life of that patient. On another day or in another context, that patient may appear very different to me. One can observe this in patients who appear to be one way—for example, passive—in a conjoint session but very lively and assertive in individual and group therapy. A holistic view of the patient takes into account not only the interactions at a given moment but a view of the person over different contexts of time and situation.

Creative Adjustment

People have to react to the current conditions in their field—to needs, resources, and dangers of self and other. People adjust by conforming to their circumstances but also create change in their circumstances by taking action in the field. The latter is creative and changes adjustment from mere conformity to healthy self-regulation.

People react to current conditions by aware contact in the contemporaneous field or by habitual responses largely determined by a repetition of past adjustments. Habitual responses vary in how effective they are and are often heavily influenced by introjected "shoulds." In organismic self-regulation, current field conditions organize experience and action, and they inform the person of the needs of self and other. The person can then creatively adjust to these field conditions. Although habits are modified by changes in field conditions, structural or significant change happens by aware contact in the field. As people live, they act and learn from the results. The field forces that determine this change include biological maturation, interpersonal interactions, and creative adjustments of the individual and/or the environment.

Identification With One's State

At each moment, thoughts, feelings, needs, impulses become salient—that is, figural. At each moment, people can identify with or alienate (disown) these configurations of experience. Identification with the emerging figure allows awareness and allows action to be organized and energized by the dominant need. Alienating the emerging figure means preventing it from reaching awareness and/or from energizing and organizing action.

Identification with one's state is a self-supportive whole process that leads to growth; alienation or disowning of the emerging experience creates psychological conflicts—which means the individual is divided and not whole. Attempting to change before knowing, feeling, and accepting oneself is very different from attempting to change after self-acceptance. In the former case, individuals base change attempts on self-rejection, disowning of self, and self-hate; in the latter case, individuals identify with the reality of who they are and what situation they are in and then are in a position to grow by taking action, by experimenting with new behavior, and by seeking and taking in what is needed from the environment.

Self-acceptance in aware contact with the rest of the organism-environment field is the means of growth. Frequently, self-knowledge, self-acceptance, and growth are limited by introjected messages from past relationships—that is, "shoulds." These are messages that are relatively unresponsive to change in the field. They undermine a person's actual experience, such as his or her affect, felt need, beliefs, and thoughts, even attack the essence of a person, and as a result undermine spontaneity and necessary actions. These messages lead to criticism of the status quo, but in a way that creates only resistance and not forward movement. Self-rejection does not support growth.

How does one improve and make necessary changes based on self-acceptance? Patients often believe that if they accept themselves their undesired behavior won't change, that self-acceptance means condoning or reinforcing the painful, the dysfunctional, and the immoral. Gestalt therapists, to the contrary, believe that only by accepting and owning how one is, by knowing and accepting the reality of the conditions one lives or has lived in and the choices one makes under these conditions, and by accepting that one makes the choice to be as one is can the individual truly change self or environment. This belief is inherent in the paradoxical theory of change. In fact, not only is aware self-acceptance the means to growth; it is, in itself, growth. The moment of full recognition is a moment of good contact and wholeness—it is a process that has the built-in corrective of experiment and learning. This can be verified by experiential work but is hard to appreciate from an abstract discussion.

People regulate their behavior with varying degrees of awareness. Most transactions are regulated by habit, by repeating previously learned behavior. In this mode, choices are made with a minimal amount of awareness and without second-order awareness—that is, without consciousness or awareness of awareness. For example, a person may stroke himself (contact and sensing) but not be aware of that small act or the meaning it holds. Many situations require focal awareness. This is true when the situation is novel, complicated, or dangerous or has multiple possibilities that require complex processing.

There is a natural or organismic process in which the field seeks the best possible organization. Individuals notice what works and what does not work. They naturally continue the behavior that works toward satisfaction of their needs and the needs of the environment. When behavior is not working, focal awareness is especially needed. With awareness people can learn, can change behavior that does not work, can be creative and experiment with new behavior and be aware of the results, and can strive to change the environment so that the individual's and the environment's needs are better met.

AWARENESS AND THE PROCESS OF CHANGE

To understand the Gestalt therapy theory of change, one must understand the awareness concept. Awareness is the very heart of the Gestalt therapy philosophy and methodology. Awareness in the Gestalt therapy framework is relational; it is a self-process that happens at the interface of the individual and the rest of the field. Awareness intends toward some otherness, and otherness is part of what and how one is aware. Awareness is sensory, affective, and cognitive. It includes observing self and other and knowing the choices that are being made. This is what Merleau-Ponty (1962, 1963) called "aware agency," and it is at the heart of what we mean in Gestalt therapy when we talk of responsibility.

Awareness is characterized by contact, sensing, excitement, and Gestalt formation (Perls et al., 1951, 1994). *Contact* refers to what one is in touch with. If I am sitting with someone and thinking of the things I must do, then I am in contact with my "to-do" list and not the other person. One can be in touch with something without being aware of it. So, in this example, I might not realize that I am sitting with a person but in contact with my list. Sometimes in therapy people believe they are "aware" when they experience only some aspects of awareness. Frequently patients will know about something but not fully sense it, feel it, be in contact with it, and know what they do not allow to become figural.

REINHARD: Awareness! You use the concept of awareness in a very broad sense. As far as I know, it was originally used in a much narrower sense by Perls and Goodman. I am glad at your use of this concept as I think self-reflection and rational considerations should by no means be excluded in the therapeutic process (which relates to my above point concerning the other pole of change). The question that I ask here is: Should we not use different terms for—in my view—qualitatively different activities of human mind? *Awareness* in the original sense means the "glowing light" inside a person, the inner witness of what I feel and think, the presence in the here and now. This I suggest to distinguish from cognitive reflection or processing of thoughts. The latter is "about" what I may or may not experience; the former would be an engaged but not entangled witnessing of my experiences and my thinking. I would again suggest a polar extension to your position relative to phenomenology: empirical exploration of what is objectively given.

GARY: I do use the term *awareness* in a very general sense—and have written about this usage elsewhere (e.g., Yontef, 1993). I believe that Perls, Hefferline, and Goodman also used the term *awareness* in a general sense, as an

The second characteristic, *sensing,* refers to how one is in touch—that is, by distant receptors such as hearing; by proprioception; by close sensing, such as touching, smelling, and tasting; or by intuition. Sensory data are used to orient and organize our internal processes (e.g., urges, provocations, desires, impulses, appetites, needs) and our experience of the field or environmental influences.

Excitement in Gestalt therapy refers to emotional and physiological excitation. It does not refer only to happy or pleasant excitement, as in general usage. I may be physically touched by someone (feeling the touch on or in my body), and I may be stimulated. This emotional quality of the excitement/arousal may be joy, sexual excitement, pleasure, disgust, or fear.

The fourth characteristic of awareness, *gestalt formation,* will be discussed in the next section.

CHANGE AND MEANING: THE FIGURE-GROUND PROCESS

Gestalt therapy is interested in change that is meaningful. An important part of the change process is helping patients increase their awareness of what is meaningful for them. To understand the change theory, one must also understand the Gestalt therapy theory of meaning and the role of the figure-ground process.

Gestalt therapy uses a process definition of meaning, starting with an assertion that our existence in the relational field is always meaningful. Meaning is the relationship between figure and ground. The figure is what stands out from the background—that is, what is salient to us. The background is the whole context of that figure. When we are in contact with something, and sense it, and have excitement about it, this figure/ground configuration is meaningful. Any behavior, event, or content is meaningful if someone is aware of it in this way. For example, I go to the opera, and the experience is very meaningful for me. If someone else goes to that

overarching term not restricted to the specific kind of awareness of "glowing light" awareness that you discuss. My use is consistent with their usage, although I draw out some implications that are not entirely clear in their classic text. When you refer to the "glowing light" inside the person as an "inner witness," I have some disagreement. The glowing light awareness is not inside, it is a total organization of the phenomenological field and includes all phenomenological data—as an organized whole. There is no separate observer in this state.

We seem to agree on including cognitive reflection and focus on the thinking process as part of the therapeutic process in Gestalt therapy. I am glad we agree on the importance of self-reflection, the rational, and observation in the therapeutic process. I suggest the use of clarifying adjectives and adverbs to be clear about what kind of awareness is being referred to. I do not favor using a different word for different kinds or phases of awareness. I think that the cognitive reflection and so forth and the "glowing light" awareness are parts or phases of an overall awareness process and are best considered as part of one whole. That would emphasize the importance of being aware of the various kinds of awareness and would assert that they are incomplete without a more holistic awareness. I suggest we work for clearer delineation of how we are using a particular concept at any one time or context.

You also refer to "empirical exploration of what is objectively given" as another pole to be added. As a phenomenologist, I do not dichotomize the subject and object or the subjective and the objective. As I understand phenomenology, it is not the study of the subjective but a systematic study that includes what might be referred to in a more traditional framework as the subjective (e.g., the meanings of the perceiver) and the objective (e.g., systematic sensory observation). The total phenomenological experience includes the "objective"—that is, sensory observation,

same opera but hates opera, it has a different meaning. On the other hand, someone might sleep through the opera and it might have very little meaning to that person. Meaning is not objective; it is the experience of a figure in relation to the ground.

For another example, think about the meaning of a man saying to a teenager, "Boy, you have to think before you act." The background might be a loving father helping a teenager who has been impulsive and is unhappy with the results. But in the same figure, if the man is someone in authority who is talking to a black teenager, the meaning will be different; the word *boy* will have a very different meaning in that context.

systematic formulation of the observation, testing hypotheses by repetitive phenomenological focusing, observation, and experimentation. But experience, observation, memory, and a sense of reality are always from some perspective and not just objective.

In health, our orientation in the world, including our perception, is always in meaningful wholes. The figure and ground form a gestalt, an organized and meaningful whole. A figure arises from the background at each moment and then recedes into the background to make room for another figure. This is a constantly changing process. This process of gestalt formation and destruction is a central part of awareness. In health, the gestalten—the figure/ground process—is formed by the dominant need of the person and the environment. What is meaningful to the person in the context stimulates and organizes the process of figure formation, causes what needs to be in awareness to be figural, and organizes action. When a person does not experience in wholes, or figures are not allowed to change with changing field conditions, that is an indication of psychological dysfunction.

When the figure/ground process is functioning well, the individual musters all his or her resources to identify needs, scan for resources, and become absorbed in the task; then the need is met, the gestalt is completed, and the person is no longer occupied with that figure. When the gestalt is completed and awareness no longer needed, related behaviors can operate automatically, by habit, until figural awareness is needed again. When this process is interfered with, unfinished situations occupy attention or distract. When a person is hungry, he or she is likely to think about food. When this need is met, it is no longer necessary or desirable to think of food. One might say, "When I eat, I lose my appetite." This is ordinary change, creative adjustment.

When a need is not allowed into awareness—not allowed to become figural—it becomes background noise or demand. This demand may be experienced in bodily tension, affect, or a cognitive preoccupation. Similarly, if the need is not allowed to energize and direct action, then frustration rather than satisfaction is likely to occur. This would be an unfortunate interference with growthful change. If a person is in contact with an urge to eat, and does eat, but is not aware that the primary need is actually for comfort or love rather than food per se, the eating is not likely to satisfy the underlying need.

THE IMPORTANCE OF THE HERE-AND-NOW CONCEPT

Change happens at every moment. Awareness happens at a moment. The act of remembering the past or anticipating the future occurs in the present—but the object of awareness may not be happening contemporaneously. At every moment a figure emerges that is a result of these various influences in the field. In the now, at a moment, the past flows into the future. In the now, people can experience needs and resources. This is a dynamic organismic process in which ideally that which is most relevant comes into awareness. This is the importance of "being in the now," a key concept in the Gestalt therapy theory of change.

As these figures flow one to another, as one figure recedes into the background and another becomes salient, larger gestalten form, and insight is possible. The awareness process takes place through this figure/ground process. This awareness process, including refinements and the movement of the awareness into action, is not a one-person phenomenon; awareness is relational. We learn which figures lead to good outcomes from the experience of interactions with other people and also from interactions with the general environment. Interaction, contact with others, is the sandpaper that smoothes out behavior, and awareness shapes it. In the best cases, it is shaped in the direction of greater satisfaction and/or safety. In other cases, the relational field creates dysfunction (discussed in the next section).

Through awareness of the figure/ground process, people learn and improve, grow and integrate, broaden and deepen wisdom. With this wisdom, people can maximize their growth; they can make the best possible life considering their biology, the environment and political conditions, and other factors. When awareness does not develop, conditions are not maximized and stasis or deterioration occurs. When awareness does not develop as needed, psychotherapy is indicated.

IMPEDIMENTS TO HEALTHY CHANGE

Interrupted Self-Regulation

How does it happen that awareness does not develop as needed or does not activate creative new behavior? Of course, there are factors of individual rates of maturation, cultural opportunities for learning about self-regulation, individual characteristics, factors that make life easier or harder, and so forth. But these do not fully account for situations where awareness that is needed for self-regulation persistently and repetitively does not develop—when what is needed to be in figural awareness does not adequately arise from the background. Sometimes what is felt or needed is not allowed to become figural at all; sometimes it becomes figural only fleetingly, with the figure changing too rapidly for real insight to develop or activate new behavior; and sometimes a figure is kept in awareness and not allowed to recede to allow subsequent needed figures to emerge.

Imagine an infant looking up and smiling at mother. What happens if the mother smiles back, compared with what happens if the

REINHARD: You probably have noticed that I tend to emphasize a multiperspective position, as was elaborated very clearly by Ken Wilber in his many books. This means, of course, that I certainly accept the mostly subjective and intersubjective view of change represented, I think, in your chapter and in Gestalt in general, and consider this to be an absolutely vital and underrated or even ignored perspective—yet it is only one side of the coin. When I add this perspective to my understanding of change, it opens up the possibility of doing justice and integrating two concepts of change: one that I call horizontal change and one that is vertical.

Vertical change means the expansion of consciousness/awareness, of loosening egocentricity, of triggering creativity, reducing anxiety, et cetera. *Horizontal change* means an increase in competence and knowledge on the same level of consciousness/awareness. Whether the vertical change is described in terms of stages

mother is too busy, too tired, too depressed, too sick, or too angry? The lively and mutually regulated interaction between mother and infant supports the development of organismic self-regulation—and supports the development of a child who is transparent to self, is harmonious in the balance of complex emotional states and needs, and has healthy self-esteem.

In the formation of a sense of self, the reaction of others provides a mirror and is an indispensable part of normal growth and development. We learn who we are and what we can expect in the world from the mirror that others provide for us. Although this is true throughout life, it is especially true in infancy and early childhood.

When the spontaneous behavior of the infant is not met with love and receptivity, this natural development of organismic self-regulation is interfered with. When a toddler or preschool child jumps with joy, turns red with anger, or is frightened and the environment is negative, rejecting, condemning, shaming, punishing, or ignoring, the result is that the emergence of these figures, and the energizing by them of sustained behavior, is inhibited. The child takes in—introjects—beliefs and expectations for self and the world that strongly influence the formation of character. The sense of self then is usually permeated with globalized shame and guilt that interfere with health and growth.

or waves (as most developmental theorists would describe it, including Gebser, Erikson, Kohlberg, Piaget, and of course Wilber) is not so important for me here. But I would prefer to believe in a telos, a developmental goal perspective, instead of restricting to horizontal change only (which of course prevails more or less exclusively in our times). I do not insinuate that you do not consider these two dimensions of change, though I think they are not differentiated in your text.

GARY: I find your multidimensional discussion, including the concept of the horizontal and vertical, consistent with my understanding and my practice—and a very helpful way to conceptualize it. I do not think that Gestalt therapy when well practiced is limited to the horizontal. You are right that I do not include this conception in my discussion, but it is not contradictory, and given more space I would certainly add it to this section. I think that integration is an inherent part of our concept of growth. To be complete and effective, awareness does have to be realized in everyday life. Awareness without action is not complete awareness, just as action without awareness is not complete.

Guilt and shame are chief means of socialization (Lee & Wheeler, 1996; Yontef, 1993). When a child does something that is truly bad, such as hurting another child, the environment teaches the child that this behavior is bad. When the child crosses boundaries of appropriateness, fails, or disappoints others, the feeling reaction is shame. Shame is the affect about the person's being or essence. These are part of the change process in ordinary development. When the shame and/or guilt are well matched to the situation and are not exaggerated, too harsh, or global indictments of the person, they are a part of normal growth and development. In such cases, the standards taught can become assimilated—that is, integrated—rather than being just introjects or fear of punishment. However, often the shame has the meaning of the person not being acceptable, lovable, and/or worthwhile as a person; often the guilt creates an unreasonable limitation on behavior. This becomes a significant barrier to awareness, self-acceptance, experimentation, movement toward wholeness, and transparency to self. In some cases, the person gets caught in a shame-guilt bind. If the person does the behavior (e.g., acts assertively), he or she feels guilty; or if the person does not do the behavior (e.g., does not act assertively), he or she feels inadequate—that is, ashamed.

One question that arises for the psychotherapist is: How can people be helped to change without giving or confirming their sense that they are bad, not enough, not acceptable, or defective? How can one work with people whose change toward increasing wholeness is interfered with by excessive guilt, shame, anxiety, or depression without confirming that they are indeed defective? In the next section, I will discuss the Gestalt therapy therapeutic attitude and methodology that flows out of these considerations.

CHANGE IN PSYCHOTHERAPY

Change happens in Gestalt therapy by a practice methodology that follows three principles: (a) field process thinking; (b) experimental phenomenological method of awareness work; and (c) existential dialogic attitude in contact and ongoing relationship. Together these form an overall therapeutic methodology within which specific interactions, acts, interventions, procedures, and techniques have meaning. Without this overall methodology, therapy can be reduced to a series of ad hoc or even chaotic techniques. Gestalt therapy has sometimes been erroneously identified with such a collection of techniques. Although people sometimes refer to "using Gestalt therapy techniques," such an approach is anathema to Gestalt therapy theory and to the attitude and practice of well-trained Gestalt therapists.

Unfortunately, some Gestalt therapists treat Gestalt therapy as a collection of techniques. This tends to go with an attitude in which expression of affect is the be-all and end-all of therapy and confrontation is the order of the day. This is not good Gestalt therapy theory or practice.

Well-trained modern Gestalt therapists are concerned with the relational field of the patient and with phenomenological awareness work. These two are entwined. Contemporary Gestalt therapists have two main concerns. The first is for the quality of the contact and the ongoing relationship. The Gestalt therapist understands and is committed to dialogic existentialism, discussed below, and contact with the patient is guided by the principles of dialogue. Second, the Gestalt therapist is guided by the therapeutic task of using the experimental phenomenological method to explicate the essence of a patient's functioning by increasing awareness and awareness-ability (discussed below). In this way, the Gestalt therapist works with the patient to establish conditions favorable to healing and growth. The Gestalt therapist helps set up the conditions that enable growth consistent with the paradoxical theory of change.

Any approach to change in psychotherapy that does not include both experimental phenomenological awareness work and a caring and respectful dialogical attention to the relational contact is incomplete. Some traditional Gestalt therapy approaches have emphasized change through awareness work only, without attention to the relational aspects of the process that enhance or inhibit the chance to develop awareness. Needless to say, ignoring the effect of the therapeutic relationship on the client restricts the possibilities for development of rich awareness. Renewed interest in the intimate correlation between the therapist's effect upon the patient and the patient's capacity for broadening awareness has brought the relational focus inherent in Gestalt therapy back to center stage.

What is important is the whole field of the patient and therapist and how they work together in creative ways to increase awareness, good contact, and the learning of more satisfying ways of being.

Field Process Thinking and Change in Therapeutic Practice

1. *Change in treatment is determined by the patient-therapist field as a whole.* When the treatment flows well, the patient, the therapist, and their system together are all responsible.

Importantly, on the other hand, when there is a disruption or failure, this is also caused by the patient, the therapist, and their system together.

2. *Perception is relative and not absolute or objective.* A field is always seen from some vantage point, rather than being an objective or universal truth. In the therapy situation, at least two viewpoints need to be taken into account and respected. The "truth" of the therapist is only one of many possible perspectives; it is not privileged.

3. *A field viewpoint always involves space and time.* Because all phenomena are space and time events, any valid observation must specify the time and location and the development over time and space. The generality of the observed behavior over space and time is an important diagnostic consideration. A patient may come into the therapist's office with intense emotions spilling over and creating a certain amount of chaos. Any generalization must take into account that this is happening in this space, the therapist's office, and at this time, on this particular day. The patient may not show such emotionality in other settings. The chaotic quality may not be an ongoing quality but be occurring at this time because of contemporaneous events. Or this moment may be a typical one for this patient.

4. *Field thinking is holistic.* Being holistic, Gestalt therapists take into account and work with the body, the environment, contemporary systems, and residue of childhood systems. Gestalt therapists can use a wide range of interventions, various ways of bringing the field forces into awareness.

Phenomenology and Awareness

All perception is interpreted. People make sense of their world as best they can, and the sense they make of it becomes a filter for viewing the world. In health, these filters are changed with the changing field, new information, new experience, and knowledge of what works and does not work. However, much of this filtering is not in awareness—that is, it does not become figural as needed.

Take John, for example. John learned early in childhood that he was not loved, and he assimilated a sense of himself as not being lovable. He tends to interpret another person's shyness, tiredness, or anger as evidence that this other person does not like him, and this confirms for John that he is not lovable. Not being aware of this bias, he treats the behavior of the other as confirming his reality of being unlovable. Actually, as John and I explored this in several instances, it turned out that the shy, tired, or

---

REINHARD: And another question of mine would be: Is it not possible to experience directly and immediately without interpreting too? What would be the meaning of awareness (in the narrow sense) if this were not possible? We experience reality immediately if we are aware, we interpret it subjectively, and we co-construct reality culturally, and additionally there are objective facts that may support or hamper or even block any changes. Don't you think so?

GARY: You ask if it is possible to experience directly and immediately without interpreting. This depends on semantics, what you mean by *interpreting.* From a phenomenological and field-theoretical position, all experience is from some time/space personal perspective. The organization is according to needs, expectations, observations, and so forth. The "glowing light" awareness does not have an interpretation separate from experience, but it is from a particular perspective. Phenomenologically, this is referred to as interpretation; all perception, all reality, all experience is interpreted. The "glowing light" awareness is awareness in the mode of an experiential whole, but that does not mean it is not from a particular perspective, is objective, or is not interpreted.

---

angry other person actually liked or loved him. John's filter, his customary interpretation, interfered with assimilating new interaction, new data, and interfered with a chance to change his sense of himself.

"Reality" is co-constructed by an interaction between what is out there and how the person constructs it. In psychotherapy, "reality" is co-constructed by the patient-therapist system. In phenomenological theory, all awareness is of something. If the patient goes away from a session feeling bad about him- or herself, attributing negative thoughts or feelings to the therapist, this is an event in which the therapist plays a part. Patient awareness does not happen in a vacuum.

The phenomenological method has been an important part of Gestalt therapy. The method, *epoché,* starts by putting aside (in "brackets") as much as possible all preconceptions about reality, about what the data are, and about the task at hand, so that there can be a less contaminated co-construction between what is out there and the perceiver. Phenomenologists refer to this as being open to the "given," which has been referred to in Gestalt therapy as the "obvious." The term *given* is a technical phenomenological term. The term *obvious* is an unfortunate choice for this concept because what is obvious is not obvious and seems to imply an objectivity that is not consistent with phenomenological theory or empirical investigation.

The first awareness, or given, is only a beginning of a phenomenological investigation. Phenomenological exploration works systematically to understand and reduce the effects of bias. The first awareness, before the phenomenological reduction, is only the start of the process. The first impression of the therapist or the patient, or an initial interpretation, is only a tentative start. When this is violated—when a therapist believes his or her impression is an objective observation—there is a significant danger of a partial and contaminated viewpoint becoming generalized as the whole.

The initial perception is tested by repeated observations. The results are reported to others, and further observation and testing take place. In phenomenological research, generalizations are reported to the profession, but more important in terms of therapeutic methodology is the routine reporting of observations to the patient in order to solicit disconfirmations, confirmations, and corrections of the therapist's interpretation. Together the researcher/therapist and the subject/patient refine their understanding.

This phenomenological work is traditionally done by observation and focusing. The therapist inquires about the patient's actual experience on a rather continuous basis. The prototypical question is "What are you experiencing now?" or "What are you aware of now?" The inquiries of the Gestalt therapist tend to be questions of what is experienced and how it is experienced rather than why it is experienced. Questions of "what" tend to be more productive of observation, and questions of "how" focus on the details of how the patient does or experiences what he or she does. "Why" questions tend to lead to speculative responses, defensive responses, intellectualized responses, and guesses rather than highlighting actual felt experience.

Gestalt therapy is an experimental phenomenology. This means that the focusing often takes place through the therapist's suggestion that the patient try something new—focus on it and see what he or she experiences. An accurate understanding of the phenomenological basis of these techniques protects against making the experiment into an instrument of directed change, as in behaviorism. This awareness focus is the true purpose of the Gestalt therapy techniques, *not* guided behavior change.

EXISTENTIAL DIALOGUE: CONTACT AND RELATIONSHIP

In Gestalt therapy theory, change happens through the contact between therapist and patient. The emphasis is on "meeting" the patient, on contact without aiming. The quality of the contact and the quality of the ongoing contact or relationship largely determine the effectiveness of the therapy. Historically, an important aspect of Gestalt therapy's evolution from psychoanalysis was the nature of the relationship. At first, Gestalt therapy contrasted an active and authentic presence of the therapist, including the therapist's creative process, with the neutral and impassive face of the classical psychoanalyst, but it was not very specific about the qualities of contact that were therapeutic. This has been clarified in the evolution of Gestalt therapy. The kind of contact and relationship that furthers growth in psychotherapy is contact that has the characteristics of an existential dialogue.

The following four principles or characteristics of contact are explicated by Martin Buber and discussed in the Gestalt therapy literature (Jacobs, 1995a, 1995b).

Inclusion

When therapists practice inclusion, they throw themselves as much as possible into the experience of the patient, even feeling it as if it were happening in their own body—without losing a sense of self. This has been called "imagining the real." Inclusion goes a bit further into the experience of the patient than some definitions of empathy and also is much clearer about the maintenance of the autonomous sense of self by the person practicing inclusion.

Confirmation

By practicing inclusion, the therapist confirms the existence of the patient. Confirmation is of the whole person, not just the present manifestation of

---

REINHARD: Growth! Which brings me to my last point. I must admit that I have difficulties with this term *growth,* which is so closely connected with Gestalt therapy and the humanistic movement. Of course, it is a question of definition, but I still think that growth is first and foremost a biological metaphor. And then growth is absolutely necessary up to a certain point—when it becomes destructive. Too much growth, as we all know, may be disastrous. Therefore, I would suggest to at least complement the idea of growth—which makes much sense when some aspects of our personality have not had the chance to develop organically, by integration, which, as you certainly agree, is also an original Gestalt concept. We have to integrate whatever we lost or had to split off or repress on our way after we have become aware of it, have let it grow organically—but then we also have to realize it in everyday life by making use of it in a healthy way for ourselves and for others. Even awareness in whatever sense may be too much at times if it just grows and grows.

GARY: In Gestalt therapy, and humanism in general, growth as a goal refers to optimal development and not to increase in size regardless of context. My dictionaries confirm this usage and do not identify growth as "first and foremost a biological metaphor." Of course, there is pathological or unfortunate growth, which the dictionaries delineate as a different definition of *growth,* as in a tumor or a city or organization grown too large. Living in Los Angeles, I know that very well. I think that integration is an inherent part of our concept of growth. To be complete and effective, awareness does have to be realized in everyday life. Awareness without action is not complete awareness, just as action without awareness is not complete. I agree with you when you refer to a healthy way for "ourselves and for others." It is important that the "for others" is added.

---

the person. It includes acceptance but also a validation of the growth potential of the patient. Confirmation supports the self-recognition and self-acceptance that is at the heart of the paradoxical theory of change.

Presence

The therapist is authentically present as a person. For this authenticity to be useful in psychotherapy, the caring has to be genuine, the therapist must show him- or herself as a person, and the caring must be real. Presence is contrasted with "seeming"—that is, an appearance of authenticity as opposed to a congruence between what is manifested or expressed by the therapist and the therapist's real experience. Inclusion requires this kind of presence if it is not to deteriorate into a mechanical technique.

Commitment to Dialogue/ Surrender to the Between

The key to understanding a therapeutic dialogue is that the therapist meets the patient and does not "aim." In a true dialogue, in therapy or in a wider context, the parties to the dialogue give up control of the outcome by being themselves and interacting with the other person, who does the same. The outcome emerges from this interaction. Phenomenological bracketing enables contact, dialogue, and openness to something emerging from the dialogue that was neither planned nor predictable.

The phenomenological dialogue can be thought of as a meeting of the phenomenological experience of two people. If one aims to control the outcome, the principles of phenomenological exploration and dialogic contact are both violated. One frequent example is when the therapist experiences the patient in a more positive way than the patient experiences him- or herself and the therapist tries to convince the patient of the truth of the positive experience and the distortion of the patient's sense of self. Not only is this very tempting endeavor usually unsuccessful, but it communicates only that the "reality" of the patient's negativity is too much for the therapist to bear—and that the patient must feel better to take care of the therapist's need.

In the true therapeutic dialogue, both the patient and the therapist are changed. The therapist's sense of self, other, and the relationship is changed by the dialogue. If the therapist maintains a position standing above learning from the interaction, this condition of the dialogue is violated.

POSITIVE AND NEGATIVE INTERACTION IN PSYCHOTHERAPY

Benefits of the Dialogical Relationship

Much of the outcome in effective psychotherapy comes from the kind of relationship discussed above. When patients feel understood and cared about, the situation becomes safer to acknowledge their true selves, including true feelings, desires, and past experience. When patients invest respect in the therapist and the therapist understands them, the attitude of the therapist toward them becomes very important. If the therapist not only understands and cares about them but respects and likes them as they really are, their fixed and negative sense of self usually starts to transform by the interaction of these field forces and the new data.

Disruptions in the Dialogical Relationship

Frequently in the course of therapy there are moments of disruption in the meeting of therapist and patient. The outcome of the therapy depends greatly on whether these are recognized and how they are dealt with. If the therapist does not recognize these disruptions, or if the patient brings up the disruption and the therapist does not respond well, then the best that can happen is a compromise relationship. More commonly, the lack of recognition and healing of the breach in the relationship creates iatrogenic difficulties—that is, the shame discussed in the next section.

Several principles of the change theory we have been discussing are critical to a good resolution of the difficulty:

1. The experience of the patient as well as that of the therapist is accepted as a valid phenomenological reality.
2. Responsibility for the interaction is attributed to both participants and their interaction. Difficulty in the relationship is not due just to the patient's pathology or distorted perception.
3. The outcome that emerges from true dialogue is the best possible in the circumstances.
4. True dialogue is the relational context used to explicate the emerging therapist/patient contact and developmental and characterological themes as they arise.

Iatrogenic Shame Induction

The recent Gestalt therapy literature has discussed the induction or reinforcement of shame in the patient by the influence of the therapist (Lee & Wheeler, 1996; Yontef, 1993). Patients usually come to therapy in a state of not feeling good about themselves, and on top of that they often feel shame at needing and asking for the help of a therapist. If conditions supportive of change are to be created, the therapist must understand the shame process and how to work with it. Of course, shame created, triggered, or enhanced by the therapist's attitude or behavior, if not acknowledged by the therapist, is antithetical to maximal therapeutic effectiveness.

Multiple shame triggers occur in therapy. Each triggered shame event is organized by the contributions of the therapist and of the patient and the interaction between them. If the therapist uses

REINHARD: I appreciate your response to my comments, Gary, in particular as it became clear to me in the ways we agree and differ. I believe our differences to be in the general position in relation to Gestalt. Whereas you support any further developments that can be integrated in the framework of Gestalt (including its expansion), I plead for a development that *transcends* Gestalt and integrates Gestalt into something more encompassing. Such a difference in the general position is, I think, based on one's biography, living circumstances, experiences, et cetera—and both positions are of course legitimate and need no justification as such, as it is a very personal decision (which does not exclude that there may be arguments pro and con for one or the other position).

sarcastic humor, gives the message of having a privileged knowledge of the patient superior to the patient's knowledge of self, exposes the patient before he or she is ready, or is emotionally withdrawn or intrusive, this is likely to trigger the patient's shame process. Shame is one of the biggest impediments to the development of skill at attending to one's awareness process without judgment. And it is only through such attending that the paradoxical theory of change is manifest. If the therapist responds to such incidents by treating the patient's shame reaction as a weakness created solely by the patient's fragility, thereby denying his or her own role in creating the shame incident, this shames the patient for feeling shame. In contrast, when the therapist can acknowledge his or her own part in the interaction, can recognize the validity of the patient's experience, and can share his or her own experience without being defensive, the shame and the rift in the contact can be healed.

SUMMARY

The Gestalt therapy theory of change is that change happens as a result of the forces of the field. When the field supports the emerging experience of children, they learn that they can identify with who they really are, can "be themselves," and can then learn from the experience. When the emerging experience is not supported, when children are not met in this way, they learn to limit their awareness to something accepted by the parents. When this becomes introjected and part of the sense of self, future situations that could be opportunities to learn and change are limited by the fixed sense of self that cannot adapt to the new field conditions.

In psychotherapy, the therapist has the opportunity to meet the patient by identifying and respecting the validity of the patient's experience while simultaneously manifesting his or her own experience. From this interaction, both the patient and the therapist can change and

If you/we could both accept this difference, our disagreements are easily explainable concerning the attitude—for example, toward goal-oriented approaches or toward the meaning of *awareness* or *growth*. (By the way: My new Webster's Dictionary says that *growth* means "an increase in the size or amount of something (an organism, a crystal, or wealth.") Though you legitimately state that you *are* a phenomenologist, I would say: I *use* phenomenology (or empirical studies or hermeneutics or systems approaches, etc.) in the frame of a multiperspective view. The question may be raised, of course, whether my position may legitimately be called "Gestalt" any longer. I would not mind, though, calling it "Gestalt-based," while I can well respect your position as a Gestalt approach proper. Kindest regards, Reinhard.

GARY: Reinhard, I think we are clear that our major difference is that your preference is for transcending Gestalt therapy and mine is for assimilating new possibilities into Gestalt therapy. Most of what you want to establish as an alternative to Gestalt therapy I assimilate into Gestalt therapy. I have not seen any framework that works better as an integrating framework for me as a psychotherapist than Gestalt therapy. So I want to expand it, have it grow and mature. It does not meet all of my personal needs for a theory (e.g., spiritual, religious), but it serves the function I see for it. I understand now that phenomenology (psychological phenomenology, not transcendental phenomenology) is more central for me than it is for you. I believe we differ more on the semantics of the word growth than on substance. I have been increasingly uninterested and suspicious of discussion of orthodoxy and arguments, essential jurisdictional arguments, of who is and is not a Gestalt therapist. So I am fine if you call yourself a Gestalt therapist or "Gestalt based." I like the latter phrase as a phrase, but I continue to think of you as a Gestalt therapist. Warmly, Gary.

grow. Out of these interaction opportunities to try something new, to experiment, further opportunities come up and present for phenomenological exploration, experimentation in contact, refinement of understanding through experimentation, and exploration of new possibilities.

REVIEW QUESTIONS

1. Define change from a Gestalt perspective. In what manner are Gestalt therapists "agents of change," as contrasted with what, in psychotherapy literature, are often referred to as "change agents"?

2. What is the role of awareness in the Gestalt approach to change?

3. Yontef identifies paradox as the key principle that guides Gestalt therapists as agents of change, stating, "The paradox is that the more one tries to be who one is not, the more one stays the same." How is the principle of paradox related to and connected with the concept of awareness? Think of a way in which the paradoxical principle of change has manifested in your life, and bring notes on this example to discuss with your class.

4. What does the author mean when he states, "Not only is aware self-acceptance the means to growth, it is, in itself, growth"?

5. What are the five principles of field theory that the chapter author identifies as integral to a Gestalt theory of change? Define and describe each.

6. Describe how the four principles or characteristics of contact as adapted from the work of Martin Buber are utilized in Gestalt therapy. More information about these principles can be located in publications by Jacobs (1995a, 1995b).

7. On the basis of the dialogue between Drs. Fuhr and Yontef in which alternative voices are recorded here, discuss a couple of ways in which their views of Gestalt therapy differ. Include in your discussion your own feelings about these differences.

EXPERIENTIAL PEDAGOGICAL ACTIVITIES

ACTIVITY 1: Organismic self-regulation is one component that contributes to change theory from a Gestalt perspective. In small groups, identify an object that could metaphorically represent organismic self-regulation—such as a balanced scale or a mobile at rest. Attach pieces of paper or pictures to your metaphorical object that could represent some of the life events or stressors that could cause the object to go out of balance. As a group, discuss the ways people work to self-regulate and maintain balance and how this "balancing act" functions in relation to ways they desire to and choose to change.

ACTIVITY 2: In journal, prose, or poetry format, describe a time in your life when you made a creative adjustment to a field event or circumstance. Include how your creative adjustment compared with your habitual response style and what the new process elicited.

ACTIVITY 3: In a classroom fishbowl arrangement, role-play two therapy sessions. In both sessions, ask the "client" to discuss with the "therapist" a time when he or she was in the midst of enacting change or doing something differently in his or her life. Yontef states in your chapter that "one question that arises for the psychotherapist is: How can people be helped to change without giving or confirming their sense that they are bad, not enough, not acceptable, or defective?" In the first session, the "therapist" selects mildly shaming language (e.g., indicating that the "client" may not be capable of making such changes), and in the second session the "therapist" selects supportive and nonshaming language. The observers in the outer ring discuss the differences they perceived and felt in the two different sessions, and the "client" and "therapist" also debrief by describing their experiences.

ACTIVITY 4: Identify a global/world change you would like to see occur in the next 5 years. Using the Gestalt principles for change described in this chapter, create a presentation addressed to world leaders to help them become catalysts for change so that the world will be closer to the one in which you would prefer to live.

CHAPTER **6**

Gestalt Therapy Methodology

JOSEPH MELNICK AND SONIA MARCH NEVIS

DIALOGUE RESPONDENT: NORMAN SHUB

Joseph Melnick is a clinical and organizational psychologist and a member of the professional staff of the Gestalt Institute of Cleveland and the Gestalt International Study Center, where he teaches in the Center for the Study of Intimate Systems and co-facilitates the annual Gestalt Writers' Conference and the Gestalt Research Symposium. He teaches/trains internationally, is the editor-in-chief of *Gestalt Review*, is the author of numerous articles on Gestalt therapy, and has a private practice in Portland, Maine.

Sonia March Nevis is a clinical psychologist, the director of the Center for the Study of Intimate Systems at the Gestalt International Study Center, South Wellfleet, Massachusetts (both of which she co-founded), and senior faculty of the Gestalt Institute of Cleveland. Besides providing training and supervision, she has a private practice on Cape Cod working with individuals, couples, and families and has authored numerous articles on Gestalt therapy. Her expertise in couple and family therapy is known and honored worldwide, as exemplified in her video training tape *Gestalt Family Therapy* (1995), and she is chair of the Couple, Family and Small System Training Program.

Norman Shub founded the Gestalt Institute of Central Ohio (GICO) in 1971 and has served as its clinical director since then. He is also president of Gestalt Associates, his group practice in Columbus, Ohio, and of Business of People, an international Gestalt-based organizational consulting firm. Chief among the firm's recent endeavors is a contract with USA's prominent clothing design and retail store, Limited 2, in their "TWEEN" Project—providing Gestalt-based group experiences for girls, ages 9 to 11, to enhance their self-esteem, with the goal of reaching 30,000 girls in the United States in 2004. His special interest in differential diagnosis and the treatment of character disorders has led to numerous publications, consultations, and teaching opportunities. Clinicians, institutes, and universities in many countries use his Gestalt Working Paper Series.

When we are doing psychotherapy, it is easy to become overwhelmed by the amount and complexity of the data in any encounter: the story being told, the body language, the voice tones, the questions, and the emotions being expressed, as well as the thoughts, feelings, and memories evoked in ourselves as therapists. We can take numerous potential directions in any piece of therapeutic work. Because of this, all psychotherapy theories have highly developed approaches concerning what behavior to attend to, how to make sense out of behavior, and how to be in relation with the client. This is called *methodology.*

Because of the complexity of therapeutic work, a well-grounded methodology is essential. Without a method, a therapist is adrift, lacking direction and organization in how to proceed, perhaps lacking a goal (or, if having one, having no idea how to attain it) and a sense of a beginning and an end.

Therapeutic methodology deals with principles and procedures, where to go and how to get there. It is the bridge between abstract theory and the actual psychotherapy. As such, it provides the theoretical and operational underpinnings of one's therapeutic work. A sound methodology allows one to make explicit the rules under which therapy is to be conducted, enabling the translation of theoretical insights into more concrete and workable forms (Melnick, 1980). A well-articulated methodology outlines a structure that highlights the data to be attended to as well as categories for codification, analysis, interpretation, and feedback.

NORMAN: I am pleased to share with you my thoughts and reactions to your work in a nonhokey and nonpsychobabble way. As I read your chapter, I smiled because it was clear to me as I was reading it that students and people interested in Gestalt would really understand methodological concerns, and that made me happy. I enjoyed your chapter and think it is well done.

While I was reading this section, a phrase kept floating around in my head, and that phrase was "how we are together, how are we together." I really understand the emphasis on the continuum of experience and, in my words, on accessing the inner world of the client. What I was looking for was more of an emphasis on *how* we are together and *what* we do together. It's as if we are standing in a snowy forest on a cold winter's day where the snow is coming down lightly. I am coming out of the woods and you are standing at the end of a field, and we can barely see each other. As we walk toward each other, we begin to notice and see more clearly who the other person is and to hear what we are yelling to one another, beginning to experience more sharply how we are coming together.

Regarding Gestalt methodology, a Gestalt therapist, when working with clients, is doing two things, sometimes at the same time. The therapist is engaging in an authentic encounter with the client, while at the same time watching how the client is organizing the encounter, most often for an hour. A good analogy is using two hands to play the piano.

Gestalt methodology is based on a belief in the elements of a healthy therapeutic encounter. It has a certain process and aesthetic to it. Our model for a healthy encounter is called the continuum of experience.

In this chapter, we will discuss six aspects of Gestalt therapy that form the basis of our methodology and end the chapter by presenting a case study to illustrate our approach. The six methodological components we consider as vital or integral to Gestalt therapy are (a) the continuum of experience, (b) the here and now, (c) the paradoxical theory of change, (d) the experiment, (e) the authentic encounter, and (f) process-oriented diagnosis.

For me, Gestalt is the process of co-creating moments in time where we pay a great deal of attention to the co-creation, the context, and what is happening as we come together. I believe your section on the authentic encounter is one of your key points. For me, your emphasis is on accessing the inner world of the client through the cycle of experience, yet as we are walking together in the snow, as we are walking toward each other, it is my job to help you learn how to pay attention to yourself so you can explore what it would be like to *run* in the snow instead of *walk* in the snow. You can look all around you and see the beauty of the forest, the birds, and the trees and not just focus on me. Or you can be less anxious about what I might say to you as we come closer. Or you can move your body so that you can fully dance, run, touch and taste the snow, and smell the cold, sharp air. All those things are true. But as we come together, there is something magical that happens for me—called *contact.* Gestalt, for me, is about learning to use the *how* of our coming together to make the therapy about that, and accessing the inner world is a part of that process—no question—but the connection is the process. So I was looking for more flavor of connectedness in your discussion of Gestalt methodology.

SONIA: I want you to know how grateful I am that you took such a detailed look at our chapter. A big part of my gratitude is that, with your words added to the book, our chapter will be vastly improved.

THE CONTINUUM OF EXPERIENCE

The continuum of experience (COE) was created to provide a pictorial schema of an ideal organization of experience. This provides a template for the observations of the therapist as he or she attends to how the client is organizing the encounter. It is here that the COE is most useful. It is also useful for diagnosis, as we will discuss later.

The COE, as shown in Figure 6.1, is a schema of an ideal encounter. All of us have a characteristic way of organizing the field of the present moment of our existence. We will naturally deviate from what is ideal. This deviation from the ideal is, in fact, our *creative adjustment* between what is available to us in the moment and our skills for marshalling our resources to obtain what we need at that time.

The concept of creative adjustment implies that at every moment we are doing the best that we can. Therapy does not aim for perfection. It aims for a "good enough" process to enable clients to use the resources they have with awareness, with the potential for repeated satisfying experiences.

The continuum starts with *sensation*—seeing, hearing, feeling—and then tracks how this is organized into a growing field of what is and what is wanted. The rise in energy (called

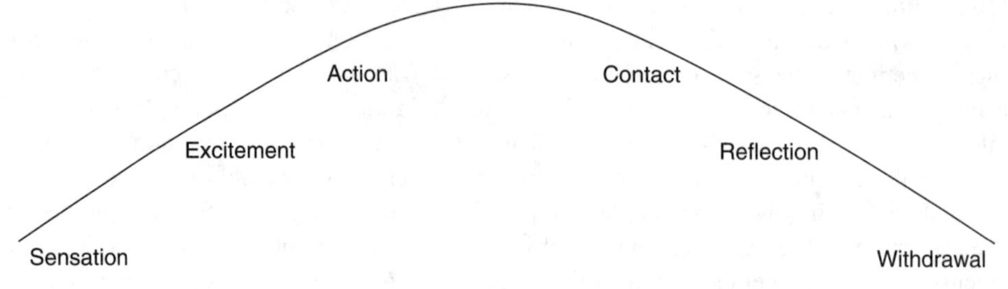

Figure 6.1 The Continuum of Experience

excitement in the early Gestalt writings) is shown as the rise in the diagram. The organizing continues as a clear want emerging from the sensory data: wanting to reach out or to withdraw, to speak or to be silent, and so forth. The energy at the highest point of the schema is then used to *act,* to *contact* the environment in a way that promises satisfaction. *Reflection* on the success of the action completes the continuum. To repeat, we are aware, which leads us to knowing what we want, which leads us to act, to be contactful, and then to reflect on our experience. This is how we learn and become wiser in the next moment. It is how we organize experience.

The interruptions, the places where clients' energy gets stuck, are noted. At times clients limit sensory data, cannot articulate their wants, are reluctant to act or act too quickly and are thus unsupported, fail to reflect and therefore learn little from their experience. These interruptions are the material for our work as Gestalt therapists. The interruptions are also the basis for our diagnostic insights, which we will talk about later.

THE HERE AND NOW

A basic belief of Gestalt therapy is that the present encompasses the past and helps

NORMAN: I have always had a reaction to the COE. We say as Gestaltists (and we do many times) that we are a relational therapy, and our history and literature all support that. And the truth is that as our work validates that, somehow for me, the COE smacks of too much attention to the therapist focusing on the internal process of clients and not enough on the actual external interpersonal process of the client with others. I understand that action is the issue [in the COE], but for me, contact and interactional qualities are what seems absent from the COE. I understand that the action an individual takes is not always about somebody else. The action also involves a reaction that allows me to do something *for* me, *about* me, or *with* me. It doesn't mean it is about you. Somehow, it still bothers me that it seems to focus on the internal world of the client and not the engagement process of the client with the world. That subtlety always seemed to be missing from the COE. Though it is a matter of emphasis, it is still in my training and my thinking something that we try to stress.

SONIA: Norman, your description of "how" an experience is co-created is very helpful. As you may know, Joe and I, and others, have tried to draw the interactive cycle, without enough success. It would be the addition to the continuum of experience, which is really a depiction of the interpersonal experience. Both are needed.

influence the future. Everything that we have learned, everything that we have experienced is carried in the present moment. The Gestalt therapist conducts the work with the data of the *here and now.*

This stance of privileging the present, when first expounded by Gestalt therapists, was revolutionary to Western psychotherapy. Rather than exploring the past, as is done in most depth psychotherapies such as Freudian and Jungian approaches, we focus on the present moment where the past is embedded and therefore alive and obvious.

JOE: I agree with you, Norman. The COE was originally conceptualized when all depth therapies, not just Gestalt, were intrapsychically oriented. In fact, the Gestalt approach was one of the driving forces, along with other humanistic approaches, that saw the process as interpersonal and field based. That is why we have expanded the COE to look at couples, families, groups, and organizations.

During the therapeutic encounter we listen and we watch. Using the image of the COE, we pay attention to what our clients do well and how they limit their satisfaction by not using their energy for a desired goal. As we look and notice, we are gathering data. This is the key to the formation of hypotheses about the client's ability to organize an experience. For example, Mary speaks with a soft voice, without awareness as to whether she is heard or not heard, and thus cheats herself of the continuous feedback that would be available to her. The reasons why she lives in the world this way can be many. For example, she may have been told, "Children should be seen and not heard," or "Good girls speak softly." However, when this stance is carried over into adulthood without awareness, a vital resource is lost.

But Mary also has many strengths. She is able to articulate her feelings when she is asked, and the therapist notices this and tells her about it. In time she will appreciate her soft voice as one of her resources and be able to use it when it is appropriate to do so. She will broaden her vocal range to respond appropriately when a loud or angry voice is more contextually correct.

Our stance of privileging the present has important implications for how we approach the therapeutic encounter. For example, when a clinician from a different therapeutic discipline notices that a client asks questions but does not wait for an answer, the clinician may explore how this characteristic behavior is rooted in past experiences. The Gestalt therapist will explore how this characteristic exists in the present. For instance, it may signify ambivalence between curiosity and a reluctance to hear something the client may not want to hear. Because this ambivalence is enacted in the room with the therapist in the here and now, it becomes data for useful work. Resolving this ambivalence in the present frees the impulse to embrace one's curiosity so that it can develop into a more mature form.

The Gestalt therapist's focus on the present does not reflect a lack of interest in how a given pattern of interaction developed, for we all wish to make sense of our lives. Our emphasis reflects the belief that all change takes place in the present. Many times the client will provide the connection of the work with earlier life experiences, filling in a picture of how the past connects with the present.

NORMAN: I agree with you that contact creates the here-and-now opportunity for growth. The interactive process is the vehicle for the self to fully emerge and for growth to take place. However, for me, the essence of being in the here and now with the client involves the integration of methodological factors.

SONIA: I agree with the point you emphasize, that all Gestalt work is a here-and-now process of growth and that it is the process, not the outcome, that is the solid and important growth; your point is a valid one.

THE PARADOXICAL THEORY OF CHANGE

According to Perls, Hefferline, and Goodman (1951), "The self only finds and makes itself in the environment" (p. 248). This belief was the basis for Arnold Beisser's (1970) oft-quoted statement of the paradoxical principle of change: "Change occurs when one becomes what he is, not when he tries to become what he is not" (p. 77).

As indicated previously, theory provides the rationale for what we do. Methodology helps theory come alive and describes what the therapist does and what happens in the therapy session. All psychotherapeutic theories address change, but they differ widely on the process involved because principles help define the process.

Central to Gestalt theory is the concept of awareness. Much of what happens in the authentic encounter, in the here and now between therapist and client, involves *bringing into awareness* thoughts, feelings, gestures, beliefs, and memories. The bringing into awareness is fundamental for change and is often called the paradoxical principle of change (Beisser, 1970). It is not paradoxical but logical: Awareness, by definition, changes us. It seems paradoxical that to change we first have to get acquainted with our dysfunctional ways, but this is so. As Beisser (1970) said, "To heal a suffering one must experience it to the full" (p. 78).

Most approaches to change that are based on intention alone—for example, not doing something or doing something differently—usually result in failure. We all know that most New Year's resolutions to eat less, be nicer to our neighbors, complain less, stop smoking, exercise more, or drink less are soon forgotten. The Gestalt approach is based instead on heightened awareness of "what is," of "how we eat," of our experiences of "niceness," of noticing how it feels to "complain," of what it is like to "taste a cigarette," of our body stretching "itself," or of the experience of reaching for a drink.

For many, if not most, life is conducted with minimal awareness, which is a good thing when all is going well. For example, we walk without attending to *how* we walk. Instead, we attend to our destination and the sights along the way. We eat, unaware of *how* we eat but rather tasting the food, liking it or not liking it. But as Beisser (1970) pointed out, to change we must heighten our awareness and "enter" our experience.

The stuff of life is the walking, the eating, our conversations; the stuff of life is its content. The background of life is its processes, and if we need to change something that does not work well for us, we paradoxically have to bring it into awareness and get to know it well; then and only then can we change.

THE EXPERIMENT

> Experiment derives from *experire,* to try. An experiment is a trial or special observation made to confirm or disprove something doubtful, especially under conditions determined by the experimenter; an act or operation undertaken in order to discover some unknown principle or effect, or to test, establish or illustrate some suggested unknown truth, practical test, proof. (Perls et al., 1951, p. 12)

One can say that all of life is an experiment because with every choice the outcome is unknown. However, in the flow of life we are usually unaware of this uncertainty. Living with minimal awareness is useful when life is going well but problematic during difficult times when some change seems necessary. It is dissatisfaction that provides the motivation for many people to seek psychotherapy.

Prior to deciding to undertake therapy, most have tried to solve their problems alone, without success. Therefore, they courageously try this novel approach full of uncertainty. Those of you who have experienced psychotherapy probably remember the sensation of not knowing what will happen next. This heightens the difference between psychotherapy and everyday life. In everyday life, we usually try to minimize uncertainty. In psychotherapy, this uncertainty is brought into awareness and becomes the focus of the work.

Our goal is to support uncertainty. We create the conditions for growth to occur without having any commitment to a specific outcome. The commitment is to create a climate that allows the client opportunities to explore and to discover his or her own outcome. In this way, the client acts from experienced awareness rather than following a direction imposed by the therapist.

Gestalt therapy as described by the COE is a blend of Eastern and Western thought (Crocker, 1999). It combines the Eastern emphasis on being in the here and now and the Western orientation toward action. We have just described the Eastern aspects of Gestalt methodology: being in the here and now and heightening awareness. Next, we will turn to the Western orientation toward action as it is incorporated in the use of experiment.

Experiment is a teaching method that creates an experience in which clients can learn something that is part of their next growth step. Experiment is what transforms talking into doing, reminiscing and theorizing into presence and action (Zinker, 1977). The purpose of experiment is to assist the client in active self-exploration. Every experiment has a strong behavioral component. According to Zinker (1977), the goals of creative experiments are

- To expand the person's repertoire of behavior
- To create conditions under which the person can see his life as his own creation (take ownership of the therapy)

NORMAN: I really like this section on experiment—it is clear and extremely helpful, and anyone can benefit from reading it. That is a real response, not gratuitous praise. You say that the experiment "creates an experience in which clients can learn something that is part of their next growth step." What occurred to me when I read this was that Gestalt methodology talks about incremental growth, boundary stretching, and the process of change. In all of this, the experiment *is* the next step, *must* be the next step, and *will* be the next step because of the boundary situation. Because of the incremental nature of change and because an individual can only do so much at any given moment, the wonder and magic of the experiment is that it flows. It is like a bridge that is built halfway over a river. You take a step and get to the edge of where the bridge is built. The experiment allows you to take the next step and put your foot down on a firm foundation that holds you up. Now you can stand on that part of the bridge that wasn't there before and not fall. You feel solid there (in the new place), and eventually the bridge is expanded. The experiment *is* the next step because of boundaries, because of incrementalism, and because of how change takes place in the human. I loved the way you talked about the experiment and wish that it was emphasized as the next step. Perhaps you don't see it that way, or perhaps you see experiments producing change that is bigger than that. That was just something that I thought about as I read it and that is intrinsic to the way I view Gestalt and change.

JOE: Your point is well taken, Norman, that we did not emphasize the interactive or co-creation of experience but seemed to focus more on the interpersonal.

SONIA: You make a valid point that our focus was on a two-person system. We certainly recognize that Gestalt is applicable to all kinds of groups.

- To stimulate the person's experiential learning and the evolution of new self-concepts
- To complete unfinished situations and overcome blockages in the awareness/excitement/contact cycle
- To integrate cortical understandings with motoric expressions
- To discover polarizations that are not in awareness
- To stimulate the integration of conflictual forces in the personality
- To dislodge and to reintegrate introjects and generally place "misplaced" feelings, ideas, actions where they belong in the personality
- To stimulate circumstances under which the person can feel and act stronger, more competent, more self-supportive, more explorative and actively responsible for himself (p. 126)

JOE: I also agree with Sonia that contact is always a co-creation, and of course contact occurs in larger systems such as families and groups. Gestalt methods can be applied far beyond the field of psychotherapy, to corporate organizations, political systems, athletic teams, spiritual practices, and as Norman writes, even orchestras.

NORMAN: I like your ideas about the use of experiment as incremental. Of course, we can add that the Gestalt approach is experimental by definition. We are always looking at the impact of our mutual interaction and always playing with the question "What would happen if?" What would happen if you exaggerated that gesture, talked more quickly, really tasted the orange, experienced your whole body sitting in the chair, etc. I agree that a good experiment flows. It is really a co-creation of the therapist and the client. Although the therapist originally suggests it and the client agrees, once it is begun they are in fact both doing it together. When done well it is like a marvelous dance.

Historically, experiments have been confused with techniques. Methodology incorporates techniques, and all schools or models of psychotherapy use a variety of them. For example, psychodrama has much in common with role playing, assertiveness training, and behavioral rehearsal. A technique is a preformed experiment with specific learning goals. It is like an off-the-rack suit as opposed to a custom-made one designed to fit the individual. The same technique can be "worn" by different schools of psychotherapy. An experiment, on the other hand, flows directly from psychotherapy theory and is crafted to fit the individual as he or she exists in the here and now.

When psychoanalysis was the dominant form of depth therapy, action was underemphasized. In fact, one's actions were deliberately excluded. The emphasis stayed on insight through the interpretation of the therapist. Because of this lack of actions and because Gestalt experiments were often brilliantly conceived, they were popularized and often used for teaching purposes not particularly tailored to the needs of the individual in the moment. An example of this is the two-chair technique, used as an exercise to heal splits between parts of oneself. This experiment's power for healing is still impressive. For example, a person comes to therapy because he cannot control his eating. It soon becomes evident that one part of the self would like to control eating and another part is not cooperative. By having the client imagine each of the parts of the personality in separate chairs and asking the client to have them converse by changing chairs from one part of the self to the other, integration can occur. However, therapists who were minimally exposed to Gestalt theory routinely used this creative method in a stereotypic manner, and in some circles Gestalt therapy became characterized as empty chair work.

An excellent opportunity to use another kind of Gestalt experimentation comes ' client presents a dream in therapy with the hope of gaining awareness and understa. its meaning in his or her life. The most common method, introduced by Fritz Perls, was . have the client experiment by stating the dream in the here and now, as if the dream were happening *now.* The therapist encourages the client to experiment with being the parts and processes of the dream—as if each part of the dream had a voice—and facilitates dialogue between the various elements. This technique was based on Perls's belief that because every bit of the dream is a production of the dreamer, the various parts and processes are projections. In the words of Downing and Marmorstein (1973),

> Your dreams *are* you. They don't just *belong* to you—they *are* you. . . . In the dream, as in life, I am the microcosm. . . . Each and every one of your dreams is an expression of an infinite number of associations, harmonies, conflicts, and contradictions which make up you. Each of your dreams may be used as a starting point on an endless road of self-awareness. (p. 8, italics in original)

The elements of a dream may represent aspects or fragments of one's persona; as Perls (1969b) said, "I believe we are all fractionalized. We are divided. We are split up in many parts, and the beauty of working with a dream is that in a dream every part—not only every person, but every part is yourself" (p. 89). Another Gestalt view, presented by Isadore From (in Müller, 1996), was that the events of the dream can be retroflections, suggesting that the work of therapy is to help the client understand and undo the retroflections of what he or she cannot express in waking life. Here the therapist watches and listens for avoidance behavior and notices where the client becomes stuck. Joseph Zinker (1977) introduced an additional Gestalt method of working with dreams in group therapy: "dream work as theatre." This is a very innovative method, providing for ample experimentation in groups in which the dreamer (identified client) assigns various aspects of his or her dream to members of the group and gives them a line from the dream. He or she then acts as the director, orchestrator, or conductor of the unfolding drama as the elements of the dream enact dialogue with one another and with the dreamer, thereby providing the dreamer with broadened awareness of potential meanings in the dream and serving the goal of personal integration.

AUTHENTIC RELATIONSHIP: CRITICAL TO A SUCCESSFUL METHODOLOGY

> The therapist, according to his own self-awareness, declines to be bored, intimidated, cajoled, etc.; he meets anger with explanation of the misunderstanding, or sometimes apology, or even with anger, according to the truth of the situation. (Perls et al., 1951, p. 148)

A Gestalt therapist has a unique and complex job: He or she is asked to do two tasks at once. One, as already noted, is to watch the organizing process of the therapeutic session, noticing what the client does well and what is blocked and will therefore be the focus of the work. The other is to be available for an authentic relationship because genuine connection with others is a basic human need. Martin Buber (1923/1958) is probably the best-known philosopher to highlight this hunger to be seen, heard, and related to as a person rather than as an object. Buber's concept of the I-Thou relationship requires a Gestalt therapist to be continually working on his or her presence. To be present is to be focused on the here and now, to be aware of oneself, and to bring the self into the therapist/client encounter.

At one time this was interpreted as a requirement to be transparent to a client. To be transparent means to be fully open and honest at all times. This belief was a misinterpretation of the meaning of the here and now. In a therapeutic alliance, the therapist is transparent only in service to the client because the tasks are different for each of them. The client is asked to learn to be aware and to be transparent and genuine in the service of his or her growth. The therapist is asked to be genuine and to be selectively transparent where it serves the growth of the client. All awareness not related to that task should be bracketed out of the session.

This authenticity puts a responsibility on the therapist to be highly aware of potential and actual countertransference issues. Countertransference is feelings arising in a therapist that are evoked by the therapeutic work with the client but are not necessarily useful for the client's growth (Melnick, 2003).

Supervision is encouraged in almost all psychotherapeutic disciplines. It is particularly important for Gestalt therapists because they use their self as part of the genuine contact that they believe is an essential ingredient in building trust and in setting the groundwork for growth. An authentic relationship is, by definition, psychological nourishment that enables us to grow.

DIAGNOSIS—EVOLVING FROM AND GUIDING GESTALT METHODOLOGY

Often it has been said that diagnosis is contrary to the methodology and the spirit of a here-and-now therapy such as Gestalt therapy. This comes from a misunderstanding of the word *diagnosis.* As a Gestalt therapist gathers data,

NORMAN: As I read this section, a phrase that kept coming to my tongue and that I kept wanting to say was "doing *to* and doing *with.*" One of the things I love most about Gestalt is that the methodology allows someone who is really skilled to work with conductors to teach them how to bring the orchestra together, how to deal with difficult members, how to enhance their ability to deal with conflict, and how to explore the differences in the composition of groups. We work with CEOs in helping them understand how to work with themselves to be leaders, with individuals to experience the world more fully, and with couples to really open up and experience their relationship. One of the powerful conceptualizations of Gestalt for me is the use of methodology in all different kinds of endeavors. Part of that is the idea that once clients learn how to access their inner self and pay attention to the contact, they become more and more true partners in the process. So, for me, another question that I want to ask is, "How important was the idea of doing *with* as opposed to doing *to?*" Psychotherapy historically is something we have done *to* the patient and *to* the client, as opposed to a conjoint experience where we work *together:* By learning awareness skills and how to pay attention to contact, clients can begin to work *with* us to co-create experiences they use to learn about themselves and can become partners in the process. Ultimately, if clients have had a good Gestalt experience where the methodology was sound, they can take what they learned and use it on their own. That is another part of what is exciting for me about Gestalt, Gestalt principles, and Gestalt practices.

JOE: This is an interesting point, Norman—your distinction of "doing with" versus "doing to." I think that the phrases are tricky and can be misunderstood. We agree that Gestalt tends not to value a heavy emphasis on "doing to." However, we also tried to emphasize in our chapter the possible transferential dilemmas of "doing with." We believe that in addition to

he or she assesses the strengths and the weaknesses of the client's organizing process of the COE. This is how the Gestalt therapist diagnoses, for the process data suggest the trajectory of the needed work and the desired goal of the therapy.

For some therapists, diagnosis implies that the therapist "knows" what blocks a client and therefore "knows" the cure. When diagnosis is seen in a different way, as an ongoing process of exploration between the client and the therapist and as the development of an authentic relationship over time, the idea of the therapist as an all-knowing expert is no longer tenable.

The therapist and the client are engaging in a continual assessment of what is known and are working together to shed light on blocks of which the client is unaware. They create ways to proceed, often with the use of experiments, and to reach their desired goals jointly. The therapist has faith that an authentic relationship is healing in itself and that it provides the basis of support for growth. The therapy becomes a journey, and diagnosis is the tool that points to the directions to explore. Thus Gestalt diagnosis does not label an individual; rather, it identifies a process.

Often, when working with a client, you will be called on to confer with a mental health professional from a different psychological discipline. Therefore, it is important to be able to converse in psychologists' common language: the *DSM-IV* (American Psychiatric Association, 1994). At first glance, this diagnostic manual will look alien to practitioners of Gestalt methodology. However, a closer look will show that the conditions described are the human conditions; although different disciplines use different words, we are all talking about the same types of suffering. The translation will not be difficult, and you will be well served if you become familiar with the manual (see Melnick & Nevis, 1997).

A CASE STUDY

What follows is a segment of a session from a psychotherapy group consisting of eight members

"doing with," "doing to" is necessary in Gestalt therapy. There is always a hierarchy present in that the therapist is not a peer and has the ultimate responsibility for the session. Although the client and clinician each have responsibility for creating the music that we call therapy, more of the responsibility falls on the therapist; just as, in your example of the orchestra, more responsibility for creating real music falls on the conductor of an orchestra. Although the orchestra "does with" in the co-creation of the music, the conductor must, at times, exhibit some "doing to" behavior.

SONIA: I agree with what Joe said in making some clearer distinctions between "doing to" and "doing with." I also like what you said, Norman. This is a good example of "different voices"—our theory and practice never being exactly the same.

NORMAN: For me, from a Gestalt perspective, diagnosis is a description of the present functioning of the self. I think it is true that diagnosis in the Gestalt framework has a process orientation. Part of my reaction and part of my experience when I was reading your chapter was a question that formed: "How do you experience the self of the client in the encounter?" Further, "What is the method for clearly defining a diagnostic experience in the moment—not as a label, but in the moment?" "How do you capture the snapshot of the self and understand it?" Perhaps it is my bias that is keeping me from seeing clearly what you are saying, as I have a very defined point of view on this subject. If so, I welcome your response and would love to clarify my reactions and thoughts about this. Perhaps it isn't clear and we need to talk about it a little more and see if we can make that more clear. As I think about diagnosis in Gestalt therapy, I ask, how is the self experienced? Without going into an extensive bibliographic discussion, there is certainly a great deal of support in literature that has the

and two co-therapists. Please see if you can notice the therapist utilizing the five aspects of Gestalt methodology: the here and now, the paradoxical theory of change, experiment, authentic encounter, and diagnosis.

By way of introduction, Amanda had been a member of a psychotherapy group for more than a year. She took the same seat every week, sitting uncomfortably on the end of a sofa. She appeared unaware of her seating posture. She sat with her shoulders stooped and her eyes peering up, in a frightened "deer in the headlights" pose. She had spent much of the last year looking at her highly developed friendly side. She described life and people as agreeable, yet reported a cardboard quality to her existence. On this particular day, after reporting being rejected by a man, she requested (something she rarely did) some time to look at her agreeable personality.

Therapist: To be able to agree and notice what is good in the world is a beautiful thing.

Amanda: Yes, that is what my mother taught me. I guess I learned it too well. There just doesn't seem to be much excitement in my life. I experience myself as a victim. I never seem to get what I want.

Therapist: (Returning to the theme of "agreeability") Well, I'm still fascinated by your ability to be so agreeable. I was wondering if you would be interested in exploring an aspect of it.

Amanda: What do you mean?

Therapist: Well, sometimes when we are very good at something we are less developed in its opposite. For example, you are very good at telling us what you like. My guess is that you might find it interesting to explore the opposite, the polarity of what you don't like. Would that interest you?

Amanda: (Hesitantly) Yes.

self unfold in contact. In any given moment I feel there is a picture of the self (of the client) in the mind of the therapist. Yes, this is a process experience, and yes, we are co-attending to that process—the client and the therapist. But there is a picture in the moment of the self of the client, and that picture has something to do with the diagnosis—a momentary X ray that describes the current state of the self as contact is happening. Sometimes the elements of that picture continue to be the same and sometimes they change. I agree with the transitory nature of diagnosis. That makes sense, and it is true to Gestalt theory. It is a reality in my life, my work, and in most Gestaltists—and you explained it beautifully. However, I also believe that in any given moment we do have some idea of how the self is functioning and that the picture relates to the diagnosis. Part of the skill of integrating the methodology is being able to experience that picture, understand it, co-understand it (perhaps in the moment), and give it up and embrace a new picture. I agree that the relationship is a healing form in itself and that it underlies the whole question of diagnosis.

SONIA: You ask a very important question, Norman: "How do we experience the other, the client?" I like this question because it points to the idealism of our theory and how we try to live up to it. However, I think we can never truly know the experience of the client. Even when the client works to tell us, we still don't really know. We settle for diagnosing the process, which transforms the customary diagnoses (fixed gestalts) into a moving, changing figure that accentuates the changes from moment to moment.

NORMAN: I agree that the concept of diagnosis as attention to the nature of the unfolding process is true; my only addition, which I think is important here, is that by attending to the unfolding process you develop a changing mental picture (or I do) about the evolving self of the client. That picture is transitory, not a rigid fixed imprint, and it informs me about how the self of the client is currently functioning.

Therapist: You sound a little hesitant to me. I'm not sure whether you really want to do this or you are just being agreeable.

Amanda: (Smiles as if she were caught with her hand in the cookie jar) You're right. I was just being agreeable. Let me think if I really want to do this. (After a brief hesitation, smiles a genuine and full smile) Yes! I really want to learn about it.

Therapist: Great. My suggestion is that you go around the room in your head and pick out something about someone that you don't like and notice what happens.

Amanda: (Complies and, as she goes around looking at everyone, becomes noticeably uncomfortable)

Therapist: What did you notice?

Amanda: I became aware of something I did not like about you. I am getting nervous.

Therapist: I find that interesting. We could continue in a number of ways if you wish. However, one suggestion is that you tell me what it is that you don't like about me, and we see what happens.

Amanda: (Appears frightened, but catches her breath and blurts out) I don't like your arrogance. You always seem so sure of yourself. (A second later) I can't believe I said that. Are you okay?

Therapist: I am fine. I am glad that you noticed my arrogance. I have worked hard to develop it.

Amanda: (Looks totally confused) You like it? What is there to like about it?

Therapist: Well for one thing, it allows me to not be so concerned about others. Second, I experience a sense of power. Rather than looking up to people like you do, I find it invigorating to sometimes look down at them. I've got an idea. If you are interested I'd like you to explore your own arrogance.

Amanda: Maybe. But I need you to tell me more.

Therapist: I notice that you always seems to sit huddled on the edge of the sofa, looking up at the world. I would like to suggest something simple. I would like you to just practice sitting on a chair that is slightly above the other ones, and rather than pulling in your shoulders, fluff them out. Are you still with me?

Amanda: (With some hesitation) Yes, I am willing to give it a try. (The group joins in the experiment, helping her to find a chair and contracting to pay attention to what they experience as she works.)

Therapist: Now that you are looking down on us with your feet planted, what are you aware of?

Amanda: I notice that you all don't look so fragile. I never realized that. I always thought that I was the fragile one, but I also experience others as fragile. I also notice that I feel more powerful. I don't feel so frightened anymore. It is as if I can say things without having to be so concerned with hurting or being hurt.

Therapist: That's great. Would you be willing to sit in the chair for the remainder of the group, and when you have a disagreeable thought experiment with saying it?

Amanda: (Thinking for a moment) Yes!

SUMMARY

Methodology is what helps transform theory into action. Gestalt methodology combines an Eastern focus on awareness and being in the here and now with a Western emphasis on action and doing. We focus on how the client organizes his or her experience, while at the same time we are engaged in an authentic encounter with the individual. In turn, a diagnosis evolves that points the way to the best process for a given client. In this chapter, we have suggested the COE as a template to help the therapist make sense of the client's organization of his or her experiences.

NORMAN: The integration of the methodological components that you articulate in this chapter is a part of the unattended-to and unspoken art of the methodology. Though you both talk about playing the piano with two hands, for me the *integration* of the methodological factors is the essence of being in the here and now with the client. The integration of those factors into a whole that flows is part of what the training in the methodology is really about. And learning how to do that in a smooth way and call on the methodological resources, both as a model and without thinking about them, is what helps make a great Gestalt therapist. In closing, I want you both to know that I have enjoyed this process and, as always, enjoy both of you. I look forward to more dialogue with you.

REVIEW QUESTIONS

1. What is the purpose of methodology in counseling and psychotherapy?

2. What does the continuum of experience represent? How can it be useful in understanding what a client is experiencing or avoiding in a therapy session?

3. Differentiate between the following words that are often used as synonyms with *authentic*: *transparent, truthful, genuine, real, natural, honest, actual, open, straightforward,* and *trustworthy*. According to your authors, what is the danger of thinking they all mean the same thing as their definition of *authentic* when counseling a client?

4. Identify the five components of Gestalt methodology in the client-therapist dialogue in the case presentation of "Amanda": (a) here and now, (b) paradoxical theory of change, (c) experiment, (d) authentic encounter, and (e) diagnosis.

5. How is the Gestalt approach to diagnosis different from the standard models used in the medical models of psychotherapy? What is meant by the statement "Diagnosis is a description of the present functioning of the self"? How can this concept be useful in the conduct of psychotherapy?

EXPERIENTIAL PEDAGOGICAL ACTIVITIES

ACTIVITY 1: Reflecting on *how* you read this chapter and using a large piece of paper, draw a time line that begins with the time you began reading (beginning of line on left) and the time you finished it (at end of line on the right side). Using the terminology of the continuum of experience (COE), identify along your time line the various facets of the COE that you experienced as you read. Also identify any interruptive activities, slowdowns, blocks, stoppages, resistances, or defenses that interrupted your interest and reading.

ACTIVITY 2: Pair off with another class member into a dyad and practice staying solely in the "here and now" in everything you say and do for 10 minutes. While doing this, be aware of the ways you naturally tend to move out of present-centeredness, and discuss this for 5 minutes with your partner when the 10 minutes are finished. Then, with your partner, join another dyad and observe them doing essentially the same thing (practicing "here-and-now" interaction for 10 minutes), only while observing them, keep notes (mental or written) on ways you see and hear them staying present centered and moving away from it. Afterward, give them feedback for 5 minutes. Reverse the process so that the other dyad observes you and your partner and gives you feedback.

ACTIVITY 3: In small groups of three to five, take approximately half an hour to try to establish an "authentic dialogue" about this chapter and/or the class/training program in general. While you are all working at being authentic, "slip in" some inauthentic comments without announcing that is what you are doing, paying attention to both your own feelings in doing it and the group's response (if any). Wait until the end of the group experience to discuss your observations and feelings about the difference between trying to be "authentic" and "inauthentic."

ACTIVITY 4: Ask someone in class to share a dream with you (this can also be done in small groups or as an entire class). Using the guidelines for Gestalt dreamwork in this chapter's section on experiment, facilitate therapeutic encounter with the dreamer by having him or her first repeat the dream in present tense (as if it were happening now) and then speak as if he or she were the different parts of the dream. Be curious and ask the parts questions that will facilitate phenomenological exploration of their potential relation in the dreamer's life. Keep in mind Downing and Marmorstein's assertion that "[e]ach and every one of your dreams is an expression of an infinite number of associations, harmonies, conflicts, and contradictions which make up you. Each of your dreams may be used as a starting point on an endless road of self-awareness." Whatever you do, try to encourage the dreamer to "play it up" and put energy into acting out the parts as he or she engages in the dream encounter.

CHAPTER 7

Cultural Influences and Considerations in Gestalt Therapy

SABIN FERNBACHER

DIALOGUE RESPONDENT: DEBORAH PLUMMER

Sabin Fernbacher is a candidate for the professional doctorate in public health at LaTrobe University, Melbourne, Australia, where she completed her graduate diploma in Gestalt therapy. Originally educated as a teacher in Austria, she completed her BA at Paedagogische Akademie des Bundes in Vienna. Since 1989 she has lived in Australia, where she has worked as a crisis counselor and coordinator in a range of community organizations dealing with sexual assault, domestic violence, housing, and mental health services. In more recent years she has worked as an organizational consultant for mental health services, as a researcher for a statewide project in mental health, and as service development coordinator for an area mental health service in Melbourne. She has as a small private practice where she also provides supervision. Her presentation on cultural diversity was acclaimed at the Fifth International Conference of the European Gestalt Therapy Association in Stockholm, Sweden, and served as the impetus for inviting her to author this chapter.

Deborah Plummer is a practicing counseling psychologist and professor in the Psychology Department at Cleveland State University, where she directs the Diversity Management Training Program. Following her doctoral studies at Kent State University with Ansel Woldt as her adviser, she was on the Oberlin College Counseling Center staff. She has completed the 3-year Post-Graduate Program at the Gestalt Institute of Cleveland and the Diversity Management Program at NTL Institute for Behavioral Sciences. She serves on the editorial board for the *Gestalt Review* and has several publications, including *The Handbook of Diversity Management: Beyond Awareness to Competency Based Learning* (2003) and *Racing Across the Lines: Changing Race Relations Through Friendships* (2004).

In recent years we have started to realize that the so-called minority problems are in fact majority problems. (Lewin, 1948/1997, p. 151)

Every person belongs to a culture, no matter how obvious or how hidden that culture is. Many possibilities depend on our status within the culture, society, or country in which we live. We may choose to pay attention to our own culture, or we may feel forced to (by ways of inclusion and exclusion) show and be proud of our culture or hide (if possible) and be ashamed of our culture. We may be interested in cross-cultural work as practitioners, or we may see it as an area of specialization. We may know a lot or little about our own heritage, culture, practices, and rituals. We may live speaking our first, second, or third language, or we may speak only one language. We may live within or far away from our own cultural communities of origin. We may belong to a First Nation/indigenous community. Maybe we are immigrants of the first, second, or third generation. Our family may have lived in the same place within the same culture for many generations. We may find it difficult, interesting, exciting, or harrowing to live among cultures and communities that we are very new to, or we may find it easy to become accustomed to a new culture. Our reasons for staying, migrating, going back, or never leaving are many, and the stories behind those reasons are as colorful as they are painful. They may be full of joy and at the same time sad. We may move to another side of a country because of a loved one or may need to move to another continent in order to be safe.

As Gestalt practitioners, whether we are therapists or organizational consultants and whether we work with individuals, couples, families, or groups, we frequently relate and work across a spectrum of cultural differences. Even if we work with someone from the same ethnic culture as our own, there may be differences in class, generation, gender, education, ability/disability, sexuality, or age between us. The primary focus of this chapter will be on *ethnic culture* and its impact on Gestalt theory and practice.

I will attempt to provide a connection between Gestalt therapy theory and its possible applications to working across different ethnic cultures. Practitioner awareness, as one of Gestalt's foundations, will be explored within an ethnically focused field. Discussion will center on concepts of relevance to Gestalt therapy, namely field theory as it applies to Gestalt practitioners and their "ethnic being," the phenomenological method within a cultural frame; the use of the paradoxical theory of change to explore one's awareness about ethnicity; and the importance of the dialogic relationship between client and practitioner. Suggestions for further exploration to raise Gestalt practitioners' awareness will conclude the chapter. The content of this chapter is based on research I have undertaken that contributes to understanding the issues involved in cross-cultural situations when the therapist belongs to the "dominant" culture. Much cross-cultural practice focuses on working with people from "other"—that is, nondominant—cultures (often nonwhites or immigrants). In keeping with Gestalt theory and concepts, I have applied to this situation the exploration of the (cultural) self. The analysis I used in my research was based on two Gestalt therapy principles, phenomenology and field theory, so I will use them to explain what happens in such cross-cultural therapeutic situations. I will begin by presenting definitions of culture from a range of cross-cultural, counseling, and psychotherapy literatures.

CULTURE DEFINED

> *Culture . . . refers to milieu, the process of living, and the system of values and practices shared by particular groups of people. Culture, by distinction, is dynamic. It is ever changing and includes a whole gamut of experiences and learning and includes all the distinctive practices of daily living, customs, and attitudes. Culture encompasses all of everyday life, from the mundane, such as the type of food eaten, even mealtimes, and clothes, to religious practices and important attitudes to others in terms of age, sex, and social roles. Along with these, it includes the extent to which one can adapt to social change. (Acharyya, 1992, p. 74)*

The cross-cultural literature offers an array of definitions of culture. For example, according to d'Ardenne and Mahtani (1998), culture includes "shared history, practices, beliefs, and values of a racial, regional or religious group of people" (p. 4). Sue and Sue (1990), two of the most referenced researchers in this field, described culture as the things that people have learned to "do, believe, value and enjoy in their history" (p. 35). Ember and Ember (quoted in Segall, Dasen, Berry, & Poortinga, 1990) defined it as the "shared customs of a society" (p. 3). Rawson, Whitehead, and Luthra (1999) claimed that it is the particular beliefs and social practices that guide people's lives.

Concepts of culture vary from narrow to broad descriptions and can include a wide range of characteristics. Culture defines people who belong to a particular group but at the same time is always changing. The influences of migration, globalization, and the mix of cultures in many countries around the globe highlight the contested nature of culture. Culture used to be seen as much more static, whereas now each culture is seen as maintaining certain characteristics while also being fluid and open to a degree of change.

If culture is broadly defined, any situation has a cross-cultural aspect. In a situation where a gay or lesbian practitioner works with a heterosexual client, the cultures of both the gay/lesbian and the heterosexual person will interact. Cultural difference is present when a practitioner who is able-bodied works with a person who has a physical disability or when a female practitioner works with a male client. The practitioners and clients in each scenario have certain characteristics or have developed within a certain culture.

The broad sociocultural definition of culture by Acharyya (1992) quoted at the beginning of this section both includes and excludes cultural markers. For the purpose of this chapter I will be focusing primarily on *ethnic culture,* while keeping in mind that many other common markers, such as class, gender, dis/ability, religion, and sexual preference, intersect with ethnic culture. Whenever I refer to *culture,* I am referring to ethnic culture unless stated otherwise.

BRIDGING GESTALT THEORY AND CROSS-CULTURAL THEORY

Gestalt therapy concerns itself with how people make contact with others and with bringing to awareness how contact can be hindered or enhanced. Those training to become Gestalt therapists or practitioners are encouraged to apply Gestalt theory to themselves in order to explore their style of increasing and decreasing contact; how to bracket preconceived ideas; how to describe rather than interpret; how to pay attention to the broader field; how to pay attention to the dialogic relationship; and how to bring the process back to the "space between" practitioner and client.

DEBORAH: I read your chapter with great interest and appreciate the focus on whiteness and its relationship to the "use of self" as an instrument of change in the therapy process. Since I am not white, I am always curious about the thinking that supports behavior when one is in the privileged position. In teaching, I use the example of a fish in water that does not need to understand the concept of wetness to explain privilege. White people are the fish in water when it comes to race/culture.

SABIN: I like your "fish in water" expression; what's "natural" to a fish is so alien to a land creature that lives in the middle of the desert!

Cross-cultural literature has had a tendency to research and analyze the "Other." The term *Other* is capitalized to redress the oppressiveness of naming people as the Other (Dominelli, 2002; Fine, Weis, Powell, & Mun Wong, 1997; Frankenberg, 1993; hooks, 1995; McConville, 1997; McIntosh, 1998; Putnis & Petelin, 1996). Numerous writers have attempted to understand people from other cultures. Multiculturalism has seen a flurry of inquiry, publications, opinions, and suggestions on how to live "with difference." Generally, little attention is paid to the foreground against which the Other is measured or from which it is looked upon. However, a growing number of theorists have started to turn their gaze to the other side of this inquiry. Whiteness studies, discussed later in this chapter, have turned the gaze toward the self (i.e., the white majority) rather than exploring the Other.

What lies ahead in this chapter is a look at the often unquestioned and unexplored assumptions and practices of people who belong to the *dominant culture.* Although this approach may appear to exclude people from nondominant cultures, many of the observations and questions can be applied equally to those who identify themselves as belonging to nondominant groups. It is my intention to bring into the foreground what tends to be left out of cross-cultural encounters, namely the cultural awareness of people who belong to the dominant culture. It is in this light that the reader is invited to engage with this text.

AWARENESS

According to Mackewn (1997), "Awareness is the way in which we understand ourselves and what we need and also the way in which we organise our field and make meaning of our experience" (p. 113). Perls, Hefferline, and Goodman (1951) offered one of the most profound statements about awareness:

> Awareness is the spontaneous sensing of what arises in you—of what you are doing, feeling, planning; introspection, in contrast, is a deliberate turning of attention to these activities in an evaluating, correcting, controlling, interfering way; . . . Awareness is like the glow of a coal which comes from its own combustion; what is given by introspection is like the light reflected from an object when a flashlight is turned on it. (p. 31)

The Gestalt approach consistently emphasizes understanding the processes of awareness. Awareness is seen as the road to understanding the *how* of behavior. It is subjective and has two kinds of foci: inner and outer. We are aware of ourselves through our bodies, emotions, and insights. Awareness of the world around us comes from our perceptions of what is outside our skin using our senses of seeing, hearing, touching, smelling, tasting, and intuiting. People are responsive to internal promptings and external events, both of which they experience with interested excitement when healthy. Gary Yontef (1993), who has written extensively about awareness, stated:

> Insightful awareness is always a new Gestalt and is in itself curative. . . . The formation of the new Gestalt, in which "the significant relations are apparent" and the "relevant factors fall into place with respect to the whole," is a process that happens naturally without Gestalt training. When it does not, when habit patterns and un-self-conscious efforts do not yield insight, Gestalt training can use phenomenological exploration to gain an understanding of the insight/awareness process. The ability to form this insightful new Gestalt is essential to successful organismic self-regulation. (p. 250)

Development of awareness is one of Gestalt therapy's main aims in interaction with clients. Similarly, Gestalt training encourages trainees to develop their own awareness. To develop awareness of one's cultural identity, one must attend to its influence not only in training but also as part of ongoing development as a Gestalt practitioner.

People who belong to the dominant culture pay far less attention to investigating their own cultural background and its associated beliefs, behaviors, and worldview than people of nondominant cultures do. White people, in particular, tend not to examine their background or have a clear understanding or awareness of what it means to be white, whether they are Australian, American, German, British, Swedish, South African, or Dutch (Dominelli, 2002; Hage, 1998; Krause, 1998; McIntosh, 1998). In all cases, their cultural background affects their life and work. Perls et al. (1951) described the Gestalt awareness process as one of figure-ground formation:

> Awareness is a figure against a ground. Such awareness is possible only of a whole-and-parts, where each part is immediately experienced as involving all the other parts and the whole, and the whole is just of these parts. The whole figure could be said to be the background for the parts, but it is more than ground for it; it is at the same time the figure *of* the parts, and they are ground. . . . In such a whole-of-parts the figure provides its own boundary. . . . In all contacting, there is an underlying unity of perceptual, motor, and feelingful functions: there is no grace, vigor, dexterity of movement without orientation and interest; no keen sight without focusing; no feeling of attraction without reaching, etc. (pp. 416–417, italics in original)

In situations where cross-cultural issues are present between practitioner and client, the Gestalt practitioner will bring just as much of his or her "cultural self" to the encounter as the client does. The Gestalt approach provides practitioners with a useful way to investigate the often unmentioned "other side" that is in the foreground. Gestalt promotes working holistically with the other person while simultaneously being aware of one's self. As Mackewn (1997) reminded us, "To work holistically you need to be aware of your own whole person in relationship to clients, paying attention to all your own reactions and responses" (p. 47). Hycner (1991) similarly remarked that "[t]he therapist's self is the 'instrument' which will be utilized in therapy. This 'instrument' needs to be kept 'tuned' in order to be responsive to the ever-changing rhythms of the human encounter" (p. 12).

In the 1990s, there emerged not only an emphasis on the need for therapists to become more culturally aware but also a growing literature that invited us to reflect on our own theoretical underpinnings and personal positions as therapists (Ancis & Szymanski, 2001; d'Ardenne & Mahtani, 1998; Dominelli, 2002; Jacobs, 2000a; Krause, 1998; McConville, 1997). Pedersen (1997) provided suggestions about how to examine one's own culturally learned assumptions and "manage cultural assumptions" (p. 27).

This approach fits well with Gestalt theory and methods. Both Gestalt trainees and experienced practitioners need to be aware of their own biases and assumptions, including those of their culture. This is especially important if they belong to the dominant culture.

Kareem and Littlewood (1992) advocated that any therapeutic practice ought to be "self-reflexive practice which examines its own prejudices, ideology and will to power, which is aware of the ironies and contradictions in its own formation, and which is prepared to struggle with them" (p. 13). Gestalt training pays attention to practitioners' awarenesses and ways of making contact with other people. If we attend to ourselves fully, each of us needs to include our cultural self. People who belong to the so-called minority in the country they live in are generally asked to or forced to identify their culture and its impact on the way they live and relate to others. For example, they may be asked by others who are trying to understand how they see or experience a situation, and if they are different from the bulk of employees in an agency they will be asked whether they observe the same or different

---

DEBORAH: My question here is: In order to keep one's instrument of self "tuned," how does one use field theory to increase awareness when you are a member of the dominant culture (fish in water)? When teaching multicultural psychology, we encourage the students to design and conduct a "multicultural experience"—in other words, to place themselves in an experiential stance and intentionally change the field and shift the boundary. Your ideas about the relationship of field theory to our work as Gestalt therapists reminded me of this assignment.

SABIN: I suppose one way to keep one's self in tune about majority issues is to try out things that you might use in your workshop. I have used similar experiences/experiments, such as:

1. Ask people, just for the time of the 2-hour workshop, to put their watch on the other hand or similar things (just a small-scale idea to find out how they react within themselves to a sense of doing something out of the ordinary).
2. Reflect on a situation in which they were not sure what the right thing to do was, or how to behave, or of the rules of a situation. Generally, people can think of an example and reflect on how they felt, what happened, etc., and then discuss the experience with others, especially what happened, what was missing, etc., on a more cross-cultural level. I ask the students to reflect on a situation in which they were in the minority as a white/dominant/culturally dominant person and what happened for them. Did they know the rules? How did they pick up cues?
3. Ask students to make connections with other situations. For example, in Australia, Aboriginal people have to do translation work all the time if they live within white Australian places (as most do). How does that experience connect with their own experience?

holidays or rituals or have the same or different family responsibilities. People who do not belong to a cultural minority group but belong to the dominant cultural group rarely need to define their culture, its impact on their daily life, or its influence on how they relate to others. Hence, they are less likely to investigate their own cultural self and tend to be less aware of this part of themselves. Generally they see themselves as the norm against which everything else is measured. It is necessary to bring this area into focus because it has been out of focus for a long time.

The training of Gestalt practitioners has traditionally included a requirement of considerable therapy to facilitate awareness and understanding of what has shaped their worldview and to know their limitations and boundaries. This is because Gestalt practitioners, seeing themselves as instruments of change, bring all of themselves into the therapeutic encounter. All of the aspects of their personality and life are right there in the room with the client. So their cultural self is in the room as well, whether they are aware of this aspect of themselves or not.

4. On another level, ask students to refle[ct on] how white/dominant-culture people [benefit] from cultural capital, whiteness, etc. This example has been pretty tricky in my experience; not many white people like to admit to benefiting from their position (getting them to read Peggy McIntosh's 1998 article on white privilege can be challenging!).
5. Ask them to reflect on situations in which they are not in a dominant cultural group, such as a woman in a male-dominated job or situation, a lesbian in a heterosexual environment, or a working-class person in a middle/upper-class environment. I use myself as an example: I am white, lesbian, and a first-generation immigrant with English as a second language. There are many situations/times when I am part of the dominant white group of people and other times when I am in one of the other groups (such as at work, where most people are heterosexual). Being in a nondominant group gives me some indication of how I feel when everybody else is of the dominant group and I am not of that group.

DEBORAH: I like your examples for supporting people to move into new awarenesses because you offer graded experiences in a Gestalt sense. These experiments allow people to shift the boundaries of the field bit by bit, thus increasing their comfort zone.

FIELD THEORY

> *Gestalt's insistence upon the fact that the individual cannot be understood in isolation but only as part of their historical and social context means that in theory at least we have the capacity to take into account and attend to cultural difference, historical background and social perspectives. (Mackewn, 1997, p. 51)*

> *There is a link between where one stands and what one perceives. (Frankenberg, 1993, p. 8)*

Field theory is a crucial Gestalt concept for understanding and dealing with cross-cultural situations. It reminds us that every person needs to be seen in the broader context of his or her life, which includes culture. If we apply this to ourselves, with a specific focus on our cultural self, we need to start investigating and asking ourselves questions if we have not done this already. (See Chapter 3 of this book for a thorough presentation on field theory.)

Field theory also reminds us that we need to see the other person, the client, as well as ourselves within the broader context of culture, society, and the political system in which we operate. Krause (1998) pointed out that it is necessary to see culture within the broader field, rather than solely within the relationship between therapist and client, in particular when the cultural differences between therapist and client are noticeable. "Culture is a social construction and is therefore maintained, reconstituted and changed through social relationships both public and private, general and intimate" (p. 4). She claimed that it is impossible to divorce culture from the broader field and make it into an entity that exists only between practitioner and client.

Generally, as Gestalt trainees, we are taken through a process of applying field theory to ourselves by exploring what is figural, such as life themes that have shaped our experiences. Less common tends to be the application of field theory to exploring our cultural field, especially those aspects of culture that give us membership in the dominant group. When field theory is applied with rigor to the cultural self, areas that have been in the ground are likely to be discovered or brought into awareness—that is, made figural. The following are examples of how some Gestaltists have documented their discoveries and how field theory has been the vehicle for their discoveries.

Mark McConville (1997) shared his personal experiences of bewilderment about cross-cultural encounters and interactions at the *color boundary* while working as a therapist with adolescents. He described how his "Well Intended Whiteness" (p. 3) was challenged as he became aware that the impact of well-intended actions could still be hurtful to another person, and he pointed out the need to take responsibility for the impact of one's own actions, no matter how well intended they may be. He drew parallels about the figure/ground relationship and his experience that "the figure ends up *bearing the weight of the ground*" (p. 12, italics in original), and he strove to "learn to see the invisible" (p. 13): In other words, he argued that even if what is in the ground is not acknowledged, it can have an impact on the person and the dialogic relationship. For example, he noted that "power achieved . . . is power forgotten, power which has receded into the ground, power which has become invisible as an organizing context of perception" (p. 13). McConville used field theory to understand the complexity of cross-cultural encounters and to bring into focus what is often in the ground. His examples included the *invisible* power of privileged people (including himself), of white people, who are often seen as the norm against which everything else is measured. He suggested that even though this power has been moved into the ground, it is ever present in what is figural. It was exactly this privilege and the assumptions made about the norm that McConville sought to uncover and confront within himself. Gestalt, he asserted, provides a possibility to recognize one's own positions (e.g., that of dominance or power) and the ground into which one is born.

In sharing her experiences of working across culture and color, Lynne Jacobs (2000a) found field theory to be one of the basic tools to better understand these encounters. She wrote about her (and others') assumption that a person is white unless otherwise stated; again, this correlates with what white people see as the norm. She recognized her own assumptions and how much her worldview was shaped by her whiteness. She described both her struggle to be mindful of the wider, racially structured field when working across ethnic/cultural boundaries and the need to acknowledge this within the dialogic relationship. At the same time she strove to be aware of her own needs to "engage in talk about race matters" (p. 8) and when this need was clearly hers and not her client's.

Jarosewitsch (1997) shared his cross-cultural experience or "clash of two cultures" (p. 2) from being German and a new immigrant to Aotearoa (the Maori word for New Zealand). His previously encouraged style of confrontation and challenge did not fit with his new environment, and it took some time for him to change his way of interacting as a response to, and reflection on, the broader field.

These are just three examples of how field theory can be applied to one's self when confronted with cross-cultural situations. Field theory provides us with the opportunity to investigate what is unsaid and unknown, what we are unaware of, and the parts that are not figural. We can do this by applying everything to ourselves that we think of asking someone who comes from a different ethnic culture. Do we know our own ancestry? Do we know how and why we do things? Do we know which of our practices are culturally determined? Do we know which culturally determined practices we are not comfortable with and whether we are trying to get rid of them or trying to do things differently? If we observe that someone else is doing something in a way that is unfamiliar to us, we can stop ourselves and ask, Why am I doing this in my particular way? Am I expecting everybody else to do it in the same way? The phrase "We've always done it like this" is familiar to most of us. When we apply it to ourselves as practitioners, we need to ask if we are behaving in fixed patterns that we are not aware of.

In summary, field theory offers an opportunity for Gestalt practitioners to investigate our own assumptions, biases, and preconceived ideas. When we examine the issues that are under the surface, that are more hidden, we are likely to uncover our convictions and beliefs, to know their origination and how they may affect how we see the world and relate to others.

PHENOMENOLOGY

Though Chapter 4 thoroughly discusses the role of phenomenology in Gestalt therapy, I want to highlight here some of the ways in which it is relevant to cultural considerations. Phenomenology reminds us to temporarily bracket our assumptions (*rule of epoché*) in order to "focus on the primary data of our experience . . . [and] impose an openness to our immediate experience" (Spinelli, 1989, p. 17). The *rule of description* recommends that the therapist track and describe rather than interpret the client's processes as well as his or her own impressions. The *rule of horizontalization* reminds us to treat all aspects of the field as potentially relevant and of equal importance. Phenomenology provides a ground from which therapists can inquire about, rather than interpret, the other person's behavior as well as their own. The phenomenological method of describing, applied to ourselves, can be a wonderful way to learn about our own assumptions, noticing what comes up in a cross-cultural encounter and what meaning we give to our experience.

DEBORAH: You speak of the rule of horizontalization that "reminds us to treat all aspects of the field as potentially relevant and of equal importance." In working with differences, how do we see the "isms"—those destructive beliefs or attitudes that one holds about differences—being managed by this rule?

SABIN: I think one way of applying the rule of horizontalization to oneself, the "isms," or other thoughts, feelings, and beliefs that we hold (and sometimes hide from ourselves when we want to trick ourselves into being "politically correct," or worldly or unprejudiced) is that we need to acknowledge those "isms" and do our own work on them (McConville and others talk about needing to do the work as a white person by talking to other white people) so that we can acknowledge and then bracket these things off. In this way we know they are there but don't bring them in as much (or at all?) into the interaction with the other person. I have friends who are Aboriginal who say, "You know, you can smell

Phenomenology applied to cross-cultural encounters urges therapists to be entirely open to what emerges for them. Becoming aware of feelings and opinions that may not have previously surfaced can be both exciting and challenging. At times we may become aware of feelings that we didn't know we were capable of having, and we may be ashamed of feeling a particular way or just not want to admit it to ourselves or others. Jacobs (2000a) described a number of such phenomena that she noticed in other therapists who belong to the dominant culture: "When such notions [those of white privilege] are raised in gatherings of whites, one can often detect an uncomfortable shifting of chairs in the room" (p. 6). She described dealing with her feelings of anxiety and guilt (which she felt at times) when working across color and cultural boundaries. In the process of recognizing these feelings and in recounting her struggle to come to terms with what was going on with her, she asked which parts were necessary and important to disclose to her client and which were necessary to discuss with other (white) therapists. As a result of this self-examination, she emerged changed. One of the important things Jacobs made figural in her process of describing her awareness was the importance of letting surface what lies underneath.

them [white people] when you walk into a room." The way I understand that comment is that I believe as white people (dominant-culture people) we have intrinsically racist attitudes, feelings; I think people, like my [Aboriginal] friends, can tell when someone has not done any thinking or work around those issues. Such work still doesn't make the "isms" go away, but at least there is greater awareness.

DEBORAH: That is true. I still remain curious about the connection/correlation with awareness and behavior change and how the environment "pushes" toward awareness for an individual when there is not a felt need on the part of the individual. You also refer to bracketing and its potential to lead to a color-blind approach. I find your insight helpful for how individuals can maintain a lack of awareness or believe they are "sufficiently" aware of differences. In the area of emotional intelligence, they have had an amygdala hijack (the part of the brain that deals with feelings) when they encounter differences. Differences do not successfully translate into brain language, and thus one acts as if differences do not exist.

If feelings deriving from privilege, color, or cultural boundaries are unrecognized or suppressed, they will still affect the dialogic relationship between therapist and client. The therapist may not notice this, but the client may well be aware of it. D'Ardenne and Mahtani (1998) warned that therapists (like anybody else) carry assumptions and preconceived ideas and that "all counsellors have historically held attitudes and expectations about their own culture, which are inevitably biased. . . . Counsellors should be very careful when insisting that they are non-judgmental with all their clients, regardless of colour or creed" (p. 36). Such statements may mean only that uncomfortable feelings are covered up and internal racial conflicts are denied. Sometimes these feelings and assumptions can be buried so deeply that they do not make their way to one's awareness easily. Therapists need to discover exactly those deeply held assumptions and opinions in order to step out of their comfort zone—particularly if they belong to the dominant culture.

Color Blindness

An extreme position is the color-blind approach that some white people take (d'Ardenne & Mahtani, 1998; Dominelli, 2002). People who take this approach claim, "I don't see color,

I just see the person." This obviously denies racial or color differences while simultaneously denying a whole history of experiences. It can minimize the other person's experience and contribute to oppression and a growing chasm between people of different cultures. Dominelli (2002) identified it as one of the more subtle forms of racism—a resistance by white people to confront issues of privilege and skin color. She stated that this attitude, with its emphasis on *just seeing people,* denies the structural and interpersonal oppression and racism that black people and other people of color experience. She further argued that it promotes a unifying approach that tries to point out sameness rather than acknowledging difference. She stressed a need for change at the personal as well as the broader level of society. Merely being a trained practitioner does not shield one from making assumptions about others and unintentionally bringing these assumptions into the therapeutic relationship, thereby lessening the potential for contactful interaction with the client.

So what does this have to do with phenomenology? The Gestalt recommendation to bracket preconceived ideas about the other person may be seen as requiring a color-blind approach. Just as there is danger in making cross-cultural encounters too difficult, there is danger in making them too easy. Bracketing potentially important information about a person could lead to a naive approach by the therapist. This is not to say that phenomenology in itself suggests that we take a color-blind approach; it is merely a reminder that bracketing one's assumptions while still using one's knowledge can be a fine balancing act.

Phenomenology encourages both the client and therapist to describe rather than interpret behavior. If the therapist and the client have very different cultural norms and the associated behaviors, it may be too laborious to check out every move, word, and gesture: The therapist would be educated about the client, but therapy might grind to a halt. Phenomenology provides us with a wonderful opportunity to inquire, not interpret, and to describe and let be described. However, we need to be aware that at times we may still be interpreting and that sometimes questions, for example, about what a certain gesture might mean may take away from what the client wants to work on. In this case, the focus could be for the benefit of the therapist, rather than the client.

Paradoxical Theory of Change

> *In the process of wending my way through contextualising my whiteness, my interest in "culture" has expanded, and I feel some excitement at the possibility of working with people of other cultures and ethnic groups. This is a confirmation, once again, of the paradoxical theory of change. By staying with my experience as it evolved, twisted, turned, by not throwing anything away, I end up changed, and to my delight more open to, and inclusive of, otherness. (Jacobs, 2000a, p. 13)*

The paradoxical theory of change suggests that it is only when we "give up trying or struggling to be what we would like to become, only once we fully become who we are, [that] change will occur" (Mackewn, 1997, p. 63). If the paradoxical theory of change is applied to working on the color and culture boundary, then for change to occur we must uncover, become aware of, and sit with the feelings, assumptions, and preconceived ideas discussed in the previous section rather than pushing them aside because they may be disconcerting.

Jacobs (2000a) and Doerschel (1993) shared their stories about staying with their experience and ending up changed with regard to cross-cultural work. Cross-cultural encounters, by bringing up uncomfortable issues, can spur therapists to distance themselves from their own experience. Therapists may feel anxious out of a sense of indebtedness to the Other or uncertainty of what may emerge if they "stay with" the experience. Of course, they may also feel excitement, exhilaration, curiosity, and blessedness to be working across cultures, all of which may also induce anxiety. Therapists may feel "uneasy in intercultural interactions because, unlike many of our other meetings, they are not routine and predictable. We cannot fall back on habitual ways of thinking and behaving, not, at least, if we are going to be genuinely tuned in to the conversation" (Putnis & Petelin, 1996, p. 77).

Jacobs (2000a) openly shared the challenges she faced in working cross-culturally in her therapy practice. She described her heightened concern about her professional competence when working with a person from a different cultural background, in particular when working with black clients. She called this *white anxiety.* She also wondered how white people come to terms with being compliant with the broader context of society, which oppresses Others but not them, calling this *white guilt.* She pointed out that white therapists, when confronted with a less privileged person, may feel what she called *white shame,* or feelings of guilt because of their privileges. Jacobs's therapeutic process involves openly discussing race and racism with her clients. She relies on the paradoxical theory of change to understand her own processes and values in staying with feelings, including those she discovers in her journeys through uncovering white identity markers.

WHITENESS

> *I have always thought of race as something belonging to persons of colour, defined by differences between us. (Carter, 1997, p. 198)*
>
> *A recurrent finding in the study of whiteness is the fact that white respondents do not consider their "whiteness" as an identity or a marker of group membership per se. That is, whiteness is a "natural" identity because it has not been problematic and therefore salient to most respondents in these studies. In fact, most white respondents are hard-pressed to define whiteness and the privileges that it brings to those who own it. (Hurtado & Stewart, 1997, p. 298)*

Whiteness studies have numerous implications for Gestalt practitioners (and really any white helping professionals). Examples in previous sections have illustrated how writers such as Jacobs, McConville, and Jarosewitsch have used Gestalt theory when exploring not only cross-cultural work but also the necessity of investigating one's own cultural self.

Within most First World nations, whiteness in general is not recognized as a marker of an "ethnic" or "racial" group. People who vary from the dominant "white" are generally referred to as "the Other" or "the culturally different" (Dominelli, 2002; Frankenberg, 1993; Hage, 1998; hooks, 1995; Hurtado & Stewart, 1997; McIntosh, 1998). There are many examples of this phenomenon: One is that Band-aids and pantyhose are called skin color when really they are designed for white people. Dyer (cited in hooks, 1995, p. 36) observed that although white light is generally associated with safety whereas darkness is associated with danger, one could just as readily see it the other way because darkness can provide cover and lightness exposure. People are socialized into a division of whiteness representing goodness and blackness evil. One need only think of examples such as blackmail, black magic, and white magic or little white lies to realize how these terms are "colored."

Some researchers are content to use the term *whiteness* to claim that white people are an ethnic group (Apple, 1997). Others, such as Frankenberg (1993), have suggested that one must address the privilege that accrues to people who have white skin rather than simplistically focus on skin color as a marker of ethnic difference. Her work has opened up significant new lines of inquiry in the investigation of structural privilege. Informed by feminist and cultural theories, it shows how white women's lives are shaped by race and whiteness. She argued that "white stands for the position of 'neutrality,' or the racially unmarked category" (p. 55). Her research indicates that "whiteness lacks form and content" (p. 199), as shown by many white people's lack of clarity in being able to describe their own culture.

Hurtado and Stewart (1997, p. 299), like Frankenberg (1993), found that whiteness is considered not as an "identity or marker" but rather as "natural." They argued that privilege attached to whiteness (or cultural dominance) goes widely unquestioned. McIntosh, in her influential work *White Privilege and Male Privilege: A Personal Account of Coming to See Correspondences Through Work in Women's Studies* (1998), also addressed these issues. In analyzing her own cultural privilege, she offered a list of 46 privileges that she claimed are attached to being white and heterosexual, stating, "whites are carefully taught not to recognize white privilege, as males are taught not to recognize male privilege" (p. 1). She warned against the assimilationist approach of trying to get other people to become more like the dominant class. Rather, she took the approach that one has to start with oneself to investigate the privilege associated with one's color and status. She asserted that simply recognizing one's privilege is not enough; the next step is to consider what therapists might best do with this newly acquired knowledge.

Like McConville (1997) and Thomas (1997), both Frankenberg (1993) and McIntosh (1998) concluded that one needs to become aware of oneself before being able to change. Even though Gestalt theories have not, as yet, focused on the privilege of whiteness per se in the dialogic encounter, the paradoxical theory of change seems well supported within this broad field of inquiry into white privilege. A growing number of theorists and writers have advocated investigating the phenomenon of whiteness instead of focusing on Otherness (see, e.g., Dominelli, 2002; Frankenberg, 1993; hooks, 1995; Jacobs, 2000a; McConville, 1997; McIntosh, 1998; Thomas, 1997). Gestalt therapy, with its focus on practitioners' awareness and its underlying theories, provides rich possibilities for the practitioner to engage in such self-exploration.

CROSS-CULTURAL COMMUNICATION

> *Unless we are culturally self aware, we may fall into the trap of assuming that particular communicative behaviour (usually our own) is universal and so be blind to cultural differences. We may also fall into the trap of assuming that our way of seeing a problem or understanding a situation is the obvious "logical" one and must surely be shared by everyone else. (Putnis & Petelin, 1996, p. 61)*

The application of Gestalt theory to any work between practitioner and client involves verbal and nonverbal communication. Verbal and nonverbal expression in English, or via an interpreter/translator, includes normative behavior and culturally learned rules. Like normative beliefs and ways of seeing the world, communication is grounded in culture. Sue and Sue (1990) found in their research that "for effective counseling to occur, both the counselor and client must be able to *send* and *receive* both *verbal* and *nonverbal* messages *accurately* and *appropriately*" (p. 51, italics in original). Therefore, it is important to understand the *content* as well as *how* something is said, remembering that as much of the message is in the medium as in the content. Gestalt, with its encouragement of inquiry rather than interpretation, provides the opportunity to explore different meanings of nonverbal communication. It is also critical for all helping professionals to investigate their preconceived ideas about what others' nonverbal behavior means and what it evokes in them. The therapist may be sitting with feelings that are difficult to process, and direct questioning of the client is not always possible.

According to Sue and Sue (1990), nonverbal communication has three major components: (a) *proxemics,* which refers to personal and interpersonal space; (b) *kinesics,* which refers to body movements and includes facial expressions, posture, eye contact, and characteristics of movement and gestures; and (c) *paralanguage,* which refers to vocal cues, such as loudness of voice, pauses, silences, and hesitation. How much distance people need or want, how close they stand, how loudly or softly they talk, and the permissibility of touch are very much grounded in cultural norms. Of course, there are additional reasons why people use or prefer certain ways of nonverbal communication.

Participants in nonverbal exercises that my colleagues and I conducted (see the five experiential activities described in this chapter's second dialogue box) demonstrated that, in general, people can have difficulties if a nonverbal communication style differs sharply from their own style. In my master's thesis research, participants found it challenging when the other person did not keep eye contact with them. Participants reported being worried about what might be going on for the other person. Without eye contact, some thought that the other person was not interested in what they had to say and wondered if they were making sense. Participants reported that these were familiar feelings that they had experienced before when confronted with similar situations beyond the artificial situation of the experimental exercise. They spoke of a "lack of connection when contact was made differently from their expectation" and stated that they were "leaving their comfort zone when contact was made that was unfamiliar to them" (Fernbacher, 2002, p. 61). Literature on cross-cultural communication confirms these findings (Pedersen, 1997; Putnis & Petelin, 1996; Sue & Sue, 1990).

D'Ardenne and Mahtani (1998) argued that counselors who work with people who have different ways of conducting nonverbal communication need to "adjust their own gaze accordingly to establish non-verbal congruence" (p. 2). Obviously practitioners would find it useful to recognize their own nonverbal behavior and to uncover its values and meaning. It can be a difficult and challenging process to uncover behavior that has previously been taken for granted and never questioned.

One way of making sense of what may happen when people from different cultures interact is the concept of *culture shock* (Pedersen, 1997; Ward, Bochner, & Furnham, 2001). Pedersen sees culture shock as an "anxiety resulting from losing one's sense of when and how to do the right thing" (p. 54). The person experiencing culture shock becomes uncertain about the rules and what specific behaviors may mean. Even though this concept is usually applied to situations such as migration, it has also been useful for understanding uncertainties about new situations in which people find themselves. The unfamiliarity of another person's (e.g., the client's) behavior can be so great that the therapist becomes uncertain and unsure of the meaning of the nonverbal behavior. Wondering or worrying about a client's nonverbal cues or communication style distracts the therapist's attention. At best, we may overcome our uncertainty by checking out the meaning clients give to their nonverbal communication and by sharing whatever feeling they have with regard to our inquiry.

In summary, it is necessary to examine our preferred nonverbal communication style in order to discover its meaning. Furthermore, it is important to learn about the meanings that people from other cultures give their nonverbal behavior, while refraining from oversimplification or stereotyping. Rather than relying on schemas or stereotypes about other people's nonverbal communication styles, it is important to be aware of the impact our clients' nonverbals have on us, the therapists. With this awareness, we can hope to grow more flexible in our own behavior as well as the interpretation of others' behaviors.

CONCLUSION

> *It is not the therapist's theoretical orientation that is as crucial in the healing process as is the wholeness and availability of the self of the therapist. Only then can there be a meeting of self and self. In that meeting, wholeness is engendered in the client, which was absent before this meeting. (Hycner, 1991, pp. 12–13)*

If the wholeness of the Gestalt therapist is the ground that gives rise to the opportunity of wholeness for the client, this wholeness needs to include an awareness of the cultural and colored ground, the cultural self of the therapist, and the dominant culture. Gestalt theory and its various applications contribute to and are encapsulated in the dialogic relationship. The broader field in its cultural sense is the landscape of societal structure. This field is colored by dominance and marginalization, belonging and not belonging. Hierarchies of difference are just some of the field conditions present between therapist and client in the dialogic relationship.

DEBORAH: Thank you, Sabin, for the opportunity to engage in this dialogue. I appreciate the freshness of your approach to cultural concerns for Gestalt therapists.

To undertake work across cultures from a Gestalt perspective, it is essential that we explore our own cultural selves. What are we influenced by? What are we aware of? What is hidden but nevertheless present? Which of our behaviors are culture bound? Given Gestalt's aim to be aware, to support people in making authentic contact, and to grow with and from awareness, it is essential that we acknowledge and fathom the importance of culture in relationships by welcoming the challenge of difference and investigating our assumptions and ways of relating—especially if we belong to the dominant cultural group. To make contact and encourage contact in and with others, we need to know about ourselves.

REVIEW QUESTIONS

1. Define the word *culture.* In what way is culture a factor in the Gestalt therapeutic process?

2. Field theory is applicable to cultural experiences within the context of Gestalt therapy. How is field theory a useful construct for Gestalt therapy practitioners?

3. How do phenomenology and the phenomenological method influence the Gestalt therapeutic approach?

4. How is the paradoxical theory of change useful for Gestalt practitioners when they are exploring their own awarenesses about ethnicity?

5. What other cultural communications between the Gestalt therapist and client may come into the session besides verbal communications?

EXPERIENTIAL PEDAGOGICAL ACTIVITIES

ACTIVITIES 1–5: The chapter author has included five experiential activities in this chapter's second dialogue box. Please refer back to that box and experiment with her suggested activities if you have not already done so.

ACTIVITY 6: Visit the Web address www.Department.bucknell.edu/rescolleges/socjust/Readings/McIntosh.html to read Peggy McIntosh's (1998) piece on white privilege and male privilege. Regardless of your race or gender, identify areas in your own life where you believe you possess privilege. In small groups, compare and contrast the privileges that each group member identified.

ACTIVITY 7: Construct a family tree of your own family going back several generations. For each relative, identify his or her degree of understanding of cultural/ethnic difference. Look for patterns across generations, genders, and/or sides of the family. Can you identify any changes across generations?

CHAPTER 8

Gestalt Therapy and Spirituality

R. ELLIOTT INGERSOLL

DIALOGUE RESPONDENT: BRIAN O'NEILL

R. Elliott Ingersoll is a professor of counselor education and department chairman at Cleveland State University, having been mentored in Gestalt therapy by Ansel Woldt. He was a charter member of the Kent Gestalt Writers' Group. His doctoral research focused on spiritual well-being, and he has numerous publications in that realm. He is coauthor of four major textbooks: *Explorations in Counseling and Spirituality: Philosophical, Practical, and Personal Reflections* (2001), *The Mental Health Desk Reference: A Sourcebook for Counselors* (2001), *Becoming a 21st Century Agency Counselor* (2001), and *Psychopharmacology for Helping Professionals: An Integral Approach* (2004).

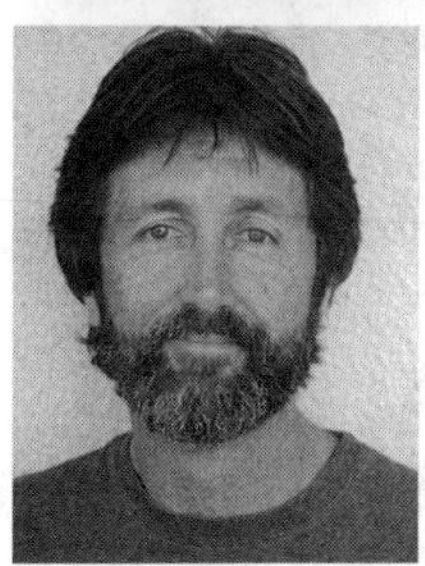

Brian O'Neill is the founder, co-director, and head of training of the Illawarra Gestalt Centre in New South Wales and the South Australian Gestalt Training Institute. He is a senior fellow in mental health at the University of Wollongong and part-time faculty in their College of Counselling Psychologists. As chair of the directors of Gestalt therapy training for Australia/New Zealand and as a registered psychologist with over 25 years' experience, he has been actively involved in policy making for counselors and psychotherapists. He assumed the presidency of the Association for the Advancement of Gestalt Therapy for 2004–2006, and is a board member of Gestalt Global, and an editorial board member of the *Gestalt Review.* He founded the *Australia Gestalt Journal* and was the founding editor of the *Gestalt Therapy Forum* (New York).

No paradise of the East,
No paradise of the West—
Seek along the way you have come.
They are all within you. (Sohl & Carr, 1970, p. 51)

This chapter addresses various aspects of spirituality and Gestalt therapy. The first part of the chapter provides some understandings of spirituality in the context of counseling and psychotherapy and then summarizes one approach to compare Gestalt therapy and spirituality. The second part contains general approaches utilized in Gestalt therapy and esoteric spiritual practices. The chapter ends with a discussion of translation versus transformation in both Gestalt and spiritual practices. Like the work of Kennedy (1998) on Gestalt spirituality, this chapter grows out of the awareness that spirituality and Gestalt therapy, more than parts of a life, can both be ways of life. I am hoping the chapter will offer you, the reader, a challenging way to understand spirituality as well as some guidelines on how to explore your own spirituality with Gestalt processes and methods.

THE PROBLEM OF DEFINING SPIRITUALITY

Some readers may wonder if trying to represent spirituality with words (and Gestalt therapy for that matter!) is an absurd undertaking. I share their wonderment but am still drawn to anything that induces wonder—so here goes. A decade ago, I wrote that spirituality could be described but not defined (Ingersoll, 1994). How can one define as a construct what is the apex of human development and one of the most meaningful lines of human development? Perhaps the only way to do it is to place the subject of spirituality like a living specimen in an academic killing jar (a peer-reviewed journal), where, under the necessary influence of caffeine, students ponder its corpse and imagine they have grasped its essence.[1] I believe there is a better way, though.

Over a decade ago, the senior editor of this book, Ansel Woldt, and I noted that there are two ways to use language to operationalize constructs (Woldt & Ingersoll, 1991). Drawing on the Taoist Tai Ji symbol of yin/yang, we noted that there are "yang" descriptions that seek to operationalize constructs and "yin" descriptions that seek to immerse the reader in an experience that may convey a meaning deeper than words. "Yin" language is what Taylor (1997) and Wilber (1995) have called the language of subjective or interior experience, having much in common with Fritz Perls's conceptualization of awareness. This is the dominant language of Gestalt therapy and spiritual experience, but unfortunately, as Taylor pointed out, such language does not have credibility in modern culture. Despite this, we have seen a slow increase of spiritual constructs in counseling and psychotherapy in the past 10 years, and although these constructs tend toward the "yang" or positivistic, there is an increasing presence of "yin" descriptions. The Gestalt construct of awareness incorporates much of the "yin" of human experience in contrast to the current "CBT" (cognitive behavioral therapy), which relies heavily on "yang" experiences. The following oft-quoted statement of Perls depicts some of these "yin" elements that are in some ways descriptive of the essence of spiritual experience:

> Awareness is the spontaneous sensing of what arises in you—of what you are doing, feeling, planning; introspection, in contrast, is a deliberate turning of attention to these activities in

> an evaluating, correcting, controlling, interfering way; which often, by the very attention paid them, modifies or prevents their appearance in awareness. . . . Awareness is like the glow of a coal which comes from its own combustion; what is given by introspection is like the light reflected from an object when a flashlight is turned on it. In awareness a process is taking place in the coal (the total organism); in introspection the process occurs in the director of the flashlight (a split-off and highly opinionated *part* of the organism which we shall call the deliberate ego). (Perls, Hefferline, & Goodman, 1951, p. 31, italics in original)

To begin, I would like to summarize some of what has been said about spirituality in the context of counseling and psychotherapy. The reader will notice that I do not make any assumptions about what is referred to as "God." I do maintain that whether one uses the image of "God," "Goddess," or "great Void," this must be affirmed in one's experience. Belief is certainly part of spirituality, but beliefs that have not been confirmed in experience remain only beliefs. Further, evidence from Western and Eastern mystical traditions indicates that when a person progressively experiences the Divine (whether "God," "Goddess," or "Void"), the experience and image of the Divine frequently evolve and change. This issue is also addressed in the dialogue boxes with Brian.

As noted, the problem of describing spirituality has not been solved. Even when it includes powerful experiences with a Divine Being, it does not lend itself to operational definitions or "yang" language. This may explain why most attempts to describe it occur in books and not peer-reviewed journal articles. I recommend the following sources to the curious reader as noble efforts to "get the ball rolling." West (2000) admitted the continued difficulty of defining spirituality, and Wiggins-Frame (2003) noted that trying to capture the concept is almost antithetical to the idea itself. She offered a general conclusion that spirituality is concerned with meaning, purpose, and value in life and may or may not include a "higher" power. Sperry (2001) offered a similar description stating that spirituality is focused on one's search for meaning, belonging, and the core values that influence one's behavior. He added the notions of interconnectedness, self-transcendence, and integrity. I (Ingersoll, 1994) claimed (echoing the transpersonal psychologist Frances Vaughan, 1995) that spirituality must be endemic to all human beings and must serve as the animating force of life. Miller (2003) followed this up by describing spirit as an animating life force and spirituality as the drawing out and infusion of spirit in one's life. Though I (Ingersoll, 1994, 1998) and others (e.g., Ellison & Paloutzian, 1982; Moberg, 1971) have stated that spirituality can be broken down into more measurable components of spiritual wellness, this has not resolved the essential dilemma of using words to describe that which transcends words.

A SOLUTION

The philosopher Ken Wilber has treated this topic most comprehensively and admits to the difficulty of capturing spirituality with words. His work has sought to unite orienting generalizations from diverse perspectives and disciplines; however, spirituality has always been a primary theme in his writings. Wilber described spirituality as a line of development and a level of development. Though acknowledging the difficulty of defining spirituality as a line of development, he wrote that it is the trans-ego or transpersonal levels ("post-postconventional" levels in developmental language) of any line of development (Wilber, 1997). At this point he "[threw] his hat in the ring" with theologian Paul Tillich, agreeing that the spiritual line of development, whatever else it may be, is "that line of development in which the subject holds its ultimate concern" (Wilber, 1997, p. 221). When we conceptualize spirituality as a line of development, it becomes easier to understand how images of and experiences with the Divine ("God," "Goddess," or "Void") could evolve.

In an effort to avoid the problem of relying solely on words, Wilber (1998) developed a set of steps that, though not defining spirituality, help us at least reproduce the experiences that others are saying are "spiritual." These steps also work in exploring Gestalt therapy and provide a natural intersection between Gestalt and spirituality. Wilber (1997) seems to believe that it is far more productive to rely on experiences than to squabble over whose words to use to label and point to those experiences. For what it's worth, I agree with him, and this is why I do not emphasize particular images of "God" in my work. Drawing on the scientific method, Wilber distilled the following three steps of scientific inquiry, stating that they work as well in assessing and confirming spiritual experience as they do in laboratory experiments. I believe these steps are also followed in the Gestalt process.

1. *The Instrumental Injunction:* This is a practice or experiment stated in the form of "If you want to find out this, do this." For example, if you believe in a particular manifestation of the Divine, you are instructed as to how to make contact with the "God," "Goddess," or "Void," depending on the tradition.
2. *Direct Apprehension:* This is an immediate experience resulting from engaging the injunction. This immediate experience becomes the data, whether one is looking through a microscope, meditating, or engaging in an "empty chair" technique. This is where people have the experience of a Supreme Being, whether "God," "Goddess," or some variation of these two.
3. *Communal Confirmation:* This is checking the results of those who have completed the instrumental injunction and experienced the direct apprehension. For example, a Christian who has had a powerful experience of Jesus compares this with the experiences of her spiritual director or others in her faith. Equally, a Wiccan who has had a powerful experience of the Goddess compares it with the experiences of others in her coven.

As noted, I think this is enough said. Here is an epistemological structure compatible with both Gestalt and spirituality. If you want to find out if your ego really exists, then meditate, record your experience, and compare it with the experiences of a community of other meditators. If you want to find out how to be more contactful, engage the Gestalt experiment, record your experience, and compare it to the experiences of others practicing Gestalt. This solution allows for incorporating the language of subjective experience ("yin" language) while also comparing it in an objective ("yang") manner with the experiences of others.

BEING A BIT MORE PRECISE—SPIRITUALITY

So at this point we have a three-step method to record experiences and compare them with similar experiences had by others. As stated, this method can be used to explore both Gestalt and spiritual experience. Astute readers will here point out that I have "ducked" the problem of saying what spirituality is, so I must be more precise. I just wrote "experiences." Experiences, the second component of Wilber's steps, are the elements by which we may compare Gestalt and spirituality. To make this comparison, I must write more precisely about common "injunctions" used in spiritual practice that lead to these experiences. Toward this end, we must distinguish exoteric and esoteric spirituality.

Every spiritual path has exoteric and esoteric aspects. The exoteric aspects involve the external forms, creeds, rituals, and dogmas generally related to religions and religious practices. This is where one frequently finds particular images of Divinity emphasized. Although not much has been published in Gestalt journals on exoteric spirituality, numerous doctoral dissertations have explored this area, including Walker (1970), Richardson (1976), Plummer (1986), and Killoran (1993).

The esoteric aspects of spirituality are those practices designed to give the aspirant a direct encounter with the Divine, or, in this case, that serve as the injunctions designed to bring about particular experiences (Smith, 1976). Here the experience may confirm the image of God, Goddess, or Void emphasized in the tradition, or it may depart substantially from what the person expected. It is these esoteric aspects of spirituality that I find most relevant from a Gestalt perspective. The esoteric traditions range from Eastern Hindu, Buddhist, and Taoist practices to Western contemplation. For the sake of narrative flow in this chapter, I will refer to these esoteric practices simply as "spiritual practices." These practices are found in what Huxley (1945) called the perennial philosophy, his term for the common ground of all spiritual traditions. Wolfert (2002) has pointed out that Gestalt shares the central elements of this philosophy. These elements are basically the practices (injunctions) that lead to an experience (direct apprehension) of transcending one's sense of individuality that may then be compared with the experiences of others (communal confirmation).

GESTALT

Recall that a gestalt is a form, configuration, or totality that, as a unified whole, has properties that cannot be derived by summation from the parts

BRIAN: As I read your chapter, Elliott, several thoughts and feelings are figural. I am reminded of the notion that a person's bookshelf will say a lot about him—what he's read and what areas he's covered—and that the books beside his bed tell more of what is current and present. As such I am interested in the common areas we share in the topic of Gestalt therapy and spirituality and the authors you reference and the notions about these topics that you share with me, the reader.

At times, I am excited to find you've read books that are less well known and feel a warmth when I find authors I enjoy mentioned and listed in the bibliography—it's like we have the same friends and acquaintances. At other times you mention authors that I do not enjoy, and I feel less connected to the writing and you. I also notice authors are missing for me whom I'd wish to be present in your chapter, and I get excited at the thought of bringing these friends into our conversation.

ELLIOTT: I have written a great deal in different venues. I guess I can't cite every influence on me in a short chapter—perhaps another book somewhere along the line. I can share some influences in our dialogue here. I have actually been away from clinical practice and much Gestalt work since I took an administrative job about 4 years ago. To complete this chapter I had to call up the ways I thought about things 4 years back when I worked with my client Frank. This left me a bit more focused on the traditions I was studying then—different forms of Buddhism in particular.

BRIAN: Alongside this walk along your "bookcase," I begin to be touched by the themes you develop and consider them both with my head and with my heart. My heart is warmed as I read how you present a humble perspective of yourself and your writing without being self-deprecating. I hear you accept the challenge to write and translate that which

(English & English, 1958). Any gestalt cannot be defined simply in terms of summation of its perceived parts because it is supple and flowing, so that the relationships between the parts and the environment constantly change. In this sense, spirit and spirituality start to sound suspiciously like gestalts. With the formation of any gestalt, one is faced with the same problem of representation that we faced in trying to represent spirit with fixed, linear symbols.

is transformative, and I like your use of these terms. They remind me of Roberto Assagioli's distinction between the two types of religion—religion that is a direct experience of spirituality and a second type [that] is the organizations that develop around these experiences.

I recall a client I worked with shortly after becoming licensed, whom I will refer to as Frank. Frank's presenting problem was a feeling of staleness, a feeling of being what he called "the walking dead." Certainly he showed many symptoms of depression, but his chief problem was a fear of engaging (making contact with) the opportunities to live that presented themselves to him regularly. Figures of opportunity (to sing in a choir, for example) would emerge from the ground of Frank's daily life, and he would deflect them for fear of not having enough time to do the work he was paid for, but for which he could not have cared less. Again, Frank's problems were not merely in the symptoms that plagued him daily but in the disrupted cycle of contact that occurred every time he shied away from another opportunity to make his life more interesting and worth living.

BRIAN: As I read I find myself moving into the translation of the material (the work of the head to understand what you are writing about), and then I am brought back to the heart of what you are saying (the work you see with Frank, the courageous struggle to live and manifest ourselves as human beings, to experience and share these experiences of the connection of self and another in equal form beyond the roles yet aided by them).

What to do? Why not just refer him for an antidepressant and be done with it? That would have been an appropriate mirroring of his deflection but would not have solved the problem. In this case, when Frank asked me if I thought he was depressed, I said "no" and told him I thought he suffered from a spiritual problem. His problem was that he was deflecting contact with the very things that, for him, were the animating force of life. I noted that I felt that spirit was the animating force in life and that his problem was a spiritual one. That caught his attention. Notice that I had no need to direct Frank to a particular image of the Divine. My belief is that if clients have an image of the Divine they prefer, they will work with it. If they do not, one may emerge.

We worked with Wilber's three steps. If he wanted to feel alive, he needed to engage (or at least put himself in contact with) those things that were life giving. Once he relearned how to do this, he had an experience—an apprehension. Frank returned the interests of a female co-worker and began spending more time with her and less time working overtime at his job. The results: He reported making less money and fearing the woman would break off the relationship, but he said he felt better—we were getting somewhere. Though there was quite a bit of work left to do, he was able to identify what "turned him on," so to speak, and move toward that while giving less attention to those things that were not terribly life giving. The reader may say, "So what?" The point here is simple and requires neither constructs nor a PhD to make sense of it. When a client tells you he or she feels dead, there is a spiritual problem. Though there was more to treatment than this summary, I will allude back to Frank's case throughout the rest of the chapter, where I will explore how trust in nature, the here-and-now orientation, direct pointing, and transcending of polarities are shared by Gestalt therapy and spiritual practices.

TRUST IN NATURE

Both Gestalt and spiritual practices exhibit a trust in nature and express it in a trust of the organism of the person and a reverence for that organism's natural processes. Watts (1957) noted that this attitude is basic to Eastern spiritual practices. He added that from that standpoint mistrust of nature seems pathological. Here is a dilemma. Though Frank presented with symptoms of depression, the construct of depression was too impoverished to explain his situation. A clinician who mistrusted nature (and the client in this case) would assume that poor Frank had some undefined chemical imbalance in his central nervous system and that the best thing to do would be to load him full of expensive drugs that no one really understood. Not this time. A client whose symptoms are primarily vegetative may be a good candidate for an antidepressant, but Frank was not such a client. His symptoms were atypical (feeling "numb," feeling "dead," diagnostically referred to as anhedonia, complicated by an acute awareness that he might in some way be responsible for it).

Gestalt's trust in nature focuses on human nature and is illustrated in the concept of organismic self-regulation. Latner (1973) defined self-regulation as organisms doing their best to regulate themselves given their own capabilities and the resources in their environment. This is a far cry from psychopharmacological solutions to problems. Organismic self-regulation is related to Gestalt's foundation in holism. Like Lewin's (1951) field theory, holism suggests that people cannot be viewed except in relationship to their environmental field (Cartwright, 1951; Clarkson, 1989). Understanding this as a starting point, Gestalt, like many spiritual practices, encourages the individual to focus awareness on the processes occurring in each present moment and to trust these processes as they occur. This was certainly important with Frank—I had to trust he could still recognize when he felt "turned on."

Two basic questions about life that propel one into a spiritual path are "Is life basically safe?" and "Can it be trusted?" In the spiritual path, these questions must be lived in the context of practices that help the aspirant discern the truth of the situation. This search for truth must engage us with the experience of life, including other people. If, in trying to answer the question "Is life safe?" one is tied to "yang" language, it is unlikely that life will appear safe or even worth going through. The brutality of nature, acts of inhumanity, and the incredible amount of human suffering will make it appear (as Jung once quipped) that life is a terminal condition with the poorest of prognoses. Frank had certainly frightened himself into this posture. He believed that one could never overplan for the future and that money equaled security. He did not, however, continue his logic to question whether security purchased with money was the only kind worth having.

A prime example of Gestalt's trust in nature is illustrated therapeutically in the Gestalt experiment. In the "experiment," clients are encouraged to increase self-awareness through enactment, directed behavior, fantasy, dreams, and homework (Polster & Polster, 1973). It is felt that the individual engaging in the experiment has the necessary elements to enhance his or her life experience and that these elements will spontaneously emerge if the environment is safe. To paraphrase Fritz Perls, Gestalt therapy allows for the safe emergency in the therapeutic situation. Clearly, safety relates to trust. For example, if you do not trust life, life will not feel safe—ask Frank. He actually said that in one session. We engaged in an experiment (of the "topdog/underdog" sort), and he had an apprehension that his (then current) brand of safety was stifling. Further, he realized that if he could not trust life, he could not trust the products of life, ergo he could not trust himself. What a pickle. No wonder he assumed I would refer him to an expert for an antidepressant. What else can someone who does not trust him- or herself do? Go to an expert, of course.

So often we are trained away from trusting life, and many Gestalt therapeutic and spiritual practices are spent "unlearning" this training. Therefore, the first injunction in Gestalt or spiritual practice is to either act as if life is ultimately safe or act as if it ultimately does not matter. Although these initial injunctions must be taken as leaps of faith, they are followed with injunctions that allow the full experience of life to emerge. With Frank we decided that because he already felt dead, things could not get too much worse, so he might want to "try on" an attitude of trust to at least engage with the therapy for a few sessions. This is in keeping with Perls's sage advice to therapists in the original text:

> We propose as the structure of the interview: to excite a safe emergency by concentrating on the actual situation. . . . As the contact becomes closer and the content becomes fuller, his anxiety is aroused. This constitutes a felt emergency, but the emergency is safe and controllable and known to be so by both partners. . . . The goal is that in the safe emergency, the underlying (repressed) intention—action, attitude, present-day object, memory—will become dominant and re-form the figure. . . . The patient accepts the new figure as his own, feeling that "it is I who am feeling, thinking, doing this." (Perls, Hefferline, & Goodman, 1994, p. 64)

"Here-and-Now" Orientation

Where does the full experience of life emerge? Gestalt and spiritual practices will state flatly that it emerges in the "here and now." Wolfert (2002) noted that the basic experiment in Gestalt therapy is attending to awareness moment by moment and derives from the Buddhist practices of mindfulness. According to Latner (1973),

> [W]hile we cannot help but live in the present, we all know it is possible for us to direct most for our attention away from it. . . . It is impossible to overemphasize the importance of the awareness of the present in Gestalt therapy. To be in the present, "in the now," brings into being all other aspects of healthy functioning. (p. 61)

In searching for the answer to the question "Is life safe?" our willingness to participate in present-centered awareness is related to our health or "dis-ease." In Gestalt and spiritual practice, disease is strongly related to our ability to dissociate from the present, and many of the injunctions of Gestalt and spiritual practice are designed to bring us back to the present. Take, for example, Frank, who had decided life was unsafe. He was constantly vigilant, on the lookout for potential threats. In his vigilance, he was constantly removing himself one step from what was going on to attend to his increasingly paranoid intrapsychic dialogue.

THE EGO MIND AND THE HERE AND NOW

A common way to distract ourselves from the present is to focus on our egos. This results in the odd sensation that we are subjects separate from objects that we observe and interact with.

Although in Gestalt this is a disruption in the cycle of contact, in spiritual practices it may be a symptom of overidentification with the ego mind (Brannigan, 1988). Ego mind is a trick of consciousness that when sought mysteriously becomes that which is doing the seeking (Powell, 2000; Wilber, 1999). In Zen it is said that trying to find the ego mind is like beating a drum in search of a fugitive. The very desire to find or destroy one's ego mind is so rooted in ego mind that the one attempting to get rid of ego gets more stuck with it. One is truly like a bird flying in search of air. If, on the other hand, one is able to fully enter into the present moment, the experience of ego mind disperses like fog in sunlight.

According to Huxley's (1945) perennial philosophy, the experience of "ego mind" is a mirror of "God" playing an eternal game of "hide-and-seek" with her- or himself. The "hide" portion of the game is the identification with concrete, apparently separate forms (people, rocks, trees, etc.), and the "seek" portion of the game is the search and discovery that all these forms are intimately connected expressions of the "dis-membered" self that "hid" or "forgot" itself (Watts, 1966). Metaphysically speaking, the latter discovery that *YOU ARE IT* is enlightenment, satori, nirvana, Buddhahood, *moksha,* salvation, Christ consciousness, and an awareness in and of the here and now. In spiritual practice and Gestalt, the awareness is transpersonal, meaning beyond the personal or beyond ego (Naranjo, 1978).

Gestalt recognizes that an existential dilemma for people is the proclivity of "ego mind" consciousness to become hypnotized by memories of a past and anticipations of a future (Brannigan, 1988; Perls, 1969b). In Polster and Polster's (1973) description of the Gestalt framework addressing this hypnosis, "[G]estalt therapy recognizes the acts of remembering and planning as present functions even though they refer to a past and a future" (p. 7). It is in memory and anticipation that we see in individuals a microcosm of the game of "cosmic hide-and-seek." In this sense, any organism can produce a state of self-alienation inasmuch as she associates herself with memories or forms an identity from anticipation as experienced through cognition. The self-alienation is akin to the above example of "self in hiding," the dis-membered self or the ignoring of the self/environment field as they interact in each unfolding moment. The interaction that occurs in every "here and now" is "re-membered" in the therapeutic process as clients are guided to include the forgotten awareness of the present in their experience. As clients allow present-centered awareness to blossom in therapy, they are allowing the "re-membering" of "self" forgotten or "dismembered." Thus, in spiritual practice and Gestalt therapy, the injunction to dwell in the here and now can lead to the apprehension of oneness that unifies the self with consciousness at large and shows the separate, threatened ego to be just an illusion. All well and good, but how do we direct ourselves (and our clients) to the here and now?

THE USE OF DIRECT POINTING

In Gestalt therapy and spiritual practice, the client is guided in the experience of self-discovery in the here and now by the technique of direct pointing. Brunink (1976) revealed a number of interesting findings that relate to direct pointing. Chief among these was that Gestalt therapists used significantly more directed interventions than either psychoanalysts or behaviorists. Gestalt therapists also used significantly more initiative in conducting therapy and made significantly more self-disclosures than the others.

For the purposes of this discussion, a correlation will be shown between the use of direct pointing in Gestalt and Zen, as the latter stands out among spiritual practices in its use of direct pointing. Watts (1957) stated that the "special flavor" of Zen is in its directness. Other Buddhist disciplines allude to "awakening" as something almost beyond the grasp of the ordinary individual. But in Zen, Watts noted that there is the feeling that "awakening" is natural and could occur at any moment. "Direct pointing ('chih-chih' in Chinese) is the open demonstration of Zen by non-symbolic actions or words" (Watts, 1957, p. 77) and usually appears to the novice to be related to the most ordinary of everyday affairs or to be completely crazy.

Zen and Gestalt share a history much richer in "doing" than in writing. It is a tenet of both disciplines that the written word should not be set up as a deity to be worshipped; rather, individuals must, through their experience, come to their own understandings. Watts (1936) stated that in Zen, scriptures or doctrines are to be viewed only as aids; Zen masters liken them to "a finger pointing at the moon . . . and he is a fool who takes the finger for the moon" (p. 50). Equally, Gestalt is "a psychological approach based on a philosophy which works away from concepts and towards pure awareness" (Clarkson, 1989, p. 3). Levitsky and Perls (quoted in Fagan & Shepherd, 1970) reminded us that rules in Gestalt therapy are

> not intended as a dogmatic list of do's and don'ts; rather they are offered in the spirit of experiments that the patient may perform. . . . When the intention of the rules is truly appreciated, they will be understood in their inner meaning and not in their literal sense. (p. 140)

In a Zen story,

> Master Po Chang once set a pitcher before two of his disciples, saying, "Do not call it a pitcher, but tell me what it is." One of them answered, "It cannot be called a piece of wood." But Po Chang considered this answer beside the point, whereupon he asked the other the same question, and in reply he came forward, pushed the pitcher over and walked away. As a result Po Chang appointed this disciple his successor. (Watts, 1957, p. 55)

We see similar stories in Gestalt. During a seminar, a woman asked Fritz Perls what he meant by differentiating words from actions. In response, he left the podium, went to the woman's seat, and kissed her (Perls, 1969c, p. 22).

In these two passages, we can see the present-centered dynamic woven into the technique of direct pointing. Watts (1936) discussed this dynamic with the following analogy emphasizing the importance of participating in the experience rather than using one's intellect or ego mind to distract from the experience.

> [Direct pointing] . . . is in many ways similar to the art of listening to music; if one stops to consider one's emotional or intellectual reactions to a symphony while it is being played, to analyze the construction of a chord, or to linger over a particular phrase, the melody is lost. . . . To think over what has passed, to wonder about what is to come, or to analyze the effect upon oneself is to interrupt the symphony and lose the reality. The whole attention must be directed to the symphony and oneself must be forgotten; if any conscious attempt is made to concentrate upon the symphony the mind is led away by the thought of oneself trying to concentrate. . . . Therefore Zen went further than telling the man to listen to the symphony instead of thinking about his reaction to it, for even to tell someone not to think about his independent reactions is to make him think about them! Therefore, Zen

> adopted the positive method of emphasizing the symphony of life itself. . . . It was this to which the Zen masters pointed; they simply demonstrated life without making any assertions or denials about it. (pp. 53–54)

In *The Gestalt Therapy Book,* written nearly 40 years later, Latner (1973) echoed Watts, stating:

> Once we begin to judge, we can no longer allow the gestalt to emerge fully. Our thoughts and opinions about what we experience interfere with the experience itself, narrowing the possibilities. To the extent that we limit ourselves in this way, the gestalts we form are likely to be weak and inept, and our experience will be correspondingly colorless. (pp. 58–59)

Latner was describing how we cultivate the illusion that we are separate subjects interacting with objects. Recall that this is the primary experience of the "ego mind" consciousness described above. Perls (1969c) commented on this experience of ego mind:

> Once you have a character you have a rigid system. Your behavior becomes petrified, predictable, and you lose your ability to cope freely with the world with all your resources. You are predetermined just to cope with events in one way, namely, as your character describes it to be. (p. 7)

He also noted that "[m]any people dedicate their lives to actualize a concept of what they should be like, rather than to actualize themselves. This difference between self-actualizing and self-image actualizing is very important. Most people live only for their image" (p. 19).

Kronsky (1975) also commented on how we avoid happiness by using our ability to self-reflect to apparently distance ourselves from experiences. She noted the uniqueness of Gestalt's approach in dealing with this particular problem:

> The moments we remember as our happiest are those in which we become totally one with our experience and do not question it. Questioning whether or not we are happy is itself a sign of alienation, and definitions of happiness reinforce the alienation that produces them. . . . Gestalt therapy . . . was the only approach to therapy that attempted to deal with . . . man's tendency to impose his abstractions upon his experience. It was the genius of Fritz Perls that he attacked the tendency to abstraction as itself at fault. (p. 32)

Kronsky went on to state that Perls's brand of direct pointing took the form of calling his client's attention to abstraction, thus allowing the client to see it as an act occurring in the present moment.

Now, back to my client, Frank. One of the ways Frank kept himself isolated from any source of inspiration was to deflect contact and then ruminate on the potential risks, talking himself into his sense of deadness in the process. Granted, there was a powerful psychodynamic component related to growing up with an alcoholic father who apparently, with drunken outbursts and violence, spoiled any fun the family was having. Understandably, Frank had a lot of anger about that. When the anger came close to the surface, he would deflect it as he had learned to do as a child. In response to direct pointing at anger that started surfacing in sessions, Frank finally took the opportunity to "let me have it" in the sense of a good yell and some fairly articulate cursing. At first he began to punish himself for "losing control," but, with more direct pointing, he stayed with the feeling long enough to realize that, though not entirely pleasant, it was quite animating and almost inspiring.

TRANSCENDING POLARITIES

One of the guiding apprehensions in both Gestalt and spiritual practices is the transcendence of polarities. In Gestalt we move through a series of shifting figures and grounds to what Perls called final contact. This final contact is "a relaxation of conscious considering, the dissolving of boundaries, and a unity of figure and ground in which splits of mind, body and external world are healed; and in the aftermath, growth occurs" (Perls et al., 1951, p. 197). This dissolving of boundaries in final contact is similar to the dissolving of boundaries in spiritual apprehension. It is not a breakdown of the ego but a breakthrough from the ego. The ego is not obliterated but transcended and included in a greater awareness that one is connected to all human beings, to all living creatures—one is essentially the same and single consciousness that looks out upon the world through billions of eyes (Powell, 2000; Wilber, 1999). In this moment one transcends one of the most tenacious perceptions of the ego mind—that of polarities.

My friend Kevin Prosnick's (1996) research on Gestalt contact processes involving spiritual and transformational qualities followed on the heels of my own dissertation on spiritual well-being (Ingersoll, 1995). His findings are especially relevant here, as he established the presence of two styles of contact that interplay with and extend Perls's construct of final contact. Using factor analysis, he found that two primary Gestalt constructs/factors emerged, both with high construct, convergent, concurrent, and discriminant validity. His hypothesis was clearly confirmed that many people experience a process that extends beyond final contact into the spiritual realm. Thus the title of his dissertation, *Final Contact and Beyond in Gestalt Therapy Theory and Transpersonal Research: A Factor Analytic Study of Egotism and Transfluence.* He named his primary construct *transfluence,* "[a] dimension of human experience involving non-ordinary transpersonal experiences, a spiritual worldview, heightened mental experiences, and . . . a capacity to mentally separate from and become a spectator of experience [that] may be indicative of . . . out-of-body experience" (p. 97). Not surprisingly, he also found that the major interruptive force, or style of resistance, that blocks this transformational flow is egotism—the lesser-studied Gestalt resistance. This construct describes a person (not unlike my client Frank when he began therapy) who is "disengaged from life, has extensive control issues, reports neurotic-like symptoms, denies a spiritual worldview, does not report heightened mental experiences and is self-centered" (Prosnick, 1996, p. 98).

At root, polarity is to be understood as a pair of opposites that work in a complementary fashion (Woldt & Ingersoll, 1991). According to Polster and Polster (1973), "There is nothing new about looking at polarities in man. What is new is the gestalt perspective that each individual is himself a never ending sequence of polarities" (p. 61). It should also be noted that although polarities are opposites working in a complementary fashion, they are rarely experienced that way from the perspective of the ego mind. The ego mind typically sides with half of a polarity, condemning the other half as "different from" or "threatening to" the half it is identifying with.

Perls (1969c) commented on the importance of polarities in Gestalt, stating, "Modern man lives and moves between the extreme poles of 'concreteness and abstractions'" (p. 141). This is congruent with Jung's work advocating recognition of, participation in, and creative synthesis between the pairs of opposites in each individual's experience. Perls et al. (1951) seemed to see the participation in polarity as the process of contact and withdrawal, which he called "the rhythm of life." In elucidating polarities in Gestalt, Latner (1973) asserted that

> [p]olarities are deeply rooted in organismic functioning. . . . Gestalt formation is itself the organization of the field into poles of figure and ground. These are biological phenomena, part of our self-regulation. The relationship of the opposites is that the existence of one necessarily requires the existence of the other. . . . The interaction between polarities functions as a dialectical process. (pp. 36–37)

This attitude toward polarity is also reflected in Gestalt's use of dialogue, or what Naranjo (1978) referred to as the transpersonal operating in the interpersonal. Gestalt recognizes the natural interaction and emergence of polarity in human experience in much the same way as in Chinese and Japanese thought. In these systems, polarity is not something to be escaped or transcended but rather a reality to be recognized and utilized in the growth of the individual.

Polster and Polster (1973) stated that any aspect of oneself implies its antithesis. This antithesis serves as background to present experience and can be powerful enough to emerge as figure in its own right if it gathers enough force. The aim, as stated in Gestalt therapy, is not merely recognizing the polarities but rather contacting and experiencing each part to its fullest while also making contact with its polar counterpart. Polster and Polster stated that therapists must be sensitive to guiding clients into awareness and contact with both poles as they are expressed. As noted, the "appearance of the other" is often perceived as a threat by the ego mind.

BRIAN: As you talk about polarities, I am reminded that I feel both drawn to what you have written and also like moving away. The "toward" motion comes from the common ground I sense between us and the ideas that we hold in common. The moving away relates to a sense of what is missing for me in your chapter and what I'd like more of—to hear the Sufi poets, bathe in the Christian mystics, revel in the Kabbalah, languish in the Gita and the Hindu Vedanta, and share authors such as Wilson Van Dusen, Evelyn Underhill, Bede Griffith, and William James. In essence, I'd like to share my library with you and see if there is another library you have that holds these other books that are also my friends.

ELLIOTT: I was not sure how much to quote from different traditions in this chapter. I don't feel compelled to give equal voice to all traditions because their esoteric cores are the same. What we have in common we have in common with all that is. How aware of it we are depends on us. How attached we are to the labels we use to describe it also depends on us. Right now I really can resonate with various ways to describe this but tend to rely more on experiences. I think those experiences wherein we understand what unites us may be helpful.

As I read your comments, I was aware that I don't revel or languish much these days. Sometimes I think I would like to do more, and then I wonder, "Who is it who is thinking this?" I am playing a game right now where I think I am killing off an image of myself by working that image to death. I slowly let go of that image in the crucible of a very intense schedule that serves the function of paying the bills and walking me through some of the imperfections I have weighted myself down with. I am aware of the witness who asks, "Who is it who is working so much?" "Who is it who wants to know?" In some ways it is an insanely sadistic game—in another way it doesn't matter.

This was certainly the case with Frank, who viewed his angry outburst in our session as a failure and a dangerous expression. Granted, some people do not know how to express anger without severe violence, but this was not the case with Frank. The anger was a glimmer that he did have strong feelings about things, and not just bad feelings but positive ones as well. Latner (1973) supported this in his explanation of gestalt formation processes:

> The opposites become distinguished and opposed; then, in their conflict, a resolution is achieved that is greater than the combination of opposites—it is a new creation. . . . In dialectic thinking in Gestalt therapy, dialectics are not irreconcilable contradictions, but distinctions that will be integrated in the process of gestalt formation and destruction. (p. 37)

If we can allow the full expression of our various psychic or organismic functions, we are in a position to center ourselves between the pairs of opposites. But this is much more difficult in the West, as Watts (1975) pointed out in the following passage. After commenting on the conceptualization of polarity in the Chinese yin-yang, he stated,

> In metaphors of other cultures, light is at war with darkness, life with death, good with evil, and positive with negative, and thus an idealism to cultivate the former and be rid of the latter flourishes throughout much of the world. To the traditional way of Chinese thinking, this is as incomprehensible as an electric current without both positive and negative poles, for polarity is the principle that + and – . . . are different aspects of the same system and that the disappearance of either one of them would be the disappearance of the system. . . . People who have been brought up in the aura of [exoteric] Christian and Hebrew aspirations find this frustrating, because it seems to deny any

When I really slow down now is in my morning meditation. This sets the tone for the day, and even when I am in the middle of "administrivia" at work, I can tap into that awareness that I recognize in my practice. It is everywhere, always, and it is amazing how often I forget that. When I am exhausted, it is easier to see through the veils to that incredible awareness—that is life's little joke on me. I'd much rather find insights and be able to sleep in at least until 6 or 7—maybe later on. Though I dislike the macho American idiocy of "no pain, no gain," there does seem to be a grain of truth in it where my own growth is concerned.

BRIAN: And I want, in the end, to share and discuss the other big "G"—not Gestalt but God—and what place this has for you in describing the spiritual, as I notice much of the writing is about spiritual practices that are not theistic. Though I enjoy these writings, I find a greater sense of being at home with those that are theistic also and miss this in your chapter. Not that I need that you be theistic, either, for I like the notion of Martin Buber when he says that even if a person abhors the name of God and still lives by an Eternal Thou greater than himself (the egotism you mentioned in Prosnick's study) then he still lives the reality of I-Thou. I sense this in your writing—what Sylvia Crocker refers to as being able to stand in the presence of mystery.

ELLIOTT: It is interesting that you mention this. I just finished another chapter for a book that really wanted each contributor to share his or her own personal narrative. I must admit I really enjoyed doing that, although it was risky for me. I shared an experience of being 4 or 5 years old and absolutely loving the feeling of air on my skin. I would run around naked, which upset the adults—but oh well—it kept them on their toes. I was raised in the Anglican faith and even contemplated the priesthood, but my mentor in the church knew that Christianity would not be a lifelong container

> possibility of progress, an ideal which flows from their linear (as opposed to cyclic) view of time and history. Indeed the whole enterprise of Western technology is "to make the world a better place"—to have pleasure without sickness. But, as is now becoming obvious, our violent efforts to achieve this ideal with such weapons as DDT, penicillin, nuclear energy, automotive transportation. . . . and compelling everyone, by law, to be "good and healthy" are creating more problems than they solve. (pp. 19–20)

Even for Westerners who claim to be "nonreligious," the categories of light and dark are often misinterpreted as mutually exclusive and have such an impact on linear thinking that the idea of the two being complementary may seem inconceivable. For Frank, anger was his "dark side" and something that he was terrified to trust.

This is, however, the point made in the treatment of opposites in both Gestalt and spiritual practice. The resolution of the opposites into a new figure created from their dynamic and their tension is an aim of Gestalt therapy. Therapy should guide the individual to own both poles and allow him or her to act in complementary fashion to elicit new, creative adjustments to life situations. These adjustments are difficult precisely because the ego mind is not conditioned to recognize the complementary nature of "yin" and "yang," light and dark. Polster and Polster (1973) noted that "no personal need yields gracefully to its antithesis within the individual any more than one country or one individual welcomes the existence of its antithesis" (p. 66). In this sense, the Gestalt therapist's task parallels the task of the teacher of a spiritual practice in that individuals must be guided into more flexible attitudes to help them increase their range of responses to life.

Polster and Polster (1973) cautioned the therapist that for the client merely to make contact with the antithesis or polar opposite is not enough; the client must be guided through contact with both poles to the point where the poles are working together in an integrated way. They referred the

for me. I had several experiences in the subtle and (I think) causal realms both in and outside of Christianity. I left the Christian path in the late 1990s, feeling I had outgrown what it could offer and having too many experiences that ran counter to many of Christianity's exoteric theologies. It wasn't that I left angry, I just didn't see the point in pursuing it any longer. In 2001, I was initiated into Wicca, and that has nurtured me ritualistically. To the extent that I report an anthropomorphic image of the Divine, it would be the Goddess, whom I have seen the most in the subtle realm. This realm has its limits, though—it is a way station where that which is the source of life may "tone itself down" into images that we can bear to perceive.

I have practiced yoga and meditation for a little over 20 years now, and those have been my staple practices in both my Christian and Wiccan periods. The big "G"—this has only been an experience for me. Earlier in my life I felt a glimpse of this during a session on psychedelic drugs. These were fine for peeking through the gates, but I needed the yoga and meditation to have a passkey. I don't even know what name to use to refer to this. I say them and they all immediately leave me cold, and I shake my head saying, "No, that's not it." I guess that is normal.

I think that yoga and meditation help till the ground, so to speak, for experiences that move one a bit closer to some awareness of the truth. One stands out for me right now. I was sitting in a very boring meeting about a month ago, feeling annoyed with some co-workers and wishing the time for the meeting was over. Slowly, I felt my awareness expand to encompass the whole room. At first I got scared, and it shrank back to "normal." Then I relaxed, and it expanded out again—I felt deeply in touch with everyone present, including those who annoyed me. It wasn't like I knew what they were thinking or anything—it was just this awareness that bred an incredible compassion

therapist to the Gestalt faith in organismic self-regulation to negotiate this task.

CONCLUSION: TRANSLATION VERSUS TRANSFORMATION

The reader at this point is fully justified in again asking, "So what?" These are just more words that have failed to capture the essence of the experience. We might all do better using an Internet conference program to sing renditions of children's songs together.

> Twinkle, twinkle Dr. I
> You have made me wonder why
> Even with your years of school
> You still sound to me a fool.

Although that is an appealing alternative, let me conclude with an injunction that may justify the paper that has gone into this chapter. The injunction is that any approach (spiritual or Gestalt) must absolutely be taken up as a practice requiring effort, commitment, and the intrapsychic equivalent of blood, sweat, and tears (cue violins). In choosing a therapeutic or spiritual path (or recognizing that one has chosen us), we take the first step to greater awareness and a greater ability to witness. In doing so, I believe we take one step closer to the Divine—however conceptualized. Our therapeutic and spiritual practices help us make sense out of our current developmental levels and transform as we move to new levels.

Though I echoed Wilber's statement in the opening of this chapter that spirituality is the highest level of any line of development, it is the animating force of spirit that is the inspiration for transformation, for growth to whatever our next level is. Gestalt therapy and spiritual practices help us adjust to certain levels of development, but, like Frank, we can get stuck and then deflect those things that would truly transform us. As Wilber (1983) rightly pointed out, many spiritual movements and pop psychologies are just offering new ways to keep thinking about the same things. They are a smorgasbord for translation. Few and far between are the practices that aim at transformation, at taking the client or aspirant to the next level of his or her development. Spiritual practices (as I have defined them here) and Gestalt therapy are designed to effect transformation.

What was Frank's transformation? In bringing to full awareness his style of deflection, he made the courageous choice to change that style—"courageous" because it is far easier (even if one is miserable) to stay with a style one knows well. As the spiritual teacher Andrew Cohen has noted, everyone wants to get enlightened but no one wants to change. I have no doubts that had Frank continued with his previous style he would have become suicidal.

and love. Whatever the big "G" is, this is an essential part of the experience of it—compassion and love. They are the direct result of a feeling of intimate connectedness, though not a philosophy or policy.

I still am engaged in psychotherapy as well. As Frances Vaughan said, meditation is for waking up from the dream and psychotherapy is for keeping the dream from becoming a nightmare. The polarities I really struggle with are both extreme—the yang tendencies that easily turn paranoid and aggressive and insist on telling me to keep vigilant. At their best they help me get a heck of a lot done, at their worst they create the illusion that the world is only scarcity and competition. The yin tendencies still nurture my musical side (I work part-time as a folk musician) and help me tune in to the rhythms of my life, my wife and our 10-month-old son. At their best they keep me receptive, at their worst they derail into seeking the return to the womb or cheap imitations of it (e.g., alcohol).

Frank's transformation allowed the freeing of his own life energy. He was no longer a "dismembered head" reflecting on and directing the activities of an untrustworthy, wayward body. He had become "whole" or "holy" in the truest sense of the word. The last I heard, he had also committed his life to the practices that led to this initial breakthrough. While continuing his therapy with a Gestalt therapist, he was also studying philosophy part time. He was actively translating at this new, life-giving level of development. His Gestalt journey had been a spiritual one. So what is spirituality anyway?

NOTE

1. I owe the metaphor of "the academic killing jar" to philosopher Ken Wilber, whom we shall hear more about in a moment.

REVIEW QUESTIONS

1. What does the chapter author mean when he states that awareness (as used in Gestalt therapy) is a "yin" element as opposed to a "yang" element?

2. What is the three-step method Wilber (1998) has recommended for reproducing "spiritual" experiences, and how can this be applied to Gestalt therapy experiences?

3. What is the distinction between exoteric and esoteric spirituality, and how do they both apply to Gestalt therapy?

4. Why is it important in a Gestalt therapeutic approach to recognize polarities?

EXPERIENTIAL PEDAGOGICAL ACTIVITIES

ACTIVITY 1: The chapter author distinguishes between "yang" descriptions (those that seek to operationalize constructs) and "yin" descriptions (those defined by interior experience, meaning, subjectivity). In a small group setting, have the first individual describe a situation from his or her life by relying on "yang" language and have him or her attempt to stretch the description of the event using "yin" language. The second individual then begins with a "yin" description and adds the "yang," with additional members alternating modes.

ACTIVITY 2: Divide your large classroom or training group into several smaller groups to continue dialogue about the case of Frank. Have each group adopt a different theoretical orientation (such as cognitive behavioral therapy, a psychoanalytic approach, or a brief solution-focused approach), and conceptualize Frank's presenting concern of feeling dead using the constructs of the assigned theoretical approach. In the larger group format, compare each conceptualization to a Gestalt therapy conceptualization.

ACTIVITY 3: In journal format, answer the chapter author's questions "Is life basically safe?" and "Can it be trusted?"

ACTIVITY 4: In this chapter, the author refers to Watts (1936) and Latner (1973) as providing guidelines for remaining present centered and for using the technique of direct pointing. It is possible to take their descriptions and adapt them into a spiritual "experiment." Select a classical orchestral piece (perhaps Barber's Adagio for Strings, or the fourth movement of Beethoven's ninth symphony, or a Mozart piano concerto), and let go of judgments that come into your mind while you are listening to the recording. Focusing on letting go is, itself, not remaining with the experience. "Just" try to maintain the posture of being in the here and now with the sound of the recording, without thinking about or cataloguing the feelings of the experiment.

ACTIVITY 5: Most resumés contain an account of our career development and state our purposes and objectives for a new career path. Instead of constructing (or revising) your career resumé, compose your spiritual resumé and reflect on the process.

Part II

GESTALT APPLICATIONS WITH SPECIFIC POPULATIONS

CHAPTER **9**

Gestalt Therapy With Children

CYNTHIA REYNOLDS

DIALOGUE RESPONDENT: PETER MORTOLA

Cynthia Reynolds is a licensed psychologist, a licensed professional clinical counselor, and associate professor of counselor education and school counseling coordinator at the University of Akron, Ohio, where she applies much of what she learned in her years of working with children and families as an elementary school counselor and teacher of gifted children. She is a member of the Kent Gestalt Writers' Group and was mentored in Gestalt therapy by Ansel Woldt, who directed her research on Gestalt coping skills used by children of divorce. She has numerous publications on Gestalt play therapy, filial therapy, and school counseling. She is highly sought after as a workshop presenter on child therapy, parenting skills, and family relations.

Peter Mortola is a licensed clinical psychologist and associate professor of counseling psychology at Lewis and Clark College's Graduate School of Education in Portland, Oregon. He is currently leading elementary school counseling groups for boys and teaching classes on human development, assessment, and counseling. After many years of assisting Violet Oaklander with her summer intensive Gestalt training program, he has completed authoring a book on Oaklander's approach to both counseling children and teaching adults to work with children from a Gestalt orientation. He has also authored several articles for professional journals and book chapters on Gestalt therapy with children.

The process of learning how to use Gestalt therapy with children can be likened to going on a journey. In this chapter, I am offering some guidance to assist you with your journey by laying important groundwork so that your particular journey may be more meaningful and rewarding. This groundwork is based on years of personal and professional journeying, finding my own way to integrate Gestalt work with children. And, I might add, it has been an exciting and lively journey. During it, my experiences have varied from voyaging to planting my feet, roving to searching, strolling to marching, sauntering to motoring, walking to running, prowling to navigating. My approach to this business of playing, working, and being with children developed from the integration of my personality and my experiences of Gestalt therapy. While reflecting on my own professional development as I write this, I am aware that the journey you, the reader, will experience will be unique. You are likely to develop your own style of journeying. You will also create your own skills to cope with the roadblocks and detours.

PREPARING FOR THE JOURNEY

A savvy explorer has an intimate knowledge of his or her physical, emotional, and psychological stamina. Charting a route demands awareness of one's strengths and weaknesses, joys and pleasures, fears and trepidations. Exploration of your boundaries will help set an appropriate pace. Awareness of the self is indispensable when using the Gestalt approach with children, as we, ourselves, are instruments of influence and change.

The benefit of spending time on your own personal growth is that you will be able to be more fully present in your work with children, assisting them to deal with their issues instead of being preoccupied with your own. Knowing one's own values, beliefs, and biases about children is a good place to start. Most children readily see through phoniness, condescension, and incongruence. With self-confidence and self-efficacy, the risk of countertransference and projecting your unfinished business into your therapy relationship is greatly diminished. Activity #1 at the end of this chapter is an invitation to pursue a comprehensive self-evaluation.

CHILD THERAPY AS A CROSS-CULTURAL EXPERIENCE: EXAMINING THE GROUND/FIELD

Learning about counseling children may be a trip into uncharted territory. Every child has unique cultural, environmental, and generational influences that affect who he or she is in ways we must be willing to discover and honor. Unfortunately, having a comfort level in working with adults does not guarantee success in working with children. There are specific characteristics of a culturally skilled counselor (Sue & Sue, 2003) that can be adapted to counseling children. It is crucial that the child therapist be able to understand and share the worldview of children. A professional working with children should have specific knowledge and training in understanding human development and the sociopolitical system's operation with respect to children. Awareness of the institutional barriers that prevent or hamper children from using mental health services is also a must. There is much to be learned about the *culture of childhood* that is necessary for entering the world of childhood and being effective in counseling children. Becoming a culturally skilled counselor is an active, ongoing process that never really reaches an end point (Sue & Sue, 2003).

Wheeler (1998) asserted that the use of a field phenomenological model assists Gestalt therapists in constructing an understanding of the child in the field, which *I consider to be the field of childhood.* The domain of that field may include the inner and outer worlds of the child's developing self-process, such as inner experiences, family dynamics, peer and adult relationships, and educational/institutional experiences such as school, church, community, clubs, culture, and politics. Wheeler stated, and I concur, that

> ultimately our concern in working with children is a concern with their worlds: the *interior world* (of intuition, creativity, developing thoughts and feelings) and also the *outer world* (of political and social realities, economic conditions and cultural practices and values). (p. 124)

If you list the differences between children and adults, as suggested in Activity 2 at the end of this chapter, you will probably identify examples that are developmental in nature. The following discussion gives assistance to understanding how to assess a child's functioning (e.g., behavior, comportment, deportment, demeanor) from a Gestalt perspective, focusing on processes rather than stages (as most developmental theorists do). Having a clearer picture of the child with whom you are about to embark on this journey will help you select interventions and techniques that will have a greater likelihood of success. Understanding the inner strengths and capacities available to the child is essential, especially during difficult parts of the journey. Awareness and knowledge of the child's reserves—what he or she has available to call upon, both internally and externally—will help you determine which challenges this child has a good chance of resolving, mastering, or just learning to cope with. This awareness will also assist you in choosing interventions to apply in the *field of the child* (e.g., with parents, teachers, siblings).

ASSESSING THE CLIENT'S STRENGTHS: VIEWING HUMAN GROWTH AND DEVELOPMENT FROM A GESTALT PERSPECTIVE

Gestalt therapists view human development as a process involving movement from total environmental support (complete confluence in the womb) to optimal self-support (interdependent adulthood in which one can ask for help when needed). Though a solid grounding in traditional developmental theory is an asset in understanding children, their development does not always occur in the precise phases presented by Piaget, Maslow, Freud, and Erikson (although these are useful reference points). Many therapists have felt uncomfortable in applying these models in working with children. Gordon Wheeler (2000, 2003c), Peter Mortola (2001), and Felicia Carroll (2002) have become the prominent Gestalt therapists writing about child development, taking much of their lead from David Stern's (1985) and Mark McConville's (1995) field theory basis for understanding infants and adolescents, respectively (refer back to Chapter 3 for an in-depth discussion of field theory).

PETER: I am excited that you have introduced me to Woldt's Gestalt Experience and Observation Guide for Children, which looks at the areas of a child's development. I am excited by this tool for a couple of reasons: First, in the discipline of school psychology we are always looking for assessment systems that reflect the "best practices" of understanding the whole child in both personal and interpersonal contexts. Woldt's system allows us a window into all the realms of a child's experience. In so doing, it is a lovely example of how the "holism" that is at the heart of the theory of Gestalt therapy can also be reflected in the practice of Gestalt therapy through the use of this applicable tool. (See Appendix B)

Second, too often in the practice of assessment in school psychology we are caught up in paradigms of pathology, of trying to discover what is "wrong" with a child. Implicit in the construction of Woldt's system, and in Gestalt therapy theory in general, is an emphatic emphasis on what constitutes healthy development in a child: How can we know how to help a child if we don't know what healthy development looks like? Thank you, Cynthia, for weaving this helpful tool into your chapter. Can you give us an example of how you have used it in your own practice and how it has been helpful to you?

The Gestalt Experience and Observation Guide for Children (see Appendix B at the end of this book) developed by Woldt (1990) is an invaluable aid to use with children to obtain Gestalt-oriented developmental assessments. Using the instrument is an ongoing process co-created by the therapist and the child in the present moment. As a therapist who is at the moment interacting with the child in a co-created field, I am fully aware that what is observed regarding the child's process may vary significantly depending on who else is in the child's field or in what other field the child is immersed/embedded.

The guide covers the following spheres: emotional and affective development; sensory, perceptual, and proprioceptive development; physical and behavioral development; intellectual and cognitive development; social and interpersonal development; and aesthetic awareness, intuition, creativity, and spirituality. Each of these will be explicated in the following sections.

CYNTHIA: Peter, one of the first things I look for when beginning to work with a child is whether there is any "light on" in his or her eyes—sparkle, twinkle, glow, responsiveness, et cetera. When I cannot see any, I know that I must work very slowly and patiently to establish some kind of contact with the child. I will focus much of my time with the child engaging in desensitization activities, and I will watch closely and monitor for any evidence of a flicker of light in the eyes. I will be using music, clay, finger painting, even food or drink, to see what will stir a glimmer in the eyes. I remember a poignant moment when working with a first-grade girl who had witnessed domestic violence and was selectively mute. Her first words to me, after I had worked with her for 15 minutes a week for 3 months, were "Where's the music today?" I had forgotten to turn on the tape recorder of music that I played each week when working with her!

Emotional and Affective Development

In the areas of *emotional and affective development,* I look and listen for evidence that feelings are in contact with lively figures and varying backgrounds. For example: Does the child have the ability to experience pleasure, pain, frustration, and fear? Is his or her affect appropriate to the situation? Has the child developed cathartic and expressive processes for tension release, for reality testing, and for feeling alive, free, autonomous, empowered, and focused? Is the child's sense of personal well-being and mastery an "I'm okay—you're okay" and "I can do it" attitude/feeling? I also pay attention to what stands out about the child's affective domain and to my predominant feelings experienced while I am with him or her.

Sensory, Perceptual, and Proprioceptive Development

I want to explore the child's *sensory, perceptual, and proprioceptive* development to discover if perceptions and senses create figure/ground differentiation. For example: Does the child have clarity of sight, hearing, smell, touch, contact through muscles and motion, taste processes, and culinary, digestive, and alimentary processes? Again, I pay attention to what stands out most about the child's sensory and perceptual domains and what senses I experience most in making contact with him or her.

Physical and Behavioral Development

In terms of *physical and behavioral development,* I observe whether the child contacts the environment for support and whether the child can create, alter, restructure, or destroy figures.

For example: Is the child aware of his or her size, shape, appearance, and presentation and/or displaying any feelings about it? Does the child have fluid body movement and experience the ability to make contact with his or her environment? Is he or she aware of handedness/sidedness, balance, movement forward and backward, and symmetry? Does the child have eye-hand coordination, and if not, is he or she self-conscious about it? Does he or she have a sense of personal space and boundaries that are self-regulated? I pay attention to what stands out most for me about the child's physical/behavioral presence and what I am most aware of about my own body as I am with him or her.

Intellectual and Cognitive Development

In terms of the child's *intellectual and cognitive development,* do reality- and fantasy-based figures emerge? Or are they created from an energized ground/field? For example: Does the child have representations of language to facilitate classification and expression of knowledge and awareness? Does the child display an awareness of and the ability to create and/or experience schemas and gestalten, including concepts of self, other(s), and environment with and without people and potential for actual interaction/contact? Is he or she able to problem-solve or predict cause-effect relations by thinking divergently and predicting outcomes? I want to be aware of what stands out most for me about the child's cognitive processes and what cerebral processes and fantasies I experience with him or her.

Social and Interpersonal Development

In *social and interpersonal development,* I attend to the child's person-to-person interactions to see how they emerge and if they are created from an energized field. For example: What is the child's awareness of self? Does he or she display self-confidence with high self-esteem, or is he or she self-conscious, insecure, anxious, or easily embarrassed? Does the child acknowledge real/authentic thoughts and desires? Is he or she considerate and accepting of others who are both similar and different? Is the child aware of personal boundaries and secure enough to assert self and receive others, making the I-Thou relationship possible? Is the child sensitive to feelings, boundaries, and concerns of others? Does the child understand what kinds of behavior bring approval and disapproval? Does he or she derive meaning from social contact with others whether it is positive or negative? Is the child able to be alone and with others, displaying neither confluence nor confluence phobia? Is he or she open to sharing, including, and excluding? Is the child able to accept responsibility for his or her own actions and yet not assume responsibility for others? Again, I want to be aware of what stands out most for me about the child's relating with others and what I personally experience in relating to and with him or her.

Aesthetic Awareness, Intuition, Creativity, and Spirituality Development

In observing for *aesthetic awareness, intuition, creativity and spirituality,* I watch for figure/ground clarification, differentiation, and expression in order to sense the child's capacity for growth in these areas. For example: Is the child aware of and does he or she attend to sensations and feelings, perceptions, and ideas, creating and allowing tension and excitement to emerge? Is the child in contact with commotions and emotions? Is the child open to self, others, and environs and willing to take risks? Is the child free (not controlled by fear) and able to create opportunities for exploration, experimentation, and experience? Is the child open to being guided by "the spiritual" and "energy forces"? Is he or she intuitive and able to sense purpose and direction? Is the child able to appreciate natural and manmade beauty and to relate to/with the environment, not against it? Is he or she guided by processes essential to form content that feels complete? Is the child able to produce good gestalten—products that demonstrate elaboration, variety, originality, and unity? Is he or she able to finish the process begetting the "aha" experience and closure, making withdrawal possible? I want to be aware of what stands out for me about the child's aesthetic and creative self and what is touched in me that is creative, aesthetic, and/or spiritual while I am with him or her.

A ROAD MAP FOR THE JOURNEY: THEORETICAL UNDERPINNINGS

Gestalt therapy is an experiential and process therapy rather than a strictly verbal, interpretive, or content therapy. This aspect of Gestalt therapy makes it perfectly suited for children, many of whom may have not yet developed the verbal sophistication to communicate feelings, desires, and needs directly through words. Experimental play can be a very effective language to use in communicating with children.

Gestalt therapists believe that all children are fundamentally healthful, that each child is striving in his or her own unique way toward wholeness, integration, fluidity, adaptation, and growth. There is an "innate wisdom" inherent in the organism. Upon further examination, every symptom that a child displays can be seen as a creative effort to make life better. Symptoms and styles of resistance are viewed as creative adjustments to challenges without sufficient support. The clinical task becomes one of embarking on a discovery-based journey to find out what supports are missing for the child and how to provide supports now that will allow him or her to change behavior, develop more effective coping skills, and/or live a more satisfying existence.

Authentic Encounter and the Paradoxical Theory of Being

Thus the child therapist joins the child in an authentic encounter in which the goal is to "be who you are, not who you are not." This rests on the paradoxical theory of change, which in essence states that change occurs when one becomes what one is, not when one tries to become what one is not. By identifying disowned aspects of self and one's experience, conditions are created that make ownership, integration, and change possible. This is the basis of choiceful living.

Gestalt methodology for children supports their experiencing as much of themselves as they can in the here and now. As they experience the ways in which they make contact with their environment and how they interrupt themselves, they will also begin to experience the self they have interrupted. In this paradigm, the act of remembering is in the present moment; thus it takes place in the immediacy of their now. The beauty of Gestalt therapy (especially with children) is that it provides experiences, not explanations. The objective is to heighten the experience of life, self, and others through direct interaction, contact, and experiencing oneself differently in one's world.

Gestalt therapy allows new concepts of the self to develop by inviting and inventing new experiences of the self in the therapeutic situation. Gestalt therapists use the self in creative and experimental ways, with awareness of how this can propel children toward health and wellness. This requires therapists to be comfortable with "not knowing" and trusting "what is" while acting upon their curiosity, interest, and intuition in the present therapeutic experience. This demands balancing their active and receptive energy guided by intuitive knowing.

Gestalt therapists respect the notion of multiple realities in which each child's experience is viewed as valid and real. The clinical stance is one of profound curiosity and wonderment regarding each child's unique experience. Though developing a therapeutic liaison involves considerable "I-It" interaction, Gestalt therapy provides an existential meeting place in which the child and therapist engage in a lively exchange of energy and essence at the boundary of contact between two human beings. This can evolve into an "I-Thou" relationship (Buber, 1958). I-Thou relationships with children involve much more person-to-person contact than is typical of adult-child relationships. Although adults are older, more experienced, probably bigger, and more powerful, in the I-Thou therapy relationship both parties are of equal value, and both the child and the therapist feel honored, valued, and appreciated, not judged or analyzed.

There is a spiritual dimension to this relationship in that the life forces of both separate beings connect in a beautiful and powerful way. For many children, this is the first time they have felt this kind of soul connection with an adult. This can be a very empowering, awesome, and healing experience for both the client and the therapist.

Gestalt therapists believe that behavior is best understood by appreciating the "field" or system in which it exists (McConville, 1995, 2001b). The field approach offers a framework for a holistic, dynamic, and comprehensive understanding of human events and patterns of interaction. Of course, children do not exist in a vacuum. All is connected, and the whole is greater than and different from the sum of its parts. Interpersonal events are not linear but occur in patterns or configurations that involve the parts of the whole. Understanding the pattern of relationships is essential to knowing something about a single part.

Gestalt therapists do not view the child client as a person with a disease or psychopathology needing a cure. Healing in Gestalt therapy is a process of growth, of reestablishing the natural process of growth and development that has been truncated, misdirected, rigidified, or fixated in and by a nonsupportive, incongruent, or toxic environment. Healthy children can complete unfinished situations and experience meaningful patterns of awareness that are integrated in such a way that needs are clear at any given moment. This allows for and supports meaningful gestalts to form.

The Gestalt Cycle of Experience

A healthy child can move with fluidity through a need satisfaction cycle known in Gestalt circles as the *cycle of experience* or *continuum of experience* (COE, as expressed in Chapter 6 of this book). As self-regulating entities, children maintain their homeostasis by fulfilling acknowledged needs through contacting their environment. Organismic self-regulation is seen as the ability to run smoothly and stay in balance. Perls (1973) stated,

> [W]e might call the homeostatic process the process of self-regulation, the process by which the organism interacts with its environment. . . . The organism has psychological

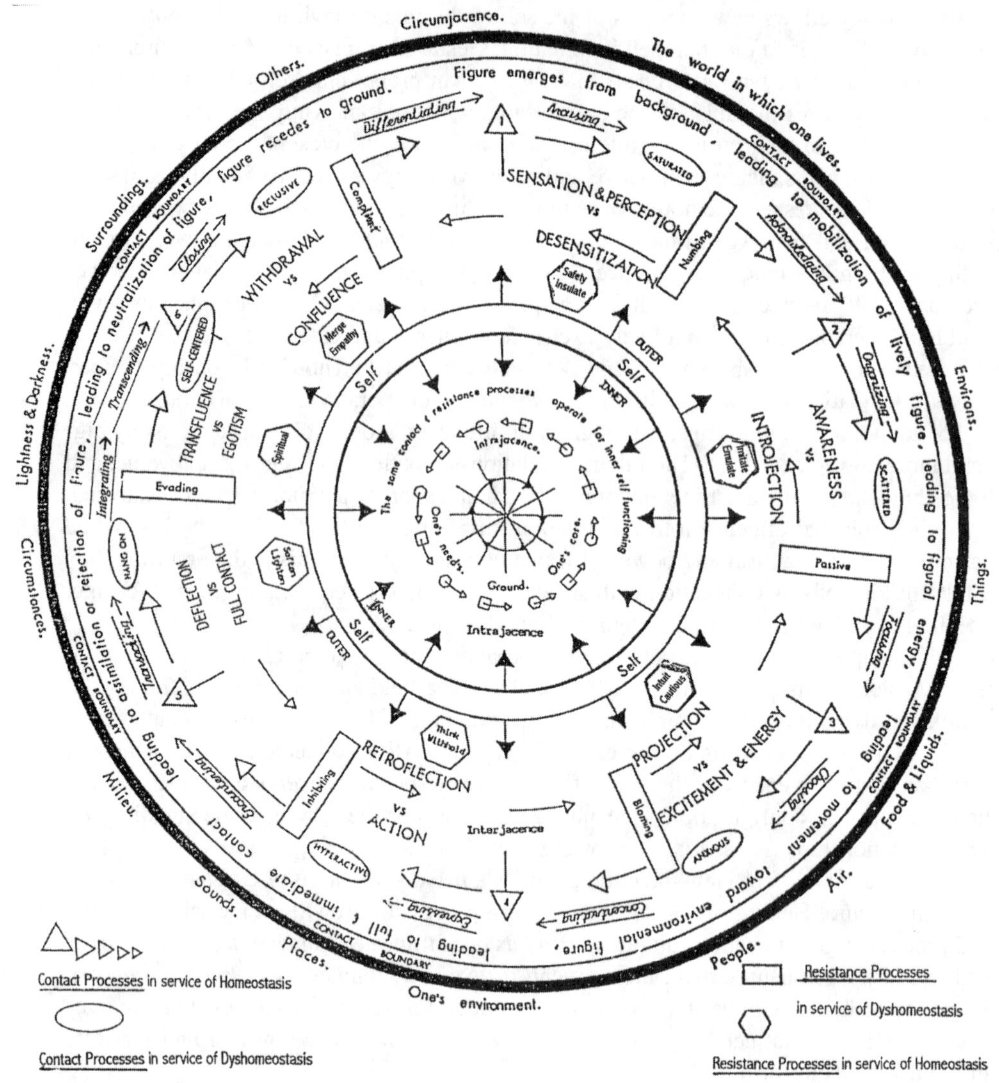

Figure 9.1 The Gestalt Homeostasis Cycle

SOURCE: Ansel L. Woldt, 1984, revised 1993

contact needs as well as physiological ones; these are felt every time the psychological equilibrium is disturbed, just as the physiological needs are felt every time psychological equilibrium is disturbed. These psychological needs are met through what we might call the psychological counterpart of the homeostatic process. Let me make it very clear, however, that this psychological process cannot be divorced from the physiological one; that each contains elements of the other. Those needs that are primarily psychological in nature

> and the homeostatic or adaptive mechanisms by which they are met constitute part of the subject matter of psychology. . . . The more intensely they [needs] are felt to be essential to continued life, the more closely we identify our selves with them, the more intensely we will direct our activities towards satisfying them. . . . [Unfortunately,] the whole instinct theory tends to confuse needs with their symptoms, or with the means we use to achieve them. . . . Formulating this principle in terms of Gestalt psychology, we can say that the dominant need of the organism, at any time, becomes the foreground figure and the other needs recede, at least temporarily, into the background. . . . For the individual to satisfy his needs, to close the gestalt, to move on to other business, he must be able to sense what he needs and he must know how to manipulate himself and his environment, for even the purely physiological needs can only be satisfied through the interaction of the organism and the environment. (pp. 5–8, italics in original)

We can see how this functions in a cyclical manner with children in the process of maintaining balance, organismic self-regulation, and homeostasis. The child first becomes aware of a need (figure) that affects his or her equilibrium (ground); the child then moves to make contact within the self, environment, and/or other to satisfy that need. The child returns to a state of balance/homeostasis when either the need is met or another satisfactory alternative is discovered. Gestalt therapy theory defines psychological health as the consistent self-enhancing flow of contact with the internal aspects of the child and/or between the child and his or her environment. Thus the behavioral choices of the child can range from conscious and aware choices that are creatively spontaneous adjustments or unconsciously rigid patterns, what we refer to as "fixed gestalts."

Similar to the COE, the Gestalt homeostasis cycle (see Figure 9.1) is a more elaborate representation of the various human processes involved in seeking and maintaining contact and balance in one's life—generally referred to in the Gestalt lexicon as creative life adjustment and organismic self-regulation. In Woldt's cycle, the seven contact-making functions are paired with the seven Gestalt resistances or styles of interruptive functioning that support either homeostasis or dishomeostasis. These processes can function at the aware and unaware levels, conscious and unconscious, and can result in both validating and invalidating experiences.

The cycle begins with a primary awakening of a *sensation and perception* within the child to an internal or external stimulus in his or her field. As the child focuses on the stimulus by experiencing it affectively and cognitively, a figure emerges from the ground, at which point *awareness* of feelings or possible choices develops. As the meaning of the figure is experienced and realized,

PETER: As in my last comment regarding how Gestalt therapy theory focuses on both holism and health, I have always loved the way that the Gestalt cycle of experience describes the ongoing moves of an organism as it strives toward health and positive development. One aspect of this cycle that I have sometimes been confused about is how, as you describe, the child "restructures and processes the experience." Cynthia, could you give an example, perhaps from your practice, of what it means for a child to "restructure" an experience in order for a need to be met? I know that Piaget (1977) described the cognitive process of how a child creates new internal schemas in order to accommodate the new experiences he or she is having. In other words, I think Piaget describes how children build more accurate internal maps that more closely resemble the world and their experience in it. Is this akin to the way we think of "restructuring" from a Gestalt perspective?

a fuller sense of choice becomes available to the child.

When *awareness* is sufficiently supported, *excitement and energy* are mobilized to either pursue the need or abort it in favor of a competing figure, fixed gestalt, or creative response to demands in the field. With *mobilization of energy,* there tends to be a natural movement toward engagement or abrogation. The transformation of energy into *action and contact* results in fuller engagement and encounter between the child and his or her environment to satisfy the need or meet the demand, or if the environment is unsatisfying or frightening the child is likely to disband this figure. When internal or external contact progresses through *action* toward figure completion, the child restructures and processes the experience, culminating in the needs being met or resolved. On the other hand, if there is insufficient support for *contact,* or if the figure is experienced as negative or too difficult to fully encounter and restructure, the child's *action* is likely to result in aborting contact. During this time of *action,* whether positive or negative, the child *assimilates* various aspects of the experience. Awareness of *completion,* whether through accommodation or rejection of the figure, propels the child toward *differentiation and closure* leading to *withdrawal and zero contact* (Mraz, 1990; Woldt & Ingersoll, 1991). The child then becomes available for movement into another cycle around a new figure.

The Gestalt Resistances and Styles of Disruption in the Continuum of Experience

At any point in the cycle or continuum, the child or his/her environment can arrest or deflect the flow of the present experience with a variety of interruptive functions or styles of resistance. Though we name and briefly describe these interruptive processes, it is of utmost importance to understand that the very process of interrupting, resisting, or blocking

CYNTHIA: There seems to be some similarity between Piaget's cognitive restructuring and the Gestalt meaning. In the Gestalt terminology, *restructuring* refers to a wide range of human and interpersonal processes, not just the cognitive domain. Restructuring is the primary effect of taking action toward the environment. Fritz and Laura Perls give the classic example of the child taking appropriate aggressive action to chew food to satisfy his or her hunger. In *Gestalt Therapy,* Perls, Hefferline, and Goodman (1951) said, "[T]he process . . . by which one arrives at a differentiated unity is one of taking things apart and putting them back together—a kind of *aggressive destructiveness and reconstructiveness!* . . . For any kind of creative reconstruction to occur there must be first, to some degree, a *destructuring* of what already exists. The present parts of a given object, activity or situation must be recombined in a fashion more adequate to the requirements of the here-and-now actuality. . . . Destruction and reconstruction refer here not to literal reduction to fragments of the *physical object,* but to *our own behavior with respect to the object"* (pp. 67–68, italics in original). Sylvia Crocker (1999) described the necessity of "restructuring the ground" in order for people to enhance their contact with others by changing behavior patterns, which is done through action in their "whole-making capacity." In her book *Brief Gestalt Therapy* (2003), Gaie Houston referred to this process as "deconstruction"—the need to "separate to integrate" (p. 21). In his discussion of "contact and creativity," as well as in earlier writings about "structured ground," Gordon Wheeler (1991, 2000, 2003c) emphasized the importance of *restructuring* and the role of "experiment" in therapy to help clients unlearn old patterns of behavior and learn more fulfilling interactive processes.

An example of facilitating a restructuring experiment could be when children are reticent to engage in play or conversation, where we first meet them in their resistance (where they are currently at) and support their contacting that resistance to engage with us.

contact or interactions with one's field or environment is in itself a form of contact (Reynolds & Woldt, 2002; Tudor, 2002; Wheeler, 1991). Additionally, it is critical to remember that Gestalt therapy, more than any other theory or model of therapy, advocates viewing "the resistance as the energy, not the enemy" in the conduct of therapy.

Through the dynamic boundary process of *desensitization,* the child slows down, or even shuts off, the sensation, perception, and/or proprioception functions, essentially blocking both internal and external stimuli from affecting his or her sensations. The boundary process of *introjection* refers to swallowing whole certain beliefs, attitudes, or expectations that remain foreign to or incongruent for the child. Introjects usually result in children blindly following many "shoulds" and "oughts." As a style of resistance, introjection commonly interferes with the awareness phase of the COE, particularly interrupting feelings and creative ideas. It is difficult for this introjected material to become assimilated as an integrated part of the organismic functioning of the child without some type of therapeutic or educational experience to help process it through. *Projection* is an interruptive function in which the disowned aspects of the self are attributed to others or some aspect of the child's environment.

As a style of resistance, projection plays considerable havoc with the mobilization of energy and the excitement phase in the cycle of experience. *Retroflection* involves keeping things to oneself and/or turning one's action back onto or into oneself. We see children doing to or for themselves what might profit them more if they received it from their environment. This process of turning the energy back in or toward the self is a primary interruption of the action phase of the cycle. *Deflection* is the redirection of action and the veering away from direct contact. Though it functions to disrupt contact in various phases of the homeostasis cycle, its primary adaptation by children is to avoid full and final contact, thus thwarting commitment and integration. A child's *egotism* also disrupts the integration and assimilation of the final contact as the child "holds out," paying more attention to his or her identity and boundaries than to the other. The process of *confluence* is an unbounded merging of aspects of the self with the other/environment—a process that sustains contact beyond what is healthy and prevents or avoids withdrawal from the figure of interest. The confluent child blunts individuation, lacks appreciation of individual differences, and

The first level of engagement might be to help them acknowledge how good they are at what they are doing (e.g., being quiet, silent, stubborn, standing their ground) and see if they can experiment with creative ways to express their reluctance or reticence more fully. This can become a "game" in and of itself and often provides ample support for them to engage more fully in typical therapeutic dialogue—a restructuring of their resistance as contactful.

PETER: Right! Thanks for reminding me of the important role that restructuring plays in the everyday process of better differentiating and integrating the self toward more complex levels of organization. We do this (as you helpfully noted that Perls pointed out) by "taking things apart and putting them back together." Your reminders and well-chosen quotes made me think of examples of restructuring in my own work with children. I learned from Violet Oaklander (aptly described in *Windows to Our Children* [1969/1978] and even more so in her training programs), how to ask children to pick an image from a stack of random pictures to represent how they are feeling. I have seen how, paradoxically, children are able to better identify and own their feelings and experiences by first projecting them outwardly. In other words, they are able to get closer to their own experience by first getting some distance on it. That is, by first "taking apart" their experience they are able to better put it "back together" in a more complete and restructured whole. I appreciate your helpful thoughts, Cynthia, on this valuable topic.

wants everyone to be alike and to appreciate him or her. Children who have adapted to a confluent style have difficulty "letting go." They avoid individuation and differentiation, expending considerable energy in trying to be accepted and liked. One of the ways they do this is by imitating others, saying the "right" things, wearing the "right" clothes, and being extra nice to please others. Their motto is "Don't ruffle the waters, much less create waves."

When Gestalt contact/resistance processes evolve into contact/resistance styles, they change from figure to ground. These adaptive contact styles are considered to be response patterns developed within the context of the child's most meaningful relationships (Kepner, 1982; Oaklander, 1969/1978). The child's lack of awareness and inability to choose alternative responses at different points of the cycle may result in the displaying of various symptoms. Three Gestalt child therapists have reported that children coming to therapy often present with a lack of integration (Carroll, 2002), boundary disturbances (Ownby, 1983), and an impaired sense of self (Oaklander, 1982).

Felicia Carroll (1995) likened the process of therapy to what Pinocchio, the wooden puppet, experienced when becoming a real little boy. The lack of personality integration is evidenced by behavioral, affective, and/or interpersonal symptoms that reveal inner conflicts, fragmentation, or artificiality within the developmental process. Carroll believed that without therapeutic intervention unintegrated children are more like glued-together puppets (Pinocchio) than lively human beings.

Ray Ownby (1983) wrote that therapeutic interventions with children should be guided by the therapist's awareness of the disturbance with the contact boundary between the child and the therapist in the here and now. In his work as a school psychologist and later as a neuropsychologist, he observed confluence, projection, introjection, retroflection, and deflection as the primary resistances in children.

Gestalt therapists work to assist children in making progressively better contact with what they are experiencing at the moment. The tools of contact identified by Polster and Polster (1973) are looking, talking, touching, listening, smelling, and tasting. These tools need to be developed in a manner that provides for awareness of both process and content. Once children are able to do this, they can have more choiceful awareness of using the contact/resistance functions in the Gestalt cycle of experience.

According to Oaklander (1992b), the goals of Gestalt therapy with children should be to help them gain self-support, self-acceptance, self-nurturance, and integration. She sees growth occurring as children learn to accept the various aspects of the self without judgment. Children experience integration through uniting the unaware/unconscious aspects of self with the nurturing self.

Expressive and Impressive Therapeutic Interventions

Much of the literature about using Gestalt therapy approaches with children focuses on expressive techniques, in which expression and expressiveness are viewed as necessary for normal development and as essential processes for healing and growth. In part, the emphasis on expression appears to reflect the time period when Gestalt therapy theory was developed. Expression was viewed as a healthy way to overcome much of the repressiveness of child-rearing methods common in the 1950s and 1960s. In today's society, many children's adjustment problems are caused by or closely related to being too expressive, having not learned how to suppress their excitement, restrict their emotionality, or retroflect their actions. These children need help with learning how to restrain their spontaneity and modulate their expression into more mature, appropriate, and acceptable avenues. This part of our work is called *impressive therapy* and includes methods of great importance to Gestalt child therapy. The child's choiceful use of both contact and resistance processes in service of integration, without being at the expense of others, is an equally appropriate goal of Gestalt child therapy. Therefore, I want to make a case for child therapists knowing as much about impressive therapy interactions as expressive ones.

Basically, "impressive" methods involve using therapeutic dialogue, activities, and experiments that help the child learn the resistance processes so as to have them at his or her disposal when he or she experiences an overabundance of sensation, awareness, excitement, energy, and contact in the field at a given time. For example, in the early phase of the cycle, when the child is becoming aware of spontaneity and is flooded with feelings that are difficult to contain, I might experiment with trying out some introjective processes, such as "I will not jump out of my seat at this time no matter how excited I am, and maybe I'll get to talk about what that was like when I show I can do it," and "I'm going to see if I can keep my mouth closed while the other person is talking, and later I'll get to share how it felt to be quiet and listen." If the child is hyperactive, I might experiment with interventions such as:

> Now that you are ready to run around the room, I'd like you to try stopping and tell me what you are aware of in your legs. Stop and stand still. Now pay attention to the muscles in your legs and tell me what they are doing right now. If your legs could speak, what might they say? Maybe we can have a conversation between the boy who wants to run around the room and the boy who knows how to stop and be still. Let's try that. What might be the first thing your active self would want to say? Next, speak as the one who knows how to stop and be still.

PETER: I am impressed with this idea of "impressive therapy"! To me, your idea brings to mind a couple of points. First, it shows how Gestalt therapy, though often stereotypically thought of as "me" centered, actually addresses both the individual and the larger "field" that surrounds the individual. In your writing, "impressive therapy" addresses the way in which our culture has changed over the past 50 years or so from being more repressive to more expressive. In this way, your idea of "impressive therapy" gives us a way to address changing individuals within a larger context that is also changing.

I am also impressed with the way that, in your approach, you playfully help the children you are working with to gain a broader repertoire of social, emotional, and behavioral skills. Your approach reminds me of how Vygotsky (1934/1962) described how children act "a head above themselves" in play. That is, in play they can practice not only what is currently within their repertoire but also that which is just beyond their reach. Paradoxically, children also can act with more self-control in play than in real life. Your approach, then, builds on a developmental strength of childhood, helping them address serious "impressive" content in appropriately expressive ways.

CYNTHIA: I found that many times just assisting a child to better express him- or herself did not help to improve behavior. To help a child learn how to both impress and express, and to be able to be more choiceful about that process, really empowers children.

Most children do not have the sophistication of language and intrapsychic insight to be able to discuss their issues logically like adults. But through play they are able to metaphorically communicate, express, and release interruptions in the cycle of experience. I am always amazed at the inner wisdom of children and do trust that many times they can lead the way to their own recovery and health.

This type of "topdog and bottom dog" dialogue provides support for both contact and resistance functions and facilitates integration so that true learning takes place that will provide choiceful behavior in the future, not just new introjects.

PREPARING THE BACKPACK: GATHERING EQUIPMENT FOR THE JOURNEY

What equipment is needed for this journey? If we honor the developmental levels of children, therapy with them will look much different than it does with adults. To take advantage of play, the natural language of children, toys and art materials are essential. Play therapists have common ideas about toy selection in their work with children. I believe that all therapists would concur that play materials should be reflective of the cultural and ethnic group of the child and parents. Play therapist Gary Landreth (1991) recommended that toys and play materials used with children facilitate a wide range of emotional and creative expression by children, engage the interest of children in some way, encourage verbal and nonverbal investigation and expression by children, provide mastery experiences in which children can experience success, and be sturdy and safe for children to use in play.

Virginia Axline, the original child-centered play therapist, stated that better results are obtained when the play materials are in view and accessible to the child to choose his or her own medium for expression, rather than being selected and placed by the therapist on the play table or in the sandbox. In her book *Play Therapy,* Axline (1947) suggested the following play materials:

> Nursing bottles; a doll family; doll house with furniture; toy soldiers and army equipment; toy animals; play house materials, including table, chairs, cot, doll bed, stove, tin dishes, pans, spoons, doll clothes, clothesline, clothespins, and clothes basket; a didee doll; a large rag doll; puppets; a puppet screen; crayons; clay; finger-paints; sand; water; tow guns; peg pounding sets; wooden mallet; paper dolls; little cars; airplanes; a table; an easel; an enamel-top table for finer painting and clay work; toy telephone; shelves; basin; small broom; mop; rags; drawing paper; finger painting paper; old newspapers; inexpensive cutting paper; pictures of people, houses, animals and other objects; and empty berry baskets to smash. . . . All playthings should be simple in construction and easy to handle so that the child will not be frustrated by equipment which he cannot manipulate. . . . Sand is an excellent medium for the children's aggressive play. It can readily keep pace with most elastic imagination. The materials should be kept on shelves which are easily accessible to the children. (pp. 54–55)

An Adlerian play therapist, Kottman (1995), recommended toys that represent five distinct categories, including family/nurturing, 'scary, aggressive, expressive, and pretend/fantasy toys. In a later publication (Kottman, 2001), she discussed two trends in toy selection based on the theoretical orientation of the therapist—maximalist and minimalist. She classified Gestalt therapists as having minimalist playrooms, meaning that they "contain a few play materials selected especially for a certain child, for a specific intervention, or to attain a particular goal" (p. 85). She went on to describe playrooms that are relatively empty, with materials stored in other rooms or in locked cabinets. Though Kottman's minimalist playroom does not reflect the practice of the Gestalt child therapists I have known, it can be valuable for certain children. For example, it may be ideal for playing/working with children who are hyperactive or hypervigilant because these children have difficulty focusing their awareness, making choices, staying with a process or figure, and ending a piece of work/play. On the other hand, delimiting choices in the playroom for many children robs them of the very processes they need to develop in their contacting skills.

When child therapists talk about their collections (backpacks) of toys, games, hand puppets, media, and so on, most recount adventures such as visiting garage sales and flea markets, revisiting their children's playrooms, and watching for special buys at toy stores. Reynolds and Stanley (2001), both of whom are Gestalt counselors who have worked with children in school settings, described several different possible arrangements for Gestalt child therapists in terms of toys and equipment, including sharing a room with other school personnel, using a whole classroom, and traveling to two or more buildings. They also recommended that school counselors avoid toys that they feel uncomfortable with, as children may pick up on the counselor's nonverbal cues that can create an unnecessary dynamic. They are in agreement with Oaklander that some traditional games or toys such as "Don't Break the Ice" or "Connect 4" are valuable to have on hand to allow the child to decompress and relax before leaving the session. Their final reminder is, "No toys should be used that cannot be replaced" (p. 358).

Another issue regarding selection of toys to be used in a school setting revolves around the adoption by many school districts of "zero tolerance" policies in reaction to recent school shootings. Therapists and counselors in schools are faced with the dilemma of whether to include toys that have traditionally been used for expression of anger, such as rubber knives, toy guns, dart guns, bop bags, and handcuffs. I believe that if these items are not included in the playroom, children are robbed of their ability to express angry and aggressive feelings, thereby eliminating the possibility of healthy release of anger in a session that can lead to a decrease of aggressive acts in daily life. In contrast, others believe quite strongly that allowing violent toys at school socializes children to believe that violence is an acceptable alternative. It is important to develop a sound rationale for your choice of toys and gain support from administration, faculty, and parents.

INCLUDING PARENTS/GUARDIANS/ SCHOOL ON THE JOURNEY

Parents play an integral role in the journey to wellness for their child. Communication with parents is a part of every session with a child because parents are valuable sources of information regarding what is happening at home and at school. Educating parents about the therapy process and encouraging them to support the changes the child is making enhance the likelihood of success of the therapy. Working with parents to enhance their own level of awareness and expression of emotions supports their growth process as well as that of their children. Increased parental functioning can clear the way for children to continue on their own rightful, healthy path of growth (Oaklander, 1994, p. 156).

Because many of the symptoms children exhibit are related to the context of their environment, it is important to include and interview the caretakers who are responsible for those environments. Private practitioners and agency counselors can benefit from communicating with the school. Likewise, school counselors can benefit from connecting with the private practitioner, the aftercare program or babysitter, and even the child's friends, if deemed appropriate. For children whose time is divided between divorced or separated parents, it is important to understand how they cope with and adjust to these differing environments. Looking through Gestalt eyes, we would want to assess their contact functions in both environments. These are all valuable resources to assist in providing support for the child or information regarding the child's functioning. It is essential that all ethical and legal guidelines be followed to contact these sources.

THE BEGINNING OF THE JOURNEY: FIRST CONTACT

First contact with a child client may begin in a variety of ways depending on your setting, style, reasons for referral, and so forth. You may begin by meeting with the child alone, the child and both parents, one parent, stepparents, a guardian, a teacher, a sibling, or even a best friend. Regardless of who is present at the first meeting, the legal and ethical guidelines of your state and profession must be followed in terms of permission and informed consent.

It is important for me to determine how the child views the therapy process. If I have met with the parent(s) alone before seeing the child for the first time, I will have already coached them about what to say about bringing the child for the first session. But I still am curious about how the child has perceived our visit(s), and I will often begin by asking, "Do you know who I am?" and "What did your parents tell you about coming here to meet with me?" At this time, I can correct any misconceptions and attempt to normalize the experience for the child. If the child has referred him- or herself (as is often the case in a school setting), I might ask, "Who are you?" "Could you tell me a little about yourself?" or "What would you like help with?" At some point I would ask, "What have you told your parent(s)/guardian about coming here to see me?" This is important if permission is needed before counseling a child in a school. For a child who is very resistant or who does not want to talk, I may not ask any questions at all in the beginning, as questions might increase the child's defensiveness. Instead, I'd consider introducing myself and what I do, followed by inviting the child to draw a picture or pick a toy he or she was interested in playing with.

Sometime during the first session, I am likely to ask the parent and child, "How would we know if you were doing better and not needing counseling anymore?" or "How could we tell if this issue had been resolved?" or "How could we tell things were better for you?" The answer to any of these questions may be useful in the future to help decide when it is time to terminate the counseling.

My main goal in the first session of counseling is to make good contact with the child and begin building a mutually respectful relationship—the groundwork for the "I-Thou" relationship. My hope is that the child will leave the first meeting with a desire to return to see

PETER: I noticed, Cynthia, that you switched at this point in the chapter to using the word *counseling* instead of *therapy* regarding the kind of work we can do with children in schools. I am aware of the debates and tensions regarding the terms *therapy* versus *counseling*. I know that many school-oriented professionals argue that we can't and shouldn't do "therapy" in schools (not enough time or resources, it is argued) and that the best we can do is "counsel" in ways that address shorter-term and less involved issues. I'm curious about your thoughts on this: Do you do "therapy" with children in schools or "counseling"? How do you think about these different terms and the contexts and audiences in which you use them?

and be with me. I expect that the child will have experienced me fully present in the here and now, will have found the experience validating, and will want more of the same. Although I may have certain activities that I would like to try or subjects that I would like to cover, there is no lesson plan or agenda for this meeting. I will trust the process and witness what unfolds. The Gestalt therapist can be both directive and nondirective. For me, part of the session may be following the child's lead if there is interest or excitement regarding the toys, media, and art materials. I may ask the child to draw a picture of a safe place and an unsafe place and when finished, invite him or her to tell me a story about each of the pictures. However, because I believe we should never try activities with children that we have not experienced ourselves, I suggest that before using this medium with children you do Activity #2 (at the end of the chapter) yourself and share it with a partner.

The role of the therapist is twofold—directive and nondirective. In the nondirective component, the Gestalt therapist works on developing the "I-Thou" relationship with the child. This happens largely by being in the here and now, staying in the present moment with the child. Gestalt therapists are not afraid to be "real" in the session. Although Oaklander (1997) stated that some of the other basic play therapy skills of tracking, restating content, and reflecting feelings are not particularly helpful in establishing the relationship, I beg to differ. These are ways to demonstrate "I am here, I see you, I understand, I care," especially with younger children. Tracking can be a powerful technique in mirroring the self for the child. I have found these play therapy skills to be readily integrated into Gestalt therapy and used successfully.

The Gestalt child therapist is also directive in his or her relationship with children. These types of interaction generally fall into the category of "I-It" contact. They consist of such things as preselecting play media and art materials and games while designing activities and experiments to provide children with experiences that are different from those they have encountered with other

CYNTHIA: I was trained, Peter, to differentiate between counseling and therapy by viewing counseling as a more short-term, educational approach and therapy as a long-term, remedial approach. But in working with children (especially using Gestalt interventions) in the schools for 16 years, I found that boundary to be quite blurry. Ideally, as a school counselor, I would refer any child with serious problems to an outside agency. My experience has shown that of those referrals, only 10% of parents or guardians follow through with actually scheduling an appointment, and then perhaps only 10% of that 10% ever go to therapy for more than one session. And now most insurance companies limit therapy to six sessions! In the meantime, with deinstitutionalization, the public schools must deal with all children, even those with many serious emotional, physical, social, and intellectual challenges. Even if the child is one of the few to get good therapy outside the school, the child still comes to school every day bringing all of the problem behaviors with him or her. The scope of practice for a school counselor does not include diagnosis and treatment of mental and emotional disorders, but it does include helping students to overcome impediments to learning and to become successful in the areas of academic, career, and personal/social skills. I have found Gestalt approaches can be successfully used doing short-term counseling with children in schools. And I can assist children with more serious problems to strengthen their sense of self, become more aware, choiceful, and response-able, without doing labeling that is destructive to the child. I also had the pleasure of working in the same elementary building for 13 years, so I was able to work with certain children throughout their childhood years, maybe not for the traditional therapy hour once a week, but for a significant amount of time spread out over the K–6th-grade years—in classrooms, small groups, individually, or with their parents in psychoeducational groups.

people and in other environments. Therapists might direct children to use materials and to engage in experiments to learn how to increase or decrease their contact with the environment, improve their ability to make choices, enhance their sense of self, express and impress their emotions, and nurture themselves. Gestalt therapists also use many advanced play therapy skills, including creative dramatics, role plays, empty chair, video enactments, mutual storytelling, therapeutic metaphors, art projects, confrontation, sand tray, drama work, and guided imagery, to name a few (Lampert, 2003; Lederman, 1969; Oaklander, 1969/1978, 1992). In addition to the advanced play therapy skills listed above, the Gestalt therapist may create games or experiments to help the child access and use the senses. So an actual session may involve games and experiments designed by the therapist especially for the needs emerging during the here and now of the session.

As child therapists, we must be reminded that most children will not sustain intense therapeutic work for an entire 50 minutes, so a typical session may flow from a quick reacquainting and checking-in time, to a warm-up time involving making contact with the senses, relaxation, or a guided visualization, followed by a brief piece of intense therapeutic work, and ending with play directed by the child that allows for decompression before returning back to the classroom or to the parent in the waiting room.

THE ACTUAL JOURNEY: THE THERAPY PROCESS

As a kind of road map for the journey, I will give examples and descriptions of types of experiments and activities that can be used with children with issues at different phases of the Gestalt homeostasis cycle or continuum of experience.

Therapeutic Processes for the Sensation/Desensitization Phase

In the *sensation/desensitization* phase, I suggest different experiments to the child in order to facilitate his or her tuning in to or tuning out bodily sensations, depending on what is needed for growth. Many children have learned to cope with trauma by desensitizing the body, whereas others have become desensitized due to lack of environmental support for honoring and addressing everyday body sensations. If children hear statements like "You can't possibly be hungry/tired/thirsty right now. Be quiet and settle down" often enough, they will hear only these adult messages and disregard their own internal sensations. Given enough adult mandates, eventually they can lose all contact with those sensations.

I might suggest that the child put one hand over his or her heart and the other hand just above the navel area, and then ask the child to simply pay attention to the breath coming in and out of the lungs, reporting sensations that are experienced. If I notice some particular frozen or excessively active part of the body, I may ask the child to close his or her eyes and focus on that part of the body. I may further suggest shaking or stretching that part of the body or making it very still. I frequently use the waterfall breath (one deep inhalation followed by three short exhalations) as an experiment on tuning in to how breath can cause or inhibit other sensations. Throughout these activities with children, I communicate in a respectful manner how valuable these sensations can be, and I model honoring them appropriately and valuing the wisdom of the organism. Sensations are an important foundation in the development of a sense of self.

Some children overreact to sensations and may not have learned to modulate their reactions to them. In these cases, it may be valuable to experiment by staying with the sensations more fully in the present moment with my support. At times, the child may need to be taught how to desensitize in order to function more fully in some environments and situations. For example, an experiment with an uneasy stomach sensation may involve pushing that energy down the torso, into the legs, through the legs into the feet, and then down into the ground like roots.

Colleen (a second grader who was being seen because of her high-strung, perfectionistic, anxious behavior) came for an appointment right after dance class one evening, complaining of a funny feeling in her legs. She spontaneously broke out into an Irish jig and smiled and said, "This is my dance!" Then she suddenly changed her dance into a slow ballet, saying, "And this is a Mommy dance." I encouraged her to show with her legs each member of her family. Daddy's dance was a march, and her younger sister's dance was like a butterfly flitting across the room. She left the session with a smile and said, "We each have our own style, but sometimes I wish my Dad would have a little ballet with his march."

Therapeutic Processes for the Awareness/Introjection Phase

At the *awareness/introjection* phase, I want to help the child fully develop the senses, such as touching, hearing, seeing, and smelling. I might begin a first session with a child with a game of "I Spy," requesting that the child describe an object within sight in the room and then give me three chances to guess what the object is. When a correct guess is made, the one who guessed correctly gets to be the one spying. This game helps to develop powers of visual observation and description and can be a fun icebreaker for children. Two other favorite activities I learned from Hendricks and Wills (1975) are ear centering and eye centering, which I do along with the child, and then taking turns reporting to each other our experiences. I have also used 8 to 12 unmarked containers with different fragrant items, making a game out of guessing what is in the container on the basis of smelling it. I may suggest a trust walk with a blindfold in certain cases, which can be a rich experience if there is enough support for the child to take the risk to do it. Finger paints, watercolors, clay, and sand are also great media to include when designing experiments for awareness.

Madison was a 10-year-old whose parents were divorced when she was a year and a half. She became a "parentified" child, acting as if she were 32 years old by the time she was 6. Her mother, who liked a very orderly and neat household, was concerned that Madison had missed some important stages growing up because of the disruptions that occurred so early in her life. Initially, Madison talked to me as if she were an adult, looking upon the toys in the playroom with great disdain. When her eyes glanced over at the paints, I asked her what she was aware of. She replied, "I was looking at the paints and thinking they were just for babies." When I mentioned that many adults like to work with the paints, she decided to give them a try, drawing a stereotypical house, with tree in front, yellow sun, blue clouds, and flowers in the yard. At one point, paint began dripping off the brush and she wiped it on her finger and then smeared it on the paper, then stopping all movement for a minute, her eyes glazed over. When I asked her what she was aware of at that moment, she began to spill out a story about being left alone in a car in front of an apartment building on a cold winter day when she was very young. She amused herself by drawing with her finger on the steamed-up windshield for an hour before police found her. (Her mother later confirmed the story as fact.) In future sessions, Madison wanted to finger paint and then suggested toe painting. We spent time brushing each other's toes and feet with paint, then skated, stamped, and tiptoed on large butcher-block paper spread on the floor. Madison shouted with glee, giggling and laughing like a 2-year-old. Within 6 weeks, she was able to be in touch with her toddler self and was acting more like a 10-year-old than a 32-year-old at home.

In working with introjecting children, I have invited them to draw a life-size picture of themselves on paper, later asking them to give me a word that others in their life would use to describe them, as I write those descriptors on separate pieces of paper. Then I ask the children which of these descriptive words truly fit their own view of self. Children can then attach or remove the descriptive words based on what they believe fits for them. This activity can also be done by taking a Polaroid picture, gluing it to a large piece of construction paper, and letting the child take it for a week, soliciting descriptive words for a week. The next session involves sifting through the descriptors to see if the child accepts all of the words or if there are any words that family or friends did not say that should be included. Beverly came back with her picture with 10 different adjectives scrawled around it. She immediately scratched one out, saying, "My brother may think I am stupid, but that is just not true!"

Children with ADHD may experience the world as a satellite receptor dish rather than a single receptor, becoming aware of so many stimuli as to be overwhelmed and unable to focus fully on any one of the signals. Games that introduce a child to a task and make a contest out of focusing on the task can increase the ability to attend. This game can be particularly helpful when started with very small segments of time that gradually increase to 5 or 10 minutes. The therapist and child can take turns being the distractor.

Therapeutic Processes for the Mobilization/Projection Phase

Owning projections is an important aspect of Gestalt work with children that Oaklander has written extensively about. Asking the child to give voice to his or her creations in clay or sand tray is a powerful technique. Eric was a 13-year-old boy whose parents had been divorced for 4 years. He was an excellent student, artist, and athlete and was well behaved both at school and at home. He was brought for therapy because both parents felt he had not dealt with the finality of the divorce and seemed preoccupied with getting his parents back together again. He refused to talk to anyone about the divorce, behaving very stoically. He told me he had nothing to say about it. I requested he create a world in the sand tray because he didn't want to talk. He sat for 15 minutes before creating the scene. I waited patiently without expectations. His tray was divided into two sections. On the right was a house surrounded by lush trees, a pond with a boat. There was a family of four happily playing and sunning themselves. A gray and white dog watched over the right side of the tray. The left side of the tray contained a mountain surrounded by a moat of water. A small cabin perched on the top of the mountain beside a scraggly tree. A lone wolf sat to the left side overlooking the moat. When asked, Eric told me that he was both the dog and the wolf. The right side of the tray was how things used to be for him, the left side of the tray was how things were for him now. When asked if he could give voice to the animals, the wolf said, "I am lonely and isolated. I do not belong anywhere. My world has been destroyed." As Eric began to own his loneliness and isolation, tears streamed down his face. (His parents had not seen him cry over the divorce at all!) We spent the rest of the session processing his grief and some time in future sessions on developing new family traditions in his two homes with each of his parents separately.

Therapeutic Processes for the Action/Retroflection Phase

Activities or experiments may be designed to undo retroflections that prevent the child from taking action to achieve contact. A child may be doing to or for the self what he or she would secretly like to do to or for others. Katie was a 6-year-old who had been diagnosed with cancer at the age of 2. Most of her life had been spent in chemotherapy. As she was finishing her treatment, her mother was diagnosed with a serious illness. Throughout all of these ordeals, Katie smiled and never complained. She referred to the regular spinal taps that the doctors used for diagnosis as "back checks" (which were excruciatingly painful) and endured them without crying. Katie's mother brought her for therapy because Katie had told her that she wished she would die. Mother could not understand this attitude, as they were "almost out of the woods" with the cancer. In my work with Katie I was aware of her high need to please me, often cutting off her spontaneity and emotional expression. I also believed that she was retroflecting the anger and pain she must have had regarding the violations of her body by doctors and nurses for 4 years. During our fourth session, I decided to create a puppet show just for Katie. I selected three puppets: a doctor, a nurse, and a child. I proceeded to put on a show in which the doctor and nurse attempted to perform a medical procedure on the child and the child resisted with statements like "Forget it, I'm getting out of here. What do you mean it doesn't hurt? Do you think I'm crazy? You can't catch me." The medical puppets responded to these refusals with placating responses and then chased and tried to catch the child puppet. Katie roared with laughter and approval. "Do it again, oh, please do it again!" she begged me. I continued the puppet show with even more exaggerated behaviors by the puppets. She asked to be the doctor puppet herself once, then the child puppet. After several weeks of this puppet play, the death statements at home stopped. Mother reported that Katie was a little more spunky than usual but that she seemed more like a child who had never been sick. Katie did not refuse any medical treatments in the future, but she did express her dislike of the invasive procedures more often.

Therapeutic Processes for the Contact/Deflection Phase

Role playing is an excellent way to work with the *contact/deflection* aspect of the cycle. Rachel complained bitterly about being used as a spy by her father in a rancorous divorce battle. Rachel wanted her father to stop asking her to report on her mother's behavior. We role-played various solutions to the problem, and Rachel was able to succinctly and directly state her case in the role play. Then we discussed the benefits and risks of actually doing that with her father. Rachel decided that she felt much better just making the direct contact in the role play and didn't want to experience the consequences of being so direct with her father in real life. She role-played her usual ways of deflecting his questions by looking down, making a joke, changing the subject, and so forth. Rachel left the session empowered as she had different options that she could choose from the next time her father put her into that situation.

Therapeutic Processes for the Assimilation/Egotism Phase

As a therapist, I will almost always attempt to verify assimilation after successful contact has been made by asking questions such as "Is there anything in this sand tray scene, picture, or clay figure that reminds you of your real life?" or "What did you learn from this role play?"

or "How are you different because of this experience?" At times I may infer that assimilation has taken place when I witness changes in behavior, actions, emotional expression, or body language. Even young children can make the leap at times. After a particularly poignant role play, Leon (a first grader) told me that he learned that "not all white people are bad, and not all black people are good. There are good and bad people of all races." His teacher's report of his attitude at school further verified that assimilation had taken place.

Therapeutic Processes for the Closure/Confluence Phase

Once the cycle of experience is completed, it is valuable to notice if the child is able to let go or continues to hang on. Children can be shown how to say goodbye and how to establish rituals that facilitate closure and moving on. Jose came home from school to find that his precious gerbil had died. I had Jose draw a picture of his gerbil and then speak to the picture of the gerbil as if it were alive. I prompted him to say anything that he did not have a chance to say to the gerbil before it died. Jose made a list of all the things that he loved about the gerbil as well as what he didn't like about the gerbil. Jose planned a burial ceremony for his family. These activities assisted Jose in saying his farewells and being able to move on.

This part of the journey would not be complete without further reference to Violet Oaklander's (1969/1978) work with children, particularly the model she developed for how to work with drawings (or other creations such as sand tray, clay sculpture, etc.) from a Gestalt perspective. To facilitate the child's sharing him- or herself, she begins by having the child draw how he or she feels about being asked to draw. She encourages the child to stay with his or her feelings and continue the task as she follows along, noting her own process of being present with the child. This begins the sharing of the self. The next step is to have the child share the drawing, describing the picture, thus furthering the process of sharing the self. She promotes the child's further self-discovery by asking him or her to elaborate on parts of the picture by making parts clearer and more obvious, describing shapes, forms, colors, representations, objects, and people. She then asks the child to describe the picture as if it were the child and the child were it, using the word *I*. This is followed by selecting specific things in the picture for the child to identify with. Asking the child questions can aid the process. These questions grow out of "getting into" the drawing with the child and opening yourself up to his or her existence.

Focusing the child's attention sharpens awareness by emphasis and exaggeration of parts of his or her picture. Subsequent interventions may include having the child dialogue between different parts of the picture, encouraging him or her to pay attention to the colors, the sizes of things, and how the picture is organized. We also watch and listen for cues in the child's voice tone, body posture, facial and body expression, breathing, movement, and silences. Other types of process interventions that often serve as ground for experiments that derive from children's drawings are missing people and empty spaces in the pictures. Of utmost importance is staying with the child's foreground flow and attending to what is interesting and exciting. These process interventions facilitate identification and help children "own" not only what has been said about their picture but also their experience of the therapeutic process. At some point it is important to set the drawing aside and invite the child to address his or her life situation. If unfinished business emerged from the drawing, this should be addressed.

During the therapeutic journey, the therapist, child, and play media can interact in ways that create a synergy of healing. Although this section describes only a few examples of ways to work with children using different media, the possibilities are limitless. Being open to intuitive flashes and trusting the process can assist in finding unique and individual ways of touching children's lives, bringing both of you closer to the chosen destination.

PARTING WAYS: TERMINATION OF THE JOURNEY

If I am seeing the child in private practice or an agency, the parent's insurance and schedules would ideally allow me as the counselor to work with him or her for as long as necessary to attain our goals. However, in these days of managed care, combined with the daily demands of school counselors and business of parents, limits are often placed on the number of sessions, so progress toward therapeutic goals needs to be assessed and discussed frequently. In preparing for termination, it is useful to assess reports of improvements in school, in aftercare programs, and at home. Reflecting back upon the question asked during the first session regarding how parent and child would know that things were better also is especially helpful.

I like to be able to involve the child in the termination decision. Children seem to be able to tell when they don't need to come anymore. A good sign of health is when playing with their friends is deemed more desirable than playing with the therapist. As children's contacting processes improve and therapy nears completion, children readily move on. What has been precious time with you becomes less figural, their involvement in play and work is less intense, and there are fewer emotionally charged issues. It is not unusual for children who have been in therapy to have a good sense of when it is time to return. Some children will actually inform their parents a year or more after therapy was terminated that they need to return "for a tune-up"!

TRAVELOGUE

Many travelers detail the events of their travels with a journal or slide show upon completion in order to present a summary of the excursion to those who have never had the opportunity to journey. For me, after completion of the therapeutic journey with a child, it is time to let go, to take time to contemplate the lessons learned, to relish the fertile void, and to become renewed and ready for the next potential traveler. This time is an opportunity for a self-reflecting kind of travelogue detailing how I have changed and grown in the I-Thou relationship with the child, how the child has affected my life, how I have affected the growth and development of the child, and what new and creative experiments I was able to develop. Where I perceive that I have fallen short, I look at what I need to work on and what I need to do to more fully develop my skills as a child therapist and my qualities as a human being. It is a time for appreciation and celebration of the joys and struggles of helping children become more fully present, contactful, choiceful, and resourceful, knowing that Gestalt therapy enlivens and enriches these life-altering processes.

PETER: Cynthia, I want you to know what a pleasure it has been responding to your wonderful chapter! It is always encouraging for me to connect with others who are working from a humanistic and Gestalt orientation with children, especially children in the school setting. I hope that we can meet sometime soon and further the connection started with this cool book that Ansel and Sarah are putting together. I have had it in mind to start some kind of informal group of those of us who are doing this kind of work with kids in schools. I know a handful of folks from Violet's training programs, both nationally and internationally, who would describe themselves as coming from a Gestalt orientation while practicing school psychology and/or school counseling. Would you be interested in such a group?

In conclusion, thank you for a fine piece of writing that moves fluidly from theory to experience and from our adult way of thinking about our work with children to the necessarily different experience of actually working with children in practice! Thanks again for allowing me to "dialogue" with you.

CYNTHIA: And thank you, Peter, for your expressed interest in my chapter. Gestalt has been the foundation of my work with children and has made the process an exciting, productive, challenging, and rewarding experience!

REVIEW QUESTIONS

1. What are the six major spheres of child development used by Woldt in his Gestalt Experience and Observation Guide for Children? Identify at least one aspect of each sphere that appears to be more uniquely identifiable as Gestalt when compared with the usual theories of development (e.g., those of Freud, Erikson, Kohlberg).

2. What are the major considerations in setting up a child therapy room that are different from those for an adult-oriented setting? Other than play materials, which of these are most critical to anticipating therapeutic success with children, and why?

3. Your author makes a strong case for Gestalt being the therapy of choice for children. What are her main arguments? Do you agree or disagree? On the basis of your knowledge and experience with other approaches, make a case or argument against at least one of her points.

4. Identify the Gestalt terminology used to understand the resistances on the continuum of experience or Woldt's Gestalt homeostasis cycle, and list at least one way in which each of them interrupts the flow of experience or a person's contact with what is figural.

5. What is meant by your author's advocacy of "impressive therapy" and "impressive interventions"? How does this differ from the common conception of Gestalt therapy? When and with what types of client situations should such interventions be used?

6. The author has identified, as the heart and soul of Gestalt therapy with children, a number of types of Gestalt interventions for each of the stages of the Gestalt homeostasis cycle. Select at least one intervention in each of the stages that has the most meaning for you, and tell why it is meaningful.

EXPERIENTIAL PEDAGOGICAL ACTIVITIES

ACTIVITY 1: Your Inner Child—A Self-Assessment of Your Childhood. Create an exposition in which you present your awareness, reflections, explorations, analysis, re-explorations, and current understandings of your own childhood from a Gestalt perspective. You may want to assemble a narrative or lifeline in which you examine the development of your personality using the Gestalt cycle of experience. You may want to examine in detail five or six life-altering events that occurred in your childhood, how you chose to make meaning from them, and how this has affected who you are and what you believe as an adult. You are encouraged to be creative in assembling and writing your presentation of your life as a child. You may incorporate selections from such things as your childhood and family photos, early drawings, poetry, report cards, art work from elementary school, meaningful music, awards, and any other medium that might help you make better contact with the vitality of your inner child. If you have done a similar activity before, do it again, but this time add some new dimensions to your autobiographical statement, have some fun doing it, and create it in such a way that you are gaining a fresher, broader, deeper perspective on your life from ages 3 through 12.

ACTIVITY 2: Draw a Safe Place and an Unsafe Place. Using art material, create a picture or depiction of a safe place. It may be a real place where you feel safe or would like to go to in order to feel safe. It may be a fantasy or imaginary place that you can go to only in your mind's eye. As you begin drawing your safe place, also try to imagine how it smells in your safe place, what the temperature is, what sounds you experience there, even how it tastes, and so on. When that is finished, draw an unsafe place on another sheet of paper or on the back of the safe place sheet. Discuss with a classmate what you drew as well as what it was like to do the actual drawing.

ACTIVITY 3: Differences Between Children and Adults. Divide into groups of four to six and brainstorm ways that children are different from adults. Have someone in your group write every suggestion down, and ask for examples to clarify. Each group's list is written on the board, and the whole class then discusses how each of the listed differences might play out during the counseling process. Recommendations for how to make accommodations for differences are then solicited from the class. Example: Consider size differences between adults and children—one way this might play out is that the child sits in an oversized chair with feet dangling. A way to accommodate that difference would be to have some child-sized furniture in the office.

ACTIVITY 4: Applying the Gestalt Experience and Observation Guide for Children. Using the six spheres of child development explicated by Woldt— (a) emotional and affective development; (b) sensory, perceptual, and proprioceptive development; (c) physical and behavioral development; (d) intellectual and cognitive development; (e) social and interpersonal development; and (f) aesthetic awareness, intuition, creativity, and spirituality development—identify at least one strength or trait in each sphere that you remember developing during your own childhood and your approximate age and memorable experience(s) when that quality or characteristic was figural in your young life.

ACTIVITY 5: Rank-Order Ideas for Developing as a Gestalt Therapist with Children. The following suggestions are for furthering your professional growth. From your perspective, rank-order them from #1, what you believe would be the most important activity for you, to #12 or #13, what would be the least important for you, in the process of developing your Gestalt talents in working with children. Of the top five, which would you be most likely to do? Pick one of the top five, and develop a plan for how you can pursue growth in that way.

______ Respect and honor your resistances.

______ Take risks to expand your boundaries.

______ Enroll in a Gestalt training program or institute.

______ Join a professional Gestalt organization.

______ Develop a client relationship with a practicing Gestalt therapist.

______ View videotapes or listen to audiotapes of Gestalt therapy with children.

______ Read books and articles about using Gestalt therapy with children.

______ Attend a Gestalt conference or workshop.

______ Sift through what is presented in this chapter and see what fits for you.

______ Reject outright those things that do not fit for you in this chapter.

______ Keep a journal of the process of becoming a Gestalt therapist with children.

______ Be prepared to change and grow.

______ Other(s) not listed here, please identify.

CHAPTER **10**

Adolescents: Development and Practice From a Gestalt Orientation

Sarah M. Toman and Ann Bauer

Dialogue Respondents:
Mark McConville and Bruce Robertson

Sarah M. Toman is an associate professor at Cleveland State University, a graduate of the Gestalt Institute of Cleveland (GIC) Post-Graduate Training Program, and a licensed psychologist in private practice in Medina, Ohio. She worked briefly as a therapist in Ansel Woldt's practice while completing her postdoctoral internship. She was a founding member of the Kent Gestalt Writers' Group and has participated in the GIC Writers Group and in the "Cape Cod Writers' Group" at the Gestalt International Study Center. She has numerous textbook chapters and journal publications in the area of career development and counseling. She is past-secretary of the Association for the Advancement of Gestalt Therapy.

Ann Bauer is an assistant professor of counselor education at Cleveland State University and a certified school counselor and special education teacher. She received her mentoring in Gestalt therapy from Ansel Woldt, who was her major adviser in graduate school. Working with children and adolescents has been a lifelong interest for her: She has 20 years' experience in public schools as a teacher and counselor. Her debut as a crisis responder in the aftermath of the shootings at the Jonesboro, Arkansas, Middle School coincided with her supervision of master's-level school counseling students from Arkansas State University. She has since received advanced training and certification as a crisis responder and trainer of trainers by the National Organization for Victim Assistance and has served as membership co-chair for the Association for the Advancement of Gestalt Therapy.

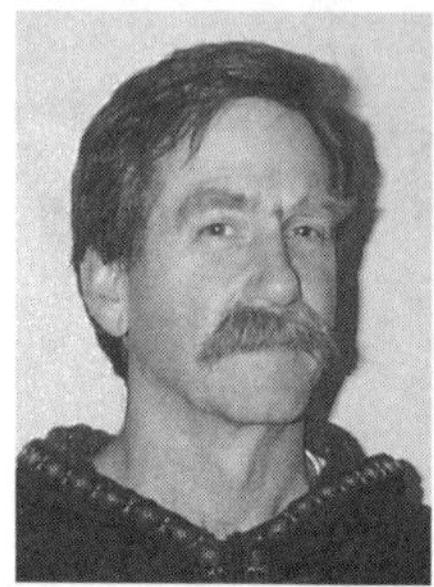

Mark McConville is a senior faculty member in the Gestalt Institute of Cleveland's Center for Clinical Theory and Practice and is co-founder of the institute's Advanced Training Program in Child and Adolescent Psychotherapy. As a clinical psychologist in private practice in Cleveland, he specializes in therapy with adolescents and their families. He is the author of *Adolescence: Psychotherapy and the Emergent Self* (1995); co-editor of *The Heart of Development: Gestalt Approaches to Working With Children, Adolescents and Their Worlds,* Vol. 1, *Childhood* (2002), and Vol. 2, *Adolescence* (2001); a member of the editorial board of *Gestalt Review;* and the author of numerous book chapters and articles. He is currently working on a book for parents of adolescents and young adults.

Bruce Robertson left a thriving private practice, a Gestalt training center, and a university teaching position in Dallas/Ft. Worth, where he specialized in adolescent therapy, to join the staff at Kanner Academy in Florida. He is a licensed clinical social worker whose job now is directing and providing direct services in the counseling and psychotherapy program for Sarasota Community School (formerly Kanner Academy), a private school for disturbed/disruptive youth. His wealth of experience using Gestalt therapy with adolescents and their families has made him a valuable resource for training and consulting in the United States, Australia, New Zealand, and elsewhere. Bruce is a past-president of the Association for the Advancement of Gestalt Therapy and continues to provide leadership for the greater Gestalt community.

The writing of an introductory textbook chapter dedicated to a Gestalt conceptualization of adolescent development and clinical applications is tricky business. First, there is no one, true, universally accepted Gestalt developmental model that can help us understand the teens that walk into our offices or high school counseling offices. We could wish for a blood test that predicts how many months or years remain in the transition from childhood to adulthood, but a Gestalt approach requires that, instead, we acknowledge the environmental field or contextual influences of adolescents' surroundings. We could wonder if any developmental model could ever adequately address the range of possible variations inherent in individual life fields. As a result, most of the writing on adolescent development from a Gestalt perspective is, itself, in its own adolescent phase of searching for identity and a voice, resulting in a mix of creative reframing and rebellion against what might be perceived as old school. Our task in this chapter is to offer one perspective for consideration in the ongoing search for a Gestalt developmental approach. We also include recommendations for, and examples of, clinical applications.

We start with the theories familiar to most of us working with adolescents in the context of Western industrialized society. Most models of human development devote a stage or two to specific aspects of adolescent functioning. For example, Piaget's (1952, 1966, 1972) model is useful for identifying stages of cognitive functioning, with most teens exhibiting formal operational thought. Erikson's model (1963, 1968) described the task of the teen years as identity development. Freud's (1966) model of personality development, focusing on psychosexual functioning, placed adolescence at the genital stage. Kohlberg's (1966, 1975, 1981) model of moral development described teens as approaching conventional to postconventional stages of morality. We suggest that you read Mortola (2001, 2003) for a comparison of these classic developmental models with the Gestalt notion of disequilibrium.

In this chapter, we assume that you are already familiar with the stages of cognitive development (Piaget), psychosocial development (Erikson), psychosexual development (Freud), and moral development (Kohlberg). Though each model contributes to our understanding of a specified area of development, none of them offers a sufficiently holistic perspective. In contrast, Gestalt theory is more focused on the configuration of the whole. That whole could be considered development of "the self" (McConville & Wheeler, 2001, p. 10), or, more specifically, the process of the self-in-relation to the world or field.

Philippson (2001) unearthed a lecture presented by Fritz Perls that may be one of the earliest attempts at a Gestalt-oriented theory of development. Perls provided an introductory view of development in one of his 1957 lectures at the Cooper Union Forum Lecture Series on "The Self," entitled "Finding Self Through Gestalt Therapy." In the publication of this lecture in the first volume of the *Gestalt Journal* (1978), Perls stated:

> There is the first basis. Let us call it the "animal self." Here we are like little children, merely organic beings with their needs, their primitive functions, though often very differentiated functions and their feelings. . . .
>
> The next layer would be a diminished layer. I call this the "as if" layer or social layer. In the social system the loss of nature is replaced by rules of games. . . .
>
> The next layer is the "fantasy layer," often called "mind." Please realize when we talk about "mind," in this context, we don't mean something opposed to the body. . . .
>
> Now the next layer would be covered by the isolation or ratification, or "objectivation layer." Here you tear sounds and tools out of their context and make them ready for a new organization. . . .
>
> Now the next stage, the final stage, is where we combine and organize these symbols and tools into machines and language. The essence of a healthy person is that there is unity, an integration of all the layers; he does not live merely in one level. (quoted in Philippson, 2001, pp. 104–109)

The linear stages, levels, or layers are obvious in Perls's model of development and, as Philippson (2001) pointed out, are reminiscent of psychoanalytic developmental models. Perls's identification of levels or layers also coincides with one focus of this chapter: to merge Anna Freud's (1963) notion of developmental lines with the Gestalt notion of levels of ground. Although some in the Gestalt community may argue that Gestalt concepts are unique to Gestalt theory and practice, others, a group in which we include ourselves, believe that Gestalt theoretical concepts have their roots and foundation in other disciplines. This chapter borrows from a psychoanalytic developmental model, as did Perls in 1957.

McConville (1995, 2001b, 2003) described Lewin's field theory (1948/1997) as integrating biological, psychological, and social aspects of adolescent development. In this chapter, we describe field theory and define some important elements of the field, context, or ground to consider when selecting relevant counseling interventions for adolescent clients. In particular, we have found Anna Freud's (1963) notion of parallel lines of development helpful for articulating the range of adolescent/field interactions.

FIELD THEORY

McConville (2001b) stated that, in working with adolescents, the field, or "life space," includes the "genetic and physiological givens, the familial, social, cultural, political and geographical aspects of development, and the experiential domains of thought, need, fantasy and personality organization" (p. 30). This acknowledgment of the field as consisting of the external or outer world of the client, along with his or her internal world, is reminiscent of the philosophical categorizations of Ken Wilber (2000), also discussed in Chapters 4, 8, and 14 of this text. Wilber explained that everything can be divided into the dichotomy of external or internal and further divided into quadrants of individual or group, resulting in the combinations of external/individual, external/ group, internal/ individual, and internal/ group. All are possible when considering the makeup of any client's experience.

MARK: Well, the first thing is that it is kind of a strange experience seeing myself quoted in a textbook. I mean, I love writing, but I'm always a little surprised when someone reads it.

SARAH: Your book *Adolescence* has been one of the primary influences on my thinking about and work with adolescent clients. I think of your book as an example of a trickle-down effect. There are many therapists who have read your book, whose adolescent clients benefit from it, along with those teens' teachers/parents who may now understand their students/children better because of your writing. And here is your book trickling down again to another audience.

Gestaltists typically consider the whole, or the self, in the context of the field, as it exists here and now. Yet development implies that the self, and even the field, is changing and shifting over time. In one moment a teen may seem very mature and adult, whereas in other moments he or she may seem 10 to 12 years old or even younger. Often the family does not easily tolerate such shifts, trying to maintain the homeostasis or equilibrium of an earlier developmental stage. Eventually, the teen may find that his or her "self" needs to function differently in the contexts of school, work, free time, and family. As clinicians, we need to consider that our clients may play yet another role in the context or field of the therapy office. During adolescence, the peer group becomes a figural field of influence while adults often become background—or at least that's what most teens wish they would do! As Levin (2003) stated, "[W]hat adults take seriously is not serious for the adolescent" (p. 248).

Although Gestalt theory's focus on the here and now seems contradictory to identifying stages of development, Gestalt theory also endorses change (see Chapter 5 of this book). McConville (1995) described the changing developmental tasks of adolescence as maintaining a place in the family field (a place of belonging) while also forming a "self" separate from the family. This can occur through rebellion, disowning, separating, or what he called "disembedding" (p. 35). As teens disembed from the family field, they often become very critical of family members and replace them by forming relationships with trusted others outside of the family. Next, adolescents turn inward to find their own voice and develop their own "self," often finding, too, their first true love or intimate partner. Eventually, adolescents learn how to shift from field to field, connecting and disembedding by choice. These notions parallel the family system theory concepts of emotional connectedness, emotional independence, and differentiation of self as defined by Bowen (Kerr, 2003).

> The implication of a field approach to development is that utilitarian psychological constructs, such as "self," "symptom," and "personality," and even developmental constructs, such as "adolescence," must be defined in field terms. . . . Symptoms, personality traits, and even adolescence itself, traditionally viewed as phenomena of the encapsulated self—the self conceived in isolation—must be understood to be creative adjustments to conditions of the field. (McConville, 2003, p. 216)

McConville (2001b) noted three aspects of Kurt Lewin's field theory relevant for conceptualizing the life space of our adolescent clients: "(1) the extension of the life space; (2) the increased differentiation of the life space; and (3) the change in organization of the life space" (p. 31). The first concept, "extension of life space," is the widening or expanding field of the developing individual over time. The life space of an infant or toddler is very narrowly defined compared to that of the typical teen. The second, "increased differentiation of the life space," refers to increased differentiation in experience, in behavior, and between parts of the self. The third, the "change in organization of life space," explains the notion of organizational interdependence or the reassembly of the differentiated parts into a more mature whole.

The developmental process from a Lewinian perspective has been described as "an unfolding that includes the de-structuring of childhood unity, expansion and differentiation of the life space, and transformation of the boundary processes that organize and integrate the field" (McConville, 2001b, p. 38). All the aspects and components of an adolescent's field can be a large entity for any one therapist to hold. We have found that it can be useful to take note of some of those destructured aspects of childhood and to trace their development, change, or adaptation over time. This effort can give clinicians a better sense of a client's field and can assist with the selection or creation of experiments or interventions that coincide with the aspect or level of ground that is surfacing or becoming figural in the moment. To that end, we have adapted from the child analyst Anna Freud the notion of parallel lines of development as one way to conceptualize and work with adolescents. As Gestaltists, we could think of these lines as a way to frame developmental aspects that run simultaneously through the growth and maturity process, as well as providing markers or definitions of the depth of the ground or field.

DEVELOPMENTAL LINES

To assist clinicians with their therapeutic endeavors with adolescents, we recommend considering the psychoanalytic concept of developmental lines as an organizing construct. The developmental lines can provide a framework for naming and noticing aspects of developmental progress. The notion that multiple developmental lines exist as "consequences of a child's separation from the mother, the parents or the home" (Freud, 1963, p. 14) has relevance for the ways adolescents disengage or disembed from the family field, as well as how they may present in psychotherapy. These lines can be considered elements in the field, each of which can become figural at some times and drop into the background at others. The task of informally noticing the degree of development along each line can help therapists to understand the adolescent's progress and maturation.

The convergence of field theory and use of Freud's notion of developmental lines occurred for me (Toman) during my own training at the Gestalt Institute of Cleveland. During one activity, we were all sitting on the floor in the Laura Perls room, stretched out with our pads of paper, crayons or markers, water bottles, and pillows for an experience of the notion of ground. Included in that introductory exercise was the concept of levels of ground. The trainers suggested that the concept of ground is not as simplistic as it seems; it is not merely the background face in the vase/face graphic. Rather, the ground contains a rich complexity of experiences and elements. Any element from this rich background may surface as figural at any given moment, but some elements lie at deeper levels within the ground whereas some elements ride more on the surface. During the moment when that definition was offered to us, I had one of those classic Gestalt "aha" moments, a sense of "I know something about that." The works of Anna Freud I had been reading surfaced, and I began to combine the notions of levels of ground with her notion of lines of development. For me, those lines offered one way of organizing the complexity of the developmental process.

Anna Freud (1963) presented four developmental lines, or tracks, to follow when assessing childhood disturbances. She also discussed the importance of reaching correspondence between the lines toward the goal of a "harmonious personality" (p. 28). The four lines are (a) dependency to self-reliance, (b) development toward body independence, (c) egocentricity to companionship, and (d) play to work. When looked at as a whole, the value placed on balance is clear. Because each line exists in the context of the others, self-reliance supports companionship (and vice versa) as dependency fosters egocentricity, and so on. Applying these developmental lines as one way to understand the experiences of adolescence can provide clinicians with a working map, giving structure or definition to the Gestalt field-based approach.

MARK: The central notion of Gestalt therapy (GT), in my opinion, is *contact*—deceptively simple but theoretically powerful and complex. This is important because all I've written about development boils down to the idea that it is the child's/adolescent's capacity for contact that develops. It is the evolution of this capacity that a Gestalt developmental psychology ought to be tracing and describing.

The magical thing about this simple word—contact—is that it implies pretty much the rest of Gestalt theory. Contact implies boundary (and thus we speak of a contact boundary), and boundary implies meeting—joining and separating. Another word that we use to designate this precise reality—and here Goodman was absolutely his most radical—is *self*. Self in GT, and in GT developmental theory, is really "selfing," a process of the person's necessary transcendence of him- or herself, completing him- or herself in the environment. So the question developmentally is, How does this process evolve over time? How does it mature? Certainly the contact process of a 6-year-old looks very different from the same child at 15, or again at 22. The challenge for Gestalt theory is how to talk about these changes.

From Dependency to Self-Reliance

In psychoanalytic terms, the successive stages along this line progress from (a) "the biological unity between the mother-infant couple . . . the need fulfilling relationship . . . based on the urgency of the child's body needs"; (b) "object constancy"; (c) the "ambivalent relationship of the preoedipal . . . rivalry with the parent of the same sex"; (d) the "latency period"; (e) the "adolescent revolt"; and (f) the "adolescent struggle around denying, reversing, loosening, and shedding the tie to the infantile objects . . . transferred to objects of the opposite sex outside of the family" (Freud, 1963, p. 14). Gestalt theory shifts from the focus on the individual to the notion that the change occurs within the context of a field, between the individual and the field. Freud's stages are apparent in the process McConville (1995) described as disembedding from the family field, yet the line from dependency to self-reliance also includes tasks accomplished during infancy and continuing into adolescence.

On the basis of contact style, resistance, and boundary formations, families can differ in their responses to adolescents' progress toward self-reliance or disembedding. McConville (1995) described healthy disengagement from the family field as being supported by the recognition that thoughts and feelings belong to the adolescent, whereas "outward behavior is very much family business" (p. 136). He also listed prototypical family resistances (introjecting, confluence, projecting, retroflecting, deflecting, and desensitization) that can influence an adolescent's process of disembedding.

Introjecting parents expect their teens to reflect the same worldview they hold, without any room for individual thoughts and interests. The "fight for control of mind and heart" (McConville, 1995, p. 141) leaves adolescents feeling unknown and alienated if they succeed in developing an independent "self." The only road to self-reliance is escape. "Confluent families are more concerned with feelings than behaviors" (p. 145), and conflict is considered a family failure. No one is allowed to disagree, everyone is nice, and discipline is accomplished with a plea rather than with authority. Projecting families often blame or "scapegoat" (p. 154) the adolescent for what is dysfunctional in the family field. The teen blames the parents while the parents blame the teen, both recognizing a problem without being able to identify the source. The retroflecting family is often very reserved and turned inward, restricting the opportunity to reach outward; "conflicts are swallowed and internalized" (p. 156). Deflecting families focus on superficial issues, without acknowledging feelings or "the heart of the matter" (p. 161). These families dilute contact through "humor, excessive talking, or politeness" (p. 159). Finally, the desensitized family seems dead, withdrawn, or hopeless. Risky behaviors may help the adolescent feel more alive and separate from the family.

Adolescents in therapy may come from any family contact style and may present almost

The concept of contact locates the "action" in the here and now, in the concrete, experiential boundary between person and person, and between person and environment. Herein lies the simple genius of GT. Everything that other psychological systems talk about—childhood influences, trauma, cognitive schemata, character structure, reinforcement history, etc., etc.—is present in some sense in the actual present moment of contact. Whatever has made a person what he or she is today (which is to say, all of his or her development) is present in this present, concrete moment of contact, in the way that the person engages others and environment. These influences may be present as the *ground* of contact, but they are nevertheless in the concrete present process of contact. Insofar as something has *not* shaped present experience and behavior, it is not relevant to the field of psychology, or at least psychotherapy.

So, you can see from this little homage to contact that I regard contact as being to psychology what the speed of light is to physics—the constant, or framework, that relativizes all the rest. This points to the other essential aspect of GT that is contained already in the word *contact,* and that is field theory. Field theory is really just a way of theoretically underscoring the belief/fact that the person, and indeed the self, is self-transcendent, requiring an environment for its actualization and therefore as part of its essential structure. In my writing, all I was trying to say was that it is this capacity for contact that develops. How to describe that development is the challenge.

SARAH: I also believe that the notion of contact is very important to understanding the process of being in a therapeutic relationship with an adolescent client. I think there may be some misperception out there, that establishing and maintaining contact with adolescents is *very* difficult. Yet I have found the willingness of adolescents to be contactful (and their experience of my willingness as an adult to

anywhere along the developmental line from dependency to self-reliance. Our premise is that the explanation for their location on this developmental line may lie in the awareness of the contact style of the family field. Separation from the family of origin is one task of adolescence, yet we need to consider, too, how well the field tolerates the separation and redefinition. Brafman (2001) described, through case examples, how "child and parent influence each other in such a way that it may be impossible to establish what is cause and what is effect in their interactions" (p. 2), or, in other terms, what is figure and what is ground.

From our clinical experiences, we contrast two clients, both 17 years old, whose family contexts put them in very different locations along the developmental line from dependency to self-reliance. The first client had recently learned of the sudden death of her friend at a time when she was also tolerating the divorce of her parents. A degree of lack of object constancy returned for her in the form of wondering if her mother would leave her too. Because the family style of resistance could be described as confluent, conflict was not acceptable, and the divorce was experienced as a failure. Disembedding from the family and establishing self-reliance had to be postponed until mother and daughter first separated from the father. The second client, who firmly believed that his father, a respected professional, was stupid and had no understanding of the client's musical talents, was attempting to sever all connections with his family. The family, because of their introjected contact style, devalued his interest and talent in music. The client believed he had no option but to completely disengage from his family as quickly as possible in order to establish his self-reliance. These two clients offer examples of differing expressions of development from dependency to self-reliance and show how identifying developmental progress is often impossible or even meaningless if done separately from the context of the field.

even want to be in contact with them) as perhaps the most therapeutic aspect of the "work." I wish I could better get across to my students and colleagues the excitement created in the session when contact is the primary objective.

MARK: I agree with what you have said. I think that so many adults have difficulty making contact with adolescents because they have lost contact with their own adolescent history and wisdom. Most adolescents are hungry for adult contact; they just don't want it at the expense of being judged and invalidated. Most adolescent clients, once they feel known and accepted for who they are, will take in even very challenging therapeutic dialogue.

SARAH: I think your words "being known" have given me another way to understand why the notion of Freud's developmental lines has been so useful for me in my work/contact with adolescents: The lines help define some of the ways in which I want to know my adolescent clients. I am interested in knowing about their self-reliance, their relationship to their body, their friends, their activities at school, and jobs/hobbies, as well as anything else they want me to know about them. I am not so interested about where they reside on a particular line, but rather I'm interested in their unique process of how they "do" the line. For me, I think of the lines as the content and process pieces around which we can have contact.

MARK: Yes. I liken it sometimes to the work of a field anthropologist. We're entering unfamiliar territory, and we want the locals to teach us about their world. Sometimes you're working with a kid and getting nowhere, and then he mentions something about skateboarding, or music, or trail biking. And you let yourself get genuinely curious, and whoosh! The next thing you know, you're inside his world, and it's like you are meeting him or her for the first time. And it's very much like you say when you talk about developmental lines: My client may have a dramatically different sense of self and way of making contact when the meeting point changes from, say, schoolwork or family problems to some area of interest that feels more uniquely personal.

Developing Toward Body Independence

Freud (1963) wrote that "although for the whole of early childhood, the child's life will be dominated by body needs, body impulses, and their derivatives, the quantities and qualities of satisfactions and dissatisfactions are determined not by himself but by the environmental influence" (p. 16). The markers for development along this line are progressions in the areas of "feeding, sleeping, evacuation, body hygiene, and prevention of injury and illness" (p. 17). Although these topics during the infancy stage may manifest as weaning from breast-feeding, sleeping through the night, potty training, cleanliness, and biting or scratching, further development along this same line has been observed in our experiences of working with adolescents. Parents frequently initiate therapy due to their adolescent's manifestations of problematic body-related issues.

One way the feeding issue can present in adolescence is as an eating disorder. Blaney and Smythe (2001) described a Gestalt model for the treatment of adolescents diagnosed with anorexia nervosa, acknowledging that "the Gestalt model's emphasis on the role of context in the development of the emerging adolescent self, is compatible with our own emphasis on the role of context—family and society—in the development and treatment of an adolescent eating disorder" (p. 201). It is also common to hear parents describe their frustrations with their teens staying up all night online and sleeping until noon on weekends, with messy rooms full of dirty clothes and dishes, and with biting and scratching progressing to cutting, piercing, and self-mutilating behaviors. Though such behaviors can be problematic to the parent, none have meaning on their own, without a consideration of the context or field and developmental implications.

One client who displayed a disruption along this line was a 15-year-old high school freshman who bathed only when forced to by her parents, pulled out her eyebrows, chewed her fingernails to the point of bleeding, binged and purged, and littered her bathroom with used tampons. For this particular client, the developmental disruption along this line could be linked to early childhood sexual abuse; having had her physical body disrespected by others created the potential for her to continue that behavior toward herself. Another client, age 13, had daily difficulties establishing body independence. She dealt with her anxiety by wearing the same clothes every day and by controlling her food. A power struggle ensued with her home economics teacher, who insisted that all students eat what they cooked in class, starting with something as simple as cinnamon toast. As the client's development along this line progressed, she began to wear lipstick for the first time, select new blouses to wear, and eat new foods in her home economics class, though extensive support was required to help her handle her fears and anxieties.

From Egocentricity to Companionship

Along the developmental line of egocentricity to companionship, Freud (1963) described progression as moving from a "selfish, narcissistically oriented outlook" to relating to other children as objects, then helpmates, then as partners. This line is about socialization, and social development can occur only in contact with others. B. Robertson (personal communication, May 15, 2003) suggested that an essential part of development, which we believe coincides with this line, is a growing awareness of self and others. Robertson stated that during an initial phase adolescents turn a critical eye toward family and peers, operating under a heightened awareness of human behaviors and interactions, in a process similar to that described by McConville (1995). At first, this awareness can have a strong flavor of projection into the field as teenagers detect and identify in others the feelings and attitudes that they cannot as yet identify within themselves. A metaphoric image for this process can be drawn from the old adage that when I point one finger at you, I am pointing four fingers at myself. Teenagers who are actively pointing accusing fingers at others are often initially unaware of how much of the accusation originates as feelings toward themselves. At this point, adolescents will often lay responsibility for their choices and behaviors on others within their field and lack awareness of the part their own choices play in the events that occur and the consequences they receive.

At the next level of deepening awareness, adolescents begin to explore an understanding of self and the power of that self to influence events, responses from others, and consequences. This phase can begin with a somewhat exaggerated, dramatic, and highly critical focus on self. In a healthy developmental process, teenagers move past this point of critical self-focus and learn to identify their own strengths and weaknesses, become aware of times they need support, and learn to articulate needs in a way that mobilizes support. Teens' awareness of the part they play in the responses and reactions in the surrounding field empowers them to be responsible (response-able) for self-change. A lack of awareness can leave adolescents stuck in misdirecting their efforts toward changing others and in a blind and futile pursuit of happiness.

BRUCE: I think that it is important that we not just settle for the concepts that come from other theories and that we stretch ourselves to bring a way of describing how an adolescent develops from a Gestalt theory perspective. The majority of existing theories start from an assumption of seeing the self in an isolated way and thus assume the basic process is internal, while Gestalt theory brings the idea that the self is continually being formed in relation to the other, to what is outside as well. This interrelationship and how it forms is "who" we are. It is both individual in its creation and collective in that we are all going through the same process. Kurt Lewin talked about this process in his concept of life spaces.

ANN: Talk to me more about a life space model.

BRUCE: Lewin wrote about the interconnectedness of the self-other process and especially about what is developed in the "in-between" of that process. Not so much the either/or of the self/other but the process of what is developing and how we organize our "self-sense" (self-gestalt) as we move into our different life spaces, including how we organize the transitions between these spaces.

ANN: It would be like having a different personality in different places.

BRUCE: Not so much completely different personalities as different organizations of our repertoire of who we are (which is continually being added to). It is important to emphasize that it is not simply that we alter who we are with regard to our situation, it is that we are continually developing who we are as we do this. We are often attempting novel ways of being. This is why adolescence stands out. Almost all of the process and the situations are new, and thus we are witnessing this self-other formation in an intense way. This process doesn't stop with adulthood, it just becomes less obvious. The understanding of an adolescent's

The gifts of a deepening level of awareness include an ability to recognize personal needs, mobilize support to meet those needs, and be responsible (response-able) to and for self. When this level of awareness is not achieved, it becomes difficult to be in and/or maintain relationship with others, and a deficit is created along this developmental line toward companionship.

Relationships, companionship, friendships, and intimate partners are frequent topics of conversation during any given therapy hour with teens. Frequently, the wishes of the family field and school fields are in contrast to what adolescents wish for themselves. One client, adopted by her current parents when she was 9 years old, denied any relationship or attachment to her adoptive parents, replacing this relationship with multiple sexual partners and friends of questionable influence. Her adoptive parents' deep wish to be experienced by her as good parents suggests one explanation for her heightened degree of rebellious individuation. Other teens form strong friendship bonds that last a lifetime. As therapists, we frequently get to hear about how teenagers experiment with differentiation by behaving differently when with their parents, in school, and with their friends and partners. Development along the companionship line is important not only during infancy and toddlerhood, as outlined by Freud (1963), but also in the differentiation and individuation process during the stage of adolescence.

Some adolescents begin to establish companionship by identifying with a group or clique. Teens who do not find a group often struggle with feelings of rejection and alienation. Some teens believe they can be accepted by their peers by using drugs and alcohol or joining a gang, whereas others find acceptance by participating in sports or playing a musical instrument in the high school band. Some teens who have felt rejection express their pain through homicidal and/or suicidal behaviors. The need every human feels for companionship or acceptance by a group seems most salient in the developmental stage of adolescence.

process is complicated because we no longer have access to the majority of their life spaces.

ANN: And what is developmental about that?

BRUCE: They are carrying their developmental process much more independently. The developmental aspect of life spaces has to do in a practical way with how aware we are of our process of organizing. In the process of developing our self-other sense, we all develop patterns that work for us in some way. The problem is that what we used in the past may not be a great fit for the current situation. So we have the continuum of experimenting with something new or holding on to what we know. In many ways we are constantly doing both.

ANN: For me as an adolescent, it was trying to figure out what people wanted me to be and to try and be that. Now I don't do that so much anymore.

BRUCE: So for you an important developmental organization that you carry is how you experience your "self" in relation to what people want from you. You have experimented with "figuring out" what people want and changing what you do and somehow that did not work for you in the way you were doing it. So now you say you do something different. I imagine that process is still going on for you as an adult. That is a good example of how we can explore how we see our process as "self," not so much that the self exists in some static way. Teenagers have moved from childhood and its more predictable life spaces to a new arena of social life spaces that are often very separate. This separateness is significant because it means that certain life spaces now can be hidden and not shared. So now adolescents have the possibility of holding on to some experiences and making a decision about what they want to share and how they share it. So as teenagers come home from being with their friends and move into their family life space, they now carry a new

From Body to Toy Parallels—From Play to Work

Freud (1963) outlined progression along the line from play to work as development from infants' play with their own fingers, mouth, or the mother's body to a transitional object (like a blanket or stuffed animal), and then to the generalizing of toys as symbolic representations. She compared this body/toy transition to the later developmental task on the same line, of progressing from finding pleasure in play to finding pleasure in academic achievement and work. The transition from play to work takes on even more meaning in the lives of adolescents who are achieving some independence by earning their own spending money and by establishing a sense of identity outside home and school. One teenager comes to mind whose father was a local sports celebrity. This adolescent was almost unable, given the context of his family, to separate play and work, believing that he too would be famous and should get paid for activities others his age viewed as play.

organization of the "in-between." How teenagers negotiate those in-between spaces is one of the primary aspects of adolescent development from an individual standpoint. How the "others" around them react to that process is the "other" part of that process. Getting both, with those interrelated processes, to make contact when they haven't been able on their own is what therapy is about.

Other aspects of the transition from play to work, according to Freud (1963), include daydreaming, games (often requiring rules, equipment, competition, and frustration tolerance), and hobbies (for pleasure, existing in reality rather than imagination, requiring planfulness). Adolescence can be a time of exploration, but only if the family field is open to the outside world. Some teens have difficulty accepting the academic and vocational dreams their parents have for them or engaging in family-approved hobbies. Recently in a counseling session it was easy to laugh with a parent who could not tolerate her daughter's choice of listening to the music of Jimi Hendrix, Janis Joplin, and the Rolling Stones. Mom stated that she had hated that music as a teen herself, still hated it as an adult, and could not understand her daughter's attraction to "that noise."

Disembedding from the family and finding a job can require teens to acknowledge what they do well, what they are interested in and enjoy, what their parents expect versus what they expect of themselves, and also what they do not like to do. These awarenesses often translate into career exploration. Along this developmental line, teens move from fantasies of becoming rock and roll stars or professional athletes to career choices that express a sense of their personal strengths, interests, values, achievements, and talents.

Integration and Assessment

"If we examine our notions of average normality in detail, we find that we expect a fairly close correspondence between growth on the individual developmental lines" (Freud, 1963, p. 28). Often the figure in therapy becomes the developmental aspect that falls behind the rest, whether it is self-reliance, body independence, companionship, or work. As clinicians, we hold these lines in mind as areas for assessment or evaluation while listening for the context in which they are presented. Current Gestalt theory and practice with adolescents have adopted a focus on field and context, yet we wish to add these developmental lines as ground definitions or levels to better define the field and the quality of contact. To borrow another concept from child analysts, parents are advised to first do *for* their infants, then do *with* their toddlers, and then to stand back and admire. As parents or therapists, we may need to stand even further back from adolescents than we would from young children, but we also need to express our admiration for their creative solutions to individuation and self-reliance.

WORKING WITH ADOLESCENTS

Conceptualization of clients' development, of their degree of disembedding, and of the different selves they embody in different fields or contexts can help guide the focus of the work with adolescents. Beginning therapists often ask for specific techniques to use in specific situations. However, techniques can be meaningless without a reason or explanation for the intervention. This chapter has provided several ways to form explanations or conceptualizations, but we do not present here Gestalt interventions specifically designed for the adolescent client. Developmentally, some adolescents may need a style that incorporates "expressive and impressive therapeutic interventions," as described in Chapter 9 on therapy with children, whereas other adolescents may respond best to the approaches described in Chapter 6 as the six methodological components integral to working from a Gestalt perspective: (a) the continuum of experience, (b) the here and now, (c) the paradoxical theory of change, (d) the experiment, (e) the authentic encounter, and (f) process-oriented diagnosis. However, one element that may assist us in working with adolescents is careful attention to the quality of the contact and the nurturance of a relationship.

Most clients enter therapy wanting to be heard, hoping their perspectives will be considered important, or not wanting to be judged for their actions. This can be especially true of adolescent clients. Many adolescents experience the adults in their lives as critical and always telling them what to do. As a therapist, it is important not to perpetuate criticism and lectures and to be instead a very different type of adult. Being an adult who is interested in hearing about their world, their thoughts, feelings, and decisions, without imposing adult values or opinions is primary before any intervention stands a chance of being beneficial. Providing support for their experience is more about the process of therapy than about the content.

Growing up is hard work, and the developmental process can cause varying degrees of stress for the adolescent and within the family system; neither emerges from the process unchanged. Support for the adolescent undergoing this transformation exists along a continuum of care from supportive others to residential treatment. Movement along the continuum brings an increase in the intensity of support, increase in time, money, and effort invested, and finally, increase in risk. The lower end of the continuum (similar to the notion of the least restrictive environment) consists of resources often readily available to the teen. Some adolescents seek and receive sufficient support from accessible sources, such as peers, school counselors, teachers, relatives outside the immediate family, and youth ministers. Acquiring support can affirm adolescents as they struggle to emerge from total familial dependence to the development of an independent and functional self with their own unique resources.

Unfortunately, not all teens have access to supportive others within or outside their family field. Individual, group, and/or family therapy may represent the next step on the continuum of care. The most restrictive end on the continuum of care requires the teenager to attend classes in a therapeutic school environment, to reside at the school, or even to reside in a locked-down residential facility. We will first describe working with adolescents in the individual/family therapy setting and then follow with school and residential approaches.

Individual and/or Family Therapy

Adolescents typically do not seek psychotherapy on their own; referral sources can be parents, school, court, or sometimes peers. Often teens do not have an interest in establishing a relationship with an adult, for we can be seen as the enemy, people who will never understand or support their point of view. The therapist may be perceived as aligned with the parents. Therefore, initial sessions with adolescent clients can be fraught with hazards.

Trust and confidentiality, important with all clients, are crucial in work with adolescents. We recommend that all stakeholders be present during the first session, with the parents and the teenager (and sometimes siblings) all together in the room with the therapist(s). The second half of the first session is best dedicated to meeting with the teenager alone to hear his or her perspective. To encourage trust, we suggest that after the initial session the flow of information should not go both ways; the teen hears everything said by the parents to the therapist but has final approval over the information that the parents receive. The only exceptions to that are when the teenager expresses potential harm to self or others. Confidentiality and duty to warn must be clearly explained to both parents and adolescents during the initial meeting.

The initial contact also includes the first opportunity to build a relationship with the teen. Neutrality and being nonjudgmental must begin during the very first second of the very first meeting. McConville (1995) explained that adolescents want to know

> am I likeable, will I be taken seriously, will I have anything to offer when I enter the adult world. In a therapy situation, the experience of being liked, being confirmed and acknowledged, and having one's value and potential confirmed amount to experiencing support. (p. 200)

Troubled teenagers will not directly ask for support or confirmation but may test your empathy and tolerance to the limits. For example, one of our clients could fake belches for 5 minutes, another would ask repeatedly to use the phone to call his girlfriend, and another had an extensive vocabulary of four-letter words. The testing of the therapist may be to get attention (negative attention being better than no attention) or to see if you will react like all the other adults in their world.

The phenomenon of just "being with" another is often therapeutic. The willingness to listen to teens' stories, to understand that their words have meaning and power, and to convey that they matter to you is often the work of individual therapy. How many others (especially adults) are willing to merely "be with" a teen for an hour and devote their attention to the teen and his or her story?

Working with adolescents is often a mysterious business; as with most clients, you do not often learn the results of the therapy. You seldom receive feedback about what worked and what didn't work. Occasionally, an adolescent client will return to your practice as an adult, but most will not. As this is being written, one of us (Toman) is working with a 24-year-old who was also a client from the ages of 14 to 18. When the client was a teen, we had formed together goals for achieving high school graduation, maintaining a job, and establishing friendships and relationships. After high school graduation, she continued her work outside of therapy. She returns to therapy now with concerns of raising her toddler but also offers insights as to how her family of origin and her adoptive family contributed to the acting out of her feelings of inadequacies and insecurities during adolescence. She now wants her daughter's life to be different from her own.

As therapists, we can formulate interventions or experiments based on clinical "data" combined with a bit of intuition. One source of data, as described in this chapter, is our informal assessment of the adolescent's maturation along each of the four developmental lines. We include here two case examples to help illustrate how informal developmental assessment can guide intervention.

The Case of Elise

I first met Elise in her senior year of high school, when most of her peers were getting ready for prom and graduation. She was an honors student and gifted writer. While other seniors were attending high school sports events, dating, and working to pay for their first cars, Elise was reading the latest fiction and writing short stories for teen magazines. She seemed comfortable with her life until not being invited to the senior prom prompted the first in a series of depressive episodes.

As we assess Elise's development along each of the lines, we can easily determine that she had accomplished the task of transforming play to work. She enjoyed reading and was well on her way to a career in writing. On the line from dependency to self-reliance, Elise may have been more "mature" than most of her peers. As an only child, she was quite capable of caring for herself and was even making strides toward financial independence. When assessing her development toward body independence, she demonstrated no difficulties or developmental delays. Her "disruption" was clearly on the third developmental line of egocentricity to companionship. What had been a discomfort through high school (not being invited on a date) turned into a crisis in the context of senior prom. Living in a family as the only child may have contributed to her lack of familiarity with forming relationships. The temporary manifestation of the disruption was resolved by going to the prom with the son of a family friend, but the longer-term concerns with friendship and intimacy continued through her years in college. Elise offers us an example of healthy development along three lines, with a delay on the developmental line from egocentricity to companionship.

The therapeutic process with Elise included hearing her story and being with her in her experience of depression. Friends had never been important to her, as she had previously found companionship in her books. She used our time together to define what was missing for her at this stage in her life and to formulate a dialogue with her newly discovered need for companions. Drawing on her skills in writing, she kept a journal of her thoughts and challenged some of those thoughts during sessions. As well, the therapeutic alliance may have provided an experimental opportunity in forming a relationship. The process of being with her was far more important than the content.

The Case of Michael

While working in a college counseling center, I (Toman) met Michael, a 19-year-old African American college freshman. He attended only one counseling session but conveyed through tears his angst over his career choice. He explained that his friends from high school were criticizing him for going to college and ridiculing his choice to major in mathematics. They conveyed that he was selling out. Michael stated that he had a choice to make—his friends or a college degree. His dilemma was not related to self-reliance or body independence but was a conflict between the developmental lines of companionship and work. I do not know the outcome of his decision, but I remember feeling amazement that he was willing to even discuss the issue with me. My hope is that in the process of telling his story he was able to formulate a decision.

School and Residential Facilities

As we move further along the continuum of care, we encounter those teenagers whose histories of interactions with adults have created a vast reservoir of distrust and nearly impenetrable barriers to accessing support. A supportive and therapeutic community may be necessary to break through patterns created by years of opposition and resistance. Alternative schools, day treatment centers, and residential settings can provide a variety of treatment approaches and supportive processes. The Sarasota Community School (formerly Kanner Academy) in Sarasota, Florida, is an example of one such therapeutic community for teenagers that combines elements of an alternative school, day treatment, and residential setting while operating from a Gestalt perspective.

B. Robertson, in a discussion about his perspective of the advantages of the Sarasota Community School/Kanner Academy setting (personal communication, May 15, 2003), described the school as providing a container in which students are in a continuous experiment with behaviors and interactions that limit opportunities for continued resistance. Students are challenged to be in the moment and in their bodies, to develop awareness about the ways they make choices, and to be responsible for the consequences of those choices for themselves and others. The academy's field is rich with opportunities for reflective feedback from administrators, teachers, staff, and peers as the community as a whole assumes responsibility for the growth and development of each of its members. The reverse is also true, as each member of the community is challenged to take responsibility for the welfare of the community as a whole.

During a consultation visit at Kanner Academy/Sarasota Community School, one of the authors (Bauer) had the opportunity to experience an intervention complicated by a high degree of resistance and denial: We sat as a group for 10 hours to bring one student to an increased awareness of the consequences of his behavior. Confronted, in turn, by therapists, teachers, staff members, a psychiatrist, one of his parents, and peers, he progressed from "I didn't do it" to "I did it; what's the big deal," to an offer of support and apology to one of the persons who had been hurt by his actions. During this long and intense day, other parents came and went, and the attention turned toward other students and other adults working through various issues. The theme of the day was fostering a sense of awareness of and responsibility for choices.

Certainly, the idea of a therapeutic school is not new. Even in the United States, the therapeutic preschool notions developed by Anna Freud were instrumental principles in the establishment of Hanna Perkins School in Cleveland, Ohio. Included in the preschool curriculum is an attention to complementary growth along each of the developmental lines. In contrast to Hanna Perkins's psychoanalytic approach, the impact of Gestalt precepts on a therapeutic school setting enriches the degree of contact possibilities as all members of the community, adults included, work to increase awareness of self and self in relationship to others. Instead of avoiding multiple relationships, adults and students work, learn, eat, and play together so that numerous points of contact are created. B. Robertson (personal communication, May 15, 2003) proposed that this process of working within multiple relationships, in addition to revealing the parallel developmental process of the adults in the community, provides access to a more whole experience with students, as well as making it possible to assert stronger influence on the school field or community. To learn more about the Sarasota Community School/Kanner Academy, visit their Web site: www.kanneracademy.com.

Further along the continuum of care are the locked-down units typically located in hospitals and residential settings, often the last attempts at keeping adolescents safe, usually from themselves. These facilities can offer the advantages of safety, along with intense attention to medical and psychiatric concerns and security from outsiders providing inappropriate resources and environments. Usually, teens find themselves in locked-down residential units because of extreme risk to self or others; such units also provide the necessary structures or supports for teens who may be in the custody of the state.

THE HIGH COSTS OF FAILURE TO TREAT

Growing up not only is hard work but can prove hazardous as well. The Centers for Disease Control (2003) stated that the second most frequent cause of death in teens is homicide and that the third is suicide. The At Risk Web site (2003) reported that 1,942 suicides occurred in 2002 among youth 15 to 24 years of age. Given the genuine possibility that some single car accidents could have been disguised suicide attempts, the number of young people that chose death is likely higher. The continuum of care and support can provide a safety net for some young people, but statistics provided by the Centers for Disease Control clearly show that there are holes in the net and that some adolescents are falling through.

Small in number but mighty in impact are other teenage events that point out another cost of an inadequate support system. As a part of the Safe Schools Initiative, psychologists working with the Secret Service identified 37 cases of school-targeted attacks from 1975 through 2000 (Fein et al., 2002). Interviews with the school shooters who survived their targeted attacks revealed powerful and tragic similarities. Each of them was driven to a drastic problem-solving method by enormous pain, and none of them could identify a single adult who was safe to talk to and whom they believed would help. Fein (2003) explained that if there could be only one change that would make a difference, it would be to provide each

MARK: I attempted to describe disembedding, interiority, and integration in my book. I conceived those three movements as aspects of a "reorganization of the contact boundary," whereby fuller and more differentiated contact between the self and other selves evolves through the course of the adolescent years.

Now, this distillation also reflects how I conceive of therapeutic work with adolescents, which is all about how to support and promote and catalyze this developmental process. Whether I am working with a kid one-on-one, or counseling his parents, or sending him off to the Kanner school, I am thinking about one thing: What matrix of specific environment supports and challenges will act to promote the development of contact process? What will help this kid to learn the fluid interplay of joining skills and separating skills that makes for healthy adult enterprise and relationship?

SARAH: I can imagine that those supports to contact could be different from adolescent to adolescent and different from setting to setting. The environments with which I have the most

teenager with a trusted adult who offered listening ears and supportive advice. A school system in California chose to address this issue by posting during a staff meeting the names of all the students in their school. Faculty members identified those on the list with whom they had a close relationship. The process highlighted those students who were not identified by any teacher (Fein et al., 2002).

Another similarity among these tragedies is that although the adults involved were unaware, peers knew about the shooters' plans. That they chose to keep the code of silence is terribly unfortunate but not surprising. It is chilling to learn that some peers actually encouraged the shooters to act, at times pushing them to increase the level of violence. For example, in one case that ended with several deaths, a student planned to bring a gun to school to frighten his tormentors into backing off and leaving him alone. Several of his peers told him he would actually have to shoot someone for his plan to work and helped him construct a list of targets. Education about the important role peers can play in facilitating safe or tragic outcomes needs to continue as part of a larger agenda toward the creation of safe school climates.

The Center for Prevention of School Violence (Riley, 1999) identified the nonprofit organization Students Against Violence Everywhere (2003) as an effective proactive approach that offers methods for involving and empowering students to create safe schools. Peer support groups that hold everyone accountable for the progress of individuals within that group, such as those found in alternative schools like the Kanner Academy, use the potent power of peers to promote health.

It seems simplistic to say that what is needed are caring adults and peers, but supportive adults, a safe school climate, and a positive peer climate can provide valuable help with the stress of the teenage years (Bauer, 2000). The continuum of care begins with connected and caring adults within the school, neighborhood,

experience are middle/high school settings and the private practice setting. I wonder if you could add some examples of supports to contact from your experiences with adolescents?

MARK: My experience likewise derives primarily from office practice and from work in schools. The essential ingredients for promoting contact development are the same regardless of context. First, kids must feel that they have someone in their corner—someone who knows them and likes them. It may sound trite, but let's face it: That is what all of us were looking for when we were adolescents. Second, the environment must push kids to challenge their own resistances to fuller contact: self-centeredness, reluctance to assert, need to be liked, tendency to blame others, and so on. A lot of the growth in therapy for adolescents comes from being pushed to become aware of and experiment with these patterns—but this has to happen in the context of a nonjudging, fundamentally accepting relationship.

SARAH: This reminds me of the "conditions" for a therapeutic relationship introduced by Carl Rogers: empathy, genuineness, and positive regard. When putting those notions into a Gestalt framework, is it too simplistic to suggest that those may also be the conditions that help make "contact," "challenging resistances," and "being known" possible within the "field" of our offices, school counseling centers, or alternative schools?

MARK: I think that's exactly right. Rogers describes the necessary starting point for working with adolescents—the posture of interest and openness. But it's also important to note that when it comes to working with adolescents, a strictly Rogerian approach of acceptance and reflection doesn't go far enough. Gestalt therapy encourages us to use the foundation of empathy and positive regard as a supportive platform for actively engaging the adolescent in constructive give-and-take—which is to say, in an active contact process.

and community. The next step of additional support is individual or group counseling provided by mental health personnel. If more support is needed, alternative schools and residential settings can provide intense attention and contact. Unfortunately, not all of these support formats are available to, or utilized by, those struggling to master the tasks of adolescence. If those who needed care and support were given access to the complete array of supportive functions, more teens could safely navigate the stormy seas of adolescence and prevent the painful and tragic results for those who do not make it safely through to shore.

SUMMARY

Models of adolescent development and applications were offered here to assist the practitioner in understanding and working with clients in this intriguing phase of life. We hope we have shed some light on working with teens by providing a description of the developmental lines that we believe help define the field or context; by merging the notion of developmental lines with the more traditional Gestalt theory concepts of awareness, resistances, contact, boundaries, and field; and by presenting case examples from our own experiences with clients. We also discussed a continuum of care and support for working with adolescents as they undergo developmental changes and struggles and the potential costs of not adequately utilizing the array of resources.

Working with teenagers will never be dull: They have incredible potential for good or ill and a madcap exuberance for experimenting with all that life has to offer. For those drawn to this work, we recommend you tap into your own memories from adolescence and "be with" your clients in a contactful manner during their time of growth and development. We also ask that you add your own voice to the ever-developing conceptualization or model of a Gestalt theory of development, for we are all adolescents in that endeavor.

BRUCE: One of the fundamental principles of Gestalt is contrast, often referred to as a polarity. Part of the forming self-gestalt as a teenager is creating a contrast (or, as Sarah Toman and Mark McConville write, about "disembedding"), forming an opposite of me so I am not like my parents, for instance. The self-sense is often tied to who they imagine their parents are. In therapy, if I sit a mother and daughter across from each other and we start to do some basic grounding work, then they begin to look at each other. First, as they see each other, I have them stop and look and describe what they see. They begin with what they already know, and all the projections start to show up. That is one layer. But at some point the possibility exists that they begin, in the moment, to relate in some novel way with each other. I can't describe what happens, but every Gestalt therapist knows that moment of something exciting and novel and new, the experience of anxiety and excitement. In working with a teenager, it's working through that anxiety/excitement and then supporting staying there so that they can move through the anxiety/excitement. They may have a patterned way of moving off that. The mom and daughter may have a patterned way of doing that, a mutual cueing, or through sustaining the contact and feeling the interruptions they can begin to move and develop. Contact is required for development—the simple skill of anything human. One step is trying out new ways of self in relation to others and then doing it in new places, experimenting with peers—pretending to be somebody else, and then coming back home. Then there is the self that shows up with adults who are not the parents. These are all subtle shifts, being done all day, and it is pretty complex. And what is mature is how they carry self between them all and stay in contact, everywhere. The flow is what is developing.

ANN: It is like a shifting kaleidoscope. I was thinking too about teaching kids and how one

REVIEW QUESTIONS

1. Describe the notion of "disembedding" from the family field (as identified by McConville, 1995), and provide a rationale for its relevance to the tasks of adolescence.

2. List the four developmental lines outlined in this chapter, and describe each line's usefulness in understanding an adolescent's context or field.

3. Compare and contrast what you know from other classes about the developmental tasks of adolescence, as outlined in Piaget's (1952, 1966, 1972) stage model of cognitive development, Erikson's (1963, 1968) description of psychosocial stage tasks, Freud's (1966) personality development focus on psychosexual functioning, and/or Kohlberg's (1975, 1966, 1981) model of moral development. Describe each of these models' unique contributions to the notion of adolescents' experiences of individuation from the family field.

4. McConville (1995) described how families can differ in their responses to adolescents' attempts to disengage from the family field. Describe each of the six family resistances he identified as relevant to adolescents' attempts to disembed.

5. Describe the continuum of care available for therapeutic work with adolescents. Identify some strengths and weaknesses you believe exist at various points along the continuum.

EXPERIENTIAL PEDAGOGICAL ACTIVITIES

ACTIVITY 1: On a long sheet of shelf paper or newsprint, draw a visual representation of the four developmental lines outlined in this chapter. Along each line, identify significant events from your own life, indicating each with a representative drawing, a cutout from a magazine, or significant words/phrases. Take particular note of where

classroom has a particular feel to it that changes when one or two students aren't there, and learning to be in that is the developmental process. So in therapy, you support kids to stay with who they are in any interaction.

ANN: So Bruce, did you agree with anything that we wrote?

BRUCE: The fact is that you wrote it—Gestalt therapy is very hard to write about; it is very hard to describe what we do. But I want to offer the challenge to let go of going to something else to describe what we can't. It seems as if no new thoughts get written when you write in an academic style, supporting a point of view with the writings of others. I'd rather we write about the *struggle* of describing what we do; the struggle has not been written about enough.

ANN: It's like taking a great piece of artwork that stands your hair on end and then trying to write about it, describing what it is about when no words convey the power of the actual artwork.

BRUCE: What I find particularly difficult in writing about what we do as Gestalt therapists is that the readers do not get to experience themselves as members of the field resonating with what is going on. One problem is that our model is so fundamentally based on the mutuality of relationships and not on a therapeutic hierarchy. Psychotherapy is one subset of relationship—a particular relationship. An adolescent in psychotherapy is simply forming a new sense of self in a new situation with the therapist. It is just the latest in many. One of the great limitations of this new relationship is that the therapist has limited access to the teenager's movement from one life space to another. Often I would meet with a teenager alone for a few sessions and then bring in one of the parents. I would have the parents sit

progress along each line may have been accomplished at different ages/stages. Complete this exercise by writing an essay, poem, or storied description of the developmental experiences you identified on your shelf paper or newsprint.

ACTIVITY 2: In a small-group-discussion format, discuss the various methods each of you used when attempting to disembed from your families. Also, describe the success of those attempts.

ACTIVITY 3: Take a field trip to a location where there are significant numbers of teens (such as a mall, a high school football game, or a high school or middle school classroom), and note the variety of apparent developmental stages accomplished by adolescents of the same chronological ages. What are the markers or cues that indicate each teen's level of maturity?

outside in the waiting room and have the teenager start to describe what changes in him or her as he or she begins to consider including the parent in our new life space. Then I would invite the parent in and ask the teen to describe what changes in his or her body, and conversely the same process with the parent. This is the closest we can get to the in-between in therapy. This is why I have moved into working in a community-based environment at Sarasota Community School. I am able to work "therapeutically" at the spontaneous moments of teenagers in all of their varying life spaces: in the hallway, on the basketball court, at lunch, in their room at night. With all of their various life processes.

ACTIVITY 4: Identify an adolescent who would be willing to participate in an interview (we recommend you not select your own child or sibling for this exercise). Establish a series of interview questions you would really like to discuss with your interview participant. You may want to ask for his or her perspective on school, clothes, the importance of friendships, how he or she coordinates school and work responsibilities, and his or her understanding of school violence. Please remember, though, that you are getting only one teen's perspective and that the answers you receive may not be generalizable to other teens.

CHAPTER 11

Family and Couples Therapy From a Gestalt Perspective

J. EDWARD LYNCH AND BARBARA LYNCH

DIALOGUE RESPONDENT: JOSEPH C. ZINKER

J. Edward Lynch is an associate professor and chairman of the Department of Marriage and Family Therapy at Southern Connecticut State University, a graduate program specializing in applications of Gestalt therapy theory and practice. He is an active member of the New York Institute for Gestalt Therapy, where he trained with Laura Perls and Isadore From for over 10 years. In addition, he has Gestalt therapy training with Erving and Miriam Polster, Joseph Zinker, Michael Vincent Miller, and training in object relations therapy with Salvador Minuchin at the Washington School of Psychiatry. He is a respected trainer and workshop facilitator throughout the United States and Europe and is the coauthor, with his wife, of *Principles and Practices of Structural Family Therapy* (2000).

Barbara Lynch is professor and director of the Marriage and Family Therapy Graduate Program and Director of the Family Therapy Clinic at Southern Connecticut State University, having trained with Jay Haley, Milton Erickson, and Salvador Minuchin to develop her specialty in systemic family and couple therapy. She is on the board of directors of the National Supervised Visitation Network. A certified supervisor, clinical member, and accreditation officer of the American Association of Marriage and Family Therapy, she has numerous publications and is a frequent presenter at professional conferences. She is the author of *Structural Family Therapy* (1989) and numerous chapters and articles on family therapy and is coauthor, with her husband, of *Principles and Practices of Structural Family Therapy* (2000).

Joseph C. Zinker trained with Fritz Perls in the 1960s and has had a significant influence on the development of Gestalt therapy since. He was a co-founder of the Gestalt Institute of Cleveland. His present affiliation is with the Gestalt International Study Center, where he is senior faculty in the Center for the Study of Intimate Systems. His books, articles, and book chapters are among those most frequently referenced in Gestalt therapy, especially *Creative Process in Gestalt Therapy* (1977), *In Search of Good Form: Gestalt Therapy With Couples and Families* (1994), and, most recently, *Sketches: An Anthology of Essays, Art and Poetry* (2001).

Gestalt therapists have struggled to integrate systemic couples and family therapy with Gestalt therapy, with varying degrees of success. The collection of essays in *On Intimate Ground,* edited by Gordon Wheeler and Stephanie Backman (1994), represents the comprehensive views of well-respected Gestalt therapists and should be considered required reading for those who wish to work with this approach.

What is Gestalt couples and family therapy? The answer is predicated on a definition of couples and family therapy. For some it is having a couple or family in the room and working with the *individuals* in each "grouping" while other members of the system are present and witnessing, responding, and reacting to what happens between the therapist and the individual. This, of course, has value. As one family member gains awareness, others, with the assistance of the therapist, can restructure their responses to the new information and behaviors. In this example, however, the *individual* is the focus of intervention, with the *system* being the secondary focus. The contrast is similar to the contrast between classical Gestalt theory and practice (see Chapter 2) and contemporary/field theory (see Chapter 3) or between Perlsian group therapy using the hot seat and contemporary group work as exemplified in Elaine Kepner's model (see Chapter 12).

Systems therapists hold to the principle that the focus of intervention must be the system—couple or family. Whereas some Gestalt therapists have drawn on the concept of Paul Dell (quoted in Kaplan & Kaplan, 1994) that "individuals function as primary systems in ways that produce the secondary coherence of an interactional couple or family system" (p. 112), such a focus on individual function is in direct contrast to the focus of systems therapists, who believe primarily that the larger system, couple or family, functions in ways that organize, limit, support, nurture, and hinder individuals.

Therefore, the first summons to those desiring to work with couples and families might be to combine the general principles of systems and systemic functioning with a Gestalt therapy perspective. Both Gestalt therapists and systems therapists (using any one of the major models—Salvador Minuchin's structural model, Jay Haley's strategic model, Carl Whitaker's experiential model, etc.) explain family organizational patterns as the family itself sees them. According to editors Wheeler and Backman (1994), "[I]nvisible rules and structures make up the 'ground' and the therapist presents a new figure (an intervention, experiment) and then sees how the system deals with it" (p. 124). This invisible set of rules and structures *is* the system—a concept at once familiar and basic to all systemic treatment models. In this regard, Gestalt therapists and the systems therapists begin at the same point. They also converge in understanding that psychotherapeutic phenomenology is working from within the experiences of the system (Wheeler, 1994).

The difficulty lies in attempting to minimize the divergences between Gestalt therapists and systems therapists. Traditionally, the differences stem from Gestalt therapists' focus primarily on the individual as an interactional system and on the family as a collection of individual systems in interaction with each other. Systems therapists tend to view the system as a whole, with minimal attention to individual "parts" as singular entities. Both approaches are concerned with a "figure-ground" model, albeit with different perspectives. The intent of this chapter is to harmonize the two in a manner that allows the therapist to work with a system and maintain the integrity of the primary modality.

BACKGROUND PREMISES

A basic axiom of systems therapy is to work with and stabilize the largest system before moving on to working with "parts." However, this idea must be held in conjunction with the understanding that even what appears to be the largest system possible still remains a fractional system. Each individual in the adult system, couple or parent, is an amalgamation of the characteristics, experiences, and historical context of ancestors who carries legacies, unfinished gestalten, and an incomplete ledger into present and future systems. Individuals tend to find partners with compatible intrinsic emotional motivations who at the same time offer hope for completion or change within the new system they form. Systems mesh in all aspects of functioning, even when it appears on the surface that there are vast disagreements. Often these disagreements represent failures to fulfill (unexpressed and often unknown) expectations, breaching a contract that the system's members maintain without awareness. Whatever system is present as the therapeutic focus is but a microcosm of larger systems, such as families of origin, ethnic and religious groups, and groups of people who reside in the same geographical area.

The unit of the family system is usually made up of two main subsystems. One system, the adult system, is made up of each of the individuals as a system in him- or herself, the couple as an intimate system, and the parental system. This "three-in-one" composition has the potential for intra- and intersystemic contaminations. The other main subsystem in the family is the child system. The two main subsystems, adult and child, are organized first on generational differences. A general rule is that a subsystem consisting of one generation of individuals has the greater chance of functioning with only minor difficulties. Therefore, an adult system made up of a grandparent and parent has more likelihood of experiencing problems than one made up of a couple with 15 years' or less age difference between the individuals.

The adult system and child system are the primary "fixed" systems in the family. However, less fixed systems based on interest, gender, and compatibilities can functionally exist while ignoring the generational system's expectations. A parent and child can become a subsystem for limited periods of time engaged in common pursuit of sports, art, music, or other shared talents or interests. These interest systems are not gender restricted and are relatively fluid, existing without expectations of long-term commitment. It is important that these systems do not take *long-term* precedence over the primary, couple, parent, and sibling subsystems.

Subsystems are maintained by a regulatory process that creates boundaries—"the invisible fences," Minuchin would say (1974)—that regulate who participates (when, where, and how). Functional systems have clear rules that govern these transactions, and these boundaries allow for the safety and growth of the members of the system. Actions and reactions are constrained within these boundaries. There is a clear expectation that as children grow up there is a functional lessening of adherence to family rules and that members will both leave the primary unit and stay connected, differently, to the family.

The couple system is the most complex human system—and the one with the most opportunity for *personal* growth. When the couple system is stressed by the need to also function as a parental system, the complexities multiply. Here are two individual systems often struggling to form a system of two, elementally bound by their family systems and at the same time inherently yearning for the intimacy potential of a dyadic system made up of two peers. Concurrently the physical and emotional demands of child rearing compete for attention and offer a convenient rationale for abandoning the couple system in deference to the child's needs when the tension of being a couple is too great. The paradox of the couple system is that partners must be able to find primary satisfaction of emotional needs and resolution of difficulties and tensions *within their couple system.* And when that is seemingly impossible, at least in part due to their individual unfinished business, they most commonly turn to focusing on functioning as a parental system. They must constantly regulate the often-competing needs of their couple system and their family (of procreation) system. When these decisions are made conjointly, based on the genuine needs of the family as a rationale for the temporary relegation of the couple system to second place, both systems are sound. Problems are resolved without the need for outside assistance. Input may be sought from outside sources, but the executive functioning is not abdicated. In addition, the balance of power between the adults is based on perceived equality—the recognition that each is "better than" in some instances while overall there is a balanced power structure. The relationship is one without competition for power and/or control of the other.

JOSEPH: Before we begin to dialogue about this piece, I'd like say that this is a beautiful dissertation, integrating Gestalt and family therapy. You demonstrate cognitive clarity with respect to the boundaries that delineate the subsystems.

Connecting and integrating systemic and Gestalt models of family and couples therapy has a considerable history. Virginia Satir (1964, 1972) was one of the earliest family therapists to work at integrating systemic and experiential family therapy models. More recently, Leslie Greenberg and Susan Johnson (1988) addressed the integration of Gestalt-experiential and systemic perspectives in their book *Emotionally Focused Therapy for Couples.* Presenting their case for producing a theoretical synthesis of the two models, they argued that

> both [models] view the person as a fluid system constantly in process of change rather than as possessing a fixed core or a rigid character based on psychogenic determinants. Both approaches also focus on current functioning rather than on historical determinants as important causes of specific behaviors . . . [simultaneously focusing] on both intrapsychic and interactional factors. (p. 35)

With these basic concepts in place, we can move on to the process of therapy.

THE PROCESS OF THERAPY

Individuals, couples, and families have many therapeutic experiences in the process of normal living. They are even able to make significant moves toward more satisfying and healthy functioning *without the benefit of a therapist*. However, when a couple or family elect to enter therapy, it must be determined whether this is a quest for enrichment, enhancement, or personal growth or an attempt to find relief from suffering and to make major changes in their fixed gestalts, uncreative adjustments, stuck patterns of relating, maladaptive coping processes, and feelings of lostness or hopelessness in dealing with chronic symptoms. Without detracting from the value of personal growth work, therapy as discussed in the following section will be limited to the process that occurs when a couple or family present for therapy as being stuck in their attempts to resolve difficulties that do not bring about the desired results. Further, they are so entrenched in unsuccessful problem resolution, in unsatisfying fixed gestalten, that the system has developed a symptomatic individual (commonly referred to as the "identified patient"), the harbinger of the need for change.

Systems therapists see "problems" as metaphors for a *system's* inability to find functional ways of obtaining support, nurturance, and a sense of satisfaction. These "problems" are symptoms of systemic malfunctioning, including failed attempts at contact and resolution of difficulties that have become entrenched ways of being, supported by *all members of the system* despite the lack of success. As such, the symptom is the catalyst for therapy and the means of monitoring the progress of therapy. It is the medium through which all of the system's functioning becomes visible. It is the therapist's "ticket" to working with the family, the reason for being in therapy. Furthermore, the symptom organizes the therapist's work with the system and provides a window into understanding where basic functioning has been neglected. The symptom tells the therapist if this is a family with a weak hierarchy, a family with boundary difficulties, a family with basically sound structures that is having difficulty negotiating developmental changes. Most families won't come into therapy without a significant symptom, one that has defied all usual means to be eliminated.

Therapy follows an orderly progression, and this schema helps to keep both the therapy and the therapist on track. Figure 11.1 depicts the process of systemic family therapy that moves from initial meeting through termination.

Joining, or fore-contact, requires the therapist to engage with each member of the system *and* with the system as a whole. Joining is a shared felt experience where the family (or couple) feel respected by the therapist and in turn respect the therapist's ability to help them. The process includes the formation of a "new field" that includes the therapist. The therapist is the carrier of hope, without directly or formally stating it. Rather, the therapist brings inspiration into the system, an experiential glimmer of success. General small talk that reflects a genuine interest in family members begins the joining process. It continues through a statement of the

Joining	Reframing	Change Takes Hold	Termination
/ Assessing the System /	Intervening /	Supporting Change /	
Therapeutic Fore-Contact	Therapeutic Contact	Therapeutic Final Contact	Therapeutic Post-Contact

Figure 11.1 The Process of Systemic Family Therapy

circumstances that bring the family into therapy, during the recitation of which the therapist links behaviors to responses and reactions of others, using observations of the phenomenological experience that is happening in the room. Underlying this process is the therapist's intent of gaining as full an understanding as possible of the function of the unfinished business in maintaining the homeostatic system and, at the same time, knowledge of how the system maintains the symptom. Because this is an outgrowth of the appreciation of the self-regulating mechanism of systems, there is no judgment or criticism inherent in the observations. Furthermore, the therapist adopts an acceptance of the system as it is in the present and a willingness to meet the system where it is currently.

As the system gradually relaxes the boundaries to include the therapist, the therapist gains experiential data to understand the family's processes. This is the ground from which the therapist assesses the system, looking primarily for strengths and possibilities for movement. From this frame, the therapist is interested in contact processes within the family. A distant position facilitates accurately seeing the system. According to Zinker and Nevis (1994),

> Being able to see the couple [or system] as a "third entity" is essential for doing Gestalt couple [and family] therapy. After all, a couple [and family] is a system, a gestalt in its own right. To begin experiencing a couple [system] in this way, the therapist must first "move away" from them, both intellectually and experientially. The therapist begins by seeing both partners in the visual field and watching their physical movements—their swaying and tilting—in relation to one another. (p. 360)

The therapist becomes aware of the system's contact style, the predictable ways family members arrange themselves in terms of boundaries and hierarchy in an isomorphic ebb and flow around different situations. Also, the therapist looks for instances in contact making where the system comes closest to optimal functioning. The "job" of therapy is much easier when the therapist supports healthy functioning, as compared with attempting only to correct dysfunction.

In this assessment phase of treatment, the therapist works to enlarge the focus of the presenting problem, being sure to include everyone in the system, their reactions to symptomatic behavior, and their responses to it. The system's goal for treatment should be clearly understood, and the therapist should convey his or her goal for therapy to the couple or family. This jointly negotiated goal-setting process assures the couple or family that solutions will be co-created; however, this is not an exclusive Gestalt therapy understanding. Therapists consider this shift in thinking from a linear, cause-effect mode to an interdependent frame of reference a therapeutic reframe. At the point in the process when this shift occurs, the therapeutic unit composed of the therapist and system coalesces, and a commitment to change emerges.

The hallmarks of systemic therapy are the interventions. Because the overall goal of treatment is resolution of a painful way of being together, interventions should facilitate the couple or family in finding new and more satisfying ways of being with each other. The enactment, or experiment, is at the heart of all interventions, allowing change, and the contact disturbances, to be monitored in the present. The most frequent, and effective, enactment is for the therapist to remove him- or herself from being the recipient of all conversations, the gatekeeper of interactions between family members. The ease with which this is accomplished is usually a function of the experience of the therapist. Statements directed at the therapist can be rerouted to another family member with as simple a move as the therapist's looking at *who should be the recipient of the comment* and attending to the contact boundary between the dyad. Most new therapists are intent on maintaining eye contact with the speaker, and in individual therapy this is, of course, important. But when working with a couple or family, the therapist is least effective when engaging one member of the system in an interaction while excluding others. The therapist, uncontaminated by the system's dysfunction and well trained in the art of listening, can become a better listener than other family members, subtly setting up a competition where there are losers and winners, a situation that does not foster the process of therapy.

When interaction between system members begins to occur, the therapist (with nonverbal language) signals support. He or she can accomplish this by moving back, slightly away from the couple or family (e.g., subtly by sitting back in the chair or moving the chair a few inches away from the speaking dyad), with the message being, "You are doing fine." Such a withdrawal offers the couple or family the experience of being able to "do it on their own." To complete the message of support of the members' interaction, the therapist should avoid looking at the dyad speaking and should instead, in the case of families, watch how other members react. When working with a couple, where there is no one else to observe, the therapist can look down and away. Jay Haley, a well-known family therapist, claims that therapists need to have excellent peripheral vision. It certainly helps to be able to avoid direct eye contact and unobtrusively note nonverbal behaviors.

A common mistake made in the process is to interrupt the dyadic interaction at a time when the dyad first attempts to engage the therapist. Often one of the two members will use deflection and look away from the other toward the therapist. If the therapist makes him- or herself available at this time, the transaction between the dyad will likely cease. Before responding to this invitation to interrupt, the therapist should consider either not being available or indicating with hand gestures, not words, that the interaction can continue. In general, individuals will end a transaction too soon. By allowing them the opportunity to sustain the interaction, they get the chance to increase the potential for resolution and contact. These are essential elements of the enactment that are often overlooked by zealous therapists eager to intervene. In Gestalt terms, they may be considered as miniexperiments.

Though Gestalt experiments are generally approached as open, creative processes that evolve from clients' present therapeutic experience without specific behavioral objectives or directional goals (Polster & Polster, 1973; Zinker, 1977), in couples and family therapy experiments should have as their goal the restructuring of a component of relating that has possibly been one of the root causes for other dissatisfactions or dysfunctions. For example, after listening to a family (we'll refer to them as C Family) that consisted of a single parent (Mrs. C) and three daughters and who presented with a problem of the second daughter (Carrie, a 15-year-old who was sneaking out of the house to be with her boyfriend despite all parental efforts to curtail this behavior), the therapist set up an experiment to explore a dyadic interaction. Prior to this, the family's dialogue went as follows:

Mother: I forbid you to see that boy!

First Daughter: You're making Mom sick with your behavior.

Second Daughter: Sure, goody-two-shoes, like you're perfect.

[The third daughter, a 12-year-old, plays with her hair.]

Second Daughter: At least when I'm with him, there's no fighting!

First Daughter: You're the cause of all the fights in this family. If you'd just drop that creep and act like a normal person, there'd be no problem.

The therapist hypothesized that in addition to engaging in *normal* adolescent rebellious behavior, this girl might not be getting her need for nurturance, support, and validation met within the family and, at the same time, might be acting out her mother's unaware desire to run away from the rigors of parenting her three adolescent daughters alone. The therapist set up the dyadic experiment with this introduction:

> I have an idea. It's just an experiment that may or may not tell us something. I think it's worth a try. If Mrs. C (mother) and Carrie (second daughter) would attempt to negotiate when and how often she can be with Bill (the boyfriend) while the three of us just watch and note how often both of them says "no" in some way, I think we all might learn something.

This is simply the skeleton of the experiment. Following the metaphor of running away and going outside the system for need satisfaction to a degree that it is contrary to functional system behavior, the therapist attempted to block attempts by the mother-daughter dyad to go outside their system or to deflect their conflict. At the same time, anticipating that the first daughter would *automatically* offer herself as a deflection, the therapist blocked her. The effect was to heighten the intensity, afford the dyad a new opportunity to compromise, and possibly bring to awareness the potential for sustaining tension within the system without negative outcomes.

In this example, the therapist utilized strategic interventions as experiments to block the first and third daughters from providing either their mother or their sister with avenues of escape out of the interaction. The therapist huddled with them and kept them occupied. At the same time, the therapist listened to the cadence of the dyad's interaction and learned that even though they seemed frustrated and at times hesitant, they picked up again when no outside interference provided them with a reason to end.

Each time the interaction momentarily stopped (usually by the mother announcing that they weren't getting anywhere), the therapist would respond with a statement acknowledging their difficulty, while continuing to support the need to make more attempts. The therapist did not offer solutions but instead asked the family to decide who in the family might have the most valuable information that they could use to resolve the difficulty. As was not at all surprising, the girls thought their father should be brought into the mix. Even though the mother indicated that she wanted nothing to do with her former spouse, the girls offered a solution that was agreeable to their mother. In the spirit of their own experiment, the girls proposed a session with just them and their father to see if he had any insights into what they might do.

The overt goal of therapy with this family was to help the mother set appropriate limits that were consistent with her daughter's (Carrie's) developmental level and her need for differentiation. At the same time, the therapist held another objective in mind, that of supporting the family's competence in finding viable solutions within their system, while at the same time fostering awareness of appropriate ways of going outside the system for assistance and solutions. The experiment used in this case held the possibility for both objectives to be met. In several modifications of the original enactment, which made up the entire intervention phase of treatment, the family eventually left treatment satisfied and better than when they arrived. Over the course of treatment, the boyfriend "dumped" Carrie. Distraught, she turned to her mother for nurturance. Mrs. C, with support from the therapist, arranged some appropriate distractions and support, some for just Carrie and her, some for just the sisters alone, and one for the girls and their father. In an isomorphic manner, the intra- and intersystemic boundaries were renegotiated in several instances.

The experiment or enactment is the mainstay of Gestalt family therapists. However, the goal of the experiment must be formulated with awareness and with attention to systemic principles of couples and families. These principles include restructuring boundaries to become more flexible or more defined, realigning the hierarchy, validating strengths and competencies, and/or supporting selected subsystem functioning. How effectively the therapist implements the enactment will depend on his or her level of awareness of self and family of origin and ability to differentiate between the family in the room and the therapist's own family of origin or family of procreation. The degree to which the therapist's own family is projected onto the family in treatment will determine in large part the lack of therapeutic success.

Creating a series of experiments that are similar at the core and different on the surface is likely to result in a discernible change in the system *in the room.* When this is followed by reports of changes outside treatment, the therapist concludes that change has taken hold. The next step in the process is to support change. This is a crucial aspect of systemic as well as Gestalt therapy. The principle of balance must be maintained. There are equally weighted fears of change and delight with the changes. Often the family have survived with their symptom and have fears that the therapy has robbed them of a valuable tool that has served them well, albeit painfully, in the past. The challenge presented at this post-therapeutic contact point in treatment is to support both the change and the fear of change. The frequent temptation is for the therapist to compliment the family on their changes, predict smooth functioning, and otherwise be the container of all the positives. To counterbalance this, the system then must be the container of all the resistance to change and all the negatives. The solution is deceptively simple and must be executed with exquisite care. The therapist must either skillfully be the holder

JOSEPH: The aspect that most interests me is the similarity and difference between the concepts of the enactment and the experiment. This is illustrated in the case study of the mother and her three daughters. You have set up a situation where two generations have been involved, and you gave the adult a parental function. The children were supported as a subsystem that attended to them as a distinct sibling system. Also there was an inclusion of the therapist, as an adult, engaged with the two sisters in the task of noting the number of times either the mother or the sisters used some form of "no." The first difference I noticed is in how you two set up the experiment. You two seem to give a general directive, where you give the observers, the two daughters, a task. I wonder what your purpose was in doing this.

BARBARA: Basically, the idea was to give them a task that would keep them involved but at the same time encourage them to stay out of the interaction between their mother and their sister. What we were thinking was that since the mother and daughter deflected their conflict onto anybody outside their subsystem, the therapist who was included in the observer system would have opportunities to block any attempts at deflection.

JOSEPH: In the same situation, I would have been more active. I would coach the mother and the child. My motive would be to create an encounter in the moment where they could move toward resolution. I would join them, and the three of us would be working together.

ED: I think this might be a stylistic difference—a matter of style. I think we stand back more and follow their process—let the system tell us what the solution is. We set up the enactment, the experiment, and stay out of it.

JOSEPH: What I notice in the three of us is a respect for the boundaries. Consistent with Gestalt therapy is this abiding respect for the change that takes place in the process of respecting boundaries. Individuals are supported to make individual boundaries, giving them permission to say no, and stay out of each other's business. We are each

of resistance to change or expect to become the harbinger of the relapse. To complete the healthy gestalt in this miraculous balancing act, the family is left to support change and to resist the relapse.

In the case of the C Family, the therapist began supporting change with the following statement:

Therapist: I've noticed over the past few weeks that there seem to be some changes in the family. I'm both pleased with this and a little bit suspicious. Sometimes families change when they're in treatment with some unaware desire to please the therapist while really there are no lasting changes. I don't know which is true with your family, though. I'd like to think our work has had some results.

attempting to strengthen the intergenerational system. I would be more inclined to create an encounter in the moment, while you create a context for the encounter to occur.

ED: I think you might say that we see the solution and set up an experiment where it is possible for the subsystem to reach a resolution. This comes out of a belief that the system actually recognizes the solution inherent in the difficulty and that our function is to be bystanders to the process.

JOSEPH: I'm not likely to give them that. I would set up an existential encounter and then support whatever happens. I would stay in the moment and encourage them to do the same.

Mrs. C: I'm not sure how permanent the changes are either, but we really seem to be doing better as a family. I'm less tense, the girls seem to get along better, and there haven't been too many situations where I am screaming at them with no effect.

Second Daughter: I think things are just better because I got dumped and there is nothing to fight about. But at least for now, things are really better. My little sister is beginning to get into trouble, so Mom will pay attention to her and leave me alone.

Some healthy, normal, bickering among the siblings ensued. The net result was that the family agreed with each other and disagreed with the therapist's negative predictions. This is more productive in that the family reinforce their own progress without being dependent on the therapist to contain and support their changes. They are free to go on with their lives without therapeutic interference; at the same time, should they need therapy or desire personal growth work, they have the foundation of a respectful and successful process in their experience.

Once the changes have been supported and relapse possibilities have been resisted and reframed, treatment, per se, can be finished and termination can occur. Watzlawick, Beavin, and Jackson (1967) pointed out that one of the primary distinctions between "pure" systems therapy and Gestalt therapy is that systems therapy is for the "relief of suffering," whereas Gestalt therapy has personal growth as a primary goal. Systemic family therapy is bounded—when the system is changed, therapy is complete. *Individuals* may choose to go on to do individual work. In general, the therapist allows the desire for personal work to emerge from any of the individuals in the system and supports a "digestive" period of time to allow for the integration of systemic changes prior to beginning individual work. At that point, care is taken to ensure that the system can support the changes in the individual that will invariably take place through Gestalt therapy.

There is always potential for more therapeutic work if the family or couple desire and have the resources to continue. Continuation would likely result in a deeper exploration of the root causes of dysfunction, personal growth, and enhanced awareness for members of the family or couple. As many Gestalt therapists have been known to say, "You don't have to be sick to get better." Or, as Polster and Polster (1973) affirmed in extolling the virtues of the Gestalt approach, "Therapy is too good to be limited to the sick" (p. 23).

FACTORS SPECIFIC TO COUPLES THERAPY

Gestalt couples therapy will vary from therapist to therapist and be dependent on which theoretical concepts form the foundation of the therapist's work. Within the framework of Gestalt therapy, there are unique views about the goal of treatment. Richard Borofsky and Antra Kalnins Borofsky's (1994) definition facilitates organizing interventions and measuring progress:

> The health of a relationship, like the health of an economy, depends on the ease and frequency of exchange. When this exchange goes well, relationships thrive. Both partners [be]come increasingly present, alive, and aware. They become deeply connected with each other yet are respectful of their separateness. Partners are able to freely share with each other the unique truth of their experience and both are able to value, receive, and learn from the contact with each other's otherness. (p. 327)

Zinker and Nevis (1994) presented the paradoxical theory of change as the basis for Gestalt work with couples.

> Gestalt couples therapy asserts that change occurs paradoxically in the heightened awareness of "what is." . . . What does it mean when we say we look at "what is" in a couple? We give the couple an opportunity to examine what is experienced, what is done, what actions occur, what feelings and sentiments are available and expressed, as well as what may be held back. We encourage the couple to see and to experience the goodness, the usefulness, the creativity of what they discover when they examine themselves. Our basic position is that couples and families are generally unable to see the goodness and competence of their present positions. They receive little if any affirmation of what they do well in their relationship; foreground for them is the discomfort of their predicament. (p. 363)

Certain unifying principles organize couples therapy. First, it should be held as a possibility that the couple often will come into therapy with a hidden agenda. Frequently there is an unacknowledged and unaware desire to thwart the process of therapy, a need to defeat the therapist. This is most true when a couple comes into therapy "too late," when there has been a (sometimes unspoken) agreement to end the relationship. In this case it is common for one member to expect the therapist to be a miracle worker while the other one expects him or her to fail. On the other hand, couples coming to therapy "too soon," when there isn't yet a crystallization of the difficulty between them, often find enrichment. This can be a valuable means to take them through or over a temporary hurdle, resulting in enhanced functioning and a greater capacity for intimacy.

An initial assessment of the couple can readily reveal what modality would be most fitting to their situation, therapy or enrichment. Because a dyadic system is by definition one that is *mostly* without outside interference that *detracts* from its functioning as an intimate system, Gestalt therapists utilize "a variety of process assessments" of the degree of boundary breaks or disturbances in the relationship. For example, if the primary disruptions of the dyadic system occurred due to an affair, chemical substance or behavior addictions, or extraordinary interference from career/work, important activities, close friends, or families of origin, therapy would be indicated. By "extraordinary interference," we mean that there have been precipitating complaints and that the interference has resisted intrasystemic efforts to change. These are situations where relative *outside* factors have detracted from dyadic functioning and have become substitutes for intrasystemic satisfactions. Children in the system, including stepchildren (Papernow, 1993), are most prone to being the carriers of dyadic dissatisfactions. In the exploratory phase of therapy, the therapist can ask the couple about the symptoms that are manifest in their family system; what symptoms are evident in their children? If the children are symptom free and there is an absence of outside detractors, the couple have demonstrated that they can contain their dissatisfaction within their system and can benefit from enrichment efforts to maximize their potential for satisfaction within their system. Improved communication, awareness of self and other, and shared insights are legitimate and valuable goals for working with these healthy couples. Zinker and Zinker (personal communication, 2000) developed a model that reaches into the heart of a couple system to allow for the emergence of increased intimacy and understanding. Having witnessed their model in action, we consider it to be worthy of study and replication.

In work with couples in general, it is important to continue to see the relationship as the unit of treatment. Zinker and Nevis (1994) called it the "relational organism" and addressed the need to form observations from this perspective with language that attends to phenomenological observations of the dyad through phrases that link them, such as "we notice the two of you . . ." and "both of you are . . ." Zinker and Nevis stated, "These simple yet direct (and phenomenologically validated) observations lead the couple to increasing levels of awareness about themselves as individuals and their 'being together' as a couple. In the Gestalt model, awareness of process leads to change" (p. 360).

In our work with couples, we have found that understanding that there must be a system of equality between the partners is crucial (Lynch, 1992). Therefore, any rigid hierarchical organization that is evident in the couple becomes a focal point for experiments and interventions. The Zinkers' approach brings this aspect into focus, although at first glance it does not seem to be the central focus of therapy. The importance of *perceived* equality held by both members of the couple system is strengthened and highlighted through interventions that encourage and support emotional equality. The following are some possible "leading" instructions, which should always be directed at the couple rather than individuals:

- I'd like to hear the two of you describe your relationship looking at it from the point of view of a stranger. How would a stranger know you were a couple?
- Together, I'd like you to reminisce about a time when your relationship was just the way you both dreamed it would be.

- Relationships seem to need a purpose, a reason for being. I'm interested in you two coming up with an agreement about the objectives of your relationship.
- Most relationships have individuals outside of their couple who support them as a couple. That might be true for you two also. Together, come up with some individuals who really support you as a pair.
- If there was one thing about your relationship that you both wouldn't want to change, what would it be?

Though each of these statements implies that the couple will work together to come up with a response, there are also additional potential benefits to using them, or similar ones. Each directive or experimental intervention pinpoints strengths and presents an opportunity for positives to emerge—both of these being cornerstones of Gestalt therapy theory and practice. Because this is undertaken only in response to a therapist's directive, the couple should not be threatened by too sudden moves toward change. However, the therapist should introduce the experiment with the understanding that the difficulties that brought the couple to therapy are not ignored.

The pace of therapy is important. In maintaining this new field, where the therapist is incorporated into the system, there should be intentional assimilation. This is crucial in the therapeutic forecontact phase of therapy but cannot be ignored anywhere in the process. Experiments will be more readily accepted if the dyad experiences the therapist as being in sync with them. The therapist's presence must never be an irritant. There must be smooth, seamless transitions between therapist-driven experiments and the couple's moves toward contact. This process allows for genuine co-creation of solutions and resolutions. The therapist is not solely responsible for the couple's changes. Instead, the therapist devises experiments where the couple can emerge as engineers of their own progress, however that is defined.

Most therapists automatically think that couples in therapy are in need of more intimacy. We believe that this is rarely the case. Couples maintain whatever degree of intimacy their

---

JOSEPH: When you two talk about couples therapy, I see some distinct stylistic differences in the way we work and what guides our interventions. I emphasize being intimate. The strategy is background, they fall in love.

BARBARA: I think with us the strategy is in the foreground. We're more directive, using strategy to get the couple to a place where they can be more intimate. Another facet that seems to guide our work with couples is a focus on how the couple achieves distance. Rather than allowing hurtful or damaging actions to bring about functional or necessary distance, we would support bringing the need for distance to awareness so intentional choices can be made.

ED: We would tend to remove the blocks to intimacy and clear the way for intimate relating to occur.

JOSEPH: I think we all agree on a wide range of highly functional relating, allowing the dance of coming together and moving apart to be fluid and healthy. We're motivated by the same goal, and we come at it differently. I think one of the primary differences is that you two support the resistance to maintaining the changes that take place in therapy. You do things like prescribing the relapse, or being doubtful about the strength of the change. In response to a couple or family reporting the changes they've made in therapy, I've heard you say something like "I'm not so sure that these changes are really a part of you." I would be more inclined to praise them and support them, saying, "This is great!" Yet I can see the value in not being so invested in the changes they've made.

---

past experiences allow for. In general, as a couple live together over time, experiencing challenges, difficulties, and disappointments, they usually will expand their capacity for intimate relating, and they do this in their own ways, in their own time frame that is uniquely constructed out of their own past and current experiences and that is predicated on their level of differentiation and their finished and unfinished family-of-origin issues. What usually causes couples most difficulty is their unrewarding means of creating necessary distance. Therapists should trust couples to manage their intimacy tolerance when functional "distance producers" are in place.

Couples have an infinite variety of distance producers at their fingertips. The easiest and most convenient means of distancing are fighting with each other, finding fault, discarding a benevolent perspective, and acting in displeasing ways. With remarried couples, criticizing and finding fault with the partner's children is a great distancer. These means readily create barriers and distance, and with it emotional wounds that in time become fixed gestalts. If these common means do not produce enough distance or if, in time, the ordinary means of distancing become incorporated into the couple's usual communication patterns and "way of being," there are infinite possibilities for escalating. Common among them are addictions and overinvolvement with work, family of origin, hobbies, or friends, all of which can become fixed gestalts and entrenched distance producers.

From this viewpoint, it is vital for the therapist to respect the couple's need for distance and refrain from imposing personal distance tolerance levels onto the couple. This requires the therapist to show some awareness and sensitivity in allowing the couple to hold onto their need for distance while making the possibility of less painful means of attaining it available for their discovery. The couple that is not threatened by the therapist's "demand" to be more intimate (especially if the partners have identified that as their goal) will be less resistant to experiments and more easily supported in movement toward a more satisfying relationship.

SUCCESSFUL THERAPY—WHAT REALLY MATTERS

To become an effective Gestalt couple or family therapist, an individual should have a thorough grounding in systems theory, a full understanding of how couples and families are bound by the principles of systems across generations and within a context—or, in Gestalt terms, their "field." The basic principles and concepts are:

1. A system is an interactional unit made up of individuals with shared history, containing elements of power, intimacy, anxiety, differentiation, and need satisfaction that are transmitted intergenerationally.

2. Under stress, individuals and the system will repeatedly attempt to deal with a problem in old ways, even if those methods have failed in the past.

3. The system is composed of various subsystems formed by generational commonality, gender, shared interests, and compatibility.

4. The primary subsystems in a family are the couple system, the parental system, and the sibling system. Other subsystems, such as those formed by interests and gender, are secondary.

5. Subsystems are regulated by boundaries, with intra- and intersystemic rules (most often unstated).

6. There is a natural hierarchy in the system. In general, the adults are in the executive position in the system, and children are the subordinates.

7. Each subsystem has a unique function and purpose:
   A. The function of the marital subsystem is to provide emotional nurturance and support between peers. Intimacy within this subsystem includes sex.
   B. The function of the parental system is to provide limits, protection, nurturance, support, place, permission (to be male or female, to differentiate appropriately, etc.), respect, and love.
   C. The function of the sibling system is to learn to relate to peers, to be recipients of the parental offerings, and to learn to negotiate with adults in authority. The eventual function of the sibling or child system is to differentiate and leave home.

Learning to become an effective systems therapist involves a process that begins with intensive attention to the therapist's family of origin, including a thorough investigation of the therapist's unfinished business relative to his or her family of origin. This investigation provides therapists with warnings about potential projections that would contaminate their work with couples and families. It is well known that therapists become stuck with families at the same point where they have unfinished business in their own families. This becomes even more evident in work with couples, where there is an inherent tendency to project the therapist's parental dyad, the therapist's own unresolved dyads, and current intimate systems onto the dyad in treatment. When the therapist's vision is cluttered with unfinished business with intimate partners of the past and present, successful therapy is rarely possible.

If the therapist intends to work with couples and families using a Gestalt model, it is crucial that the therapist *experience* Gestalt therapy firsthand—a common requirement in Gestalt institutes and other psychotherapeutic training programs with a Gestalt focus. This is an opportunity to learn by doing and to begin to work on the disturbances to contact that will also negatively influence therapy. It is not enough to learn by reading or listening. Gestalt therapy is present centered and active—a relationship between therapist and client. It must be experienced to become part of a therapist's way of being. Because effective systemic couples and family therapy is focused on the relationship between the therapist and the couple or family system and, in an isomorphic manner, the relationship between subsystems, Gestalt and systems therapies are intricately connected.

A body of theoretical background and practical knowledge predicates effective work with couples and families. This knowledge should include:

1. The basic principles that guide couple systems, such as projective identification, the developmental cycle of couple systems, power and intrasystemic hierarchy, and birth order factors that affect mate choice and marital satisfaction

2. The concepts of normal family development, including developmental crises

3. The ancestor "syndrome": that is, how patterns are transmitted across generations

4. The impact of race, ethnicity, gender, socioeconomic, and cultural factors on couples and families

5. The effects of adoption, divorce, remarriage, being gay and lesbian, chronic and critical illnesses, and other unique factors affecting couple and family systems.

Last and perhaps most important is work on one's self and family of origin. As indicated in one of the earliest (if not the first) contributions to Gestalt family therapy, Walter Kempler (1981) reminded us that all therapy is transmuted through a person and therefore that the self of the therapist is the most significant impediment or effective instrument of change. With extensive work on the multigenerational family of origin, self-introspection with attention to the barriers to contact, and a foundation of systemic couple and family theory, the therapist should be ready to begin the exciting and awesome process of facilitating couples' and families' progress toward a more rewarding way of being with each other.

JOSEPH: This brief discussion has just reinforced what I always knew, that we are basically similar and that our differences are those of style. The three of us are manifestations of a combination of Gestalt and systems modalities where our core beliefs are stronger than any surface differences.

It is important to add that the process is incomplete without an experienced supervisor, one who has years of experience—hopefully in both Gestalt therapy and systemic family therapy. The changes that emerge from the field of a skilled Gestalt family therapist in contact with couples and families, under the guidance of a challenging and supportive supervisor, are limitless.

REVIEW QUESTIONS

1. Where do Gestalt therapy and general systems therapy converge? Diverge?

2. How do systems therapists and Gestalt therapists differ in their views of presenting problems?

3. Describe the unique complexities of the couple system within the larger family system.

4. What is the focus of intervention for the systems therapist? Provide theoretical support for the origins of this focus.

5. How are interventions in the systemic therapeutic process comparable to Gestalt therapy?

6. Describe ways in which couples produce distance in their relationship.

7. How do individuals in an intimate system actualize their equality?

8. What is meant by Zinker and Nevis's identification of the couple or family system as a "third entity"?

9. Describe how support of system change is accomplished so that the therapist becomes "the holder of resistance to change" and not the "harbinger of the relapse."

10. What are the basic conditions necessary to be a successful Gestalt couple or family therapist?

EXPERIENTIAL PEDAGOGICAL ACTIVITIES

ACTIVITY 1: Family systems function with family-specific styles—for example, limiting, organizational, supportive, nurturing, or unique styles. Think back to your own family of origin, and identify the primary or automatic style of functioning used during a stressful family event. Provide examples that support your functioning-style selection. Generate other examples where your family engaged in a contrasting functioning style, and note your awareness of any differences in the process and/or outcome.

ACTIVITY 2: Select a system of your choice (family, couple, work associates, school cohorts, church committee, etc.), and draw a model that includes a representative symbol for each individual within the system. That identified system is embedded within larger systems or fields that you can draw as increasingly larger consecutive circles around the identified system. There may also be subgroupings within the identified system, based on gender, age, similar interests or motives, personal styles or preferences, or a vast variety of additional identifiers. With a different color for each subsystem, draw a circle around the individuals within the identified system that constitute the various subsystems. Get together with another class member to discuss the awarenesses you both gained from identifying the various levels of systems and how each has had an impact on you. If a class member is not available for discussion, you could process the experience through journaling.

ACTIVITY 3: The Lynches stated in this chapter, "[T]he enactment, or experiment, is at the heart of all interventions, allowing change, and the contact disturbances, to be monitored in the present." Discuss and select an appropriate family dilemma to reenact in the classroom from experiences briefly introduced by volunteer class members. For this experiment, the individual student becomes the director, describes the details of the family's dilemma, and selects class members to play the roles of the family. No clinician or therapist is necessary in this experiment but would be an option for an advanced class. In a fishbowl formation, other class members can take on roles as observer(s), secretary, mediator, and/or monitors of the interests of family subsystems. The student director can stop action or make redirections at any point in the reenactment. When the conversation reaches a natural stopping point (not necessarily a resolution), the director and all class members describe their experiences of participating in or observing the family system and its struggle with the dilemma.

ACTIVITY 4: This activity has a "couples focus." Think of an individual with whom you have had a significant relationship, and keep that person in mind as you respond to the suggestions below. By yourself, respond to the following intervention recommendations, which have been modified from those presented in this chapter. Choose a response method that feels most comfortable to you (such as written dialogue, two-chair dialogue, tape recording, or journaling).

A. Describe your significant relationship, looking at it from the point of view of a stranger. How would a stranger know you were a couple?

B. Reminisce about and describe a time when this relationship was just the way you both dreamed it would be.

C. If there was one thing about your relationship that you wouldn't have changed, what would that have been?

D. Identify at least one thing you might have done differently in your relationship if you had previous knowledge from this chapter.

CHAPTER **12**

Gestalt Therapy in Groups

PAUL SCHOENBERG AND BUD FEDER

DIALOGUE RESPONDENTS: JON FREW AND IRWIN GADOL

Paul Schoenberg is a licensed professional clinical counselor who works as an outpatient psychotherapist at Coleman Professional Services, a community mental health center in Ravenna, Ohio, where he has effectively researched and proven the value of Gestalt group therapy for persons diagnosed with borderline and other personality disorders. He currently serves as an adjunct faculty member, supervising graduate students in counseling practicums and internships at both Kent State and Cleveland State Universities. An excellent facilitator, he has delivered presentations and workshops on Gestalt therapy to national and international audiences. He was a master's and doctoral advisee of Ansel Woldt and is a charter member of the Kent Gestalt Writers' Group. His writing interests also include the art of self-healing from trauma.

Bud Feder completed his PhD in clinical psychology at Columbia University Teachers College and has practiced Gestalt therapy for over 30 years, primarily in New Jersey. He appreciates the several years of Gestalt training and group therapy that he had with Laura Perls. His special interest is group therapy; he has written *Peeling the Onion: A Gestalt Therapy Manual for Clients* (1975; 2nd ed., 1990), has co-edited *Beyond the Hot Seat: Gestalt Approaches to Group* (1980), and is writing another book on group therapy. He leads a Gestalt training group in New York City; is past treasurer and current president of the Association for the Advancement of Gestalt Therapy; and is an actively involved "full member" of the New York Institute for Gestalt Therapy.

Jon Frew is co-director of the Gestalt Therapy Training Center–Northwest and is an associate professor in the School of Professional Psychology at Pacific University in Portland, Oregon. He is graduate of the Gestalt Institute of Cleveland's Post-Graduate Program and a doctoral advisee of Ansel Woldt at Kent State University, where he researched the interpersonal contact processes of couples. He has been training Gestalt therapists since 1982, has published numerous articles on Gestalt therapy in professional journals, and serves on the editorial board of the *Gestalt Review.*

Irwin Gadol is a licensed clinical psychologist practicing in Dallas/Ft. Worth, Texas. He is an adjunct professor at the University of Texas Medical School, where he teaches group therapy to psychiatry residents. He is co-founder and senior faculty trainer of the Gestalt Training Institute of Dallas and a regular contributor to the Association for the Advancement of Gestalt Therapy and to the growth and development of the Gestalt community.

THE ORIGIN OF GESTALT GROUP THERAPY: THE HOT SEAT MODEL

Gestalt group therapy can be traced back essentially to the work of Fritz Perls, one of the founders of Gestalt therapy. Perls utilized both his background in theater and his monolithic ego (Kitzler, 1980) as tools in creating a stage from which to both present and demonstrate the application of Gestalt therapy to and for both small and large groups. His own expressed intolerance for individual therapy (Kitzler, 1980; Perls, 1975) became the rationale for his eventual choice of a group model as the favored forum for his stylized approach. Perls (1975) averred that

> [i]n the group situation something happens that is not possible in the private interview. . . . Somehow trust in the group seems to be greater than trust in the therapist. . . . In the safe emergency of the [group] situation, the neurotic discovers that the world does not fall apart if he gets angry, sexy, joyous, mournful. Nor is the group's support for his self-esteem and appreciation of his achievements toward authenticity and greater liveliness to be underestimated. . . . There are other advantages of working with a group. A great deal of individual development can be facilitated through doing collective experiments—talking jibberish together, or doing withdrawal experiments, or learning to understand the importance of atmosphere, or showing the person on the spot how he collectively bores, hypnotizes, or amuses the environment. . . . The group soon learns to understand the contrast between helpfulness, however well-meaning, and true support. . . . It is always a

> deeply moving experience for the group and for me, the therapist, to see previously robotized corpses begin to return to life, gain substance, begin the dance of abandonment and self-fulfillment. *The paper people are turning into real people.* (pp. 13–15, italics in original)

It is important to note that the group therapy model Perls is most remembered for (and frequently most castigated for) was primarily a demonstration or teaching model, created to quickly and dramatically demonstrate the possibilities and potential of Gestalt therapy. It was not designed to reflect the more deliberate and thoughtful process usually practiced by Perls and other early disciples when conducting actual therapy in a private setting. Perls's demonstration model of group therapy was typically presented in a training or institute setting (such as the Esalen Institute) as opposed to a private therapist's office or clinic, was performed with therapists and other clinicians serving as clients (as opposed to real clients), and was short term, lasting often only for a day or a weekend (as opposed to the longer-term process of actual group therapy).

Within the practice of Perls's original model, the facilitator works primarily with one person at a time, sitting on the focal chair or "hot seat," while the rest of the group quietly listens. Group interaction is kept to a minimum and in fact is often discouraged or even criticized (Perls, 1973). Dialogue flows through the facilitator only, in what Zinker (1977) described as the "broken wagon wheel model" (p. 159). The group more often than not serves to provide a Greek chorus for the facilitator, an audience that he or she can utilize to support the particular focused awareness that the facilitator and client are seeking to sharpen.

As noted above, Perls used the group primarily as a blank screen on which the individual working could project his or her present fears or "catastrophic expectations" in encountering a particular neurosis (Perls 1973, 1975). Usually these fears were of group humiliation (embarrassment) or social condemnation (shame). In using the audience as a nonresponsive and nonjudgmental screen, the working member could be taught to recognize his or her projections as just that, self-generated (and often inaccurate) assumptions reflective of his or her own innate aggressions and fears. From this awareness, the individual could then move into developing his or her own form of internal autonomous support to manage those aggressions and fears, rather than relying on the group members to provide support. Perls viewed the latter as antithetical to the integrity and responsibility of the individual (Clarkson & Mackewn, 1993). However, when the group was used in this limited fashion, the experience rarely engendered member interaction or accessed dialogical possibilities contained within the fullness of Gestalt therapy.

In response to this particular demonstration model, some observers strongly criticized Perls (and by default Gestalt therapy) as an alleged therapeutic bully who used the audience to shame working members into believing and mouthing his personal values under the guise of a therapeutic transformation (Clarkson & Mackewn, 1993; Kitzler, 1980). In addition to this personalized criticism, Perls's style of group therapy led to the frequent rejection of Gestalt group therapy as a genuine group approach. Yalom (1985) summarily dismissed Gestalt group therapy as simply "individual therapy in a group" and added, "I feel that Perls' group therapy technique is ill founded and makes inefficient use of a group's therapeutic potential" (p. 453).

ALTERNATIVE MODELS OF GESTALT GROUP THERAPY

Two recent studies (Feder, 2002; Frew, 1988) revealed that Gestalt group therapy in the United States is, on the whole, practiced in quite a different style from the one originated by Perls. Frew's (1988) research noted that most Gestalt therapists practicing in the United States utilize an approach that integrates the Perls hot seat model with a broad range of other group approaches. He found that a majority of the surveyed therapists combined the use of different levels of individual, dyad, subgroup, and whole-group work within their approach. Feder (2002) corroborated Frew's research with almost parallel results. In addition to these quantitative data, other contemporary Gestalt group therapists such as Earley (1996), Aylward (1996), and Handlon and Fredericson (1998) described theoretical and anecdotal models of group therapy that valued real relationships between members, peer dialogue, a broader range of present-centered experience, a sense of the group as a whole, and emphasis on intimate contact between members to create acceptance and support for experiment and risk.

This integrative and more comprehensive approach to Gestalt group therapy was developed and enhanced by numerous Gestalt clinicians. Elaine Kepner described an integrative interpersonal approach in her chapter in *Beyond the Hot Seat* (Feder & Ronall, 1980), a seminal text that brought Gestalt group therapy to new understandings and expansion from the hot seat model. Whereas Perls focused primarily on work done by the individual client in the hot seat, Kepner (1980) identified three major levels of opportunity for work within a Gestalt therapy group: the intrapersonal (self-exploration); the interpersonal (exploration of in-group relationships such as dyads); and the group as a whole (exploration of larger group patterns or themes). Ideally, the therapeutic process moves smoothly among all three levels.

JON: The thesis of my subsequent remarks is that the practice of Gestalt therapy in groups involves an array of complex and challenging choices, and the choices cannot be mutually exclusive. As you so clearly explicated in your chapter, "stand-alone" hot seat or demonstration models are only remotely related to the philosophical and theoretical foundations of Gestalt therapy.

Fritz Perls's "use" of the group as a nonresponsive blank screen defies the principles inherent in "field theory" and "dialogue." To ignore the group or use it as a "Greek chorus" denudes the richness and very existence of the field, and to *use* the group as only an object in the service of individual work robs the experience of any I-Thou potential. Indeed, a hot seat model that serves the agenda of moving an individual to what you called "internal autonomous support and away from any group support" is patently antithetical to a field theory perspective, which embraces the dance of dependence and independence, the perennial polarity that bounds and defines interdependence. If our only goal as Gestalt therapists is heightening awareness, the notion of promoting independence has no place in Gestalt therapy practice in or out of groups.

The demonstration/hot seat model employed by Fritz Perls (and by a small percentage of Gestalt therapists to this day) does have a place in the history and evolution of Gestalt therapy. But practiced as a freestanding and exclusive model, it cannot be considered or categorized as group work. In the chapter you use the term *alternate models of Gestalt group therapy* to describe group work that departs from the demonstration model. I would argue that hot seat work, which transformed the fertile field into a frozen tundra, was the departure from the essential philosophical and theoretical foundations of Gestalt therapy.

The choice of the level of work at any given moment is influenced by facilitator(s) and group members alike. Kepner labeled this alternative approach to the Perlsian hot seat model "Gestalt group process" (sometimes known as the Cleveland model).

In addition to broadening the use of the varied levels of group work, Kepner (1980) redefined the facilitator as a "manager," one who accesses and supports transitions between the different levels of work to provide group members with rich and diverse learning opportunities and who notices and honors the group's choices. This style of facilitation is in contrast to the hot seat model, in which the facilitator functions more as a leader or director.

Not all contemporary Gestalt therapists subscribe to Gestalt group process (Feder, 2002; Frew, 1988). Some 10% of Gestalt therapists in the United States continue to utilize the Perls model exclusively. Others integrate elements from the two primary models and their own personal experience to create their own eclectic styles.

EVOLUTION OF GESTALT GROUP PROCESS

Though the original Perls model has remained fairly constant, Gestalt group process has continued to evolve. Huckaby (1992) provided a succinct synopsis of this evolution. She described modern Gestalt group process as the integration of three theoretical systems: systems theory, group dynamics theory, and Gestalt theory.

The first of these, systems theory, is essentially an organized reaction to Newtonian science theory, which proposed that phenomena could be studied only when broken down into their smallest observable parts. Systems theory suggested instead that all organisms can be understood only in context of the system(s) or field(s) (field theorists may take issue with the lumping of systems theory and field theory together) within which they operate and that what is important are the relationships between organisms, not just the individual organisms themselves.

BUD: Jon, you make some cogent points regarding the gap between the hot seat method and Gestalt therapy theory and philosophy. Yet I wouldn't go that far, particularly after having recently watched some tapes of Fritz's work. I see it more as a matter of emphasis, since when the therapist/client work takes place in a private setting, as compared to within a group setting, there is a felt difference—at least for me watching. The clients' reactions and concerns often reflect their awareness that there are group members around them, supporting or judging or ignoring or whatever, depending on the clients' perceptions. And in all fairness, Fritz does [or did], at times, bring these aspects into the work. And almost always at the end of the work, the films show various interactions between the person leaving the hot seat and the rest of the group, usually support and affection. So in addition to having a place in history, the demonstration/hot seat method planted the seed of later work and in my view was a "poorly cultivated field" rather than a "frozen tundra." It took later workers, notably Elaine Kepner and others from Cleveland, as well as some of us from NYC to recognize that the field was much more fertile than the demo/hot seat method.

JON: Bud, I agree that Fritz would bring aspects of the "group field" into his individual work in groups. I believe that Fritz worked exclusively with one person at a time in his demonstration model because of his training and his interest, not as a matter of emphasis. He was, of course, a psychiatrist and an individual psychotherapist, not a group or interpersonal psychotherapist. He acknowledged this at an American Psychological Association meeting in 1966. As you note, a number of Gestalt therapists who followed him into group work began to experiment with alternating between attention to individuals and intrapersonal awareness, interpersonal relationships and dynamics, and group issues and themes. These are all avenues that can lead to individual

Within systems theory, several core beliefs are relevant to the development of Gestalt group process. First, systems theory emphasizes holism, the concept that the whole is different from and greater than the sum of its parts. Holism, as applied to small groups, suggests that knowing the members as individuals within the group is not enough. The group itself is an organism with a complexity not accounted for by individual input. Holism then proposes that each configuration of a group will provide its own unpredictable and unique nature and that subtle or not so subtle changes to individual composition within the group may have dramatic effects on the group as whole. For instance, if a group introduces one new member, the group's process may become radically different, even if the remaining membership and facilitation remain the same.

A second component of systems theory is the idea that systems are more or less closed or open. Closed systems seek to be self-contained, whereas open systems are constantly taking in new energy and information. How a small group establishes and experiences itself as either closed or open (or, more commonly, somewhere in between) affects its ability to grow and flourish or to exhaust itself and die. Rigid efforts to keep the group closed may result in the group rapidly depleting its energy and losing members due to attrition and abrupt termination. Exaggerated attempts to sustain openness may result in the group remaining diffuse and distanced and experiencing dissolution. For example, constantly introducing new members to a group makes it difficult for members to build a sense of safety and trust and achieve deeper levels of work.

growth and change. Kurt Lewin was known to say that sustainable changes with individuals occur only when the groups and communities they inhabit change. It could be said that Fritz drove a car in one gear that was equipped with at least three. I do not disagree that Fritz was truly a master at attending acutely to an individual's intrapersonal process as he or she sat in the hot seat and reacted to Fritz and other aspects of the field. My objection is to categorizing his model as group therapy.

IRV: Jon, basically I agree with you that Perls was not doing "group" work in the sense that he was using a dyadic model, just the "patient" and him, and that he was, therefore, not focusing on or using the group as a whole or utilizing group process or group dynamics. I also agree, Bud, with you, and your comments in general, but I do feel that we don't have to choose between the "hot seat" or the field; and of course, as Gestaltists, we work with the three major levels all of the time.

PAUL: As Irv notes, a focus on individual awareness is one level available for therapeutic process in a group. Perls deserves credit, in my view, simply for publicly introducing Gestalt therapy into a group setting, no matter how narrowly or broadly he used that setting.

A third aspect of systems theory proposes that a group's ability to grow is based on its ability to self-regulate or move toward homeostasis (a state of group levelness and calm based on creation of consistent roles and norms within the group) in the face of the universal process of entropy (the tendency of systems to lose energy or become disorganized over time). Gestalt group facilitators and responsible members foster the integration of the natural entropic process and the concurrent process of organismic self-regulation by attending to how the creation and dissolution of norms and roles within a specific group (e.g., disrupted by a change in facilitation) affect the group's ability to self-regulate.

Finally, systems theory utilizes the concept of equifinality, or, in simpler language, the concept that there are many ways to get things done. Contemporary Gestalt group process depends not only on a leader-driven path to group satisfaction and goal achievement but also on the creative input and curiosity of its members and any other contextual field that influences the group (setting, enveloping institution, surrounding community, etc.). Responsibility for group progress then becomes diffused among the members and other outside forces, instead of being placed solely upon the shoulders of the facilitators.

Huckaby (1992) also identified that modern Gestalt group process integrates a second core theoretical base, that of group dynamics. Group dynamics was originally developed as a theory by Kurt Lewin (1951), who, while at the Research Center for Group Dynamics at Massachusetts Institute of Technology, became interested in the process of how small groups operate. Although the initial intent was to discover how groups solve particular problems or tasks, Lewin and his colleagues rapidly discovered that there were underlying dimensions of group process common to each group. His initial work and subsequent research provided much of the foundation for research and practice of group work today.

Lewin (1951) believed that group dynamics contained five core elements. First, each group develops goals or outcomes appropriate to the needs of the group. Each individual group is responsible for determining its goals and adapting them as desired. Second, each group develops specific norms, or parameters of behavior that establish both overt and covert rules for behavior within the group. Once again, all members of the group take on responsibility for maintaining awareness and determination of these norms. Third, groups develop and establish roles for group members. This assignation occurs both overtly and covertly and creates characteristics and specific group functions for different members. The group must also seek to take responsibility for increasing awareness of both the existence of roles and the processes of developing, sustaining, and modifying them. Fourth, groups seek to progress through developmental stages, building intimacy, trust, and depth of work in a consistent manner. All types of groups seek this development. Though fundamentally linear in theory, stage development may also move in a circuitous or even reverse fashion, depending on unanticipated factors or changes in the group, such as introduction of new members, disruption of trust, or change in facilitators. Lewin proposed that, in addition to facilitator awareness, group members must be aware of and take responsibility for their own movement through stage development (or stuckness in a particular stage). Lewin's fifth and final essential element of group dynamics theory was that of group levels of interaction. As previously described by Kepner (1980), each group contains a number of possible levels of interaction. The group chooses to focus at any time on the intrapersonal level, the interpersonal or subgroup level, and/or the whole-group level (of course, in some dimension all of these levels operate simultaneously). Once again, Lewin suggested the group must take responsibility for selecting the particular level of engagement at any one moment in the session.

As can be observed in the description of these essential elements of group dynamics, awareness of and taking responsibility for the choices inherent in all of these elements need to occur through the facilitators, individual group members, and all of the other levels of group for effective functioning. Awareness, contact, and responsibility, as noted in previous chapters in this book, are also critical elements of Gestalt group theory.

The third essential theory that affects modern Gestalt group process is that of Gestalt therapy theory (Huckaby, 1992). Previous chapters in this text have described the key terminology and theoretical constructs in Gestalt therapy theory as applied to the individual organism and in the context of Gestalt therapy applied to individuals. These same constructs are also applicable to Gestalt group process, although they take on a more complex nature due to the greater number of interactive possibilities.

GESTALT CONSTRUCTS APPLIED TO GROUP PROCESS

Organismic Self-Regulation

The first Gestalt construct applied to group process is organismic self-regulation—a process that has been described as the organism's efforts to sustain an internal homeostatic (also described as balanced or satisfied) state of existence (Perls, Hefferline, & Goodman, 1951). Gestalt theory applied to individual organisms proposes that this process initially takes place through the gradual or sudden awareness of individual needs within the organism that become figural or highlighted against the surrounding environment or ground. The satisfaction of each need results in the destruction of the figure, or completion of the gestalt, so a new figure can then arise, be satisfied, be destroyed, and so on. Needs that go unmet (or incomplete gestalts) result in unfinished business or internalized figures that then press for resolution within the organism, even as new figures arise and also demand attention. Woldt (1993) described and labeled this process as the Gestalt homeostasis cycle. New and old figures then compete with each other; in the most severe case, this results in places of stuckness, incompleteness, and ambivalence. Resnick (1995) described this exaggerated competition between unfinished business and present need satisfaction as the creation of fixed gestalts, or frozen patterns of phenomenology that we also know as character.

In Gestalt group process, organismic self-regulation occurs not only within the individual as he or she goes about seeking completion of individual needs but also within other levels such as subgroupings or the group as a whole (in fact, these levels can also include lesser-noticed systems, such as facilitator to facilitator or group to the outside system of the agency or institution). The addition of these different levels of organismic self-regulation provides a broader, more complex experience of the self-regulatory process and also one that is more reflective of the dazzlement, interruption, and confusion of competing needs (figures) within everyday life.

Contact Processes

Gestalt theory's contact processes within a group, as in life, become more complex as membership increases. More contact boundaries between individuals or systems are brought to attention within a group, and the unique process occurring at each boundary becomes more influenced by the invested and concerned field (other members, facilitators, institutions, etc.). Rather than one cycle of experience (or contact cycle) occurring during any one time period (as within any one organism), multiple cycles of experience weave and entwine with each other, creating a richer, denser, and sometimes more frustrating (from a standpoint of individual satisfaction) experience. Within this plethora of

JON: The three theoretical systems described in the chapter, which inform Gestalt therapy in groups, also support the thesis that individual work alone is not consistent with Gestalt therapy theory. As a *systems theory,* the whole group is an organism that cannot be accounted for by attending only to individual group members. *Group dynamics* (à la Kurt Lewin) requires that we understand that groups are communities that develop goals and norms and proceed (though not in a strictly linear way) through different stages. Finally and most importantly, Gestalt therapy theory brings us the key concepts of *organismic self-regulation* (which in a group setting could be called

contact processes, the individual figure or need diminishes in significance (although, of course, the figure does not become insignificant), and the large system or field figures become more prominent.

As the group functions as a whole unit, the group's organismic self-regulation process itself influences the selection of figure resolution from among the many figures (or subjects/topics) available at any one time. Rather than having any one individual choose a specific need to satisfy, the contemporary Gestalt group as a whole selects the particular figure of interest to work on. Of course, in reality, other levels of system (such as demanding, curious, or needy individuals, dyads, or facilitators) also seek to influence the choice of figural resolution, resulting in the lively and demanding tapestry of figural creation and completion (and frequent incompletion!) within the group process.

Gestalt Styles of Contact and Resistance in Groups

Specific contact and resistance styles exhibited within the contact cycle of experience are manifested in group therapy much as they are in individual therapy; in fact, the number of possibilities of contact/resistance is exponentially increased within the group. In Gestalt group process, members and facilitators alike will encounter most of their familiar contact and resistance styles or habits and may choose to experiment with or try on a broad range of other styles as well. Though the possibilities of experimentation in contact and resistance styles increase in a group, so, too, may the use of frozen or rigid contact and resistance styles. Rigidity or increased defensiveness is predictable, given the increase in potential challenges or perceived threats to personal boundary styles, especially with the addition of more individuals to the group therapeutic arena. It is the excitement and potential of these possibilities and challenges that draws some therapists to this very arena of group work, whereas the anxiety and workload scare others away!

organismic self, relationship, and group regulation); *contact processes,* or as you stated, "multiple cycles of experience"; and *present-centeredness,* which inspires attention both to members' awarenesses and to the group and interpersonal dynamics and opportunities.

IRV: I guess that your "short but pregnant" paragraph just about covers it all and succinctly at that. What I would embellish is the concept of organismic self-regulation. When I am working with patients, what I point out is that we are all interacting within the external environment (or field) and we are trying very hard to "flourish" by trying to get our needs met at any given moment. Here the concept of "support" becomes crucial. In Gestalt we discriminate between self-support and environmental support. These two concepts have been very useful to me when dealing with patients and helping them to grow. Gestalt group psychotherapy can be a wonderful opportunity for patients to become aware of what differences there are between supporting the self and getting support from the (group) environment. Encouraging the patient to assume greater and greater self-support is one of the most important aspects of group function.

PAUL: I would quibble slightly with you, Irv, on your last statement, as I understand it. As valuable as learning self-support skills is, I would argue that, even more importantly, the group setting provides an ideal (and often necessary) opportunity for the individual client to learn balanced and reciprocal support skills within the surrounding and responding environment of other people: in other words, learning how to "act in concert with," rather than "act upon." The organismic self-regulation of the group environment as a whole helps support this learning process, which, hopefully, the individual can then apply or adapt to all of his or her other "environments."

Awareness

Awareness remains the cornerstone of Gestalt group process, just as in individual therapy. What is different in Gestalt group process is that awareness is not merely focused on any one contact boundary between a single individual and his or her field but becomes focused, diffused, and then refocused from among the broader variety of contact boundaries possible within the group. Thus attention is not paid just to self-awareness, or awareness of the relationship between therapist and client, as in individual therapy; it also includes awareness of the functioning and satisfaction present within group member to group member boundaries, subgroup to group boundaries, group to facilitator(s) boundaries, and so on. In Gestalt group process, awareness of boundaries and of reasonable satisfaction is necessary for the smooth functioning and continuity of the group's existence. However, it is equally important that the larger system's/field's boundaries receive attention. As in our social institutions, if the larger frameworks fail, the smaller boundaries are inherently doomed ("If the boat is sinking, who cares where you get to sit!").

Present-Centeredness: Here and Now

The focus of Gestalt theory on the primacy of the here and now, as opposed to past experiences or future possibilities, does not change in moving from individual therapy to Gestalt group process. Group dialogue is still focused on remaining in the here and now and utilizing the present experience of group interaction. In fact, Gestalt group process provides an even greater opportunity for using the present as an opportunity for awareness and change than does individual therapy. The quantitative increase in present-centered interactions between group members offers a greater chance to awaken some unresolved issues (unfinished business) in members and offers a correlating increase in opportunity to use group process to finish those historically incomplete figures.

In summation, the practitioner of contemporary Gestalt group process seeks to integrate these three theories (systems theory, group dynamics theory, and Gestalt theory) from both an observational and a participatory perspective and to develop interventions based on perception of need and appropriateness to the group's position within the triangulation of the three theories. The authors propose that the actual development and implementation of specific interventions during individual and ongoing group sessions can also be described as a series of interconnected and overlapping process goals and objectives.

GESTALT GROUP THERAPY PROCESS GOALS

Within an actual group session, Gestalt group facilitators attend to several primary and coherently linked process goals and objectives, which emerge from this integration of theories. Any and all of the subsequently developed specific strategies, interventions, and techniques are designed to serve these process goals and objectives. Contemporary Gestalt therapists utilize facilitative interventions that focus largely on interpersonal processes, not the heavy-handed, coercive, or demanding style depicted in some of the films of Fritz Perls.

The primary and overarching process goal is the generation of increased awareness within the different levels of the group. As Simkin and Yontef (1989) stated, "In Gestalt therapy the goal is always awareness and only awareness" (p. 294). This overall goal of awareness includes individual recognition, description, and ownership of sensations, thoughts, memories, emotions, behaviors, and all other functions of the self. Within Gestalt group work, the awareness goal also includes recognition, description, and ownership of different dynamic processes occurring within the group's subsystems and the group as a whole. Increased awareness allows members and the group as a whole to recognize and take responsibility for both their current practices of initiating contact or responding to the initiation of contact from others and the consequences of how these styles work for or against the satisfying completion of figures or needs raised within the group. Gestalt group therapists, as process facilitators, seek to heighten and sharpen all levels of group awareness, particularly in the recognition of thematic and intrusive unfinished business and repetitious contact and resistance styles that interfere with members' accurate awareness of present experience.

Within this overarching goal of awareness, a series of objectives occur that (in the ideal sense) often represent a completion of a whole-group cycle of experience or a complete cycle of contactful processes—in other words, a group gestalt. Let us move through an idealized version of this cycle as it occurs within a specific session.

As an individual group session begins, members and facilitators seek to simultaneously sharpen and "fatten" the present sensations and awareness of all present. Sharpening is when members heighten their focus on their current experience of entering and being in the group on that given day. Fattening is when members attend to awareness from a multitude of sources, including sensory instruments, cognition, and affect. This process may include initial pleasantries and group practicalities (e.g., "Who's making the coffee?" or "Are there any Kleenex?"), focusing activities, brief statements of current awareness, expression of personal and other levels of desire for the particular session, and identification of anything clouding or blocking present awareness or ability to attend (including unfinished group business). Some of this work may occur internally, whereas some may need to be expressed verbally within the group to support initial present awareness at the broader level. Role induction may occur through the description, teaching, and modeling of these awareness skills by group facilitators.

With these "fattened" awarenesses and recognition of incomplete gestalts in place, the group selects, or sometimes slides into, a figure or piece of unfinished business. In other words, the group selects what it wishes to do in that moment. Examples of work selection could include a problem one member brings in from outside the group, a conflict between two group members, or members' concern about how the group is functioning as a whole. The selection process is influenced by group and individual desires and the facilitators' observations of stuckness or movement within different levels of the group.

Gestalt group process facilitators then seek to create an environment conducive to working on that consensually selected piece. Zinker (1977) called this process the development of the Perlsian "safe emergency" (p. 59). *Emergency,* in this context, means that the working member or members are faced with a situation similar to and reminiscent of previously difficult or traumatic events. The term *safe* indicates that this reenactment takes place in the relatively secure and protected therapeutic environment. Depending on the functioning level, the group may spend the entire session getting to the "safe emergency," and that may be where the work takes place.

The creation of a dimension of safety is the process objective of the provision, enhancement, or withdrawal of support for group members by the facilitator(s) and other group members. The primary purpose of this process objective is to increase the group's ability to tolerate the anxiety that occurs during contact with the unfamiliar or familiar "emergency." For example, this process could occur when an individual member "tries on" a new or exaggerated contact and/or resistance style. Support may be presented or withheld in numerous modalities, including verbal, nonverbal, body language, use of space, and member proximity. Specific strategies could include the use of encouragement and/or challenge, reminders of past success, noting of possible gains, pats on the back, and applause. Support needs to be provided or offered with discretion and respect for the individual's and the group's ability to generate their own support. Sometimes environmental support may be purposefully diluted or withdrawn with the intention of encouraging the process of self-support, or what Perls (1967) and Simkin (1976/1990) called "frustrating" clients to let them discover their own strengths and skills. These methods could include using silence, turning away, reducing eye contact, or denying or discouraging the member's request for assistance. In using environmental support, Gestalt group facilitators are encouraged to observe the guidelines of Laura Perls, who often reminded us to "[g]ive as much support as necessary and as little as possible" (quoted in Feder & Ronall, 1980, p. 45).

When a sufficient level of support has been established for working on a relevant figure of unfinished business, the next process objective of experimentation begins. Obviously, as Wheeler (1988) noted, "getting to" the experiment may be experimental in its own right and may create and close existing figures or needs as it goes. The facilitators and members join in achieving the experimentation process goal by creating a verbal, behavioral, and interactive group process. This might entail, for example, reenacting the original event of unfinished business or generating a representation (as in fantasy, drama, or dialogue) of the particular thematic style in which the individual or group experiences contact is stuck, dissatisfying, or even psychologically painful.

Unfamiliar, unexplored, or underdeveloped polarities of contact and resistance styles are identified as alternatives to the original, known, or familiar contact or resistance style. In the therapeutic setting, the appropriate level of group is invited to experiment with, play with, or try on these different alternatives of contact or resistance styles. Experimentation with contact styles might include the use of paradox, such as exaggerating and owning the familiar style, practicing an alternative approach, role-playing polarities, dialoguing within the group, and a variety of other means. All of the possible strategies of experimentation serve the larger process goal of increasing and enlarging awareness within the appropriate group level and thereby enhancing the potential for authentic contact. An example of experimentation is when two members are invited or choose to speak directly to each other about their resentments and appreciations rather than talking obliquely to the facilitators about similar past situations.

A final objective of Gestalt group process is the reporting to the group of any assimilation or changes in awareness, both during and immediately after the experiment, by the involved level of system. This post–contact stage objective is an essential part of the larger process in that it allows participants to consider and absorb the novelty of the experiment rather than swallowing it whole or spitting it back out abruptly. Facilitators and observant group members may verbally offer their own awarenesses and phenomenological experiences of the experiment, but the final choice of value and meaning of the experiment is left to the participants. For example, the group as a whole could discuss what it was like to work with the experiment of reduced verbal intervention from the facilitator.

Perls believed that interpretation often deadens the actual experience by primarily valuing awareness of the cognitive properties and diminishing the other dimensions of human awareness (Perls et al., 1951). However, many contemporary Gestalt theorists disagree. For example, Crocker (1999) placed great emphasis on the therapeutic process of "assimilation" and the use of cognition and language to facilitate this process. Shub (1992, 2000) also stressed the importance of the cognitive assimilation process to sustain change when working with persons with entrenched character disorders or with low self-esteem.

With the experiment and resultant dialogue fully explored, and the group having had opportunities to experience and assimilate this new awareness, the Gestalt cycle, or a unit of work, is finished. Perls et al. (1951) proposed that an increase in awareness creates change in itself. They suggested that further development be left to the self-regulating process (i.e., if the experience is satisfying and valued, it is likely that the organism will seek to re-create it). However, we believe singular inspiration is often only the beginning of change. More often than not, it is necessary for an awareness to be experienced numerous times for it to "stick." Facilitators and members alike may wish to notice and encourage the process goal of practice and repetition of a desired experience and subsequent satisfaction until the process becomes so familiar that it becomes fully assimilated. For example, a member who notices excitement and pleasure in making full eye contact with other group members may need to practice this "experiment" during repeated sessions of group until it becomes an integrated process.

IRV: Another element of Gestalt group psychotherapy is an existential component. It emphasizes the reality that we are all unique and that at any given moment we are creating events and processes that are unique. So what attracted me to "Gestalt" was the "permission" to be different and not have to be like every other therapist doing the work of therapy. It was fantastically liberating to know that I didn't have to be punched into a pigeonhole and it was okay to let the creative juices flow. Group work is exciting because there are even more opportunities from inputs within the group for the creativity and uniqueness to flow. There may be "silent therapizing" in the group, but most of the time there is an abundance of vocal "therapizing" in the group—between the members of the group—and it gets really challenging and gratifying when the group is really rolling. Watching the group evolve, à la Elaine Kepner's article (and others' conceptualizations), is really a treat. When I'm teaching group psychotherapy at the medical school, I have the students read Elaine's chapter and also Joseph Zinker's on the awareness continuum (from that "seminal work," *Beyond the Hot Seat*), since I think that both articles really can be helpful to the novice in getting a good overview on how groups are likely to evolve on a longitudinal and also cross-sectional basis.

PAUL: I think you've "nailed" it, Irv. Facilitating/participating in Gestalt therapy with an individual is exciting; and facilitating/participating in Gestalt group therapy is *really exciting!*

When one unit of work has been completed, the group is free to select and move toward the next figure of interest. It is often useful for the facilitator to publicly notice when such a cycle has been completed. Therapeutic facilitation may include inviting the group to cleanse and refresh their therapeutic palate by encouraging them to "take a breath," have a moment of silent appreciation for the work achieved, or take a bathroom break. Sometimes one completed figure may evoke a strong response in some other level of group, thereby influencing the next choice of focus and speeding up the movement into the next unit of work (e.g., an awakened traumatic association that may demand support and additional work by affected members). As in life, the above phases do not occur cleanly and smoothly but often involve interruption, tangential input, and even full redirection. The facilitators and (hopefully) group members are responsible for noticing interruptions and the potential for redirection into a different unit of work, thereby providing input into the group's choices of movement (or pause).

For those budding therapists wishing to utilize the Perlsian "hot seat" model, many, if not all, of the above process goals can still be utilized. The primary difference is that the focus remains at the individual level or directed at the intrapsychic boundary and possibly the boundary between the individual and the facilitator(s). As Frew (1988) noted, it is also possible to integrate the two models as desired.

GESTALT GROUP FACILITATOR TASKS AND ROLES

Though the above-mentioned process goals may represent an idealized group session, in actuality the interactive work cycle in a group in any given session (let alone over the life of the group) is much less predictable and linear and much more erratic, circular, and even reversible. The Gestalt group facilitator has many roles and tasks within this work cycle. The most essential is the public support of multidimensional awareness within individual members and all subsequent levels of the group in order to optimize interpersonal and intrapersonal contact. A secondary but still essential task is to both observe and participate within the broad range of possible group directions and movements.

A facilitator also has the responsibility to intervene in a timely and choiceful fashion when overt resistance or blockage of the group's organismic self-regulation process is observed if, and only if, the group itself is unable to resolve the blockage (other than through dissolution). One of the unique attributes of Gestalt group therapy is its ability to paradoxically use these blockages and periods of stuckness or stagnant repetition as opportunities for creative intervention, not simply something to be removed, as in psychodynamic approaches. However, this demands considerable facilitator ability to utilize theory-driven observations and intuitive artistic creativity in the form of experiments. The facilitator must also notice the various levels within the group, range of awarenesses, and patterns of rigidity or fluidity. Gestalt facilitation involves caution and discretion in how we influence group process. Facilitative expression of our observations may at times be dramatic to foster the creation of other possibilities of contact. As facilitators, we must also attend to our own experiences in the group and utilize our self-awarenesses to influence the process. Another caution here is to maintain awareness and respect for the implicit power differential we have as therapists. All of these activities must also flow from within our own unique patterns of awareness, phenomenology, and contact styles. It is no wonder that the task of Gestalt group facilitation is complex and demanding (Zinker, 1980).

On the basis of complexity of the above tasks, it is useful to weigh the benefits of having a co-facilitator. There is no right answer on this issue. Perls, of course, worked alone, as did many of his disciples and as do many contemporary therapists. The primary advantage of a single group facilitator is that you have fewer "cooks" stirring and possibly overspicing the therapeutic soup. Direction is clearer, and group members need to look in only one direction for leadership and intervention. Members may more quickly become comfortable and willing to work with a predictable style and value set offered by the solo facilitator. Finally, the solo facilitator is usually less expensive. One of the means of reducing the expense of having co-facilitators is to have an intern or trainee as a junior partner.

However, co-facilitation offers many benefits as well. In the traditional "tag-team" co-facilitation model, one therapist works with the group while the other observes group process (or even regroups for the next piece of work). The observational stance within a group allows for increased awareness and the notice of subtle changes too difficult to perceive when the facilitator is in the middle of group process.

Some contemporary co-facilitators utilize overt discussion between themselves about their own internal and dialogical therapeutic process, as well as the group's process, and offer (in the ideal) a living model of cooperative dialogue and resolution of difference. One facilitator may notice and compensate for the blind spots and limitations of the other and vice versa. Access to the richness of style and depth of both professional and personal experience of two facilitators also adds to the possibilities of experiment and learning within the group.

On the basis of this discussion, the choice of the number of facilitators for any given group is just that, a choice that takes into consideration the above advantages and disadvantages. This choice can then be evaluated according to group, facilitator, and organizational satisfaction.

GESTALT GROUP MEMBER TASKS AND ROLES

In the hot seat model, group members' tasks were basically to sit quietly and wait their turn. In contrast, within the above-mentioned goals and objectives of Gestalt group process, group members have a number of diversified tasks and roles. Primary, of course, is attending to awareness both as an individual and as a member of the varying levels of the group. Such awareness itself occurs through utilizing the differing functions of self at the contact boundary and can be noticed internally or expressed within the group. Members are encouraged to take responsibility for the functioning and satisfaction of all levels of the group and for achieving a balance between their individual needs (e.g., why they came to group) and the needs of the other levels of the group. Members are also encouraged to give active feedback to the facilitator(s) during all phases of group process, both in response to and in shaping of interventions suggested by the facilitators. Members can be encouraged to suggest their own interventions, to be assessed and incorporated as desired by the group as whole. As in most groups, members are discouraged from monopolizing group time or dialogue; shifting group work to their own needs without group input; offering other members excessive advice, criticism, or questions; and pontificating on abstract issues or focusing outside the present group experience.

SUMMARY

Contemporary Gestalt group facilitators can choose from the clarity and focus of the traditional hot seat model and the richness of modern Gestalt group process, which integrates elements of systems theory, the theory of group dynamics, and Gestalt theory (both traditional and contemporary). These models do not need to be mutually exclusive. Facilitators can utilize the resultant integration of theories as a framework for noticing and developing opportunities for greater awareness and subsequent change for the individual member, larger levels of systems contained within the group, and the whole group or, in some cases, even beyond.

Facilitator involvement and prior need for training are based on two primary principles. First, facilitators need to be able to generate accurate awareness and recognition of how the integration of the above theories emerges within group process. Second, facilitators need practice and experience in using awareness skills in the application of timely and intentional choices of creative and theoretically grounded interventions, linked to the primary process goal of heightening present awareness.

New group facilitators encountering Gestalt group therapy for the first time and wishing to improve their skills would be wise to focus on the first principle and spend ample time honing their ability to notice and describe awareness occurring at various group levels. After a base of these skills has been developed, the new facilitator can slowly and cautiously begin to introduce intervention ideas. In other words, build a foundation of observation and perceptual skills before leaning into techniques and experiments.

If at all possible, the novice facilitator should seek to work with a seasoned facilitator and spend time after each session debriefing and processing both of their experiences and learnings. It is also essential for the prospective group facilitator to have experienced Gestalt group therapy as a member of a group (or, at minimum, a Gestalt training or supervision group) to more fully understand the perspective and challenges of being a group member. If feasible, doing both concurrently is even better.

Finally, as in all learning experiences, new facilitators must rely on their own repetitious assimilation of the experiences and new awarenesses that results from experiment. In simpler language, if you have an opportunity to be a group member, take it! Then take it again, and again and again. In the unpredictability and excitement of group process, you will find your own excitement in being a group facilitator. And isn't excitement why you became interested in Gestalt therapy in the first place?

JON: Paul and Bud, I commend you both for a very comprehensive, coherent, and clear discussion and description of the history, evolution, and current practice of Gestalt therapy in groups.

IRV: Your chapter is a good one, and I like the emphasis on the intrapersonal, interpersonal, and whole-group levels. Shuttling from one to the other and having the group look at any particular work from all three points of view always turns out to be enriching for each individual in group and the group at large. I also agree that the chapter ought to be useful to students who want to get a good overview of what might be considered the "Gestalt approach to group psychotherapy." I put that in quotes because it is clear that Gestalt approaches to group will vary. They have to vary because the people will vary and always there will be different "versions" created. And that is not only acceptable but desirable.

PAUL: Thank you both, Jon and Irv, for your thoughtful input.

REVIEW QUESTIONS

1. The chapter authors describe how Gestalt work in groups is an integration of three theories: systems theory, group dynamics theory, and Gestalt theory. How does each of these integrate Gestalt group work theory and practice?

2. The chapter authors and dialoguers explain how organismic self-regulation is an important process for both Gestalt individual therapy and Gestalt group work. How does the process of organismic self-regulation differ when applied in individual work and group work?

3. Explain why awareness is such a central concept to Gestalt group therapy and explain its relevance to Gestalt's major focus on the here and now.

4. How are the Gestalt processes of contact and contact resistances utilized in working with groups?

5. What are the facilitators' and the group members' tasks and roles within a Gestalt therapy group?

EXPERIENTIAL PEDAGOGICAL ACTIVITY

ACTIVITY: (compliments of Jon Frew). This experience is intended to provide an opportunity for a majority of individuals in a training situation to practice formulating interventions reflecting the intrapersonal, interpersonal, and group levels of process in Gestalt groups. The following are the steps in the activity:

Step 1. Four to six individuals volunteer to form a "self-directed" group. They are instructed either to role-play a certain type of group (e.g., a divorce support group) or to "play themselves" and discuss something of common interest (e.g., feelings about workload, the impending holiday season). Generally it is not recommended that an individual adopt a role, as this may cloud the intervention-making attempts that follow.

Step 2. The "inside" groups are instructed to carry on a dialogue as if they were beginning a group meeting. The instructor/trainer also tells the group to anticipate periodic interruptions. The remainder of the class/training group forms an outer circle around the group.

Step 3. After a few minutes (usually 5 to 10), the instructor/trainer stops the dialogue in the inside group. Participants in the outer circle are instructed to formulate the intervention they would make at that moment in the group's dialogue as if they were inside the group as a leader and are asked to respond to these questions:

1. What level(s) and type(s) of process would your intervention highlight?
2. To whom (e.g., individual, dyad or subgroup, whole group) would you direct the intervention?
3. What would be your intention (e.g., heighten awareness, support interpersonal contact, seek information, identify a group theme)?

Step 4. People in the outer circle who have an intervention are instructed to "make the intervention as if they were the leader," instructing the leader to say what they would actually say if they were leading the group.

Step 5. After several interventions are "hurled" into the group, the instructor asks the inside group which intervention is most appealing or attuned to their present experience as group members. At this stage, the instructor reinforces all of the intervention possibilities as reasonable and valid to diminish any sense of competition among the intervention authors and to inspire others to participate in these exercises at later stages of the activity.

Step 6. The inside group chooses an intervention (the instructor ensures that this step does not take too long), and the "author" of that intervention joins the inside group, becomes the leader, and makes the intervention again, thus beginning the second phase of the activity. In this second phase, the designated leader continues to make interventions as appropriate.

Step 7. After a few minutes, the instructor/trainer stops the dialogue again and has the class repeat Steps 3, 4, 5, and 6. When the next intervention from the outer group is chosen, that intervention author joins the group, becomes the leader, and makes the intervention. The former leader remains in the group as a member.

Step 8. Continue this process for several rounds to give as many people as possible opportunities to formulate interventions.

Step 9. Optional: If time allows and you have enough participants, give the members who volunteered initially to be group members an opportunity to formulate interventions by forming a new group and positioning them in the outer circle.

Note for Instructors/Trainers:

Try to time your interruptions of the group dialogue with attention to allowing enough discussion and interchange between members so that the group develops and matures and with sensitivity to not leaving the designated leaders on the point too long. Also, try to stop the group dialogue at a moment ripe for a "fresh" intervention.

Possible Discussion Questions for Debriefing the Activity:

1. Which levels of interventions were the easiest or most difficult for you to formulate?
2. As the group developed, did the opportunities for intragroup-level and intergroup-level interventions increase?
3. How closely did the intent of certain interventions match the impact as reported by group members?
4. How do interventions at various levels of group process serve the goals of a Gestalt group experience, such as increasing awareness, promoting contact between members, and identifying salient group themes?

CHAPTER **13**

Gestalt Approaches With Organizations and Large Systems

RICK MAURER

DIALOGUE RESPONDENT: SEÀN GAFFNEY

Rick Maurer was a graduate of and is now a faculty member in the Gestalt Institute of Cleveland's Organization and Systems Development Program. He is an organizational change consultant in Arlington, Virginia, serving clients such as MCI, Bell Atlantic, International Monetary Fund, Fannie Mae, Deloitte & Touche, and the U.S. Department of Defense. He serves as an associate editor of *Gestalt Review* and has authored several articles and books, most prominently *Beyond the Wall of Resistance: Unconventional Strategies That Build Support and Change* (1996), *Feedback Toolkit: 16 Tools for Better Communication in the Workplace* (1994), and *Caught in the Middle: A Leadership Guide for Partnership in the Workplace* (1992).

Seàn Gaffney grew up in Ireland, spent some years in England, and has lived in Sweden since 1975. He is a Gestalt therapist and organization and systems development (OSD) consultant who is on the training faculties of the Gestalt Akademie of Scandinavia, Gestalt Trust of Scotland & Northern Ireland, the Gestalt Institute of Cleveland, and the Gestalt International Study Center's International OSD Program. He is well represented in publications and is an esteemed lecturer in cross-cultural management at SDA Bocconi University, Milan, Italy, and at the Stockholm School of Economics near his home in Sweden.

A church owned two hospitals and a number of small ancillary care units in a densely populated metropolitan area. Pressure was mounting to contain costs. Leaders decided to merge all of these operations. They believed that if they centralized functions such as the lab, human resources, marketing, public relations, and some expensive but highly specialized medical procedures they could save money. Six months into this merger, they could see little benefit.

I had consulted with the person who was now CEO of the new health care system. When they decided to hold a daylong meeting of all managers, I was invited to speak to them. They hoped that my talk would turn things around.

What would you do if you had received that call? Would you take the assignment? Turn it down? Offer an alternative? Ask for more information? Refer the work to someone you didn't like? (I will discuss this request further at the end of this chapter.)

RATIONALE FOR GESTALT THEORY IN ORGANIZATIONS

The theory developed by Fritz and Laura Perls, Paul Goodman, and others provides the foundation for a sound and rigorous way to respond to requests, assess situations, develop interventions, monitor progress, make adjustments, and evaluate our work, not only with individuals and groups, but also with organizations. The power of awareness as a way to facilitate contact is as important in organizations as it is with individuals and groups. Looking at resistance as creative adjustment, rather than a force that needs to be obliterated, applies as well at home as in international relations. The notion that contact occurs at the boundary between self and the environment is just as true when two departments try to merge as it is when a single person comes to grips with the fact that he is no longer single but needs to be willing to be influenced by his partner.

Some argue that Gestalt therapy principles apply to individuals and couples but not to groups and organizations. They might say that because Perls, Hefferline, and Goodman did not discuss these larger configurations in the classic *Gestalt Therapy* (Perls, Hefferline, & Goodman, 1951), they are not a suitable subject for exploration. I disagree. Experience suggests otherwise.

Even though those who work from a Gestalt orientation in organizations are deeply

SEÀN: On the sometimes sensitive subject of Gestalt therapy and its applications to OSD (organization and systems development), I am of the firm opinion that our Gestalt principles and philosophy actually do readily apply—and always have—to other than individuals and even therapy. The more I think about it, the more I can place the text *Gestalt Therapy* as specifically an *application* of Gestalt psychology, existentialism (especially Kierkegaard), Lewin's field theory (a social psychology theory), and phenomenology to individual therapy, influenced by the fact that both Fritz and Laura Perls were trained psychoanalysts—though others were not psychoanalysts—not Goodman, the social critic, and not Shapiro, who was perhaps the first to apply his integration of Gestalt to an organization and system, namely schools in New York City.

RICK: I agree, and Lewin in particular is a very strong link to our work in organizations: for example, his concern over the question of what supports democratic process, his experiments in group dynamics, and the practical application of how our own phenomenology creates the ground that influences how we interpret figures. By the way, I like that you use the spirit of the Gestalt Institute of Cleveland's term *OSD* to describe our work. I think it reflects our Gestalt orientation better than the more common term *OD* (organization development) used to describe

indebted to the theory of Gestalt therapy, the work performed in organizations is not therapy. People such as consultants, managers, and project leaders who apply the principles of Gestalt therapy in organizations are not practicing therapy. They do not (or should not) do deep intrapsychic work inside corporations, agencies, or any other type of organization. The employer-employee contract seldom requires people to submit themselves to deep internal exploration, so to engage in a therapeutic intervention would be a breach of that contract. And many of us who work in organizations are not licensed therapists; in fact, it is unethical for us to practice therapy, if not illegal. Given these parameters, I hope to provide an explanation of how Gestalt theory and methods inform the practice of those who work in organizations.

the type of consulting we do. I acroynm *OSD* casts a broader accurately embraces the rang influenced work.

SEÀN: Your review of our theory as it relates to OSD nicely captures the sound knowledge base that we integrate and express in our work, the shared thinking that informs what we do and how we do it. So my comments will be in the context of the sameness of our Gestalt ground and the distinctiveness of our figures. Gestalt OSD is not a distant cousin; rather, it is a sibling—maybe even a twin—of Gestalt therapy, and both were parented by the same core concepts!

GESTALT IN CONTRAST TO OTHER APPROACHES

Consider the example that opened the chapter. Trying to get people to actually join operations after a merger can be difficult. Here are some of the common ways organizations handle such a challenge.

- A leader demands that people comply. In a long-term major change, such as a merger, the command-and-control approach often fails. This approach often ignores people's fears as well as any cultural differences, and the oversight often leads to massive resistance.
- The organization provides training. There is nothing wrong with training, but it is most useful as an approach to help people develop skills. Because resistance to merging is usually not a skills issue, training often costs a lot of money with little to show for all the expense. Training works best once people are convinced that the training is something they truly need to learn.
- The organization attempts to inspire motivation. Everyone is brought together (in this case all the managers) for an inspirational revival meeting. A former test pilot or aging athlete is trotted out to talk about the importance of grit and determination to little avail. Inflicting bromides on people fails to respect their own desires and fears.

None of these approaches coincide with a more Gestalt-oriented view. In fact, none of the approaches respect where the organization is at the moment of intervention. All imply that wherever people are isn't good enough and that forcing change from the current state (whether through force, education, or inspiration) is the preferred approach. So how do you lead or facilitate change and still respect where people are today? The answer isn't easy to implement, but Gestalt theory can point the way.

Gestalt theory and practice provide a way to look at situations like this and develop interventions that have a chance of succeeding. I divide this chapter into three major parts: foundation, intervention choice points, and the Gestalt stance.

GESTALT FOUNDATION FOR ORGANIZATIONAL CONSULTING

What is the work of a Gestalt organization development (OD) or organization and systems development (OSD) person? In *Organizational Consulting: A Gestalt Approach,* Edwin Nevis (1987) offered the following: "I see the major objective of consulting relationships as being the education of the client system in how to improve its awareness of its functioning and to enhance its ability to take actions that improve this functioning" (p. xi).

Notice that Nevis doesn't say that our job is to make leaders more powerful, or to inspire and motivate, or to throw canned solutions at problems. Our job is to assist in heightening awareness in a way that supports the organization to take action work, whatever that may be, from a new project, to reorganizing, to dealing with the nuts and bolts of running a business.

If we take Nevis's statement as our objective, how do we orient to the work? I believe that three concepts provide the foundation for the work: phenomenological field theory, the paradoxical theory of change, and the cycle of experience. In combination, these form a powerful way to examine and engage with others in organizations. Details about foundational concepts can also be found in Chapters 2 through 6.

Phenomenological Field Perspective

The field theory used by Gestalt practitioners is based on phenomenology, so some have given it the title *phenomenological field theory* to distinguish it from other field theories, such as the ones used in physics, economics, ecology, and chaos theory (Nabozny & Carlson, 2001; Yontef, 1993). According to Nabozny and Carlson,

> A field perspective views all phenomena as inextricably linked, part of a network of interactions, which form a continuous whole called the organism/environment field. Field theory assumes that the organism and the environment co-regulate one another and change of the organism happens as a result of interactions at the boundary of the organism/environment field. Everything affects everything else as the field is viewed as a unitary whole. (p. 1)

When a situation occurs in an organization, there is no objective truth, no true right answer. Reality is in the mind of the beholder. The following are some of the significant implications of field theory for our work, as adapted from the work of Nabozny and Carlson (2001), and Yontef (1993).

Organizations Are Made Up of Multiple Realities

Someone once said that where you stand depends on where you sit. When an organization attempts a major change, there is no single truth. People view the proposed change through their own eyes and make meaning based on how they construct reality. Imagine a CEO's desire to introduce a new software system that gives access to financial information to all departments. From her vantage point, this seems sensible. However, the accounting department believes the software will give too much information to people who will not be able to interpret it correctly. Middle managers across the organization are afraid that this could result in downsizing.

Who is right? As viewed from a field perspective, they all are. The question for Gestalt practitioners is this: How can we bring all of these multiple realities to light in such a way that others can hear and understand them?

The Field Is Constantly Changing

Because the field is a mass of influences from internal psychological experiences to events inside the organization and extending out to events in the marketplace and the world, any change in one part of the field will have an impact throughout the field. In explaining chaos theory, people often say that a butterfly flapping its wings in Brazil can have an effect on weather in Seattle.

The implications are immense. An employee survey that was completed 2 weeks ago is already at risk of becoming outdated because of some event that occurred in the field. We cannot afford to allow our own views to become fixed gestalts. We need to stay open to the shifting nature of the field.

We Are of the Field, Not Just in It

Everything in the field is *of the field.* Those of us who work as consultants become part of that field by the mere fact that we have been hired and have entered the system. When a manager flies to a regional office to conduct a meeting, his or her presence has an impact on what is said and done. Our work is to be aware of the impact that we have on the field and the impact that the field has on us. It is a reciprocal process.

There Is No Hierarchy to the Data

If everything affects everything else, then a butterfly flapping its wings is potentially no less important than the bulldozer that is mowing down an acre of a rain forest. Everything in the field affects everything else and, in return, is affected again. The challenge is to stay open to data from everywhere and not place a hierarchy on where opinions and data come from. If we put more value on data from one place, we are likely to get unintended resistance from other parts of the field.

Bracketing Perceptions Is Essential

Because everyone, including us, creates his or her own version of reality, understanding our own biases and trying to put them in brackets temporarily is critical if we hope to try to understand the other person's point of view, assumptions, values, and beliefs. Though it may never be possible to fully bracket our perceptions, just the act of trying can make a significant difference.

The challenge for the Gestalt practitioner is twofold. First, we need to understand our own biases well enough so that we can put brackets around our own preconceived notions. Second, we need to find ways to support members of the organization so that they can hear how the world looks different from another's vantage point. This can be especially difficult, for one group's reality often is threatening to that of another group. When people feel threatened, they often respond defensively, and that works against the ability to put aside our own perceptions long enough to fully take in what the other person is saying.

Everything Is in the Present

The past is prologue to the present moment. History, real and imagined, plays itself out in the field today. A Gestalt practitioner needs to find ways to allow people to voice some of these conditions that create the ground, without the conversation shifting the focus from present to past. Imagine two people who must work together but who have developed strong antipathy toward one another. That history contaminates the ground. We need to support them in examining how the past is alive—and influencing how they work—today.

Paradoxical Theory

In 1970, Arnold Beisser made a major contribution to Gestalt theory when he wrote "The Paradoxical Theory of Change." Even though he was writing about the therapeutic relationship, he speculated, "I believe the same change theory outlined here is also applicable to social systems, that orderly change within social systems is in the direction of integration and holism" (p. 80). Though this textbook contains an entire chapter of the Gestalt theories of change, Beisser explained the paradoxical theory in a nutshell as *"Change occurs when one becomes what he is, not when he tries to become what he is not"* (p. 77, italics in original). Following are some of the implications of this theory for those who work in organizations.

Actions Heighten Awareness of the Current State

The concept of heightening awareness is fundamental to Gestalt therapy. But many organizations take a "ready—fire—aim" approach to challenges. Armed with a limited amount of data, or showing preference for particular types of data, such as financial projections, people tend to act quickly.

Helping action-oriented people stay in the present is tough but essential. The challenge is finding ways to respect the sense of urgency within the organization and finding ways to help the organization see itself more fully.

The War Between What Is and What Should Be

Beisser (1970) suggested that there is a constant struggle between the poles of what is and what should be. Our work as consultants is to support all parts of the organization in staying interested in both what is present today and the excitement that leads them to envision a picture of what should or could be.

People's Reluctance to See How They Contribute to the Problem

The work is to help individuals in the organization see and own what they might not be seeing. Often people in organizations recognize a problem but don't understand it in their bones. They don't see how they are part of the field that created this mess (or this opportunity). Managers may see the impact of their company's poor management-labor relations but not really accept how management practices have helped create the problem. On their side, union members fail to see that their 1930s style of labor negotiations actually widens the rift. The challenge, then, is helping individuals in the company to stay open not only to listening to the stories others tell but to examining their own beliefs and actions. We, as OSD consultants, must be adept at meeting this challenge.

Avoiding the Savior Trap

Nevis (1987) suggested that our job is to educate our clients and not to save them. For consultants, this can be difficult. We are usually hired because people aren't pleased with the status quo. Our reputation (not to mention paycheck) rides on making something happen. It can be tempting to give in to this pressure. For managers or project leaders, the challenge is no less great. Their performance review may rest on the ability to make things happen. The temptation to forget our theory can be great. It can seem as if everything in the field is inviting us to save the day. As tempting as it may be to be the savior (if only for a moment), our theory provides a more helpful alternative.

When we look at how we work in organizations to facilitate desired movement and change, our good intentions can be contrary to Gestalt's paradoxical approach. As Beisser (1970) said, "The patient comes to therapy because he wishes to be changed. . . . [A] therapist who seeks to help a patient has left the egalitarian position and becomes the knowing expert, with the patient playing the helpless person" (p. 78).

When we collude with the system (the "what is"), it becomes contaminated by the difference in status between us and our client and by our desire to move away from the current situation and find a cure. Inadvertently, our well-intended actions make attention to the paradoxical theory difficult because, when we collude, we are joining with the client to move into the future.

SEÀN: You really capture that indefinability of Gestalt in OSD, the special paradox of knowing from our experience what we do—yet knowing also that we are clearest about it afterwards! We are better at describing what we have done than what we usually do or will do next. And the other paradox: You and I would certainly not "do" the same things, nor make the same interventions—yet we are still recognizably (and proudly) Gestalt OSD practitioners.

RICK: Apparently, Sonia Nevis once said that she can't describe what she is doing in the moment but can do just that on reflection. I think her comment reflects what the worldly philosopher Yogi Berra once referred to as "deep depth." Her knowledge of Gestalt theory and practice is so deep that it creates an incredibly lively ground for her work. This allows her to be fully present with her clients and with what is occurring in the present moment.

The Gestalt Cycle of Experience

The cycle of experience is a graphic way of showing how energy builds and dissipates in a system. The cycle describes a natural movement from sensation to awareness to mobilization of energy to action to contact to withdrawal. It simply identifies a flow that occurs when we make contact. See Chapter 6 for a graphic depiction and further elaboration of the cycle of experience.

Although the cycle was originally described in reference to a process that an individual or a couple might go through, the process can also be helpfully applied to organizations. Although not presented graphically here, the following is the sequence of cycle stages as described in language more appropriate to groups and organizations: (a) random incidents (sensation), (b) recognition (awareness), (c) initial actions (mobilization of energy), (d) implementation (action), (e) integration into the system (contact), and (f) waning activity (withdrawal) (Maurer, 1996).

A paper manufacturing plant was losing money. The owners would put money into this aging facility only if management and its six unions could agree to work without the disputes that often crippled their productivity. This wake-up call took senior leaders from random incidents to recognition, but before they could take any action they needed the support of the unions. Some of the unions didn't trust management and therefore didn't trust what management told them. In an effort to increase recognition of the problem, management opened the books. Unions were skeptical, but over time they began to believe that the problem was real. Once this happened, they collectively began to take initial actions to address the challenge given to them. They implemented the solution they proposed by telling owners the ways in which they planned to work more cooperatively. In time, this new way of working became integrated into the way the plant operated. But nothing lasts forever: Eventually something will interfere with the way things are working, and it will be time to move on (waning activity).

It is common for leaders (or those people who sense a need for change) to want to move to action quickly. As individuals, we may find this situation challenging because we may act before we are fully in touch with the current state. Urgency can tempt us to forget the paradoxical theory of change. This problem is compounded when others are involved. The leaders are ready to act, but some others are still in the dark and see only some unrelated random incidents. Others have ideas of their own (they are on different cycles), and still others see the leaders' actions as a threat to their own approach to the situation.

The cycle of experience can help us and our clients calibrate. A simple question like "So where do we suspect people are on the cycle?" can be eye-opening. It is common for me to hear a client say, "We've got to watch out, we're getting ahead of Chicago on that one."

People seem to understand the cycle. Once they do, it is easy for me to talk about the importance of the paradoxical theory of change. (However, I rarely use Gestalt language when I am working with clients. I think it is my responsibility to be bilingual and not make them learn my arcane lingo.)

The Gestalt cycle of experience has numerous implications for organizational work. These are outlined below.

Diagnosing the Situation

When someone says, "We need to do something," he or she has already passed the stages of random incidents and recognition and has moved to some initial action. Energy is mobilized. But that does not necessarily mean that anyone else is where this person is on the cycle. For example, it is quite common for executives to have access to critical data that no one else sees. The data can prompt recognition that there is a severe problem. Let's say customers are leaving at an alarming rate. When the leadership team tries to roll out changes associated with retaining customers, few see the need to change from the status quo. According to Lewin

(1951), once a figure is formed, people resist changing it. So for the middle managers and staff there is no compelling reason to make a shift.

Work in Each Stage

Each stage of the cycle has within it the seeds of its own destruction. For example, implementation will not last forever. It will inevitably lead to integration or failure. Waning activity leads to either renewal or an ending. And on it goes. This is why attention to the paradoxical theory of change can be so helpful. Heightening awareness at any stage of the cycle can help the organization fully understand and own where it is. It is in the paradox of this profound recognition that organizations are freed to move.

A Way to Monitor

Movement around the cycle occurs best when individuals and subgroups are aligned. For example, when a critical mass of people recognize a problem or opportunity, it is relatively easy to mobilize sufficient energy to consider various possible actions to alleviate the disruption in the status quo. As work continues on a project, it is important to pay attention to these issues: Are people aligned? If not, where are various key individuals or groups on the cycle?

Avoiding the Biggest Mistake

Getting out ahead of others on the cycle is the biggest mistake some consultants make when trying to influence an organization. It is common for some groups in power to feel a sense of urgency, make plans, and then try to enlist support for something that has already been decided. People react to such manipulations, asking questions such as: Will the change cost me my job? Will I lose control? How might this affect my status? Will my own project die? What has become figural for these groups is not the proposed change but their resistance to it. Someone working from a Gestalt perspective looks for these differences on the cycle and heightens awareness of the differences.

Using the Cycle to Help Pinpoint Where to Intervene

If most of an organization is in the random incidents stage with regard to some issue, then the intervention might be to support ways to heighten awareness of these seemingly unrelated events. For example, one organization had lost a major contract for work with a state government. During a planning meeting to determine "where do we go from here?" a contracting officer from the state government was invited in to talk with everyone about why they had been rejected. So problems that seemed random before (e.g., slow billing cycles, occasional service breakdowns, indifference to the concerns of the customer) suddenly took on new meaning. People began to recognize the patterns perpetuated by the administration.

CHOICE POINTS FOR INTERVENING

With field theory, the paradoxical theory of change, and the cycle of experience as our foundation, Gestalt consultants have choices to make. Where and how will I intervene? Although there is no cookbook approach, there are choices to be made. Following are some major considerations in intervening in organizations.

What Level of System?

In any organization there are many levels of system, including the individual, interpersonal (an individual in relation to another person or in relation to a group), dyad (pairs of people whose connection holds some particular force for the whole), subgroup (teams, departments, and regions, as well as various alliances), full organization, and larger community or environment levels. Using a Gestalt stance, you might find yourself moving from level to level depending on where you believed you could best support the client system. For example, in a meeting of an entire department, you might find yourself addressing the full group, subgroups, or individuals depending on your sense of what seemed to best serve the figure they were working on.

Figural Choice Points

As figures emerge in organizations, we have many choice points with regard to level. We must constantly shuttle among levels to determine where to intervene. We are searching, not for the perfect level, but simply for one that is likely to draw attention and create more awareness for the figure. We then put a sufficient boundary around it so that work can be done. If we choose incorrectly, our comments may be met with confusion, or we will find that the ensuing discussion lacks much vitality. We can learn from that feedback and allow that information to inform our next intervention.

Units of Work

Joseph Zinker (1994) has written about creating an aesthetic in our work that he refers to as good form. He envisioned the therapist as artist, and I refer you to his work for more on developing that deeper aesthetic.

> A clear and powerful observation emitted from one's loving heart is magnetic, compelling, difficult to brush aside, and beautiful to behold. . . . We learn to make the "dance" inside of us so that through our creativity we can evoke changes in "human choreography" to empower a couple or family [or organization] to move with sure footing on the solidity of anchored strength. (p. 4)

With this, we can see that attention to a unit of work is a good place to start on an aesthetic intervention. (See also Chapter 12 for more about units of work.)

Think of it this way—every encounter with a client, staff, or your colleagues can be a unit of work. A meeting, training session, or coaching session works best when it has a clear beginning, middle, and end. Without this attention to form, the experience is like going to see a three-act play and arriving late, leaving early, or pulling away during the second act to return a phone call. Something big is missing when this happens, but getting to experience the play *Death of a Salesman* from beginning to end can be a riveting evening. We leave the theater feeling as if something happened, and the experience feels complete. That is what a unit of work can do.

Attention to the unit of work is especially important in organizations because people often rush from meeting to meeting with little time to breathe. There is a tendency to hit the ground running and end when the last agenda item is crossed off the "to-do list" or when another group demands access to the conference room. Just making sure that people know why they are meeting and ensuring that there is sufficient ground for people to do the work at hand help move the group toward forming a gestalt. Some of the issues to consider and questions to ask that can help support meaningful units of work and lead to gestalt formation are:

- *Appropriateness.* Is this the right group to do the work? Can they handle this task at this time? Do they have the resources they need to be effective? Have they been given sufficient authority so that they can complete this work successfully?
- *Timing.* Is this a good time for work on this task? For example, if people are still asking themselves, "Why are we reorganizing?" and you convene a group to work on implementation strategies, you may find that little work gets done.
- *Sufficient Support for This Work.* It can be tempting to plan an intervention, say a meeting that will attempt to get important issues out in the open. But the need for this conversation and our own enthusiasm aren't enough; we must ask if the people in this system can handle it. If we hold the meeting, will people feel free enough to speak candidly? If not, then we probably should find another way to begin the conversation. Perhaps one-on-one conversations or an anonymous staff survey would be a better way to open the door.
- *Time Allotted for the Work.* Has sufficient time been allocated to complete this task successfully? If not, the quality of the work will suffer, but also people are likely to feel incomplete when the project or meeting ends.
- *Closure.* Have you determined a way to close the work, allowing the group to enter the withdrawal phase of the cycle of experience? It is important for people to express what worked, what didn't work, and what was left undone; consider whether there are unfulfilled expectations; and, if appropriate, identify what comes next.

Experiment

A cornerstone of Gestalt therapy is the experiment—a real-life experience during the meeting that allows for a more complete examination of the data than merely talking about the issues. Introduced by Fritz Perls in his first book, *Ego, Hunger and Aggression* (1947/1969a), the concept of deeper experience in the therapeutic relationship was extended by Perls et al. (1951) in their seminal book *Gestalt Therapy: Excitement and Growth in the Human Personality.* Polster and Polster (1973) did an excellent job of explicating the essence of Gestalt experimentation:

> The experiment in Gestalt therapy is an attempt to counter the *aboutist* deadlock by bringing the individual's action system right into the room. Through experiment the individual is mobilized to confront the emergencies of his life by playing out his aborted feelings and actions in relative safety. A safe emergency is thus created where venturesome exploration can be supported. Furthermore, both ends of the safety-to-emergency continuum can be explored, emphasizing first the support and then the risk-taking; whichever seems salient at the time. (pp. 234–235)

The "safe emergency" in organizational consulting can allow various parts of the organization to explore issues in a way that heightens awareness in a safe environment. The experiment might focus on just heightening awareness of an issue facing the organization, or it could explore a polarity. For example, I sometimes introduce clients to role playing, acting as they think others might who have a stake in the outcome. I might ask the characters to describe their reaction to the new reorganization. All I know going in is that this experiment will probably heighten awareness of the resistance. I cannot predict what clients will say or how they will react to saying it. Will they be deeply moved? Blasé? Will they change the subject? Will they stop short of completing the experiment? Good experiments have an unknown element, and that is what gives them vitality. The safety in this "safe emergency" comes from collaborating with the clients in the development of the experiment by not going beyond their own support and by not doing something so routine that it lacks any life.

An experiment can be quite simple. After interviewing workers in a plant, I was pretty sure that they believed their organization was doing fine financially. However, the leaders saw things differently: They were worried about the future of their operation, and they wanted to make dramatic changes quickly. I said that workers were likely to resist these changes because they didn't see a need to do anything differently. The leaders pushed back. They told me they were certain that workers understood the situation. I didn't think their assumptions were correct, but they didn't think mine were either. I asked if they would do a simple experiment. Would each of them spend 30 minutes over the next week talking informally with a few employees? I suggested that they ask the workers about their views regarding the financial health of the operation. They agreed. When the leaders reconvened, they learned that the hourly workers did not see the challenges. On the basis of this heightened awareness, the leadership team developed an extensive communication strategy to let people know the threats facing them.

In considering whether to introduce an experiment, the same list of considerations apply from the previous section on units of work, namely appropriateness, timing, sufficient support for this work, time allotted for the work, and closure.

THE GESTALT STANCE

An executive once told me, "I don't know what it is, but there is something different about people who have training in Gestalt." If we look at the tools that "Gestaltists" use, we won't find it there. And, if we're lucky, we won't find it in their use of some specialized language. We will find it in their way of being—a way of presenting oneself—a way of life. This may seem ineffable, but it's not. This stance can be observed, and fortunately it can be learned.

Essential to Gestalt work is the ability to work in a way that embraces the paradoxical theory of change, the appreciation for where individuals, groups, and organizations are with regard to the work (the cycle of experience), and a field perspective, as well as other basic tenets of Gestalt. Things work best when these concepts are part of the ground, allowing us the freedom to make contact with the client, thus allowing us to support contact among various parts of the client system.

Effective work from a Gestalt perspective is not a collection of recognizable tools and techniques; rather, it encompasses a way of being. When we are at our most effective, we embody the values and theory of Gestalt theory. I cover some of the most important elements below.

Open Curiosity

Anyone attempting to work by Gestalt principles in an organization needs to be interested and curious about what he or she observes without judgment and without a need for anything to be other than as it is at that moment. This can be extremely difficult to do. Many organizations have a "we're late, we're late for a very important date" urgency. Attending to heightening awareness of "what is" can seem frivolous and a terrible waste of time. It is easy for the Gestalt consultant to get caught up in moving to action and showing some tangible result. When you couple that with the consultant's desire to show that he or she is productive, you can say goodbye to the paradoxical theory of change.

Curiosity extends to an interest in the various ways in which people see a situation. We need to be committed to helping organizations find ways to begin to see those various ways of making meaning of the present situation.

Traditional union-management relationships create strong projections that can span generations. It becomes difficult for someone on one side to imagine that her counterpart on the other side has a credible or even legitimate point of view. This phenomenon can be true in the division between field and headquarters, between global headquarters and offices in other countries, or between the different races, cultures, genders, ages, sexual orientations, and classes that make up a large organization. And, of course, we bring our own biases to that table as well.

Not only is the paradoxical theory of change an important guide, but also just remembering Beisser's (1970) model can often help us stay open and curious when we desperately want to give in to our own projections or our desire to get on with things.

Laura Perls and other founders of Gestalt therapy were influenced by Martin Buber's "I-Thou" philosophy. To say the pronoun *I* implies a relationship—I in relation to someone or something else. This can be I in relation to Thou, or I in relation to an inanimate object—an It. The challenge of Gestaltists is to treat the other person as a Thou and not as an It. Salespeople who call our homes at mealtime are seldom interested in us; rather, they want to make a sale. They listen for signals that will help them close a sale. They don't care about us, our needs, our finances, or our dinner plans. They have turned us into "Its."

Many organizational procedures are built on an I-It foundation. Most performance evaluation systems provide one-way feedback that includes

---

SEÀN: I have been engaged by how you grapple with "I-Thou" in an organizational context, surely the core challenge of our work as Gestalt OSD practitioners. Part of the complexity of this issue for me is that I meet not only people but also functional roles in OSD. Relationships are not only interpersonal but also interfunctional. As a result, the "It" is pervasive and often dominant. My perspective is to regard the client system (people + functions) as my environmental other, a "Thou" to my "I." Equally vital is that I do not support the system to treat me as an "It," just any consultant doing what he's told or what he usually does. If we can be fully present, our approach and skills well integrated, then our work flows through us, rather than being done by us. In this way, our "I-ness" can evoke a "Thou-ness" in whole or in part in our client systems. We know we're there when the feedback from individuals in the system is given on behalf of the whole. As always, everything comes back to our use of self as our core competence.

RICK: I agree. Sometimes it seems that the phenomenological field of an organziation supports "It" and punishes or disregards the "Thou." And though that makes our work as practioners in organizations more diffiuclt, it also makes it all the more needed.

---

quantitative rankings (to give the illusion of some objective and scientific truth). Organizational changes usually are top-down affairs with others expected to go along. What makes these procedures I-It is the lack of reciprocal influence. The employee has no way to challenge the grade or to explore field conditions that might have caused this poor performance. Departments have no way to challenge corporate decisions. An I-Thou relationship implies that both sides can be influenced by each other. It is impossible to be influenced by an It.

Maintaining a commitment to I-Thou can be challenging in organizations. Those who work as consultants may find that their clients want to get things up and running with little regard to being influenced by others. Fortunately, the field of organizational development has developed or adapted many tools to support I-Thou relating. Many of these tools are deeply rooted in dialogue, a type of conversation that puts a strong emphasis on inquiry over action and on supporting all sides to make contact with the ideas, fears, wishes, values, and opinions of others.

Commitment to Dialogue

Judith Brown is credited with saying that dialogue is at the heart of all good Gestalt practice. Consultants sometimes forget this. Current authors are bringing our attention back to this I-Thou way of being and working (Crocker, 1999; Hycner & Jacobs, 1995; Yontef, 1993). These authors suggest that the therapist be open to being influenced by clients. I have heard Gary Yontef (1993) say, "When a client tells me that I don't understand him, and I think I do—I am wrong." He goes on to say that neither party holds full knowledge of the situation and that this awareness is co-created between therapist and client. Of course, we do not give up our knowledge of theory and practice, but in the moment of contact all of that experience and knowledge becomes ground and the relationship becomes figural. The therapist enters into and experiences the world through the eyes of the client.

Though the organizational development approach to consulting supports I-Thou contact, the practitioners may keep themselves outside that loop, choosing to support I-Thou contact between parts of the client organization. For example, the consultant might create a forum where people from all levels and departments can engage in congruent dialogue over matters of importance. During this exchange, the consultant remains on the boundary of this dialogue, helping facilitate this process.

As yet, we do not have a literature that explores if and when a consultant should cross that boundary and become part of the I-Thou exchange. Because everyone is a part of the phenomenological field, there is a good argument to be made for the consultant being part of the deeper exchanges. In practice, I have known some consultants who engage in the I-Thou realm with clients, but it appears to be more of a personal choice than a part of Gestalt's theory or teaching of practice. However, our major work remains inside the client boundary. If we do cross that boundary, how do we maintain the marginality that is so necessary for our work? I believe there is a rich vein to be mined by further study of the I-Thou stance in organizations.

Being Aware of Our Impact

Our own presence is critical to the work we do. Who we are, the projections people place on us, and how we present ourselves have a significant impact on the work. If people are intimidated by our presence (even though we see ourselves as gentle lambs), it will be difficult for us to make decent contact. Understanding the reactions people have to us is important. Without this self-awareness, we are left with only our techniques and tools. We may miss the real reason why our interventions work or fail. We may miss how our presence influences people in ways that support or detract from the work: in other words, being aware of how our presence affects interpersonal contact.

Shifting the focus inside ourselves, it is important to understand our own way of making meaning and to be aware of where we feel at ease and where we feel reluctance to explore. For example, imagine someone who can't stand conflict. This reluctance may create such a strong block that it could limit his or her ability to even see the need to explore conflict inside an organization.

Lack of awareness of bigger issues can also stand in our way. It is common for therapists to be in therapy and/or supervision as a way to understand their own issues and receive feedback on their practice. No such requirements are demanded of consultants, managers, or project leaders. For example, it is quite possible (and common) for consultants to hang out a shingle and develop a practice without paying any serious attention to the impact that their presence, unfinished personal business, and skill have on the work. Imagine a consultant who doesn't recognize his or her own biases with regard to diversity or cross-cultural issues in an organization. It is quite possible that these issues can be screaming for attention, but his or her scanning doesn't even pick up the signals. Without this awareness, the practitioner cannot support people making contact with diversity issues or any other issues where he or she lacks self-awareness.

I distinguish I-Thou from Gestalt's notion of "use of self," in which the practitioner allows his or her own sensations and awareness to inform meetings with clients. For example, it is not uncommon for someone with Gestalt training to express her physical discomfort as a way to intrigue and perhaps provoke a client to examine his or her own sensation. Still, this is done in the service of heightened contact among people in the organization. The consultant is not acknowledging that she herself is fully a part of this field.

Encouraging Support for Contact

It is extremely difficult for people to tell the truth to each other in organizations. Chris Argyris (1990) has written extensively on this problem and on what he calls defensive routines. A major contribution of Laura Perls (1992d) to Gestalt theory and practice was her attention to support for contact. She believed that contact could occur when sufficient support was available; otherwise, people would resist going where the wise might fear to tread. In a series of training workshops conducted shortly after her arrival in the United States in 1953, she addressed contact and support in this way:

> Contact is the recognition of "otherness," the awareness of difference. It is the boundary experience of "I and the other." I would differentiate between "being in contact" and "making contact." *Being in contact* indicates a continuing state, which gradually tends toward indifference (confluence). *Making contact is a foreground* function, alert, awake, etc. . . . Support for making contact comes from what has been assimilated and integrated. (L. Perls, 1992d, p. 84, italics in original)

Knowing what supports good contact and what detracts from it is a critical set of skills for the Gestalt practitioner. I have seen meetings turn from civil discourse into finger-pointing recriminations, and I have watched other meetings grow eerily silent when someone asked a question that was too hot to handle.

Organizations are political. People are usually wise to carefully consider what they say. Attention to this political reality interrupts good contact. The dilemma is: "How can we support good dialogue around critical issues in a way that the participants feel safe?" Though challenging, this is an essential process. If we demand that people speak when they don't feel supported or we create the illusion that things are safer than they really are (often through our own charisma), we put people at risk.

I recall one executive team that desperately needed to hear the voices of people in their organization. There are some wonderful large systems change interventions that can get a hundred people in a room to address critical issues. As good as these techniques are, they would have been the wrong approach for this team. I didn't believe they could take in the criticism that would have come at them without getting defensive and lashing out. Instead, I chose a much simpler and slower way of supporting them to make contact with the staff. For example, we did some simple surveys, we held town hall meetings limited to single topics, and I asked the executives to conduct small focus groups. These interventions allowed the executives to begin to make contact with what the employees were telling them.

Attending to Emerging Figures and Themes

Figure and ground work together. As figures emerge, they have an effect on the ground, just as the ground influences how and what figures emerge. This fluctuation is part of the field. Part of our work is to help organizations pay attention to this dance and to the multiple and sometimes competing figures that appear. Our task is not to choose the figure for clients but simply to help them look at the choices they are making and support their view. As a figure picks up steam, energy gets mobilized, and themes emerge. A theme is often a combination of the goal and the resistance to this goal. By focusing on and drawing attention to these themes, we support the development of the work.

Appreciating Resistance

A significant difference between a Gestalt approach and other approaches to change in OSD consulting is that we respect resistance and take it seriously. We see resistance as "the energy," not "the enemy." The larger field of OD, with which we have a close kinship, often misses the primacy of resistance. For example, the fifth edition of *Organization Development* (French & Bell, 1995), a classic OD text, devoted only one-half page to resistance.

We draw on the earliest writing of Gestalt therapy to guide our work (Perls et al., 1951). Resistance is creative adjustment to a situation. In other words, it is not a bad thing or something to be overcome. It is simply a natural way of responding to situations that either are threatening in themselves or evoke some unfinished business in the organization. Our work is to allow people to voice their views. Drawing on phenomenology, we recognize that our reality, or how we see things, is no more or less valid than realities created by others in the organization.

Case Example: "The Hospital Request for How to Bury a Cat"

A hospital where I was consulting regarding a possible merger made a simple request/demand: "Give a speech and turn things around." Though most of us might see warning flags in a similar situation, it was Gestalt theory that helped me articulate why I was uncomfortable, so I reframed the situation in a way that I could respond.

The cycle of experience suggests that resistance often comes when one group is out ahead of others on the cycle. Certainly what I knew about the reasons why so many mergers failed in the United States (part of the field conditions) suggested that this might be a reason for the problem. I knew that a speech would not create sufficient support for contact to get people to change. Plus, I didn't even know if the merger was a good idea. I knew that my best work would come from helping them heighten awareness of the current state of affairs.

I needed more information, so I invited a colleague to join me on the project. Regina and I interviewed a cross-section of the new entity. When she and I met to discuss what we had heard, she said, "These people haven't had a chance to grieve." I agreed. She then said, "I think they need a funeral." I spoke with my client and suggested that we facilitate the entire day. I made no promises other than that by the end of the day the management team would have a clearer picture of where they were and why they were stuck.

Although the retreat was not called a funeral, that metaphor was figural as Regina and I planned and facilitated the day. After some brief opening remarks by the CEO, we began our work. Shortly before this event, I had facilitated a meeting of the executive team. George, one of the members, said, "We've got to bury the cat." Others looked quizzical. His explanatory comment went something like this: This merger is like running over your neighbor's cat. You feel bad, so you bury the cat and tell your neighbor how sorry you feel. The next day, you are still feeling bad, so you dig up the cat and give it a better grave. And this goes on day after day. At some point you've just got to bury the cat.

I asked George if he would tell that story during the retreat. As he told it, people nodded. Some laughed. Regina and I had decided to invite him to tell the story because we knew the power that metaphors can sometimes have—and we just liked the story.

For the first event of the day, we asked managers to meet in their regular work groups. Each group was asked to identify what it gained from the merger and what it lost. When each group reported, it was striking how similar each list was—including the list compiled by the executive team. Most groups had assumed that the new executive team had the most to gain and little to lose, so when their report looked like other lists, people were quite surprised. The executive team was amazed to learn that their position was seen as so favored. People asked questions about items on the various lists and commented on the similarities and differences. This simple exercise led to a rich conversation.

In the spirit of the paradoxical theory of change, we continued with other similar activities. All we wanted was to heighten awareness. By the early afternoon, we formed a fishbowl that included two representatives from each of the facilities and a couple of

> empty chairs. The empty chairs allowed people to enter the group when they had something to add. The focus: Where are we today? As the conversation began, we noticed a shift in the use of language. People had been talking about "them" and "their idea" and "their merger." Now people were speaking in the first person. There seemed to be an acceptance that the merger was real, and the focus of the discussion shifted to the future. People discussed what needed to happen if the merger was going to succeed.
>
> Energy was mobilizing around the figure of making this merger work. It seemed that a lot of people were ready to move to action. We asked if they wanted to discuss next steps. They formed mixed groups so that each facility was represented in each small work group. One of these groups left the room. We didn't know where they had gone, but neither Regina nor I had much interest in tracking down a group of adults who probably could do just fine without us. When it came time to report, the group made a surprise and triumphant entrance into the room. Led by the chaplain, the group intoned an improvised chant. Some were carrying a small shoebox coffin with a cat's tail sticking out the back. (By the way, no real animals were harmed during this intervention.) They stopped and mimed digging a grave once and for all. The entire management group was on its feet laughing and cheering during this scene. Months later, people referred to the "bury the cat" incident as a turning point in their work together. In meetings, it was not uncommon to hear someone say, "Wait a minute, let's not dig up that cat again."
>
> We could not have forced the group to move to action, nor could we have orchestrated the "bury the cat" scene. All we could do was choose work that could be reasonably completed given the time, respect where they were, try to create sufficient support for contact so people could engage in candid dialogue, and be attentive to the aesthetic of when it was time to support the group moving to another phase. In doing all of that, we supported them in completing a unit of work. In choosing to affirm the new order, we could support the completion of a unit of work—the formation of a new gestalt.

Is that all there is to it? Of course not! The "bury the cat" example simply illustrates how Gestalt theory and practice influenced our work with one relatively small intervention.

CLOSING: SPEAKING PROSE ALL OUR LIVES

John Carter (personal communication, 2004) points out that intervening from a Gestalt perspective is not a series of separate techniques but the integration of the theory into our practice that makes it come alive. A character in Molière's play *The Bourgeois Gentleman* bursts into the room with great excitement. He has just learned that he has been speaking prose all of his life. Gestalt is a lot like that. Our day-to-day activities don't look a lot different from those of our colleagues. Prose is prose. It is the integration of this rich theory that makes our prose sound so different.

REVIEW QUESTIONS

1. Describe the differences and similarities between Gestalt *therapists* and *organizational consultants* who apply Gestalt perspectives to their work with large systems.

2. Explain field theory in the context of working with organizations. Who/what constitutes the field? How does a consultant operating from a field approach differ from a consultant taking the stance of "expert"? What are the significant implications of field theory for the work of organizational consulting from a Gestalt perspective?

3. What does the author mean when he states that understanding our own biases and bracketing them is an important goal or skill of the organizational consultant? Provide your own example of how effective bracketing can positively influence organizational change.

4. What are some of the implications of the paradoxical theory of change for those who work in organizations? In considering the organizational setting of your present Gestalt training program and/or graduate course, discuss with your peers how the paradoxical approach might be applied to implement desired changes in your program.

5. Maurer adapts the terms used in the traditional Gestalt cycle of experience to make them more relevant to movement and change in organizations. Identify and define the organizational terminology used for *sensation, awareness, mobilization/energy, action, contact,* and *withdrawal.*

EXPERIENTIAL PEDAGOGICAL ACTIVITIES

ACTIVITY 1: This chapter contains descriptions of common ways that organizations handle challenge. In small groups, generate and discuss "real-life" examples of each approach listed below:

A. The leader demands that people comply by issuing verbal and written orders.
B. The organization provides staff development and training.
C. The organization takes a motivational approach in which everyone is brought together for an inspirational (revival) meeting.

ACTIVITY 2: The author states that none of the approaches outlined in Activity 1 coincide with a more Gestalt-oriented view; "[i]n fact, none of the approaches respect where the organization is at the moment of intervention. All imply that wherever people are isn't good enough and that forcing change from the current state (whether through force, education, or inspiration) is the preferred approach." Continue your small group discussion to brainstorm other ways change could be approached that would be more aligned with Gestalt principles.

ACTIVITY 3: One principal component of endorsing a field theory approach with organizations is that every member in the field has a relevant perspective to share and that all views are accurate. To illustrate this in the classroom setting, select an insiders group and an outsiders group and assign each individual a specific role to play, with an assigned perspective or viewpoint. Provide a dilemma (perhaps one in the news) for the group to merely discuss. The "hidden" objective of the exercise is not the actual resolution or perspective the group may generate but the process of honoring each individual voice. Ask each participant to describe his or her degree of comfort and experience of feeling heard by the others. The outsiders can participate either as process observers or as individuals outside the organization who may have a perspective or invested interest.

ACTIVITY 4: In the section entitled "The Field Is Constantly Changing," the author explains that events both inside and outside the organization can influence the organizational field and that "any change in one part of the field will have an impact throughout the field." To provide a visual representation of this phenomenon, each individual class member (or small clusters/groups of class members) can design and construct organizational mobiles. The materials you will need include string for hanging the mobile pieces, sticks to be used as the crossbars to which the strings are tied (small wooden meat skewers for kabobs work well for this), and objects to represent various aspects of the organization. Those aspects could be (a) personnel (for which you can cut pictures from magazines that resemble specific people in the organization); (b) levels of the organization (for which drawings or pictures of different-sized desks represent power or lack thereof); (c) tools of the trade (icons cut out of cardboard or paper that could represent powerful internal influences, such as computer systems and financial structures); (d) unions (for which symbolic representations could be identified); or (e) unique aspects of the organization that could be a combination of any or all of the above. After the mobile is completed, the entire class could be asked to generate the external winds that blow change into the organization/mobile. As your author states, those changes could be due to fluctuations in the marketplace or in the world. After identifying a variety of potential external influences, shift the position of the mobile figures to illustrate how it, the organization, might reconfigure.

ACTIVITY 5: The felt distinction between I and Thou is the difference between being related to as an "It," or relating to another in an equally respectful relationship. Identify a time in your own life when you felt like an "It" within an organization. In journal format, generate the thoughts and feelings you had being in that "It" position. Describe what would have had to be different in the organizational field for you to feel you were in relationship with other aspects of the organization as an "I." Discuss your experiences in a dyad or small group with classmates.

CHAPTER **14**

Gestalt Therapy in Community Mental Health

PHILIP BROWNELL

DIALOGUE RESPONDENT: KAREN FLEMING

Philip Brownell received his Gestalt therapy training at the Portland Gestalt Therapy Institute and is in private practice in Portland, Oregon, at Western Psychological & Counseling Services, but he will have joined the psychology staff of Ashton Associates in Bermuda when this is published. He is a licensed clinical psychologist in Oregon and North Carolina and an ordained clergyman. He has worked in community mental health since 1967, when he was a corpsman in the psychiatric units at Oak Knoll Naval Hospital, and he has had experience since then in residential treatment centers in California and Oregon and in state-funded outpatient centers and juvenile courts in North Carolina. His name is widely recognized in Gestalt circles as an author; as senior editor of the electronic journal *Gestalt!* (www.g-gej.org); and as manager of the worldwide Listserv discussion group known as Gstalt-L (www.g-gej.org/gstalt-l).

Karen Fleming is a licensed counseling psychologist who graduated from the Gestalt Institute of Cleveland's Post-Graduate Program and has since served on their faculty, where she specializes in training couple and family therapists. Her full-time position as director of Outpatient Services at Coleman Professional Services, Community Mental Health Center in Kent, Ohio, provides ample opportunity for her to supervise clinicians in the application of Gestalt therapy with a diverse population. In addition, she provides supervision for pre- and postdoctoral psychology interns as assistant professor of psychology (part-time) at Northeastern Ohio Universities College of Medicine.

The goal of this chapter is to help Gestalt therapists who work in agencies and other community-based mental health organizations to support themselves in those settings. A secondary objective is to encourage the use of Gestalt therapy in such work.

Community psychology has been defined as the discipline

> oriented to developing psychological theory, values, and research methods and to creating innovative social interventions, all for the purposes of: preventing social, economic, health, and mental health problems; improving the quality of life and well-being, particularly for marginalized groups; and building the sense and reality of community and empowerment. (Walsh-Bowers, 1998, p. 280)

Considering the work in community mental health, however, is like sighting a moving target because it is always changing and one has to sense where it has been in relationship to where it is going if there is to be any hope of hitting it on the fly.

To accomplish this, with respect to the practice of Gestalt therapy within various systems of community mental health, this chapter first identifies the ground of community mental health and then describes focal points in community work. This ground is the developmental history of community mental health, serving as context for current situational units in mental health's dependency upon public policy. The chapter incorporates how subsystems' clinicians can manage as they move across levels within specific community mental health organizations, pointing to relational structures, performance demands, and diverse experiences of self. Moving to the figure of Gestalt therapy practice within this field-theoretical perspective, the chapter encompasses consideration of acceptable treatment planning, documentation of Gestalt therapy processes, assimilation of evidence-based interventions, and a Gestalt therapy theoretical matrix to guide clinical judgment. It concludes by listing pragmatic concerns for individual therapists desiring to practice Gestalt therapy within the organizational framework of community mental health.

THE GROUND OF COMMUNITY MENTAL HEALTH

Community mental health was strongly influenced by the social concerns and group dynamics research of Kurt Lewin and others (Holtzman, 1997). Lewin's initial work in Berlin following World War I was largely a phenomenological investigation of everyday life; thus it was rooted in very mundane events. He articulated the major ideas for field theory from his experiences as a soldier in the war. In summarizing Lewin's accomplishments, Paul Shane (1999) saw him "asserting that humans organize their perception and experience—indeed, their personal 'worlds'—around things that are of personal interest or concern" (p. 59). Lewin's method was revolutionary: For example, he made films in Berlin that captured the life space of children, and to communicate what that was like, he lowered the perspective of

> **KAREN:** The biggest appreciation I have is the attention you paid to the ground of field theory in community mental health. That follows through the chapter when you discuss the focal points in community mental health and even the pragmatic concerns.

the camera to the eye level of his subjects. When Lewin came to the United States, he attracted inquisitive, intelligent, and assertive colleagues. He lived out his field theory by establishing the *Quasselstrippe* (wandering string), a loosely structured series of seminars and meetings of faculty and students in which topics were encountered and discussed as they came up in the group interaction. Lewin's *Quasselstrippes* created lively discourse and gave birth to interesting focal points for new research (e.g., fascism, anti-Semitism, poverty, intergroup conflict, and minority issues). In the center of Lewin's theory was "the interaction between an active, initiating self and an equally active, demanding environment" (Richan & Kleiner, 1990, p. 283).

Thus social psychology, as influenced by Lewin, emerged strengthened by the interest and resources of those who had experienced the World War, supported and encouraged by the enthusiastic intellectual magnitude of Kurt Lewin himself, and realized out of the direct curiosity and freedom of younger colleagues and students, who extended Lewin's influence by adopting his approach. Ron Lippitt, for example, ended up studying aggression in autocratic versus democratic leadership styles (with direct applicability to Germany's Nazi government) because he had first been interested in discovering a balance between autocratic and democratic styles in the leadership of community small groups such as the YMCA and the Boy Scouts in Springfield, Illinois (R. White, 1990)—practical and mundane interests arising from his own developmental field.

Field theory became a backbone of social psychology and the application of psychological principles in social settings. It was the fundamental principle in community psychology, which took seriously Lewin's assertion that behavior is a function of the person, the environment, and the interaction between the two (Orford, 1992). Field theory remains prominent today and can be seen as a member of a set of person-in-context theories, all of which are often referenced in language such as "complex systems" or "multisystemic" work (Henggeler, Melton, & Smith, 1992) and are wonderfully described by Wayne Holtzman (1997):

> Community psychology is based on systems and ecological thinking that integrates health, human resources, education, social interventions, citizen empowerment, and cultural values into one strategy, focusing in particular on well-defined communities. This integration recognizes the mutual adaptation and interdependence of individuals and social structures so that both individual and collective needs are met. (p. 3)

More specifically, however, community mental health evolved along its own developmental path. It became influenced by social psychologists, but it has a more common antecedent in everyday life. The history of community mental health follows the practical question of what to do with the mentally dysfunctional people in our midst.

Before 1830, mental health care in the United States was largely a private matter, and people with psychological disorders did not usually fare well. Dorothea Dix (1802–1887), a retired schoolteacher, succeeded in removing those with severe mental disorders from jails and almshouses and initiated the movement for their placement in hospitals at public expense (Shore, 1992). Clifford Beers (1876–1943) also mobilized public awareness of mental health by trying to educate the public. His efforts to improve the care of mental health patients led to the formation of the National Committee for Mental Hygiene in 1909, which in turn led to what is now the National Association for Mental Health (NAMH).

Public opinion evolved into the belief that mental health was a social issue deserving public attention (Bickman & Dokecki, 1989). State-run asylums were built to house the mentally ill, but until the middle of the twentieth century they were mere domiciles with deplorable conditions. Various providers and local hospitals were trying to meet the needs of the mentally ill, but they were overlapping and duplicating their efforts, without any coordinated approach or guiding philosophy. When World War II occurred, the high rejection rate for psychological disorders among those considered for the military (over 1,000,000) and the high psychiatric casualty rate from the war (40% of all discharges were psychologically related) made mental health a visible and important concern in the United States. This provided incentive for the creation of a national program for mental health, resulting in the passage of the Mental Health Act in 1946, which in turn created the National Institute of Mental Health (NIMH)—a federally funded program built on three commitments: research, training, and services.

During the 1940s and 1950s, in both the United States and Europe, people continued to lay the ground for what would later become community mental health care. In Europe there were efforts at establishing small therapeutic communities, emergency services, and partial hospitalization, and in the United States efforts were made to assist local communities in establishing community-based settings for the mentally ill, but there was no comprehensive plan for a national strategy. In 1955, the government passed the Mental Health Study Act, which established the Joint Commission on Mental Illness and Health. The commission published several volumes of its findings between 1955 and 1961, representing a broad scope in mental health and providing information on research, personnel needs, schools, churches, public attitudes, economics, epidemiology, and community resources. On the basis of the 1963 reports of the Joint Commission, Congress passed the Community Mental Health Centers Construction Act (Kennedy, 1990). That legislation divided communities into catchment areas, each of which was to develop a plan based on an evaluation of its specific needs. Community mental health centers were to be constructed in each area, and these centers were to be central pivots around which a variety of essential community-based services were to be organized. Each center was mandated by law to provide five essential resources: (a) inpatient services, (b) outpatient services, (c) partial hospitalization, (d) emergency services, and (e) consultation and education to community agencies and the public at large. This was all organized by a guiding philosophy of comprehensiveness, coordination, and continuity of care, with special emphasis on acceptability, availability, accessibility, and awareness.

The Joint Commission on the Mental Health of Children was established in 1968, and the public health concerns arising from a consideration of developmental influences on children began to resonate with the entire field, resulting in a value being placed on advocacy for all populations. By 1980 there were over 700 federally funded community mental health centers; however, the public policy that resulted in federal funding, with the plan to eventually shift to local revenue sources, became obviously unrealistic, leading to an overall rethinking of the feasibility of the community mental health system. Its ambitious beginnings became increasingly scaled back because community mental health did not seem to have delivered on its promises, never dealt adequately with the issue of the severely mentally ill, never sufficiently funded prevention research and strategies to affect the etiology of various disorders, and never developed adequate research on service delivery to sharpen the efficiency and effectiveness of service provision (Shore, 1992). The last of these failings left the door wide open for managed care to step in and assume that role.

FOCAL POINTS IN CONTEMPORARY COMMUNITY MENTAL HEALTH

Community mental health is often associated with adult populations and a focus on substance abuse, severe and persistent mental illness (SPMI), and homelessness. In more recent years it has grown to include concern for children, youth, families, and the developmentally disabled. When thinking about how to work within community mental health, people usually go immediately to the direct provision of service for these various populations. But wherever community mental health exists, it is a complex system that cannot be understood by considering the clinical populations alone. Community mental health is also related to public policy, the managed care movement (including a preference for evidence-based treatment), and the desire to promote health as a priority over merely identifying and treating illness.

Public Policy

Community mental health is linked directly to public policy. That is evident from its evolutionary history but also from the testimony of those who participate in its current support through political activism (Miller, 2002). As such, community mental health has come full circle, moving from the private sector to the development of a community system administrated at public expense, and now back to the privatization of direct service. In North Carolina, for instance, the state-run system of area programs (designed to provide direct service for the developmentally disabled, the mentally ill, and those with substance abuse problems) has been changed to require the various community mental health agencies to function as Local Management Entities—that is, managed care organizations conducting case management and contracting with the private sector for direct service. This has become a national trend implemented in various ways according to regional demands.

Public policy has developed in other substantial ways to reflect a growing preference for consumer-community collaborations as creative alternatives to old-style provider-run programs (Pomeroy, Trainor, & Pape, 2002). In many areas, community initiatives, faith-based programs, and partnerships with school systems have provided resources when the traditional community health organization reduced direct services. Interestingly, with politics and economics now determining psychotherapeutic relationships and treatment regimens, clients are no longer called "clients" or "patients" but rather "consumers" or "customers," and clinicians no longer do "counseling" or "psychotherapy" but rather "deliver a *product*."

In the face of such changes in public policy, it is necessary for individual therapists working with clients to be aware of field dynamics affecting both the therapists and their clients (Richan & Kleiner, 1990). Politicians and social activists influence what gets funded and how those funds get utilized, which, in turn, affects the viability of therapist employment and professional practice in community health systems and the availability of therapists for client-consumers requesting psychological and social services.

Managed Care

As managed care exerts its powerful influence on the delivery of mental health care, it defines mental disorder, the criteria by which people are referred to services, the nature and the length of treatment, and the treatments of choice. These influences affect society's understanding of health and illness, healing, the scope of human nature, and what is possible for human beings (Cushman & Gilford, 2000).

Even though objections to managed care can be seen in popular culture (Miller, Shander, & Cohen, 1999), and many established Gestalt therapists have refused to operate within its scope, managed care is an accepted aspect of wider professional life and must be assimilated by those working in community mental health. Three figures drive the daily decisions of managed care organizations: efficiency, effectiveness, and accountability.

Efficiency

The primary consideration in managed care is fiscal. One example of this is the preference, in some agencies, for "stepped care," indicating the practice of starting therapeutic efforts with the least expensive and least intrusive intervention and moving up to more expensive and perhaps more intrusive interventions only when that is absolutely necessary in order to reach the clinical objectives (Davison, 2000).

Managed care executives want to make a profit, and when their strategies are employed in nonprofit organizations, they are aimed at preventing a loss. Consequently, one of the most salient figures in managed community mental health work is cutting costs and becoming profitable. On several occasions I have listened to administrative supervisors announce changes from a system of therapist productivity to a system of therapist profitability. In the first, employees make sure they are engaged in various kinds of work deemed to be associated with client contact for a majority of their overall time; in the second, employees opt for the most profitable kinds of client-consumer contact for a majority of their time. In such situations, it is easy to see that the most efficient use of one's time equals the most profitable time management.

KAREN: The new expectation, again to increase efficiency, is for therapists to do everything client related with the client present. That includes writing the progress note and any treatment planning. So our shift in modes now needs to take place within the session, and we need to teach clients this skill.

PHIL: The need to do everything in the presence of the client does not account for (and contaminates) all those elements laying ground for the face-to-face meeting; it ultimately does not serve the consumer well. To draw an analogy to another marketplace, this would be like telling people at the door of the grocery store that clerks would be happy to check out customers but customers could only purchase food that had been seeded, grown, harvested, and packaged while the customer was in the store.

What I experienced in one community mental health organization is that it was top-heavy with fiscal managers and that the fiscal matters (such as eliminating paybacks to Medicare and Medicaid or obtaining and keeping contracts) drove the figures of interest for the overall organization. Clinical interests were constantly minimized or ignored, and I believe that's because business-minded individuals essentially misunderstand them. This situation constitutes an ethical dilemma. The clinician must support good business practice or the organization cannot survive, but good business practice often undercuts good clinical practice; with an imbalance either way the consumer suffers, and the clinician tiptoes along a stressful tightrope trying to support organizational equilibrium. Virtually every licensing board has ethical principles that licensed clinicians are expected to follow. To be a social advocate is usually one of them, so that licensed Gestalt practitioners are obligated to work for the good, for justice, for equity. Such a person would be obligated to assert clinical interests within a community mental health

Effectiveness

As early as 1997, those keeping a research watch on the development of managed care realized that cost may have been the catalyst for its emergence, but the future of managed health care would be found in a concern for quality (Steenbarger, 1997). That judgment has proven accurate and crucial for the credibility of the health care industry; it has been implemented through an emphasis on careful treatment planning and case management that is supposedly grounded in empirically supported practice (Deegear & Lawson, 2003; Garland, Kruse, & Aarons, 2003). Treatment planning has become increasingly constructed utilizing cognitive and behavioral language to describe measurable goals, indicate time-and-date-stamped interventions, and accomplish symptom reduction.

Accountability

To protect against accusations of fraud and the need for payback to insurance companies and government auditing agencies, the community mental health system in most places has constructed deeply layered departments overseeing records. They have created redundant documentation procedures that usurp time and energy from direct contact between client and therapist, and in many situations the needs of the records department for careful documentation actually intrude on the clinical process. Therapists often find themselves asking questions and gathering data that they themselves do not need but that their supervisors demand and that the organization needs to appease auditors and maintain accountability. It is a stressful situation for everyone concerned, as quite often the community mental health organization experiences a breakdown in documentation that results in expensive paybacks and losses of revenue.

organization. The tension between fiscal solvency and clinical effectiveness requires Gestalt therapists to self-regulate, to find the balance, and to take responsibility for what they are doing.

KAREN: I agree with you that forces for efficiency and for profitability exist in the move to complete progress notes and treatment plans with the client present. Other forces support this movement. For example, at our company (and at large and small medical facilities in the area), we have moved to an electronic record; intakes, notes, and plans are completed online. I have an electronic signature, and eventually clients will sign their plans with their own electronic signatures. To be in compliance with our state regulations, clients must participate in designing the plan. In some ways clients are open to this. Our intakes, for example, are like structured interviews, and my hope is that clients see them as thorough. I admit that I put it all aside in some crisis situations. In addition, the HIPAA (Health Information Portability and Accountability Act of 1996) laws have made chart access more of an expectation for clients.

HOW TO PRACTICE GESTALT THERAPY IN COMMUNITY MENTAL HEALTH

As one can imagine, there are no cookie-cutter templates with which to produce formulaic applications of Gestalt therapy because there is no one-size-fits-all Gestalt therapy or any truly generic community mental health center. Every position in the environmental context is relative to another, and each is unique, with its own set of characteristics, affected by its own influences. What follows is a general consideration regarding how one might practice Gestalt therapy within a contemporary community mental health organization (CMHO), but this model would have to be adapted to the specific therapist and setting. One must fit in with the organization and find one's way of conducting Gestalt therapy in that place. The basics of Gestalt therapy practice (such considerations as field theory, phenomenological method, dialogical relationship, and experiment) would be present but applied uniquely by the therapist-in-context.

Any functional CMHO is a system composed of subsystems, all operating within the therapist's field. "Although it is common to describe aspects of the total life-space as fields unto themselves, in actuality everything that affects a person is their field, the totality of coexisting facts all mutually interdependent and providing context for life" (Brownell, 1998, p. 144). It is the way organizations or individuals perceive and organize their relationship with, and interaction within, an environment (Kleiner & Okeke, 1991). For the purposes of this chapter, "field" is relative to the individual, consisting of proximal effects and thus distinct rather than environmentally all-inclusive (Brownell, 2002). A system is a closed, or bounded, portion of one's field (Crocker et al., 2001). Thus one's place of employment, one's practice, is a bounded portion of one's life and is a system.

Michael Lewis (1997), in writing about the developmental field of the child, stated that current context is a greater predictor of behavior than early attachment; we perceive and remember according to the needs we anticipate in the future or those we experience in the present. We reconstruct our various stories to support our contacting in any given present context. This is what is meant when people recognize that in therapy the clinician is presented with a "situation" rather than merely with a person, and the situation is the person-in-context (McConville, 2001b). Although Lewis (1997) was writing about child development, what he said is true of present context for adults as well. Thus the current context is a mix of what the environment brings to the organism and what the organism brings to the environment. It changes from one situation to the next, so it is not uncommon for any given therapist to have to regulate his or her experience while moving among different subsystems and relating to people with diverse needs, expectations, and purposes, flexibly distinguishing one situational unit from another. When person-in-context is considered, that situation applies to therapists operating within a CMHO as well as consumer-clients coming into a CMHO for help.

Consequently, there are various organizational obligations and situations the staff must navigate. They need to attend staff meetings, converge with colleagues in the medical records department while going over documentation, and meet with supervisors, both administrative and clinical. They encounter clients. They attend in-service training workshops together. They interface with the community for case management, networking and support, and public education.

CMHOs can be regarded as functional or dysfunctional systems according to the degree to which good contact and fluid satisfaction of figures can be maintained across the various levels of their organization and to the degree that they operate in accord with public policy wherever they exist (Nevis, 1987). If the systemic operations, which are organizational in structure, actually impede gestalt formation and satisfaction, people will experience frustration, heightened stress, and lack of support. It will become difficult for therapists, who are agents of organizational contact, to move easily among the various levels of the system and accomplish their work.

A Gestalt therapist would be wise to study Gestalt processes in organizational development (see Chapter 13 of this book) and to "step back" while at work in order to utilize a modified phenomenological method applied to organizational processes. One needs to be able to observe and describe what the organization is doing at any given level of its system. It is important to be able to observe the processes involved with any given CMHO and to take note of differences as one moves from one level to another. Most Gestalt therapists learn how to support themselves for therapeutic encounter during their training, but when one is working in a CMHO, self-support extends to doing what needs to be done so that one's standing in the organization does not weaken one's ability to be present with colleagues and clients. It is a matter of becoming more aware of self-in-relation, the "other" being the portion of one's field that is bounded by time, space, purpose, and agency (the other people who are also agents of the system). The contact boundaries in every subsystem bring demands consistent with those unique contexts, and therapists must be able to identify and adjust accordingly.

KAREN: It is not so much whether Gestalt therapy works or does not work in a community mental health setting. It does work. It's that the type of reality we emphasize is so much different. We teach, and perhaps value, the subjective realms in our training programs and for the therapy itself. At the same time, we exist in agencies, among funding agents, and within a medical-model culture that demand objective accounting in order for us to exist. It is often difficult to translate between those subjective and objective realities. We might do better to recognize the difference and learn with our clients to shift from subjective to objective modes.

So the question remains, Can a Gestalt therapist function as an agent of health, growth, and change in a CMHO? In general, yes, we can practice Gestalt therapy principles in our contact within the organization. Just as the development of community mental health began with a concern for the field, the field is a first concern for any Gestalt therapist desiring to succeed in community mental health today.

What are the factors having effect? How is one's field being organized by the environmental context, and in what ways can one act purposefully, even when trying experiments, so as to become an effect in the fields of others in the organization? The principles of dialogue, including appreciation for the "I-It" mode of interaction, can help one support oneself organizationally and interpersonally while attempting to get that task accomplished. There is a job to be done as well at any given level in the organization, and, of course, there are expectations that must be met. This is no different because one is a Gestalt therapist. Paying attention can help a person adjust accordingly and meet the performance demands inherent in each context. Making these adjustments results in differing experiences of self as therapists interact with differing relational structures, meet various performance demands, and experience divergent aspects of their phenomenology. It can be troubling if some of these experiences do not accord with therapists' self story, ideals, values, and preferences regarding themselves and their work. One way around that experience is to realize that any given subsystem in the organization is not the whole; it is merely a part contributing to the whole.

I used to work at a CMHO in rural North Carolina. On a typical day I might have a client or two scheduled for the early morning, followed by a 2-hour block for staff meeting, followed by lunch, followed by an hour for supervision, followed by more clients scheduled for testing and therapy, one after another until quitting time. In between, I would often have to attend to documenting my work, perhaps conferring with people in admissions and finance or medical records, and calling on the phone to interface with various service providers, school officials, and/or parents for case management. Sometimes I would have to work on community presentations or attend a community meeting across town over some issue such as a school violence initiative, teach an in-service training class, write a column for a local newsletter of the community collaborative, or pick up supplies for my play therapy stockpile. In each situation I would meet with differing kinds of people and experience a different relational structure, try to satisfy differing performance demands, and ultimately have a different experience of myself in the process. It is very important for a therapist in a CMHO to understand that this is normal and that no single level of system defines the therapist as a person or as a professional. Furthermore, ability to see the differences and understand the intensity of need on the part of others, with regard to performance demands, can help one set priorities and reduce stress. Table 14.1 compares the various subsystems, relational structures, performance demands, and experiences of self one might find in a CMHO.

Table 14.1 Example of CMHO Subsystems and Related Process Variables

System	Relational Structure	Performance Demands	Experience of Self
(level of system)	***1 = social feel*** ***2 = relational style*** ***3 = dialogical mode***	***(behavioral expectations)***	***(internal dialogue)***
Front desk/appointments	(1) Casual (2) Superficially personal (3) I-It	Be on time, be pleasant, pick up appointment schedule, get working space ready	Am I punctual and responsible? Am I friendly? Am I professional?
Staff meetings	(1) Casual to formal (2) Superficially personal (3) I-It	Be on time, contribute to discussions, pay attention, present cases, identify changes in procedures, take instruction, be a team player	Do I know what I'm talking about? Am I friendly? Was I listening? Does this feel good? Am I taking anything away from the meeting that I can use?
Clinical supervision	(1) Formal (2) Impersonal to professionally personal (3) I-It to I-Thou	Be on time; bring cases, questions, frustrations, blocks to process, successes, clinical issues, procedural matters; demonstrate constructive use of supervision	Am I safe? Can I get help with those things for which I need help? Am I competent? Am I authentic or a people-pleaser?
Administrative supervision	(1) Formal (2) Impersonal to professionally personal (3) I-It	Be on time, account for time and resources, attend to documentation, professional responsibility, organizational cooperation, staff relationships	Am I safe? Am I a good worker? Am I open to critical feedback?

Table 14.1 (Continued)

System	Relational Structure	Performance Demands	Experience of Self
Medical records	(1) Formal (2) Superficially personal (3) I-It	Correct mistakes in documentation, keep charts current, attend to billing, use proper forms, maintain current/timely records	Am I intelligent? Am I frustrating? Am I capable, responsible, and competent?
Therapy	(1) Casual (2) Professional personal (3) I-It and I-Thou	Establish therapeutic relationship, keep appointments, implement treatment plan, maintain boundaries, evaluate progress, update treatment plan, terminate appropriately	Am I helpful? Am I competent? Do I know my own issues and not confuse them with the client's? Do I like the client? Do I like conducting therapy like this? Who am I?
Case management	(1) Formal (2) Impersonal to professionally personal (3) I-It	Provide accurate diagnosis, treatment plan, consult with community providers and agents of various kinds, broker services, determine length of service and next steps to treatment	Am I correct? Is this a waste of time? Am I competent? Am I a therapist or a case worker?
Community involvement	(1) Casual to formal (2) Superficially personal to professionally personal (3) I-It to I-Thou	Provide community resources, participate on community action committees	Am I interested? Am I a therapist, public speaker, or politician? How am I going to find time for this and everything else I have to do?
Staff relationships	(1) Casual (2) Superficially personal to authentically personal (3) I-It and I-Thou	Acknowledge one another interpersonally, provide and receive support, fulfill professional responsibilities	Am I likable and socially competent? How can I get out of this? Or, how can I get more of this? Why did I choose to do this?

Healthy functioning takes into consideration the particulars of both a person and his or her situation, and it has been described as the ability to cope with anything capturing one's attention (Crocker, 1999). Another way of saying this is that it is the awareness required to solve one's problems (Yontef, 1993). Aware functioning increases with contact at the boundary of person-in-context. So healthy functioning as an agent in a CMHO requires attending to contact as it changes with the context across levels of system.

Just as a fluid identification and fulfillment of figures is one aspect of such health, an ability to move fluidly among the various levels of system in a CMHO will enable a Gestalt therapist to maintain a healthy, vigorous, and valuable relationship to the organization. Becoming a valued part of the problem-solving processes of the organization, thus fulfilling one's responsibilities as an agent, strongly affects one's experience of self and ability to practice. Without understanding these organizational matters and system requirements, a person bent on just doing Gestalt therapy in community mental health will not fit and will usually move on for one reason or another.

KAREN: As you know, I work in a community mental health setting, and in reading your table I more fully realize the *multiplexity* of systems to which we respond.

PHIL: Supervisors could use this table to discuss performance at various levels and to break multiplexity down so as to develop capacity by supporting staff in focused areas: for instance, a supervisor discussing with supervisees the correlation between their internal dialogue in "experience of self" and their behavioral expectations in "performance demands."

KAREN: I had not thought of using your chart in supervision, but it makes sense. We operate in this vast relational field and often only explicitly think through our relationships with our clients or with our supervisees. Related to this is your observation that a therapist needs to learn skills to be able to shift in and out of different modes in the community mental health setting. I suppose this is true in an academic setting as well, where you shift from teaching, advising, to research and writing. In the community mental health setting, however, there is so much emphasis on production and doing what pays that it takes special skill and discipline to set up a schedule supporting our different activities—that is, therapy, supervision, assessment, peer review, and utilization management.

GESTALT THERAPEUTIC PROCESS IN COMMUNITY MENTAL HEALTH

A Gestalt therapist will find a few critical rivers to cross in order to make a place for his or her practice of Gestalt therapy in a community mental health setting. These include acceptable treatment planning, documentation of Gestalt therapy processes, and assimilation of evidence-based interventions. Once these have been mastered, the practice of Gestalt therapy in a CMHO flows as the natural product of finding one's place in the organization and utilizing the clinical judgment one has attained in one's Gestalt training.

Many people do not believe that Gestalt therapy is a viable, contemporary approach. Often, they are open to a colleague's justification for using Gestalt therapy and interested to even learn something about it, but sometimes the bias against Gestalt therapy among colleagues in a CMHO is so strong, a Gestalt therapist might as well move on. I have worked in both situations.

Regardless, recent research indicates that Gestalt-based, experiential therapy is as effective as cognitive-behavioral therapy for the treatment of depression and may be preferable when interpersonal issues are involved (Watson, Gordon, Stermac, Kalogerakos, & Steckley, 2003). As more research is generated, one is likely to see a corresponding rise in support for the use of Gestalt therapy. As things stand now, those who have been using Gestalt therapy in various spiritual, educational, and clinical contexts have written about their work and reported anecdotal evidence of both effectiveness and client and therapist satisfaction (Clemmens, 1997; Engle & Holiman, 2002a; Garcia, 1998; Hamilton, 1997; Imes, Rose Clance, Gailis, & Atkeson, 2002; Kepner, 1995; Mackewn, 1997; McConville, 1995; O'Leary, Sheedy, O'Sullivan, & Thoresen, 2003; Papernow, 1993; Wheeler & Backman, 1994).

I started using Gestalt therapy with dual-diagnosed patients on a locked intensive care unit at a psychiatric hospital serving substance abusers who also had diagnosed psychological disorders. Along the way, I have used Gestalt therapy with children, adolescents, families, couples, sex offenders, victims of sexual abuse, the traumatized and dissociative, the paranoid and psychotic, those diagnosed with anxiety disorders or mood disorders, and the elderly, and I have done all of this within the systems of community mental health.

In 1997 Brian O'Neill, director of a community mental health agency in Australia, started a discussion at Behavior OnLine (www.behavior.net/forums/gestalt/) regarding the use of Gestalt therapy with psychotic and bipolar clients. He and several responders provided anecdotal attestation to *their* positive experiences while using Gestalt therapy with clients diagnosed with those disorders (O'Neill, 1997). In the same year, Abraham Luchins (1997) explored the field perspective in dealing with paranoia, reflecting all the way back to Wertheimer and showing that from the beginnings of Gestalt theory the serious disorders commonly thought to reside outside the scope of Gestalt therapy have been very much within it.

With discernment in case conceptualization, diagnosis, and treatment planning, appropriate adjustments in the practice of Gestalt therapy can accommodate a variety of clinical demands. I have used Gestalt therapy in community outpatient clinics, inpatient hospitals, partial-hospitalization programs, and child and family community resource centers, as well as in the juvenile justice system. Speaking from experience, I can readily attest that *it is possible!*

I rely on three ways of working as a Gestalt therapist, alternating as the moment seems to indicate: (a) *tracking* the client's experience through a phenomenological method, (b) *connecting* with the client interpersonally through dialogue, and (c) *experimenting* to move from mere talking and knowing to experience itself in some event, some kind of behavior. Having these ways of working has provided some flexibility. Moving from one to another at choice points in therapeutic process over the years has enabled me to identify four content areas around which the work seems to organize in the figures of the client: first, *context,* the client's field; second, *individual experience,* the client's phenomenology; third, *adaptation,* the way the client chooses and adjusts in various contexts; and fourth, *holism,* a recognition that all things are related for the person of the client. Figure 14.1 contains a Gestalt theoretical matrix in which I have selected examples of these ways of working and focusing (Brownell, 2000, in press). This matrix can serve as a heuristic guide for case conceptualization and the process of therapy itself.

Ways of Working → Focuses for Work ↓	Connecting	Tracking	Experimenting
Context			
Individual Experience			
Adaptation			
Holism			

Figure 14.1 A Gestalt Theoretical Matrix

SOURCE: Adapted from Brownell (2000).

Treatment Planning

To get the job done as a Gestalt therapist, one must be able to provide competent treatment planning (Mackewn, 1997; Maruish, 2002). This requires establishing a diagnosis, writing measurable treatment goals, linking Gestalt interventions to goal attainment, expressing a strengths-based perspective, and setting up a connection between treatment planning and outcomes evaluation.

Some Gestalt therapists might wince at such things, believing that measurable goals and behavioral evaluation are not what Gestalt therapy is about. I have addressed this general concern in a different context (Brownell, 2002), but in this case it is helpful to understand that such things are precisely what community mental health is about, because it has become managed and evaluated for its effectiveness and efficiency. If one is to attempt Gestalt therapy in a community mental health setting, one must adapt one's Gestalt practice to the dynamics operating in one's field, which means that basically the CMHO will organize the Gestalt therapist, not the other way around. Does this mean that it is impossible to practice Gestalt therapy in an agency of community mental health? No. It just means that we must be flexible, creative, and less rigid with regard to our idealism. For example, even though Gestalt therapy is an elegant option for long-term work with personality disorders or the severely and persistently mentally ill (especially in processing their rehabilitative, social adjustments), funding sources, including Medicare, will not authorize long-term treatment, so one must use brief Gestalt therapy (Houston, 2003).

Diagnosis is the starting place for strategies in treatment. Put in general terms, it is the investigation of something to ascertain its nature. Specifically, it is a clinical procedure by which a therapist investigates the client as well as the product of that investigation (Yontef, 1993). The purpose is to discriminate between conditions relevant to the client, providing an assessment of the client's strengths and weaknesses. Traditionally, this sets up treatment planning and provision of services because it identifies a disorder that needs to be remedied; however, it can just as easily identify a set of assets available in a model of positive psychology. It may include psychological testing, and when it does it can utilize testing instruments focused exclusively on categories of pathology as well as those providing more dimensional scaling, resulting in a range between both pathology and health (Brownell, 2002; Sprock, 2003). These positive elements are important to note for those wishing to practice the growth approach evident in Gestalt therapy.

The diagnosis can refer to figure-ground processes and nominal categories considered to be true of the client. The first represents a fluid range of experience, whereas the second stands for a more static identity. Those in community mental health are familiar with diagnostic categories to identify diseases, deformities, injuries, and dysfunctions, but they are not so familiar with process diagnosis that observes and describes the characteristic manner in which a person does something, and they are certainly unfamiliar with the language by which a Gestalt therapist would conceive of these processes (Mackewn, 1997). The nominal categories listed in the *Diagnostic and Statistical Manual of Mental Disorders* (*DSM*) are constructed around criteria sets, and they conform to the traditional method established and followed by all systems of medical diagnosis (American Psychiatric Association, 2000). The process diagnoses inherent in Gestalt therapy have not been so clearly delineated but have been addressed by Melnick and Nevis (1992), Shub (1992), Yontef (1993), Mackewn (1997), and Greenberg (2002), among others. They identify how a person self-regulates in the approach to performance demands, identifying and accomplishing goals, making decisions, consummating or interrupting contact in relation to others, managing life, and interpreting experience.

A dimensional perspective is inherent to process diagnosis. Dimensional scaling in assessment has been shown to be as valid as categorical methods (Costa & Widiger, 1994; Sprock, 2003); however, thus far, dimensional approaches have not become widely utilized by clinicians. Here is an opportunity for Gestalt therapists to contribute to the discipline of clinical psychology if they assimilate dimensional assessment procedures and adopt and document dimensional methods more purposefully, more rigorously, and with greater understanding. Actually, because of the needs of CMHOs to track and document progress in treatment outcomes, Gestalt therapists who practice in community settings are particularly positioned to accomplish this very thing.

Gestalt therapists must become proficient at the use of the *DSM* without losing their Gestalt distinctiveness in order to conduct mental health evaluations; indeed, the establishment of a *DSM* diagnosis is the basic starting point in case management and provision of services, and without this a therapist choosing to use the Gestalt approach will not be allowed to proceed to case conceptualization according to a process model. Yet, to practice Gestalt therapy, a clinician must be able to evaluate the client's phenomenology, relationships, and patterned behavior. As Jennifer Mackewn (1997) spoke of this, one needs to be flexible in Gestalt diagnosis so as to be able to move from contact styles in the moment-to-moment process to familiar patterns (fixed gestalts and structured ground) relevant to a client's field. Elinor Greenberg (2002) described how the different personality disorders, for instance, can be distinguished from each other by the characteristic ways people have of relating to their interpersonal wishes and fears, thus organizing their interpersonal fields. These are the kinds of distinctions that set Gestalt-based, process diagnosis apart from *DSM*-based categorical diagnosis, but both are necessary, and each sets up diverse, yet important treatment strategies that can be written down in the treatment plan and evaluated in outcome research.

Treatment goals identify symptoms or situations that will change in some observable way, by some measurable amount, and by a certain time. They are figures of interest for the client. Though the client may begin in therapy without much clarity regarding these figures, the Gestalt therapist can utilize phenomenological methods, coupled with experiment, to bring them into more clarity. This will facilitate not only the writing of important treatment goals but also the achievement of positive outcomes. When people have clear figures for why they are in therapy, they achieve more positive gains. Poor outcomes in family therapy, for instance, are thought to result from disparate or foggy figures among family members regarding why they came for therapy in the first place (Yeh & Weisz, 2001). Thus treatment goals can be thought of as aspects of a budget; one has only so many sessions available, and by a certain time, having spent a certain number of meetings, both therapist and client estimate that they will achieve something. They will spend time and effort to "purchase" results. Perhaps a somewhat more Gestalt-friendly way of thinking about this is to wish something good for the client; treatment goals are one's good wishes, and Gestalt therapists can help make them more clear from the very beginning by helping the various people involved identify what is figural for them, how that interacts with others' figures, and the ways in which such awareness might be put to good use (Nevis, 1987; Papernow, 1993).

Treatment goals are more than mere wishes, however, because both therapist and client will try to work toward them, and the way in which they will work, what they will do in the effort to achieve them, composes the interventions that will be utilized. Gestalt therapists need to operationalize Gestalt therapy theory in order to indicate what they will actually do in the effort to obtain their good wishes, and they need to give what they are doing a name that will stand for the operation in question. An example might be the *Gestalt dialogues* employed by Leslie Greenberg and his associates in helping clients work through their unfinished business of forgiveness (Greenberg & Malcolm, 2002). One might use *experiments* to provide in-session experiences that develop self-understanding and help clients choose actions to reach identified goals (Engle & Holiman, 2002b). Other examples might be the use of *phenomenological tracking* to increase the client's awareness of angry responses or the *experimental use of homework* to increase the client's investment in the process of therapy.

Though one cannot actually predict the direction of the results of any given Gestalt intervention, one can write treatment goals that describe Gestalt processes, and this can be done using Gestalt constructs. Gestalt therapy involves training in a way of living and relating, experiencing life, and interpreting experience. Several Gestalt therapy terms derive from our history and theoretical development (see Chapters 1–6), some of which are grounded in somewhat esoteric philosophical traditions. These terms are used by Gestalt therapists to refer to a range of meaning and a continuum of application in practice (Brownell, 2003). In turn, Gestalt constructs need to be fleshed out in behavior and described in common language so that other people will know what is being attempted, the good wishes to which they are connected, and the nature of that connection.

Treatment planning in many CMHOs is often a contradiction. On the one hand, they espouse a preference for strengths-based treatment goals and the avoidance of pathological, deficit-based labels, but on the other hand they are required to operate within the structure of the American Psychiatric Association's (2000) *Diagnostic and Statistical Manual (DSM-IV-TR)* and to utilize symptom/deficit-reducing treatment goals rooted in behavioral interventions. This is a polarity most clinicians do not actually resolve. Pragmatically, before funding can take place, every client must have a *DSM* diagnosis, which establishes a baseline of disorder, including negative symptoms and loss of function, so writing strengths-based treatment goals is counterintuitive.

Many clinicians compartmentalize the need to diagnose, maintaining the polarity instead of resolving it through an investigation of the ground between strengths and weaknesses. Here is where a Gestalt therapist can utilize Gestalt theory to an advantage, for Gestalt practitioners are trained to experiment with holding both ends of a polarity in order to explore what exists in the "between." The challenge comes in finding language that expressly addresses the connection between strengths and weaknesses, assets and deficits. The ability to write a treatment plan demonstrating the synthesis in question puts a Gestalt therapist on solid ground as therapy proceeds. Indeed, having Gestalt therapy woven naturally and essentially into the fabric of the treatment plan legitimizes the use of Gestalt therapy during review and reauthorization of services.

Assimilation of Evidence-Based Interventions

Assimilation is not simple eclecticism; it is not a matter of adding a few interventions gleaned from another therapist's practice. It involves case conceptualization according to a theoretical model. For example, what are called objects in object relations theory, or automatic thoughts in cognitive-behavioral therapy, are seen as topdog-underdog self dialogues in a Gestalt therapy approach (Webb, Stiles, & Greenberg, 2003). When assimilation moves into practice, a therapist understands how the method of an intervention accomplishes clinical objectives in keeping with a particular therapeutic theory and then implements a similar technique but in accordance with his or her own theoretical orientation. What is called empty chair work in Gestalt therapy is called rational-emotional role play in cognitive-behavioral therapy (Simos, Simos, & Beck, 2002); yet in each case these are assimilations and not mere eclectic adoptions because they are consistent with a respective clinical theory. Such an assimilative approach absorbs practices with established theory (Greenberg & Brownell,

KAREN: In regard to assimilating interventions, I would be interested in examples of how you "break down and assimilate CBT (cognitive behavior therapy) into an expanded Gestalt approach." Are you moving from CBT to Gestalt?

PHIL: I was not thinking of moving from an established and comprehensive CBT approach. Rather, I contemplated "evidence-based" practice as often conducted, which amounts to picking from research projects or lists of best practices to piece together a number of interventions, each having some empirical support. However, if a Gestalt therapist wants to expand his or her practice by assimilating a few "best practices," then CBT is a good place to start. I think an example of this is Iris Fodor's (1998) article in *Gestalt Review* about working with schemas in the "dance" of meaning making. Another example might be using reframing or counterfactual thinking, but doing so as experiment and approaching these interventions as preliminary to a phenomenological inquiry following the reframing event or counterfactual consideration.

1997), expanding one's clinical range while maintaining the integrity of one's theoretical base.

This is what Gestalt therapists, in general, must learn to do. Thus, if a client is feeling particularly disappointed because his girlfriend left him, one can suggest reframing that as an opportunity for more freedom and opportunities to meet other people. As a cognitive therapist, the suggestion might be made to produce a change in the client's cognitive map, to brighten his thinking and subsequently lighten his affect, and the therapist might have the direction of such change in mind from the beginning. Such would be the result expected. A Gestalt therapist, by contrast, might ask, "What happens if you think of it this way?" It becomes an experiment in which the therapist cannot predict change but invites the client to pay attention to his experience when he thinks of the situation in that novel fashion. In both cases a cognitive reframing takes place, but the process around its implementation may be quite different. Assimilated by Gestalt theory, such remapping can lead in various directions, as the awareness of the client touches on influences from the past perceived to be present in the current interaction, figures associated with the person of the therapist or the feel of the client's contact in the moment, creative adjustments the client may choose, or threats from imagined consequences in the future. In all of these, the Gestalt therapist invites paying attention to the process, as it unfolds around the use of the intervention, and chooses to follow the work relying on his or her understanding of Gestalt therapy theory.

Each Gestalt practitioner needs to be able to operationalize what is done so that he or she can put that into a treatment plan, but the overall and comprehensive map of one's total Gestalt system will surely differ from one person to another. I may do something I call "phenomenological inquiry" or something else I call "dialogical support," but I will use those things to accomplish various purposes when the situational unit seems to call for it, and that will depend on field forces present at various choice points in the process. I need to be able to describe these Gestalt interventions in ways that relate them to established research and best practices and to anticipate the need for them in the therapeutic process I see ahead as I meet with the client to construct a treatment plan.

Because community mental health relies so much on empirical support and evidence-based clinical interventions, it is wise for Gestalt therapists to routinely consult research literature that supports our approach. It helps to be conversant with "best practices" and to carry out aggressive assimilations of these findings in order to create acceptable treatment plans and documentation pleasing to the organization. The upside of this is that such information helps expand Gestalt practice.

Documentation of Gestalt Therapy Processes

This subject corresponds with that of writing treatment goals around an assimilative practice; one must learn how to document what one does in terms of Gestalt therapy theory, but in keeping with customary documentation procedures. It is very important to maintain the integrity of the organization, prevent paybacks when auditing sources call for accountability, and furnish a record of services provided. However, more to the point for a Gestalt therapist in a CMHO is the ability to describe Gestalt therapy process in very direct and behavioral ways, providing the operational definition of Gestalt therapy as it plays out in the life of therapist and client.

Clinical Judgment in the Application of Gestalt Theory

Clinical judgment will call for a focused use of the phenomenological method in order to clarify treatment issues, a strategy of working the field so as to change the context of the client, a flexible application of dialogical principles to purposefully distinguish I-Thou from I-It contact, and an expanded use of experiment so as to stimulate awareness and creative adjustment.

The use of the phenomenological method to clarify clinical figures of interest has already been addressed. Beyond that, however, it is an exquisite way to provide the client something he or she rarely gets in the typical, much less purely cognitive behavioral world. That is because the phenomenological method integrates the body and the mind through observation and description of the whole person in action, as present to the therapist. Ironically, the usual feedback I have received by applying it is that I make the client *think.* What clients mean is that I come to them with questions and statements, all rooted in simple observation and description of what they are doing, and my statements stimulate their reflection. They usually find this approach very fresh and, even though sometimes challenging, solid. They experience the sense that they are actually getting somewhere because, through being described, they obtain a new experience of themselves. This is consistent with Gestalt's use of paradox, helping clients get in touch with who they are, supporting and challenging them to be present with themselves, not trying to get them to be something they are not—in other words, getting somewhere by not running away.

Working the field can be thought of as touching on developmental aspects in the client's current process. However, and especially in community mental health with children and families, working the field means changing something in the general context of the client. This might be accomplished by meeting with the team of faculty and administration at a child's school, referring a client for a psychiatric evaluation and medication management, arranging for the client to attend a Dialectical Behavior Therapy group, setting up services for the client in the community, or doing couples therapy with a child's parents. It is an indirect move aimed at bringing something new into the client's context, based on the realization that when something new enters the field of the client it will effect an adjustment.

Gestalt therapists in the decades of the 1980s and 1990s came alive to the significance of dialogue. Though dialogue had been in the theory from the beginning, it gained in emphasis during these years. The I-Thou moment became a prized trophy, often stalked even though the very attempt to attain it prevented it from happening. Corresponding to this, the I-It interactions were relegated to a second-class status, and that is unfortunate, because very much of the therapy in a CMHO is aimed at getting something accomplished; it is goal oriented. Others have extolled the value of the I-Thou interaction, and it is essential, but the practical value of learning skills should not be lost. In community mental health, taking care of business has many practical rewards and often creates a structure in which the I-Thou moment can occasionally take place and be experienced against a solid background of support.

This accompanies the expanded use of experiment, for the process of learning a new skill is a series of experiments. In fact, any behavioral component in therapy can be seen as an experiment as long as the therapist gives the client (and him- or herself) permission for the result to go in any direction that it goes. There is no failure in experiment—only more experience to explore.

CONCLUSION

KAREN: I have enjoyed reading your responses, Phil, and thinking through my own. Because of this conversation I plan to apply some of your suggestions for supervision, and I will continue to think through our treatment planning. Thank you.

Gestalt therapy in the hands of a trained Gestalt therapist can be an especially effective tool for the work of community mental health. That is because it has built into its essential theoretical development the very concerns that were at the core of the origin of community mental health. Gestalt therapy brings together an appreciation of the person-in-context, the relationship between self and other, and an essential respect for the whole person's individual experience, which includes what they do as well as what they think and how they feel. Gestalt therapy also places a high value on the experience of the therapist, and the therapist-in-context, which means an understanding of how public policy and the organizational health of any given CMHO affect clinical processes.

REVIEW QUESTIONS

1. What has prompted the change in terminology from patients/clients being referred to as consumers and the practice of counseling or psychotherapy being called delivery of a product?

2. Why might it be useful for a clinician working in a community mental health system to be familiar with Gestalt applications in the field of organizational development (as discussed in Chapter 13)?

3. Identify and define at least six roles or responsibilities of the clinician within the context of the community mental health system.

4. Using the roles noted in your response to review item #3, explain how each role may evoke an I-It or I-Thou relationship.

5. How is the process of treatment planning often experienced as conflictual for Gestalt therapists working in the community mental health setting?

6. Discuss how case conceptualization and clinical methodology relate to the assimilation of evidence-based interventions in Gestalt practice.

EXPERIENTIAL PEDAGOGICAL ACTIVITIES

ACTIVITY 1: Divide into groups of three or four. Using the table in the chapter, fill in the squares of the grid with the various kinds of interactions that students experience in their graduate or training program. Present your grid to the other groups, and follow up with class discussion.

ACTIVITY 2: Divide the class into two sides and hold an impromptu debate, pro and con, on the following proposition: Public policy is destroying community mental health.

ACTIVITY 3: Treatment plans for clients seen in the community mental health setting are typically expected to follow a strengths-based model, while including a *DSM* diagnosis. Practice writing such treatment plans for your current cases or for cases with which you possess some familiarity. Design a treatment plan that merges a strengths-based approach, Gestalt principles, and a *DSM* diagnosis. Share the treatment plans in small groups, and have members compare/contrast and discuss any differences.

ACTIVITY 4: The clearest research support being generated for Gestalt therapy and its efficacy can be found in the activities of Professor Leslie Greenberg at York University, Toronto, Ontario, and his colleagues. It can be referenced in literature searches under his name or under the subjects of "process-experiential" or "emotion-focused" work. Do a literature search for this research on PsycInfo or through a search engine like Google. Select an interesting article, and then summarize its content and value in Gestalt practice for class discussion. As a group, create a short bibliography of evidenced-based practices consistent with Gestalt therapy.

ACTIVITY 5: Create a list of potential research projects that might extend the base of evidence in support of Gestalt therapy. In this list include research questions and any operational definitions that might be useful.

ACTIVITY 6: Divide into pairs in which one person takes the role of a therapist and the other a consumer. The therapist utilizes a phenomenological method to clarify and articulate what the consumer wants to achieve as a student in the class. As a pair, identify two problems/goals and develop interventions that can be articulated in terms of Gestalt therapy theory (as each student best understands it). Share in class discussion what it was like to attempt this. For reference to Gestalt methodology, use the theoretical matrix in Figure 14.1 to help in choice points during the process, and, if you need to, refer to the text of this chapter and other chapters in the book for expanded descriptions of these tenets.

CHAPTER 15

Gestalt Approaches to Substance Use/Abuse/Dependency: Theory and Practice

MICHAEL CRAIG CLEMMENS

DIALOGUE RESPONDENT: HELGA MATZKO

Michael Craig Clemmens is a licensed psychologist in Pittsburgh, Pennsylvania, working with individuals, couples, and groups, and is senior faculty of the Gestalt Institute of Cleveland's Center for Clinical Theory and Practice. His 20-plus years of working with chemical dependency and personality disorders provided ample experience to write *Getting Beyond Sobriety: Clinical Approaches to Long-Term Recovery* (1997), plus book chapters and journal articles on the subject. He uses his interest and training in Gestalt body/somatic therapy to augment his interest in consulting with therapists to develop and maintain self-support.

Helga Matzko is the founder and director of the Gestalt Institute of Rhode Island. She is prominent in the New England area for her dynamic workshops on Gestalt therapy with addicted clients. She has authored professional articles on her Gestalt-oriented treatment of chemically dependent persons, called the Multiphasic Transformation Process. Her most recent contribution is the development of a training DVD, entitled *Synthesis of Dialectical Behavior Therapy (DBT) and Therapeutic Community Treatment (TCT) for Addiction/Mental Health Troubled Clients: DVD Training Video and Manual* (2003).

Gestalt therapy focuses on patterns of human experience and the field context in which these experiences occur. It is the belief of Gestalt therapists that behavior is both uniquely individual and inseparable from the relationships and the world surrounding the individual (Parlett, 2000). So too, the drug user exists not in isolation but in continual interplay with the field, however intoxicated and seemingly "alone" he or she may feel.

The field is the ground in the moment (Wheeler, 1991). The field is the present context. The field is those aspects of ground that exist in the present. For the drug user the field conditions might include the present physical environment, such as music playing in the room, the presence of others who are using drugs, and emotional or physical states (anger, sadness, feeling "hung over").

HELGA: Michael, I admire your work with addictions and feel privileged to be included in this dialogue process with you. Our approaches are rather out of the mainstream of treatments offered, and we both know how effective and respectful (and often lonely) our phenomenological approaches can be.

MICHAEL: I remember a time when working in a detoxification unit late at night when I felt the loneliness that you speak of here. I also appreciate your work and all that has gone before us in working with drug use. It is easier to just decide and categorize people, but this approach (our approach) requires truly "being with" another human being who happens to live in relation to drugs.

The progression from drug use to abuse and dependency is related to the person's capacity to interact with others and his or her ability to tolerate sensations such as frustration, anger, and fear (Clemmens, 1997). To understand and treat the drug user's process, we must apply and utilize an approach that allows for an observational and a phenomenological perspective. Gestalt therapy focuses on the patterns or processes of a client's behavior while valuing their meaning for the client.

This chapter moves from an overview of the continuum of drug use, abuse, and dependency (addiction) to an outline of Gestalt theoretical and treatment approaches to substance use, abuse, and dependency and then closes with a discussion of recovery from substance dependency.

OVERVIEW OF SUBSTANCE USE, ABUSE, AND DEPENDENCY

The range of treatments historically applied to drug use range from 12-step programs to hydrotherapy (hosing patients with alternate hot and cold power hoses). Treatment interventions have also included the use of prefrontal lobotomies, convulsive therapies, hypnosis, tranquilizers, LSD, carbon dioxide, therapeutic communities (e.g., Synanon, Daytop), religious conversion (e.g., Christian groups, Nation of Islam), psychoanalysis, Rational Recovery, nutritional treatments, and many more (W. White, 1999). The most well-known treatment programs have been the 12-step programs: Alcoholics Anonymous (AA) (2001) and Narcotics Anonymous (NA) (1988).

Psychotherapists frequently can see the impact of alcohol and drug use gone awry. Domestic violence–fractured family systems, drug-induced depression and other affective disorders, financial conflicts, and loss of income are often related to the drug use of one or more members of a family system. Corporations have developed Employee Assistance Programs to support workers whose alcohol or other drug use affects the company. All levels of public employees (e.g., airline pilots, police personnel, physicians, fire workers) have contracts that provide for their potential impairment by drugs. This sensitization and mobilization reflects our cultural awareness that alcohol and other drug use can be problematic and socially destructive. Modern responses to alcohol and other drug use, from that of AA to, more recently, that of the American Psychiatric Association and the World Health Organization, have identified its extreme forms as a disease. In a framework borrowed from religious and disease models, alcohol and drug use has been viewed as an "either/or" phenomenon: Either you are a "social user" or you are an "addict" or "alcoholic." This dichotomous diagnosis has been useful in helping to identify the addict.

Recently, the *Diagnostic and Statistical Manual of Mental Disorders: DSM-IV-TR* (American Psychiatric Association, 2000) has distinguished between *substance abuse* and *substance dependency,* with the latter fitting the traditional description of addiction or alcoholism. Substance abuse is less severe in the impact on the individual's functioning. This distinction has been useful because in the past substance abusers sometimes received inappropriate treatment based on the substance dependence model. Treatment facilities are designed to treat, not the range of alcohol and drug behaviors presented, but only those that fit the classic definition of "addict." This may account for many of the "false positives"—that is, individuals who were diagnosed and treated as if they were more progressed, and in some cases as if drug use were their primary treatment need.

THE CONTINUUM OF SUBSTANCE USE

Disease is a medical and epidemiological term. It is a view of human behavior from the perspective of illness and its patterns in a population. From this macro perspective, we focus on the pathways of a disease. If we are to work with individuals, couples, and families embroiled in problematic drug use, our focus needs to be on the experience itself. From this perspective, how is using the drug useful, or what function does it serve for the user? Our perspective then becomes the functionality of behavior. This is a key ingredient of Gestalt therapy, that all behavior has some intrinsic function or purpose. Put simply, all behaviors serve a function for the individual, and therefore change processes must include an appreciation of that function. I emphasize that change in dependent or addictive behavior can occur only if the individual is interested in changing. It is not enough that we, as observers, can chart all the symptoms of substance dependence in our client. He or she may continue in this behavior because, as a client pointed out to me, "It works for me!" As a Gestalt therapist, I am interested in how or in what ways the behavior works and does not work for my client. Because drugs affect the entire system—physical, emotional, and cognitive functioning—I am especially interested in how use of the chemical regulates or modulates one's physical, emotional, and cognitive experiences: that is, how the use of alcohol or other drugs decreases certain sensations or emotions, relaxes the person's body, and even creates different thought patterns. An example of this might be a student who smokes a "joint" or drinks a little before an examination to decrease his or her anxiety.

Rather than relying on a dichotomous division of "normal users" versus "addicts," we can look at drug/alcohol ingestion along a continuum. The continuum begins with *substance use,* followed by *substance abuse* in the middle of the continuum and *substance dependence* at the far extreme. In all of these modes, the individual is using the substance to modulate sensations and/or influence feelings and behaviors. The movement from use to abuse to dependence accounts for the dominance of drug-using behavior and its disruption of everyday life. As the user becomes more dependent, the primary relationship is between the person and the drug, and all other relational experiences become secondary or irrelevant (Clemmens, 1993, 1997; J. R. White, 1999).

Following the continuum in Figure 15.1, we can see that in *substance use* the basic processes of managing self and interacting with others are intact. The person's drug use is just another aspect of his or her life, finding expression in recreational/social use, and is a creative adjustment in his or her field. "Using" does not negatively affect the person's relational or occupational functioning. In the next stage, *substance abuse,* the drug becomes "the cure," and intoxication becomes intentional. Though we summarily call this substance abuse, it is not so much the chemical that is abused as one's relational and occupational functioning. As people begin to abuse drugs, their style of interacting with others and managing self may become extreme. This often represents a lack of self-support or emotional/affective struggles. The roots of a potential substance dependency style are present in this pattern. In the next stage, *substance dependency,* the person is engaged in a process that is the main focus of his

Stage of Dependency	Behavior	Figure Dominance	Functioning
Substance use	Creative adjusting, recreational use for relaxation and enjoyment or coping	Drug use is not the dominant figure, enjoyment is figural, intoxication is rare	Relational or occupational functioning is not affected by drug use
↕	↕	↕	↕
Substance abuse	Avoidance of sensation or uncomfortable feelings	Some social using but intoxication is more frequently the intention. Heavy partying is figural	Relational and/or occupational functioning are often affected by frequent use/abuse
↓	↓	↓	↓
Substance dependency Alcoholism and/or Drug Addiction	Maintenance use Self-destructive behavior, broken patterns, collapse	Intoxication is the dominant figure Diminishing new figures as inebriation is fixed figure	Relational and occupational functioning are noticeably impaired Dysfunctional in relations and occupation

Figure 15.1 The Continuum of Substance Use, Abuse, and Dependency

or her life. A behavior that may have been functional and a creative adjustment at some point is now reducing and inhibiting relational and occupational functioning. Substance dependency eventually is neither creative nor an adjustment. The dependent user behaves in a habitual pattern with little or no awareness and has to adjust the rest of his or her world and self around the drug use.

The differences between the three rows on the left are more process and behavioral than quantitative. The substance-dependent person has a different process with the drug. The average drug user functions on an everyday basis. He or she goes to work, engages in meaningful relationships, and is able to take or leave the drug. The drug and its resulting intoxication is not the dominant figure in his or her life. Some individuals begin to use drugs in college or the military, become more drug abusive, and later return to normal drug use. Other people seem to move quickly from use to dependence on a rather steep curve. And still others become chemically dependent immediately; in the recovering community, they are described as "instant alcoholics."

Referring back to Figure 15.1, note that the arrows between the first and second rows go both ways, illustrating the movement or progression between use and abuse, which is common during adolescence, stressful situations, and life changes. There are many clinical examples of this occurrence. However, it appears to be much less common for individuals in a drug-dependent process to return to substance use, or "normal" drug use. This has been debated in research (Pendery, Maltzman, & West, 1982; Sobell & Sobell, 1978). Though some study findings support chemically dependent people reverting to normal use, the preponderance of research on "controlled drinking" does not support these claims (W. White, 1999).

HELGA: My 20 years of clinical experience have taught me that most "addicted" individuals have experienced trauma, deprivation, and neglect to various degrees and have learned to organize their experience around avoiding the deep well of pain and shame that has accumulated in their lives. Once clients are made aware of how they slowly found their way into addiction or substance abuse, they feel tremendous relief, since their behaviors begin to make sense to them. This approach does not foster excuses and blaming; rather, it provides an "aha" experience and an unveiling appreciation of one's personal wisdom, self-regulation, and integrity. It helps lay the foundation for the co-creation of our therapeutic experience. In addition, I gain an immediate, if basic, sense of my client's available skills to regulate affect, skills of self-care, and ability to tolerate relationships—an invaluable tool, even if perceptions require modifications thereafter. As long as I can keep clients involved in their process, they will remain interested.

MICHAEL: I agree, as I have stated previously (Clemmens, 1993, 1997), that addiction is a developed contact style, a way of managing one's experience that develops over time in relation to both environmental and physiological/emotional conditions. Where I differ from the commentary is the timing of focusing on these roots of the pattern. My view is that the timing of attention to these early life patterns depends on the individual and his or her stage of recovery.

THE PROCESS OF FIGURE FORMATION

Gestalt therapy is based on the view that the individual is constantly responding to his or her internal sensations and the field in which he or she exists. The individual's primary orienting principle is organismic self-regulation—attending to primary needs and adjusting behavior to meet those needs (Perls, Hefferline, & Goodman, 1951). Perception of needs is based on the figure/ground phenomenon (Kepner & Brien, 1970).

Perceptual experience is organized in a relationship of ground (background) and figure (foreground: i.e., whatever we are focusing on at any given moment). What becomes figural out of ground varies according to our need in the moment. The individual attends to sensations, which support his or her need at any given moment. As these sensations become sharper, an awareness of need begins to emerge, or, as we say, becomes figural. This process of self-regulation moving smoothly is a continuum of experience as depicted in Figure 15.2, also represented in our literature as the cycle of experience (Carlock, Glaus, & Shaw, 1992; Kepner, 1987).

Figure 15.2 contains a description of the uninterrupted development of sensation, awareness, action, satisfaction, and integration. This process can serve as a template for experience. Clearly, not all experience is uninterrupted or as full and satisfying as this example indicates. Individuals develop patterns or styles that uniquely influence their typical and immediate patterns. The cycle or pattern of their experience will vary according to contact episodes and circumstances. This is a momentary snapshot of the individual experiencing his or her process behavior at this moment. Individuals interrupt or modify the emergence of these figures. People who become dependent upon chemical substances learn to interrupt other needs and sensations, and they experience the need to be intoxicated as a constant figure.

HELGA: Gestalt therapy has as its basic premise the concept of self-regulation in the context of the environment. All creative adjustments serve that purpose, and therefore the adjusted behaviors have meaning and purpose for each individual, whether or not they make sense to anyone else. Adjustments also require support from the environment to continue.

MICHAEL: There is so much variation among individuals. I work with these factors at different stages in treatment. If the client continues to use, the process of intoxication and avoidance continues during the therapy. Frequently clients are desensitized (less able to feel) due to their history of drug use. So the creative adjustment of using drugs can impede clients' attempts to experience themselves.

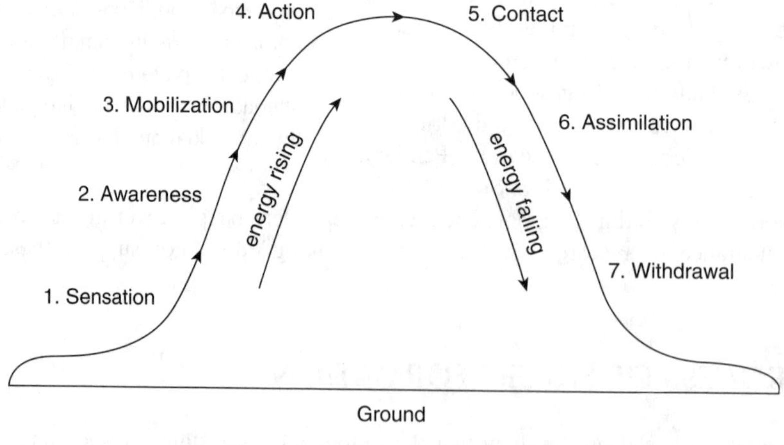

Figure 15.2 Figure Formation as a Continuum of Experience: Figure Emerges out of Ground and Recedes to Ground

GESTALT APPROACHES TO WORKING WITH THE CLIENT

In each of the case examples in this chapter, I will describe four Gestalt approaches in working with the client. These are (a) co-assessment or development of the client's interest/figure, (b) experimentation, (c) meaning making, and (d) the dialogic relationship.

1. *Co-assessment* is the collaborative discussion and attention that both the therapist and the client(s) direct toward the client's functioning and interest. This approach is different from one in which the therapist is a detached observer who arrives at assessment or diagnosis by him- or herself. Part of the co-assessment process is determining the type of treatment needed for the client, such as the need for detoxification.
2. *Experimentation* is a hallmark of Gestalt therapy (Zinker, 1977) through which the client experiences the dilemma in the present rather than just talking about a problem. The therapist's role is one of guide and partner who may see aspects of the client's experience or behavior to add to the experience. The therapist is attending to the ground. An example of such experimentation would be to put the alcohol or other drug in an empty chair and to have the client dialogue with the drug. Such an experiment would support the client to "own" and integrate his or her drug-using behavior and its function in his or her life.
3. *Meaning Making* is the process whereby clients make sense or develop understanding of what they have experienced in the experiment and the session. Relating back to the cycle of experience (Figure 15.2), meaning making occurs in the second half of the cycle as an individual is assimilating and withdrawing from a contact experience.
4. *Dialogic Relationship* is the interactive, respectful use of oneself as a therapist and participant in the sessions with the client. At the core of Gestalt therapy is the relationship between the therapist and the client. This relationship, at its best, has a quality of appreciation of the client as a whole person. Rather than "figuring out" the client or reducing the client to a diagnostic category to be worked on (Hycner & Jacobs, 1995), the therapist tries to understand him or her and to be in contact together. This relationship creates a context in which techniques such as experiments can flow out of a genuine interest and spontaneity. Therefore, in the Gestalt approach described here, the therapist's behavior, feelings, and meaning to the client are crucial aspects of the healing process. To appreciate the uniqueness of the other person, my client, I attempt to suspend my knowledge about people in general and my client in particular. I think of this as trying to become curious about the client's experience and the meaning he or she is making.

SUBSTANCE USE

Gestalt Theory and Substance Use

Substance use can be a form of creative adjustment. A drink at the beginning of a party (cocktails) loosens the inhibitions of the group, allowing people to become uninhibited. Loosening inhibitions is one of the effects of the drug alcohol. Using Novocain numbs the gum, thus allowing the toothache sufferer to manage or modulate the pain. A strong cup of coffee in the morning is used by many people to "get going," the effects of the drug caffeine modulating any sense of fatigue or sluggishness. These are examples of common socially acceptable ways that we use drugs to adjust to our sensations. There is no limitation in functioning; the person can choose to use the drug or not with little difficulty.

The importance of the drug and/or intoxication is substantially the same as that of any other interest. The individual may enjoy a drink with her meal or smoke some marijuana at a concert as part of a day filled with other activities. Returning to the figure formation model, the figure of the drug naturally emerges within the context of daily behavior and does not dominate the person's awareness. The use of the drug is not symptomatic of some pattern or style; sometimes, to paraphrase Freud, "a beer is just a beer."

Gestalt Treatment of Substance Use

Because clients' substance use is not figural for them or the therapist, it rarely becomes the focus of therapy. Sometimes clients may have developed some concerns about their substance use, based on what they have read or been told by others. The following case example illustrates such a situation and the Gestalt approaches in working with this client and substance use.

Case Example—John

John was a client whose father literally drank himself to death. John would feel guilty every time he took a drink. As we explored this in our sessions, he talked about reading a book on children of alcoholics. What John took from this book was that if he felt guilty when he drank he "was an alcoholic." I asked John if he could pay attention to what effects he experienced after he drank: In particular, did he want to drink more? Did he feel he lost control or became intoxicated? I did this because John did not trust his own experience; instead, he trusted something someone else had told him. For the next 3 months, John focused more on other issues in life. We looked at these other issues and his process of swallowing or "introjecting" statements or feelings that other people made "as if" they were true. My approach with John was to encourage him to explore how he knew something to be true about him.

After 3 months, John began a session by laughing. I asked him what was so funny. He said he had had another date where he had left his only drink half-empty after an entire evening. This was the third time he had done this in the last month. John said he was amused at how different his behavior was from his father's but that he still worried that somehow he was an alcoholic. I then asked John to imagine his father drinking, and he closed his eyes and sat quietly for a few minutes. John now looked tearful and said, "My drinking is nothing like his—he never left a drop and ended up smashed every time he drank!" What became figural for John was not his drinking but his fear that he would be like his father. My sense was that John had swallowed or internalized his father's behavior "as if" it were his own. He was also able to experience his sadness from witnessing his father's drunkenness. The last focus of John's therapy was on developing skills to discriminate his own experience from that of others.

John's story is not unusual in our culture of self-help books and prescriptive TV doctors. He tended to attribute information to himself without discrimination. In our addiction-focused culture, many people seem to worry that they may have some sort of disease. This case illustrates the Gestalt approach to working with substance use through building the client's awareness. The following is a description of the Gestalt approaches I used with John.

Co-assessment: Co-assessment involved developing the client's initial interest and sensations. We did this through collaborative dialogue on what interested John or "stood out" for him as opposed to my beginning with an agenda or plan. We began with him talking about and feeling his feelings of guilt and fear that he might be an alcoholic like his father. I did not offer any opinion to him as to whether that was true. Instead, I explored his experience as the starting point, following his interest. In this sense we were co-assessing what the focus or nature of his figure was for the therapy.

Experimentation: Experimenting provides clients with a pathway to answer their own questions. The experiments John tried, at my suggestion, were to observe and experience his own drinking behavior over time for numerous trials and to picture his father drinking. He used his awareness from these experiments to conclude that he did not drink like his father but that he was very concerned about being like him. His other awareness was how profoundly affected he had been by his father's behavior.

I chose to encourage John to experiment with his experience, rather than perhaps giving him a checklist of the characteristics of alcoholism, for two reasons. First, he had already talked about taking in from others definitions of his behavior. I did not want to replicate that pattern by giving him more to swallow. Second, by learning to explore his own experience directly, John could develop this skill and apply it to his everyday functioning.

Meaning Making: Throughout any experience, and notably at the end of a cycle, people make meaning by understanding, integrating, and internalizing this experience. Meaning making is a result and a part of ongoing experience. We are always making meaning of our experience (Kepner & Brien, 1970). In working with clients, my role as a Gestalt therapist is both to support their meaning and to help them devise supports to make fuller and richer meanings out of fuller and richer sensations and awareness. In these experiments, John made his own meanings out of his experience. He began to understand that he was not alcoholic and that he felt unfinished with his father. I did not interpret this to John but supported him to come to his own conclusion through attention to his process.

Dialogic Relationship: What occurred between John and me was a collaboration based on my trusting of his capacity to "know his truth." I did not offer some definition of his behavior but rather stayed with him and his experience of sorting through what was his father's and what was his own. This sense of tracking allowed me to focus on what the problem was and to stay in relation to what John experienced.

SUBSTANCE ABUSE

Gestalt Theory of Substance Abuse

From my perspective as a Gestalt therapist I have observed five developmental stages of accommodating behavior that become habitual. The stages, which develop as the drug or alcohol use and dependence become more severe, are (a) avoidance of sensation/discomfort, (b) maintenance using, (c) diminishing new figures, (d) unfinished business, and (e) collapse. As you read on in this chapter, you will see how the stages are inserted into the descriptions of the various levels of dependence/addiction.

Stage 1 of what may become a dominance of the drug in the individual's process in the world is *Avoidance of Sensation/Discomfort.* Although individuals who are merely using a substance may occasionally do so partly to avoid sensation or discomfort, abuse involves a pattern of reliance on the substance primarily for this purpose. This may be the early development of substance dependence. As the individual begins to use drugs more frequently, the figure of the drug and intoxication dominates awareness. The abuser may use socially (with others), but his or her intention is the drug effect, with social interactions being secondary. An example of this is the man who goes to a party to meet women and who ends up drinking all night. When he has become intoxicated enough he tries to "find someone," but often it is too late, or he may not be attractive in his drugged state.

Initially, taking a drink or drug modifies awareness, such as awareness of discomfort when meeting people. The normal excitement of initial contact is reduced. Each drug has a particular effect on the user; this effect is what the user feels, not the excitement of normal life. The stimulating effect of drugs such as cocaine and amphetamines is a pharmacologically induced excitement. What the person does not feel are the usual sensations we feel when beginning an experience. This interruption of contact can occur between sensation and awareness (see Figure 15.2) so that the person barely feels anxiety; alternatively, a person may drink at the mobilization/action phase so that drugs are substituted for talking to others. Drinking then serves the additional purpose of "something to do." This can be a large attraction for adolescents and young adults who frequently experience themselves as "bored" and having "nothing to do." Intoxication can provide the stimulation that they may be struggling to develop for themselves.

An example of using drugs to avoid sensation/discomfort would be a high school student attending his first dance. A few sips of beer can minimize the normal fears of being rejected and being observed. The adolescent then temporarily circumvents the developmental crisis of socialization by using the drug.

An adult example would be the salesperson under enormous pressure to deliver sales. She has had some difficulty lately and has taken to having a drink before meeting customers. As if by magic, the sinking feeling in her stomach has gone away, and she feels as if she can sell anything. Each sale reinforces her belief, and she may even appear self-confident to her customers. Her difficulty occurs when she does not have a drink before meeting customers because she has relied on "liquid" confidence rather than developing a sense of her own ability.

In both cases, a lesson has been learned—certain feelings and awkward experiences can be avoided or even mastered with drugs. If this learning is repeated, the teenager's or salesperson's tolerance for that same anxiety will be less because there is a way out.

Gestalt Treatment of Substance Abuse

In moving to *substance abuse,* the person begins to use drugs more frequently, thereby influencing more his or her emotional, cognitive, and interpersonal state. The person may now be using the drug to influence this state to the degree that it is now becoming part of his or her style. The person's way of being in the world is increasingly to not feel certain feelings through drug use. This is the first stage of substance dependency, which I describe first because avoidance of feelings can begin at this point on the continuum and determine potential work in therapy. The following section describes this in more detail.

The major question when working with a client who is abusing drugs is the degree of severity: how much the figure of the drug and its resulting effect dominate the client's life and awareness. We can assess this in different ways. First, what is the client's present capacity for sensation and awareness? If he or she is "numb" from using drugs regularly, we will not be able to do any meaningful therapy that involves feeling and insight. An extreme example of this occurs when a client comes to a session intoxicated.

A second evaluative criterion in assessing the dominance of the client's drug use is how often he or she uses drugs (frequency), for what period of time he or she uses drugs (duration), what activities are secondary to drug use or revolve around it, and what significant life activities (family, career, health, other relationships) are being affected by drug use.

Case Example—Eileen

Eileen had come for therapy for 3 months, attending weekly sessions. The focus of her therapy had been on her romantic relationship with a man. After 3 months, she began to cancel sessions, complaining of car problems and "that nagging flu bug." When she canceled an hour before a session by cell phone, I informed her that she would need to pay for it. At the appointed time, she did show up at my office, obviously intoxicated, slurring her speech and speaking loudly in my waiting room about "your dumb cancellation policy." I asked Eileen to come into my office. Almost as soon as she entered, she began to cry and looked visibly shaken. I asked her to tell me what she was experiencing. After a few minutes, she talked about feeling frustrated that I wanted her to pay for the session and about being scared of how fast she had been driving. Her eyes were bloodshot, and I could smell the rich, pungent odor of marijuana smoke. When I asked her about this, she acknowledged that she had been smoking and drinking for a few hours. We then talked about how often she was high; she slumped in the chair and said, "A lot more lately." After a few minutes, Eileen said that she had wanted to talk about her drug use lately but had felt "embarrassed." I told her that I appreciated her being honest with me. We ended the session with Eileen getting a friend to drive her home; we both felt she was too upset to drive home.

Eileen began the next session talking more about her feelings of embarrassment and fear. This was the way she had felt most of the time lately after she had been drinking and smoking pot. I asked Eileen what drinking did for her. She held her breath and then exhaled her response that she did not know but frequently felt "sad" after losing her relationships. When she drank, her sadness "went away for a while." I asked Eileen if she could feel her sadness now that she had not been drinking for a few days. She sat still and looked out the window. After a few minutes of silence, a tear rolled down her face. I told Eileen that I saw her tears and was also feeling sad as I sat with her. She began to move more in her chair and talk about how she had "finally found a relationship with Jim that she had thought would last but it had not." The focus of our session had moved from Eileen's drinking and drug use to the feelings she had managed by using these drugs.

As Eileen continued to explore her feelings and develop internal supports to tolerate them, her drinking decreased significantly. She no longer drank to bury her feelings and then "pour" them out when drunk. She described the change in her life as moving from "running away, or better, driving away with booze and dope" to "knowing me." Another aspect of our work was Eileen's focus on her relationship with me. Our relationship became a model for how she might be with others. This involved her talking to me about how she felt toward me, confronting me when I looked inattentive, and asking me about my feelings. These were qualitatively different behaviors for Eileen in relating to another person. Alcohol and other drugs were no longer significant aspects of her everyday life. She had a drink at times but did not drink to get drunk, and intoxication was no longer her focus.

Co-assessment: In working with Eileen, I found it important to assess her drug behavior over time. I collected enough data (frequently canceled sessions, chronic illness, frequent calamities, and finally coming to a session intoxicated) to set a limit about sessions and then confront her about her intoxication when she did come to the session. Confrontation is important with a client actively using substances; it is a way of stating what is in the present. Nothing could be more vivid than a client who comes to a session drunk or high. In this way, Eileen made her drug use both of our businesses or figures. It was as if our session was a slice of her everyday life.

Experimentation: In these sessions the experiential aspect was for Eileen to come to the session "as she was," intoxicated, and for both of us to know her process in that moment. A more direct experiment occurred when I asked her to stay with or feel her feelings when she returned to therapy without drugs. This led her to feel her sadness and loss in the presence of another person. It also helped to clarify the "what for" of her drug abuse: anesthetizing her sadness. The use of experiment or experiential enactment is a cornerstone of the Gestalt approach of bringing feelings and behavior into the present, where they can be assimilated.

Meaning Making: Eileen became clear that her drug use was a solution gone awry. As she was able to attend to her feelings and make some changes, it became clear to us that her drug and alcohol use was not the primary issue. We worked on her emotional experience, feelings of embarrassment, and patterns of using relationships to decrease these feelings. When Eileen first entered the session intoxicated, my working hypothesis (diagnosis) was that she was possibly an alcoholic (substance dependent). As she continued in the therapy work and her drug and alcohol use diminished, I saw her more as someone who had been abusing drugs but was not dependent. This is sometimes difficult for both the therapist and client to determine because some people move from substance abuse to dependency, in which the drug is no longer a means to an end but the end itself.

The figures of interest or need emerge not out of thin air but out of the person's ground. This ground is out of our awareness but includes our biological processes (such as respiration and digestion), personality, past and immediate history, temperament, and nervous system. The (back)ground influences and organizes what comes into our awareness. In Eileen's case we collaboratively made the meaning that she was managing her feelings with drugs. She also agreed to pay attention to any increase in her use of alcohol and other drugs as a means of managing her feelings.

Dialogic Relationship: The most significant aspect of our relationship was my inclusion of myself as part of the process. I did this first by holding Eileen to her responsibility to me to pay for her sessions if she did not cancel by a certain time limit. Not only was this my policy, but I wanted her to comply with it out of consideration for me, another person who was in relation to her. It did matter to me that Eileen attended sessions. The second example of inclusion was my sharing of my feeling of sadness that emerged when I sat with her as she cried. Both of these acts of inclusion brought to the foreground Eileen's relationship with others and me. In this way, our interaction was authentic and continued to be part of the working focus for her in therapy.

SUBSTANCE DEPENDENCY

Gestalt Theory of Substance Dependency

What begins as a creative adjustment to situations can evolve into a habitual response to most situations. The substance-dependent client has a particular style of managing experience. This style includes but is not limited to the use of drugs and may continue when the client is not using drugs. Because this pattern develops over time, it can be seen as similar to the patterns described by developmental theories of alcoholism and addiction (Brown, 1995; Clemmens, 1997; Wallace, 1974). The drug is now the primary and most frequent figure, and the user's cycle is more rapid and stereotypic (same behaviors and outcomes). The user is frequently agitated or impatient. There is less awareness because the person's behavior is redundant and because the drug's effect narrows the potential world, an effect some addicts refer to as "the gray world."

Using has become limiting and problematic when an individual does not know how to adjust without drugs. Using drugs can also become the individual's only response. At this end of the continuum, the drug is the primary source of comfort. The process of using the drug has become more automatic. The person has less awareness of his or her behavior. Sometimes, the drug seems to appear in his or her hand.

The following stages of the progression of substance abuse are associated with what has traditionally been referred to as addiction or alcoholism. Traditionally, in the beginning of substance abuse treatment (early AA), it was thought that people needed to go through the stages until eventual collapse in order to get treatment and therapy. What now appears clear is that individuals can be assisted at any point and that some do not progress through these stages but stay at one stage for their entire life (W. White, 1999).

In Stage 2, *Maintenance Using,* users attempt to maintain the sense of comfort they have achieved through use of alcohol or other drugs. This sense of comfort is both within themselves and interpersonally with others. This is the contact modulation of confluence. Polster and Polster (1973) defined confluence as "a phantom pursued by people who want to reduce difference so as to moderate the upsetting experience of novelty and otherness" (p. 92). Users of alcohol/drugs have had some success at this by modulating their feelings through intoxication. To maintain that success, they will need to use more regularly and eventually to increase their quantity and frequency.

Stage 3 is *Diminishing New Figures.* After some pattern of attempting to maintain a state of comfort through maintenance use, addicts have less tolerance for the energy and excitement of new (novel) situations. Alcohol and/or drugs are used earlier in the contact cycle. Users become habituated to warding off the increasing energy of sensation and awareness. Progressively, all sensations are experienced as intolerable or "too much." This experience is like that of a burn victim who is missing an outer layer of skin so that the slightest breeze or bump produces pain.

The act of using is now gulping, snorting, smoking, or injecting. The drug crosses the contact boundary without any discrimination. At this point in the process, using has become introjective. The drink or drug is usually not tasted or experienced at the point of contact.

Once a person reaches Stage 4, *Unfinished Business,* in the progression of dependence, he or she is using more frequently, and the substance strongly affects his or her life. By interrupting countless opportunities for completing interaction, the substance-dependent person creates an enormous backlog of unfinished business. Taking a drink can eliminate awareness before the rising figure of needing to pay a bill; plans to travel are seemingly forgotten as the person smokes away the money to do so; the original intention to take a niece or nephew out for a birthday just vanishes due to being hung over. These are very short-term and mild examples of the impact of continuing to use drugs in a consistent pattern. The cycle between sensations grows shorter, and the substance-dependent user literally has no time or attention for the everyday functions of life. Promises are made and intentions are felt, but the pattern of using is now pervasive.

Substance-dependent users spend an increasing amount of time by themselves, both by choice, out of discomfort, and as a sheer function of their lifestyle. Most people have numerous commitments and relationships that they maintain as a priority; these are their dominant figures. But for substance-dependent users, the dominant figure is the drug.

At Stage 5, *Collapse,* the user's world has mostly narrowed to self and drug. Increased tolerance to the substance demands greater consumption. As a client of mine put it, he had to "feed the beast" on an hourly basis, his euphemism for warding off discomfort and possible withdrawal symptoms. The cycle of sensation-action is now almost automatic. Users frequently move toward a horizontal position, often passed out or lying down, rarely moving about in the world except for basic needs.

Users so fully organize their life around getting, using, and having drugs (NA, 1998) that there is little involvement in the rest of life. It is during this stage that users' physical deterioration is so pronounced that they have numerous physical ailments and may enter treatment through a medical emergency. Such people rarely, if ever, come to individual therapy. This is really the final and logical conclusion of constant drug use. This is the world of the lying-down drunk, the crack user passed out with her pipe, and the parent who passes out daily after the children go to school.

Substance Dependence Cycle

Figure 15.3 shows how the continuum of experience is altered by substance dependence, both in the difference in the pattern of the wave and in the characteristics (Wheeler, 1991) of the ground. The substance-dependent person tends to move from sensation (Stage 1) to action (Stage 4) and back again—repeatedly. This jumping in the cycle becomes like "hot-wiring" a car, where the normal starting mechanism is bypassed and an action abruptly occurs without preliminary orienting. The orienting parts of experience—awareness (Stage 2) and mobilization (Stage 3)—are rushed through, creating a kind of immediate or impulsive pattern of action.

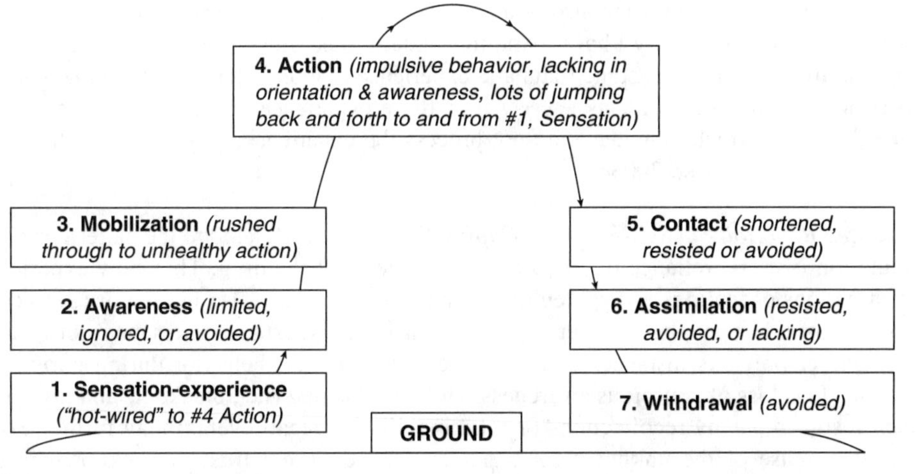

Figure 15.3 Substance Dependence Cycle

Any contradictory sensations that might lead to a different action, such as memories from the last drinking episode, do not emerge in the addict's awareness. In the movement back to sensation, the contact functions of contact (Stage 5), assimilation (Stage 6), and withdrawal (Stage 7) are shortened and avoided. This results in the addict learning little from his or her experience. Because the user is intoxicated, there is a lack of withdrawal and assimilation. A style eventually funnels all experiences though the same action, drinking or using drugs. It is obvious, but seldom stated, that addiction is a mobilization of energy with the wrong action.

This cycle illustrates not only the present behavior of most addicts but the potential for others. It is a useful template for understanding the ways that substance-dependent people behave and organize their experience. They behave this way between periods of drug use and long after abstinence. They may experience themselves and others in this pattern or develop it through their use of drugs and alcohol.

Substance-Dependent Ground

Certain characteristics of substance-dependent individuals either existed prior to their drug use and/or developed through drug use—I call them the *substance-dependent ground.* These characteristics are part of the ground out of which the desire for (figure) the drug continues to emerge. By repeating this pattern, users experience emotional, physical, and cognitive impacts that influence their sense of self and style of interacting with others. The predictable figure of drug use or avoidance emerges from this ground.

Overstimulation—Agitation/Anger. Over time (and, for some people, prior to using drugs), substance-dependent individuals move quickly from sensation to action, with agitation and anger mounting due to overstimulation. When frustrated in the attempt to do so, they tend to become angry. Such intolerance of staying with the feelings of normal resting or no action is characteristic of substance-dependent users. It is also the initial figure in treatment because they literally cannot sit still to let feelings or awareness emerge.

In relating to others, they are also in a hurry, moving toward either a kind of fusion with others or conflict. Frequently I have found this pattern to be true of the substance-dependent user's family of origin or of some traumatic experience (childhood abuse or trauma, combat experience, automobile accidents, etc.). All of these experiences have the same sensation-action pattern in which individuals do not process the experience; they feel something and must take action (Kepner, 2003b).

Limited Repertoire of Self-Soothing/Coping Skills—Fear. Related to the pattern of overstimulation is users' reliance on the predictable effects of the drug. They now experience new situations or feelings as frightening. Conversely, they may also use the drugs to cope with fears of other people. Another aspect of fear is that substance users may not be able to remember previous instances of taking the drugs or their behavior during periods of drug use. This loss of conscious awareness while intoxicated (i.e., blackouts and grayouts, which result in patchy recollections or total inability to recall events) may further exaggerate the sense of the unknown for a person who does not trust the unknown in the first place.

History of Failures and Noncompletions—Guilt. From a Gestalt perspective, guilt is the result of unfinished business. According to Perls et al. (1951), unfinished business occurs when we do not have the resources to attend to an experience or interrupt our process. Substance-dependent people are constantly interrupting their process and do not experience having the resources to attend to situations. They have much unfinished business and then often use the substance to avoid feeling guilt.

Discomfort With Self-Shame. Wheeler (1991) described shame as the feeling, thought, and belief that there is something bad about one's self. Substance-dependent users frequently feel this way prior to using drugs. By continuing in this pattern of using drugs, they can magnify the feeling that "there is something wrong about me," as a client of mine put it. Paradoxically, they may use to avoid this feeling, thus creating more dread.

Gestalt Treatment of Substance Dependency

As with substance abuse, the major concern is determining the degree of severity of drug use and the resulting impact on the person's life. The treatment interventions need to be based on the client's stage of dependency. As substance users continue through the stages, their capacity to experience sensation and be present enough for therapy is diminished. The following case example illustrates how the Gestalt approach can be useful in working with a substance-dependent client.

Case Example—Martha

Martha scheduled an appointment with me because, as she put it, "My partner decided I needed help." Martha's partner, Anne, was very worried about Martha losing her job because of so many sick days. When I got this information from Martha in the initial phone consultation, I thought she might have some organic physical difficulty because of the controlled and almost mechanical pattern of her speech. We scheduled an appointment.

Both Martha and Anne arrived for the appointment, and I asked them if they both wanted to come into my office. Anne replied that she was only there to make sure Martha made it to the appointment. I asked Martha to come into my office and had her fill out some basic intake forms. As she did this, I looked at her and felt shocked. Although she said she was 32, Martha looked almost 60 years old. Her cheeks were sunken; she appeared underweight, yet puffy in her body. As she had walked into my office, her gait was that of a teetering newborn colt, as if her legs could barely support her. As we began to talk, I became aware that Martha appeared to gaze through me as if she did not see me.

I asked Martha about her physical health, and she vaguely made a comment about "being fine." I told her that she did not look fine but rather ill. She said nothing more until I asked her about her history of drug and alcohol use (one of many initial assessment questions I ask all clients in the first session). At this point, she became agitated, speaking about how some people can use drugs and others do not understand that. We determined quickly that she was the person who used drugs and that Anne and all her "bullshit friends" were the ones who did not understand that. I asked Martha what drugs she was talking about and in what frequency she was using them. She looked at me coldly and said, "Percodan, some Percocet, alcohol, and some pot now and then." She had been using these drugs in combination for over 4 years with little or no break. Percodan and Percocet are extremely powerful upload analgesic drugs similar to morphine.

I again asked Martha what she wanted in therapy. This time she answered, "I want to be left alone and do my thing!" I suspected Martha's thing was to numb out from the extremely powerful drugs she was using on a daily basis. The irony was that Martha had been a nurse and was on disability due to a car accident. This is how she had gotten started on the pain medication, and she had never returned to work. She later told me that she knew that if she returned to work she would be required to give a urine sample as part of her employment contract and that her use of drugs would be revealed.

Because Martha only wanted to "do my thing" and would not explain what she meant, I asked her if we could bring Anne into the session, given that Anne was the reason she had came to see me. Martha waved her hand and said, "Sure." At this point, I could not tell how intoxicated Martha was, but I knew we needed to do

HELGA: In the case of Martha, who is in an advanced stage of addiction, I would become more directive, following Laura Perls's dictate "to help a client only as much as is necessary" (personal communication, May 1975). When people are so involved in taking heroin derivatives that they cannot recall when or how many pills they take, the addictive process has become life threatening and calls for action. Nor can they be expected to have any sense of what to do and how to do it. Important to remember here is that no behavior can be maintained unless it is supported. The common verbiage is that "no addict exists in isolation." In such a case I have found it useful to have an intervention (I use interventions even if the addiction is only heavy abuse). In Martha's case she had a significant other, perhaps also friends and family members who may have been willing to join in such a venture. It is a painful

something different to work together. Anne entered the session, and Martha began to get angry with her for bringing up her drug use. Anne was persistent, and I supported the conversation. As the conversation became heated and loud, I stopped the conversation and asked Martha what she thought was going on. She said, "We're fighting again!" I wondered aloud if this was what they usually fought about, her drug use. She literally glared at me but stopped talking to me and instead told Anne she could not or would not stop, she did not know which one. I persuaded both Martha and Anne to come back in a few days to continue this dialogue and asked Martha if she could keep track for me how many times she thought about using the drugs before she used them. I did this to heighten her awareness about how automatic her drug use was. I also asked if she could notice if there were any times she wanted not to use but still took the drugs.

undertaking for all and is fueled by caring and love for the afflicted person. Friends/family relate their experiences of seeing the individual suffer from their addiction *and* say that they can no longer stand by without intervening. Preferably a plan of action is in place that can be activated immediately. I have never yet had anyone not go to treatment in response to an intervention. There is such a fine line between supporting and enabling. Eventually, each individual still chooses his or her own path toward recovery or not. While addicted individuals in their end stages seek only to drink, one cannot forget that drinking still serves the same purpose—not to feel pain.

MICHAEL: As I write this, I am aware that we are talking about clients (even substance-dependent clients) as if they all are attending therapy in a similar state. But many addicts, because of their lifelong history, need some period of time without drugs to be emotionally and physically available to do the developmental tracing.

Surprisingly, they both showed up for a session two days later. Martha began the session angrily, but I persisted in asking her how the experiment of paying attention to her drug use went. She said she wanted to use but frequently did not remember taking the drugs; at least half the time she knew she had taken them only because of the bottle being empty. Anne began to cry, and Martha looked at me almost helplessly. This was a turning point for Martha—the combination of my attention to her and Anne's tearful presence built up enough sensation that she could feel some sense of her own despair. She eventually talked about this and agreed to attend an NA meeting with a nurse friend who had offered to take her. On the way out of my office, she told me, "It's not going to do a damn thing!" After coming for two individual sessions, Martha ended therapy with a promise to get back to me when she was "ready." I did not hear from either of them for almost a year. Martha called me at my office to tell me that she had been without any drugs for 6 months. It had taken her a while to stop using, and she had relapsed one time, but she had been able to decrease her drug use enough to feel how miserable and frightened she felt. Following my initial suggestion, she had begun attending NA meetings for support, including one meeting specifically for recovering medical professional addicts.

Co-assessment: Initially I was concerned that Martha was physically ill or had some form of neurological problem. Her gait was somewhat a result of the car accident but became exaggerated when she was intoxicated. She had no interest in being in therapy and had come only to appease her partner. Her level of sensation was so muted due to the powerful drugs she had been using that she was not available for work in therapy. It was also important to take a history and background with Martha that allowed me to appreciate the quantity and frequency of drugs that she had been using. The other clinical consideration for Martha and clients who appear to be substance dependent is whether they need some form of detoxification. Detoxification is the process of providing initial education and supervised withdrawal from the substance as part of a treatment.

Experimentation: Gestalt therapy focuses on "what is," what is present and available in the here and now (Perls et al., 1951). What was available to work with was Martha's relationship with Anne. Martha could become angry and defensive with Anne if Anne even mentioned her drug use. I used this relationship as an emotional pressure point to bring Martha emotionally into the room. This allowed the importance of their relationship to be part of the field. By herself, Martha would have just given me the cold shoulder; I was of no consequence to her. The other experiment was for Martha to witness Anne's reaction to her drug use. This sensitized her enough to realize her own behavior. Anne's pain was the mirror for Martha's drugged behavior.

Meaning Making: The meaning that Martha made during these sessions was that she was behaving in a way that profoundly hurt her partner and might cost her this relationship. The other meaning she made, after a number of trials, was that she could no longer remember how much Percodan she took in a given day. She later reported that this was the most alarming reality of her drug use, but she needed to be off those "sensation-inhibiting drugs" to feel alarm.

From my perspective, Martha was clearly in the later two stages of substance dependency. She was isolated, using drugs constantly, and withdrawn from any meaningful work. Her drug use was about to cost her the only significant relationship that remained in her life. Yet she had no desire or interest in stopping her process.

Dialogic Relationship: In working with Martha (and to an extent Anne), I tried to understand what was happening without jumping to conclusions. This "bracketing" of my assumptions (of her neurological damage and advanced drug addiction) was intentional. My goal was to stay interested in Martha's experience of her drug use and her experience of Anne as "nagging." I did this despite Martha's obvious degree of physical distress. It is easy to reduce a client to a "sick" person and then not bring his or her voice into the room. Martha really did not include me in her emotional experience. My goal was to have Martha be interested in her use of drugs, to have her diagnose herself through following the experiment of tracking dosage (as all experienced nurses do).

Substance dependence is an experience qualitatively different from that of other drug use. The use of drugs to such a degree, whether in daily (and even multiple times per days) or "binge" periods, affects every aspect of the whole person. Martha was engaged in a process that literally seemed to be "eating" her from the inside out. Her only significant relationship was at risk and damaged by her drug use. She had given up her career in nursing because it threatened her drug use. This is the pervasive impact of living out this style. Life shrinks down to periods of intoxication. To make any significant changes in such a life (if this client wants to), the process of using must be interrupted. The dependent user (addict) has lost the capacity to choose the drug over other aspects of life, including his own or her own health.

The Gestalt approach focuses on working with the client's behavior and highlighting behaviors as choices. By developing awareness and inhibiting the drug-using process, clients such as Martha can experience a sense of choice in their lives. As part of the recovery and treatment, I usually refer clients to 12-step programs of recovery (AA and NA).

SUMMARY

I have focused on the application of Gestalt therapy approaches and interventions to the range of substance use behaviors. The notion of substance use as occurring on a continuum from use to dependency is different from the dichotomous view of either addiction or nonaddiction. Additionally, the usefulness of drugs for the user in managing experience is an important part of working with any client. It is our job not to take away behaviors from our clients but rather to help them experience and become aware of the impact of these behaviors. What is unique about substance dependency is the habitual and all-encompassing impact of using drugs to manage experience and sensation. If we understand that clients are doing something for themselves by using drugs, we can then help them develop supports to accomplish these goals through means other than ongoing intoxication.

Working with substance abuse and dependency in therapy needs to begin with an assessment by the therapist of the client's severity of use and functioning. What is important from a Gestalt perspective is how much the figure of the drug dominates the client's perceptual field. Dependency occurs when the drug dominates the field; the drug becomes the figure and ground. This occurs because the person has a limited repertoire of managing his or her experience. The focus of Gestalt therapy is to help the individual broaden that range and develop alternative processes for managing experience and feelings.

HELGA: I begin with a different assessment with the substance-abusing/addicted population. In addition to the usual, I explore early experiences and their response to them. I see the creative adjustments of taking a drug or a drink as a continuation and intensification of earlier creative adjustments that follow a developmental progression beginning with a young child's developmentally available repertoire of possible responses to painful experiences. These early creative adjustments, let's say withdrawing when parents fight or humiliate the child, will work adequately until the child's social environment calls for more sophisticated adjustments once the child enters school. The child may then learn to dissociate, daydream, become depressed, develop ADHD symptoms, or become a bully for self-protection. In high school, these adjustments may become insufficient, and the loner or aggressive kid may find cocaine or alcohol and learn to fit in or join a gang or use heroin to calm down and thus exit the pain of his or her young life. I do not suggest immediate termination of drug use, since this would be foolhardy and create denial. My definition of denial is the vehicle by which the individual attempts to secure continued use of substances when there is a perceived threat aimed at elimination of the drug of choice without prior preparation.

MICHAEL: I have worked with addicts to help them stay in therapy until they discovered the reason for their drinking in order to make an "awareful" choice. In other situations, the individual needed to stop the substance-dependent process in order to make this choice. As Gestalt therapists we need to make this capacity part of the ongoing co-assessment process with our client. I use the term *co-assessment* since our clients have expectations of what they want from the therapy. Involving them in a dialogue of what I see in their behavior allows me to avoid the problem of being the expert who decides (diagnoses) what the client needs.

Many individual differences and diagnostic issues have not been mentioned in this chapter. Therapists can work with individual differences among clients by using the principles outlined in this chapter. The Gestalt approach of developing and working with the client's interest and meaning making creates a working relationship that supports client change and ownership. By using experimentation to bring their experience into the present, clients can experience themselves and their choices. Other diagnoses add more complexity to the ground in working with substance-using and recovering clients. Attention to the ground is the guiding principle that will support work with dual-diagnosed clients. Practitioners need to be familiar with both substance use and these other processes.

HELGA: In closing what has been an interesting and challenging dialogue with you, Michael, I would like to take this opportunity to say a bit about the addiction treatment training material that I just finished producing. I receive many requests from Gestalt therapists regarding addiction treatment approaches from a Gestalt therapy perspective. So recently I videotaped a 30-hour workshop that we've condensed into a 1 hour and 45 minute DVD and a companion trainer's manual entitled *Synthesis of Dialectical Behavior Therapy (DBT) and Therapeutic Community Treatment (TCT) for Addiction/Mental Health Troubled Clients: DVD Training Video and Manual* (Matzko, 2003). DBT is philosophically so similar to Gestalt therapy that one could, without reservations, call it by that name. However, the contract was to teach DBT, hence the title. While TCT is referenced, the DVD and manual are equally applicable to any addiction/mental health treatment settings.

For Gestalt therapy (or any other therapy) to be useful, clients must be interested in working with their experience. Through the dialogic process, it is possible for the client and therapist to co-diagnose the focus of therapy. When this occurs, therapy has the best chance of creating change and growth. However, the therapist needs to be aware of the process of substance dependency and the stages of progression into it, as well as the process of recovery and its stages, in order to intervene effectively with the substance-using client.

The process of recovery from substance dependency is more than this chapter can encompass. Readers who are interested in exploring addiction recovery therapy can refer to *Getting Beyond Sobriety* (Clemmens, 1997). Students and readers can also gain enormous insight into both addiction and recovery processes by attending "open" meetings of both AA and NA. Such attendance is often a regular part of psychology, social work, and medical degree programs.

REVIEW QUESTIONS

1. What is the continuum of substance use, abuse, and dependency, as described by the chapter author?

2. How is the Gestalt continuum similar to and different from the AA or NA (Alcoholics Anonymous, Narcotics Anonymous) 12-step model?

3. What are the definitions of co-assessment, experimentation, meaning making, and the dialogic relationship, as used for the purposes of the chapter?

4. Why is it important for clients to be interested in their own substance use, patterns, and meaning making?

EXPERIENTIAL PEDAGOGICAL ACTIVITIES

ACTIVITY 1: Clemmens presents a model of how using alcohol/drugs can have some intrinsic function or purpose. In journal format, reflect on some coping mechanisms you have used during times of stress or pain, the affect you experienced, the usefulness of your coping style, and any benefits or deficits of your coping choice.

ACTIVITY 2: Many classic and contemporary Hollywood films depict use and/or abuse of substances. Examples include *Days of Wine and Roses, Leaving Las Vegas, Clean and Sober, Requiem for a Dream,* and *The Lost Weekend.* Using the chapter author's stage model (Stage 1, avoidance of sensation/discomfort; Stage 2, maintenance use; Stage 3, diminishing new figures; Stage 4, unfinished business; and Stage 5, collapse), view the main characters in one of the films, and identify the progression of the stages from scene to scene.

ACTIVITY 3: In your journal and/or in a small group, discuss the positives and negatives of working with clients who present with continued alcohol and/or drug use versus those who are requested to first be "clean and sober."

ACTIVITY 4: *Co-assessment,* in this chapter, refers to a collaborative process between the client and the practitioner. In dyads, with one individual representing the client and the other individual taking the part of the practitioner, role-play examples of both a Gestalt co-assessment model of collaboration with the client to explore the meaning of an event or a "symptom" and a model in which the practitioner offers an interpretation or diagnosis *to* the client. Discuss the differences for both members of the dyad.

CHAPTER **16**

Gestalt Educational Therapy

CARA GARCIA, SUSAN BAKER, AND ROBERT DEMAYO

DIALOGUE RESPONDENT: GEORGE ISAAC BROWN

Cara Garcia is professor of education at the Graduate School of Education and Psychology, Pepperdine University, Los Angeles, where she supervises the Educational Therapy Services in their clinic. She came to the university with classroom teaching experience in the Los Angeles Unified School District. Since her certification by the Gestalt Therapy Institute of Los Angeles in 1981, she has researched Gestalt principles in regular instruction and educational therapy, with particular interest in academic anxiety, specifically reading and writing blocks, math and test anxiety, and stage fright. Her book *Too Scared to Learn: Overcoming Academic Anxiety* (1998) and her articles in professional journals (including the *Gestalt Review)* have been enlightening for psychotherapists and educators.

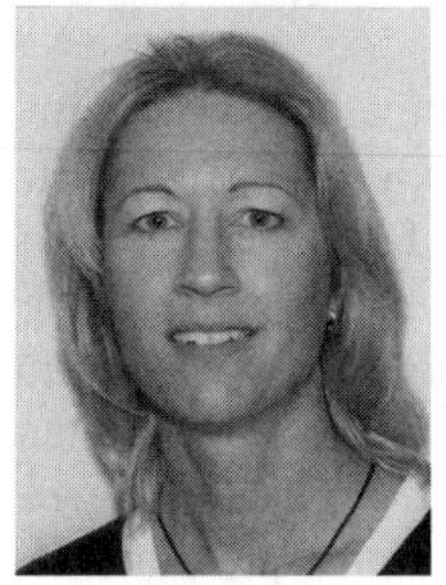

Susan Baker is the director of Clinical Services at Interface Children & Family Services in Camarillo, California, where she manages a division of more than a dozen clinical and social services. She is a certified Gestalt therapist and a faculty intern with the Gestalt Therapy Institute of the Pacific, and she maintains a private practice in Los Angeles and Ventura. As an adjunct faculty member in the clinical psychology program at Pepperdine University, she provides relational Gestalt training and supervision for graduate students and interns.

Robert deMayo is associate dean of the Psychology Division and professor of psychology in the Graduate School of Education and Psychology at Pepperdine University in Los Angeles. He is a licensed and practicing clinical psychologist with offices in Santa Monica and is a past president of the Los Angeles Society of Clinical Psychologists. He was the honored recipient of the Shepherd Ivory Franz Distinguished Teaching Award in Psychology at the University of California, Los Angeles. His research has focused on mood disorders, professional practice issues, health psychology, and Gestalt therapy's interface with clinical education.

George Isaac Brown, with his experience as an elementary school teacher and principal, and his PhD from Harvard University, taught organizational leadership, Gestalt therapy, and educational change at the University of California, Santa Barbara, for over 30 years, retiring as an emeritus professor in 1995. His books *Human Teaching for Human Learning: An Introduction to Confluent Education* (1971) and *The Live Classroom: Innovation Through Confluent Education and Gestalt* (1975), combined with his Confluent Education Graduate Program, contributed significantly to the human potential movement of the 1970s and 1980s. He and his wife, Judith, who is a couples therapist, travel internationally to conduct Gestalt workshops and leadership training.

The process by which learning occurs has been a central interest of Gestalt therapy from its beginning. Learning, say Gestaltists, like all human activity, is a process, often more valuable than the outcome. Miriam Polster's (1999) eloquent statement about Gestalt therapy serves as a backdrop for our better understanding of its place in the classroom and in education generally. "[Gestalt therapy] is a blend of clinical exigencies and philosophical insight, of learning theory and psychotherapeutic technique, of psychological inquiry into the nature of experience and one person's simple concern with another" (p. 364). Though education has always purported to be for the "whole" person, the obvious focus has been on academic and intellectual development, not emotional or social development, which in most schools is left to chance. As proponents of psychological education, Gestalt therapists and educators value holistic education and view the classroom situation as a means for promoting personal growth, self-understanding, and interpersonal contact to maximize learning and healthy development.

In the earliest days of our history, when the foundations of Gestalt therapy were being established, innovative educators were vitally involved with the "founding fathers," Fritz Perls and Paul Goodman, and "founding mother," Laura Perls. In fact, Laura Perls's (1939/1992b) article "How to Educate Children for Peace" (which she wrote as a psychoanalyst in South Africa) provides evidence of her lifelong interest in education. Her involvement in the very foundation of Gestalt therapy through her contributions to Fritz Perls's first Gestalt book, *Ego, Hunger and Aggression* (1947/1969a), was from a preschool educational perspective. The Perlses' observations and experiences with their first baby prompted them to examine the human oral functions of aggression, dentition, digestion, assimilation, and rejection as metaphors of mental metabolism and psychological health (Wysong & Rosenfeld,

1982). Their interest in educational applications of their ideas led the Perlses to invite Dr. Elliot Shapiro, one of New England's most prominent innovative educators of that time, to their foundational meetings. Shapiro's prominence was due in part to his creative ideas for educating minority children in Harlem and, as described in *The Lives of Children* by George Dennison (1969), in part to his work as a consultant to the First Street School in New York City. Speaking of the Perlses' early professional life in New York City, Laura Perls said, "A whole line of people came to us through Elliot. Elliot gave the first training in Gestalt therapy for educators" (quoted in Wysong & Rosenfeld, 1982, p. 12).

Early in the development of Gestalt therapy, 1964 to be exact, Fritz Perls became a scholar in residence at Esalen Institute at Big Sur, California, where he conducted Gestalt therapy training groups. Fritz had a profound influence on George Brown, then a professor at the University of California, Santa Barbara, who had been leading Esalen workshops on creativity and awareness training. Though Brown was also influenced by such notables as Abraham Maslow, Carl Rogers, Arnold Toynbee, Paul Tillich, Buckminster Fuller, Rollo May, and Joseph Campbell, his primary thrust became one of integrating Gestalt principles into educational processes. As a result of this interest, Brown wrote and received a project grant from the Ford-Esalen Foundation to create a variety of experimental projects in school districts to demonstrate the potential of applying Gestalt principles and methods in education (Castillo, 1974; Lederman, 1969; Yeomans, 1975), in universities (G. I. Brown, 1971; J. H. Brown, 1996; Shapiro, 1998; Woldt, 1976), and in the Gazebo School, which was begun at the Esalen Institute itself (Esalen, 2002). George Brown's work in the area of confluent education was part of the heart and soul of the human potential movement. His two primary books, *Human Teaching for Human Learning* (Brown, 1971) and *The Live Classroom: Innovation Through Confluent Education* (Brown, Yeomans, & Grizzard, 1975), are classics in the field. Two other classics that emerged from these early applications of Gestalt in the classroom were Janet Lederman's *Anger and the Rocking Chair* (1969) and Gloria Castillo's *Left-Handed Teaching: Lessons in Affective Education* (1974). Castillo was one of George Brown's students in the Ford-Esalen Project who developed the Confluent Education Program in the Winnipeg Schools, which led to implementing a Gestalt-based confluent educational program in classrooms throughout the entire Canadian province of Manitoba and other parts of Canada.

Gestalt therapy as translated for school use has been described in several ways—as confluent education (Brown, 1971; Castillo, 1974), Gestalt approaches in psychological education (Passons, 1975), Gestalt educational therapy for academic anxieties (Garcia, 1998), resilience education (Brown, D'Emidio-Caston, & Benard, 2000), Gestalt interventions to reduce anxiety (Shraga, 2000), Gestalt teacher education (Copelend, Birmingham, Caston, DeMuelle, & Natal, 1994), Gestalt approaches to resistances among adult learners (Okere, 1984), Gestalt role playing for language instruction (Horwitz & Young, 1991), and psychoeducational therapy (Daniel, 2004). The term that became most commonly used to capture the essence of the Gestalt approach in education was *confluent education,* meaning "the integration or flowing together of the *affective* and *cognitive* elements in individual and group learning" (Brown, 1971, p. 1, italics in original). In addition to the Gestalt approaches mentioned above, a number of educators drew on Brown to forge their own approaches to applying Gestalt principles and methods in elementary, secondary, and higher education (Blumenthal, 2001; Brown, Cline, & Necochea, 2003; Fodor & Collier, 2001; Hendricks & Wills, 1975; Woldt & Ingersoll, 1991). Some Gestalt practitioners have integrated educational therapy into their private practices (Hopkins, 1999; Lampert, 1969), and some have integrated it into agencies (deMayo & Garcia, 1997; Garcia, Baker, & deMayo, 1999; also see the American Educational Research Association's Confluent Education Special Interest Group at http://members.aol.com/confluent/). The following history of the Esalen Institute illustrates Brown's influence:

> 1967 to present: A Ford Foundation grant led to the creation of the Ford/Esalen Project in Confluent Education, joining affective and cognitive learning. Dr. George Brown, a regular Esalen workshop leader and Professor of Education at UC–Santa Barbara, spearheaded the program. His work was summarized in an Esalen book entitled *Human Teaching for Human Learning,* which sold more than 50,000 copies in the education field and was republished in 1990 as a Penguin paperback. Brown also published a subsequent book called *The Live Classroom: Innovations Through Confluent Education and Gestalt.* This project gave rise to 3 full-time faculty positions in the Confluent Education program at UC–Santa Barbara's School of Education, which has conferred more than 80 doctorates and 300 master's degrees. . . . Graduates from this program have taken Confluent Education all over the world. More locally, the State University of California at Bakersfield now uses Confluent Education as its official philosophy. (Esalen Center, 2004)

CONFLUENT EDUCATION IN THE CLASSROOM

Confluent education classrooms looked different, sounded different, and felt different. Sometimes called "the human potential movement in education," they implied many changes in behavior. The inclusion of the affective domain meant that students were learning to articulate feelings in the give-and-take of relationships. The pecking order was routinely processed: Class meetings were a time when powerful personalities were called to task for their putdowns and the meek were supported to be more forthcoming and engaging. Similarly, the inclusion of process education facilitated learning the "how" in education in addition to the "what." "Magic circle sessions" and "classroom meetings" were commonplace as the media for emotional and process education. In fact, "the medium is the message" was often cited as a focal point of education.

Another inclusion was attention to the body in relation to the learning process. The basic was learning how breath is a support—shallow when anxious and deep when centering and focusing. The moment just after recess, when students calmed down and got ready to work, was a natural time to center and focus. Students also learned to discover tensions in muscles and shake them out as a means of improving concentration.

Finally, there was a shift to include fantasy and art to express what was being contacted in one's inner life. Creative writing, fantasy role playing, and the manual arts were avenues for expression from the inside out.

GESTALT APPROACHES TO LEARNING DIFFICULTIES

Having reviewed and illustrated the history of Gestalt approaches to learning, we turn now to ways the Gestalt approach differs from other approaches to learning difficulties.

Although Gestalt psychology has long been interested in the process of learning, Gestaltists are a distinct minority in school-based settings. The Gestalt approach to understanding the learning difficulties people experience differs significantly from the two approaches that have recently come to dominate the field of education. One dominant approach is the medical model approach to learning problems. This approach examines learning difficulties from the framework of identifying deficiencies in functioning, attributing these deficiencies to abnormalities in neopsychological functioning, and attempting to correct these abnormalities through medical/pharmacological interventions. For example, children who have difficulty reading and writing are assessed for deficits in visual processing such as dyslexia, children who have difficulty staying on task are assessed for attention deficit disorder, and so on. Such approaches have been helpful for many children with demonstrable deficits that can be addressed with medical or pharmacological interventions. Unfortunately, children often acquire these diagnoses on the basis of only the most rudimentary evaluation without any consideration of the contributions of other potential emotional and environmental variables. Also, within the medical model, differences in functioning are labeled as abnormalities or deficiencies, leaving little room for exploration of the potential benefits of divergent ways of processing information.

The second dominant approach to understanding learning difficulties comes from the field of cognitive psychology, which has been heavily influenced by information-processing notions of human learning. These models have frequently looked at the learning process as distinct from emotional or social functioning. They frequently examine how educators can present information in a way that will optimize the rapid assimilation of information. Unfortunately, they have often focused on the assimilation of information devoid of emotional content or context, neglecting that most school-based learning takes place within an emotion-laden context.

When applied to school-age children, both of the above models focus on the identification and remediation of deficiencies relative to standardized norms. These models frequently leave little room for the valuing of divergent styles of learning. In contrast, Gestaltists evaluate learning difficulties from the perspective of trying to understand and value individual variations in the process of learning. Thus the Gestalt approach is an idiographic one, in which the basic assessment process involves evaluating the factors that both facilitate and impair the individual's experience of learning, while being much less concerned with identifying areas of divergence from normative functioning on standardized measures.

Rather than describe abstract learning problems, we now wish to conduct a Gestalt experiment with

GEORGE: My first comment relates to your comments on the medical model and cognitive psychology as approaches based on theories. Theories are nothing but extrapolations of experience, and because of this, I think Gestalt is much more powerful. Gestalt theory is idiosyncratic and holistic, as you point out, with an emphasis on the now. The problem with the medical model and cognitive psychology and the way they approach problems in education is that they're very normative and quantitative, as opposed to qualitative. If you look at the normal curve of distribution, what they tend to ignore are the upper and lower quartiles, which Gestalt doesn't even consider—each case is individual. Therefore, we get much more pertinent information with regard to individuals. So I am agreeing with you and reinforcing what you are saying in your chapter.

ROBERT: When talking about how the normative approach excludes people at the far ends of the continuum, I think, to be fair, people using the medical model approach would say, "Why, no, actually we're quite interested in

you, the reader. Please reflect on your experience of reading this chapter so far. Has it been a comfortable, relaxed experience for you? If asked, could you summarize what you have read so far, or would you have to read it a second or third time? Have you found yourself thinking about other things, wondering how long the chapter is, pondering what you might have for dinner? If you have been daydreaming, what were the contents of the daydreams? Did you notice any distractions to your learning process? Were the distractions related to the material you were reading (e.g., thinking about a relative who has been diagnosed with a learning disability) or with external demands (e.g., being anxious about whether you would be tested on this material)? Do you find yourself interested in the topic, or do you find you have to force yourself to continue with the chapter because it is a required assignment?

Conversely, if you found your attention wandering, how did you recover your concentration? Did it happen easily, or did you feel a strain in paying attention? Did you use a technique such as note taking or highlighting to focus your attention on relevant points? If you lost your concentration, did you go back and read the section you had glossed over, or did you infer the content from the material you read later?

The questions above illustrate the basic areas Gestaltists explore when analyzing the learning problems of the people who seek help. When the process of learning is going easily, what we are learning is in the foreground and other things are in the background. This represents uninterrupted concentration or attention. Unfortunately, the people who seek our help with learning problems are often overwhelmed by the many internal and external sources of interruption that disrupt their process of learning. Often they have gotten into unproductive struggles regarding interruptions, and they view these interruptions as a sign of their deficits. Consequently, they often feel helpless and hopeless and avoid the learning process as

abnormalities and deviations from the norm. When we assess that a child is showing significant deficits that put them several standard deviations below the norm, we intervene very actively." My main concern about the medical model is that it tends to be a very symptom-based approach.

GEORGE: That is actually what I was commenting on. I agree with you. When the medical model is generalized, in the way it often is, this is what I object to. So I think we are actually in agreement.

ROBERT: Yes. One of the things that I hope is clear to the readers is that when we write about the approach of cognitive psychology, many students may confuse that with cognitive behavior therapies (CBT—as developed by Aaron Beck, Albert Ellis, and so forth), whereas the discipline of cognitive psychology has had a place in experimental psychology departments for many decades and has nothing to do with cognitive therapy.

GEORGE: Even when you are considering cognitive psychology, it is easy to make the error of ignoring affective components and how they relate to cognitive psychology.

ROBERT: Yes, I agree. It is almost as though there is a belief that all we need to attend to are the cognitive aspects. If we don't pay attention to the affective, it doesn't exist.

GEORGE: And some of the recent studies of the brain point out that there can be no cognitive functioning without an emotional component and it shows in the brain measurements.

CARA: Hmmmm! We can't have a thought without an emotional experience, just as we can't have an emotional experience without a thought.

GEORGE: Absolutely! I wish we had had that research when we were doing our Confluent Education Program, and of course, Gestalt approaches are built around that notion too.

much as possible. We encourage these people to view their interruptions as an opportunity to explore their process of learning rather than as an indication of their deficits. In other words, rather than becoming angry with yourself when you notice your attention wandering, it might be more useful to become curious about what happened.

Often people with learning problems have learned to hide the difficulties, to pretend they are reading and concentrating when their attention has drifted. We ask them to not pretend to themselves or others but rather to honestly acknowledge when they have become distracted. The sooner one becomes aware of the distraction, the sooner one can become aware of the myriad strategies useful to regain attention. So as you, the reader, continue with this chapter, allow yourself to notice the difference between attention and distraction, and when the distraction comes, take this as an opportunity to notice how you usually regain your concentration.

KEY PRINCIPLES IN GESTALT EDUCATIONAL THERAPY

A key concept in understanding the concepts of concentration and distraction involves what we refer to as academic anxiety. In Gestalt theory, anxiety is not a state but a process. The term *academic anxiety* refers to the emotional and cognitive processes of vacillating between being on and off task.

The Gestalt approach to addressing academic anxiety is holistic. It acknowledges the student's mind, body, and spirit and treats the whole person as an integral part of his or her interpersonal, social, and physical environment. Gestalt educational therapy emphasizes the individuality of the student and unique style of each therapist.

The Whole Is Different From the Sum of the Parts

Gestalt loosely translates to "the whole" or "a configuration" and includes the tenet that the whole is different from the sum of its parts. It is the relationship of a figure or thing to its context or environment that becomes the whole. In this case, a gestalt evolves through a focus on the relationship between the student and his or her learning process. We attend to this focusing process through an emphasis on various figures that emerge in the learning process. Do you remember the vase/faces optical illusion in Figure 16.1 from psychology classes?

The vase/faces and other optical illusions were depictions of how the early Gestalt psychologists showed that human perception is limited. In their research on problem solving,

Figure 16.1 Gestalt Psychology's Vase/Faces–Figure/Ground Perception

they noted that whatever is figural (in the foreground) eclipses other material that resides in the background of attention. One cannot see both the vase and the faces at the same time—one of them must fade into the background for the other to be seen. Similarly, we cannot attend to more than one figure at a time without compromising our focus. The more clearly we attend to one figure, such as reading this chapter of the book, the more other competing figures, such as the reader's hunger or comfort, will shift into the background, out of awareness for the moment. The more distracted the reader is by his or her hunger or discomfort, the less focused and attentive he or she is to understanding the material.

Figure and background apply to learning situations as well. When a student is "on task," other potential figures are lying in the background. When competing thoughts/figures come to mind, he or she can choose to acknowledge them and move back to the task or can choose to attend to them more closely, compromising his or her focus on task. Despite the teacher's description that a student is off task, we would describe him or her as simply attending to a task other than the learning lesson. The student may become more interested in thinking about an after-school activity and noticing some emerging anticipatory excitement. In other cases, the student may start thinking about how difficult the assignment was last night and worrying about not being able to complete tonight's assignment as well. This latter experience describes some emerging academic anxiety that the educational therapist will attend to with the student.

The concepts of figure and ground can also be used to help describe the polarities of concentration and interruption. When the student is concentrating and fully engaged in the learning process, the educational therapist will notice few interruptions. When the student becomes anxious or worried, the interruptions become figural and the concentration recedes to the background. This process can alter back and forth, but when it becomes fixed, the student may lose touch with the hope of succeeding at the learning and instead feel scared, frustrated, and even hopeless. The student struggles to recover enough concentration to move forward or stays stuck in anxiety or fear.

To negotiate and recover concentration and to slow down the anxiety process, an inner conflict resolution process is useful. This is a dialogue between the concentration and interruption parts of the student. The student can learn what each part needs from the other in order to recover concentration. We call this a "dialectic dialogue." To restate how it works in other vocabulary: *"Concentration → Interruption → Recovery" is the dialectic of "Thesis → Antithesis → Synthesis."* This theory, when internalized by the educational therapist as a belief about the human experience, orients the therapist to the client's process and prevents him or her from getting lost in the content of the client's issues.

Learning Is Different From the Sum of Its Parts

These theoretical concepts are best understood in the process of learning. Gestalt therapy is known for its use of "experiments" with clients. Experiments are thought of as a way to help clients experience more of themselves, to take a risk of doing something different in a supportive, therapeutic environment. Through the use of experiments, the educational therapist will help students get to know themselves better as learners. He or she may ask students to role-play parts of themselves, such as the part that wants to learn, is interested in the subject material, and can concentrate on the assignment. Even the most "lazy" students (as described by teachers or parents) have a part that is trying, and this is seen simply by their physical presence in your office. If these students were not at all interested, they would not be in your office. An opposing role may be the part that is interrupting the student's work on the assignment, is not interested in the subject matter, does not think he or she wants to learn, or believes he or she cannot learn.

For purposes of illustration, let's say that the educational therapist or facilitative teacher asks a student to talk aloud as the interrupting part of herself and to give that part of herself a name—let's say, "the lazy me," "the goof-off"—whatever term has meaning for her. Once that part of her has been clarified in a few statements, the therapist/teacher asks to hear from the other side, the part that wants to learn or try. Sometimes this part needs some coaching or prompts from the facilitator. Validation of the student's concentrating side can be done by pointing out her presence in your office, coming to the appointment on time, and bringing her schoolwork. That part of her should also be given a name—for example, "the learner," "the on-task me." It would be well to then ask the student whether she knew that she had these two opposing parts inside of her and whether she has ever considered having them talk to each other.

The second experiment might be to have the student begin a dialogue between the two parts. Each side now begins to speak to the other. It does not matter which side speaks first, just as long as it is speaking to the other. Often the "concentrating" part will speak in terms of "shoulds," like "You should do your homework, it is good for you. You want to go to college someday, don't you?" This is fine at first, but at some point it will become important to challenge whose voice that really is—it may not be the "concentrating" part of the student but rather a parent or teacher's voice. Help the student find her voice as one who wants to learn rather than simply as someone else's introjection.

Keep in mind that the only goal of an experiment is to give students a new experience of themselves, of possibilities that they may not have considered for themselves before. The exact outcome or format of the experiment does not matter. It is more important for the therapist to adopt an "experimental attitude" than to worry about the exact protocol of conducting an experiment. Again, the purpose is not the outcome. The outcome of an experiment is almost irrelevant, compared with the process and freedom of having an experimental attitude about the "problem." The therapist's attention is focused on being curious about the student's learning process, without judgment or a need to "fix it" (as if that could be done). The student is the expert on his or her experience of learning or not learning. The therapist is the expert on helping the student discover that process.

Sometimes the first revelation in the work is helping the student discover that learning is a process, not a static outcome or a grade on an assignment. The answers to the test questions do not just appear inside the heads of the "smart kids." When students realize that getting the correct answer involves a series of steps that are under their control, they begin to become more invested in the process and are able to take some responsibility for it. They become able to identify themselves as learners, who attend, attempt, sometimes succeed and other times fail, but then attend and attempt again. Learning is not about whether they knew the right answer to a particular question. Rather, the approach is like that of a scientist who gathers data, makes an assumption or hypothesis, tests it in the environment, and notices the outcome, which then becomes new data upon which to develop a further hypothesis, and so on.

A RUNNING ANALYSIS OF AN INTERRUPTED PROCESS

Figure 16.2 illustrates a Gestalt approach, using dialectic dialogue, with an interrupted learning process. We define an interrupted process as one in which the learner is no longer

(Text continues on page 314)

COUNSELOR–CLIENT DIALOGUE	OBSERVATIONS & PROCESS COMMENTARY
C: So, Steve, as I understand it, you're wanting help with stage fright in speech class.	We reframe the description as a dialectic of concentration and interruption.
S: (Nods in agreement.)	
C: You look sad to me. Is that how you're feeling?	
S: Ya. (Looks away.)	
C: (Softly) So can you just be sad and see what happens?	Although Steve is physically present, where are his thoughts and feelings?
S: (Angrily) I want to get a grip on this speech block.	
C: Oh! Well, here's a pad of paper that could be your speech notes. Grip this!	It is common that a person is fearful when taking a risk to achieve something. He may wish to obliterate the fear rather than accept that fear is a natural part of one's experience when taking a risk. Gestalt theory suggests that change is paradoxical and that if Steve can accept his fear as part of himself, he will change (Beisser, 1970).
S: (Rolls up paper into a tube and wrings it.)	
C: Tell the block what you want.	
S: You've had a grip on me and I want to get a grip on you. (Pounds the tube again with the palm of his other hand.)	
C: What does the tube answer?	
S: It says, "You can beat me up but I'll just get you later."	
C: Do you believe that?	
S: Ya, I do . . . and it does.	
C: (Energized) Ah . . . so you are stuck . . . you against the block, yes?	
S: Yes.	
C: Are you open to finding another way to approach the block?	Cara delineates the two competing polarities, noticing the energy that Steve exhibits when mentioning each of them.
S: Yes.	
C: Well, I hear that you want to give speeches and on the other hand you feel doubtful because you have a block. Along with those doubting thoughts come feelings of sadness and anger. Does that seem true to you?	The polarities are a dialectic of thesis and antithesis: Speech ⟷ Doubt
S: (Resolutely) Yes.	<u>Contract</u>
C: Would you like to experiment with making some changes and seeing if you get better results?	We make a contract with the student to address his issue, stating our goal so as to take responsibility for what we want.

Figure 16.2 Case Example of Counseling Dialogue With a Client Experiencing Stage Fright

COUNSELOR–CLIENT DIALOGUE	OBSERVATIONS & PROCESS COMMENTARY
S: (Somewhat curiously) OK. C: Would you be willing to give a speech to me . . . just me right here and now? S: (Slowly) The one I couldn't give in class? C: OK. S: (Doubtfully) I don't know if I remember it. C: Well, since this is an experiment, we don't know what might happen, right? But we'll just begin and find out what might happen . . . is that OK with you? S: (Interested) OK. Should I stand up and pretend you're the class?	When conducting an experiment, it is important to set enough structure for the client to feel supported in taking the risk to experiment. At the same time, much permission is given to the client to set up the structure that will be deeded supportive.
C: You can if you want to. That might show what it's like when you're in class. Or you can just give it to me without pretending. Which would you prefer?	Note how Steve is very engaged in the experiment. It is helpful to follow his energy level and adjust the experiment as needed.
S: (Energized) I want to do it like in class. C: OK, then set it up so that you feel like you're in class. S: (Stands, walks to opposite side of room, faces Cara.) I need to hold notes. (Takes a sheet of paper that Cara hands him, plants his feet apart and looks at her. Face reddens.) C: Breathe. S: (Takes a deep breath.)	Notice how even in an "experiment," very real actions and experiences are felt. At this point, Cara intervenes in the here and now, addressing what is happening in the moment between her and Steve. This theoretical point has been made into a small saying by Gestaltists: Here and now; What and how; I and Thou.
C: Keep breathing to see if you feel a bit more comfortable. S: (Breathing, looking down at floor about 4 feet in front of him.) C: Are you calming down? S: (Nods affirmatively without looking up.) C: Your body looks rigid, like your knees are locked. Can you jiggle your knees a bit to loosen them?	Body awareness and body process are common tools used during experimentation. It may be helpful to have the student exaggerate his current body posture or take on an opposite posture to see what that feels like and to arrive at an insight.
S: (Jiggles knees.) C: How's that?	Steve may believe, "If I behave in a certain way, I will be ridiculed." This is an introjection, which he can reality-test in educational therapy.

Figure 16.2 (Continued)

COUNSELOR–CLIENT DIALOGUE	OBSERVATIONS & PROCESS COMMENTARY
S: Good.	
C: How about just shaking out the tightness? Can you just shake your head, shoulders, arms?	
S: (Reddens, apparently at the thought.)	
C: You imagine that you'll look funny and I'll laugh at you?	
S: (Nods yes.)	Again, Steve and Cara negotiate the structure of the experiment. Steve is becoming more aware of the type of support he needs from Cara in order to risk changing his behavior.
C: (Rising and begins shaking out legs and arms.) Does it help if you're not alone?	
S: (Shakes out one leg and then the other.) Ya.	
C: (Sitting back down.) So it is too intense if I see you . . . (Pauses.)	Introject. Steve seems to have a belief about how this should be done. Most likely it's a rule that he's taken in from the professor and hasn't yet examined as to whether it is true for him in the present situation. Cara engages him to reconsider his introject regarding what others are thinking when they are looking at him in front of them.
S: Ya . . . (Pauses.)	
C: But not if . . .	
S: . . . you don't stare.	
C: So let's see. When you stand up and I look at you, you think that I'm staring at you, right?	
S: (Nods yes.)	
C: But you don't really know for sure if that's what I'm doing without asking me, do you?	
S: (Nods no.)	
C: Are you staring at others when they get up?	
S: No.	
C: What are you doing?	
S: Depends. Waiting . . . just looking . . . thinking . . .	
C: About them?	
S: Sometimes . . . if it's a pretty girl . . . (Laughs)	
C: (Laughing) Sure, but your experience is different at different times, correct?	
S: Ya.	
C: So when you stand up, do you think the people sitting down are basically doing what you're doing when you are sitting there?	

Figure 16.2 (Continued)

COUNSELOR – CLIENT DIALOGUE	OBSERVATIONS & PROCESS COMMENTARY
S: Pretty much.	
C: So what do you make of all this?	
S: All what?	
C: Well, it seems to me that you get nervous when you imagine everyone is staring at you . . . what's the key word there?	Steve is considering other possibilities from his previous rigid introject about others in this situation. He has loosened the "fixed gestalt" and is better able to creatively adapt, i.e., consider other options and act accordingly.
S: Imagine.	
C: I think so, too. In fact, are they scaring you? Are they doing anything to you?	
S: Maybe, maybe not.	
C: So what's the truth?	
S: They're probably not staring at me.	
C: So . . .	
S: So there's no reason to freak out.	Cara underscores the shift in Steve, helping to raise his meta-awareness: awareness about his awareness of self.
C: And when you do freak out, it's coming from you, yes?	
S: Ya.	
C: And when it comes from you and you are aware of that, you can change it, yes?	
S: Ya.	
C: By . . .	
S: Seeing that they are just looking.	Cara verifies her contract with Steve.
C: And if someone is staring . . .	
S: Get her number later.	
C and S: (Laughing.)	They decide to continue.
C: So, you got up and faced your audience and got some insights! Bravo for you! You're looking bright-eyed and enthusiastic like a scientist who had made a discovery! Shall we meet again and continue on in the process?	
S: (Brightly) Sure.	

Figure 16.2 (Continued)

concentrating, no longer on task for learning, because other needs take precedence for his or her attention. In the vignette given in the figure, Cara is working with Steve, a 10th grader with stage fright. He presented with feelings of embarrassment because he had twice gone to the front of the room and then had sat down without saying anything. Noticing how Steve reddened when he told the story, Cara initiated a dialogue using the Gestalt principles introduced in the previous section. We have placed the dialogue in the left column and linked it to the theoretical explication in the right column.

DEALING WITH THE MOST COMMON LEARNING PROBLEMS

The most common learning problems that we have addressed in our work have been stage fright, reading problems, mathematics problems, and test anxiety, presented below.

Stage Fright

Stage fright (also known as communication apprehension) is described as fear of speaking in common situations, not just when being on a stage. Public speaking is one of the most prevalent of the social phobias (Davidson, Marshall, Tomarken, & Henriques, 2000), and speaking is performed more frequently than reading, writing, math, and test taking. One person's process of stage fright has been detailed in Figure 16.2. Any time a person has something to say is potentially an occasion for stage fright. In our counseling approach we also give considerable attention to the nonverbal aspects of communication (e.g., when a person fears being seen as having strong feelings such as sadness or anger). Some of the experiments that have helped students have been sitting down rather than standing; designing the speech in order to notice the breath; shaking out body tension before beginning; and starting by acknowledging the anxiety: "I'm really anxious, but today I want to speak to you about . . ." Debriefing after each experiment is essential for keeping the focus on awareness so that the student doesn't see the experiments as "tips."

GEORGE: I also have comments on learning like a scientist, with scientific methods. This relates very much to how Fritz Perls defined learning. He defined learning as discovering that something is possible, which I think fits right into what you are saying. With regard to your work with stage fright, there is one other possibility that I thought of: that it is possible to re-own the power projected on the audience by becoming the audience.

SUSAN: Oh cool! That would be a good experiment.

Reading Difficulties

Referrals of children and adolescents for reading difficulties are the most common in our Community Counseling Center. This may reflect the current emphasis on reading in schools as a result of No Child Left Behind (U.S. Department of Education, 2002), which is placing increased emphasis on standardized testing. Difficulties of K–12 children include word analysis, vocabulary development, and comprehension, whereas difficulties of university-aged clients include complaints about reading too slowly (and falling behind in assigned reading) and inefficient reading habits (e.g., needing repeated readings, inadequate comprehension).

It is common to find that students judge themselves using a standard of perfection. Their complaints about their reading often reduce to "I should be able to read something through once, quickly, without skipping a word, and have perfect recall." Often an examination of unrealistic expectations ("shoulds") leads to their willingness to be more who they are as readers of a particular type of material, especially conceptually dense text material in an area unfamiliar to them (Craft, 1989).

Mathematics Problems

Students having difficulties with mathematics who are referred to our community counseling center most often have problems with algebra because it serves the gatekeeper function of entrance to a college preparatory track in high schools (Atanda, 1999). One client was repeating Algebra I for the fourth time, and this time her younger sister would be in the same class, prompting opinions of failure and feelings of shame. On the other hand, she was seeking help for learning algebra and was proud of her perseverance. Another aspect of working with students with math difficulties is that it is hard to find clinicians who feel competent to take a math anxiety case. This speaks to the general discomfort that Americans have with math (Morales, 1999).

One Gestalt approach to use with children who present with math problems is the two-chair experiment. Although, in our experience, many therapists do not think it is possible for young children to conduct a two-chair experiment, our work with a second grader showed otherwise. The child was working on her conflict about learning "regrouping" (borrowing in subtraction). While sitting in one of the two chairs, she began to imply (in Gestalt terms, acting as "topdog") that she "should" learn regrouping: "Math will be fun and then it will get even more funner."

Test Anxiety

In our counseling center we have found that test anxiety very often overlaps with reading and math problems for K–12 students, especially those who must take annual standardized tests. Adult clients have been seen in our counseling center for test anxiety regarding issues of preparing for licensure exams, such as those for real estate licenses and teaching credentials. Common themes emerging from this educational therapy are procrastination, fear that no amount of preparation is sufficient, resentment about being tested or about being tested in a certain manner, fear of going blank, fear of failure, and fear of exposure (Sameto, 2001).

Stuttering

Although we do not work extensively with stutterers in our clinic, the husband-and-wife Gestalt therapist team of Woody Starkweather and Janet Givens has considerable experience working with people who stutter. Their book *Experiential Therapy for Stutterers* (in press) describes in detail their clinical applications of Gestalt-experiential therapy with stutterers. They incorporate the Gestalt cycle of experience in both diagnosis and treatment. Following are some of the key ingredients of Gestalt therapy that guide their work: (a) Experience is more important than behavior, (b) development is more important than etiology, (c) therapeutic power is in the present, (d) experience counts most, (e) the therapist is his or her own instrument of change, (f) it's all about the relationship, (g) therapy is equally important for the therapist, (h) therapy is too good to be limited to the sick, (i) control is not the goal, (j) the stutterer is in a process, (k) meet stutterers where they are, (l) expect and respect resistance, (m) therapy is out there, not in here, and (n) the process is more important than the outcome.

Writer's Block

An important aspect of our clinical work has been to offer a dissertation support group to doctoral students in organizational leadership who are at risk of not completing the degree due to issues with their dissertation. Common difficulties expressed in this group were feelings of isolation and estrangement from the faculty, imagining that there was one right way to do their dissertation, and feeling that they had to discover it because no one had yet told them.

SUMMARY

In summary, writing about the fears people express when they struggle with learning often makes them sound dumb or foolish. They are probably neither, in our opinion. Gestalt work discloses irrational introjections that have interfered with healthy learning processes and affords students an opportunity to put their thoughts and feelings in a perspective that is nourishing and self-supportive for them.

REVIEW QUESTIONS

1. What is the difference between a medical model or scientific approach to learning and an idiographic approach? Which paradigm best describes a Gestalt approach to learning and education? Why?

2. What is the theoretical relationship between the vase/face image (figure/ground) and concentrations/interruptions?

CARA: If you were using this chapter in a class for beginning counselors, what would you want your students to get from this particular chapter?

GEORGE: I think what I would be looking for is a paradigmatic shift—and I think you provide this—from thinking in the old ways to a more idiosyncratic, holistic way, requiring a shift in their experience as learners, too. I hope you have startled them into realizing that there is a hell of a lot more that can be done than is being done.

ROBERT: I think that one of the really profound challenges for people interested in working with students on the learning process is that educators will tell us that more and more they have to teach to the test.

GEORGE: And of course that's an obscenity! It's so stupid, among other things; testing should be a part of the learning process rather than a way of chastising people. That is part of the result of the value system in our culture right now.

CARA: Yes, testing is very heavy-handed in the schools right now. It seems to me that if you were to follow a Gestalt model on a schoolwide basis you would ungrade the schools.

GEORGE: Grades are a very arbitrary classification. The best schooling was probably in the one-room schoolhouse.

CARA: I actually started out in a one-room schoolhouse, and it was great because I could go and sit in different rows.

SUSAN: Similar to the Montessori approach—the opportunity to observe the child who is 3 years older do something and then gradually work at your pace toward the next experiment in learning.

CARA: I agree, you could end up with one group of students for math, another for language arts, and another for science.

3. What are some of the most common learning struggles that can be addressed using Gestalt therapy principles?

4. What is stage fright from a Gestalt perspective, and what are some Gestalt therapy experiments useful for those struggling with stage fright?

EXPERIENTIAL PEDAGOGICAL ACTIVITIES

ACTIVITY 1: You may have experienced some interruptions in your learning, whether with regard to learning page by page or the accumulative learnings of your graduate or training program. Your authors suggest that these interruptions could be considered opportunities to explore rather than deficits. In a journal, note or list things, events, and/or people that have been interruptions during the process of completing your program. You also may be able to connect each with a feeling or meaning. Looking back over your list, what was the additional learning you acquired from the interruptions?

ACTIVITY 2: Your chapter authors describe an experiment of "dialectic dialogue" between the concentrating and interrupting parts of ourselves that often emerge while we are engaged in a learning process. In the classroom setting, you can try varying versions of this experiment:

a) Set up a "fishbowl" with two chairs in the middle of a circle of observers. The two chairs will be used by one person representing the concentrating part of the learner and, switching chairs, the interrupting part. Or have two individuals play both parts in dialogue with each other.

b) Divide the class into dyads so that everyone in class has the opportunity to experiment.

c) Have one individual play the role of the concentrating part, and have all the other class members, as a chorus, represent interruptions.

GEORGE: And you could even put the three groups together.

CARA: Oh yes, for peer teaching.

GEORGE: The disciplines, too, are arbitrary, they came out of reality and all have connections to one another, because they are out of life. Furthermore—this is something I mentioned in *Human Teaching for Human Learning*—there are really two ways to look at this: Parmenides, the Greek philosopher, who believed in absolutes and being very rational, and Heraclitus (the one who said you couldn't put your foot in the same place in the river twice because the river flowed on), who was very process oriented. And Gestalt owes a lot to Heraclitus, for it, too, is process oriented and dynamic. And schooling and learning are process oriented and dynamic.

GEORGE: Well, I have no problem with anything you said—all I have done is elaborate on your points. I did experience the frustration, as you must have, of the limitations of space and time. There is so much to write about, and you have given a very sound foundational introduction that I hope will pique readers' interest to pursue this.

SUSAN: I was thinking this morning, that 15-plus pages got filled pretty quickly. It really is just an introduction, a taste of it.

GEORGE: What is needed is a textbook, just based on this issue. When are you going to write it?

CARA: Thank you George; it is very helpful to have your support on this material.

GEORGE: Thank you for the stimulation of reading your chapter and the opportunity to dialogue about your ideas.

ACTIVITY 3: Many public figures experience and deal with stage fright. Review the popular and academic literature to identify some of those individuals. Compare your own impressions of these individuals with the impressions of others in class.

EPILOGUE

ANSEL L. WOLDT AND SARAH M. TOMAN

The process of collecting chapters for this textbook was, in and of itself, an experience of many aspects of Gestalt therapy theory and practice. Most notable was the opportunity for contact. We, the editors, feel privileged to have had such rich contact with the authors, dialogue partners, and others involved with this textbook project. All have been focused on offering their expertise to you, the reader. Our shared intent has been to provide faculty and novice students with a clear, readable, and useful text and to make contact with you and your interest in Gestalt therapy history, theory, and practice.

Another Gestalt concept and process we experienced during this project was dialogue. The founders of Gestalt therapy most certainly could not have envisioned corresponding by the electronic means at our disposal today. Theirs was primarily face-to-face contact when they met to create the original masterpiece, *Gestalt Therapy* (Perls, Hefferline, & Goodman, 1951). We found that the media of e-mail, fax, immediate access to Web sites, electronic connections to library holdings, and the cell phone greatly enhanced our opportunities to share and compare viewpoints about various elements of this textbook.

The dialogue partners have provided for you not only models of ways to share themselves and their views but also examples of how considering multiple voices and multiple perspectives can add depth, energy, and richness to the learning process. There are nearly endless possibilities of viewpoints to consider in the Gestalt community; we regret that page limits restricted us from including more voices and in some cases required that we exclude some of the dialogue that had been created. Interestingly, the dialogue that began between one of our chapter authors and her dialogue partner was just the beginning of their dialogue: At the time of this writing (months later), they are still having e-mail conversations between continents about their agreements and disagreements on various aspects of Gestalt theory, enough to create a book in itself. We also extend our regrets to those who expressed interest in our project and desired to contribute as authors and dialogue partners, but we didn't have room for more. If not for page limits, this could readily have been at least a 20-chapter book. We are aware of client systems and areas of application that are not represented here. Of those that were considered but not included due to page restrictions, the most notable are research on Gestalt therapy, Gestalt approaches to supervision, Gestalt somatic/body work, Gestalt with elderly patients, Gestalt ethics, brief and crisis-centered Gestalt therapy (although touched on in Phil Brownell's chapter), Gestalt therapy with clients having chronic psychological conditions,

Gestalt applications in behavioral health and medical settings, and Gestalt applications in the economic and political spheres.

Our hope is that the materials found in each chapter will encourage continued dialogue. By including our list of online and digital Gestalt resources in Appendix A, we are attempting to offer support for those interested in further contact with some of the faces and places in the worldwide Gestalt community.

Some of the chapter authors referred to the concept of a "unit of work" and how a "unit" coincides with the cycle of experience. As editors and coauthors of the Review Questions and Experiential Pedagogical Activities at the end of each chapter, we experienced many "small units" or "cycles" similar to what we experienced in the beginning phase with the book proposal in the delight of contacting authors and dialogue partners and having them agree to write, responding to peer feedback, completing a chapter, writing review questions for each chapter, creating the set of experiential pedagogical activities for each chapter, interacting with the chapter about our suggested experiential activities, completing a dialogue, and checking all the citations in a chapter against the references to be sure they were complete and coincided. All of these provided meaningful contact and, when completed, formed a "unit" and mini-gestalt. The "larger unit" is one of experiencing the entire project from start to finish, although we may find ourselves experiencing contact withdrawal as the manuscript is converted into the completed textbook. Closure does not seem possible without information and feedback from you, the reader. We encourage you to contact others interested in Gestalt therapy to dialogue about figures that have meaning for you and add your own voice to the Gestalt literature.

As noted previously, our interest in having dialogue continue after reading our book has prompted us to include in our book, as Appendix A, a comprehensive listing of many of the resources and opportunities for continuing contact in the greater Gestalt community. Though we recognize that Web sites and Internet addresses often change and as a result the exact resource you are looking for may not be there anymore, our efforts are to at least let you know of the abundance of potential contacts to assist you with your next steps if you want to expand your knowledge and vision of Gestalt therapy.

COMPREHENSIVE REFERENCE AND GESTALT BOOK LIST

Acharyya, S. (1992). The doctor's dilemma: The practice of cultural psychiatry in multicultural Britain. In J. Kareem & R. Littlewood (Eds.), *Inter-cultural therapy: Themes, interpretations and practice* (pp. 74–82). Oxford, UK: Blackwell Scientific Publications.

Adler, A. (1956). The individual psychology of Alfred Adler (H. L. Ansbacher and R. R. Ansbacher, Ed. and Trans.). New York: Harper and Row.

Alcoholics Anonymous World Service. (2001). *Alcoholics Anonymous.* New York: General Services Office.

American Educational Research Association Special Interest Group. (2003). Confluent education today. Retrieved October 8, 2004, from http://members.aol.com/confluent.

American Psychiatric Association. (1994). *Diagnostic and statistical manual of mental disorders: DSM-IV.* Washington, DC: Author.

American Psychiatric Association. (2000). *Diagnostic and statistical manual of mental disorders: DSM-IV-TR.* Washington, DC: Author.

Ancis, J., & Szymanski, D. (2001). Awareness of white privilege among white counseling trainees. *Counseling Psychologist, 29*(4), 548–569.

Apple, M. W. (1997). Consuming the other: Whiteness, education, and cheap french fries. In M. Fine, L. Weis, L. C. Powell, & L. Mun Wong (Eds.), *Off white: Readings on race, power, and society* (pp. 121–128). New York: Routledge.

Argyle, M. (1975). *Bodily communication.* New York: International Universities Press.

Argyris, C. (1990). *Overcoming organizational defenses.* Boston: Allyn & Bacon.

Aristotle. (1962). *Nicomachean ethics* (M. Oswald, Trans.). Indianapolis, IN: Bobbs-Merrill.

Aspy, D., & Roebuck, F. (1977). *Kids don't learn from people they don't like.* Amherst, MA: Human Resources Development Press.

Assagioli, R. (1971). *Psychosynthesis.* New York: Viking Press.

Atanda, R. (1999). Do gatekeeper courses expand educational options? *Education Statistics Quarterly 1*(1). Retrieved August 16, 2004, from http://nces.ed.gov/programs/quarterly/Vol_1/1_1/4-esq11-c.asp.

At Risk. (2003). Statistics. Retrieved May 25, 2003, from www.at-risk.com.

Axline, V. (1947). *Play therapy.* New York: Houghton Mifflin.

Axline, V. (1964). *Dibs: In search of self.* New York: Ballantine.

Aylward, J. (1996). The marathon group. In B. Feder & R. Ronall (Eds.), *A living legacy of Fritz and Laura Perls: Contemporary case studies* (pp. 233–251). Montclair, NJ: Beefeeder.

Ballard, J., & Timmerman, W. (1975). *Strategies in humanistic education.* San Diego, CA: Mandala.

Banet, A. G., Jr. (1976). *Creative psychotherapy: A source book.* La Jolla, CA: University Associates.

Barnett, M. (1973). *People, not psychiatry.* London: Allen & Unwin.

Bates, C. (2001). *Pigs eat wolves: Going into partnership with your dark side.* St. Paul, MN: Yes International.

Bateson, G. (1971). The cybernetics of self: A theory of alcoholism. *Psychiatry, 34,* 1–18.

Bauer, A. (2000). Violence prevention: A systematic approach. In D. S. Singhu & C. B. Aspy (Eds.), *Violence in American schools: Practical guidelines for counselors* (pp. 139–151). Alexandria, VA: American Counseling Association.

Baumgardner, P., & Perls, F. (1975). *Gifts from Lake Cowichan* (Book I) and *Legacy from Fritz* (Book II). Palo Alto, CA: Science and Behavior Books.

Beaumont, H. (1993). Martin Buber's "I–Thou" and fragile self-organization: Contribution to a Gestalt couples therapy. *British Gestalt Journal, 2*(2), 85–95.

Beaumont, H. (1998). In the field of soul (interview by Judith Hemming). *British Gestalt Journal, 7,* 76–85.

Beisser, A. (1970). The paradoxical theory of change. In J. Fagan & I. L. Shepherd (Eds.), *Gestalt therapy now: Theory, techniques, applications* (pp. 77–80). Palo Alto, CA: Science and Behavior Books.

Beisser, A. (1989). *Flying without wings: Personal reflections on loss, disability and healing.* New York: Doubleday.

Beisser, A. (1990). *A graceful passage: Notes on the freedom to live or die.* New York: Doubleday.

Beisser, A. (1991). *The only hope: Thoughts on the meaning of friends and friendship.* New York: Doubleday.

Belzunce, P. (1994). *What really matters is the heart: A psychologist grieves the death of his mother.* North Ridgeville, OH: Bella-Tierra.

Belzunce, P. (2000). *Heart shadows.* Cleveland, OH: Gestalt Institute of Cleveland Press.

Bernard, H., & Huckins, W. (1974). *Humanism in the classroom: An eclectic approach to teaching and learning.* Boston: Allyn & Bacon.

Bessell, H., & Palomares, U. (1973). *Methods in human development: The Magic Circle curriculum.* San Diego, CA: Human Development Training Institute.

Bianco, M. W. (1994). *The velveteen rabbit.* Mankato, MN: Creative Editions.

Bickman, L., & Dokecki, P. R. (1989). Public and private responsibility for mental health services. *American Psychologist, 44*(8), 1133–1137.

Blaney, B., & Smythe, J. (2001). A Gestalt approach to the treatment of adolescent eating disorders. In M. McConville & G. Wheeler (Eds.), *The heart of development: Gestalt approaches to working with children, adolescents and their worlds: Vol. 2. Adolescence* (pp. 193–213). Cambridge, MA: Gestalt Press.

Bloom, D. (1997, January). *Self: Structuring/functioning.* Unpublished paper presented at the New York Institute for Gestalt Therapy.

Blumenthal, M. (2001). A field of difference: A Gestalt consideration of learning disabilities. In M. McConville & G. Wheeler (Eds.), *The heart of development: Gestalt approaches to working with children, adolescents and their worlds: Vol. 2. Adolescence* (pp. 153–171). Cambridge, MA: Gestalt Press.

Borofsky, R., & Borofsky, A. K. (1994). Giving and receiving. In G. Wheeler & S. Backman (Eds.), *On intimate ground: A Gestalt approach to working with couples* (pp. 325–355). San Francisco: Jossey-Bass.

Borton, T. (1970). *Reach, touch and teach: Student concerns and process education.* New York: McGraw-Hill.

Boszormenyi-Nagy, I., & Krasner, B. R. (1986). *Between give and take: A clinical guide to contextual therapy.* New York: Brunner/Mazel.

Bottome, P. (2001). *Completing the circle: Taking Gestalt to Asia.* Cleveland, OH: Gestalt Institute of Cleveland Press.

Bowman, C. (1998). Definitions of Gestalt therapy: Finding common ground. *Gestalt Review, 2*(2), 97–107.

Bradford, L. P., Gibb, J. R., & Benne, K. D. (Eds.). (1964). *T-Group theory and laboratory method: Innovation in re-education.* New York: John Wiley.

Brafman, A. H. (2001). *Untying the knot: Working with children and parents.* New York: Karnac.

Brannigan, M. (1988). *Everywhere and nowhere: The path of Alan Watts.* New York: Peter Lang.

Brentano, F. (1999). Psychology from an empirical perspective. In D. Moss (Ed.), *Humanistic and transpersonal psychology: A historical and biographical sourcebook.* London: Greenwood. (Original work published 1874)

Brown, G. I. (1971). *Human teaching for human learning: An introduction to confluent education.* New York: Viking.

Brown, G. I. (1975). Human is as confluent does. In G. I. Brown, T. Yeomans, & L. Grizzard (Eds.), *The live classroom: Innovation through confluent education and Gestalt* (pp. 99–108). New York: Viking.

Brown, G. I. (1990). *Human teaching for human learning: An introduction to confluent education* (2nd ed.). Highland, NY: Gestalt Journal Press.

Brown, G. I., Yeomans, T., & Grizzard, L. (Eds.). (1975). *The live classroom: Innovation through confluent education and Gestalt.* New York: Viking.

Brown, J. (1980). Buber and Gestalt. *Gestalt Journal, 3*(2), 47–55.

Brown, J. H. (Ed.). (1996). *Advances in confluent education: Integrating consciousness for human change.* Greenwich, CT: JAI.

Brown, J. H., Cline, Z., & Necochea, J. (Eds.). (2003). *Advances in confluent education: Connections with multicultural education.* Greenwich, CT: JAI.

Brown, J. H., D'Emidio-Caston, M., & Benard, B. (2000). *Resilience education.* Thousand Oaks, CA: Corwin.

Brown, J. R. (1996). *The I in science: Training to utilize subjectivity in research.* Boston: Scandinavian University Press.

Brown, J. R. (1998). *Back to the beanstalk: Gestalt enchantment and reality for couples.* Cleveland, OH: Gestalt Institute of Cleveland Press.

Brown, S. (1995). *Treating the alcoholic: A developmental model of recovery.* New York: John Wiley.

Brownell, P. (1998). Condensing the field: Internet communication and Gestalt community. *Gestalt Review, 2*(2), 143–153.

Brownell, P. (2000). A theoretical matrix for training and practice. *Australian Gestalt Journal, 4*(1), 51–61.

Brownell, P. (2002). Psychological testing: A place in Gestalt therapy? *British Gestalt Journal, 11*(2), 99–107.

Brownell, P. (2003). Gestalt Global's Gestalt therapy construct library: Preamble and preliminary considerations. *Gestalt! 7*(1). Retrieved August 16, 2004, from www.g-gej.org/7-1/librarypreamble.html.

Brownell, P. (In press). Contemporary Gestalt therapy theory: Organizing perspective for juvenile sex offender treatment. *Gestalt Review.*

Brownell, P., O'Neill, B., & Goodlander, M. (1999). Field in flux: Gestalt in the world through Internet technology. *Gestalt! 3*(1). Retrieved October 25, 2004, from www.g-gej.org/3-1/gestaltnet.html.

Browne-Miller, A. (1993). *Gestalting addiction: The addiction-focused group therapy of Dr. Richard Louis Miller.* Norwood, NJ: Ablex.

Brunink, S. (1976). *A phenomenological content analysis of the therapeutic verbal behavior of expert psychoanalytically oriented, Gestalt and behavior therapists.* Unpublished doctoral dissertation, Kent State University.

Buber, M. (1958). *I and thou* (R. G. Smith, Trans.). New York: Scribner. (Original work published 1923)

Buber, M. (1965a). *Between man and man* (R. G. Smith, Trans.). New York: Macmillan. (Original work published 1926)

Buber, M. (1965b). *The knowledge of man.* New York: Harper & Row.

Buber, M. (2000). *I and thou* (R. G. Smith, Trans.). New York: Scribner. (Original work published 1923)

Bugental, J. F. T. (1965). *The search for authenticity: An existential-analytic approach to psychotherapy.* New York: Holt, Rinehart & Winston.

Bugental, J. F. T. (Ed.). (1967). *Challenges of humanistic psychology.* New York: McGraw-Hill.

Bugental, J. F. T. (1976). *The search for existential identity.* San Francisco: Jossey-Bass.

Burke, M. T., & Miranti, J. G. (1996). *The description of spirituality.* Paper presented at the annual meeting of the Association for Counselor Education and Supervision Conference, Portland, OR.

Burley, T. (2001). The present status of Gestalt therapy. *Gestalt! 5*(1). Retrieved from www.g-gej.org/5-1/todd.html.

Canfield, J., & Wells, H. (1976). *100 ways to enhance self-concept in the classroom.* Englewood Cliffs, NJ: Prentice Hall.

Carlock, C. J., Glaus, K. O., & Shaw, C. (1992). The alcoholic: A Gestalt view. In E. Nevis (Ed.), *Gestalt therapy: Perspectives and applications* (pp. 191–238). New York: Gardner.

Carroll, F. (2002). The Pinocchio syndrome: Path to wholeness. Gestalt therapy with children and adolescents. In G. Wheeler & M. McConville (Eds.), *The heart of development: Gestalt approaches to working with children, adolescents, and their world: Vol. 1. Childhood* (pp. 331–345). Hillsdale, NJ: Analytic Press.

Carroll, F., & Oaklander, V. (1997). Gestalt play therapy. In K. O'Connor & L. M. Braverman (Eds.), *Play therapy theory and practice: A comparative presentation* (pp. 184–203). New York: John Wiley.

Carter, R. T. (1997). Is white a race? Expressions of white racial identity. In M. Fine, L. Weis, L. Powell, & L. Mun Wong (Eds.), *Off white: Readings on race, power, and society* (pp. 198–209). New York: Routledge.

Cartwright, D. (Ed.). (1951). *Field theory in social science: Selected theoretical papers.* Oxford, UK: Harpers.

Castaneda, C. (1971). *A separate reality.* New York: Simon & Schuster.

Castillo, G. A. (1974). *Left-handed teaching: Lessons in affective education.* New York: Praeger.

Centers for Disease Control. (2003). Causes of death. Retrieved May 25, 2003, from www.cdc.gov.

Chase, L. (1975). *The other side of the report card: A how-to-do-it program for affective education.* Pacific Palisades, CA: Goodyear.

Clark, N., & Fraser, T. (1987). *The Gestalt approach: An introduction for managers and trainers.* West Sussex, UK: Roffey Park Management College.

Clarkson, P. (1989). *Gestalt counseling in action.* Newbury Park, CA: Sage.

Clarkson, P. (1994). *On psychotherapy.* London: Whurr.

Clarkson, P., & Mackewn, J. (1993). *Fritz Perls.* Newbury Park, CA: Sage.

Clemmens, M. (1993). Chemical dependency as a developed contact style. *Gestalt Review, 4*(1), 1–6.

Clemmens, M. (1997). *Getting beyond sobriety: Clinical approaches to long-term recovery.* San Francisco: Jossey-Bass.

Cole, H. P. (1972). *Process education.* Englewood Cliffs, NJ: Educational Technology Publications.

Combs, A. (1962). *Perceiving, behaving, becoming.* Washington, DC: National Education Association.

Copelend, W., Birmingham, C., Caston, M., DeMuelle, L., & Natal, D. (1994). Making meaning in classrooms: An investigation of cognitive processes in aspiring, experienced teachers, and their peers. *American Educational Research Journal, 31*(1), 166–196.

Corlis, R. B., & Rabe, P. (1969). *Psychotherapy from the center: A humanistic view of change and of growth.* Scranton, PA: International Textbook.

Costa, P., & Widiger, C. (1994). *Personality disorders and the five-factor model of personality.* Washington, DC: American Psychological Association.

Craft, J. H. (1989). *Gestalt educational therapy: Its application to learning to read. A case study of resistance among students in an elementary school.* Unpublished doctoral dissertation, Pepperdine University.

Crawford, J. (1985). *A walk into awareness: A Gestalt approach to growth.* San Antonio, TX: Watercress.

Crocker, S. F. (1999). *A well-lived life: Essays in Gestalt therapy.* Cambridge, MA: Gestalt Institute of Cleveland Press.

Crocker, S. F., Brownell, P., Stemberger, G., Gunther, S., Just, B., Sen, A., et al. (2001). Field and boundary. *Gestalt! 5*(2). Retrieved August 16, 2004, from www.g-gej.org/5-2/1998field.html.

Culley, S. (1991). *Integrative counseling skills in action.* Newbury Park, CA: Sage.

Cullum, A. (1971). *The geranium on the window sill just died, but teacher you went right on.* New York: Harlan Quest.

Curwin, R., & Fuhrman, B. (1975). *Discovering your teaching self.* Englewood Cliffs, NJ: Prentice Hall.

Cushman, P., & Gilford, P. (2000). Will managed care change our way of being? *American Psychologist, 55,* 985–996.

Daldrup, R., Beutler, L., Engle, D., & Greenberg, L. (1988). *Focused expressive psychotherapy: Freeing the overcontrolled patient.* New York: Guilford.

Daniel, P. (2004). *Types of therapy for mental health.* Retrieved October 25, 2004, from www.medformation.com/ac/crsaha.nsf/aha/aha_kindther_bha.htm.

Daniels, V., & Horowitz, L. (1976). *Being and caring.* Palo Alto, CA: Mayfield.

d'Ardenne, P., & Mahtani, A. (1998). *Transcultural counselling in action.* Thousand Oaks, CA: Sage.

Davidson, R. J., Marshall, J. R., Tomarken, A. J., & Henriques, J. B. (2000). While a phobic waits: Regional brain electrical and autonomic activity in social phobics during anticipation of public speaking. *Biological Psychiatry, 47,* 85–95.

Davison, G. C. (2000). Stepped care: Doing more with less? *Journal of Consulting and Clinical Psychology, 68*(4), 580–585.

Deegear, J., & Lawson, D. (2003). The utility of empirically supported treatments. *Professional Psychology: Research and Practice, 34*(3), 271–277.

DeMayo, B. A., & Garcia, C. L. (1997). A Gestalt approach to educational therapy. *Educational Therapist, 18*(2), 14–17.

DeMeulle, L., & D'Emidio-Caston, M. (1996). Confluent education: A coherent vision of teacher education. *Advances in Confluent Education, 1,* 43–62.

DeMille, R. (1973). *Put your mother on the ceiling: Children's imagination games.* New York: Penguin.

Dennison, G. (1969). *The lives of children: The story of the First Street School.* New York: Vintage.

DiBella, A., & Nevis, E. C. (1998). *How organizations learn: An integrated strategy for building learning capability.* San Francisco: Jossey-Bass.

Doerschel, E. (1993). The paradox of change and the treaty of Waitangi. In Y. Starak, A. Maclean, & A. Bernet (Eds.), *More grounds for Gestalt.* Christchurch, New Zealand: Foreground.

Dominelli, L. (2002). *Anti-oppressive social work: Theory and practice.* London: Palgrave.

Doubrawa, E. (2001, Spring). The politics of the I-Thou: Martin Buber, the anarchist. *Gestalt Journal.* Retrieved August 2003 from http://ourworld.compuserve.com/homepages/gik_gestalt/doubrawa.html#text.

Downing, J. (Ed.). (1976). *Gestalt awareness: Papers from the San Francisco Gestalt Institute.* New York: Harper & Row.

Downing, J., & Marmorstein, R. (Eds.). (1973). *Dreams and nightmares: A book of Gestalt therapy sessions.* New York: Harper & Row.

Dreikurs, R. (1957). *Psychology in the classroom.* New York: Harper & Brothers.

Dye, A., & Hackney, H. (1975). *Gestalt approaches to counseling.* New York: Houghton Mifflin.

Earley, J. (1996). The interactive Gestalt therapy. In B. Feder & B. Ronall (Eds.), *A living legacy of Fritz and Laura Perls: Contemporary case studies* (pp. 221–232). Montclair, NJ: Beefeeder.

Earley, J. (1999). *Interactive group therapy: Integrating interpersonal, action-oriented, and psychodynamic approaches.* New York: Brunner-Mazel.

Egan, G. (1970). *Encounter: Group processes for interpersonal growth.* Belmont, CA: Brooks-Cole.

Ehrenfels, C. von. (1988). On gestalt qualities. In B. Smith (Ed. & Trans.), *Foundations of Gestalt theory* (pp. 82–117). Munich: Philosophia. (Original work published 1890)

Ekman, P., & Davidson, R. (1994). *The nature of emotions: Fundamental questions.* New York: Oxford University Press.

Elliott, C. (1999). *Locating the energy for change: An introduction to appreciative inquiry.* Winnipeg, Manitoba, Canada: International Institute for Sustainable Development.

Ellis, W. (Ed.). (1997). *A source book of Gestalt psychology.* Highland, NY: Gestalt Journal Press. (Original work published 1938)

Ellison, C., & Paloutzian, R. (1982). Loneliness, spiritual well being, and quality of life. In L. A. Peplar & D. Perlman (Eds.), *Loneliness: A sourcebook of current research theory and therapy* (pp. 121–140). New York: John Wiley.

Engle, D., & Holiman, M. (2002a). A case illustration of resistance from a Gestalt-experimental perspective. *Journal of Clinical Psychology, 58*(2), 151–156.

Engle, D., & Holiman, M. (2002b). A Gestalt-experimental perspective on resistance. *Journal of Clinical Psychology, 58*(2), 175–183.

English, H., & English, A. (1958). *A comprehensive dictionary of psychological and psychoanalytical terms.* New York: David McKay.

Enright, J. (1980). *Enlightening Gestalt: Waking up from the nightmare.* Mill Valley, CA: Pro Telos.

Erikson, E. (1963). *Childhood and society* (2nd ed.). New York: Norton.

Erikson, E. (1968). *Identity: Youth and crisis.* New York: Norton.

Erskine, R., & Moursund, J. (1988). *Integrative psychotherapy in action.* Beverly Hills, CA: Sage.

Esalen Center. (2004). Esalen history. Retrieved September 29, 2004, from www.esalenctr.org/display/aboutpage.cfm?ID=15.

Esalen Institute. (2002). Esalen initiatives: Education. Retrieved August 16, 2004, from www.esalen.org/air/esalen_initiativesfoldr/esalen_initiatives1.shtml.

Estrup, L. (Producer). (2000). *What's behind the empty chair: Gestalt therapy theory and methodology* [Video]. Available from Gestalt Associates Training Los Angeles, www.gatla.org/LIV_WEB-SITE/ORDER.HTM.

Fagan, J. (Ed.). (1974). Gestalt therapy [Special issue]. *Counseling Psychologist, 4*(4).

Fagan, J., & Shepherd, I. (1970). *Gestalt therapy now.* Palo Alto, CA: Science and Behavior Books.

Faiver, C. M., Ingersoll, R. E., O'Brien, E., & McNally, C. (2001). *Explorations in counseling and spirituality: Philosophical, practical, and personal reflections.* Pacific Grove, CA: Brooks Cole.

Fantini, M., & Weinstein, G. (1968). *Toward a contact curriculum.* New York: Anti-Defamation League of B'nai B'rith Society.

Fantz, R., & Roberts, A. (1998). *The dreamer and the dream: Essays and reflections on Gestalt therapy.* Cleveland, OH: Gestalt Institute of Cleveland Press.

Farrelly, F., & Brandsma, J. (1974). *Provocative therapy.* Cupertino, CA: Meta.

Feder, B. (1990). *Peeling the onion: A Gestalt therapy manual for clients* (2nd ed.). Montclair, NJ: Author.

Feder, B. (2002). *Gestalt group therapy: National survey.* Unpublished manuscript, Montclair, NJ.

Feder, B., & Ronall, R. (Eds.). (1980). *Beyond the hot seat: Gestalt approaches to group.* New York: Brunner/Mazel.

Feder, B., & Ronall, R. (1996). *A living legacy of Fritz and Laura Perls: Contemporary case studies.* Montclair, NJ: Walden.

Fein, R. (2003, May). *Preventing targeted violence in schools.* Paper presented at the Safe School Seminar, sponsored by the Cleveland Office of the Secret Service and the Division of Continuing Education, Cleveland State University, Cleveland, OH.

Fein, R., Vossekuil, B., Pollack, W., Borum, R., Modzeleski, W., & Reddy, M. (2002). *Threat assessment in schools: A guide to managing threatening situations and to creating safe school climates.* Washington, DC: U.S. Department of Education, Office of Elementary and Secondary Education, Safe and Drug-Free Schools Program and U.S. Secret Service, National Threat Assessment Center.

Feldenkrais, M. (1972). *Awareness through movement.* New York: Harper & Row.

Fernbacher, S. (2002). *The influence of dominant culture on Gestalt practice: A qualitative study.* Unpublished master's thesis, LaTrobe University, Melbourne, Australia.

Fine, M., Weis, L., Powell, L., & Mun Wong, L. (Eds.). (1997). *Off white: Readings on race, power and society.* New York: Routledge.

Firestone, R. (1988). *Voice therapy: A psychotherapeutic approach to self-destructive behavior* New York: Human Sciences Press.

Fluegelman, A. (Ed.). (1976). *The new games book.* San Francisco: New Games Foundation.

Fodor, I. E. (1998). Awareness and meaning-making: The dance of experience. *Gestalt Review, 2*(1), 50–71.

Fodor, I., & Collier, J. C. (2001). Assertiveness and conflict resolution: An integrated Gestalt/cognitive behavioral model for working with urban adolescents. In M. McConville & G. Wheeler (Eds.), *The heart of development: Gestalt approaches to working with children, adolescents and their worlds: Vol. 2. Adolescence* (pp. 214–252). Cambridge, MA: Gestalt Press.

Fogel, A. (1993). *Developing through relationships: Origins of communication, self, and culture.* Chicago: University of Chicago Press.

Frank, R. (2001). *Body of awareness: A somatic and developmental approach to psychotherapy.* Cambridge, MA: Gestalt Press.

Frankenberg, R. (1993). *White women, race matters: The social construction of whiteness.* Minneapolis: University of Minnesota Press.

Frankl, V. (1963). *Man's search for meaning.* New York: Washington Square Press.

French, W. L., & Bell, C. H. (1995). *Organization development.* Englewood Cliffs, NJ: Prentice Hall.

Freud, A. (1963). The concept of developmental lines. In A. Freud, *The writings of Anna Freud* (pp. 11–30). New York: International Universities Press.

Freud, S. (1966). *The complete introductory lectures on psychoanalysis* (J. Strachey, Ed. & Trans.). New York: Norton.

Frew, J. (1988). The practice of Gestalt therapy in groups. *Gestalt Journal, 11*(1), 77–96.

Friedman, M. (1985). *The healing dialogue in psychotherapy.* Northvale, NJ: Jason Aronson.

Friedman, N. (1984). *The magic badge: Poems 1953–1984.* Austin, TX: Slough.

Fuhr, R., & Gremmler-Fuhr, M. (1997). Shame as a normal and sometimes dysfunctional experience. *Gestalt Review, 1*(3), 245–255.

Fuhr, R., Sreckovic, M., & Gremmler-Fuhr, M. (Eds.). (2001). *Handbuch der Gestalttherapie.* Göttingen, Germany: Hegrefe-Verlag.

Gaines, J. (1979). *Fritz Perls: Here and now.* New York: Integrated Press.

Garcia, C. L. (1998). *Too scared to learn: Overcoming academic anxiety.* Thousand Oaks, CA: Corwin.

Garcia, C. L., Baker, S. M., & deMayo, R. A. (1999). Academic anxieties: A Gestalt approach. *Gestalt Review, 3*(3), 239–250.

Garfield, S., & Bergin, A. (1971). *Handbook of psychotherapy and behavior change: An empirical analysis.* New York: John Wiley.

Garland, A., Kruse, M., & Aarons, G. (2003). Clinicians and outcome measurement: What's the use? *Journal of Behavioral Health Services and Research, 30*(4), 393–405.

Gendlin, E. (1962). *Experiencing and the creation of meaning.* New York: Free Press.

Gendlin, E. (1986). *Let your body interpret your dreams.* Wilmette, IL: Chiron.

Gendlin, E. (1996). *Focusing-oriented psychotherapy: A manual of the experiential method.* New York: Guilford.

Geta, B. (1973). *Breathe away your tension: An introduction to Gestalt body awareness therapy.* Berkeley, CA: Bookworks.

Gillie, M. (1999). Daniel Stern: A developmental theory for Gestalt? *British Gestalt Journal, 8*(2), 107–117.

Ginger, S. (1995). *Lexique international de Gestalt therapie* [International glossary of Gestalt therapy]. Paris: Forge.

Ginnot, H. (1965). *Between parent and child: New solutions to old problems.* New York: Macmillan.

Glasser, W. (1969). *Schools without failure.* New York: Harper & Row.

Goldstein, K. (1995). *The organism: A holistic approach to biology derived from pathological data in man.* New York: Zone. (Original work published 1939)

Goleman, D. (1995). *Emotional intelligence.* New York: Bantam.

Goodman, P. (1947). *Kafka's prayer.* New York: Vanguard.

Goodman, P. (1977a). The father of the psychoanalytic movement. In T. Stoehr (Ed.), *Nature heals: The psychological essays of Paul Goodman.* New York: Free Life Editions. (Reprinted from *Kenyon Review,* September 20, 1945)

Goodman, P. (1977b). *Nature heals: Psychological essays of Paul Goodman* (T. Stoehr, Ed.). New York: Free Life Editions.

Goodman, P. (1977c). The political meaning of some recent revisions of Freud. In T. Stoehr (Ed.), *Nature heals: The psychological essays of Paul Goodman.* New York: Free Life Editions. (Reprinted from *Politics,* 1945)

Goodman, P. (1994). *Crazy hope and finite experience: Final essays of Paul Goodman* (T. Stoehr, Ed.). San Francisco: Jossey-Bass.

Gordon, T. (1955). *Group centered leadership.* Boston: Houghton Mifflin.

Grant, P. H. (1978). *Holistic therapy: The risk and pay-offs of being alive.* Secaucus, NJ: Citadel.

Greaves, G. B. (1976). Gestalt therapy, Tantric Buddhism and the way of Zen. In E. W. Smith (Ed.), *The growing edge of Gestalt therapy* (pp. 181–201). New York: Brunner-Mazel.

Greenberg, E. (2002). Love, admiration, or safety: A system of Gestalt diagnosis of borderline, narcissistic, and schizoid adaptations that focus on what is figure for the client. *Gestalt! 6*(3), 393–405.

Greenberg, L., & Brownell, P. (1997). Validating Gestalt: An interview with researcher, writer, and psychotherapist, Leslie Greenberg. *Gestalt! 1*(1). Retrieved from www.g-gej.org/1-1/greenberg.html.

Greenberg, L., & Johnson, S. (1988). *Emotionally focused therapy for couples.* New York: Guilford.

Greenberg, L., & Malcolm, W. (2002). Resolving unfinished business: Relating process to outcome. *Journal of Consulting and Clinical Psychology, 70*(2), 404–416.

Greenberg, L., & Pinsof, W. (Eds.). (1986). *The psychotherapeutic process: A research handbook.* New York: Guilford.

Greenberg, L., Rice, L., & Elliott, R. (1993). *Facilitating emotional change: The moment-by-moment process.* New York: Guilford.

Greenberg, L., & Safron, J. D. (1987). *Emotion in psychotherapy.* New York: Guilford.

Greenberg, L., Watson, J., & Lietaer, G. (Eds.). (1998). *Handbook of experiential psychotherapy.* New York: Guilford.

Greer, M., & Rubinstein, B. (1972). *Will the real teacher please stand up?* Pacific Palisades, CA: Goodyear.

Grof, S. (1988). *The adventure of self-discovery: Dimensions of consciousness and new perspectives in psychotherapy and inner exploration.* Albany, NY: SUNY Press.

Grossman, W. (1998). *To be healed by the earth.* Cleveland, OH: Institute of Light.

Gunther, B. (1968). *Sense relaxation: Below your mind.* New York: Collier.

Gunther, S. V. (2001). *The desperate man's guide to relationship.* Lismore, Australia.

Gunther, S. V. (2002). *How a man loves a woman: Secrets of success.* Lismore, Australia: Northern Rivers Gestalt Institute Publications.

Hage, G. (1998). *White nation: Fantasies of white supremacy in a multicultural society.* Annandale, NSW, Australia: Pluto.

Haggbloom, S., Warnick, R., Warnick, J., Jones, V., Yarbrough, G., Russel, T., et al. (2002). The 100 most eminent psychologists of the 20th century. *Review of General Psychology, 6*(2), 139–152.

Hamilton, J. (1997). *Gestalt in pastoral care and counseling: A holistic approach.* New York: Haworth.

Handlon, J., & Fredericson, I. (1998). What changes the individual in Gestalt groups? A proposed theoretical model. *Gestalt Review, 2*(4), 275–294.

Hardy, R. E. (1991). *Gestalt psychotherapy: Concepts and demonstrations in stress, relationships, hypnosis and addiction.* Springfield, IL: Charles C Thomas.

Harmon, R. (1989). *Gestalt therapy with groups, couples, sexually dysfunctional men, and dreams.* Springfield, IL: Charles C Thomas.

Harmon, R. (1990). *Gestalt therapy discussions with the masters.* Springfield, IL: Charles C Thomas.

Harris, I. (1961). *Emotional blocks to learning: A study of the reasons for failure in school.* New York: Free Press.

Harvey, W. (1993). *On the motion of the heart and blood in animals* (R. Willis, Trans.). Amerherst, NY: Prometheus. (Original work published 1628)

Hatcher, C., & Himmelstein, P. (Eds.). (1976). *The handbook of Gestalt therapy.* New York: Jason Aronson.

Havens, L. (1986). *Making contact: Uses of language in psychotherapy.* Cambridge, MA: Harvard University Press.

Heard, William. (1993). *Healing between: A clinical guide to dialogic psychotherapy.* San Francisco: Jossey-Bass.

Heck, S., & Cobes, J. (1978). *All the classroom is a stage: The creative classroom environment.* New York: Pergamon.

Heidegger, M. (1949). The essence of truth. In W. Brock (Ed.), *Existence and being* (R. F. C. Hull & A. Crick, Trans.). New York: Henry Regnery.

Heidegger, M. (1962). *Being and time* (J. Macquarrie & E. Robinson, Trans.). New York: Harper & Row. (Original work published 1927).

Heimannsberg, B., & Schmidt, C. (Eds.). (1993). *The collective silence: German identity and the legacy of shame* (C. O. Harris & G. Wheeler, Trans.). San Francisco: Jossey-Bass.

Hendricks, G., & Roberts, T. (1977). *The second centering book: More awareness activities for children, parents and teachers.* New York: Prentice Hall.

Hendricks, G., & Wills, R. (1975). *The centering book: Awareness activities for children and adults to relax the body and mind.* New York: Prentice Hall.

Henggeler, S. W., Melton, G. B., & Smith, L. A. (1992). Family preservation using multisystemic therapy: An effective alternative to incarcerating serious juvenile offenders. *Journal of Consulting and Clinical Psychology, 60*(6), 953–961.

Herman, S., & Korenich, M. (1977). *Authentic management: A Gestalt orientation to organizations and their development.* Reading, MA: Addison-Wesley.

Hester, R., Nirmeberg, T., & Bergin, A. (1990). Behavioral treatment of alcohol and drug abuse: What do we know and where shall we go? In M. Glanter (Ed.), *Recent developments in alcoholism* (Vol. 8, p. 311). New York: Plenum.

Hillman, J. (1975). *Re-visioning psychology.* New York: HarperCollins.

Hills, C., & Stone, R. (1970). *Conduct your own awareness sessions.* New York: NAL/Signet.

Hodges, C. (1997, January). *Field theory.* Unpublished manuscript presented at New York Institute for Gestalt Therapy.

Holt, J. (1964). *How children fail.* New York: Pitman.

Holtzman, W. H. (1997). Community psychology and full-service schools in different cultures. *American Psychologist, 52*(4), 381–389.

hooks, b. (1995). *Killing rage: Ending racism.* New York: Penguin.

Hoopes, M. M., & Harper, J. M. (1987). *Birth order roles and sibling patterns in individual and family therapy.* Rockville, MD: Aspen.

Hopkins, L. (1999). Starflyer. Retrieved October 25, 2004, from www.thewildrose.net/aboutme.htm.

Horwitz, E. K., & Young, D. J. (1991). *Language anxiety: From theory and research to classroom implications.* Englewood Cliffs, NJ: Prentice Hall.

Houston, G. (1993). *Being and belonging: Group, intergroup and Gestalt.* New York: John Wiley.

Houston, G. (1995). *Supervision and counselling.* London: Rochester Foundation.

Houston, G. (1998). *The red book of groups.* London: Rochester Foundation.

Houston, G. (2003). *Brief Gestalt therapy.* London: Sage.

Huckaby, M. A. (1992). Overview of Gestalt group process. In E. C. Nevis (Ed.), *Gestalt therapy: Perspectives and applications* (pp. 303–331). New York: Gardner.

Hunter, E. (1972). *Encounter in the classroom: New ways of teaching.* New York: Holt, Rinehart & Winston.

Hunter, R. (1970). *The enemies of anarchy: A Gestalt approach to change.* New York: Viking.

Hurtado, A., & Stewart, A. I. (1997). Through the looking glass: Implications for studying whiteness for feminist methods. In M. Fine, L. Weiss, L. Powell, & L. Mun Wong (Eds.), *Off white: Readings on race, power and society* (pp. 297–311). New York: Routledge.

Huxley, A. (1945). *The perennial philosophy.* London: Harper & Brothers.

Huxley, L. (1963). *You are not the target.* New York: Farrar, Straus & Giroux.

Hycner, R. (1991). *Between person and person: Toward a dialogical psychotherapy.* Highland, NY: Center for Gestalt Development.

Hycner, R., & Jacobs, L. (1995). *The healing relationship in Gestalt therapy: A dialogic/self psychology approach.* Highland, NY: Gestalt Journal Press.

Imes, S., Rose Clance, P., Gailis, A., & Atkeson, E. (2002). Mind's response to the body's betrayal: Gestalt/existential therapy for clients with chronic or life-threatening illnesses. *Journal of Clinical Psychology, 58*(11), 1361–1373.

Ingersoll, R. E. (1994). Spirituality, religion and counseling: Dimensions and relationships. *Counseling and Values, 38,* 98–112.

Ingersoll, R. E. (1995). *Construction and initial validation of the Spiritual Wellness Inventory.* Unpublished doctoral dissertation, Kent State University.

Ingersoll, R. E. (1998). Refining dimensions of spiritual wellness: A cross-traditional approach. *Counseling and Values, 42,* 156–165.

Ingersoll, R. E. (2004). *Psychopharmacology for helping professionals: An integral approach.* Pacific Grove, CA: Brooks/Cole.

Jacobs, L. (1978). *I-Thou relation in Gestalt therapy.* Unpublished doctoral dissertation, California School of Professional Psychology, Los Angeles.

Jacobs, L. (1989). Dialogue in Gestalt theory and therapy. *Gestalt Journal, 12*(1), 25–67.

Jacobs, L. (1992). Insights from psychoanalytic self psychology and intersubjectivity theory for Gestalt therapists. *Gestalt Journal, 15*(2), 25–60.

Jacobs, L. (1995a). Dialogue in Gestalt theory and therapy. In R. Hycner & L. Jacobs (Eds.), *The healing relationship in Gestalt therapy* (pp. 51–84). Highland, NY: Gestalt Journal Press.

Jacobs, L. (1995b). The therapist as "other": The patient's search for relatedness. In R. Hycner & L. Jacobs (Eds.), *The healing relationship in Gestalt therapy* (pp. 215–233). Highland, NY: Gestalt Journal Press.

Jacobs, L. (2000a). For whites only. *British Gestalt Journal, 9,* 3–14.

Jacobs, L. (2000b). Respectful dialogues (Interview with Jenny Mackewn). *British Gestalt Journal, 9*(2), 105–116.

Jacobs, L. (2003). Ethics of context and field: The practices of care, inclusion and openness to dialogue. *British Gestalt Journal, 12*(2). Also in R. Lee (Ed.), *The values of connection: A relational perspective on ethics.* Hillsdale, NJ: Analytic Press.

James, M., & Jongeward, D. (1971). *Born to win: Transactional analysis with Gestalt exercises.* Reading, MA: Addison-Wesley.

Janov, J. (1994). *The inventive organization: Hope and daring at work.* San Francisco: Jossey-Bass.

Jarosewitsch, R. (1997). Aroha, or what constitutes healing in psychotherapy? In *Gestalt! 1*(3). Retrieved August 16, 2004, from www.g-gej.org/1-3/aroah.html.

Johnson, S. (1996). *Creating connection: The practice of emotionally focused marital therapy.* New York: Brunner-Mazel

Jones, R. (1968). *Fantasy and feeling in education.* New York: New York University Press.

Jourard, S. (1964). *The transparent self.* New York: Litton Educational Publications.

Jung, C. G. (1961). *Memories, dreams, reflections.* New York: Vintage.

Kaplan, N. R., & Kaplan, M. L. (1994). Processes of experiential organization in couple and family systems. In G. Wheeler & S. Backman (Eds.), *On intimate ground: A Gestalt approach to working with couples* (pp. 109–127). San Francisco: Jossey-Bass.

Kareem, J., & Littlewood, R. (Eds.). (1992). *Inter-cultural therapy. Themes, interpretations and practice.* Oxford, UK: Blackwell Scientific Publications.

Karp, H. (1985). *Personal power: An unorthodox guide to success.* Lake Worth, FL: Gardner.

Kelly, G. A. (1955). *The psychology of personal constructs: Vol. 1. Clinical diagnosis and psychotherapy.* New York: Norton.

Kempler, W. (1974). *Principles of Gestalt family therapy.* Costa Mesa, CA: Kempler Institute.

Kempler, W. (1981). *Experiential psychotherapy within families.* New York: Brunner/Mazel.

Kennedy, D. (1998). Gestalt: A point of departure for a personal spirituality. *British Gestalt Journal, 7,* 88–98.

Kennedy, E. M. (1990). Community-based care for the mentally ill: Simple justice. *American Psychologist, 45*(11), 1238–1240.

Kepner, E. (1980). Gestalt group process. In B. Feder & R. Ronall (Eds.), *Beyond the hot seat: Gestalt approaches to group* (pp. 5–24). New York: Brunner-Mazel.

Kepner, E., & Brien, L. (1970). Gestalt therapy: A behavioristic phenomenology. In J. Fagan & I. Shepherd (Eds.), *Gestalt therapy now* (pp. 39–46). Palo Alto, CA: Science and Behavior Books.

Kepner, J. I. (1982). *Questionnaire measurement of personality styles from the theory of Gestalt therapy.* Unpublished doctoral dissertation, Kent State University.

Kepner, J. I. (1987). *Body process: A Gestalt approach to working with the body in psychotherapy.* New York: Gardner.

Kepner, J. I. (1995). *Healing tasks: Psychotherapy with adult survivors of childhood abuse.* San Francisco: Jossey-Bass.

Kepner, J. I. (2003a). The embodied field. *British Gestalt Journal, 12*(1).

Kepner, J. (2003b). *Healing tasks: Psychotherapy with adult survivors of childhood abuse.* San Francisco: Jossey-Bass

Kerr, M. E. (2003). *One family's story: A primer on Bowen theory.* Washington, DC: Bowen Center for the Study of Family.

Kierkegaard, S. (1954). *Fear and trembling* and *The sickness unto death* (W. Lowrie, Trans.). Princeton, NJ: Princeton University Press. (Original work published 1941)

Killoran, C. (1993). *A spiritual dimension of Gestalt therapy.* Unpublished doctoral dissertation, Garrett-Evangelical Theological Seminary, Evanston, IL.

Kitzler, R. (1980). The Gestalt group. In B. Feder & R. Ronall (Eds.), *Beyond the hot seat: Gestalt approaches to group* (pp. 25–37). New York: Brunner/Mazel.

Kitzler, R. (1999). *Theoretical wondering.* Unpublished e-mail conversation.

Kleiner, R. J., & Okeke, B. I. (1991). Advances in field theory: New approaches and methods in cross-cultural research. *Journal of Cross-Cultural Psychology,* 22(4), 509–524.

Koch, K. (1970). *Wishes, lies and dreams.* New York: Random House.

Koffka, K. (1935). *Principles of Gestalt psychology.* New York: Harcourt Brace.

Kogan, J. (1976). The genesis of Gestalt therapy. In C. Hatcher & P. Himelstein (Eds.), *The handbook of Gestalt therapy* (pp. 236–255). New York: Jason Aronson.

Kohlberg, L. (1966). A cognitive-developmental analysis of children's sex-role concepts and attitudes. In E. Maccoby (Ed.), *The development of sex differences.* Stanford, CA: Stanford University Press.

Kohlberg, L. (1975). The cognitive developmental approach to moral education. *Phi Delta Kappan, 56,* 670–677.

Kohlberg, L. (1981). *The philosophy of moral development.* New York: Harper & Row.

Köhler, W. (1940). *Dynamics in psychology.* New York: Liveright.

Köhler, W. (1947). *Gestalt in psychology: An introduction to new concepts in modern psychology.* New York: Liveright.

Köhler, W. (1969). *The task of Gestalt psychology.* Princeton, NJ: Princeton University Press.

Kohut, H. (1984). *How does psychoanalysis cure?* Chicago: University of Chicago Press.

Kottman, T. (1995). *Partners in play: An Adlerian approach to play therapy.* Alexandria, VA: American Counseling Association.

Kottman, T. (2001). *Play therapy: Basics and beyond.* Alexandria, VA: American Counseling Association.

Krause, I. B. (1998). *Therapy across culture.* Thousand Oaks, CA: Sage.

Krauss, D., & Fryrear, J. (Eds.). (1983). *Phototherapy in mental health.* Springfield, IL: Charles C Thomas.

Kronsky, B. (1975, January/February). Allen Ginsberg in India: Therapy, Buddhism, and the myth of happiness. *Humanist, 35*(1), 32–35.

Kurtz, R., & Prestera, H. (1976). *The body reveals: An illustrated guide to the psychology of the body.* New York: Harper & Row.

Laing, R. D. (1967). *The politics of experience.* New York: Ballantine.

Lampert, R. (1969). *A child's eye view of Gestalt therapy* [Audiotape]. Catalog #MS 90. Available from MaxSound, (562) 856-4832, maxsound@charter.net.

Lampert, R. (2003). *A child's eye view: Gestalt therapy with children, adolescents and their families.* Highland, New York: Gestalt Journal Press.

Landreth, G. L. (2002). *Play therapy: The art of the relationship.* New York: Brunner-Routledge.

Lao Tzu. (1963). *The way of Lao Tzu* (Wing-Tsit Chan, Trans.). Indianapolis, IN: Bobbs-Merrill.

Lapworth, P., Sills, C., & Fish, S. (2001). *Integration in counseling and psychotherapy: Developing a personal approach.* Thousand Oaks, CA: Sage.

Latner, J. (1973). *The Gestalt therapy book.* New York: Julian.

Latner, J. (1986). *The Gestalt therapy book* (Rev. ed.). Highland, NY: Gestalt Journal Press.

Latner, J. (1992). The theory of Gestalt therapy. In E. C. Nevis (Ed.), *Gestalt therapy: Perspectives and applications.* New York: Gardner.

Lederman, J. (1969). *Anger and the rocking chair: Gestalt awareness with children.* New York: McGraw-Hill.

Lee, R. G. (1995). Gestalt and shame: The foundation for a clearer understanding of field dynamics. *British Gestalt Journal, 4,* 14–22.

Lee, R. G. (2001). Shame and support: Understanding an adolescent's family field. In M. McConville & G. Wheeler (Eds.), *The heart of development: Gestalt approaches to working with children and adolescents: Vol. 2. Adolescence.* Hillsdale, NJ: Analytic Press.

Lee, R. G. (2002). Ethics: A Gestalt of values/the values of Gestalt—A next step. *Gestalt Review, 6*(1), 27–51.

Lee, R. G. (2004). *The values of connection: A relational approach to ethics.* Hillsdale, NJ: Gestalt Press.

Lee, R. G., & Wheeler, G. (Eds.). (1996). *The voice of shame: Silence and connection in psychotherapy.* San Francisco: Jossey-Bass.

Lennos, C. (Ed.). (1997). *Redecision therapy: A brief, action-oriented approach.* Northvale, NJ: Jason Aronson.

Leonard, G. (1968). *Education and ecstasy.* New York: Delacorte.

Levin, J. (2003). Toward a developmental Gestalt therapy: A case study. *Gestalt Review, 7*(3), 244–248.

Levin, L., & Shepherd, I. L. (1974). The role of the therapist in Gestalt therapy. *Counseling Psychologist, 4*(4), 27–30.

Levy, R. (1973). *I can only touch you now.* Englewood Cliffs, NJ: Prentice Hall.

Lewin, K. (1938). Will and need. In W. Ellis (Ed.), *A source book of Gestalt psychology* (pp. 283–299). London: Routledge & Kegan Paul. (Reprinted from *Psychologische Forschung, 7,* 294–385 [1926])

Lewin, K. (1951). *Field theory in social science: Selected theoretical papers.* New York: Harper.

Lewin, K. (1952). *Field theory in social science: Selected theoretical papers.* London: Tavistock.

Lewin, K. (1997). Action research and minority problems. In K. Lewin, *Resolving social conflicts: Selected papers and field theory in social science* (pp. 143–154). Washington, DC: American Psychological Association. (Original work published 1948)

Lewis, M. (1997). *Altering fate.* New York: Guilford.

Lichtenberg, P. (1988). *Getting even: The equalizing law of relationship.* Lanham, MD: University Press of America.

Lichtenberg, P. (1994). *Community and confluence: Undoing the clinch of oppression.* Cambridge, MA: Gestalt Institute of Cleveland Press.

Lichtenberg, P., van Beusekom, J., & Gibbons, D. (1997). *Encountering bigotry: Befriending projecting persons in everyday life.* Cambridge, MA: Gestalt Press

Lieberman, E., Yalom, I., & Miles, M. (1973). *Encounter groups: First facts.* New York: Basic Books.

Littlewood, R. (1992). Towards an intercultural therapy. In J. Kareem & R. Littlewood (Eds.), *Intercultural therapy: Themes, interpretations and practice* (pp. 3–13). Oxford, UK: Blackwell Scientific Publications.

Loew, C., Grayson, H., & Loew, G. (1975). *Three psychotherapies: A clinical comparison.* New York: Brunner/Mazel.

Lowenfeld, Viktor. (1952). *Creative and mental growth.* New York: Macmillan.

Luchins, A. (1997). On Schulte, Wertheimer, and paranoia. *Gestalt Archive.* Retrieved August 16, 2004, from www.enabling.org/ia/gestalt/gerhards/lusch1.html.

Lynch, B. (1989). *Structural family therapy.* Paris: Editions ESF.

Lynch, B. (1991). An anatomy of bonding in the dyadic system. *Journal of Couples Therapy (Haworth), 1,* 127–145.

Lynch, B. (1992). Partnership and ego equality in the marital system. *Journal of Couples Therapy, 2*(4), 11–24.

Lynch, B. (1999). Catastrophic conditions in couple systems: Managing an unwelcome pregnancy. *Journal of Couples Therapy, 8*(2), 37–48.

Lynch, J., & Lynch, B. (2000). *Principles and practices of structural family therapy.* Highland, NY: Gestalt Journal Press.

Lyon, H. (1971). *Learning to feel—feeling to learn: Humanistic education for the whole man.* Columbus, OH: C. Merrill.

MacCluskie, K., & Ingersoll, R. E. (2001). *Becoming a 21st century agency counselor.* Pacific Grove, CA: Brooks/Cole.

Mackewn, J. (1997). *Developing Gestalt counseling: A field theoretical and relational model of contemporary Gestalt counseling and psychotherapy.* Thousand Oaks, CA: Sage.

Maclean, A. (2002). *The heart of supervision.* Wilmington, NC: Topdog.

Mahrer, A. R. (1978). *Experiencing: A humanistic theory of psychology and psychiatry.* New York: Brunner/Mazel.

Mahrer, A. R. (1989). *Dream work in psychotherapy and self-change.* New York: Norton.

Martin, M. L. (1987). *Speech blocks in women: A case study.* Unpublished doctoral dissertation, Pepperdine University.

Martinek, S. (1985). *Gestalt therapy homeostasis theory: Instrument construction and validation of the Gestalt Personal Homeostasis Inventory.* Unpublished doctoral dissertation, Kent State University.

Maruish, M. (2002). *Essentials of treatment planning.* New York: John Wiley.

Maslow, A. (1968). *Toward a psychology of being.* New York: Van Nostrand Reinhold.

Maslow, A. (1971). *The farther reaches of human nature.* New York: Viking.

Matzko, H. (1997). A Gestalt therapy treatment approach for addictions: "Multiphasic transformation process." *Gestalt Review, 1*(1), 34–55.

Matzko, H. (2003). *Synthesis of dialectical behavior therapy (DBT) and therapeutic community treatment (TCT) for addiction/mental health troubled clients: DVD training video and manual.* Cranston, RI: Gestalt Therapy Center of Rhode Island.

Maurer, R. (1992). *Caught in the middle: A leadership guide for partnership in the workplace.* Portland, OR: Productivity.

Maurer, R. (1994). *Feedback toolkit: 16 tools for better communication in the workplace.* Portland, OR: Productivity.

Maurer, R. (1996). *Beyond the wall of resistance: Unconventional strategies that build support and change.* Austin, TX: Bard.

Maurer, R. (2000). *Building capacity for change sourcebook.* Arlington, VA: Maurer.

Maurer, R. (2002). *Why don't you want what I want? How to win support for your ideas without hard sell, manipulation or power plays.* Austin, TX: Bard.

Maurer, R. (2004). *Making a compelling case for change.* Arlington, VA: Maurer.

May, R. (1939). *The art of counseling: How to gain and give mental health.* New York: Abingdon-Cokesbury.

May, R. (1969). *Love and will.* New York: Norton.

McConville, M. (1995). *Adolescence: Psychotherapy and the emergent self.* San Francisco: Jossey-Bass.

McConville, M. (1997). The gift. *GIC Voice (Gestalt Institute of Cleveland), 4,* 11–15.

McConville, M. (2001a). Husserl's phenomenology in context. *Gestalt Review, 5*(3), 195–204.

McConville, M. (2001b). Lewinian field theory, adolescent development, and psychotherapy. In M. McConville & G. Wheeler (Eds.), *The heart of development: Gestalt approaches to working with children, adolescents and their worlds: Vol. 2. Adolescence.* Hillsdale, NJ: Analytic Press.

McConville, M. (2003). Lewinian field theory, adolescent development, and psychotherapy. *Gestalt Review, 7*(3), 213–238.

McConville, M., & Wheeler, G. (2001–2002). *The heart of development: Gestalt approaches to working with children, adolescents and their worlds* (2 vols.). Cambridge, MA: Gestalt Press.

McGoldrick, M., Pearce, J., & Giordano, J. (Eds.). (1982). *Ethnicity and family therapy.* New York: Guilford.

McIntosh, P. (1998). *White privilege and male privilege: A personal account of coming to see correspondences through work in women's studies.* Retrieved October 2001 from www.Department.bucknell.edu/rescolleges/socjust/Readings/McIntosh.html.

Mead, G. H. (1934). *Mind, self and society* (C. Morris, Ed.). Chicago: University of Chicago Press.

Meister-Vitale, B. (1979). *Unicorns are real: A right-brained approach to learning.* Rolling Hills, CA: Jalmar.

Melnick, J. (1980). The use of therapist-imposed structure in Gestalt therapy. *Gestalt Journal, 3,* 4–20.

Melnick, J. (2003). Countertransference and the Gestalt approach. *British Gestalt Journal, 12*(1), 40–48.

Melnick, J., & Nevis, S. (1992). Diagnosis: The struggle for a meaningful paradigm. In E. C. Nevis (Ed.), *Gestalt therapy: Perspectives and applications* (pp. 57–78). New York: Gardner.

Melnick, J., & Nevis, S. (1997). Gestalt diagnosis and DSM IV. *British Gestalt Journal, 6,* 97–106.

Merleau-Ponty, M. (1962). *The phenomenology of perception.* London: Smith, Routledge & Kegan Paul.

Merleau-Ponty, M. (1963). *The structure of behavior.* Boston: Beacon.

Merriam-Webster. (1991). *Webster's ninth new collegiate dictionary.* Springfield, MA: Author.

Merry, U., & Brown, G. I. (1987). *The neurotic behavior of organizations.* New York: Gardner.

Miller, D. (2002). Advancing mental health in political places. *Professional Psychology: Research and Practice, 33*(3), 277–280.

Miller, G. (2003). *Incorporating spirituality in counseling and psychotherapy: Theory and technique.* New York: John Wiley.

Miller, I., Shander, D., & Cohen, J. (1999, August 1). HMO woes: One way to empower Colorado's health-care consumers [Guest opinion]. *Boulder Daily Camera,* p. 3E.

Miller, J. (1976). *Humanizing the classroom: Models of teaching in affective education.* New York: Praeger.

Mills, J. C. (1988). *Therapeutic metaphors for children.* New York: Magination.

Minuchin, S. (1974). *Families and family therapy.* Cambridge, MA: Harvard University Press.

Moberg, D. (1971). *Spiritual well-being: Background.* Washington, DC: University Press of America.

Morales, M. (1999). Website helps mathematically challenged. Retrieved August 16, 2004, from www.sosmath.com/press/Prospector199911.htm.

Moreno, J. L. (1959). *Psychodrama: Foundations of psychotherapy.* Beacon, NY: Beacon House.

Mortola, P. (2001). Sharing disequilibrium: A link between Gestalt therapy theory and child development theory. *Gestalt Review, 5*(1), 45–56.

Mortola, P. (2003). Differentiating and integrating a theory of practice: A response to Mark McConville. *Gestalt Review, 7*(3), 239–243.

Moustakas, C. (1956). *The teacher and the child.* New York: McGraw-Hill.

Moustakas, C. (1974). *Children in play therapy.* New York: Ballantine.

Moustakas, C. (1995). *Being-in, being-for, being-with.* Northvale, NJ: Jason Aronson.

Mraz, T. J. (1990). *A study of the validity of the Gestalt personality theory of homeostasis and the Gestalt Personal Homeostasis Inventory–Revised.* Unpublished doctoral dissertation, Kent State University.

Müller, B. (1991). Una fonte dimenticata: Il pensiero di Otto Rank. *Quaderni di Gestalt, 7*(12), 41–47.

Müller, B. (1996). Isadore From's contributions. *Gestalt Journal, 19*(1), 57–82.

Mulligan, K., & Smith, B. (1988). Mach and Ehrenfels: The foundations of Gestalt theory. In B. Smith (Ed.), *Foundations of Gestalt theory* (pp. 124–157). Munich: Philosophia.

Nabozny, S., & Carlson, C. (2001). *Published Internet dialogue.* Retrieved October 25, 2004, from www.keypartners.ws/field_theory_and_its_implications_in_organizations.htm.

Naranjo, C. (1973). *The healing journey: New approaches to consciousness.* New York: Ballantine.

Naranjo, C. (1978). Gestalt therapy as a transpersonal approach. *Gestalt Journal, 1,* 75–81.

Naranjo, C. (1980). *The techniques of Gestalt therapy.* Berkeley, CA: SAT Press. (Original work published 1973)

Naranjo, C. (1993). *Gestalt therapy: The attitude and practice of an atheoretical experientialism.* Nevada City, CA: Gateways/IDHHB.

Narcotics Anonymous World Service. (1988). *Narcotics Anonymous.* Van Nuys, CA: Author.

Nevis, E. C. (1987). *Organizational consulting: A Gestalt approach.* New York: Gardner.

Nevis, E. C. (Ed.). (1992). *Gestalt therapy: Perspectives and applications.* New York: Gardner.

Nevis, E. C., Lancourt, J., & Vassallo, H. G. (1996). *Intentional revolutions: A seven-point strategy for transforming organizations.* San Francisco: Jossey-Bass.

Nevis, S. (1995). *Gestalt family therapy* [Video]. Cleveland, OH: Gestalt Institute of Cleveland.

Norton, R. F. (1980). *Toward a Gestalt theory of child development.* Unpublished doctoral dissertation, California School of Professional Psychology, Fresno.

Oaklander, V. (1978). *Windows to our children: A Gestalt therapy approach to children and adolescents.* Moab, UT: Real People. (Original work published 1969)

Oaklander, V. (1982). The relationship of Gestalt therapy to children. *Gestalt Journal, 5*(1), 64–74.

Oaklander, V. (1992a). Gestalt therapy with children: Working with anger and introjects. In E. C. Nevis (Ed.), *Gestalt therapy: Perspectives and applications* (pp. 263–283). Cleveland, OH: Gestalt Institute of Cleveland Press.

Oaklander, V. (1992b). *Helping children and adults to become self-nurturing* (Audiotape). Catalog #MS 4. Available from MaxSound, (562) 856-4832, maxsound@charter.net.

Oaklander, V. (1993). From meek to bold: A case study of Gestalt play therapy. In T. Kottman & C. Schaefer (Eds.), *Play therapy in action: A casebook for practitioners* (pp. 281–299). Northvale, NJ: Jason Aronson.

Oaklander, V. (1994). Gestalt play therapy. In K. O'Connor & C. Schaefer (Eds.), *Handbook of play therapy* (Vol. 2, pp. 143–156). New York: John Wiley.

Oaklander, V. (1997). The therapeutic process with children and adolescents. *Gestalt Review, 1*(4), 292–317.

Oaklander, V. (2000). Short-term play therapy for grieving children. In H. Kaduson & C. Schaefer (Eds.), *Short-term play therapy for children* (pp. 28–52). New York: Guilford.

Oaklander, V. (2001). Gestalt play therapy. *International Journal of Play Therapy, 10*(2), 45–55.

Okere, N. S. (1984). *The application of Gestalt psychotherapy principles to learning: A case study of resistance in adult education.* Unpublished doctoral dissertation, Pepperdine University.

Okum, B. (1996). *Understanding diverse families.* New York: Guilford.

O'Leary, E. (1992). *Gestalt therapy: Theory, practice and research.* London: Chapman & Hall.

O'Leary, E., Sheedy, G., O'Sullivan, K., & Thoresen, C. (2003). Cork Older Adult Intervention Project: Outcomes of a Gestalt therapy group with older adults. *Counselling Psychology Quarterly, 16*(2), 131–143.

O'Neill, B. (1997). The Gestalt approach in working with people experiencing psychotic disorders. *Behavior OnLine.* Retrieved from www.behavior.net/forums/gestalt/1998/9_5.htm.

Orford, J. (1992). *Community psychology: Theory and practice.* New York: John Wiley.

Ornstein, R. (1969). *On the experience of time.* Palo Alto, CA: Science and Behavior Books.

Otto, H. (1956). *Social education in elementary schools.* New York: Rinehart.

Otto, H., & Mann, J. (Eds.). (1968). *Ways of growth: Approaches to expanding human awareness.* New York: Grossman.

Ownby, R. L. (1983). Gestalt therapy with children. *Gestalt Journal, 6*(2), 51–58.

Packard, D. (2002). Role-playing: Language teaching methodology. *Humanizing Language Teaching, 4*(1). Retrieved August 16, 2004, from www.hltmag.co.uk/jan02/less3.htm.

Page, R., & Berkow, D. (1994). *Creating contact, choosing relationship: The dynamics of unstructured group therapy.* San Francisco: Jossey-Bass.

Palanyi, M. (1966). *The tacit dimension.* Garden City, NY: Doubleday.

Palazzoli, M. S., Boscolo, L., Cecchin, G., & Prata, G. (1978). *Paradox and counterparadox: A new model in the therapy of the family in schizophrenic transaction.* New York: Jason Aronson.

Papernow, P. (1993). *Becoming a stepfamily: Patterns of development in remarried families.* San Francisco: Jossey-Bass.

Parlett, M. (1991). Reflections on field theory. *British Gestalt Journal, 1*(2), 69–81.

Parlett, M. (1997). The unified field in practice. *Gestalt Review, 1*(1), 10–33.

Parlett, M. (2000). Creative adjustment and the global field. *British Gestalt Journal, 9*(1), 15–27.

Passons, W. (1975). *Gestalt approaches in counseling.* New York: Holt, Rinehart, & Winston.

Pedersen, P. B. (1997). *Culture centered counseling interventions: Striving for accuracy.* Thousand Oaks, CA: Sage.

Pendery, M., Maltzman, I., & West, L. (1982). Controlled drinking for alcoholics: New findings and re-evaluation of a major affirmative study. *Science, 217,* 169–175.

Perls, F. S. (1967). Group versus individual therapy. *Etc.: A Review of General Semantics, 24*(3), 306–312.

Perls, F. S. (1969a). *Ego, hunger and aggression: The beginning of Gestalt therapy.* New York: Random House. (Original work published 1947)

Perls, F. S. (1969b). *Gestalt therapy verbatim.* Lafayette, CA: Real People.

Perls, F. S. (1969c). *In and out of the garbage pail.* Moab, UT: Real People.

Perls, F. S. (1973). *The Gestalt approach and eye witness to therapy.* New York: Bantam.

Perls, F. S. (1975). Group vs. individual therapy. In J. O. Stevens (Ed.), *Gestalt is* (pp. 9–15). Moab, UT: Real People.

Perls, F. S. (1978). Finding self through Gestalt therapy. *Gestalt Journal, 1*(1), 54–73.

Perls, F. S., Hefferline, R., & Goodman, P. (1951). *Gestalt therapy: Excitement and growth in the human personality.* New York: Julian.

Perls, F. S., Hefferline, R., & Goodman, P. (1994). *Gestalt therapy: Excitement and growth in the human personality* (Rev. ed.). New York: Julian.

Perls, L. (1976). Comments on the new directions. In W. L. Smith (Ed.), *The growing edge of Gestalt therapy.* Secaucus, NJ: Citadel.

Perls, L. (1992a). Concepts and misconceptions of Gestalt therapy. In E. Smith (Ed.), *Gestalt voices* (pp. 3–8). Norwood, NJ: Ablex.

Perls, L. (1992b). How to educate children for peace. In J. Wysong (Ed.), *Laura Perls: Living at the boundary* (pp. 37–44). Highland, NY: Gestalt Journal Press. (Original work published 1939)

Perls, L. (1992c). *Living at the boundary* (J. Wysong, Ed.). Highland, NY: Center for Gestalt Development.

Perls, L. (1992d). Notes on fundamental support of the contact process. In J. Wysong (Ed.), *Laura Perls: Living at the boundary* (pp. 83–91). Highland, NY: Gestalt Journal Press.

Perls, R. (2001). Those who come after: An autobiography by the daughter of Fritz and Laura Perls. Metairie, LA: Gestalt Institute Press.

Philippson, P. (2001). *Self in relation.* Highland, NY: Gestalt Journal Press.

Philippson, P., & Harris, J. B. (1992). *Gestalt: Working with groups.* Manchester, UK: Manchester Gestalt Centre Press.

Piaget, J. (1950). *The psychology of intelligence.* New York: Harcourt, Brace.

Piaget, J. (1952). *The origins of intelligence in children.* New York: International Universities Press.

Piaget, J. (1966). *Psychology of intelligence.* Totowa, NJ: Littlefield, Adams.

Piaget, J. (1972). Intellectual evolution from adolescence to adult. *Human Development, 15,* 1–12.

Piaget, J. (1977). *The development of thought: Equilibration of cognitive structures.* New York: Viking.

Plummer, D. (1986). *Perceived and measured characteristics of adjustment of Catholic sisters: A profile study of contemporary women religious.* Unpublished doctoral dissertation, Kent State University.

Plummer, D. (Ed.). (2003). *The handbook of diversity management: Beyond awareness to competency-based learning.* Washington, DC: University Press of America.

Plummer, D. (2004). *Racing across the lines: Changing race relations through friendships.* Plymouth, MI: Pilgrim.

Polster, E. (1987). *Every person's life is worth a novel: How to cut through emotional pain and discover the fascinating core of life.* New York: Norton.

Polster, E. (1995). *A population of selves: A therapeutic exploration of personal diversity.* San Francisco: Jossey-Bass.

Polster, E., & Polster, M. (1973). *Gestalt therapy integrated: Contours of theory and practice.* New York: Brunner-Mazel.

Polster, M. (1992). *Eve's daughters: The forbidden heroism of women.* San Francisco: Jossey-Bass.

Polster, M. (1999). What's new? In A. Roberts (Ed.), *From the radical center: The heart of Gestalt therapy—Selected writings of Erving and Miriam Polster.* Cambridge, MA: Gestalt Institute of Cleveland Press.

Pomeroy, E., Trainor, J., & Pape, B. (2002). Citizens shaping policy: The Canadian Mental Health Association's Framework for Support Project. *Canadian Psychology, 43*(1), 11–20.

Postman, N., & Weingartner, C. (1969). *Teaching as a subversive activity.* New York: Dell.

Powell, R. (Ed.). (2000). *Talks with Ramana Maharishi: On realizing abiding peace and happiness.* New York: Inner Directions.

Pribram, K. H. (1991). *Brain and perception: Holonomy and structure in figural processing.* Hillsdale, NJ: Lawrence Erlbaum.

Prosnick, K. (1996). *Final contact and beyond in Gestalt therapy theory and transpersonal research: A factor analytic study of egotism and transfluence.* Unpublished doctoral dissertation, Kent State University.

Purlsglove, P. D. (Ed.). (1968) *Recognitions in Gestalt therapy.* New York: Funk & Wagnalls.

Putnis, P., & Petelin, R. (1996). *Professional communication: Principles and applications.* Sydney, Australia: Prentice Hall.

Radin, D. I. (1997). *The conscious universe: The scientific truth of psychic phenomena.* New York: Harperedge.

Radler, D. H. (1960). *Success through play: How to prepare your child for school achievement and enjoy it.* New York: Harper & Row.

Rainwater, J. (1979). *You're in charge: Becoming your own therapist.* Los Angeles: Guild of Tutors.

Rank, O. (1941). *Beyond psychology.* Philadelphia: Dover.

Raths, L., Harman, M., & Simon, S. (1966). *Values and teaching: Working with values in the classroom.* Columbus, OH: Charles E. Merrill.

Ravich, L. (2002). *A funny thing happened on the way to enlightenment.* Metairie, LA: Gestalt Institute Press of New Orleans.

Rawson, D., Whitehead, G., & Luthra, M. (1999). The challenges of counseling in a multicultural society. In S. Palmer & P. Laungani (Eds.), *Counseling in a multicultural society* (pp. 6–34). Thousand Oaks, CA: Sage.

Read, D., & Simon, S. (1975). *Humanistic education source book.* Englewood Cliffs, NJ: Prentice Hall.

Reich, W. (1945). *Character-analysis* (T. P. Wolfe, Trans.). New York: Farrar, Straus & Giroux.

Reich, W. (1960). *Wilhelm Reich: Selected writings* (T. Wolfe, Trans.). New York: Farrar, Straus & Giroux.

Resnick, R. (1995). Gestalt therapy: Principles, prisms and perspectives. *British Gestalt Journal, 4*(1), 3–13.

Resnick, R. W. (1997). The "recursive loop" of shame: An alternate Gestalt therapy viewpoint. *Gestalt Review, 3*(1), 256–270.

Reynolds, C. A. (1996). *Coping styles of children of divorce: Attitudes, personality, and Gestalt processes.* Unpublished doctoral dissertation, Kent State University.

Reynolds, C. A., & Stanley, C. B. (2001). Innovative application of play therapy in school settings. In A. A. Drews, L. J. Carey, & C. E. Schaefer (Eds.), *School-based play therapy* (pp. 350–367). New York: John Wiley.

Reynolds, C. A., & Woldt, A. L. (2002). Healing young wounded hearts: Gestalt group therapy with children of divorce. In M. McConville & G. Wheeler (Eds.), *The heart of development: Gestalt approaches to working with children, adolescents and their worlds: Vol. 1. Childhood* (pp. 239–261). Hillsdale, NJ: Analytic Press.

Rhyne, J. (1973). *The Gestalt art experience.* Monterey, CA: Brooks/Cole.

Rice, L., & Greenberg, L. (Eds.). (1984). *Patterns of change: Intensive analysis of psychotherapy process.* New York: Guilford.

Richan, W. C., & Kleiner, R. J. (1990). The social agency as a field of forces: A program evaluation strategy. In S. Wheelan, E. Pepitone, & V. Abt (Eds.), *Advances in field theory* (pp. 281–293). Newbury Park, CA: Sage.

Richardson, R. (1976). *The implications of Gestalt therapy for Christian ministry.* Unpublished doctoral dissertation, Colgate Rochester Divinity School/Bexley Hall Crozer Theological Seminary, Rochester, NY.

Riley, P. (1999). *Preventing school violence.* Paper presented at the Koch Crime Institute's National Conference on Juvenile Justice, Little Rock, AR.

Roberts, A. (1999a). The field talks back: An essay on constructivism and experience. *British Gestalt Journal, 8*(1), 35–46.

Roberts, A. (Ed.). (1999b). *From the radical center: The heart of Gestalt therapy—Selected writings of Erving and Miriam Polster.* Cambridge, MA: Gestalt Institute of Cleveland Press.

Robine, J. M. (1989). Come *pensare* la psicopatologia in terapia della Gestalt? *Quaderni di Gestalt, 8/9,* 65–76.

Robine, J. M. (1991). *La honte, rupture de confluence Gestalt.* Paris: Société française de Gestalt.

Robine, J. M. (1996). The unknown carried in relationship (G. Wheeler, Trans.). *British Gestalt Journal, 5*(1), 7–17.

Robine, J. M. (2001). From field to situation. In J. M. Robine (Ed.), *Contact and relationship in a field perspective.* Bordeaux: L'Exprimerie.

Rogers, C. R. (1951). *Client-centered therapy.* Boston: Houghton Mifflin.

Rogers, C. R. (1961). *On becoming a person.* Boston: Houghton Mifflin.

Rogers, C. R. (1968). *Freedom to learn.* Columbus, OH: Charles E. Merrill.

Rogers, C. R., & Dymond, R. (Eds.). (1954). *Psychotherapy and personality change.* Chicago: University of Chicago Press.

Rogers, C. R., & Stevens, B. (1967). *Person to person: The problem of being human—a new trend in psychology.* Lafayette, CA: Real People.

Rosenblatt, D. (Ed.). (1980). *A festschrift for Laura Perls* (From the *Gestalt Journal,* Vol. 3, No. 1). Highland, NY: Gestalt Journal Press.

Rosenblatt, D. (1989). *Opening doors: What happens in Gestalt therapy.* Highland, NY: Center for Gestalt Development.

Rosenblatt, D. (1995). *The Gestalt therapy primer.* Southhold, NY: Yurisha. (Original work published 1975)

Rosenfeld, E. (1978a). An oral history of Gestalt therapy, Part 1: A conversation with Laura Perls. *Gestalt Journal, 1*(1), 8–31.

Rosenfeld, E. (1978b). An oral history of Gestalt therapy, Part 2: A conversation with Laura Perls. *Gestalt Journal, 1*(2), 7–29.

Rosenthal, R., & Jacobson, L. (1968). *Pygmalion in the classroom: Teacher expectation and pupils' intellectual development.* New York: Holt, Rinehart & Winston.

Ross, V. (1954). *Handbook for homeroom guidance.* New York: Macmillan.

Rubin, L. (1973). *Facts and feelings in the classroom: The role of emotions in successful learning.* New York: Viking.

Rudestam, K. E. (1982). *Experiential groups in theory and practice.* Monterey, CA: Brooks/Cole.

Safran, J. D., & Greenberg, L. (Eds.). (1991). *Emotion, psychotherapy and change.* New York: Guilford.

Salonia, G. (1992). Time and relation: Relational deliberateness as hermeneutic horizon in Gestalt therapy. *Studies in Gestalt Therapy, 1,* 7–19.

Sameto, S. (2001). *Test and financial aid anxieties of teacher education candidates.* Unpublished doctoral dissertation, Pepperdine University.

Satir, V. (1964). *Conjoint family therapy.* Palo Alto, CA: Science and Behavior Books.

Satir, V. (1972). *Peoplemaking.* Palo Alto, CA: Science and Behavior Books.

Schiffman, M. (1967). *Self-therapy techniques for personal growth.* Menlo Park, CA: Self-Therapy Press.

Schiffman, M. (1971). *Gestalt self-therapy and further techniques for personal growth.* Menlo Park, CA: Self-Therapy Press.

Schmuck, R., & Schmuck, P. (1975). *Group processes in the classroom.* Dubuque, IA: William C. Brown.

Schoen, S. (1994). *Presence of mind: Literary and philosophical roots of a wise psychotherapy.* Highland, NY: Gestalt Journal Press.

Schutz, W. (1967). *Joy: Expanding human awareness.* New York: Grove.

Schutzenberger, A. A., & Utzenberger, A. (1998). *The ancestor syndrome: Trans-generational psychotherapy and the hidden links in the family tree.* New York: Routledge.

Segall, M., Dasen, P., Berry, J., & Poortinga, Y. (Eds.). (1990). *Human behaviour in global perspective: An introduction to cross-cultural psychology* (2nd ed.). Needham Heights, MA: Allyn & Bacon.

Serok, S. (1999). *Innovative applications of Gestalt therapy.* Malabar, FL: Krieger.

Shane, J., Shane, H., Gibson, R., & Munger, P. (1971). *Guiding human development: The counselor and the teacher in the elementary school.* Belmont, CA: Wadsworth.

Shane, P. (1999). Gestalt therapy: The once and future king. In D. Moss (Ed.), *Humanistic and transpersonal psychology: A historical and biographical sourcebook* (pp. 49–65). Westport, CO: Greenwood.

Shapiro, S. B. (1998). *The place of confluent education in the human potential movement: A historical perspective.* Lanham, MD: University Press.

Sheldrake, R. (1995). *Seven experiments that could change the world: A do-it-yourself guide to revolutionary science.* London: Fourth Estate.

Shepard, M. (1975). *Fritz: An intimate portrait of Fritz Perls and Gestalt therapy.* New York: E. P. Dutton.

Shore, M. (1992). Community mental health: Corpse or phoenix? Personal reflections on an era. *Professional Psychology: Research and Practice, 23*(4), 257–262.

Shraga, S. (2000). *Innovative applications of Gestalt therapy.* Malabar, FL: Krieger.

Shub, N. (1992). Gestalt therapy over time: Integrating difficulty and diagnosis. In E. C. Nevis (Ed.), *Gestalt therapy: Perspectives and applications* (pp. 79–113). New York: Gardner.

Shub, N. (2000). Gestalt therapy and self-esteem. *Gestalt Review, 4*(2), 111–120.

Sichera, A. (1997). Comparison with Gadamer: Towards a hermeneutic epistemology of Gestalt therapy. *Studies in Gestalt Therapy, 6/7,* 9–30.

Simkin, J. (1990). *Gestalt therapy: Mini-lectures.* Highland, NY: Center for Gestalt Development. (Original work published 1976)

Simkin, J., & Yontef, G. (1989). Gestalt therapy. In R. Corsini (Ed.), *Current psychotherapies* (3rd ed.). Ithasca, IL: F. E. Peacock.

Simos, G., Simos, G., & Beck, A. (2002). *Cognitive behaviour therapy: A guide for the practicing clinician.* New York: Taylor & Francis.

Sinay, S. (1998). *Gestalt for beginners* (Illustrated by P. Blasberg). New York: Writers and Readers.

Smith, E. W. L. (1976). *The growing edge of Gestalt therapy.* New York: Brunner/Mazel.

Smith, E. W. L. (1977). *The growing edge of Gestalt therapy.* Secaucus, NJ: Citadel.

Smith, E. W. L. (1985). *The body in psychotherapy.* Jefferson, NC: McFarland.

Smith, E. W. L. (1987). *Sexual aliveness: A Reichian-Gestalt perspective.* Jefferson, NC: McFarland.

Smith, E. W. L. (Ed.). (1991). *Gestalt voices.* Norwood, NJ: Ablex.

Smith, E. W. L., Clance, P. R., & Imes, S. (Eds.). *Touch in psychotherapy: Theory, research and practice.* New York: Guilford.

Smith, H. (1976). *Forgotten truth: The common vision of the world's religions.* New York: Harper.

Smuts, H. C. (1996). *Holism and evolution.* New York: Macmillan. (Original work published 1926)

Sobell, M., & Sobell, L. (1978). Alcoholics treated by Individualized Behavior Therapy: One-year treatment outcome. *Behavior Change and Therapy, 11,* 599–618.

Sohl, R., & Carr, A. (1970). *The gospel according to Zen.* New York: Penguin.

Solomon, T. (2000). History of Gestalt therapy in Canada. Retrieved September 2003 from www.psynet.net/git.

Spagnuolo Lobb, M. (2001a). From the epistemology of self to clinical specificity of Gestalt therapy. In J. M. Robine (Ed.), *Contact and relationship in a field perspective* (pp. 19–65). Bordeaux: L'Exprimerie.

Spagnuolo Lobb, M. (2001b). The theory of self in Gestalt therapy: A restatement of some aspects. *Gestalt Review, 4*(4), 276–288.

Spagnuolo Lobb, M. (2002). A Gestalt therapy model for addressing psychosis. *British Gestalt Journal, 11*(1), 5–15.

Spagnuolo Lobb, M. (2003a). Creative adjustment in madness: A Gestalt therapy model for seriously disturbed patients. In M. Spagnuolo Lobb & N. Amendt-Lyon (Eds.), *Creative license: The art of Gestalt therapy.* New York: Springer-Verlag.

Spagnuolo Lobb, M. (2003b). Therapeutic meeting as improvisational co-creation. In M. Spagnuolo Lobb & N. Amendt-Lyon (Eds.), *Creative license: The art of Gestalt therapy.* New York: Springer.

Spagnuolo Lobb, M., & Amendt-Lyon, N. (Eds.). (2003). *Creative license: The art of Gestalt therapy.* New York: Springer-Verlag.

Spagnuolo Lobb, M., Salonia, G., & Cavaleri, P. (1997). Individual and community in the third millennium: The creative contribution of Gestalt therapy. *British Gestalt Journal, 6*(2), 107–113.

Spagnuolo Lobb, M., Salonia, G., & Sichera, A. (1996). From the discomfort of civilisation to creative adjustment: The relationship between individual and community in psychotherapy in the third millennium. *International Journal of Psychotherapy, 1,* 45–53.

Sperry, L. (2001). *Spirituality in clinical practice: Incorporating the spiritual dimension in psychotherapy and counseling.* Philadelphia: Brunner Rutledge.

Spinelli, E. (1989). *The interpreted world: An introduction to phenomenological psychology.* Newbury Park, CA: Sage.

Spitzer, R. (Ed.). (1975). *Tidings of comfort and joy: An anthology of change with Virginia Satir, Fritz Perls, Sheldon Kopp and Raven Lang.* Palo Alto, CA: Science and Behavior Books.

Spolin, V. (1963). *Improvisation for the theatre.* Evanston, IL: Northwestern University Press.

Sprock, J. (2003). Dimensional vs. categorical classification of prototypic and non-prototypic cases of personality disorder. *Journal of Clinical Psychology, 59*(9), 991–1014.

Starak, Y., Maclean, A., & Bernet, A. (Eds.). (1994). *Grounds for Gestalt.* Christchurch, New Zealand: Foreground.

Starak, Y., Maclean, A., & Bernet, A. (Eds.). (1996). *More grounds for Gestalt.* Christchurch, New Zealand: Foreground.

Starkweather, C. W., & Givens, J. (2001, July). *Getting below the tip of the iceberg: Experiential therapy for stuttering.* Workshop presented at the Michael Palin Centre, London.

Steenbarger, B. (1997). The Gestalt! Editorial: The future of managed care. *Gestalt! 1*(3). Retrieved August 16, 2004, from www.g-gej.org/1-3/editorial.html.

Stepansky, P. (1999). *Freud, surgery, and the surgeons.* Hillsdale, NJ: Analytic Press.

Stephenson, F. D. (1995). *Gestalt therapy primer: Introductory readings in Gestalt therapy.* Springfield, IL: Charles C Thomas.

Stern, D. (1985). *The interpersonal world of the infant.* New York: Basic Books.

Stern, D. N. (2004). *The present moment in psychotherapy and everyday life.* New York: Norton.

Stern, E. (1992). A trialogue between Laura Perls, Richard Kitzler, and E. Mark Stern. In E. Smith (Ed.), *Gestalt voices* (pp. 18–32). Norwood, NJ: Ablex.

Stevens, B. (1970). *Don't push the river.* Moab, UT: Real People.

Stevens, J. (1971). *Awareness: Exploring, experimenting, experiencing.* Moab, UT: Real People.

Stevens, J. (Ed.). (1975). *Gestalt is.* New York: Bantam.

Stoehr, T. (1994). *Here now next: Paul Goodman and the origins of Gestalt therapy.* San Francisco: Jossey-Bass.

Stolorow, R. D., & Atwood, G. E. (1992). *Contexts of being: The intersubjective foundations of psychological life.* Hillsdale, NJ: Analytic Press.

Strang, R. (1953). *The role of the teacher in personnel work.* New York: Teachers College, Columbia University Press.

Strang, R. (1965). *Helping your child develop his potential.* New York: E. P. Dutton.

Strouse, N., & Strouse, C. (Eds.). (1993). *On heroes, hero-worship, and the heroic in history.* Berkeley: University of California Press.

Students Against Violence Everywhere. (2003). *S.A.V.E.* Retrieved May 25, 2003, from www.nationalsave.org.

Stulman, J. (1972). *Fields within fields . . . within fields: The methodology of pattern.* New York: World Institute Council.

Sue, D. W., & Sue, D. (1990). *Counseling the culturally different: Theory and practice* (2nd ed.). New York: John Wiley.

Sue, D. W., & Sue, D. (2003). *Counseling the culturally diverse: Theory and practice* (4th ed.). New York: John Wiley.

Sullivan, H. S. (1953). *The interpersonal theory of psychiatry.* New York: Norton.

Suzuki, D. T. (1956). *Zen Buddhism.* New York: Doubleday Anchor.

Swanson, J. (1984). *G.E.T.: Gestalt experiential training: A multimedia training program in Gestalt helping skills.* Corvallis, OR: G.E.T.

Tattlebaum, J. (1980). *The courage to grieve.* New York: Lippincott & Crowell.

Taylor, E. (1997). *A psychology of spiritual healing.* Westchester, PA: Chrysalis.

Teachworth, A. (1997). *Why we pick the mates we do: Ending the cycle of unhappy relationships.* New Orleans, LA: Gestalt Institute of New Orleans.

Telfair-Richards, J. (1988, Fall/Winter). Energy: A Taoist/Gestalt perspective. *Gestalt Review, 3,* 1, 8–10.

Thomas, B. Y. (1997). Integrating multicultural perspectives in Gestalt therapy theory and practice. *GIC Voice (Gestalt Institute of Cleveland), 6,* 1, 6–9.

Thomas, J. J. (1977). *The* you*niverse: Gestalt therapy, non-Western religions and the present age.* La Jolla, CA: Psychology and Consulting Press.

Thompson, J. R. (1987). *The process of psychotherapy: An integration of clinical experience and empirical research.* Lanham, MD: University Press of America.

Tillich, P. (1952). *The courage to be.* New Haven, CT: Yale University Press.

Tudor, K. (2002). Integrating Gestalt in children's groups. In G. Wheeler & M. McConville (Eds.), *The heart of development: Gestalt approaches to working with children, adolescents and their worlds: Vol. 1. Childhood* (pp. 147–164). Hillsdale, NJ: Analytic Press.

Ullman, D., & Wheeler, G. (Eds.). (1998). *The gender field: Gestalt perspectives and readings.* Cambridge, MA: Gestalt Institute of Cleveland Press.

U.S. Department of Education. (2002). *No child left behind.* Retrieved December 12, 2002, from www.nclb.gov.

Valett, R. (1977). *Humanistic education: Developing the total person.* St. Louis: C. V. Mosby.

Van de Riet, V., Korb, M., & Gorrell, J. (1989). *Gestalt therapy: An introduction.* New York: Pergamon. (Original work published 1980)

Van Kaam, A. (1966). *The art of existential counseling.* Denville, NJ: Dimension.

Vaughan, B. (1982). *Body talk: Understanding the secret language of the body.* Allen, TX: Argus Communications.

Vaughan, F. (1995). *Shadows of the sacred: Seeing through spiritual illusions.* Wheaton, IL: Quest.

Vygotsky, L. S. (1962). *Thought and language.* Cambridge, MA: MIT Press. (Original work published 1934)

Walkenstein, E. (1983). Your inner therapist. Philadelphia: Westminster.

Walker, J. (1970). *Body and soul: An essay on Gestalt therapy and religious experience.* Unpublished doctoral dissertation, Graduate Theological Union, Berkeley, CA.

Wallace, J. (1974). *Tactical and strategic use of the preferred defense structure of the recovering alcoholic.* New York: National Council on Alcoholism.

Walsh, F. (Ed.). (1993). *Normal family processes* (2nd ed.). New York: Guilford.

Walsh-Bowers, R. (1998). Community psychology in the Canadian psychological family. *Canadian Psychology, 39*(4), 280–287.

Ward, C., Bochner, S., & Furnham, A. (2001). *The psychology of culture shock.* New York: Routledge.

Watson, J., Gordon, L., Stermac, L., Kalogerakos, F., & Steckley, P. (2003). Comparing the effectiveness of process-experiential with cognitive-behavioral psychotherapy in the treatment of depression. *Journal of Consulting and Clinical Psychology, 71*(4), 773–781.

Watson, R. I. (1979). *Basic writings in the history of psychology.* New York: Oxford University Press.

Watts, A. (1936). *The spirit of Zen.* New York: Grove.

Watts, A. (1957). *The way of Zen.* New York: Pantheon.

Watts, A. (1963). *The two hands of God.* New York: George Braziller.

Watts, A. (1966). *The book: On the taboo against knowing who you are.* New York: Vintage.

Watts, A. (1975). *Tao: The watercourse way.* New York: Pantheon.

Watzlawick, P., Beavin, J., & Jackson, D. (1967). *Pragmatics of human communication.* New York: Norton.

Webb, L., Stiles, W., & Greenberg, L. (2003). A method of rating assimilation in psychotherapy based on markers of change. *Journal of Counseling Psychology, 50*(2), 189–198.

Weeks, G., & L'Abate, L. (1982). *Paradoxical psychotherapy: Theory and practice with individuals, couples and families.* New York: Brunner/Mazel.

Weinrib, E. (1983). *The sandplay therapy process: Images of the self.* Boston: Sigo.

Weinstein, G., & Fantini, M. D. (Eds.). (1970). *Toward humanistic education: A curriculum of affect.* New York: Praeger.

Weizman, S., & Kamm, P. (1985). *About mourning: Support and guidance for the bereaved.* New York: Human Sciences.

Welfel, E. R., & Ingersoll, R. E. (Eds.). (2001). *The mental health desk reference: A sourcebook for counselors.* New York: John Wiley.

West, W. (2000). *Psychotherapy and spirituality.* Thousand Oaks, CA: Sage.

Wheeler, G. (1988). *Gestalt reconsidered.* New York: Gardner.

Wheeler, G. (1991). *Gestalt reconsidered: A new approach to contact and resistance.* New York: Gardner.

Wheeler, G. (1995). Shame in two paradigms of therapy. *British Gestalt Journal, 4*(2), 76–85.

Wheeler, G. (1996). Self and shame: A new paradigm for therapy. In R. G. Lee & G. Wheeler (Eds.), *The voice of shame: Silence and connection in psychotherapy.* San Francisco: Jossey-Bass.

Wheeler, G. (1997). Self and shame: A Gestalt approach. *Gestalt Review, 1*(3), 221–244.

Wheeler, G. (1998). Towards a Gestalt developmental model. *British Gestalt Journal, 7*(2), 115–125.

Wheeler, G. (2000). *Beyond individualism: Toward a new understanding of self, relationship, and experience.* Hillsdale, NJ: Gestalt Institute of Cleveland Press.

Wheeler, G. (2003a, August). Connection and belonging: The feeling of family. *GANZ Community Newsletter,* pp. 8–9.

Wheeler, G. (2003b). Contact and creativity: The Gestalt cycle in context. In M. Spagnuolo Lobb & N. Amendt-Lyon (Eds.), *Creative license: The art of Gestalt therapy* (pp. 163–180). New York: Springer-Verlag.

Wheeler, G. (2003c). The developing field: Toward a Gestalt developmental model. In G. Wheeler & M. McConville (Eds.), *The heart of development: Gestalt approaches to working with children, adolescents and their worlds: Vol. 1. Childhood* (pp. 37–84). Hillsdale, NJ: Analytic Press.

Wheeler, G., & Backman, S. (Eds.). (1994). *On intimate ground: A Gestalt approach to working with couples.* San Francisco: Jossey-Bass.

Wheeler, G., & McConville, M. (Eds.). (2002). *The heart of development: Gestalt approaches to working with children, adolescents and their worlds: Vol. 1. Childhood.* Hillsdale, NJ: Analytic Press.

White, J. R. (1999). A Gestalt approach to working with the person-drug relationship. *Gestalt Review, 3*(2), 147–156.

White, R. (1990). Democracy in the research team. In S. Wheelan, E. Pepitone, & V. Abt (Eds.), *Advances in field theory.* Newbury Park, CA: Sage.

White, W. (1990). *Pathways from the culture of addiction to the culture of recovery.* Center City, MN: Hazelden.

White, W. (1999). *Slaying the dragon: The history of addictions treatment and recovery in America.* Bloomington, IL: Chestnut Health Systems.

Whitfield, C. (1989). *Healing the child within.* Deerfield Beach, FL: Health Communications.

Wiggins-Frame, M. (2003). *Integrating religion and spirituality into counseling.* Pacific Grove, CA: Brooks Cole.

Wilber, K. (1983). *A sociable god: Toward a new understanding of religion.* Boston: Shambhala.

Wilber, K. (1995). *Sex, ecology, spirituality: The spirit of evolution.* Boston: Shambhala.

Wilber, K. (1997). *The eye of spirit: An integral vision for a world gone slightly mad.* Boston: Shambhala.

Wilber, K. (1998). *The marriage of sense and soul: Integrating science and religion.* New York: Random House.

Wilber, K. (1999). *One taste: The journals of Ken Wilber.* Boston: Shambhala.

Wilber, K. (2000). *A brief history of everything.* Boston: Shambhala.

Wilentz, J. S. (1968). *The senses of man.* New York: Thomas Y. Crowell.

Williams, A. (1995). *Visual and active supervision: Roles, focus and techniques.* New York: Norton.

Winnicott, D. W. (1960). The theory of the parent-infant relationship. In D. W. Winnicott, *The maturational process and the facilitating environment* (pp. 37–55). New York: International Universities Press.

Woldt, A. (1976). *Confetti and capers: A cache of gems and pedagogical minutiae for counselors and fellow pilgrims.* Unpublished handbook, Kent State University.

Woldt, A. L. (1980). *Books that influenced and/or were influenced by Gestalt/confluent education.* Unpublished manuscript, Kent State University.

Woldt, A. L. (1990). *Gestalt experience and observation guide for children.* Unpublished manuscript, Kent State University.

Woldt, A. L. (2003). *Gestalt therapy graduate course syllabus.* Unpublished document, Kent State University.

Woldt, A. L., & Ingersoll, R. E. (1991). Where in the "yang" has the "yin" gone in Gestalt therapy? *British Gestalt Journal, 1*(2), 94–102.

Wolfert, R. (2000). Self inexperience, Gestalt therapy, science and Buddhism. *British Gestalt Journal, 9*(2), 77–86.

Wolfert, R. (2002). The spiritual dimensions of Gestalt therapy. *Gestalt! 3,* 1–5.

Wright, L., Everett, F., & Roisman, L. (1986). *Experiential psychotherapy with children.* Baltimore, MD: Johns Hopkins University Press.

Wulf, R. (1996). The historical roots of Gestalt therapy theory. *Gestalt Dialogue: Newsletter for the Integrative Gestalt Centre.* Retrieved August 16, 2004, from www.gestalt.org/wulf.htm.

Wundt, W. (1999). Grundzuge der physiologischen psychologie [Principles of physiological psychology]. In R. Wozniak (Ed.), *Classics in psychology, 1874* (Vol. 10). Bristol, UK: Thoemmes. (Original work published 1874)

Wysong, J. (1979). An oral history of Gestalt therapy, Part 3: A conversation with Erving and Miriam Polster. *Gestalt Journal, 2*(1), 3–26.

Wysong, J. (Ed.). (1992). *Laura Perls: Living at the boundary.* Highland, NY: Gestalt Journal Press.

Wysong, J., & Rosenfeld, E. (Eds.). (1982). *An oral history of Gestalt therapy.* Highland, NY: Center for Gestalt Development.

Yalom, I. (1975). *The theory and practice of group psychotherapy* (2nd ed.). New York: Basic Books.

Yalom, I. (1985). *The theory and practice of group psychotherapy* (3rd ed.). New York: Basic Books.

Yeh, M., & Weisz, J. R. (2001). Why are we here at the clinic? Parent-child (dis)agreement on referral problems at outpatient treatment entry. *Journal of Consulting and Clinical Psychology, 69*(6), 1018–1025.

Yeomans, T. (1975). Gestalt theory and practice and the teaching of literature. In G. I. Brown (Ed.), *The live classroom: Innovation through confluent education and Gestalt.* New York: Viking.

Yontef, G. (1992). Considering Gestalt reconsidered: A review in depth. *Gestalt Journal, 15*(1), 95–118.

Yontef, G. (1993). *Awareness, dialogue and process: Essays on Gestalt therapy.* Highland, NY: Gestalt Journal Press.

Yontef, G. (1996). Shame and guilt in Gestalt therapy. In R. G. Lee & G. Wheeler (Eds.), *The voice of shame: Silence and connection in psychotherapy.* San Francisco: Jossey-Bass.

Yontef, G. (2001). Relational Gestalt therapy: What it is and what it is not. Why the adjective "relational"? In J. M. Robine (Ed.), *Contact and relationship in a field perspective.* Bordeaux: L'Exprimerie.

Zamborsky, L. (1982). *The use of Gestalt therapy with clients expressing religious values issues.* Unpublished doctoral dissertation, Kent State University.

Zinker, J. (1977). *Creative process in Gestalt therapy.* New York: Brunner/Mazel.

Zinker, J. (1980). Developmental processes of a Gestalt group. In B. Feder & R. Ronall (Eds.), *Beyond the hot seat: Gestalt approaches to group* (pp. 55–77). New York: Brunner-Mazel.

Zinker, J. (1987). Presence as evocative power in therapy. *Gestalt Review, 1*(2).

Zinker, J. (1994). *In search of good form: Gestalt therapy with couples and families.* San Francisco: Jossey-Bass.

Zinker, J. (2001). *Sketches: An anthology of essays, art and poetry.* Cambridge, MA: Gestalt Press.

Zinker, J., & Nevis, S. (1994). The aesthetics of Gestalt couples therapy. In G. Wheeler & S. Backman (Eds.), *On intimate ground: A Gestalt approach to working with couples* (pp. 356–399). San Francisco: Jossey-Bass.

APPENDIX A

Digital Gestalt: Online Resources for the Discipline of Gestalt Therapy, A Comprehensive International Listing

ANSEL L. WOLDT, EDD, AND PHILIP BROWNELL, PSYD

This appendix begins with a presentation of Phil's history of electronic Gestalt. It is followed by Ansel and Phil's listing of several categories of Gestalt resources available on the Internet, with invited input from Lars Berg on the European and Scandinavian resources.

In 1995 Gestalt therapy entered the digital world of the Internet. The Association for the Advancement of Gestalt Therapy (AAGT) started an e-mail discussion group; the *Gestalt Journal* had a Web site; Lars Berg (a Gestalt therapist and artist in Sweden) had an article online; there were two or three other individual Web pages; and Philip Brownell hosted AAGT's first Web site.

In 1996, Phil started publishing *Gestalt!*, an online journal for Gestalt therapy with full text articles and graphics. At first it was hosted at St. Johns University under the auspices of Dr. Bob Zenhausern, who founded a network of professional-level listserv discussion groups at that university. He offered Phil space to publish an electronic journal for the discipline of Gestalt therapy, and, to support that, he set up two listserv discussion groups, Gstalt-L and Gstalt-J, giving Phil control as owner of these lists. The journal was mirrored through the Center for Psychotherapeutic Studies on the server at Sheffield University in England. Gstalt-L was conceived to be a place to discuss the contents that were published in the Web-based journal, and Gstalt-J was originally set up to be a discussion hub for all the associated editors, each of whom was supported and encouraged by Phil to begin his or her own Web publishing projects. The idea was to create a small, creative community of Web publishers, each of whom could use the server at St. Johns to build his or her own Web creations. Gerhard Stemberger was one of those people, and he went on to develop a very large site devoted to the Society for Gestalt Theory and Its Applications (GTA). Lars Berg was another, and he went on to do Web design for the European Association for Gestalt Therapy (EAGT) and to create his own Web publishing associated with Gestalt therapy. Eventually, Phil moved the journal to a registered domain reflecting his publishing interests, and Gstalt-L took off, developing a life of its own apart from the journal. It overcame the energy in the AAGT's discussion group and eventually replaced it as an online community in which Gestalt trainers, theorists, writers, trainees, and practitioners share themselves as well as their ideas. It has become a vibrant meeting place for Gestalt people where discussions of theory influence the face-to-face work being done at various training centers. Phil has managed, nurtured, and facilitated this group since its beginning. As an outgrowth of that activity, he supervised for

2 years a Gestalt therapy training group in Kyrgyzstan using an online, text-based method and has since begun to explore the use of Gestalt therapy theory in the practice of online counseling. As of this writing, the electronic journal is in its seventh year of publishing, and Gstalt-J has switched from being a place for associate editors to a discussion group available to those interested in research through the Gestalt Research Consortium.

Between 1995 and 1999, the online presence of Gestalt therapy grew by over 1000%. Brian O'Neill became the moderator for a Gestalt Forum at Behavior Online, which had become known as one of the foremost digital meeting places for professional dialogue among behavioral scientists. Many of the established Gestalt training institutes began to explore how they might come online themselves. The work of AAGT in planning its international conferences was conducted almost entirely through e-mail and repeatedly offered workshops at these conferences exploring how the traditional world of Gestalt therapy might become more digitally sophisticated. Gestalt training institutes and publishing organizations have since accomplished these goals, developing polished and helpful online presences, offering digital services as well as advertising what they provide in real time. The Manchester Gestalt Centre established a library of free articles. The Gestalt Institute of Philadelphia began offering a newsletter and helpful background explanations of Gestalt therapy. The Gestalt Institute of Cleveland offers an online bookstore reflecting its years of publishing Gestalt texts. The Gestalt International Study Center offers connections with many training centers and organizations, who are not represented otherwise on the Internet, through its individual (IAN) and organizational (OAN) affiliates networks. *Gestalt Review* offers content outlines and abstracts for its publishing history (as does the *British Gestalt Journal*). It also provides selected full-text articles of impeccable scholarly achievement in its online library. The *Gestalt Journal* offers several "classic" articles from its archives, a current listing of news and events, and a directory of Gestalt practitioners.

Gestalt therapy Web sites reflect the cultural differences and respective theoretical emphases in the understanding and practice of Gestalt therapy around the world. Taken as a whole, these are a truly impressive display of a global gestalt—a global community of Gestalt theorists, trainers, trainees, writers, and practitioners that has formed at a grassroots level in parallel to established academia but just under the radar of most institutions. Along the way, our training centers, professional societies, and Gestalt therapy practitioners and educators have learned how to offer announcements and registration portals for conferences, workshops, training schedules, and various educational opportunities.

What follows is a breakdown of the Gestalt therapy-related sites on the World Wide Web at the time of submission of this book for publication. Because we recognize that addresses are an ever-changing thing, we want you to know that there will be a continually updated version of Gestalt therapy-related resources available at Gestalt Bookmarks (www.g-gej.org/gestaltbookmarks) and at the Open Directory Project (www.dmoz.org/Science/Social_Sciences/Psychology/Gestalt/Gestalt_Therapy), which is the largest, most comprehensive human-edited directory on the Web. It is constructed and maintained by a vast, global community of volunteer editors, currently edited for Gestalt therapy by Philip Brownell. If you become aware of additional digital Gestalt resources or find any of these references to be in error, please inform us accordingly so that we can maintain an up-to-date listing of Web sites.

GESTALT ASSOCIATIONS AND PROFESSIONAL SOCIETIES

Asociación Española de Terapia Gestalt (AETG; Spain)
www.gestalt.es

Association for Gestalt in Organizations (Swedish Association for Gestalt)
www.fgo.se

Association for the Advancement of Gestalt Therapy (AAGT)
www.aagt.org

Association Gestalt-Therapie et Yoga (Central America)
www.agy.org

Austrian Association for Gestalt Theoretical Psychotherapy (ÖAGP; Austria)
http://gestalttheory.net/gtp

Centro Gestáltico de Montevideo (Uraguay)
www.gestaltinstitut-suedlingen.de

Dansk Gestalt-Akademinforening (DGA; Danish Gestalt Academy)
www.danskgestalt.dk

Deutsche Arbeitsgemeinschaft für Gestalttheoretische Psychotherapie (DAGP; Germany)
http://gestalttheory.net/dagp

Deutsche Gesellschaft für Integrative Therapie, Gestalttherapie und Kreativitätsförderung (DGIK; Germany)
www.agpf-ev.de/dgik.htm

Deutsche Vereinigung für Gestalttherapie (DVG; Germany)
www.gestalttheory.net/info/gpass.html

Europäische Akademie für psychosoziale Gesundheit—Fritz Perls Institut (Germany)
www.integrative-therapie.de

European Association for Gestalt Therapy (EAGT)
www.eagt.org

German Association for Gestalt Theoretical Psychotherapy (DAGP)
www.gestalttheory.net/info/gpass.html

Gestalt Association of the United Kingdom (GAUK)
www.gauk.co.uk

Gestalt Australia and New Zealand (GANZ)
www.ganz.org.au

Gestalt Individual Affiliates Network (IAN@GISC)
www.gisc.org/indivaffnet.html

Gestalt International Network (GTin; Peter Philippson at Manchester Gestalt Centre)
www.mgc.org.uk

Gestalt International Study Center (GISC)
www.GISC.org

Gestalt-Opleidingen Centrum voor Levenskunst (Belgium)
http://user.online.be/gestaltopleiding.cvl/index.htm

Gestalt Organizational Affiliates Network (OAN@GISC)
www.gisc.org/orgaffnet.html

Individual Affiliates Network (IAN; sponsored by Gestalt International Study Center)
www.gisc.org/indivaffnet.html

International Federation of Gestalt Training Organizations (FORGE; 30 Gestalt institutes cooperate to offer training in 18 countries)
www.angelfire.com/emo/forge

International Gestalt Therapy Association (IGTA)
http://kotisivu.mtv3.fi/igta

Nederlands Vlaamse Associatie voor Gestalttherapie en Gestalttheorie (Netherlands)
www.nvagt-gestalt.org or www.nsgestalt.nl/nvagt.htm

NPO Gestalt Network Japan
www.gestaltnet.jp

ÖAGG-Sektion Integrative Gestalttherapie (Austria)
http://www.gestalttherapie.at

Organizational Affiliates Network (OAN; sponsored by Gestalt International Study Center)
www.gisc.org/orgaffnet.html

Österreichische Arbeitsgemeinschaft für Gestalttheoretische Psychotherapie (ÖAGP; Austria)
http://gestalttheory.net/oeagp

Slovene Association for Gestalt Therapy
http://www.gisc.org/orgaffnet.html

Société Belge de Gestalt (Belgium)
http://enabling.org/ia/gestalt/gpass.html

Society for Gestalt Theory and Its Applications (GTA; Austria)
www.enabling.org/ia/gestalt

Swedish Association for Authorized Gestalt Therapists
www.gestaltterapeuterna.org

Vlaams Nederlands Gestalt Netwerk (Netherlands)
www.xs4all.nl/%7Ejrhgland/vngn.html

Yugoslav Association for Gestalt Therapy
http://solair.eunet.yu/~psihopro

GESTALT INSTITUTES, TRAINING ORGANIZATIONS, AND INDIVIDUAL TRAINERS

North America

Atlanta Gestalt Therapy Practice and Training (Georgia)
http://pages.prodigy.net/nlpatlanta/gestalttraining.htm

Center for Clinical Theory and Practice/Gestalt Institute of Cleveland On-line (Ohio)
www.gestaltcleveland.org

Center for Integrative Gestalt Therapy (New York City)
www.integrativetherapy.com

Center for the Study of Intimate Systems (Gestalt International Study Center, Cape Cod, Massachusetts)
www.gisc.org/csis.html

Center for the Study of Strategic Systems (Gestalt International Study Center, Cape Cod, Massachusetts)
www.gisc.org/csss.html

Centre d'intervention Gestaltiste (Quebec, Canada)
www.cigestalt.com

Cincinnati Gestalt Institute (Ohio)
www.gestalt.org/file27.htm

Connecticut Center for Human Growth and Development (Colchester)
www.conncenter.com

Crocker, Sylvia, PhD (Laramie, Wyoming)
www.crockergestalt.com

Earthnet Institute (Hawaii)
www.eni.edu

Esalen Institute (Big Sur, California)
www.esalen.org

Fitzmartin, Gina (Pennsylvania)
www.icubed.com/~cfitz/home.htm

Foresight Group (Cleveland, Ohio)
www.theforesightgroup.org

Gestalt and Humanistic Therapy Institute (Washington, D.C.)
www.gestalt.org/file6.htm

Gestalt Associates for Psychotherapy (New York City)
www.GestaltAssociates.com

Gestalt Associates Training Los Angeles
www.gatla.org

Gestalt Center for Psychotherapy and Training (New York City)
www.gestaltnyc.org

Gestalt Center of Gainesville (Florida)
www.afn.org/~gestalt

Gestalt Center of Long Island (Mellville, New York)
www.gestaltnyc.org

Gestalt Center of New Mexico (Albuquerque)
www.zianet.com/gcnm/AboutJohn.html

Gestalt Center of Queens (New York City)
www.gestaltnyc.org/faculty.htm

Gestalt Center of Sedona (Arizona)
www.gestalt.org/file1.htm

Gestalt Center South (Knoxville, Tennessee)
www.gestalt.org/file36.htm

Gestalt Counseling and Training Institute of Ann Arbor
www.gestalt-annarbor.org

Gestalt Growth Centers of the Bay Area (El Cerrito, Emeryville, and Albany, California)
www.gestaltcenter.net

Gestalt in Chicago Training Program
www.gestalt.org/file10.htm

Gestalt Institute of Austin (Texas)
www.Gestaltist.org

Gestalt Institute of Central Ohio (Columbus)
www.gestaltassoc.com

Gestalt Institute of Calgary (Alberta, Canada)
www.gestalt.org/file41.htm

Gestalt Institute of Cape Cod (Barnstable, Massachusetts)
www.Gestalt.org

Gestalt Institute of Georgia (Atlanta)
www.gestalt.org/file8.htm

Gestalt Institute of Missouri (St. Louis)
www.gestalt.org/file21.htm

Gestalt Institute of New England (Cambridge, Massachusetts)
www.gestalt.org/file24.htm

Gestalt Institute of New Orleans (Louisiana)
www.gestalt-institute.com

Gestalt Institute of Phoenix (Arizona)
www.gestaltphoenix.com

Gestalt Institute of Rhode Island (Cranston)
www.gestaltri.com

Gestalt Institute of Richmond (Virginia)
www.gestalt.org/file36.htm

Gestalt Institute of San Francisco
www.gestaltinstitute.com

Gestalt Institute of Santa Fe (New Mexico)
www.zianet.com/gcnm OR www.gisc.org/orgaffnet.html

Gestalt Institute of Texas (Dallas)
www.gestalt.org/file33.htm

Gestalt Institute of the Berkshires (Richmond, Massachusetts)
www.healinghearts.com/directory/WMA/Listers/GIB.html

Gestalt Institute of the Gulf Coast (Sarasota, Florida)
www.gestalt.org/file7.htm

Gestalt Institute of the Rockies (Golden, Colorado)
www.gestaltoftherockies.com/index.htm

Gestalt Institute of Toronto (Canada)
www.gestalt.on.ca/site

Gestalt International Study Center (South Wellfleet, Cape Cod, Massachusetts)
www.gisc.org

Gestalt Self-Help Interactive Program—Dr. Bea Mackay (Vancouver, Canada)
www.b-sort.com

Gestalt Sing (Susan Gregory; New York City)
www.gestaltsing.com/gestalt.html

Gestalt Therapy and Training Center (Dr. David Gorton; Woodland Hills, California)
www.gestalt.org/file44.htm

Gestalt Therapy Center of Queens (Flushing, New York)
www.gestalt.org/file25.htm

Gestalt Therapy Center of the Bay Area (California)
www.gestaltcenter.net

Gestalt Therapy Institute of Philadelphia (Bryn Mawr, Pennsylvania)
www.gestaltphila.org

Gestalt Therapy Institute of the Pacific (Los Angeles)
www.gestalttherapy.org

Gestalt Therapy Training Center Northwest (Portland, Oregon, and Vancouver, Washington)
www.gttcnw.org

Gestalt Training Center of San Diego (LaJolla, California)
www.gestalt.org/file9.htm

Gestalt Training Institute, Vancouver (British Columbia, Canada)
www.Gestalt.org (for information)

Gremlin Training Institute (Dallas, Texas)
www.tamingyourgremlin.com

Hartford Family Institute (Connecticut)
www.Gestalt.org (for information)

Houston, Gaie (United Kingdom)
www.gaiehouston.co.uk

Indianapolis Gestalt Institute (Indiana)
www.indygestalt.com

Institute for Integrative Psychotherapy (New York City)
www.integrativetherapy.com

Life Purpose Center (Larkspur, California)
www.earley.org

Marin Gestalt Institute of Western Massachusetts
www.javanet.com/~stefan/therapy/Marin_Gestalt.html

New York Institute for Gestalt Therapy (New York City)
www.newyorkgestalt.org

NLP Center and Gestalt Institute of Atlanta (Georgia)
http://pages.prodigy.net/nlpatlanta/gestalttraining.htm

Organizational and Systems Development International Program (Sponsored by GISC)
www.gisc.org/internationalosd.html

Pacific Gestalt Institute (Los Angeles)
www.gestalttherapy.org

Pennsylvania Gestalt Center (Malvern)
www.gestaltcenter.com

Portland Gestalt Therapy Institute (Oregon)
www.gestalt.org/file28.htm

Quebec Gestalt Training Program (Montréal, Canada)
www.gestalt.org/file41.htm

Sarasota Community School (Gestalt-based K-12 academy for difficult kids, Florida)
www.kanneracademy.com

School of Gestalt and Experiential Teaching (San Francisco)
www.directimpactcreativity.com/school/index.asp

Sierra Institute for Contemporary Gestalt Therapy (Sacramento, California)
www.gestalt.to

Southwestern Gestalt Center (Phoenix, Arizona)
www.gestalt.org/file1.htm

Tobin, Stephen (Portland, Oregon)
www.doctortobin.com

Violet Oaklander Institute (Santa Barbara, California)
www.violetoaklander.com OR oaklander@gestalt.org

Europe

Applicazioni Ricerche Studi, Istituto di Gestalt, Rome
www.aicounselling.it/ars.htm

Artheja (Netherlands)
www.artheja.com

Associazione per lo Sviluppo Psicologico (ASPIC; Rome)
www.psychother.com/training/aspic.htm

Centre d'Intervention Gestaltiste (France)
www.cigestalt.com

Centre for Gestalt Development in Organisations (United Kingdom)
www.gestalt.co.uk

Centro Gestalt—Genoa (Italy)
http://xoomer.virgilio.it/emileone

Centro Studi di Terapia Gestalt ed Esperenziale (CSTG; Italy)
www.psicoterapia.it/cstg

Dansk Gestalt Akademiforening (Denmark)
www.danskgestalt.dk

Deutsche Vereinigung für Gestalttherapie (Germany)
www.dvg-gestalt.de

Ecole Parisienne de Gestalt (France, Belgium, Switzerland, Italy, Russia)
www.gestalt.mgn.fr

Edinburgh Gestalt Institute (Scotland)
www.edinburgh-gestalt-institute.moonfruit.com

Fédération Internationale des Organismes de Formation à la Gestalt (Paris)
www.angelfire.com/emo/forge

Federazione Italiana Scuole e Istituti di Gestalt (FISIG)
www.mclink.it/com/cstg/page2.html

Föreningen Auktoriserade Gestaltterapeuter (Sweden)
www.gestaltterapeuterna.org/foreningen.html

Fritz Perls Institut für Integrative Therapie, Gestalttherapie und Kreativitätsförderung (FPI)
www.integrative-therapie.de

Gestalt Academy of Scandinavia/Gestalt Academin Skandinavien (Stockholm, Sweden)
www.gestaltakademin.se

Gestalt Bodymind (United Kingdom)
www.gestaltbodymind.co.uk

Gestalt Centre London (United Kingdom)
www.gestaltcentre.co.uk

Gestalt Consultancy and Training (United Kingdom)
www.gestalt.co.uk

Gestalt Counseling Training Center of Rome (Italy)
www.gestalt.org/file54.htm

Gestalt Education (United Kingdom)
www.gestalteducation.org.uk

Gestalt Education Network International (Frankfurt, Germany, and Kerala, India)
www.geni-gestaltinstitut.de

Gestalt Foundation (Thessiloniki, Greece)
www.eagt.org/conferences2.htm

Gestalt Institut de Neuilly (GIN; Neuilly sur Seine, France)
www.gestalttheory.net/info/gpass.html

Gestalt Institut Köln (GIK; Germany)
www.gestalt.de/links.html

Gestalt Institut Südlingen (Germany)
www.gestaltinstitut-suedlingen.de

Gestalt Institute for Education and Personal Development (Krakow, Poland)
www.gestalt.haller.kraknet.pl

Gestalt Institute of Houston in Europe (Leland Johnson, Rolfing and Gestalt Somatics, Germany)
http://www.living-gestalt.com/gestalt

Gestalt Praktijkschool BOLT (Nieuwaal, Netherlands)
www.gestaltschoolbolt.nl

Gestalt Psychotherapy and Training Institute (United Kingdom)
www.gpti.org.uk

Gestalt Southwest (United Kingdom)
web.onetel.net.uk/~gestaltsw/welcome.html

Gestalt Therapy in Latvia (Riga)
www.gestalt.lv

Gestalt Therapy Institute of Cologne (Germany)
http://ourworld.compuserve.com/homepages/gik_gestalt/index.html

Gestalt Training Center (Denmark)
www.gestalt.dk

Gestalt Trust of Scotland and Northern Ireland
www.thegestalttrust.com

GestaltinFormation Webplats (Scandinavian Web site offering training opportunities; edited by Lars Berg for a Swedish audience)
www.egenart.info/gestalt

Gestalt-Institut Frankfurt (Germany)
www.gestalt-institut-frankfurt.de

Gestalt-Kindertherapie (Gabriele Enders, Cologne, Germany)
www.gestaltkindertherapie.de

Gestalt-Klinik/Hardtwaldklinik I, Bad Zwesten (Germany)
www.wicker-kliniken.de/hardtwald1/psychoth.htm

Gestaltkritik—Zeitschrift für Gestalttherapie (Germany)
www.gestaltkritik.de

Gestaltowski Instytut Edukacji i Rozwoju Osobistego (Poland)
www.gestalt.haller.kraknet.pl

Gestaltpsychotherapie.de (Germany)
www.gestaltpsychotherapiede/index.htm

Gestaltteraapia Arenduskeskus (Tartu, Estonia)
www.hot.ee/gestalt/index.htm

Gestaltterapi i Sverige (Lars Berg; Sweden)
http://katalogen.sunet.se/kat/business/corporations/human_resources/training_and_development

Gestaltterapeutisk Institut (Copenhagen, Denmark)
www.gestaltterapi.dk

Gestalttherapie in Bamberg (Germany)
www.gestalt.de/links.html

Gestalt-Zentrum Gottingen (Germany)
www.gestaltzentrum.de

GIS-International (Denmark)
www.gis-international.com/frameset.php

Hamburger Institut für Gestaltorientierte Weiterbildung (HIGW; Germany)
www.higw.de

Institut Français de Gestalt-therapie (IFGT; Bordeaux, France)
www.gestalt-ifgt.com

Institut für Gestaltorientierte Organisationsberatung (IGOR; Frankfurt, Germany)
www.igor-gestalt.com/Deutsch/seite1-d.htm

Institut für Gestalttherapie und Gestaltpädagogik e.V. (Germany)
www.igg-berlin.de

Institut für Integrative Gestalttherapie Wien, Austria (IGWien)
http://members.aon.at/igwien

Institut für Integrative Gestalttherapie Würzburg
www.igw-gestalttherapie.de

Institut Gestalt (Barcelona, Spain)
http://institutgestalt.com

Institut Gestalt Viernes (Spain)
www.institutgestalt.com/index.php

Institut pro Gestalt Terapii (Czech Republic)
www.gestalt.cz

Instituto Ananda (Pamplona, Spain)
www.institutoananda.com

Instituto de Terapia Gestalt de Valencia (Spain)
www.itgestalt.com/instituto.htm

Instituttet for Krop-og Gestalttherapi (Denmark, training for bodywork and psychotherapy)
www.ikg.dk/instituttet.htm

Instytut Terapii Gestalt (Poland)
www.gestalt.pl

Integrative Gestalttherapie (ÖAGG; Germany)
www.gestalttherapie.at

Integrative Psychotherapy Training Programs (Richard Erskine; Rome, Italy; Exeter, England; Madrid, Spain; Zaragoza, Spain)
www.integrativetherapy.com/training.php

Istituto di Gestalt, Human Communication Center (with five offices in Italy, at Syracuse, Ragusa, Venice, Rome, and Palermo, all recognized by the Italian Minister for the Universities)
www.itff.org/CNSP/Scuole.CNSP/IstitutoGestalt.html

Istituto di Psicoterapia della Gestalt e di Analisi Transazionale (IGAT; Naples)
www.igatweb.it

Istituto Gestalt Firenze (Florence, Italy)
www.igf-gestalt.it/depliant-2005.htm

Istituto Gestalt di Puglia (Puglia, Lecce, Brindici, Bari, Italy)
www.apuliagestalt.it

Istituto Gestalt e Body Work (Cagliari, Italy)
www.aicounselling.it/igbw.htm

Istituto Gestalt Pordenone (Italy)
www.aicounselling.it/igp2.htm

Istituto Gestalt Trieste (Italy)
www.aicounselling.it/trieste.htm

Istituto Torinese di Analisi Transazionale e Gestalt s.r.l.
www.itat-formazione.it

Jugoslovensko Udruzenje za Gestalt Terapiju (Yugoslavia)
http://solair.eunet.yu/~psihopro/sindex.html

Kursstallet (Institute for Gestalt and Body Therapy, Ystad, Sweden)
http://w1.411.telia.com/~u41100278/english.htm

Lebenskunst (Gestalt-Labor, Sulzburg, Germany)
www.neue-ideen.de/lebenskunst.html

Liberating Potential (United Kingdom)
www.liberatingpotential.co.uk

Mainliners, Ltd., London (Counselor Certification Program)
www.mainliners.org.uk OR www.rdlearning.org.uk

Manchester Gestalt Centre (United Kingdom)
www.mgc.org.uk

Martin, Linda (United Kingdom)
www.lindamartinonline.com

Metanoia Institute (United Kingdom)
www.metanoia.ac.uk

Multi-di-Mens, Instituut voor procesbegeleiding (Olen, Netherlands)
www.multidimens.be

Multi-di-Mens, Vlaams-Nederlands Instituut voor Gestalttherapie (Ghent, Belgium)
http://gestalttheory.net/info/gpass.html

Nederlandse Beroepsvereniging van Gestalttherapeuten (NBGT; Netherlands)
www.nbgt.nl

Nederlandse Stichting Gestalt (Amsterdam, Netherlands)
www.nsgestalt.nl

Nederlands-Vlaamse Associatie voor Gestalttherapie en Gestalttheorie (NVAGT; Amsterdam)
www.nvagt-gestalt.org

Netwerk van Gestalt en Transpersoonlijke therapeuten (NGTT; Netherlands)
www.ngtt.net

Norsk Gestaltinstitutt AS (NGI; Oslo, Norway)
www.gestalt.no

Perry, Philippa (United Kingdom)
www.awareness.fsnet.co.uk

PHYSIS (Petruska Clarkson; London)
www.physis.co.uk

Practice for Gestalt Therapy in Amsterdam (Netherlands)
www.pgta.nl

Psykoterapeutisk Center (Denmark)
www.jarmsted.suite.dk/uk.htm

Riga Gestalt Institute (Latvia)
www.gestalt.lv

Saarbrücker Gestalt Institut (Germany)
www.sgi-gestalttherapie.de

Salisbury, Claire (United Kingdom)
www.clairesalisbury.com

Samtalspartner—Gestalt terapi (Sweden)
www.samtalspartner.se/gestaltt.html

SAVOIR PSY (Paris)
www.savoirpsy.com

Scarborough Psychotherapy Training Institute (United Kingdom)
www.scpti.co.uk

School of Gestalt and Experiential Teaching (Paul Rebillot European Training Programs)
www.directimpactcreativity.com/calendar/index.asp

Schweizer Verein für Gestalttherapie und Integrative Therapie (SVG; Switzerland)
www.gestalttherapie.ch

Sherwood Psychotherapy Training Institute (Sherwood Castle, United Kingdom)
www.spti.net

Site des Praticiens en Gestalt-Therapie Francophones (France)
www.gestalttheory.net/info/gpass.html

Società Italiana di Psicoterapia Integrata (SIPI; Casoria, NA)
http://www.sipintegrazioni.it/Sipi.htm

Società Italiana Psicoterapia Gestalt (SIPG; Syracuse, Italy)
www.humantrainer.com/scuole-psicoterapia/gestalt.html

Spoelstra, Susan, Praktijk voor Gestalttherapie (Netherlands)
www.xs4all.nl/%7Ejrhgland/index.html

Symbolon Institut für Gestalttherapie e. V. (Nuremberg, Germany)
www.symbolon-institut.de

Toula Vlachoutsikou Gestalt Training Site (Greece)
www.gestalt.gr

Vlaams Nederlands Gestalt Netwerk (Netherlands)
www.vngn.nl

Voies Nouvelles en Développement Personnel (Gestalt Massage et Gestalt Thérapie, Paris)
www.gestalttheory.net/info/gpass.html

York Psychotherapy Training Centre (United Kingdom)
www.yorkpsychotherapy.co.uk/homepage.htm

Yugoslav Association for Gestalt Psychotherapy (Yugoslavia)
http://solair.eunet.yu/~psihopro

South America

Anchimalén—Escuela de Psicoterapia Gestalt (Chile)
www.gestalt.cl

Associatión Gestáltica de Buenos Aires (Buenos Aires, Argentina)
www.gestalt.org/ar

Centro de Estudos de Gestalt Terapia del Brasilia (CEGEST; Porto Alegre, Brazil)
www.cegest.org.br

Centro de Gestalt de Florianopolis (Brazil)
www.gestalt.com.br

Centro Educacional de Gestalt y de Psicologia Transpersonal (Argentina)
www.transpersonalpsycho.com.ar

Centro Gestáltico de Montevideo (Uruguay)
www.gestaltmontevideo.com

Cristiane Silveira Becker Correa Gestalt Center (Santa Catarina, Brazil)
www.gestalt.com.br

Gestalt Institut—Suedlingen
www.gestaltinstitut-suedlingen.de

Instituto de Psicologia Gestalt em Figura (Rio de Janeiro)
www.geocities.com/HotSprings/Resort/2631

Instituto de Treinamento e Pesquisa em Gestalt—Terapia de Goiânia (ITGT; Brazil)
www.gestaltterapia.com.br

Instituto Gestalten (Brazil)
www.gestalten.com.br

Red Latina de Terapeutas Gestalticos
www.agba.org.ar/redlatina.htm

Mexico and Central America

Centro de Investigación y Entrenamiento en Psicoterapia Gestalt Fritz Perls (Mexico)
www.cgestalt.com/login/index.php

Centro Gestalt de México
www.mundogestalt.com

Instituto Gestalt de Guadalajara (Especialidad en Psicoterapia Gestalt, Educacion Secretaria)
http://sesicdrip.sep.gob.mx/IGG.htm

Instituto Humanista de Psicoterapia Gestalt (Mexico)
www.gestalthumanista.com/home.html

Australia and New Zealand

Brisbane Gestalt Institute (Australia)
www.gestaltinstitute.com.au

Conscious Partnership (New Zealand)
www.partnering.inet.net.nz

Gestalt Association of Queensland, Inc. (Australia)
www.gestaltqueensland.org.au

Gestalt Institute of Melbourne (Victoria, Australia)
www.swin.edu.au/sbs/pub/gestalt

Gestalt Institute of New Zealand (Christchurch, New Zealand)
www.gestalt.org.nz

Gestalt Practitioners Training Sydney (GPTS; Australia)
www.gestaltpractitioners.com.au

Gestalt Therapy and Training Center (Queensland, Australia)
http://www.gestalt.org/file44.htm

Gestalt Therapy Australia
www.gestalt.com.au

Gestalt Therapy Training Center Toowong (Australia)
www.gestaltqueensland.com.au

Gestalt Training Institute Sydney
www.g-gej.org/1-3/institutes.html

Gestalt Training Institute West Australia
www.gestaltwa.com

Illawarra Gestalt Centre
www.illawarragestalt.com

Jansen Newman Institute of Counselling and Applied Psychotherapy (St. Leonards, New South Wales)
www.jni.nsw.edu.au

Melbourne Institute for Experiential and Creative Arts Therapy (MIECAT)
www.miecat.org.au

Northern Rivers Gestalt Institute (Australia)
www.gestalt.org.au

Soul of Life Wellness Center (Melbourne, Australia)
www.souloflife.com

South Australian Gestalt Training Institute
www:jenadelaide@bigpond.com

Sydney Gestalt Centre (Australia)
www.gestaltsydney.com

Asia, Russia, Middle East

Ecole Parisienne de Gestalt (Russia)
www.gestalt.mgn.fr

Faye Ratner Gestalt Program, School of Social Work and College of Medicine, Tel-Aviv University (Tel-Aviv, Israel)
www.Gestalt.org (for information)

Israel Gestalt Training Program, Gestalt Institute of Cleveland (ISRAGIC)
www.gestaltcleveland.org/ptps/g55-isragic.html

Moscow Gestalt Institute (Russia)
www.gestalt.ru

North Western Gestalt-Center—Petersburg (Russia)
www.gestalt.sp.ru

NPO Gestalt Network Japan
www.gestaltnet.jp

South Russian Gestalt Center (Marina Aralova, Rostov State University, Russia)
www.rnd.runnet.ru/rsu/psychfac/aralova.html

JOURNALS, NEWSLETTERS, AND DISCUSSION GROUPS

AAGT Newsletter (Association for the Advancement of Gestalt Therapy; Marcy Stern, editor)
www.AAGT.org

Abordagem Gestáltica (Brazilian e-mail discussion list in Portuguese)
http://debates.hipernet.ufsc.br/foruns/gt-latina/debates/mensagem.srv?

Australian Gestalt Journal (Bruno Just, editor)
www.users.bigpond.com/justbruno

Behavior Online Forum on Gestalt Therapy (Brian O'Neill, moderator)
www.behavior.net/bolforums/forumdisplay.php?f=11

British Gestalt Journal (Malcolm Parlett, editor)
www.britishgestaltjournal.com

Cahiers de Gestalt-thérapie (Institut Français de Gestalt-thérapie; in French)
http://forum.doctissimo.fr/psychologie

Contact (Newsletter of the Gestalt Therapy Institute of Philadelphia)
www.gestaltphila.org/Newsletter/index.asp

FOROGESTALT (Lista de discusión sobre teoría y práctica gestaltica en español)
forogestalt-subscribe@yahoogroups.com

Forum École Parisienne de Gestalt (discussion list for French-speaking people)
www.gestalt.asso.fr/pages/forum.htm

Freedom Express, a Gestalt Publication for Freedom of Expression Through Writing (Lars Berg, Sharon Snir, and Marcy Stern, editors)
www.freedomxpress.net

Fritz-Perls-List (e-mail discussion list with Bruno G. Just, Australia)
fritzperls-l-subscribe@listas.hipernet.ufsc.br

Gaceta de la Gestalt On-Line (e-zine from Argentina; in Spanish, some articles in English)
www.transpersonalpsycho.com.ar/lagaceta.htm

Gestalt (Zeitschrift d. Schweizer Vereins f. Gestalttherapie u. Integrative Therapie—SVG)
http://mypage.bluewin.ch/altburg/Gestalt/1.html

Gestalt! (Philip Brownell, editor)
www.g-gej.org

Gestalt Critique (in German: *Gestaltkritik,* from Gestalt Therapy Institute of Cologne)
http://ourworld.compuserve.com/homepages/gik_gestalt/gestalt_critique.html

Gestalt dwumiesiêcznik (Journal of the Gestalt Therapy Institute, Krakow and Warsaw, Poland)
www.gestalt.pl/czasopismo/index.html

Gestalt Gallery: Artistic Expression of Gestalt Therapy Philosophy and Values (Lars Berg, editor)
www.egenart.info/gestalt-gallery/index.html

Gestalt Review (Joseph Melnick, editor)
www.gestaltreview.com

Gestalt Theory—An International Multidisciplinary Journal (Official Journal of the Society for Gestalt Theory and Its Applications (GTA); bilingual, German/English)
http://gestalttheory.net/gth

GestaltinFormation Webplats (Scandinavian Web site)
www.egenart.info/gestalt

Gestaltpsychotherapie.de (discussion board in German and English, maintained by Achim Votsmeier-Röhr)
www.gestaltpsychotherapie.de OR http://gestaltpsychotherapie.de/index_english.htm

Gestaltterapeutisk Forum i Danmark
www.gfdk.com

Gestaltterapi i Sverige (Lars Berg, Sweden)
http://katalogen.sunet.se/kat/business/corporations/human_resources/training_and_development

Gestalttherapie in der Schweiz (German Gestalt bookstore)
http://mypage.bluewin.ch/gestalt

Gstalt-J (e-mail discussion list; Philip Brownell, manager)
www.g-gej.org/gstalt-j

Gstalt-L (e-mail discussion list; Philip Brownell, manager)
www.g-gej.org/gstalt-1

gt-br—Gestalt-Terapia no Brasil (discussion board in Portuguese)
http://debates.hipernet.ufsc.br/foruns/gt-br/debates/listagem.srv

International Gestalt Journal (Frank M. Staemmler, editor)
www.gestalt.org/igjpromo

Lista de Gestalt en Español (e-mail discussion list for Spanish-speaking people, moderated by Eva Sabina Lopez Castell, Argentina)
gestalt@sorengo.com

MundoGestalt.Com (Latin American Gestalt portal originating in Mexico)
www.mundogestalt.com

Newsletter of the Association for the Advancement of Gestalt Therapy (AAGT; available as downloadable PDF files at the Web site for the AAGT; Marcy Stern, editor)
www.aagt.org

Nordiska GestaltJournalen: The Nordic Gestalt Journal (Lars Berg, editor; for back copies; journal has been disbanded)
www.egenart.info/ngj

Partners in Dialogue Newsletter
www.partnering.inet.net.nz/frame2.htm

Person-Centered and Experiential Psychotherapies Journal
www.pce-world.org/idxjournal.htm

Psicologia Humanista Existencial (Brazilian Gestalt discussion list in Portuguese)
www.cied.rimed.cu/revistaselec/ss/ss1ano1/cueto.html

Psychotherapy in Australia (journal and newsletter on training and professional development)
www.psychotherapy.com.au/index.asp

Quaderni di Gestalt (Italian Gestalt journal; Margherita Spagnuolo Lobb, editor)
www.gestalt.it/inglese/qdg-e.htm

Studies in Gestalt Therapy (Italian Gestalt journal in English: Margherita Spagnuolo Lobb, editor)
www.gestalt.it/inglese/sgt-e.htm

Voices: Journal of the American Academy of Psychotherapists
www.coe.iup.edu/aap/voices.html

GESTALT-ORIENTED RESEARCH ORGANIZATIONS AND RESOURCES

Evidence-Based Mental Health
ebmh.bmjjournals.com

Frederick and Laura Perls' Gestalt Therapy Special Collections, Kent State University Libraries
http://speccoll.library.kent.edu/other/gestalt.html

Gestalt Archives at Kent State University, Ohio
http://speccoll.library.kent.edu/other/gestalt.html

Gestalt Collections of Dissertations and Research at Kent State University
http://kentlink.kent.edu

Gestalt Research Conference (Gestalt International Study Center, Cape Cod, Massachusetts)
www.gisc.org

Gestalt Research Consortium (Phil Brownell's Internet Interchange)
www.g-gej.org/grc

Journal of Psychotherapy Practice and Research
http://jppr.psychiatryonline.org

Network for Research on Experiential Psychotherapies
www.experiential-researchers.org

Psychological Therapies Research, University of Leeds
www.psyc.leeds.ac.uk

Psychology and Psychotherapy: Theory, Research and Practice
www.bps.org.uk/publications/jHP_6.cfm

Psychotherapy Research
http://ptr.oupjournals.org

Psychotherapy Theory, Research and Practice (American Psychological Association)
www.apa.org/journals/pst/description.html

Research at the Focusing Institute
www.focusing.org/research.html

Society for Gestalt Theory and Its Applications (GTA)
www.gestalttheory.net

Society for Psychotherapy Research (SPR)
www.naspr.org

Society for Psychotherapy Research UK (SPRUK)
www.psyctc.org/spruk/default.htm

Society for the Exploration of Psychotherapy Integration
www.cyberpsych.org/sepi

World Council for Psychotherapy
www.worldpsyche.org

INSTITUTIONS OF HIGHER EDUCATION WITH A GESTALT PRESENCE

Bryn Mawr College (Pennsylvania) (MA and PhD in Social Work Professors David Henrich, Philip Lichtenberg [Emeritus])
www.brynmawr.edu

California Institute of Integral Studies (San Francisco) (Graduate degrees in Integral Counseling, Drama Therapy, Somatic Psychology, Expressive Arts Therapy, and Clinical Psychology. Gestalt contacts: Professors Lu Grey, Judith Glass, Jamie Nisenbaum)
www.ciis.edu

Cleveland State University (Ohio) (Graduate degrees in School and Community/Agency Counseling, and Clinical Psychology. Gestalt contacts: Professors Ann Bauer, Elliott Ingersoll, Deborah Plummer, Sarah Toman)
www.csuohio.edu

Fielding Graduate Institute (Santa Barbara, California) (Graduate degree in Clinical Psychology offers emphasis in TA-Gestalt. Organizational Development faculty has three Gestaltists: Marcela Benson-Quaiena, Janice Rubin Rudestam, Barbara Mink)
www.fielding.edu

Georgia Southern University (Statesboro) (MS in Clinical Psychology. Gestalt contacts: Professor Edward Smith, William McIntosh, Rebecca Smith)
www.georgiasouthern.edu OR http://class.georgiasouthern.edu/psychology/faculty.html

Indiana University of Pennsylvania (Indiana, Pennsylvania) (MA and MEd in School and Community Counseling, PsyD in Clinical Psychology. Gestalt contact: Bob Witchel)
www.iup.edu

Institute for Transpersonal Psychology (Palo Alto, CA) (MA in Counseling and Transpersonal Psychology, PhD in Transpersonal Clinical Psychology. Gestalt contact: Professor Arthur Hastings)
www.itp.edu

Kent State University (Ohio) (MA, MEd, EdS in School and Community Counseling, PhD in Counselor Education and Supervision, Nondegree Gestalt certificate program in College of Continuing Studies. Gestalt courses offered since 1970. Gestalt contact: Emeritus Professor Ansel Woldt)
www.kent.edu

La Trobe University (Melbourne, Australia) (MA in Gestalt Therapy in the School of Public Health in association with Gestalt Therapy Australia Institute. Gestalt contact: Professor Linsey Howie)
www.latrobe.edu.au/health/Health/Courses/Postgrad/Mast_Gest_Ther.html

Lewis and Clark College (Portland, Oregon) (MA in Counseling Psychology, Marriage and Family Therapy, Addictions Treatment; MS in School Psychology. Gestalt contact: Professor Peter Mortola)
www.lclark.edu

Loma Linda University (California) (PhD and PsyD in Clinical Psychology. Gestalt contact: Professor Todd Burley)
www.llu.edu/llu/grad/psychology/faculty/burley.htm

London Metropolitan University (MA in Gestalt Psychotherapy in conjunction with training at the Gestalt Centre. Gestalt contact: Jacqueline Wearn)
www.londonmet.ac.uk/pg-prospectus-2004/courses/dops/gestalt-psychotherapy-ma.cfm

London South Bank University (Department of Health and Social Care and Department of Arts and Human Sciences)
www.lsbu.ac.uk OR www.rdlearning.org.uk

Middlesex University (United Kingdom) (MSc in Gestalt Psychotherapy in conjunction with training at Metanoia Institute. Gestalt contact: Lynda Osborne)
www.mdx.ac.uk

New York University, Steinhardt School of Education (BS, MA, PsyD, PhD degrees in Applied Psychology, Counseling and Guidance, Counseling Psychology, Educational Psychology, Psychological Development, School Psychology. Gestalt contact: Professor Iris Fodor)
www.nyu.edu/education/appsych

Pacific University, School of Professional Psychology (Forest Grove, Oregon) (MA in Counseling Psychology, PsyD in Clinical Psychology. Gestalt contacts: Professors Jon Frew, Stephen Zahm)
www.pacificu.edu

Pepperdine University, Graduate School of Education and Psychology (Los Angeles) (Professors Cara Garcia, Robert deMayo)
http://gsep.pepperdine.edu

Saybrook Graduate School and Research Center (San Francisco) (MA in Marriage and Family Therapy; PhD in Humanistic and Transpersonal Psychology, Consciousness and Spirituality, Organizational Systems and Social Transformation. Gestalt contacts: Professors James Bugenthal, Eleanor Criswell, Robert Flax, Tom Greening, Richard Hycner, Maureen O'Hara, Stephen Tobin)
www.saybrook.edu

Sonoma State University (Rohnert Park, California) (MA in Psychology with specialization in Depth Psychology, Art Therapy, Humanistic/Transpersonal Psychology, Organization Development. Gestalt contact: Professor Victor Daniels)
www.sonoma.edu/users/d/daniels

Southern Connecticut State University (New Haven) (MA in Family Therapy with a Gestalt therapy emphasis. Gestalt contacts: Professors Barbara Lynch and Ed Lynch)
www.southernct.edu/grad/programs/MFT

Swinburne University (Victoria, Australia) (Graduate Diploma of Social Science in Gestalt Therapy in association with the Gestalt Institute of Melbourne. Gestalt contact: Peter Cantwell)
http://domino.swin.edu.au/cd31.nsf/Open/N0810

University College, Cork (Ireland) (Higher Diploma in Gestalt Therapy. Gestalt contact: Professor Eleanor O'Leary)
www.ucc.ie/ucc/depts/psycho/courses/hdgt.html

University of Akron (Ohio) (MA and MEd in School Counseling and Classroom Guidance for Teachers have a Gestalt presence. Gestalt contact: Professor Cynthia Reynolds)
www.uakron.edu

University of Birmingham (United Kingdom) (MA in Gestalt Psychotherapy, Humanistic Person-Centered Psychotherapy, and Integrative Psychotherapy in cooperation with Sherwood Institute)
www.spti.net

University of Brighton (Sussex, United Kingdom) (Gestalt courses offered in Departments of Applied Social Sciences, Centre for Health Care Research, and School of Healthcare Professions in association with Gestalt Centre. Gestalt contact: Jacqueline Wean)
www.brighton.ac.uk OR www.rdlearning.org.uk

University of Derby (United Kingdom) (MA in Gestalt Psychotherapy in conjunction with training at the Sherwood Psychotherapy Training Institute. Gestalt contact: Barbro Curman)
www.gestaltakademin.se/eng/terap.htm

University of South Maine (Portland) (Gestalt contact: Counselor Education Professor Maryjane Fall)
www.usm.maine.edu

University of Western Sydney, School of Applied Social and Human Sciences (Australia) (Master of Counseling and Graduate Diploma in Expressive Therapies. Gestalt contact: Professors Fiona Rummery, Jill Eastwood)
www.uws.edu.au

Walsh University (Canton, Ohio) (MA degrees in School Counselor Education and Mental Health Counseling. Gestalt contacts: Professor Judy Green, Linda Barclay)
www.walsh.edu

West Kent College (Christbridge, New Zealand) (Advanced Diploma in Humanistic Counseling. Gestalt contact: Linda Martins)
www.wkc.ac.uk

York University (Toronto, Ontario) (MA and PhD in Clinical Psychology with Experiential Psychotherapy emphasis. Gestalt contact: Professor Leslie Greenberg)
www.yorku.ca

GESTALT-BASED CONSULTING FIRMS, TREATMENT PROGRAMS, AND CLINICAL PRACTICES

Acsenture (Servaas Van Beekum Consulting, Coaching, and Training; Sydney, Australia)
www.ascenture.com.au

Akerlund, Anders (Scandinavia)
www.akerlundshelhetshalsa.com

Berg Egenart, Lars (Sweden)
www.egenart.info/egenart

Cederholm, Monica (Sweden)
www.ledarskapharmoni.se

Crocker, Sylvia, PhD (Laramie, Wyoming)
www.crockergestalt.com

Curman, Barbro and Mikael (Sweden)
www.curmans.se

Danielsson, Daniel (Sweden)
www.gestalt.is

Dannerup, Dr. J. N. (South Africa)
www.dannerup.com

Eriksson, Tina (Sweden)
www.humanresource.se

Fitzmartin, Gina (Pennsylvania)
www.icubed.com/~cfitz/home.htm

Gaffney, Seàn, Björn Magnusson, & Bertil Öhberg (Sweden)
www.granosus.se

Gestalt Sing (Susan Gregory, New York City)
www.gestaltsing.com

Houston, Gaie (United Kingdom)
www.gaiehouston.co.uk

Larsson, Boo (Scandinavia)
www.boolarsson.se

Lindblom, Ann (Scandinavia)
www.terapiochutbildning.se

Lovitt, Ken, MSW—Gestalt dream work (California)
www.dreammentor.com

Martin, Linda (United Kingdom)
www.lindamartinonline.com

Nomena, Ingrid Karhu (Sweden)
http://nomena.se.fastweb.no

Perry, Philippa (United Kingdom)
www.awareness.fsnet.co.uk

Persson & Persson Växkraft (Sweden)
www.gestaltterapeuterna.nu

Practice for Gestalt Therapy in Amsterdam (Netherlands)
www.pgta.nl

Salisbury, Claire (United Kingdom)
www.clairesalisbury.com

Sanmark Consulting, Annika Sanmark (Gestalt therapy, Scandinavia)
www.sanmarkconsulting.se

Sarasota Community School (formerly Kanner Academy, a private Gestalt boarding school)
www.kanneracademy.com

Schmidt, Ole (Sweden)
www.yogacentrum.se

Spoelstra, Susan, Praktijk voor Gestalttherapie (Netherlands)
www.xs4all.nl/%7Ejrhgland/index.html

Thrane, Susanne (Gestalt therapy, Stockholm, Sweden)
www.gestaltpsykoterapi-thrane.se

Tobin, Stephen (Portland, Oregon)
www.doctortobin.com

TWEEN Project—partnership of Gestalt Associates with Limited 2 for girls ages 9 to 11—Gestalt Institute of Central Ohio, Norman Shub, CEO
www.gestaltassoc.com/GestaltWebSite/GICO/html

Witchel, Bob, practice in psychology; Professor, Indiana University of Pennsylvania; American Academy of Psychotherapists Web site administrator
www.geocities.com/witchel

Ydremark, Louise (Sweden)
www.ordochutveckling.nu

ORGANIZATIONS LOOSELY ASSOCIATED WITH GESTALT THERAPY

American Academy of Psychotherapists
www.coe.iup.edu/aap

American Society for Group Psychotherapy and Psychodrama
http://asgpp.org

Association for Humanistic Psychology
www.ahpweb.org

Association for the Development of the Person-Centered Approach (ADPCA)
www.adpca.org

Association for Transpersonal Psychology
www.atpweb.org

Association of Humanistic Psychology Practitioners
www.ahpp.org

Australia and New Zealand Association of Psychotherapy (ANZAP)
www.anzapweb.com

British Association for the Person-Centered Approach (BAPCA)
www.bapca.org.uk

British Confederation of Psychotherapy (BCP)
www.bcp.org.uk

Center for Studies of the Person
www.centerfortheperson.org

European Association for Psychotherapy
www.europsyche.org

Expressive Therapy Association
www.expressivetherapy.com/htmls/directory2.html

Focusing Institute (New York City)
www.focusin.org

Person-Centered Society
www.existentialpsychology.org

Society for the Exploration of Psychotherapy Integration (SEPI)
www.cyberpsych.org/sepi

United Kingdom Council for Psychotherapy (UKCP)
www.psychotherapy.org.uk

World Association for Person-Centered and Experiential Psychotherapy and Counseling
www.pce-world.org

World Database on Happiness: Scientific Research on Subjective Appreciation of Life
www.eur.nl/fsw/research/happiness

APPENDIX B

Gestalt Experience and Observation Guide for Children

Human Growth and Development From a Gestalt/Wholistic Perspective

ANSEL L. WOLDT, EdD, 1990

GENERAL AREAS OF GROWTH & DEVELOPMENT	"LOOK & LISTEN FOR"	OBSERVATIONS EVIDENCE/DATA
I. Emotional/ Affective Development *****************	A. **Enjoyment & Satisfaction in "BEING" and "DOING":** Has ability to experience and express pleasure, pain, frustration, and fear (affect is appropriate to situation).	____________
***************** *FEELINGS ARE IN CONTACT WITH LIVELY FIGURES AND VARYING BACKGROUNDS*	B. **Aware, Reflective, Intuitive, Flexible, & Directed Energy:** Has cathartic & expressive processes for tension release to test reality, feel alive, free, autonomous, empowered, & focused.	____________
***************** ***************** ***************** ***************** *****************	C. **Self-Efficacy, Realistic Self-Concept, High Self-Esteem, & Aesthetic Competence:** Has a sense of personal well-being & mastery; an "I'm Okay, You're Okay" and "I Can Do It" attitude and feelings.	____________

What stands out most about this child's emotional and affective presence?

____

____

What are the predominant feelings you experience when with this child?

____

____

II.
Sensory, Perceptual, & Proprioceptive Development

****
****
****
****
****
****
****

PERCEPTIONS AND SENSES CREATE FIGURE / GROUND DIFFERENTIATION

A. Clarity of Sight—Visual Awareness:
Sees color(s), line(s), light(s), shadow(s), form(s), shading(s), parts & wholes, what "is" and "isn't" there—**The Gestalt!** ____________

B. Clarity of Hearing—Auditory Awareness:
Hears sounds, noises, tones, pitch, timbre, rhythm, cadence, pronunciation, intonation, modulation, enunciation, inflection, music, listens for subtleties, can hear "e-motion" and the "noise of silence." ____________

C. Clarity of Smell—Olfactory Awareness:
Distinguishes odors, scents, flavors, aromas, and fragrances; 7th sense—"can smell a rat." ____________

****
****
****
****
****

D. Clarity of Touch—Feeling by Touching Awareness:
Feels texture(s), temperature(s), weight(s), form(s), shape(s), density, quality, quantity, makes sensuous (not sexual) contact. ____________

****
****
****
****
****

E. Clarity of Contact Through Muscles & Motion—Kinesthetic Awareness: Aware of his/her, body image, muscles, space, boundaries, physical movement, & balance. ____________

****
****
****
****
****
****
****

F. Clarity of Taste Processes—Gustatorial Awareness:
While eating & drinking, child can differentiate flavors, tastes, textures, foods, seasonings, beverages. S/he knows what is appetizing, tasty, interesting, and palatable, as well as that which is tasteless, too tasty, &/or unappetizing. ____________

****
****
****
****
****
****
****
****

G. Clarity of Culinary, Digestive, & Alimentary Processes—Gastronomical Awareness:
Child can taste, chew, savor, swallow, & process that which is appetizing and palatable, leading to ease and regularity in elimination. S/he can differentiate, repel, pass on thru, & eliminate the tasteless, acrid, unsavory, and non-digestible. ____________

What stands out most about this child's sensory & perceptual domain?

____

____

What senses do you experience most in making contact with him/her?

____

____

III.
Physical and Behavioral Development

****
****
****

CONTACTS THE ENVIRONMENT FOR SUPPORT AND CAN CREATE, ALTER, RESTRUCTURE, OR DESTROY FIGURES

****

****
****
****
****
****

A. **Well-Organized & Directed Behavior:**
Child's body movements are fluid, experiences ability to aggress and make contact with environment. Is aware of handedness and sidedness (left/right), forward & backward, directionality—up(s) & down(s), balance, symmetry, and fluidity.

B. **Visual-Motor Coordination:**
Has eye-hand-foot coordination; body parts move in coordinated manner; has a sense of personal space and moves within that space in ways that honor his/her own and other people's boundaries. Movement seems to be self-regulated.

C. **Body Image and Spatial Relationships:**
Has a realistic concept of self in relationship to environment, with permeable boundaries support exploration & experimentation.

What stands out most for you about this child's physical /behavioral presence?

____

____

What are you most aware of about your own body as you are with him/her?

____

____

IV.
Intellectual and Cognitive Development

****

****
****
****
****
****
****
****

A. **Symbol Systems:**
Has developed representations of language (words, numbers, pictures, etc.) to facilitate classification and expression of knowledge and awarenesses.

B. **Concept Development:**
Has awareness and ability to create and/or experience schemas & Gestalten, including concepts of self, others, ideas, and environment with & without people for potential & actual interaction and contact.

****

REALITY AND FANTASY-BASED FIGURES EMERGE OR ARE CREATED FROM ENERGIZED GROUND/FIELD

****

****

****

****

****

C. **Curiosity:**
Is curious about his/her world. Has an active desire to experience, touch, feel, learn and know. Expresses interest in people and things. Makes observations and comments on them. Is inquisitive, asks questions, investigates possibilities. Looks and acts interested. Gives excited attention to the unexpected, strange, odd, different, unusual, etc.. Follows his/her sensations, perceptions & awarenesses to explore environmental possibilities. At times may be impertinent, persistent, quizzing, prying. ______

****

****

****

****

D. **Problem Solving and Cause-Effect Relations:**
Thinks divergently, imagines possibilities, has a sense of wonder, has creative solutions, is able to understand causes and anticipate outcomes. ______

What stands out for you most about this child's cognitive processes?

______

______

______

What cerebral processes and fantasies do you experience with him/her?

______

______

______

V.
Social and Interpersonal Development

****

****

****

A. **Accepts Self & Others:**
Is aware of self, although not self-conscious, insecure, anxious or easily embarrassed. S/he acknowledges real/authentic thoughts & desires, is considerate and accepting of others who are both similar and different. ______

****

****

****

****

****

B. **Trusts Self and Others:**
Is aware of personal boundaries & is secure enough to assert self and receive others; making "I-THOU" contact possible. ______

****************** PERSON-TO-PERSON INTERACTIONS EMERGE AND ARE CREATED FROM THE CHILD'S ENERGIZED FIELD

C. **Interpersonal Comprehension & Interaction:** Is sensitive to feelings, boundaries, and concerns of others: understands what kinds of behavior bring approval or disapproval; social contact derives meaning & satisfaction for all concerned, whether positive or negative. ________

****

D. **Autonomous yet Inclusionary, Responsible but Not Codependent:** Child can be alone & together, is neither confluent nor confluent phobic; is open to sharing, including and excluding; accepts responsibility for own actions. Is considerate and able to respond but does not assume responsibility for others. ________

What stands out most for you about this child's "relating" with others?

____

____

What do you personally experience in "relating" to and with her/him?

____

____

VI. Growth in Aesthetic Awareness Intuition, Creativity & Spirituality *(not religion)*

A. **Creative Attention and Awareness:** Child is aware of & attends to "vibes," sensations, feelings, perceptions and ideas. Creates & allows tension & excitement to emerge. Is able to be in contact with commotions and emotions. ________

****

B. **Flexibility and Fluency:** Displays an openness to self, others and environs. Takes risks and remains open to possibilities. Copes well with ambiguity—is able to "flow with the river," not try to control or direct it. ________

****************** *FIGURE-GROUND CLARIFICATION, DIFFERENTIATION & EXPRESSION* ******************

C. **Intuitive Identification with the Creative Process:** Is not controlled by fear; creates opportunities for exploration, experimentation & experience; can be guided by "the spiritual" &/or energy forces; intuits purpose & direction. ________

***************** ***************** ***************** ***************** ***************** ***************** *****************	D. **Sensitive to Environs, Perceptive of Form & Rhythm, Structure & Process:** Appreciates natural and man-made "beauty"; relates with the environment, not against it and is guided by , rhythm, structure, and process so that content has form reflective of child's values.
***************** ***************** ***************** ***************** ***************** ***************** *****************	E. **Good "Gestalten":** Products produced by child demonstrate elaboration, variety, originality, and unity. Completing a project is a process that begets an "AHA" experience and contains elements of good form and closure, making withdrawal possible and even enjoyable.

What stands out for you about this child's aesthetic and creative self?

What does this child touch in you that is creative, aesthetic &/or spiritual?

WHAT IS YOUR OVERALL "GESTALTEN" AWARENESS AND EXPERIENCE OF HIM/HER?

GENERAL COMMENTS, HYPOTHESES, AND/OR QUESTIONS:

Author Index

SUBJECT INDEX